faith first

Grade Three
Parish Catechist Guide

Faith First Development Team

RESOURCES FOR CHRISTIAN LIVING®

www.FaithFirst.com

"The Ad Hoc Committee to Oversee the Use of the Catechism, United States Conference of Catholic Bishops, has found the doctrinal content of this teacher manual, copyright 2006, to be in conformity with the *Catechism of the Catholic Church*."

NIHIL OBSTAT
Reverend Robert M. Coerver
Censor Librorum

IMPRIMATUR
† Most Rev. Charles V. Grahmann
Bishop of Dallas

November 15, 2004

The Nihil Obstat and Imprimatur are official declarations that the material reviewed is free of doctrinal or moral error. No implication is contained therein that those granting the Nihil Obstat and Imprimatur agree with the contents, opinions, or statements expressed.

Send all inquiries to:
RCL • Resources for Christian Living
200 East Bethany Drive
Allen, Texas 75002-3804

Toll Free   877-275-4725
Fax   800-688-8356

Visit us at **www.RCLweb.com**
             www.FaithFirst.com

Printed in the United States of America

20473   ISBN 0-7829-1065-3 (Student Book)
20483   ISBN 0-7829-1077-7 (Catechist Guide)

1 2 3 4 5 6 7 8 9 10
05 06 07 08 09 10 11 12 13

ACKNOWLEDGMENTS

Scripture excerpts are taken or adapted from the *New American Bible with Revised New Testament and Psalms*, copyright © 1991, 1986, 1970, Confraternity of Christian Doctrine, Washington, DC. Used with permission. All rights reserved. No part of the *New American Bible* may be reproduced by any means without the permission of the copyright owner.

Excerpts from the English translation of the *Roman Missal*, © 1973, International Committee on English in the Liturgy, Inc. (ICEL); excerpts from the English translation of *The Rite of Penance* © 1974, ICEL. All rights reserved.

Excerpts from the English translation of the *Catechism of the Catholic Church* for use in the United States of America, second edition, copyright © 1997, United States Catholic Conference, Inc.–Libreria Editrice Vaticana. Used with permission.

Excerpts from *General Directory for Catechesis*, copyright © 1997, United States Conference of Catholic Bishops, Washington, DC. Used with permission. All rights reserved. No part of this work may be reproduced or transmitted in any form without the permission in writing from the copyright holder.

Excerpts from *Sharing the Light of Faith: National Catechetical Directory for Catholics of the United States*, copyright © 1979, by the USCC; excerpts from *To Teach as Jesus Did*, copyright © 1972, by the USCC; excerpts from *Music in Catholic Worship*, copyright © 1972 Bishops' Committee on the Liturgy, USCC, Washington, DC. Used with permission.

Excerpts from *Pastoral Constitution on the Church in the Modern World* (Gaudium et spes), *Constitution on the Sacred Liturgy* (Sacrosanctum concilium), *Dogmatic Constitution on the Church* (Lumen gentium), from Vatican Council II: *The Conciliar and Post Conciliar Documents,* New Revised Edition, Austin Flannery, O.P., Gen. Ed., copyright © 1975, 1986, 1992, 1996 by Costello Publishing Company, Inc. Used with Permission.

Excerpts from and *Catechesi Tradendae: Catechesis in Our Time,* © 1979, Daughters of St. Paul; excerpts from *Evangelii Nuntiandi: On Evangelization in the Modern World* © 1975, Daughters of St. Paul, Boston, MA.

Excerpts from *Paschale Solemnitatis, Concerning the Preparation and Celebration of the Easter Feasts,* copyright © 1988, Liberia Editrice Vaticana.

Excerpts from *Ceremonial of Bishops,* copyright © 1989, The Liturgical Press.

Faith First Legacy Edition Development Team

Developing a religion program requires the gifts and talents of many individuals working together as a team. RCL is proud to acknowledge the contributions of these dedicated people.

Program Theology Consultants
Reverend Louis J. Cameli, S.T.D.
Reverend Robert D. Duggan, S.T.D.

Advisory Board
Judith Deckers, M.Ed.
Marina Herrera, Ph.D.
Elaine McCarron, SCN, M.Div.
Reverend Frank McNulty, S.T.D.
Reverend Ronald J. Nuzzi, Ph.D.

National Catechetical Advisor
Jacquie Jambor

Catechetical Specialist
Jo Rotunno

Contributing Writers
Student Book and Catechist/Teacher Guides
Christina DeCamp
Judith Deckers
Mary Beth Jambor
Marianne K. Lenihan
Michele Norfleet

Art and Design Director
Lisa Brent

Electronic Page Makeup
Laura Fremder

Production Director
Jenna Nelson

Designers/Photo Research
Pat Bracken
Kristy O. Howard
Susan Smith

Project Editors
Patricia A. Classick
Steven M. Ellair
Ronald C. Lamping

Web Site Producers
Joseph Crisalli
Demere Henson

General Editor
Ed DeStefano

President/Publisher
Maryann Nead

Contents

faith first® Legacy Edition

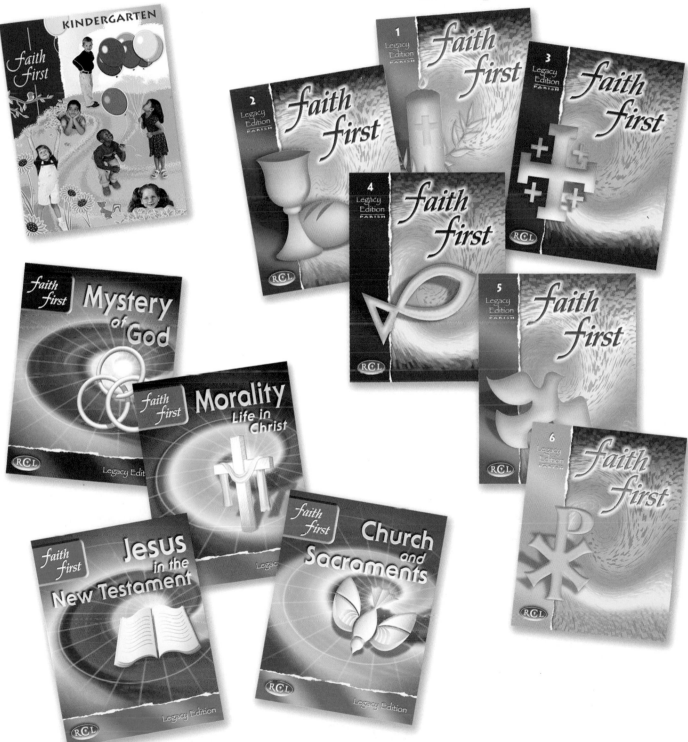

faith first®
Legacy Edition

Teaching the Timeless Truths of
Our Catholic Faith Every Year

CREED · Trinity · God Our Father and Creator · Jesus Christ, the Son of God
SACRAMENTS · Eucharist and the Mass
MORALITY · Beatitudes
PRAYER · Jesus, Model of Prayer

The Bible, the Word of God · Confirmation · Baptism · Ten Commandments · Ways of Praying

Mary · Saints · The Church, the People of God · The Church's Year of Worship · Liturgy · Loving Others · Transformation through Prayer · Virtues · Loving God · The Lord's Prayer · Grace · Conscience · Making Choices · Matrimony · Holy Orders · Anointing of the Sick · Holy Spirit · The Death and Resurrection of Jesus

Works of Mercy · Reconciliation · Tradition of Prayer · The Holy Spirit

Faith First

The spiral learning method plus Scripture
and Liturgical Year lessons make Faith First the most
comprehensive program available today!

RCL
1-877-ASK-4-RCL (1-877-275-4725)

Teaching the Timeless Truths of Our Faith Every Year

Faith First is unique, effective, and comprehensive.

The *Faith First* Kindergarten through Junior High scope and sequence* is a spiral approach to learning our Catholic faith. The four pillars of the *Catechism of the Catholic Church*—Creed, Sacraments, Morality, and Prayer—are taught and developed on every grade level every year. This ensures that the beliefs of our faith are introduced to and reinforced for the young people as they grow, develop, and mature in their faith.

This educationally sound method means that each catechist will build upon and reinforce what children have learned previously in other grades. The result is age-appropriate learning on all topics of the faith.

*See the complete *Faith First* grade 3 scope and sequence chart on pages 24–27.

Each text provides:
- **Doctrine Chapters**
- **Scripture Chapters**
- **Liturgical Season Lessons**

Doctrine Chapters
While catechesis is much more than simply "teaching religion," providing children with a comprehensive understanding of our Catholic faith is essential to good catechesis. In the *Faith First* doctrine chapters, the children come to understand what we believe as Catholics and how to live out those beliefs.

Scripture Chapters

The special Scripture chapters in each unit of *Faith First* help the children come to know and understand the word of God. Each of these complete lessons has three distinctive elements:

Bible Background

The Scripture story is put into context for the children by teaching about the author, the setting, and the background of the people in the story.

Reading the Word of God

The children read or listen to a story from the Scriptures, followed by a brief summary that recalls what happened in the Scripture story.

Understanding the Word of God

This section explores the meaning of the story and helps the children see how God's love, presence, help, and Revelation continue to guide us in our daily lives.

Liturgical Season Lessons

You can teach the liturgical seasons to their fullest with the *Faith First* seasonal lessons that give the children the opportunity to celebrate and prayerfully participate in the liturgy all year long.

Advent and Christmas

Four lessons help the children joyfully prepare to celebrate the Incarnation and Christ's rebirth in our hearts at Christmas, followed by two lessons on the Christmas season.

Lent

Six lessons guide the children through Lent and help them turn their minds and hearts to God.

The Triduum and the Season of Easter

Together, you and the children journey through Holy Thursday, Good Friday, and the Easter Vigil. Then six lessons celebrate the joy of Christ's Resurrection and conclude with a lesson on the coming of the Holy Spirit at Pentecost.

Online resources
for children, catechists,
and parents.

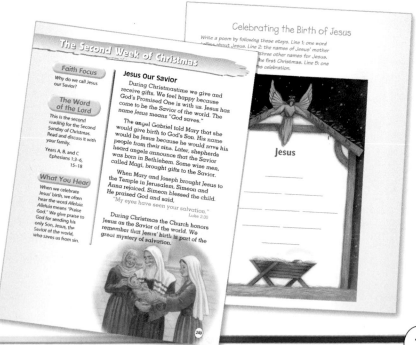

Features of the Student Book

Each chapter of Faith First *has consistent features that direct learning, develop religious literacy, reinforce content, and encourage integration of faith and life.*

Chapter Opener

The first page of every chapter features a photograph that illustrates in some way the focus of the chapter. This page also begins with an opening prayer and questions to assess the children's life experiences and what they already know about the subject to be learned.

Faith Focus

Prepares the children for learning the content of the lesson with an introductory question.

Faith Words

Assists you in helping the children build Catholic literacy by defining and explaining important faith terms and concepts.

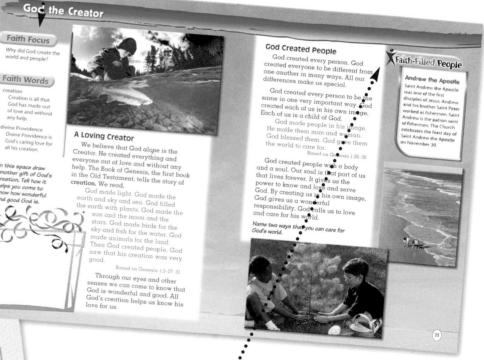

Faith-Filled People

Saints and others who have lived exemplary Catholic lives serve as models for the children.

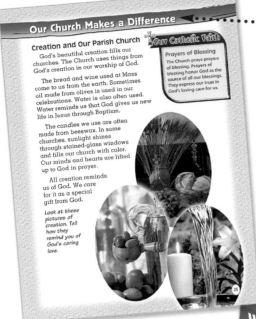

Our Church Makes a Difference

Each chapter examines the difference the Church has made and continues to make in the lives of Christians and in the world. The children's Catholic identities are developed as they learn more about how the Church expresses her faith.

What Difference Does Faith Make in My Life?

This important step helps the children recognize that faith is not meant to be isolated or compartmentalized. Faith is meant to be lived.

We Pray

Just as we began with a prayer in the chapter opener, each chapter concludes with prayer. A variety of prayer experiences help the children grow in their appreciation of the Church's rich prayer life.

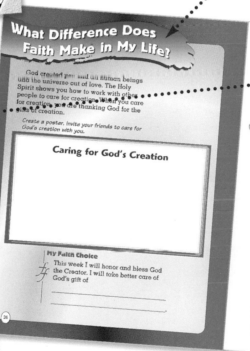

We Remember

The chapter review can be used to conclude the lesson or to begin the following week.

With My Family

Faith First offers you a way to partner with parents and help them to effectively share faith with their children. Built right into every chapter of the student book, these pages contain interesting and meaningful opportunities for making faith come alive at home.

Building Religious Literacy

Numerous resources assess the
children's religious literacy in grades 1–8.

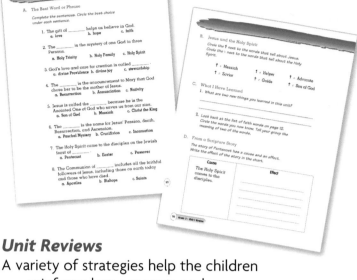

Unit Reviews
A variety of strategies help the children
- reinforce key concepts and
- identify new discoveries.

Chapter Reviews
A variety of strategies help the children review
key terms and concepts. (See page 9.)

Unit Openers
Faith First unit openers are true teaching tools that
- activate prior knowledge and
- forecast unit faith themes and faith vocabulary.

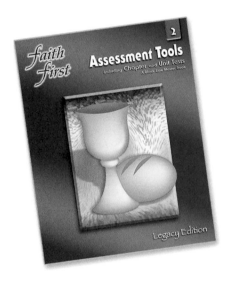

Assessment Tools
A book of reproducible masters helps you create an assessment
portfolio with chapter tests, unit tests, and other assessment instruments.

Online Chapter Reviews at FaithFirst.com ·····················➤
The children can study and review material from every chapter of every
grade level on our Web site. The children can take an interactive test and
then email the results to you. It's a great interactive way to reinforce
learning, and Mom and Dad can get involved too.

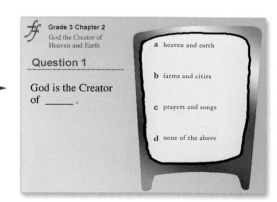

Features of the Catechist Guide

The catechist guide supports you every step of the way. Every lesson in the guide provides you with these easy-to-use resources:

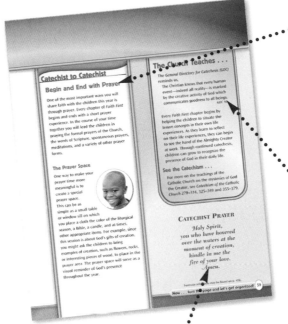

Catechist to Catechist

Thoughts from a master catechist offer both practical and prayerful ideas to get you started!

The Church Teaches

This feature introduces catechists to important quotes from key Church documents.

Background

This easy-to-read essay provides theological background on the content of the chapter. It will help you grow in your own adult understanding of our Catholic faith. Reflection questions help you connect faith concepts to your own life.

Catechist Prayer

Before you teach, you'll want to center yourself in prayer. Each chapter prayer addresses the heart of your lesson.

> The **QuickStart for Catechists** on pages 17–34 and the **Faith First Legacy Edition In-Service Video** will help you get the year off to a great start.

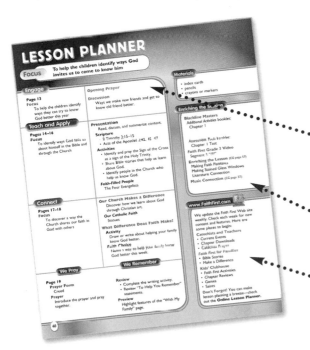

Lesson Planner

Plan Outline

Here is your lesson plan for teaching the chapter. The plan includes a chapter focus, objectives, an outline of the lesson process, and a list of materials you will need.

Enrichment Activities

A handy list of all *Faith First* enrichment materials available for this chapter is described for you.

Online Resources

And don't forget to visit **www.FaithFirst.com** for additional chapter resources and online lesson-planning tools!

Teaching Has Never Been Easier

In Faith First *you will follow this simple, effective process as you teach each lesson:*

- **Engage**
- **Teach and Apply**
- **Connect**

Engage

Each chapter begins with prayer and engages the children's interest in what you will be teaching.

Teach and Apply

On every page, first you teach, then you apply.

Teach

Focus—This simple question brings the children's attention to the core content of the lesson.

Discover—These are the building blocks of your lessons and will make the core content accessible to the children.

Apply

Reinforce—An easy way to reinforce learning. Answers to the questions are printed in the catechist guide.

Integrate—The children have the opportunity to integrate what they have learned into their daily lives.

Connect

Without a connection to real life, the content remains only head knowledge. This section helps the children understand how they can put their faith into action.

What Difference Does Faith Make in My Life?

At the heart of each *Faith First* lesson, the children are asked to apply what they have learned to their lives. Every child is asked to make a faith choice based on the content of the lesson.

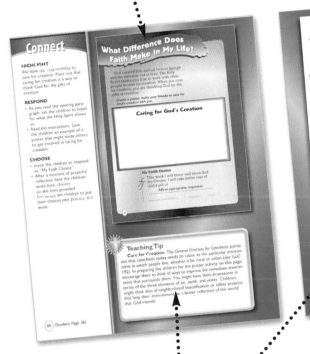

Our Church Makes a Difference

Children develop their Catholic identity by examining Catholic practices and understanding the significant place of the Church in the world.

Pray and Review

We Pray

Your lessons end as they began—with prayer.

We Remember

A short review of the core content of your lesson and an activity to reinforce it.

Background, Tips, and More

Your lessons are filled with ideas, suggestions, and additional background information to help you.

- Catholic Social Teaching
- Faith Vocabulary
- Liturgy Tips
- Teaching Tips
- Special Needs
- Background

You will find this material in boxes at the bottom of each page of the lesson plan.

Enriching the Lesson

These optional activities in every chapter offer you choices for class activities that include strategies for the many ways children learn.

Faith First Supplements

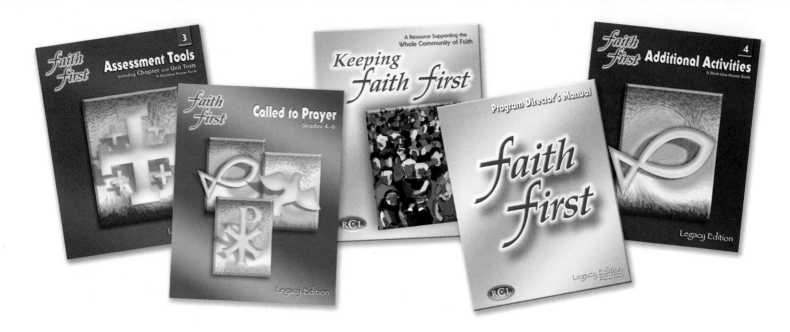

Faith First Music

For use with kindergarten and primary grades:

- **Music CD**—Twelve original songs based on biblical, liturgical, and doctrinal themes.
- **Music and Prayer Celebrations**—The booklet includes complete lyrics and accompaniment for guitar and piano, plus prayer celebrations.

Faith First Class Kits 1–6

Each kit contains:

- **Assessment Tools**—Use these reproducible masters to create an assessment portfolio with chapter and unit tests and other assessment instruments.
- **Additional Activities**—Enhance your lessons with time-saving reproducible activities that extend learning in class or at home.
- **Called to Prayer**—Touch the children's hearts with a variety of easy-to-use and practical prayer formats.
- **The Faith-Filled Classroom**—"Tried and true" tips from veteran catechists and Catholic school teachers.

Faith First Videos

Innovative videos bring your lessons to life with a variety of segments that reinforce and integrate faith formation.

Faith First Art & Environment Package

These colorful and inspiring resources touch the imagination and create a faith-filled learning environment. Each package contains eighteen posters, seven banners, including a Bible timeline, and pass-along cards (six packs of fifty in two designs). One package contains enough material for six classes (grades 1–6) plus a handy guide with suggested, age-appropriate uses.

Program Director's Manual

The manual includes everything the Director of Religious Education needs to implement *Faith First* in your parish, including ideas for catechist training, parent meetings, and for using *Faith First* as the foundation for catechesis in your whole parish community.

Keeping Faith First: A Resource Supporting the Whole Community of Faith

Bring together your whole parish community with this unique resource. Help parents and other adults explore the fundamental insights of our tradition, encourage them to share their stories of faith, and challenge them to be of service in the world. Plus visit **www.WholeCommunityCatechesis.com**.

Junior High

Four texts, twelve chapters each, can be used interchangeably and enable you to design up to a two-year curriculum for junior high students.

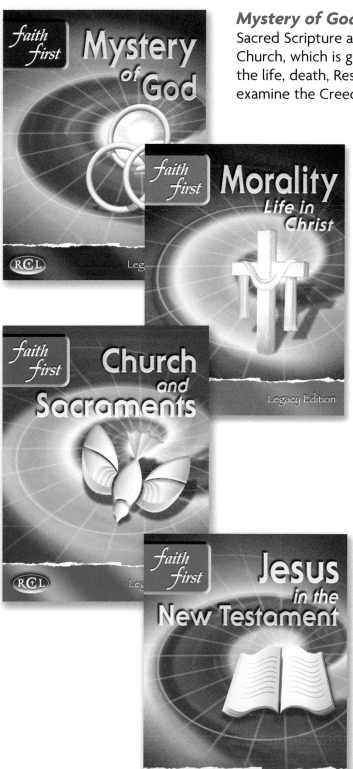

Mystery of God

Sacred Scripture and Sacred Tradition are the source of the faith of the Church, which is grounded in the fullness of Revelation that is found in the life, death, Resurrection, and Ascension of Jesus Christ. The students examine the Creed as the summary statement of our beliefs.

Church and Sacraments

The mystery of the Church unfolds as the students discover how believers take on the responsibility of continuing Christ's work on earth. The study of the sacraments centers on how they bind us together as a community of faith.

Morality: Life in Christ

As persons created in God's image, we are guided by the Ten Commandments and the Beatitudes to live a successful moral life. The principles of Catholic morality, including the social teachings of the Catholic Church, help young teens make important life choices in their daily lives.

Jesus in the New Testament

The life and message of Jesus are explored in the four Gospels with emphasis on understanding and praying the Scriptures. The students are also introduced to the writings of Saint Paul, other New Testament letters, and the Book of Revelation.

FaithFirst.com
Making a difference in people's lives

Kids' Clubhouse
Grades K-3

Kids Only Club
Grades 4-6

Teen Center
Grades 7 & 8

Faith First for
Families

Catechists and
Teachers

About Faith First

Whole
Community
Catechesis

Shop RCL

RCLWeb.com

FaithFirst.com
Highlights

 Plays & Skits
Learn the importance of
remembering our loved ones
with *Tamara Remembers*.

 Make a Difference
Discover some new ways to
respect life.

Site
Map

Find your way around
FaithFirst.com!

Sharing the
Difference

Learn how parishes and
schools around the world are
making a difference!

How to Use
FaithFirst.com

Helpful information on how
to use FaithFirst.com with
the Faith First curriculum
series.

Email
Update

Look for the green "Email
Update" buttons to sign up to
receive an email when that
section is updated.

FaithFirst.com
Correlations

Download the Lectionary (for
Year C and Year A), Music,
and Saints Correlations to
Faith First.

Points of
Interest

 Read our exciting
interactive stories:
The River Road
Adventures and Vista
Falls Junior High!

 Try our thorough
Chapter Reviews for
each grade and chapter,
grades 2-8.

The At Home Family
Guide is a visionary
approach to family-
guided formation at
home.

Learn more
about the Kindergarten
program.

 Our Current Events
section shows how you
can deal with the issues
of the world today.

RCL Sacraments
Online

Visit the web component of our
exciting Sacraments program!

 New!

 RCL Sacraments

New! for Parishes
Faith First® Legacy Edition
Transforming a New
Generation

Faith First
Legacy
Edition
PARISH

- Designed Specially for
  Parishes
- Involves Families
- Supports the Whole
  Community
- Unique Spiral Learning
  Method
- State of the Art Web
  Site
- Four NEW Junior High
  texts

Order your FREE
Faith First Legacy Edition
Review Pack today!

The National
Conference for
Catechetical
Leadership
(NCCL)
presented its
2003 Technology Award to
RCL for its innovative use of
web technology to augment
its print resources and greatly
expand the capabilities of
learners, catechists, and
parents.

 RCL
RESOURCES FOR CHRISTIAN LIVING®

FaithFirst.com brings living and learning about faith into the twenty-first century. Catechists, children, and parents visit **FaithFirst.com** every month, resulting in over four million "hits" per month. RCL is proud to have been recognized with the Technology Award by the National Conference for Catechetical Leadership.

FaithFirst.com enables you to access practical and creative resources for all of your lessons online when and where you need them—twenty-four hours a day, seven days a week.

With **FaithFirst.com** your student books are constantly updated and expanded beyond the printed pages with learning games, chapter reviews, saints, lectionary-based lessons, contemporary issues, current events, and so much more!

FaithFirst.com encourages parents to spend time online with their children, motivates children to want to learn more about their faith, and empowers you with the latest resources. And remember, every minute a child spends at **FaithFirst.com** brings faith into the home and extends your lessons beyond class time.

QuickStart for Catechists

An Interactive Workshop on the Catechetical Ministry

Welcome to Faith First!

You have agreed to serve your parish this year as a *Faith First* catechist. *Faith First* invites you, the children, their families, and the whole faith community to discover the difference that Catholic faith can make.

Faith is rooted in God's call to all people, fully revealed in Jesus Christ, guided by the Holy Spirit. *Faith First* is rooted in five principles:

- **Faith is a gift from God. It is also our free response to all that God has revealed to us.**

- **Faith includes not only an intellectual understanding of doctrine but also a conversion of heart.**

- **Faith grows and develops throughout life.**

- **Faith is lived in community.**

- **Faith-filled people look at their actions and the world differently. All life changes when seen through the eyes of faith.**

As you begin this workshop, take a few moments to reflect on your personal faith.

> **For Reflection**
>
> *In what ways do I live my Catholic faith day by day?*
>
> *Who has been a strong influence in my life of faith?*

What Is a Catechist?

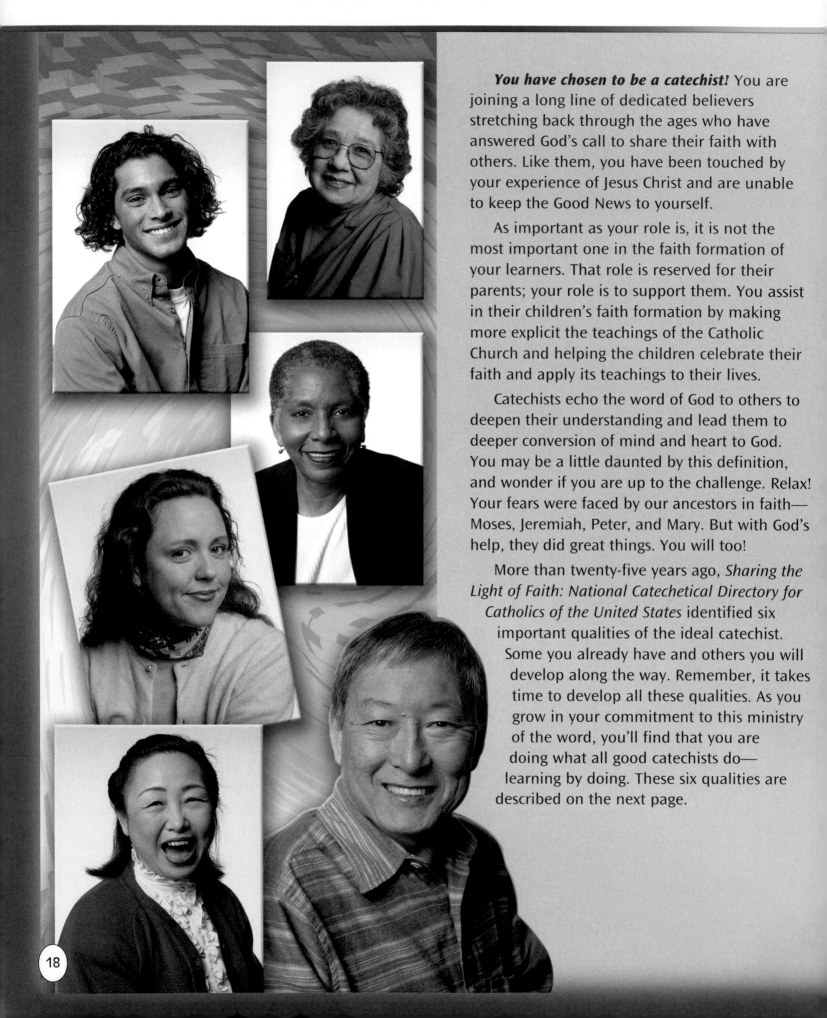

You have chosen to be a catechist! You are joining a long line of dedicated believers stretching back through the ages who have answered God's call to share their faith with others. Like them, you have been touched by your experience of Jesus Christ and are unable to keep the Good News to yourself.

As important as your role is, it is not the most important one in the faith formation of your learners. That role is reserved for their parents; your role is to support them. You assist in their children's faith formation by making more explicit the teachings of the Catholic Church and helping the children celebrate their faith and apply its teachings to their lives.

Catechists echo the word of God to others to deepen their understanding and lead them to deeper conversion of mind and heart to God. You may be a little daunted by this definition, and wonder if you are up to the challenge. Relax! Your fears were faced by our ancestors in faith—Moses, Jeremiah, Peter, and Mary. But with God's help, they did great things. You will too!

More than twenty-five years ago, *Sharing the Light of Faith: National Catechetical Directory for Catholics of the United States* identified six important qualities of the ideal catechist. Some you already have and others you will develop along the way. Remember, it takes time to develop all these qualities. As you grow in your commitment to this ministry of the word, you'll find that you are doing what all good catechists do— learning by doing. These six qualities are described on the next page.

Qualities of Catechists

1. **You are responding to a call from the Lord** expressed through your local parish. You have agreed not only to catechize others but to continue growing in your own faith and your knowledge of Sacred Scripture and Tradition.

2. **You are a witness to the Gospel** message of Jesus Christ as taught by his Church. You believe in this message and in its power to change the lives of all who believe in it.

3. **You are committed to the Church** and try to express the teachings of the Catholic Church as clearly as you can. You constantly test your own understanding of your faith against the Church's wisdom.

4. **You build a faith community among your learners** because you have experienced its power and importance in your own life. You encourage your learners to gather at the Eucharist, "the source and summit of the Christian life" (*Dogmatic Constitution on the Catholic Church* 11), and to live lives of forgiveness, reconciliation, and peacemaking.

5. **You are a servant of the Church,** seeking out the needs of others and teaching your learners to do the same. You model for your learners what it means to be a follower of Jesus.

6. **You are willing to acquire the basic skills and abilities** needed to conduct effective catechetical sessions.

For Reflection

Place a star next to the qualities that are your greatest strengths. Place a check next to the ones you want to work on this year. Discuss your assessment with another catechist and with your program DRE or coordinator, who can help you develop a growth plan for the coming year.

What Is My Task?

> [T]he definitive aim of catechesis is to put people not only in touch but in communion [and] intimacy with Jesus Christ.
>
> *ON CATECHESIS IN OUR TIME* 5

Catechists do a lot of different things. First and most important of all, you are a model for children of what it means to be a disciple of Jesus Christ. That doesn't mean that you are perfect. It means that you remember the children are watching you to learn what it means to be a Catholic. So you try your best to look, act, and sound like one. Of course, at various times you also will make short presentations, tell stories, facilitate dialogue and activities, and lead prayer.

The *General Directory for Catechesis* identifies six important tasks of catechesis (*GDC* 85–87). Reflect on the list on the next page and assess your abilities in each of these areas before you begin the year.

Tasks of Catechesis

1. **Promoting knowledge of the faith.** Catechists introduce their learners to all that has been revealed through Jesus Christ by initiating them gradually into the whole truth revealed through Scripture and Tradition. Your *Faith First* student text and catechist guide will show you what to teach this year.

2. **Liturgical education.** As a catechist you help children understand the Church's sacramental life and give them an experience of the signs, symbols, gestures, prayers, and creeds of the Church. The weekly and seasonal *Faith First* prayer experiences will give you many examples.

3. **Moral formation.** Moral catechesis involves both the announcement of the Good News through your proclamation of the Gospel call to moral living and your presentation of what the Church's Tradition teaches about this message. *Faith First* will help you with the best language and strategies to use.

4. **Teaching to pray.** As you teach the Our Father, the prayer that Jesus taught, you will introduce children ever more deeply to the forms of prayer that it includes: adoration, praise, thanksgiving, intercession, and petition and expression of sorrow for sins, all expressed with the intimacy that comes from knowing we are children of God. *Faith First* will provide you with a wide variety of prayer experiences and also offer you a complete unit exploring the prayer life of the Church, especially the Our Father.

5. **Education for community life.** You are leading children into a way of life that you are already experiencing. You invite them to join a loving community of faith, to live simply and humbly, to care for the poor and alienated, to forgive as they wish to be forgiven, and to join in common prayer. Your classroom will become a weekly experience of Christian community for the children.

6. **Missionary initiation.** Catechesis prepares children to live the Gospel in daily life and to work to prepare the way for the coming of the kingdom of God. *Faith First* is filled with suggestions for outreach activities and service projects to build in children a sense of the Church's mission.

For Reflection

For which task of catechesis do you feel most qualified? Which seems most daunting? Share with another catechist what strengths and concerns you bring to the catechetical vocation.

For Further Study

See Echoes of Faith "Roles of the Catechist" *module.* Echoes of Faith *is a video-assisted resource for the formation and enrichment of catechists in Catholic parishes and schools. It has been developed by the National Conference for Catechetical Leadership and produced by RCL. For more information call 877-275-4725.*

Teaching Others to Pray

As children experience such gestures as signing, anointing, blessing, and kneeling within the intimacy of your classroom setting, you will be preparing them to participate more fully in the worship of the whole community. Just as you have certain ways of praying with which you are most comfortable, you'll find that children have their preferences too. The many approaches that are included will provide a true school of prayer for your learners.

Liturgical formation . . . must explain what the Christian liturgy is, and what the sacraments are. It must also, however, offer an experience of the different kinds of celebration and it must make symbols, gestures, etc., known and loved. GENERAL DIRECTORY FOR CATECHESIS 87

Prayer is listening with openness to God's word, and responding in faith, hope, and love. Our response involves a willingness to spend time with God, to ponder the words of Scripture, to discern God's message to us, and to respond with our whole selves—body, mind, and heart.

Worship is simply the prayer of the Church. We gather together to lay our lives before God the Father, to praise him and give thanks for the gift of his love, and to join with his Son in offering our lives for his service. That is why the *Catechism of the Catholic Church* refers to liturgy as "the participation of the People of God 'in the work of God' " (*CCC* 1069). Liturgical celebrations weave together signs and symbols drawn from our human experience—words and actions, singing and music, and sacred images. An artful blending of these elements produces a worship experience that can evoke for us the mystery of God and lead us to a fruitful response.

How *Faith First* Will Help You

- Beginning and closing prayer experiences in every lesson
- A rich variety of prayer experiences using the signs, symbols, and gestures of the Church's liturgy whenever appropriate
- An exposition of the rich variety of the Church's Tradition of prayer, liturgy, and sacraments
- Full instructions on how to lead each prayer experience

For Reflection

How do you create opportunities in your daily life to hear the voice of God speaking to you?

What forms of prayer will you most enjoy leading for your learners?

For Further Study

See Echoes of Faith "Prayer and Spirituality" *and* "Liturgy and Sacraments" *modules.*

The Faith First Approach

Faith First lessons are built upon the three foundations: the **word of God** clearly expressed, **worship and prayer**, and the **call to service** for the reign of God.

Each *Faith First* lesson teaches as Jesus did:

- **Engage**
  Learners reflect on life experiences and recall prior knowledge about faith concepts.

- **Teach and Apply**
  On each content page, we first teach, then we apply. We teach the story of faith and challenge learners to assimilate concepts and apply them to what they already know.

- **Connect**
  Two pages, *Our Church Makes a Difference* and *What Difference Does Faith Make in My Life?*, help connect lesson concepts to the Church's life and to the lives of the learners.

A Spiral Approach

Faith First uses a spiral approach to curriculum development that incorporates doctrine, Scripture, and liturgy.

Doctrine
- Each year in grades 1–6, *Faith First* offers four units correlating to the four pillars, or sections, of the *Catechism of the Catholic Church:*
  - We Believe (Creed),
  - We Worship (Liturgy and Sacraments),
  - We Live (Morality), and
  - We Pray (Prayer and Spirituality).
- We repeat key concepts each year on the Teach and Apply pages. Core content is introduced in primary grades, then developed and reinforced in middle and upper grades.

Scripture
Sacred Scripture in each lesson and special Scripture chapters in each unit deepen understanding and challenge children to live the biblical message.

Liturgy
- Weekly prayer experiences introduce children to the rich and varied tradition of the Church's prayer and worship.
- Twenty-two special seasonal lessons help the children and their families explore and celebrate seasonal feasts and seasons of the Church's year.

On the next four pages, you will see a detailed outline of what you will be teaching this year. Study the outline of the grade 3 content on the scope and sequence chart, then respond to the reflection questions below.

For Reflection

What topics do you feel most comfortable teaching this year?

What topics would you like to learn more about?

For Further Study

The five Echoes of Faith "Theology" *modules—*"I Believe/We Believe" (Creed), "Liturgy and Sacraments," "Catholic Morality," "Prayer and Spirituality," *and* "Introduction to the Scriptures"—*will offer you an excellent introduction to the main themes of Catholic teaching.*

Scope and Sequence (Grade 3)

Unit 1 We Believe (Creed)

CHAPTER 1 — GOD SPEAKS TO US

Faith Concepts: Revelation, gift of faith, Holy Trinity, Bible, Old Testament, New Testament, Apostles, Catholic Church

Sacred Scripture: Psalm 104:1; Acts 2:42, 45–47 (life in the early Church); 2 Timothy 3:15–16 (holy writings come from God)

Faith Vocabulary: faith, Holy Trinity

Faith-Filled People: The Evangelists

Our Catholic Faith: Statues

Our Church Makes a Difference: Christian Art

Prayer: Praying the Creed

Catechism of the Catholic Church (CCC): 232–260

CHAPTER 2 — GOD THE CREATOR OF HEAVEN AND EARTH

Faith Concepts: God, loving Creator, creation of people, body and soul, caring for creation, divine Providence

Sacred Scripture: Genesis 1:3–27, 30–31 (creation of people); Matthew 6:30–32 (God's caring love for all creation); Psalm 104:1, 24, 25

Faith Vocabulary: creation, divine Providence

Faith-Filled People: Saint Andrew the Apostle

Our Catholic Faith: Prayers of Blessing

Our Church Makes a Difference: Creation and Our Parish Church

Prayer: Praying a Psalm

CCC: 279–314, 325–349, 355–379

CHAPTER 3 — MARY TRUSTED IN GOD

Faith Concepts: Annunciation, Visitation, Mary's faith and trust in God, Mary's love for God, Magnificat, Incarnation

Sacred Scripture: Luke 1:28, 31, 35 (Annunciation), 46, 47, 49 (Visitation and Magnificat)

Faith Vocabulary: Annunciation, Incarnation

Faith-Filled People: Saint Elizabeth

Our Catholic Faith: Feast Days of Mary

Our Church Makes a Difference: We Honor Mary

Prayer: The Angelus

CCC: 456–478, 484–507

CHAPTER 4 — WOMEN OF FAITH: A SCRIPTURE STORY

Faith Concepts: Sarah, Hannah, Ruth, Queen Esther, the virtue of trust, praying the Scriptures

Sacred Scripture: Exodus 15:1 (Canticle of Moses and Israelites after crossing Red Sea); Esther C:14, 25 (prayer of Queen Esther)

Faith Vocabulary: trust

Our Catholic Faith: Prayer of the Faithful

Our Church Makes a Difference: Blessed Teresa of Calcutta

Prayer: Litany of the Saints

CCC: 101–133, 144–175

CHAPTER 5 — JESUS, THE SON OF GOD

Faith Concepts: The name Jesus, presentation of Jesus in the Temple, Jesus the Messiah and Savior of the world, finding of the child Jesus in the Temple, public ministry of Jesus

Sacred Scripture: Psalm 79:9; Luke 2:30 (proclamation of Simeon), 46–47, 51–52 (finding of Jesus in Temple)

Faith Vocabulary: Jesus, Messiah

Faith-Filled People: Saint Joseph

Our Catholic Faith: Holy Childhood Association

Our Church Makes a Difference: Good News in Action: works of mercy

Prayer: Lord, Have Mercy

CCC: 512–560

CHAPTER 6 — JESUS' DEATH AND RESURRECTION

Faith Concepts: Paschal Mystery, Crucifixion, sacrifice of the cross, Resurrection, Ascension, Way of the Cross

Sacred Scripture: Psalm 33:22; Matthew 27:59–60 (burial of Jesus), 28:1, 5–7 (Resurrection); Luke 23:26, 33–34, 44, 46 (Crucifixion); 24:50–51; John 13:34 (Ascension)

Faith Vocabulary: Paschal Mystery

Faith-Filled People: Joseph of Arimathea

Our Catholic Faith: The Easter Candle

Our Church Makes a Difference: The Way of the Cross

Prayer: Praying the Scriptures

CCC: 599–655

CHAPTER 7 — THE HOLY SPIRIT: A SCRIPTURE STORY

Faith Concepts: Promise to send Holy Spirit; Pentecost; Holy Spirit: Advocate, Helper, Guide; work of Holy Spirit; fruits of Holy Spirit

Sacred Scripture: Ezekiel 36:23, 27 (promise of new heart and new spirit); Acts 2:1–4, 14, 41 (Pentecost)

Faith Vocabulary: Holy Spirit, Pentecost

Our Catholic Faith: Fruits of the Holy Spirit

Our Church Makes a Difference: Signs of the Holy Spirit

Prayer: A prayer to the Holy Spirit

CCC: 687–741

CHAPTER 8 — WE ARE THE CHURCH

Faith Concepts: Founding of the Church; Church as Body of Christ, People of God, and Temple of the Holy Spirit; Apostles; grace; sanctifying grace; Catholic Church; members of the Church

Sacred Scripture: Matthew 28:19–20 (commissioning disciples); 1 Corinthians 6:19 (temples of Holy Spirit); Colossians 3:12, 15, 17

Faith Vocabulary: Apostles, Church

Faith-Filled People: Bishops and Priests

Our Catholic Faith: Works of Mercy

Our Church Makes a Difference: The Holy Spirit in the Church

Prayer: Praying with gestures

CCC: 668–679

CHAPTER 9 — PAUL THE APOSTLE: A SCRIPTURE STORY

Faith Concepts: Saul the Pharisee, Law of Moses, conversion of Saul, faith and work of Paul the Apostle, missionaries

Sacred Scripture: Psalm 9:2; Acts 9:3–6, 8, 17–18 (conversion of Saul on road to Damascus)

Faith Vocabulary: Law of Moses

Our Catholic Faith: Missionaries

Our Church Makes a Difference: Saint John Neumann

Prayer: Memorial acclamation

CCC: 737–741, 787–795, 813–865

CHAPTER 10 — THE COMMUNION OF SAINTS

Faith Concepts: Saints of the Church, feasts of the saints, Communion of Saints, heaven, purgatory, All Saints' Day, All Souls' Day, the one Body of Christ, Saint Charles Lwanga

Sacred Scripture: Psalm 24:5–6; 1 Corinthians 12:12, 27 (Body of Christ)

Faith Vocabulary: saints, Communion of Saints

Faith-Filled People: Souls in Purgatory

Our Catholic Faith: Holy People of God

Our Church Makes a Difference: Our Lady of Guadalupe

Prayer: Prayer of Intercession

CCC: 946–959, 1172–1173, 1402–1405

Unit 2 We Worship (Liturgy and Sacraments)

CHAPTER 11 — THE CHURCH'S YEAR

Faith Concepts: Liturgy and worship of the Church, liturgical year, Advent and Christmas, Lent and Easter, Easter Triduum, Ordinary Time

Sacred Scripture: Psalm 111:1

Faith Vocabulary: worship, liturgy

Faith-Filled People: The Elect

Our Catholic Faith: Liturgical Colors

Our Church Makes a Difference: Feasts of the Lord

Prayer: Signing a prayer of thanksgiving

CCC: 1135–1186

CHAPTER 12 — CELEBRATIONS OF GOD'S LOVE

Faith Concepts: The seven sacraments, Sacraments of Initiation, Baptism, Confirmation, godparents, sponsors

Sacred Scripture: Psalm 66:1–2; Matthew 5:14–16 (disciples of Christ as lights in the world)

Faith Vocabulary: sacraments, Sacraments of Initiation

Faith-Filled People: The Apostles

Our Catholic Faith: Holy Water

Our Church Makes a Difference: Sacramentals

Prayer: A Prayer of Meditation

CCC: 1210–1274, 1285–1314

CHAPTER 13 — WE CELEBRATE THE EUCHARIST

Faith Concepts: Last Supper, sacrament of the Eucharist, Sunday Mass obligation, Liturgy of the Word, Liturgy of the Eucharist, real presence, Blessed Sacrament, sanctuary lamp

Sacred Scripture: Psalm 92:2–3, Matthew 26:26–28 (Last Supper)

Faith Vocabulary: Eucharist, Blessed Sacrament

Faith-Filled People: Blessed Jeanne Jugan

Our Catholic Faith: Precepts of the Church

Our Church Makes a Difference: Holy Days of Obligation

Prayer: Prayer based on preface of Mass

CCC: 1322–1405

CHAPTER 14 — THE PHARISEE AND THE TAX COLLECTOR: A SCRIPTURE STORY

Faith Concepts: Parables, Pharisees and tax collectors in Jesus' time, virtue of humility, divine mercy

Sacred Scripture: Psalm 25:2; Luke 18:10–11, 13 (parable of the Pharisee and the Tax collector)

Faith Vocabulary: parables

Our Catholic Faith: Prayer Gestures

Our Church Makes a Difference: Saint Augustine

Prayer: Lord, Have Mercy

CCC: 546, 2607, 2839

CHAPTER 15 — WE CELEBRATE GOD'S HEALING LOVE

Faith Concepts: Parable of the Forgiving Father, sin, Sacraments of Healing, sacrament of Reconciliation (Penance), sacrament of Anointing of the Sick

Sacred Scripture: Psalm 51:3, Luke 15:16–24 (parable of the Forgiving Father/Prodigal Son)

Faith Vocabulary: sin, Sacraments of Healing

Faith-Filled People: Saint Peter the Apostle

Our Catholic Faith: The Merciful

Our Church Makes a Difference: Pope John Paul II Forgives

Prayer: An Act of Contrition

CCC: 1420–1484, 1499–1525

CHAPTER 16 — THE WEDDING FEAST IN CANA: A SCRIPTURE STORY

Faith Concepts: Weddings in Jesus' time, miracles, the wedding in Cana, miracle of changing water into wine, presence of God and power of God at work in world

Sacred Scripture: Psalm 145:18, John 2:3–11 (wedding in Cana)

Faith Vocabulary: miracle

Our Catholic Faith: Collection at Mass

Our Church Makes a Difference: Signs of God's Love

Prayer: A Prayer for Families

CCC: 156, 515, 547–549, 1335

CHAPTER 17 — THE SACRAMENTS OF SERVICE

Faith Concepts: Last Supper teaching on service; vocation; Sacraments at the Service of Communion; sacrament of Holy Orders; ministry of bishops, priests, and deacons; sacrament of Matrimony; vocation of Christian married spouses

Sacred Scripture: Psalm 119:34; John 13:4–5, 15 (washing of feet at Last Supper)

Faith Vocabulary: Holy Orders, Matrimony

Faith-Filled People: Deacons

Our Catholic Faith: The Pope

Our Church Makes a Difference: Catholic Relief Services

Prayer: A prayer of intercession

CCC: 1533–1589, 1601–1658

Unit 3 We Live (Christian Morality)

CHAPTER 18 — JESUS TEACHES US HOW TO LOVE: A SCRIPTURE STORY

Faith Concepts: Adam and Eve, the Covenant, original sin, Great Commandment, love of enemies

Sacred Scripture: Psalm 119:33, Matthew 22:35–40 (Great Commandment)

Faith Vocabulary: Covenant, Great Commandment

Our Catholic Faith: Virtues

Our Church Makes a Difference: Teaching Communities

Prayer: Act of Love

CCC: 54–67, 2052–2055, 2083

CHAPTER 19 — THE TEN COMMANDMENTS TEACH US TO LOVE

Faith Concepts: Abraham and Moses; Ten Commandments; First Commandment: love God above all else; Second Commandment: respect name of God, use name of God truthfully; Third Commandment: Sunday Mass obligation; divine love: love of Father, Son, and Holy Spirit

Sacred Scripture: Psalm 1:1–2; Exodus 20:2–3 (First Commandment), 20:7 (Second Commandment), 20:8 (Third Commandment)

Faith Vocabulary: Ten Commandments

Faith-Filled People: Saint John the Apostle

Our Catholic Faith: Cathedrals

Our Church Makes a Difference: Churches

Prayer: Prayer of Adoration

CCC: 218–221, 253–256, 2084–2132, 2142–2159, 2168–2188

CHAPTER 20 — WE LOVE AND RESPECT ONE ANOTHER

Faith Concepts: Fourth, Fifth, Sixth, Seventh, Eighth, Ninth, and Tenth Commandments; obedience and respect of parents; caring for one's health; respecting our bodies and those of others; treating people justly and fairly; being honest and truthful; respecting families; sharing our blessings

Sacred Scripture: Psalm 119:10, Exodus: 20:12–18 (Fourth through Tenth Commandments)

Faith Vocabulary: obey, covet

Faith-Filled People: Saint Frances Cabrini

Our Catholic Faith: The Christian Family

Our Church Makes a Difference: Our Parish Family

Prayer: We Pray for Others

CCC: 2196, 2217–2246, 2258–2317, 2331–2391, 2401–2449, 2464–2503, 2514–2527, 2534–2550

CHAPTER 21 — THE PSALMS AND STEWARDSHIP: A SCRIPTURE STORY

Faith Concepts: Psalms, types of psalms, Psalm 104, caring for God's world, stewards of creation

Sacred Scripture: Psalm 67:6, 7; 104:1, 10–12, 24, 31, 33; 150:3–6

Faith Vocabulary: Psalms, stewards

Our Catholic Faith: Mealtime Prayers

Our Church Makes a Difference: Christian Farmers

Prayer: A prayer of praise based on Psalm 150

CCC: 716, 1176–1177, 2534–2550

CHAPTER 22 — GOD SHARES HIS LIFE WITH US

Faith Concepts: Sanctifying grace, actual grace, temptation, human body and soul, eternal life, heaven and hell

Sacred Scripture: Psalm 27:13; Luke 14:16, 18–21, 23 (parable of the Great Feast); John 14:2–3 ("In my Father's house there are many dwelling places.")

Faith Vocabulary: grace, heaven

Faith-Filled People: Patron Saints

Our Catholic Faith: Incense

Our Church Makes a Difference: The Funeral Mass

Prayer: Act of Hope

CCC: 1020–1050, 1716–1724, 1997–2016

Unit 4 We Pray (Prayer)

CHAPTER 23 — JESUS TEACHES US TO PRAY

Faith Concepts: The prayer of Jesus, the Our Father, Abba, praying alone and with others

Sacred Scripture: Psalm 5:2, 3; Matthew 6:9 (Our Father); Luke 23:34, 46 (Jesus' prayer of forgiveness at Crucifixion)

Faith Vocabulary: personal prayer, public prayer

Faith-Filled People: Saint Teresa of the Andes

Our Catholic Faith: Churches

Our Church Makes a Difference: A People of Prayer

Prayer: Our Father

CCC: 2558–2567, 2598–2619, 2700–2719

CHAPTER 24 — THE CHURCH IS A PEOPLE OF PRAYER

Faith Concepts: Prayers of petition and intercession, prayers of blessing and adoration, prayers of praise and thanksgiving

Sacred Scripture: Psalm 92:2, Matthew 18:20 (where two or more are gathered Jesus is there), Luke 17:15–16 (healed leper alone thanks to Jesus)

Faith Vocabulary: prayers of petition, prayers of intercession

Faith-Filled People: Blessed Damien of Molokai

Our Catholic Faith: Liturgy of the Hours

Our Church Makes a Difference: Prayer Groups

Prayer: Divine Praises

CCC: 2598–2691

CHAPTER 25 — WE PROFESS OUR FAITH

Faith Concepts: Holy Spirit, creeds of the Church, profession of faith at Mass, Nicene Creed, Apostles' Creed

Sacred Scripture: Psalm 106:12; Romans 8:26 (Holy Spirit and prayer); 1 Corinthians 12:3 (Holy Spirit and prayer)

Faith Vocabulary: creeds, Apostles' Creed

Faith-Filled People: Saint Paul the Apostle

Our Catholic Faith: Baptism Promises

Our Church Makes a Difference: Living What We Believe

Prayer: You Are God! (Te Deum)

CCC: 2650–2672

CHAPTER 26 — THE HAIL MARY: A SCRIPTURE STORY

Faith Concepts: Messiah, Annunciation, Visitation, Hail Mary, meaning of name of Mary, Mary the Mother of God

Sacred Scripture: Luke 1:30 (Annunciation), 41–42, 46–49, 56 (Visitation and Magnificat)

Faith Vocabulary: Visitation, Hail Mary

Our Catholic Faith: The Rosary

Our Church Makes a Difference: Say Yes to God

Prayer: Mary's Prayer

CCC: 2673–2679

Catholic Prayers and Practices

Sign of the Cross • Glory Prayer • Lord's Prayer • Prayer to the Holy Spirit • Hail Mary • Act of Contrition • Apostles' Creed • Nicene Creed • Morning Prayer • Evening Prayer • Grace Before Meals • Grace After Meals • A Vocation Prayer • The Beatitudes • Corporal Works of Mercy • Spiritual Works of Mercy • The Ten Commandments • The Great Commandment • Precepts of the Church • Rosary • Stations of the Cross • The Seven Sacraments • We Celebrate the Mass • Sacrament of Reconciliation

We Celebrate the Liturgical Seasons

The Liturgical Year
The seasons of the Church's year.

Ordinary Time
The Church's year, liturgical colors.

The Season of Advent
First Week: Jesse tree, ancestors of Jesus. **Second Week:** John the Baptist, the coming of Christ in glory. **Third Week:** Promise of the prophets Jeremiah and Isaiah, Jesus the Messiah. **Fourth Week:** The announcement of the birth of Jesus, the Savior of the world, to Mary.

The Season of Christmas
First Week of Christmas: The birth of the newborn King and Savior, the shepherds. **Second Week of Christmas:** Jesus the Savior of the world, the Magi, the presentation in the Temple.

The Season of Lent
First Week: Preparing for Easter and the welcoming of new members into the Church. **Second Week:** Lenten discipline of praying, fasting, and almsgiving. **Third Week:** Pray always, spending time with God alone. **Fourth Week:** A time for sharing our blessings and making a difference. **Fifth Week:** Celebrating Reconciliation, the gift of peace and forgiveness.

Holy Week
Palm Sunday of the Lord's Passion: Hosanna, Jesus' final entry into Jerusalem. **Triduum/Holy Thursday:** Holy Thursday, the beginning of the Triduum; the Last Supper, the institution of the Eucharist, the washing of the disciples' feet, and the call to service. **Triduum/Good Friday:** The Crucifixion, Jesus' prayer of forgiveness. **Triduum/Easter:** Celebrating Easter, Alleluia, Christians as Easter people.

The Season of Easter
Second Week: Witnesses for Christ, appearances of the Risen Christ to the disciples in Emmaus and to Thomas the Apostle. **Third Week:** Jesus the Good Shepherd, the Christian ministry of service. **Fourth Week:** The newly baptized, the Eucharist, Christians as lights in the world. **Fifth Week:** Love one another, putting faith into action. **Sixth Week:** The early Church grows, life in the early Church. **Seventh Week:** Sharing the Gospel with others. **Pentecost:** Work of the Holy Spirit in the Church, Saint Peter's proclamation of Jesus.

Who Are My Third Graders?

Catechesis based on different age groups is an essential task of the Christian community.
GENERAL DIRECTORY FOR CATECHESIS 171

You and your third graders can have an exciting and meaningful year together. The faith of eight-year-olds is expanding as is their ability to think logically, to make connections between events, and to understand the feelings and point of view of others. Their enthusiasm for life is unmatched. Eights welcome new challenges. They have a growing sense of competence and independence. They can do their homework, complete chores, read for enjoyment, and carry on a conversation.

Growing as Catholics

Third graders are at an exciting time in their development. More independent than in previous years, they can develop a deeper appreciation for Scripture, liturgy, community and prayer. Though they cannot yet think in abstract terms, they can understand and apply Jesus' teaching to their lives and become involved in efforts that will help them recognize their own unique gifts and their role in the Christian community.

For Reflection

What do you recall about yourself as a third grader? What experiences had you had? What did you enjoy doing?

What will be the most enjoyable aspects of serving as a catechist to third graders? What will be most challenging?

For Further Study

See Echoes of Faith "Introduction to the Learner" *module.*

Physical Characteristics

- Enjoy participating in sports, dance or gymnastics and are involved in these activities after school
- Wide variations in physical growth from child to child
- Enjoy active play during free time

Cognitive/Learning Skills

- May become frustrated if his or her work does not live up to expectations
- Enjoy figuring out solutions to problems
- Predominance of literal thinking over abstract reasoning
- Enjoy learning facts in entertaining ways, such as games and puzzles

Relationships

- Heightened interest in being a member of a group and a community
- Increasing importance of peer relationships
- May be very competitive
- Enjoy cooperative learning tasks

Religious Growth

- Understand and appreciate the community dimension of sacramental celebrations
- Enjoy stories from the Acts of the Apostles
- Inspired by Jesus' Law of Love to incorporate good works in everyday life
- Enjoy having a role in liturgical experiences
- Identify with the dramatic action and vivid images in the stories of Jesus
- Like active community service
- Relate to saints as role models who stand for morality, justice, and faith
- Comfortable with a variety of prayer forms

How Do Children Learn?

Many Gifts, One Lord

There are different kinds of spiritual gifts but the same Spirit; there are different forms of service but the same Lord.

1 CORINTHIANS 12:4–5

How do you prefer to learn new things? Do you like to attend a lecture or watch one on TV? Do you like to read novels or see movies and reflect on the life messages they hold? When you cook, do you follow a recipe or learn through trial and error? Do you just want the facts, or do you like open-ended questions with lots of possibilities? The way in which you answer these questions tells a lot about how you prefer to learn and express yourself. You may prefer to learn by listening, by seeing, by imagining, or by doing. Children, as well, have preferred ways of learning that educators call learning styles.

But there is another way to think about learning. Learning preferences may reflect only our "comfort zones." According to a popular theory, each of us is born with at least eight different ways of processing and responding to new information. A well-known theorist, Howard Gardner, calls them "multiple intelligences." You might think of them as eight different ways of being smart. All of us possess each of these kinds of "smart" in one degree or another. The particular combination that we have is one of the things that makes each of us unique. One or several of them is probably dominant in each of us.

Some children learn and express their ideas best through words, others by thinking things out or putting them in categories, and still others learn by using their bodies. Some learn and express themselves best when things are presented in a musical or rhythmic way. Some are best at writing and quiet, self-directed activities, others at group activity or sharing. Still others learn best through their contact with nature, through field trips, or by nurturing plants and animals.

In religious formation, as in classroom education, attention to the variety of gifts among the children will help them grow in an understanding of their faith and deepen their relationship with God. *Faith First* presents you with many different strategies to honor the gifts that already exist in your learners and to encourage them to express themselves in new ways. Here are some activities that support the different ways that children can learn about and express their relationship with God and one another.

Language- and Music-Related Activities

- Researching word meanings
- Word games and puzzles
- Reading and Bible search activities
- Storytelling and journal writing
- Learning hymns and Mass responses
- Writing prayers or songs
- Using background music for activities

Object-Related Activities

- Learning "how many?" of different categories: sacraments, Apostles, and so on
- Celebrating Church seasons
- "You are there" activities placing oneself in the action of a Bible story
- Using maps and models
- Graphic organizers to display information visually
- Posters and "designing" activities
- Crafts and classroom dramas
- Using gestures with songs and prayers
- Expressing response through dance
- Nurturing plants and animals
- Creating gardens or nature areas on parish grounds

Person-Related Activities

- Cooperative group learning activities
- Peer tutoring and sharing
- Teaching other students
- Games and simulations
- Quiet prayer times
- Writing and drawing in journals
- Creating autobiographies
- Self-assessment activities

For Reflection

What kinds of activities did you enjoy most as a child?

What kinds of activities are you most comfortable leading? What is a new kind of activity you would be willing to try with the children?

For Further Study

The Echoes of Faith *"Methods for Grades 3 and 4" module demonstrates a variety of classroom activities that you will enjoy leading.*

What Is a Good Climate for Catechesis?

When he saw the crowds, he went up the mountain, and after he had sat down, his disciples came to him. He began to teach them. MATTHEW 5:1–2

Through the centuries, good catechists have taught outdoors under trees, in churches, and in public places. Jesus taught seated on hillsides, walking along roads, and at dinner tables. Twenty-first-century catechists in the United States most often teach in classrooms, in homes, or in parish halls or meeting rooms. No matter how simple your space, here are some things you can do to improve the environment for good catechesis.

- **Your Prayer Center.** This is the heart of your catechetical space. You will gather the children in the prayer center each week when you pray with them. If others use your catechetical space during the week, you may wish to carry your prayer center materials in a box or plastic crate. Here are some suggestions:

- Cover the table with an attractive cloth that matches the color of the liturgical season.

- Place a crucifix at the highest point in the prayer center.

- Place a candle on the surface as a sign of the light of faith. (Light the candle only during the prayer service. Use an electric candle if fire regulations require it.)

- Enthrone an open Bible on the table. The opening lesson in your student book includes a prayer service for enthroning the Bible on the first day of class.

- Place a plant or other objects in the prayer center to symbolize the lesson themes.

- **Supplies.** Most catechists say that the most convenient way to carry their weekly supplies is in a plastic crate. Here is a checklist of typical supplies:
  - Catechist guide
  - Materials for prayer center
  - Special art supplies for scheduled activities
  - Visual aids, either packaged or those you have created
  - Your own chalk, eraser, markers, scissors, extra pencils
  - Copies of handouts, markers, and pencils for children

> ### For Reflection
> *What can I do to create a climate for prayer in my teaching space?*
>
> *How can I make my teaching space an inviting climate for catechesis?*

> ### For Further Study
> *The* Echoes of Faith *"Getting Started as a Catechist" module offers wonderful and varied ideas for creating an inviting teaching space and an attractive prayer center.*

- **Your Teaching Space.** Before your first class, visit your teaching space and evaluate its strengths and limitations. Learn the answers to these questions:
  - Is your space shared with a Catholic school teacher? If so, meet with him or her and try to build a spirit of cooperation.
  - Are chairs, desks, and tables of an appropriate size? See if it is permissible to move them. If the floor is uncarpeted, consider a stack of carpet squares to provide alternative seating for storytelling and sharing activities.
  - Can you adjust lighting and temperature for comfort?
  - Does the room have a chalkboard, a dry-erase board, or newsprint? Will you need to provide chalk or markers?
  - Find out if you will be allowed to tape or staple posters or other materials to walls or bulletin boards. Can you leave materials from week to week, or must you remove them after each class?
  - What electronic media equipment is available? Take some time to learn how to use any unfamiliar items.

Resource Bibliography

Church Documents

Abbot, Walter M., S.J., gen. ed. *The Documents of Vatican II*. New York: Herder and Herder, 1966.

Congregation for the Clergy. *General Directory for Catechesis*. Vatican City: Libreria Editrice Vaticana, 1997.

Connell, Martin, ed. *The Catechetical Documents: A Parish Resource*. Chicago: Liturgy Training Publications, 1996.

A Family Perspective in Church and Society: Tenth Anniversary Edition. Washington, DC: United States Catholic Conference, 1998.

Go and Make Disciples: A National Plan and Strategy for Catholic Evangelization in the United States. Washington, DC: National Conference of Catholic Bishops, 1999.

Hoffman, Elizabeth, ed. *The Liturgy Documents, volume 1*. Chicago: Liturgy Training Publications, 1991.

Lysik, David A., ed. *The Bible Documents*. Chicago: Liturgy Training Publications, 2001.

———. *The Liturgy Documents, volume 2*. Chicago: Liturgy Training Publications, 1999.

National Conference of Catholic Bishops. *Sharing the Light of Faith: National Catechetical Directory for Catholics of the United States*. Washington, DC: USCC, 1979.

Our Hearts Were Burning Within Us: A Pastoral Plan for Adult Faith Formation in the United States. Washington, DC: United States Catholic Conference, 1999.

Pope John Paul II. *Redemptoris Missio* (The Mission of the Redeemer).

Sharing Catholic Social Teaching: Challenges and Directions. Washington, DC: United States Catholic Conference, 1998.

Trouvé, Marianne Lorraine, ed. *Mother of the Christ, Mother of the Church: Papal Documents on the Blessed Virgin Mary*. Boston: Pauline Books, 2001.

Theological Resources

Bokenkotter, Thomas. *A Concise History of the Catholic Church*. New York: Doubleday, 2004.

Cameli, Louis J. *Going to God Together: A Spirituality of Communion*. Notre Dame, IN: Ave Maria Press, 2002.

Groome, Thomas H. *What Makes Us Catholic: Eight Gifts for Life*. San Francisco: HarperSanFrancisco, 2003.

Himes, Michael J. *The Mystery of Faith: An Introduction to Catholicism*. Cincinnati, OH: St. Anthony Messenger Press, 2004.

Huebsch, Bill. *The General Directory for Catechesis in Plain English*. Mystic, CT: Twenty-third Publications, 2001.

McKenzie, John, S.J. *Dictionary of the Bible*. New York: Macmillan, 1965. (Reprint edition: Touchstone Books, 1995.)

Catechetical Resources

Akin, Terri, and Dianne Schilling. *Everybody Wins! 100 Games Children Should Play*. Jalmar Press. (Available through Pro-Ed., Inc., Austin, TX)

Arbuckle, Gerald A. *Earthing the Gospel: An Inculturation Handbook for the Pastoral Worker*. Maryknoll, NY: Orbis Books, 1990.

Armstrong, Thomas. *Multiple Intelligences in the Classroom*. Arlington, VA: ASCD, 1994.

Cahill, Thomas. *The Gifts of the Jews*. New York: Doubleday, 1998.

Campbell, Anne, Kathryn Waite, and Anne Mikelonis. *Creative Crafts for All Seasons: Projects That Help Kids Learn*. Allen, TX: RCL • Resources for Christian Living, 1999.

Campbell, Anne, et. al. *The Faith-Filled Classroom: Top 10 Ideas That Really Work*. Allen, TX: RCL • Resources for Christian Living, 1999.

Cavaletti, Sofia, et. al. *The Religious Potential of the Child: Experiencing Scripture and Liturgy with Young Children*. Chicago: Liturgy Training Publications, 1993.

Coles, Robert, Ph.D. *The Spiritual Life of Children*. Boston: Houghton-Mifflin, 1990.

Costello, Gwen. *School Year Activities for Religion Classes*. Mystic, CT: Twenty-third Publications, 2000.

Cronin, Gaynell Bordes. *Friend Jesus: Prayers for Children (Guiding Children into Daily Prayer)*. Cincinnati, OH: St. Anthony Messenger Press, 1999.

Drew, Naomi. *Learning the Skills of Peacemaking: A K–6 Activity Guide on Resolving Conflict, Communicating, Cooperating*. Jalmar Press. (Available through Pro-Ed, Inc., Austin, TX)

Dues, Greg. *Catholic Customs & Traditions: A Popular Guide*. Mystic, CT: Twenty-third Publications, 1990.

Duggan, Robert. *Teaching Kids the Basics of Liturgy: Making Rituals More Meaningful*. Allen, TX: RCL • Resources for Christian Living, 1999.

Florian, Amy. *Sign & Symbol, Word and Song*. Notre Dame, IN: Ave Maria Press, 2001.

Gallagher, Maureen. *The Art of Catechesis: What You Need to Be, Know, and Do*. Mahwah, NJ: Paulist Press, 1998.

Gardner, Howard. *Intelligence Reframed: Multiple Intelligences for the 21st Century*. New York: Basic Books, 2000.

Gargiulo, Barbara. *How Do I Talk to God? Prayers for the School Year*. Allen, TX: RCL • Resources for Christian Living, 1999.

Gather Comprehensive. Chicago: GIA Publications, 1994.

Huebsch, Bill. *A Handbook for Success in Whole Community Catechesis*. Mystic, CT: Twenty-third Publications, 2004.

———. *Whole Community Catechesis in Plain English*. Mystic, CT: Twenty-third Publications, 2002.

Jambor, Mary Beth. *Helping Kids Live Their Faith: Service Projects That Make a Difference*. Allen, TX: RCL • Resources for Christian Living, 1999.

MacDonald, Margaret Read. *The Storyteller's Start-up book*. Little Rock, AR: August House Publishers, 1993.

Mazer, Peter. *School Year, Church Year: Activities and Decorations for the Classroom*. Chicago: Liturgy Training Publications, 2001.

McGrath, Eileen, Ph.D. *Kids Get Stressed Too: Understanding What's Going On and How to Help*. Allen, TX: RCL • Resources for Christian Living, 1999.

Mongoven, Anne Marie. *The Prophetic Voice in Catechesis*. Mahwah, NJ: Paulist Press, 2000.

Palomares, Susanna. *Lessons in Tolerance and Diversity*. Jalmar Press. (Available through Pro-Ed, Inc., Austin, TX)

Rotunno, Jo McClure. *Heritage of Faith: A Framework for Whole Community Catechesis*. Mystic, CT: Twenty-third Publications, 2004.

Singing Our Faith: A Hymnal for Young Catholics. Chicago: GIA Publications, 2001. (Accompaniment book also available.)

Vasiloff, Barbara C. *Teaching Self-Discipline to Children: 15 Essential Skills*. Mystic, CT: Twenty-third Publications, 2003.

faith first

Legacy Edition
PARISH

Grade Three

RESOURCES FOR CHRISTIAN LIVING®

www.FaithFirst.com

NIHIL OBSTAT
Reverend Robert M. Coerver
Censor Librorum
IMPRIMATUR
† Most Rev. Charles V. Grahmann
Bishop of Dallas
September 1, 2004

The Nihil Obstat and Imprimatur are official declarations that the material reviewed is free of doctrinal or moral error. No implication is contained therein that those granting the Nihil Obstat and Imprimatur agree with the contents, opinions, or statements expressed.

ACKNOWLEDGMENTS

Scripture excerpts are taken or adapted from the *New American Bible with Revised New Testament and Psalms* Copyright © 1991, 1986, 1970, Confraternity of Christian Doctrine, Washington, DC. Used with permission. All rights reserved. No part of the *New American Bible* may be reproduced by any means without the permission of the copyright owner.

Excerpts are taken or adapted from the English translation of the *Roman Missal* © 1973, International Committee on English in the Liturgy, Inc. (ICEL); the English translation of the Act of Contrition from *Rite of Penance* © 1974, ICEL; the English translation of *Rite of Confirmation, Second Edition* © 1975, ICEL; excerpts from the English translation of *A Book of Prayers* © 1982, ICEL; excerpts from the English translation of *Book of Blessings* © 1988, ICEL. All rights reserved.

Excerpts are taken or adapted from the English translation of *Gloria Patri*, The Nicene Creed, The Apostles' Creed, *Sanctus*, and *Agnus Dei*, by the International Consultation on English Texts (ICET).

Photograph and Illustration Credits appear on page 304.

2

Faith First Legacy Edition Development Team

Developing a religion program requires the gifts and talents of many individuals working together as a team. RCL is proud to acknowledge the contributions of these dedicated people.

Program Theology Consultants
Reverend Louis J. Cameli, S.T.D.
Reverend Robert D. Duggan, S.T.D.

Advisory Board
Judith Deckers, M.Ed.
Elaine McCarron, SCN, M.Div.
Marina Herrera, Ph.D.
Reverend Frank McNulty, S.T.D.
Reverend Ronald J. Nuzzi, Ph.D.

National Catechetical Advisor
Jacquie Jambor

Catechetical Specialist
Jo Rotunno

Contributing Writers
Student Book and Catechist Guide
Christina DeCamp
Judith Deckers
Mary Beth Jambor
Marianne K. Lenihan
Michele Norfleet

Art & Design Director
Lisa Brent

Electronic Page Makeup
Laura Fremder

Production Director
Jenna Nelson

Designers/Photo Research
Pat Bracken
Kristy O. Howard
Susan Smith

Project Editors
Patricia A. Classick
Steven M. Ellair
Ronald C. Lamping

Web Site Producers
Joseph Crisalli
Demere Henson

General Editor
Ed DeStefano

President/Publisher
Maryann Nead

3

Contents

5

6

We Pray

Dear God,

We think third grade will be great. Thank you for creating my friends, my family, and me. Help us show our faith in all that we do. Help us know you better each day. Amen.

Welcome to Faith First!

My Friends, My Family, and Me

Write your answers. Then tell your answers to someone you do not know very well.

My name is _____.

My friends call me _____.

I live with _____.

My family and I have the most fun when we

_____.

A game I like to play with my friends is

_____.

My favorite story is

_____.

The thing I like best about my church is

_____.

7

TO THE CATECHIST

Creating an inviting environment is an important part of everything you do with young children. Before your first meeting, prepare name tags for the children. Greet each child as they arrive. This will help them feel safe and ready to learn. This first session provides the opportunity for you to get to know the children. By setting realistic expectations, introducing them to their new books, and creating an atmosphere of prayer and hospitality, the children will know they are welcome.

INVITE

- Have the children hold hands and pray the opening prayer after you.
- Give each child a name tag and have them write on it a name they like to be called.
- Ask the children to open their books to page 7 and write their answers in the "My Friends, My Family, and Me" activity.
- Have the children draw something from the activity about themselves on their name tag.
- Ask volunteers to share some of the things they wrote or drew about themselves.

Teaching Tip

Getting to Know Your Children. This opening session provides you with the first opportunity to discover the talents and gifts of your children. It is only a beginning. Each week talk with the children about the exciting moments in their young lives and the fun things they do with their family and friends. It is important to affirm each child every session. Make this one of your goals.

DISCOVER AND INVOLVE

- Introduce the book and allow the children to look through it and find a favorite picture.
- Have them share their favorite picture with the child beside them.
- Tell the children that they will now join with a partner to complete the activity on pages 8 and 9. Let them know that you will help them.
- Have the children read "Learning About the Catholic Church."
- Read to the group the "We Believe" activity. Have them turn to page 81 and find the name of an American missionary who made a difference. Have everyone write the name on the bottom step in the activity.
- Have the children read the question and clue in the "We Worship" activity on page 9 and then turn to pages 147 and 148 to find the names of the two sacraments.
- Ask volunteers to share their discovery.
- Have everyone write the names of the sacraments on the lines on page 9.

Learning About the Catholic Church

The Church is like a house of faith. In each of the rooms we can learn more about what Catholics believe, how we celebrate, how Jesus calls us to live, and how we pray. Do the activity on these pages to discover some things we will learn about this year.

We Believe

Saint Paul the Apostle was an early Christian. He was a missionary who traveled to many places to spread the Good News.

Look on page 81. Find the name of an American missionary who made a difference. Write his name on the bottom step.

8

Saint John Neumann

Teaching Tip

Setting Expectations. The children will be curious about what they will be doing during the sessions. They will also want and need to know what you expect of them. There are many ways to set expectations. One way is to create signs using the colors red, yellow, and green. Whenever you put up the red sign, the children know they need to stop and be quiet. The yellow sign reminds them that they are learning something new and need to listen. The green sign means it is all right to talk with one another about the questions or activity. Use the signs as a reminder when the children seem to be losing focus.

We Worship

One way to worship God is to continue Jesus' work on earth. Two of the Church's sacraments help Christians serve the whole Church.

Look on pages 147 and 148. Write the names of the two sacraments on the lines below.

Holy Orders

Matrimony

We Live

Our whole parish family helps to continue Jesus' work on earth through acts of service.

Look on page 177. Write two things that parishes do on the To Do list. Put a check next to one that you or your family could do.

To Do

☐ ___Responses will vary.___

___Affirm appropriate___

☐ ___responses.___

___

We Pray

Catholics pray alone, with one another, with their families, and at Mass. The Hail Mary is a special Catholic prayer.

Look on page 227. Find out what Bible story the Hail Mary helps us remember. Write the name of the story and the two characters here.

Title: The Visitation

Characters: Mary ___

Elizabeth

9

DISCOVER AND INVOLVE

- Work with the children on the "We Live" activity.
- Have the children read page 177 in their books. Then have them complete the "We Live" activity.
- Ask the children to share their responses with a partner.
- Have the children focus on the "We Pray" activity and read the question.
- Have them turn to page 227 and discover what Bible story the Hail Mary helps us remember.
- Give them time to write the title and characters in the spaces on page 9 in their books.
- Choose volunteers to read each question and share what answer they have written in the box. This will help you make sure everyone has the correct answers.

Teaching Tip

Knowing Your Learners. Remember that everything you do with the children helps you get to know them a little more. You will have many opportunities during the sessions to get to know their learning styles, talents and gifts. Observing each of the children working in the total group, in small groups, or with a partner will help you plan your lessons and meet the needs of all the children.

PRAY

- Invite the children to prepare for prayer. Reverently hold a Bible slightly above your head and lead them in procession to the prayer space.
- Teach the children to echo, or repeat after you, the parts of the prayer marked "All."
- After a moment of silence, pray the prayer. Use a hand signal to invite the children to join in when you want them to echo their parts of the prayer.
- After the prayer, place the Bible on the prayer table and reverence it by slightly bowing your head. Invite each child to come forward and do the same.
- Thank the children for being good learners and remind them to have a fun week.

A Community of Believers

LEADER: Lord, we gather to listen to your word. Help us remember how to live as members of your Church.

ALL: **Your word is truth and life.**

LEADER: A reading from the Acts of the Apostles.

The community of believers was of one heart and mind. They followed the Apostles and respected them. Everyone shared everything they had with those in need. One of the early Christians, Barnabas, sold his land and gave the money to the Apostles to help Christians in need.

Based on Acts of the Apostles 2:42, 45–47

The word of the Lord.

ALL: **Thanks be to God.**
Come forward and reverence the Bible by bowing before it.

10

Teaching Tip

Creating a Prayer Space. Having a prayer space that is decorated in a special way will help the children realize the importance of prayer. Display the Bible in your prayer space in such a way that shows its importance. Talk about respecting the Bible. Always hold the Bible reverently when you proclaim God's word. Before you pray together, allow a moment of quiet time and share with the group that God is with them.

A Catechist's Prayer

Gracious God, I ask for your blessing as I begin this year as a catechist. I wonder if I am up to the task. Yet I am inspired by my ancestors in faith who also were surprised by God.

Give me the **courage** of Abraham and Sarah, who did not hesitate when God called them to a new land. With them as my models, surely I can face a class of energetic children once a week!

Let me be a **liberator** like Moses, setting children free from their fears and giving them the hope that comes from believing in a Provident God.

Give me the **wisdom** of Samuel to listen more than I speak. Remind me to allow the moments of silence that permit children to reflect on you.

Give me the **patience** of Job, so that when the children get beyond me, or my best-laid plans fall flat, I can believe that the next week will be better.

Give me the **justice** of Amos, so that I will challenge the children to take up the work of building your kingdom of justice and peace here on earth.

Give me the **faith** of Joseph, so that I can be a model of faith to the children in my care. Let the children learn what faith is, not only from the definition I teach them, but from the witness of my life.

Give me the **humility** of Mary, so that I will remember that you are the source of any good I do. Help me create a loving, fair, and secure environment for the sharing of faith, as Mary and Joseph did for the child Jesus.

Give me the **hospitality** of Martha and Mary, joyfully welcoming the children each week. Help me remember to be, like Mary, a prayerful person who listens to your will for me. But like Martha, help me also to do the practical work that ensures a successful session.

Give me the **enthusiasm** of Mary Magdalene, the first witness to the Resurrection. Help me enter my classroom each week with the same passion to share the good news of the Risen Lord.

Above all, let me never waver in my **respect** for the dignity of each child that you have entrusted to my care. Let me teach as your Son did, listening to them, and allowing them to grow in the ways that are best for them.

With your **love**, the example of your Son, and the power of the Holy Spirit, I think I am ready to begin!

Amen.

Unit 1 Opener

The unit opener pages are designed to assess, through a variety of questioning techniques, the children's prior knowledge about the key faith concepts presented in the unit. Processing these pages should not take more than ten or fifteen minutes.

USING ILLUSTRATIONS

Pictures help stimulate the religious imaginations of the children. The first page of the unit opener contains pictures that illustrate some of the important concepts in the unit.

- Invite the children to look at and think about the pictures.
- Ask volunteers to describe what each picture says to them.
- Invite the children to share a response to the question.

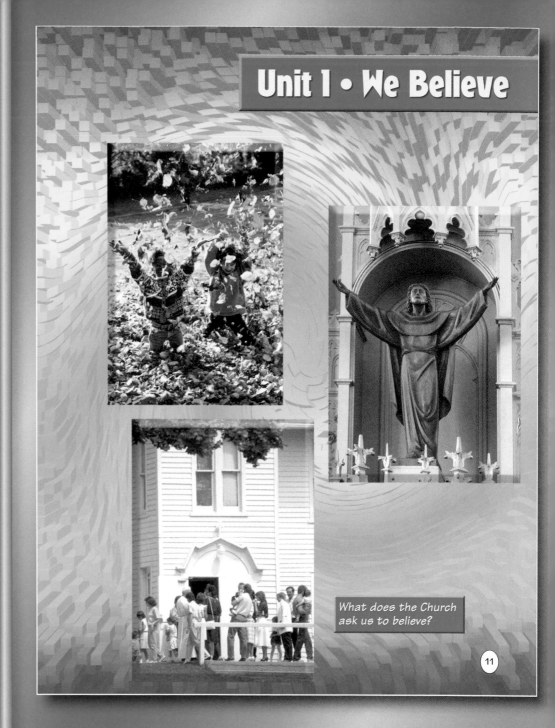

Unit 1 • We Believe

What does the Church ask us to believe?

11

Teaching Tip

Importance of Prior Knowledge. Most of the children come to their religion class with prior faith knowledge and experiences. You will want to draw on their experiences to help them build new understandings of their faith. By starting with the children's knowledge, you show them that you respect and value their thinking. There are many techniques to assess prior knowledge. Pictures, questions, the use of vocabulary, and Scripture stories have been incorporated on these pages to encourage the children to share what they already know.

Getting Ready

What I Have Learned

What is something you already know about these three faith words?

The Holy Trinity

Responses will vary.

_____

Jesus' death and Resurrection

Responses will vary.

_____

The Church

Responses will vary.

_____

Words to Know

Put an X next to the faith words you know. Put a ? next to the faith words you need to know more about.

Faith Words   Responses will vary.

_____ faith

_____ Holy Trinity

_____ divine Providence

_____ Incarnation

_____ Messiah

_____ Paschal Mystery

_____ Pentecost

_____ Church

12

Questions I Have

What questions would you like to ask about the Church?

Responses will vary.

_____

_____

A Scripture Story

The coming of the Holy Spirit

How did the Holy Spirit help the disciples?

Affirm appropriate responses.

GETTING READY

The "Getting Ready" page engages the children in sharing prior knowledge and aids you in planning your lessons to meet their needs.

What I Have Learned

Read the concepts to the children and ask volunteers to share ideas they have about each concept.

Words to Know

Read each faith term to the group. Have them put an X next to the terms they know and a ? next to the ones they may need to learn more about.

Questions I Have

• Invite the children to ask questions they have about the Church.

• Write their questions on a chart.

A Scripture Story

The story of the coming of the Holy Spirit is one of the Scripture stories in this unit. Have the children look at the picture and answer the question.

Teaching Tip

Ready, Set, Go. The unit opener pages provide you with new insights into how to plan for your lessons. As you observe the children working through the parts of the unit opener, make notes to yourself on the differences in their prior knowledge. Plan new strategies to build on their prior knowledge. Feel confident that you can help the children grow in their faith. Make teaching the children a joy in your life. You are ready to begin. As you work through the unit, you can refer back to the chart and ask volunteers to try to answer the questions the children have.

God Speaks to Us

The Word of God

To understand the importance of Sacred Scripture in the life of faith, we need to dwell on the phrase "the word of God." What does this phrase really mean?

The root of the phrase "the word of God" is the Hebrew word *dabar*. If we opened a Hebrew-English dictionary, we would see that *dabar* translates into "word." What we may not catch by reading a translation of the word *dabar* is that for the Hebrews, *dabar* is a very dynamic word. It includes the concept of "word" being a living and active communication of the person who speaks.

In the Judeo-Christian faith tradition, we understand the word of God as God's communication of himself. No wonder we reverence the Scripture in liturgy. No wonder we use phrases like "being nourished by the word of God." God's Revelation of himself in Scripture creates, produces, and ultimately redeems us.

The Revelation of God to humankind is not merely a long-ago event. While nothing essential has been added to the content of Revelation since the death of the last Apostle, we continue, even today, to deepen our understanding of that unique Revelation.

The God who spoke in the past continues to converse with the Church.

The Living Heart of Church Teaching

Sacred Scripture is food for our souls. Both the Old Testament and the New Testament are fonts from which we draw strength for nourishing our faith. For this reason the Second Vatican Council urged that all members of the Church are to have wide access to the Sacred Scriptures.

The Constitution *Dei Verbum* of the Second Vatican Council emphasizes the fundamental importance of Sacred Scripture in the Church's life. Together with tradition, it is the "supreme rule of faith," since it transmits "the very word of God" and makes "to resound . . . the voice of the Holy Spirit."[1]

General Directory for Catechesis 127

The writings of Sacred Scripture revolve around Jesus Christ. All of Scripture is thus interpreted in the light of Jesus' Passion, death, and Resurrection. Sacred Scripture, interpreted from within the Tradition of the

Church, forms the living heart of Church teaching. Under the guidance of the Holy Spirit, we continue to reap the truth of God's Covenant of love and draw strength from the living Word of the Sacred Scriptures.

For Reflection

In what ways has Sacred Scripture become a living source of faith in my life?

How often do I turn to the Bible as a source for reflection and prayer?

Catechist to Catechist

Believing

You and the children in your group are about to begin a wonderful journey of faith. Believe that your generosity in accepting the call to be a catechist will be rewarded in ways that may or may not be clear to you right away. Believe that the Holy Spirit will be with you and with the children every step of the way. You and each of them have the ability to share your faith and to grow in faith.

Learning to Believe

None of us fully understands the Trinity. But we each have our own experience of this great mystery. Some of  us feel God the Father's love cocooning us each day. Some of us ask the Spirit to help us do those things that we are afraid we cannot do on our own. Some of us turn to Jesus as our friend and confidant. Most third graders already have some sense of the Trinity. As they grow, their understanding will deepen. As their catechist, you will have a role to play in this. Do your best, and trust God to do the rest!

The Church Teaches . . .

The *General Directory for Catechesis* (*GDC*) teaches:

> God, in his greatness, uses a pedagogy[1] to reveal himself to the human person: he uses human events and words to communicate his plan; he does so progressively and in stages,[2] so as to draw even closer to man. *GDC* 38

By approaching religious studies as a mystery to unravel, you can use *Faith First* to elicit excitement in the children and help them build an enduring relationship with God.

See the Catechism . . .

For more on the teachings of the Catholic Church on the mysteries of God the Creator, see *Catechism of the Catholic Church* 279–314, 325–349, and 355–379.

CATECHIST PRAYER

God the Father, work through me and the children this week. We ask this in Jesus' name. Amen.

Footnote references for these two pages may be found on p. 456.

LESSON PLANNER

Focus
To help the children identify ways God invites us to come to know and believe in him

Engage

Page 13
Focus
To help the children identify ways they can try to know God better this year

Opening Prayer

Discussion
Ways of getting to know God better

Teach and Apply

Pages 14–16
Focus
To identify ways God tells us about himself in the Bible and through the Church

Presentation
Read, discuss, and summarize content.
Scripture
- Psalm 104:1
- 2 Timothy 3:15–16
- Acts of the Apostles 2:42, 45–47

Activities
- Identify and pray the Sign of the Cross as a sign of the Holy Trinity.
- Share Bible stories that help us learn about God.
- Identify people in the Church who help us know God.

Faith-Filled People
The Evangelists

Connect

Pages 17–18
Focus
To discover ways the Church shares our faith in God

Our Church Makes a Difference
We learn about God through Christian art.
Our Catholic Faith
Statues

What Difference Does Faith Make?
Activity
Draw or write about helping your family know God better.
Faith Choice
Choose a way to help your family know God better this week.

We Pray

Page 19
Prayer Form
Creed
Prayer
Divide the class into three groups. Introduce the prayer and pray together.

We Remember

Review
- Review "To Help You Remember" statements.
- Complete the writing activity.

Preview
Highlight features of the "With My Family" page.

Materials
- index cards
- pencils
- crayons or markers

Enriching the Session

Blackline Masters
Additional Activities booklet:
Chapter 1
Coloring
Drawing
Assessment Tools booklet:
Chapter 1 Test

Faith First **Grade 3 Video**
Segment 1: "St. Patrick/Three in One"

Enriching the Lesson (CG page 57)
Making Faith Pennants
Making Stained-Glass Windows
Literature Connection

Music Connection (CG page 57)

www.FaithFirst.com

We update the *Faith First* Web site weekly. Check each week for new content and features. Here are some places to begin:

Catechists and Teachers
- Current Events
- Chapter Downloads
- Catechist Prayer

Faith First **for Families**
- Bible Stories
- Make a Difference

Kids' Clubhouse
- *Faith First* Activities
- Chapter Reviews
- Games
- Saints

Don't Forget! You can make lesson planning a breeze—check out the **Online Lesson Planner.**

God Speaks to Us

1

We Pray

LORD, my God,
 you are great!
 Psalm 104:1

**Glory be
to the Father,
and to the Son,
and to the Holy
Spirit.   Amen.**

*How do you make
new friends and get
to know old friends
better?*

Friends spend time
talking together. They
share things and get
to know each other
better. God is always
inviting us to get to
know him better too.

*What are some of the
ways you can try to
know God better
this year?*

(13)

PRAY

- Gather the children for prayer.
- Divide the class into two groups. Invite one group to pray the Psalm and one group to pray the rest of the prayer.
- Begin and close with the Sign of the Cross.
- All say "Amen."

DISCOVER

Purpose: To assess what the children may know about ways God speaks to us

- Ask the children how they can make new friends and get to know old friends better.
- Remind them that God wants us to know him better too.
- Ask the concluding question. Affirm appropriate responses.

Liturgy Tip

Praying the Psalms. Incorporated in the Old Testament following the Book of Job, the Psalms deserve special attention. They follow a certain literary form since they were composed for worship and were meant to be sung. The type of prayer we are asking the children to do on this page is very similar to the call and response format we use when praying the Responsorial Psalm at Sunday Mass. It is important that children become familiar with this form of prayer as they will see this many times throughout the year.

Teach

FOCUS

Read the "Faith Focus" question aloud. Tell the children that in this chapter they will discover that God is a mystery who speaks, or makes himself known, to us.

DISCOVER

- Tell the children that some mysteries in life have solutions, but we can never fully understand a mystery of faith.
- Invite a volunteer to read aloud "God Tells Us About Himself."
- Ask a volunteer to find the words in the text that define *Holy Trinity* and read them aloud.
- Ask the children to look at the illustration and tell which symbols they think represent the three Persons of the Trinity. God the Father: cloud and light; God the Son: cross; God the Holy Spirit: dove and fire.

Apply

REINFORCE

Tell the children that each week they will be creating review cards for the faith words in the chapters. Have the children copy the definitions of the words *faith* and *Holy Trinity* on index cards.

INTEGRATE

Ask the children to respond to the question. Sign of the Cross. Ask the children to share times when we pray this prayer.

God Tells Us Who He Is

Faith Focus

What are some ways that God speaks to us?

Faith Words

faith
Faith is a gift from God. It helps us believe in God and all that he has revealed.

Holy Trinity
The Holy Trinity is the mystery of one God in three divine Persons—God the Father, God the Son, and God the Holy Spirit.

Baptism of Jesus (Matthew 3:13–17)

What prayer of the Church shows that there is one God in three Persons? Quietly pray that prayer in your heart.

God Tells Us About Himself

God is a mystery. A mystery is what we could never know on our own. God has to reveal, or tell us, about himself. God gives us the gift of **faith**. Faith helps us come to know and believe in God and what he reveals.

God has revealed that he is one God in three Persons. He is the **Holy Trinity**. The three divine Persons are God the Father, God the Son, and God the Holy Spirit. This is a great mystery of faith.

14

Special Needs

Using Word Walls. To help reinforce new vocabulary concepts, you may want to create a portable word wall in your classroom. At the beginning of each lesson, introduce the "Faith Words" on the board. Ask the children to give ideas as to what the words mean before you write the definitions. Then draw a simple illustration to go with the words. Refer to the word wall at different times throughout the year to reinforce the words and meanings. Keep it posted during each class and add to it as the children learn new vocabulary words.

Need: All children, especially those with learning difficulties

God Speaks to Us in the Bible

The Bible is the written word of God. The Holy Spirit helped God's people write the Bible. The Bible is also called Sacred Scripture. The words *Sacred Scripture* mean "holy writings." In the Bible we read,

> Always remember that the holy writings come to us from God.
>
> Based on 2 Timothy 3:15–16

The Old Testament is the first main part of the Bible. It tells us about the promises God made at creation and to Noah, Abraham, Moses, and the prophets. God always keeps his promises.

The New Testament is the second main part of the Bible. It tells us about Jesus and his teachings. Jesus tells us the most about God.

Write about your favorite Bible story that helps you learn about God. Share that story with a friend.

Faith-Filled People

The Evangelists

The writers of the four Gospels are called the four Evangelists. They are Saint Matthew, Saint Mark, Saint Luke, and Saint John.

15

FOCUS

Point out that God reveals himself to us in the Bible, the written word of God.

DISCOVER

- Invite the children to name some times or places where they have heard or read the word of God.
- Ask the children to read silently "God Speaks to Us in the Bible" to learn more about the distinction between the Old and New Testament.
- Emphasize that God speaks to us each time we hear or read God's word.
- Ask a volunteer to read the Scripture passage. Remind the children that the Bible is God's written word.

Apply

REINFORCE

- Write the headings *Old Testament* and *New Testament* on the board. Ask the children to help you list what each part of the Bible tells us.
- Invite a volunteer to read "Faith-Filled People" to discover who the four Evangelists are.

INTEGRATE

- Brainstorm with the children a list of their favorite Bible stories. Ask what they like about these stories.
- Present the activity and have the children complete it.

Teach

FOCUS

Point out that another way God speaks to us is through the Church.

DISCOVER

- Explain the first paragraph of "God Speaks to Us through the Church" in your own words.
- Ask the class to listen for what the early Church learned to do together as a volunteer reads the Scripture passage based on Acts 2:42, 45–47.

Apply

REINFORCE

Emphasize that the Catholic Church today helps us come to know God just as the Apostles helped the early Church.

INTEGRATE

- Invite the children to complete the activity by identifying people in their parish who teach them about God.
- After it is completed, ask volunteers to share their responses.

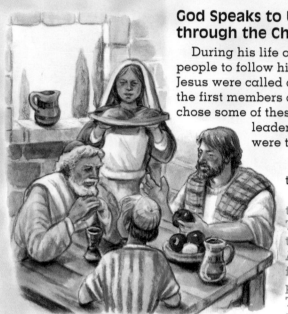

God Speaks to Us through the Church

During his life on earth, Jesus called people to follow him. These followers of Jesus were called disciples. They were the first members of the Church. Jesus chose some of these followers to be the leaders of the Church. These were the Apostles.

The New Testament tells us,

Many people came to believe in Jesus. They listened to the teachings of the Apostles. They cared for one another. They prayed together. They broke bread together. Together they praised God.

Based on Acts of the Apostles 2:42, 45–47

We belong to the Catholic Church. The Catholic Church goes back to Jesus and the Apostles.

List three people in the Church who help you come to know God. Tell how they help you.

Names	How They Help
	Responses will vary.

16

Teaching Tip

Handing on the Faith. Before teaching this lesson reflect on your own life as a catechist. Think about those people who were responsible for passing on their faith to you. You are faithful today because of those who were faithful before you. As you share your faith with the children, you are giving them one of God's greatest gifts.

Our Church Makes a Difference

Christian Art

Christians have always shared their faith in God. One way they have shared their faith in God is through beautiful works of art. God can speak to us through religious art.

Christian artists create mosaics and stained-glass windows. They decorate churches and cathedrals. These and other works of Christian art express faith in Jesus. These works of art help people come to know, love, and serve God better.

Tell what each of the pictures shows about the faith of Christians in Jesus.

Our Catholic Faith

Statues

Statues are symbols of the faith of Christians. They help us remember Jesus and Mary and the saints. Statues of the saints give honor to them. We honor the saints because of their faith and holy lives.

Mosaic

Stained glass

Wood carving

17

HIGHLIGHT

Remind the children that God reveals himself to us in the Bible and through the Church. Point out that Christians express their faith in what God has revealed through religious art.

DISCOVER

- Ask a volunteer to read aloud the second paragraph to find out different kinds of art that Christians create.
- Ask: Why do Christian artists create mosaics and stained-glass windows? These works of art help people come to know, love, and serve God better.
- Present "Our Catholic Faith" to discover another form of art that helps us know God.

INTEGRATE

- Direct the children's attention to the mosaic, wood carving, and stained-glass window pictured on this page. Invite volunteers to share where they have seen these types of art.
- Ask them to tell what each of these pieces of art tells them about the faith of Christians in Jesus.

Teaching Tip

Display Ethnic Sacred Art. Collect photographs or other images of sacred art designed by people from different ethnic backgrounds. These images can often be found in Catholic magazines and newspapers as well as on the Internet. The children will enjoy looking at images of Jesus created by Chinese or African artists and sculptors, as well as those in Eastern Europe and the United States. Point out how these various artists depict Jesus and the saints in their own unique ways. Help the children appreciate the beauty and the message about God in each piece of art.

Connect

HIGHLIGHT

Remind the children that many people help us come to know, love, and serve God.

RESPOND

- Point out that we are invited to tell others about God. The Holy Spirit, the third Person of the Holy Trinity, gives us the help we need.
- Introduce the activity and have the children complete it. Let them share their work with a partner.

CHOOSE

- Point out to the children that at the end of each lesson they will be given time to make a faith choice that will help them live as children of God in the coming week.
- Invite the children to respond to "My Faith Choice."
- After a moment of prayerful reflection have the children write their choice on the lines provided.
- Encourage the children to put their choice into practice this week.

What Difference Does Faith Make in My Life?

Many people help you come to know, love, and serve God. Most importantly, the Holy Spirit helps you.

Write about or draw yourself helping your family come to know God better.

Helping My Family

My Faith Choice

This week I will help my family to know God better. I will

Affirm appropriate responses.

18

Teaching Tip

Faith Choice Journal. The weekly faith choice is an important part of the children's faith formation. It insures that the lesson does not end when the children leave the classroom. You may wish to have the children record their faith choice in a notebook or simple handmade journal. When they return the following week, they can review the choice they made and record their progress. If the children make their journals, provide them with ten sheets of lined paper and two sheets of art paper to use as covers. Bind them with brads.

We Pray

Praying the Creed

The Church prays the creed, or professes its faith, each Sunday at Mass. Pray these words from the Nicene Creed.

All: We believe in one God, the Holy Trinity.

Group 1: We believe in one God,
the Father, the Almighty,
maker of heaven and earth.

Group 2: We believe in one Lord, Jesus Christ,
the only Son of God.

Group 3: We believe in the Holy Spirit,
the Lord, the giver of life.

All: We believe in one God, the Holy Trinity.

We Remember

In each leaf of the shamrock, write one way you come to know God.

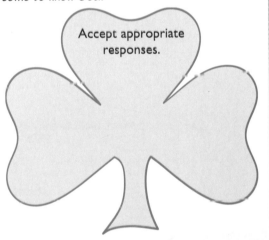

Accept appropriate responses.

To Help You Remember

1. God gives us the gift of faith to help us know and believe in God.

2. God speaks to us through the Bible.

3. God speaks to us through the Church.

Grade 3 • Chapter 1   19

Background: Doctrine

The Creeds of the Church. From her beginning the Church has expressed her faith in brief formulae known as creeds. The Church's earliest profession of faith was "Jesus is Lord." By the fourth century the western Church developed a trinitarian profession of faith that we know today as the Apostles' Creed. In the East a conciliar creed, known as the Nicene Creed, emerged in the fourth century. In the East this creed was used as the baptismal creed; In the West it was used within the celebration of the Eucharist. Together the Apostles' Creed and the Nicene Creed have stood through the centuries as symbols of the Church's faith.

Pray

WE PRAY

- Gather the children in the prayer center with their books.
- Remind the children that the Creed we say each Sunday at Mass professes our belief in the mystery of the Holy Trinity.
- Divide the children into three groups.
- Pray the portion of the Creed on page 19.
- Remind the children that all Christians should learn this prayer by heart.

Review

WE REMEMBER

- Use the "To Help You Remember" statements by asking a question about each statement and inviting the children to answer without looking at their books.
- Introduce the activity and give the children time to complete it. When they are finished, ask if they recall who used the shamrock to help explain the mystery of the Holy Trinity. Saint Patrick.
- Remind the group that we can come to know more about God by reflecting on each Person of the Holy Trinity.

At Home

ENCOURAGE

Have the children carefully tear out pages 19 and 20 along the perforation. Encourage the children to share the pages with their families and to do the activities together. If they did not complete the review activity on page 19 by the end of the session, emphasize that they can complete it with their families.

VISIT FAITHFIRST.COM

- Share with the children the many activities on the *Faith First* Web site.
- Encourage the children to visit **www.FaithFirst.com.**

---

1 With My Family

This Week . . .

In chapter 1, "God Speaks to Us," your child learned that God has revealed himself to us. God is a mystery, and we could not know many things about God unless God revealed them. Jesus revealed that there is one God in three Persons—God the Father, Son, and Holy Spirit. We call this mystery of God the Holy Trinity. This is the central belief of Christians. The Bible and the Church teach and help us understand what God has revealed.

For more on the teachings of the Catholic Church on divine Revelation and the mystery of the Holy Trinity, see *Catechism of the Catholic Church* paragraph numbers 232–260.

Sharing God's Word

Read together the Bible story in Acts 2:42–47 about the first members of the Church or read the adaptation of the story on page 16. Emphasize that the first Christians cared about one another and prayed together.

Praying

In this chapter your child learned part of the Nicene Creed. Read and pray together this part of the creed on page 19.

Making a Difference

Choose one of the following activities to do as a family or design a similar activity of your own.

- When you take part in Mass this week, plan to arrive early or stay late. Walk around the church and look at all the works of art in your parish. Talk together about what each work of art teaches you about God.

- Take time this week to become more familiar with the Apostles' Creed. You can find the creed on page 284. Use the Apostles' Creed for family prayer.

- Talk about how your family helps one another know God. Ask each family member to choose one thing they can do this week to help the rest of the family know God better.

For more ideas on ways your family can live your faith, visit the "Faith First for Families" page at **www.FaithFirst.com.** You will find the "About Your Child" page helpful as your child begins a new year.

20

Evaluate

Take a few moments to evaluate this week's lesson.
I feel (circle one) about this week's lesson.

    a. very pleased
    b. OK
    c. disappointed

The activity the children enjoyed most was . . .

The concept that was most difficult to teach was . . .

because . . .

Something I would like to do differently is . . .

Before Moving On . . .

As you finish today's lesson, reflect on the following question before moving on to the next chapter.

What child could use more praise from me?

ENRICHING THE LESSON

Making Faith Pennants

Purpose
To reinforce that God gives us the gift of faith (taught on page 14)

Directions
- Brainstorm with the children slogans that say something important about their faith in God, such as "God is speaking. Are you listening?" or "Faith is God's gift: Open it!"
- Provide the children with pennant shapes made ahead of time.
- Encourage the children to make their pennants attractive and colorful by adding illustrations.
- Arrange with the parish staff for an area in the parish buildings where the children's pennants can be displayed and enjoyed by the entire parish community.

Materials
pennants from construction paper
markers or crayons

Making Stained Glass Windows

Purpose
To reinforce the teaching about Christian art (taught on page 17)

Directions
Children this age will enjoy making stained-glass windows.
- Invite the children to put crayon shavings of different colors on a sheet of wax paper.
- Next have them cover the shavings with another sheet of wax paper.
- Then help the children melt their shavings by placing a warm iron on the top sheet of wax paper. This step should always be done with an adult present!
- Help the children cut out a picture frame from construction paper to paste or glue around the stained glass window.

Materials
iron
wax paper
crayon shavings of different colors
construction paper
scissors and glue

Literature Connection

Purpose
To reinforce the teaching that family members can help us to know God better (taught on page 18)

Directions
Children form their first ideas of God through their relationships with their parents or other caregivers. The story *Our Tree Named Steve* by Alan Zweibel (Penguin, 2005) is a heartwarming tale of fatherhood and family love.
- Read the story to the children, and show them the illustrations.
- Invite volunteers to tell what the children in the book may have learned about God from their parents' actions in the story.
- Remind the children that the Bible tells us how God's people found him in the experiences of their daily lives.

Material
Our Tree Named Steve by Alan Zweibel

Music Connection
- "Baptized in Water" (Gaelic melody) acc. R. Batastini. *Singing Our Faith (SOF)* #222.
- "Come to Us, Spirit of Jesus," M. Friedman. *Rise Up and Sing (RUS)* #183.
- "Jesus Is with Us," O. Alstott. *RUS* #274.
- "Praise to the Trinity," R. Glover. *SOF* #161.

God the Creator of Heaven and Earth

Background

God's Continuing Care for Creation

God is the ultimate source and destiny of the universe. God created all things and rules over all things. God is goodness itself, and his creation is filled with goodness, beauty, and order. Human beings, created in the divine image and likeness, are the summit of God's creation. Created to know, love, and serve him, human beings are more precious in God's eyes than all other creatures.

God continues to govern and create the world. Together, humanity and the created universe are on a journey guided by divine Providence, or God's continuing care for creation. God has not abandoned the created world, but continues to perfect and order all things.

God has vested human beings with the responsibility to share in that care for the earth and all its creatures. We are to be wise stewards of the earth, sky, waters, animals, and plants that make up the beauty of the universe. The Second Vatican Council reminds us:

Believers and unbelievers agree almost unanimously that all things on earth should be ordained to humanity as to their center and summit.

PASTORAL CONSTITUTION ON THE CHURCH IN THE MODERN WORLD 12

The Responsibility of Stewardship

Our care for the earth is a way of responding to God's providential care. His plan for creation is that we live in partnership with one another. We are united to one another because we are created in his image.

The wisdom of divine Providence asserts the interdependence of all creatures. Every creature is dependent upon the rest of the created universe for wholeness and perfection. The flower depends upon clean air, water, sunlight, and soil for nourishment and growth. We in turn depend upon plants for food and beauty.

The order and interdependence of the created world is a reflection of God's infinite beauty and profound love. We are inspired by this remarkable goodness, beauty, and unity of creation to respect the divine plan and bring the created world to perfection through our solidarity with all of creation.

God created everything for human beings. Good stewardship in turn flows from our profound gratitude to the Creator. We give honor and glory to God through the unselfish and responsible use of his wonderful gift.

For Reflection

In what ways have I experienced the interdependence of humankind with all creation?

How can I fulfill my responsibility to care for the earth and give glory and honor to God?

Catechist to Catechist

Begin and End with Prayer

One of the most important ways you will share faith with the children this year is through prayer. Every chapter of *Faith First* begins and ends with a short prayer experience. In the course of your time together you will lead the children in praying the formal prayers of the Church, the words of Scripture, spontaneous prayers, meditations, and a variety of other prayer forms.

The Prayer Space

One way to make your prayer time more meaningful is to create a special prayer space. This can be as simple as a small table or windowsill on which you place a cloth the color of the liturgical season, a Bible, a candle, and at times, other appropriate items. For example, since this session is about God's gifts of creation, you might ask the children to bring examples of creation, such as flowers, rocks, or interesting pieces of wood, to place in the prayer area. The prayer space will serve as a visual reminder of God's presence throughout the year.

The Church Teaches . . .

The *General Directory for Catechesis (GDC)* teaches:

> The Christian knows that every human event—indeed all reality—is marked by the creative activity of God which communicates goodness to all beings.
> *GDC* 16

Every *Faith First* chapter begins by helping the children to situate the lesson concepts in their own life experiences. As they learn to reflect on their life experiences, they can begin to see the hand of the Almighty Creator at work. Through continued catechesis, children can grow to recognize the presence of God in their daily lives.

See the Catechism . . .

For more on the teachings of the Catholic Church on the mysteries of God the Creator, see *Catechism of the Catholic Church* 279–314, 325–349, and 355–379.

CATECHIST PRAYER

Holy Spirit,
you who have hovered
over the waters at the
moment of creation,
kindle in me the
fire of your love.
Amen.

Footnote references may be found on p. 456.

LESSON PLANNER

To explain why God created the world and people

Engage

Page 21
Focus
To help the children identify how creation reminds us that God is good

Opening Prayer

Discussion
What creation tells us about God's goodness

Teach and Apply

Pages 22–24
Focus
To identify God as a loving creator who cares for his creation

Presentation
Read, discuss, and summarize content.
Scripture
• Psalm 104:24
• Genesis 1:3–27, 31; Genesis 1:26–30
• Matthew 6:30–32
Activities
• Draw a gift of God's creation.
• Answer the question.
• Decorate the border of the prayer.
Faith-Filled People
Saint Andrew the Apostle

Connect

Pages 25–26
Focus
To identify ways the Church cares for God's creation

Our Church Makes a Difference
The Church and its members use things from God's creation in the worship of God.
Our Catholic Faith
Prayers of Blessing

What Difference Does Faith Make?
Activity
Create a poster about caring for creation.
Faith Choice
Choose a way you will take care of God's gift of creation this week.

We Pray

Page 27
Prayer Form
Psalm of praise
Prayer
Divide the class into two groups. Introduce the prayer. Pray the verses from Psalm 104 together.

We Remember

Review
• Complete the fill-in-the-blanks activity.
• Read the "To Help You Remember" statements aloud.
Preview
Highlight features of the "With My Family" page.

Materials

• pens or pencils
• crayons or markers

Enriching the Session

Blackline Masters
Additional Activities booklet:
  Chapter 2
    Solving a code
    Writing a letter
Assessment Tools booklet:
  Chapter 2 Test

Enriching the Lesson (CG page 69)
Pantomiming the Creation Story
Planning Photos
Literature Connection

Music Connection (CG page 69)

www.FaithFirst.com

We update the *Faith First* Web site weekly. Check each week for new content and features. Here are some places to begin:

Catechists and Teachers
• Current Events
• Chapter Downloads
• Catechist Prayer

Faith First **for Families**
• Bible Stories
• Make a Difference

Kids' Clubhouse
• *Faith First* Activities
• Chapter Reviews
• Games
• Saints

Don't Forget! You can make lesson planning a breeze—check out the **Online Lesson Planner.**

God the Creator of Heaven and Earth

We Pray

LORD! . . .
the earth is full
of your creatures.
Psalm 104:24

Blessed are you, God, Creator of heaven and earth. Amen.

What parts of creation do you enjoy the most?

God is the loving Creator. God's beautiful creation tells us about his goodness.

What beautiful parts of creation remind you that God is good?

(21)

PRAY

- Gather the children for prayer.
- Divide the children into two groups. Have one group proclaim the Psalm and the other group pray the prayer.
- Begin and close with the Sign of the Cross.
- All say, "Amen."

DISCOVER

Purpose: To help assess what the children already know about God the Creator

- Ask the children what parts of creation they enjoy the most.
- Tell the children that God's creation tells us something about his goodness.
- Ask volunteers to describe how the picture reminds them of God.
- Have volunteers share what beautiful parts of creation remind them that God is good.

✝ Liturgy Tip

God Speaks Through Our Senses. God is transcendent. Yet we can come to know him through creation. We see the beauty of a leaping dolphin and are reminded of the gift of life. We listen to beautiful music and are reminded of God's majesty. We feel the brush of a breeze across our arm and remember that the Spirit of God moves in the world. God uses all of his creation to help us know his love for us. Help the children to be aware of the signs of God that come to them through their senses.

Teach

FOCUS

Read the "Faith Focus" question aloud. Share with the children that in this chapter they will discover that the beauty of creation tells us about God.

DISCOVER

- Point out that God alone is the Creator. Invite the children to read silently the first paragraph of "A Loving Creator."
- Proclaim the story of creation based on Genesis 1:3–27, 31.
- Ask a volunteer to read the last paragraph aloud. Ask the children to underline what God's creation helps us to know. God's love for us.

Apply

REINFORCE

- Point out the faith word *creation* and have a volunteer read aloud the meaning.
- Invite the children to make a word card for the word *creation*.

INTEGRATE

Read the instructions for the drawing activity at the bottom of the page and give the children a few moments to complete it. Ask volunteers to share their work.

God the Creator

Faith Focus

Why did God create the world and people?

Faith Words

creation
Creation is all that God has made out of love and without any help.

divine Providence
Divine Providence is God's caring love for all his creation.

In this space draw another gift of God's creation. Tell how it helps you come to know how wonderful and good God is.

A Loving Creator

We believe that God alone is the Creator. He created everything and everyone out of love and without any help. The Book of Genesis, the first book in the Old Testament, tells the story of **creation.** We read,

God made light. God made the earth and sky and sea. God filled the earth with plants. God made the sun and the moon and the stars. God made birds for the sky and fish for the water. God made animals for the land. Then God created people. God saw that his creation was very good.

Based on Genesis 1:3–27, 31

Through our eyes and other senses we can come to know that God is wonderful and good. All God's creation helps us know his love for us.

22

Catholic Social Teaching

Care for God's Creation. We show our respect for God the Creator by caring for all that he created. Care for creation is, in fact, a requirement of Christian faith. First of all, we are called by God to show respect for all people, since we are all created in his image. This is the foundation of our human dignity. We are to be stewards of the earth as well. Christians must measure every choice by the impact it has on human life and on the environment.

Tip: October 4th is the Feast of St. Francis of Assisi. Celebrate this patron saint of the environment with the children. Have them bring in a picture of their favorite pet or share a report on one of the five classes of animals.

God Created People

God created every person. God created everyone to be different from one another in many ways. All our differences make us special.

God created every person to be the same in one very important way. God created each of us in his own image. Each of us is a child of God.

> God made people in his image. He made them man and woman. God blessed them. God gave them the world to care for.
>
> Based on Genesis 1:26–30

God created people with a body and a soul. Our soul is that part of us that lives forever. It gives us the power to know and love and serve God. By creating us in his own image, God gives us a wonderful responsibility. God calls us to love and care for his world.

Name two ways that you can care for God's world.

Faith-Filled People

Andrew the Apostle

Saint Andrew the Apostle was one of the first disciples of Jesus. Andrew and his brother Saint Peter worked as fishermen. Saint Andrew is the patron saint of fishermen. The Church celebrates the feast day of Saint Andrew the Apostle on November 30.

(23)

Background: Faith-Filled People

Saint Andrew the Apostle. Little is known about Saint Andrew other than the fact that he was the brother of Simon Peter and one of the chosen Twelve Apostles. As one of the Twelve, he was with him during his public life, was present at the Last Supper, saw the Risen Lord, and witnessed his Ascension. Like the other Apostles, he preached the Gospel message at the risk of his own life. It is generally agreed that he was crucified by order of the Roman governor and that he was bound, not nailed, to the cross in order to prolong his suffering. The cross on which he suffered is commonly known as Saint Andrew's cross. His martyrdom took place during the reign of Nero on November 30, A.D. 60.

Teach

FOCUS

Remind the children that God alone is the Creator. Tell them they are going to learn more now about the creation of people.

DISCOVER

- Ask the children to help you list on the board all the visible differences among members of the class. Answers might include differences in ethnicity, gender, height, or color of hair.
- Ask a volunteer to read the second paragraph aloud and ask all to listen for a way we are all alike. God created everyone in his own image.
- Ask another volunteer to read the Scripture passage in Genesis 1:26–30.
- Have the children read the last paragraph silently and underline the word *soul*. Then ask: What is our soul? The part of us that lives forever.
- Tell about Saint Andrew the Apostle in "Faith-Filled People." Emphasize that when fishermen fish responsibly, they care for God's creation.

Apply

REINFORCE

Remind the children that we are special because we are made in God's image.

INTEGRATE

Divide the class into partners. Have the children brainstorm ways they can care for God's world.

Teach

FOCUS

Remind the children that all people are created in God's image.

DISCOVER

- Talk with the children about the people in their lives who care for them. Explain that these people take care of them because they love them.
- Read the first paragraph aloud to the children. Ask them to listen for the meaning of the term *divine Providence.*
- Tell the children that Jesus talks about divine Providence. Ask a volunteer to read the Scripture passage based on Matthew 6:30–32.
- Have the children silently read the last paragraph to find out how much God cares for creation.

Apply

REINFORCE

- Have the children turn to page 22 and ask a volunteer to read the meaning of *divine Providence* from "Faith Words."
- Have them make a word card for this term.

INTEGRATE

- Direct the children's attention to the activity on page 24.
- Invite the children to decorate the border of the prayer. Then read it aloud together.

God Cares for His Creation

God our Father and Creator is with us at every moment. He provides for, or takes care of, his creation. We call God's caring love for his creation **divine Providence.**

Jesus revealed how much God cares for us. He said,

"Look at the fields of grass. God clothes the fields with beautiful wild flowers. Your Father in heaven knows everything you need."
Based on Matthew 6:30–32

God always cares for his creation. He cares for the least of his creation to the greatest of his creation. He cares about everything that happens in the world. We never have to handle our problems alone.

Decorate the border of the prayer with symbols of God's creation. Pray the prayer each morning.

God our Father and Creator, you care for me. I praise your name, O God. Amen.

24

Teaching Tip

Biblical Flora and Fauna. The land where Jesus lived and taught the people about God's divine Providence was abundant with the gifts of creation. The children might enjoy knowing that the birds flying over Jesus' head might have been barn swallows. Jesus might have also seen sparrows, doves, eagles, crows, pigeons, and ravens. Wildflowers growing in the region might have included white, purple, scarlet, and blue anemones. Roses, irises, daffodils, jasmine, lilies of the valley, and almond blossoms also grew in the fields and on the hillsides of Palestine. If possible, bring in picture books or print pictures off the Internet that show some of these birds and flowers.

Our Church Makes a Difference

Creation and Our Parish Church

God's beautiful creation fills our churches. The Church uses things from God's creation in our worship of God.

The bread and wine used at Mass come to us from the earth. Sometimes oil made from olives is used in our celebrations. Water is also often used. Water reminds us that God gives us new life in Jesus through Baptism.

The candles we use are often made from beeswax. In some churches, sunlight shines through stained-glass windows and fills our church with color. Our minds and hearts are lifted up to God in prayer.

All creation reminds us of God. We care for it as a special gift from God.

Look at these pictures of creation. Tell how they remind you of God's caring love.

Affirm appropriate responses.

Our Catholic Faith

Prayers of Blessing

The Church prays prayers of blessing. Prayers of blessing honor God as the source of all our blessings. They express our trust in God's loving care for us.

25

Connect

HIGHLIGHT

Remind the children that God cares for his creation out of love. Point out that we see the beauty of creation in our churches.

DISCOVER

- Ask the children to recall a Sunday Mass or other sacramental celebrations. Ask what parts of creation they see used in these celebrations. Water, fire, bread, wine, oil, people.
- Invite volunteers to read "Creation and Our Parish Church."
- Explain to the children that all these parts of creation help to remind us of God.

INTEGRATE

- Have the children look carefully at the pictures on this page. Ask volunteers to share how the pictures of creation remind them of God's love.
- Point out that all signs of creation can remind us of God's loving care.

Teaching Tip

Children's Spirituality. As you may already be finding out, spending time growing closer to God with third graders can be fun as well as challenging. They enjoy life, learning, and being with their friends. Remember that you are nurturing the children's spirituality as you reflect on the beauty of God's creation. This helps them deepen their relationship with God.

Connect

HIGHLIGHT

We have the responsibility to care for creation. Point out that caring for creation is a way to thank God for the gifts of creation.

RESPOND

- As you read the opening paragraph, ask the children to listen for what the Holy Spirit shows us.
- Read the instructions. Give the children an example of a poster that might invite others to get involved in caring for creation.

CHOOSE

- Invite the children to respond to "My Faith Choice."
- After a moment of prayerful reflection have the children write their choices on the lines provided.
- Encourage the children to put their choices into practice this week.

What Difference Does Faith Make in My Life?

God created you and all human beings and the universe out of love. The Holy Spirit shows you how to work with other people to care for creation. When you care for creation, you are thanking God for the gifts of creation.

Create a poster. Invite your friends to care for God's creation with you.

Caring for God's Creation

My Faith Choice

This week I will honor and bless God the Creator. I will take better care of God's gift of

Affirm appropriate responses.

_____

_____.

26

Teaching Tip

Care for Creation. The *General Directory for Catechesis* points out that catechesis today needs to relate to the particular environment in which people live, whether it be rural or urban (see *GDC* 192). In preparing the children for the poster activity on this page, encourage them to think of ways to improve the immediate environment that surrounds them. You might have them brainstorm in terms of the three elements of air, earth, and water. Children might think also of neighborhood beautification or safety projects that help their environment be a better reflection of the world that God intends.

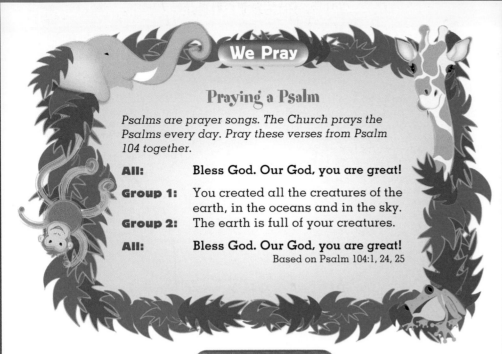

We Pray

Praying a Psalm

Psalms are prayer songs. The Church prays the Psalms every day. Pray these verses from Psalm 104 together.

All: Bless God. Our God, you are great!

Group 1: You created all the creatures of the earth, in the oceans and in the sky.

Group 2: The earth is full of your creatures.

All: Bless God. Our God, you are great!

Based on Psalm 104:1, 24, 25

We Remember

Fill in the blanks. Use the words in the word bank to complete the faith sentences.

Blessing	soul	Providence	Creator

1. We believe that God is the
   _____Creator_____.

2. Divine _____Providence_____ is God's caring love for all his creation.

3. God created people with a body and a
   _____soul_____.

4. _____Blessing_____ prayers express our faith in God's loving care for us.

To Help You Remember

1. God created everyone and everything out of love and without any help.

2. God created every person in God's image and likeness.

3. God always cares for us and all of his creation.

Grade 3 • Chapter 2   27

WE PRAY

- Ask the children to recall what Psalms are. Remind them that the Church prays the Psalms every day.
- Gather the children in the prayer center and divide them into two groups.
- Tell them to raise their hands high in praise each time they say, "Bless God. . . ."
- Pray the Psalms together.

Review

WE REMEMBER

- Write the words *created, image,* and *always* on the board.
- Write each "To Help You Remember" statement on the board, leaving out one of the key words in each. Invite volunteers to fill in the missing words.
- Introduce the activity and allow time for the children to complete it.

Special Needs

Creating an Opportunity for Movement. Cut sentence strips of appropriate length from poster board or purchase ready-cut strips at a teacher supply store. Write the sentences from the "We Remember" activity on the strips, leaving out key words. Write the word choices on shorter sentence strip lengths. Distribute sentences and words to the children. Ask them to come to the front of the class. Have the children who have sentence strips read their sentence. Students with the correct word to complete the sentence move to join them. Ask them to read the completed sentence together. You may repeat this with different students participating if you wish.

Need: Children with attention deficits

At Home

ENCOURAGE

Have the children carefully tear out pages 27 and 28 along the perforation. Encourage the children to share the pages with their families and to do the activities together. If they did not complete the review activity on page 27 by the end of the session, emphasize that they can complete it with their families.

VISIT FAITHFIRST.COM

- Share with the children the many activities on the *Faith First* Web site.
- Encourage the children to visit **www.FaithFirst.com.**

Before Moving On . . .

As you finish today's lesson, reflect on the following question before moving on to the next chapter.

Which children work well together?

---

2 With My Family

This Week . . .

In chapter 2, "God the Creator of Heaven and Earth," your child came to know God as our loving, caring Creator. God's caring love is known as divine Providence. Everything and everyone God creates is good. God creates every person to be a unique individual. At the same time, God creates everyone in his own image and shares the very life of the Holy Trinity, sanctifying grace, with us.

For more on the teachings of the Catholic Church on the mysteries of God the Creator, see *Catechism of the Catholic Church* paragraph numbers 279–314, 325–349, and 355–379.

Sharing God's Word

Read together the Bible story in Genesis 1:1–31 about creation or read the adaptation of the story on page 22. Emphasize that the diversity within creation helps us come to know that God is wonderful and good.

Praying

In this chapter your child prayed part of Psalm 104. Read and pray together the adaptation of Psalm 104 on page 27. Or choose another psalm, look it up in the Bible, and pray it.

Making a Difference

Choose one of the following activities to do as a family or design a similar activity of your own.

- This week at Mass notice all of the things from creation your parish uses to help you worship. After Mass try to name everything you saw.
- Invite each family member to share how creation helps them feel close to God.
- We honor God when we care for creation. As a family choose one thing you will do this week to take care of creation.

For more ideas on ways your family can live your faith, visit the "Faith First for Families" page at **www.FaithFirst.com**. The "Make a Difference" page goes especially well with this chapter.

28

✓ Evaluate

Take a few moments to evaluate this week's lesson.
I feel (circle one) about this week's lesson.

- a. very pleased
- b. OK
- c. disappointed

The activity the children enjoyed most was . . .

The concept that was most difficult to teach was . . .

because . . .

Something I would like to do differently is . . .

ENRICHING THE LESSON

Pantomiming the Creation Story

Purpose

To reinforce the story of creation (taught on page 22)

Directions

- Have the children work with partners and pantomime the reading from Genesis 1:3–27, 31.
- Assign each set of partners a line from the story, such as light and day, darkness and night, earth, sky, sea, plants, sun, moon, stars, birds, fish, and animals.
- Have someone read the Scripture as the children pantomime the elements of creation.

Materials

Planning Photos

Purpose

To reinforce that all creation reminds us of God (taught on pages 22–25)

Directions

- Have the children work with partners and plan a series of photos they would like to take to illustrate the parts of creation they enjoy the most.
- Have them write or draw the exact photos they would like to take.
- Encourage them to look through magazines and to think about photos that their families might have taken on vacations.
- Invite volunteers to share their favorite parts of creation. Encourage the children to bring in photos that their families have taken and share them with the class.

Materials

magazines
construction paper
markers or crayons

Literature Connection

Purpose

To reinforce that God calls us to love and care for his world (taught on page 23)

Directions

Miss Rumphius by Barbara Cooney (Penguin Putnam Books, 1985) tells the story of Miss Alice Rumphius, who resolves to travel the world when she grows up. In her old age, she returns to her home by the sea and decides to do something to make the immediate world around her more beautiful. She finds this to be the most difficult work of her life, but the most rewarding.

- Read the story aloud to the children.
- Ask the children what their dreams are for themselves when they grow up.
- Ask each child to use words, pictures, music, or rhyme to describe one thing they would like to do to create more beauty in one part of God's world.

Materials

Miss Rumphius by Barbara Cooney

Music Connection

- "All Grownups, All Children," P.J. Shelly. *Singing Our Faith (SOF)* #147.
- "All You Works of God," M. Haugen. *SOF* #157.
- "Canticle of the Sun," M. Haugen. *SOF* #145.
- "Sing Our Earth and Skies," M. Haugen. *SOF* #153.

Mary Trusted in God

Background

Mary, Model of Faith and Holiness

Mary, the Mother of God, is our model of faith and holiness. Chosen by God the Father to be the mother of the Incarnate Son of God, Jesus, Mary has an esteemed and unique place in the plan of salvation. She is our link to the saving work of Jesus. Mary, both then and now, freely cooperates in the work of our salvation through her faith and obedience. In spite of the perplexing announcement of the angel Gabriel, Mary conformed her will to the will of God (See Luke 1:38).

Mary's faith and holiness are not a result of her own merits or because of something she did. God's love drew her close and prepared her for her graced response of faith to become the mother of the Incarnate Son of God.

> This union of the mother with the Son in the work of salvation is made manifest from the time of Christ's virginal conception up to his death; first when Mary, arising in haste to go to visit Elizabeth, is greeted by her as blessed because of her belief in the promise of salvation, and the precursor leaped with joy in the womb of his mother; then also at the birth of Our Lord, who did not diminish his mother's virginal integrity but sanctified it.

> *DOGMATIC CONSTITUTION ON THE CHURCH (LUMEN GENTIUM) 57*

The Power of the Gift of Faith

The Holy Spirit is responsible for Jesus' conception in the womb of Mary. Elizabeth, filled with this same Holy Spirit, recognized the transformation in her younger cousin and greeted her with the words,

> Most blessed are you among women, and blessed is the fruit of your womb. And how does this happen to me, that the mother of my Lord comes to me?

> *LUKE 1:42–43*

Faith surrounds Mary. This visit to Elizabeth reveals the first account of another woman of faith who recognizes the profound role Mary will play in God's plan of salvation.

These two women of faith help our own belief and trust in God. When surrounded by overwhelming struggles, we believe and trust because nothing is impossible with God. In grasping the power and might of God in our midst

and acting on our behalf, we discover that God does indeed do great things for each of us—and lifts up the lowly. Joining with Mary we magnify the Lord!

God's grace pulls us into the light and life of faith, and we are empowered, or graced, to conform our lives to the will of God. We can take courage from Mary's faithfulness and seek her aid as we grow in faith and discipleship.

For Reflection

What are some tangible ways that I can grow in faith and conform my life more closely to the will of God?

When have I surrendered to the power of God? What were the results?

Catechist to Catechist

Witness Your Faith

Throughout this year, you'll have many opportunities to share your faith with the children. Third graders are very perceptive. They will look to you to model what it means to be a person of faith. The children's concept of God is greatly influenced by what they see you and other adults do. Being consistent in your positive faith-filled attitude toward life and unconditional respect for the children will help them find God in your words and actions.

Mary, A Model of Faith

Most third graders know that Mary is the mother of Jesus. In your time together this year, help them to appreciate Mary's great faith and trust in God the Father, which enabled her to accept his invitation to be the mother of his Son. Many eight- and nine-year-olds have a strong sense of a mother's love. With the right guidance they can grow in their relationship with Mary as their mother and someone whom they can count on to always be there for them.

Be sensitive to any children who may be separated from their mothers through death or other circumstances. Reassure them that Mary's love for them has no boundaries or limitations.

The Church Teaches . . .

The *General Directory for Catechesis* reminds us:

Catechesis on the Blessed Virgin Mary should always express clearly the intrinsic Trinitarian, Christological and ecclesiological aspects of mariology. In revising or drawing up materials for use in Marian piety account should be taken of biblical, liturgical, ecumenical and anthropological orientation.[1]   *GDC* 196

This is why *Faith First* uses Sacred Tradition and Sacred Scripture to teach the children about Mary.

See the Catechism . . .

For more on the teachings of the Catholic Church on the mystery of the Incarnation and the unique role of Mary in God's plan for the salvation of the world, see *Catechism of the Catholic Church* 456–478 and 484–507.

CATECHIST PRAYER

God our loving Father, you chose Mary to be the mother of your Son, Jesus Christ. Help me guide the children to know that joined to Christ in Baptism they are your adopted sons and daughters. Amen.

Footnote references may be found on p. 456.

LESSON PLANNER

Focus | **To identify that Mary showed her faith and trust in God**

Engage

Page 29
Focus
To discover that the angel Gabriel brought Mary good news from God

Opening Prayer

Discussion
Our reaction to good news and the good news the angel brought Mary

Teach and Apply

Pages 30–32
Focus
To discover Mary's response to the angel's message from God

Presentation
Read, discuss, and summarize content.
Scripture
- Luke 1:47
- Luke 1:28, 31, 35
- Luke 1:46, 49
Activities
- Retell the story of the Annunciation.
- Write a prayer of praise.
- Write a news story about the shepherd's visit to the manger.
Faith-Filled People
Saint Elizabeth and Zechariah

Connect

Pages 33–34
Focus
To discover ways the Church honors Mary

Our Church Makes a Difference
The Church honors Mary on feast days with prayer and through art.
Our Catholic Faith
Feast Days of Mary

What Difference Does Faith Make?
Activity
Design a poster that shows ways you say "yes" to God.
Faith Choice
Choose a way to show faith and trust in God this week.

We Pray

Page 35
Prayer Form
The Angelus
Prayer
Divide the class in two groups and pray The Angelus together.

We Remember

Review
- Complete the scrambled letter activity.
- Read the "To Help You Remember" statements aloud.
Preview
Highlight features of the "With My Family" page.

Materials

- Bibles
- pens or pencils
- crayons or markers

Enriching the Session

Blackline Masters
Additional Activities booklet:
Chapter 3
Singing songs
Drawing pictures
Assessment Tools booklet:
Chapter 3 Test

Enriching the Lesson (CG page 81)
Role-Playing Scripture Stories
About Mary
Making Nativity Bookmarks
Literature Connection

Music Connection (CG page 81)

www.FaithFirst.com

We update the *Faith First* Web site weekly. Check each week for new content and features. Here are some places to begin:

Catechists and Teachers
- Current Events
- Chapter Downloads
- Catechist Prayer

Faith First for Families
- Bible Stories
- Make a Difference

Kids' Clubhouse
- *Faith First* Activities
- Chapter Reviews
- Games
- Saints

Don't Forget! You can make lesson planning a breeze—check out the **Online Lesson Planner.**

Mary Trusted in God

We Pray

"[M]y spirit rejoices in God my savior."
Luke 1:47

Hail Mary, full of grace, the Lord is with you! Blessed are you among women. Amen.

What do you do when someone tells you good news?

Sometimes we can't sit still when we hear good news. The angel Gabriel brought Mary very good news from God.

What good news did the angel bring to Mary?

Mary, the mother of Jesus, the Mother of God (29)

PRAY

- Gather the children for prayer.
- Pray the Sign of the Cross.
- Proclaim Luke 1:47.
- Say, "Let us pray."
- All pray the first part of the Hail Mary together.
- Close with the Sign of the Cross.

DISCOVER

Purpose: To find out what the children may already know about Mary's trust in God

- Point out the statue of Mary on the page. Ask the children if they have noticed statues of Mary in their parish church or if they have any statues of her in their homes.
- Ask volunteers to share what they do when someone tells them good news.
- Read aloud the opening paragraph.
- Invite volunteers to respond to the question. Affirm appropriate responses.

Liturgy Tip

Praying the Rosary. Mary has a unique role in the divine plan of salvation. She is the Mother of God, the mother of our Redeemer. Time permitting, be sure to pray the Hail Mary in its entirety. Include it as part of today's closing prayer as well. The month of October is the month of the Rosary. Perhaps with enough time the children can pray a decade of the Rosary. Review the Rosary with the class, which can be found on page 288 of their text.

Teach

FOCUS

Read the "Faith Focus" question aloud. Share with the children that in this chapter they will learn that Mary is our model of faith.

DISCOVER

- Invite the children to share some good news they have heard recently.
- Point out that everyone likes to hear good news. Sometimes the news is so good that it changes our lives.
- Introduce the Gospel account of the Annunciation in your own words. Then read the words of the angel Gabriel from the text.
- Ask a volunteer to read the last paragraph. Have the children listen for the name the Church gives this story.

Apply

REINFORCE

- Have the children work with partners to retell the Annunciation story to one another.
- Emphasize that Mary had great faith in God's love for her. That is why she could say "yes" to him.

INTEGRATE

- Have the children name people they know who have great faith in God. How do they show their faith?
- Ask: How do you say "yes" to God every day?

The Faith of Mary

Faith Focus

How did Mary show her faith and trust in God?

Faith Words

Annunciation
The Annunciation is the announcement the angel Gabriel made to the Blessed Virgin Mary that God had chosen her to be the mother of Jesus, the Son of God.

Incarnation
The Incarnation is the Son of God becoming a man and still being God.

Retell the story of the Annunciation to a friend or a member of your family.

Mary and the angel Gabriel

Mary Says Yes to God

The best news that we will ever hear is that God sent his Son, Jesus, into our world. The angel Gabriel announced this good news to the Blessed Virgin Mary. Gabriel said,

"Hail, Mary. The Lord is with you. You shall give birth to a son and you shall name him Jesus. The Holy Spirit will come to you. Your son will be God's own Son." Based on Luke 1:28, 31, 35

The Church calls the announcement of Jesus' birth to Mary the **Annunciation.** Mary believed that God's word to her would come true. She had great faith in God's love for her.

 30

Background: Doctrine

Angels of God. The existence of angels is recognized in both Scripture and Tradition. Children seem to especially enjoy the knowledge of an angel watching over them as guardian and protector. The Church celebrates the Feast of Guardian Angels on October 2. The following prayer is commonly used throughout the year and is easily memorized by children:

"Angel of God, my guardian dear,
To whom God's love commits me here,
Ever this day be at my side,
To light and guard, to rule and guide. Amen."

Mary Praises God

Before Jesus was born, Mary visited a relative whose name was Elizabeth. Elizabeth was going to have a baby too. Mary's visit to Elizabeth is known as the Visitation.

When Mary arrived at Elizabeth's home, Elizabeth said, "Blessed are you, Mary!" Mary answered Elizabeth by praising God. Mary said, "My soul praises the great goodness of God! God has done great things for me!"
Based on Luke 1:46, 49

The Church calls Mary's prayer of praise of God the Magnificat. The Magnificat is a canticle, or song of praise to God.

Mary shows us what it means to believe and trust God with our whole heart. Mary is our model of faith.

Faith-Filled People

Elizabeth

Saint Elizabeth and Zechariah were the parents of John the Baptist. As Mary did, they trusted in God's promise to send God's people the Savior. Their son John grew up to announce the good news that Jesus was the Savior promised by God. The Church celebrates the feast day of Saint Elizabeth on November 5.

Write your own prayer of praise. Thank God for something wonderful he has done for you.

My Prayer of Praise

Affirm appropriate responses.

_____

_____

_____

_____

31

✦ Background: Faith-Filled People

Elizabeth and Zechariah. Elizabeth and Zechariah gave witness to the power of God. The first chapter of Luke tells us that the angel Gabriel announced to Zechariah that Elizabeth would give birth to a son, and they should call him John. Zechariah was troubled because of their age and asked how this could be. The angel told Zechariah that because he didn't believe, he would be speechless until this happened. When Elizabeth gave birth, her relatives wanted to call him Zechariah after his father, but Elizabeth said he would be named John. They didn't understand, so they asked Zechariah. Zechariah wrote "'John is his name.' . . . Immediately Zechariah's mouth was opened, his tongue freed, and he spoke blessing God" (Luke 1:63–64).

Teach

FOCUS

Remind the children that Mary had great faith in God. They are going to learn how Mary showed her faith in God after the angel came to her.

DISCOVER

- Write these three words on the board: *Visitation*, *canticle*, and *Magnificat*. Invite the children to listen carefully for these words and their meanings as you read "Mary Praises God."
- Ask the children to share the meanings of the three words on the board.
- Point out that Mary praised God for the wonderful things he had done for her.
- Have the children read "Faith-Filled People" to discover who Elizabeth and Zechariah were.

Apply

REINFORCE

Ask the children to find and underline the sentence that defines the Magnificat.

INTEGRATE

- Have the children think of some of the wonderful things God has done for them. Giving them loving families, or the ability to learn and have fun with their friends.
- List these ideas on the board.

Teach

FOCUS

Remind the children of Mary's role as the Mother of Jesus. Tell them they are going to learn more about Jesus' birth.

DISCOVER

- Invite the children to read silently "Jesus Is Born."
- As they read, ask them to look for the meaning of the word *Incarnation* and another new word about the birth of Jesus. *Nativity.*
- Emphasize that the Holy Spirit helped Mary to trust God the Father's plan for her and for her only Son, Jesus.

Apply

REINFORCE

- Ask the children to underline the meaning of the word *Incarnation.* They may add this word to their word wall and create a word card for it.
- Make a Bible available for the children to find the complete account of the Annunciation in Luke 1:26–38.

INTEGRATE

- Have the children read the directions for the activity and complete it on their own.
- Encourage them to share their news story with someone at home.

Jesus Is Born

The Bible tells us that after Adam and Eve sinned, God promised to send a savior. God chose Mary to be the mother of the Savior he promised to send. The Holy Spirit helped Mary come to believe in God. Mary trusted in God's plans for her and her only son, Jesus.

When the time was right, Jesus, the Son of God and the son of Mary, was born according to God's plan. We call the Son of God becoming one of us and still being God the **Incarnation.**

We read the story of Jesus' birth in the Gospels of Matthew and Luke in the New Testament. The Church calls the story of the birth of Jesus the Nativity.

Pretend you are a news reporter on location in Bethlehem. You visit the manger. Report what you see and hear.

Affirm appropriate responses.

News Flash!

We interrupt this program to bring you this news bulletin.

_____

_____

_____

_____

_____

_____

_____

_____

32

Special Needs

Learning By Doing. Invite all students to participate in developing a scene depicting the shepherds telling of the birth of Jesus. Allow students to take on the parts of the shepherds, townspeople, and the reporter. Students can work in small groups to write their scripts. Assign one student in each group to write down the ideas and words they plan to use. Practice the scene. Have the reporter give the "News Bulletin" describing the scene.

Need: Children with writing/learning deficits

Our Church Makes a Difference

We Honor Mary

Catholics honor Mary as the greatest saint. Mary is our model of faith. Mary's faith and trust in God help us know how to live as God's children.

Catholics show their devotion, or their love and respect, for Mary in many ways. Each year we celebrate feast days to honor Mary. On all these days we thank and praise God for choosing Mary to be the mother of his Son.

We also say special prayers to Mary. We place statues and pictures of Mary in our churches and homes. When we show our devotion to Mary, we show the world how much God loves all people.

What do these pictures tell you about Mary?
Affirm appropriate responses.

Our Catholic Faith

Feast Days of Mary

These are some of the feast days the Church celebrates to honor Mary.

January 1—Mary, Mother of God
May 31—Visitation
August 15—Assumption of Mary to Heaven
September 8—Birth of Mary
October 7—Our Lady of the Rosary
December 8—Immaculate Conception
December 12—Our Lady of Guadalupe

33

HIGHLIGHT
Remind the children that Mary is the greatest saint.

DISCOVER
- Ask the children to name times they know when the Church honors Mary.
- Divide the class into three groups and have each group read aloud one paragraph of "We Honor Mary."
- Ask the children to go back into the text and underline ways the Church honors Mary.
- Have the children read "Our Catholic Faith" to become familiar with the days the Church honors Mary.

INTEGRATE
- Ask the children to share ways they and their families honor Mary.
- Have the children look at the pictures as you read aloud the question. Invite volunteers to respond.

Teaching Tip

Important Connections. The "Our Church Makes a Difference" page highlights how the teachings of the Church presented in the chapter have made and continue to make a difference in the Church and in the lives of Christians today. This page helps the students make that important connection between what they have learned and how those teachings have been and are being lived in the life of the Church. Relate this page to the life of your own parish community. This will help the students see the lives of faith in action and the difference living the faith makes.

Connect

HIGHLIGHT

Remind the children that Mary is the Mother of the Church.

RESPOND

- Read aloud the opening paragraph.
- Have the children read the directions for the activity and complete it on their own. Ask volunteers to share their work with the class.

CHOOSE

- Invite the children to respond to "My Faith Choice."
- After a moment of prayerful reflection have the children write their choice on the lines provided.
- Encourage the children to put their choice into practice this week.

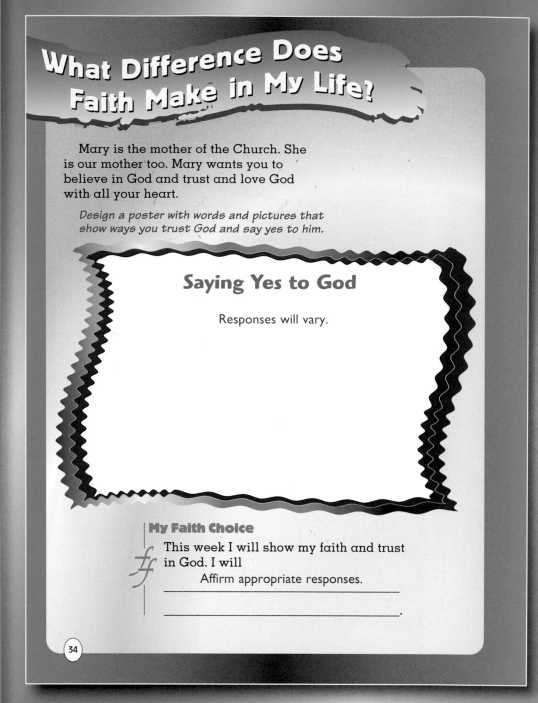

What Difference Does Faith Make in My Life?

Mary is the mother of the Church. She is our mother too. Mary wants you to believe in God and trust and love God with all your heart.

Design a poster with words and pictures that show ways you trust God and say yes to him.

Saying Yes to God

Responses will vary.

My Faith Choice

This week I will show my faith and trust in God. I will

Affirm appropriate responses.

34

Teaching Tip

Another Important Page. It is so important to give the "What Difference Does Faith Make in My Life?" pages the time the students need to process them. Processing these two pages is an integral part of the children's discovering the connection between the teachings of the Church and their personal lives. It allows the students to move from what they have learned to how they can live their faith in their daily lives. Allow time for the children to share faith stories with one another.

We Pray

The Angelus

The Angelus is a prayer that expresses the Church's faith that the Son of God became one of us and that Mary is the Mother of God.

Group 1: The angel spoke God's message to Mary,

Group 2: and she conceived of the Holy Spirit.

All: Hail Mary . . .

Group 1: "I am the lowly servant of the Lord:

Group 2: let it be done to me according to your word."

All: Hail Mary . . .

Group 1: And the Word became flesh

Group 2: and lived among us.

All: Hail Mary . . .

We Remember

Unscramble the blue letters to find the words that complete the sentences. Write the words on the lines.

1. The Son of God becoming man is called the **CANRAONINIT**.
   INCARNATION

2. The announcement of the birth of Jesus to the Virgin Mary is called the **NNUANIOTIACN**.
   ANNUNCIATION

3. Mary's visit to Elizabeth is called the **ITOVSIATNI**.
   VISITATION

To Help You Remember

1. Mary believed that God had chosen her to be the mother of Jesus, the Son of God.

2. Mary praised God for choosing her to be the mother of the Savior.

3. Mary showed us what it means to believe and trust in God.

Pray

WE PRAY

- Introduce The Angelus to the children in your own words.
- Gather the children in the prayer center. Divide the class into two groups. Each group will pray their part, and the whole group will pray the Hail Mary together.
- Conclude by praying the Sign of the Cross together.

Review

WE REMEMBER

- Review the "To Help You Remember" statements. Leave a key word out and ask volunteers to fill in the missing word.
- Read the directions to the activity and have the students complete it.

Background: Liturgy

The Angelus. The Angelus is a ritual prayer in honor of the Incarnation of Christ, which is repeated three times each day—morning, noon, and early evening—at the sound of the bell. The history of this tradition began during the late thirteenth century. Introduce the children to the Angelus and pray it together. Be sure to pray it during Advent to remind the children of Mary's trust and love for God.

At Home

ENCOURAGE

Have the children carefully tear out pages 35 and 36 along the perforation. Encourage the children to share the pages with their families and to do the activities together. If they did not complete the review activity on page 35 by the end of the session, emphasize that they can complete it with their families.

VISIT FAITHFIRST.COM

- Share with the children the many activities on the *Faith First* Web site.
- Encourage the children to visit **www.FaithFirst.com.**

---

3 With My Family

This Week . . .

In chapter 3, "Mary Trusted in God," your child listened to the Bible stories of the Annunciation, the Visitation, and the Nativity. Mary believed and trusted in God. God chose Mary as part of his plan to fulfill his promise to send the world a savior. Mary is the mother of Jesus, the Son of God, the Savior of the world. He is the Savior whom God promised to send.

For more on the teachings of the Catholic Church on the mystery of the Incarnation and the unique role of Mary in God's plan for the salvation of the world, see *Catechism of the Catholic Church* paragraph numbers 456–478 and 484–507.

Sharing God's Word

Read the Bible story in Luke 1:26–38 about the angel Gabriel's announcement to Mary or read the adaptation of the story on page 30. Emphasize Mary's faith and trust in God and her love for him.

Praying

In this chapter your child learned to pray part of the Angelus. Read and pray together the Angelus on page 35.

Making a Difference

Choose one of the following activities to do as a family or design a similar activity of your own.

- Help each other become more familiar with the Hail Mary. Make puzzles of the prayer. Write the Hail Mary on a piece of paper. Cut the paper into small puzzle pieces. Then put the puzzle together. Assembling the puzzle will help you learn the prayer.
- Elizabeth and Zechariah were the parents of John the Baptist. Their son grew up to announce the good news that Jesus was the Savior promised by God. Read about Elizabeth and Zechariah in Luke 1:5–25.
- Mary believed in and trusted God. Talk about how your family shows that you believe in and trust God. Invite each person to share one thing they will do this week to show their belief and trust in God.

For more ideas on ways your family can live your faith, visit the "Faith First for Families" page at **www.FaithFirst.com.** Share some of the ideas on the "Gospel Reflections" page with one another this week.

Before Moving On . . .

As you finish today's lesson, reflect on the following question before moving on to the next chapter.

What more can I do to make sure everyone is involved in class activities?

Evaluate

Take a few moments to evaluate this week's lesson.
I feel (circle one) about this week's lesson.

- a. very pleased
- b. OK
- c. disappointed

The activity the children enjoyed most was . . .

The concept that was most difficult to teach was . . .

because . . .

Something I would like to do differently is . . .

ENRICHING THE LESSON

Role-Playing Scripture Stories about Mary

Purpose

To reinforce the stories of the Annunciation and Visitation (taught on pages 30 and 31)

Directions

- Children enjoy role-playing some of the simple Scripture stories, such as the Annunciation and the Visitation.
- In small groups have the children role-play the Scripture stories. Read to the children the longer versions of the Gospel stories found in the New Testament: Luke 1:26–38 and Luke 1:46–55.
- Invite the children to take the parts of Mary, the archangel Gabriel, and Elizabeth. Have the children take turns playing each of the characters, while using their own dialogue to move the stories along.
- Consider presenting the Gospel stories for another class.

Materials

Making Nativity Bookmarks

Purpose

To reinforce the story of the Nativity (taught on page 32)

Directions

- Invite the children to make bookmarks using old Christmas cards.
- Have each child choose a card, cut out the religious scene, and mount their images on sheets of tag board.
- Ask the children to trim the tag board so that there is only a small border around the artwork.
- Then, on the back of the tag board, suggest that they write a message that summarizes the Nativity, for example, "Jesus is God's Son." "Mary is the mother of Jesus." "Mary is our mother too."

- As Christmas approaches, the bookmarks can be hand-delivered by the children to a first- or second-grade group of children.

Materials

Christmas cards with religious scenes
tag board
scissors
glue sticks
pens or pencils

Literature Connection

Purpose

To reinforce the importance of the life of Mary in our faith life (taught on 31)

Directions

Tomie dePaola has written a wonderful book about Mary. It is titled *Mary: Mother of Jesus* (Holiday House, 1995).

- Read the book to the children and ask them to listen for something new they did not know about Mary.
- Ask the children to share with a partner how Mary is important to their faith.

Materials

Mary: Mother of Jesus by Tomie dePaola

Music Connection

- " Ave Maria," D. Kantor. *Singing Our Faith (SOF)* #266.
- " Hail Mary: Gentle Woman," C. Landry. *Gather Comprehensive* #782.
- " Holy is Your Name," arr. D. Haas. *SOF* #269.
- "Sing of Mary, Meek and Lowly," R. Palmer. *SOF* #267.

Women of Faith
A Scripture Story

Background

The Gift of Faith

Faith is our "yes" to God's invitation to know and believe in him and all that he reveals. Faith involves the whole person. When we respond to God in faith, we freely surrender into a relationship of love with him.

In the Old Testament, faith is disclosed as obedience to the will of God. The Israelites pledged their loyalty to the God of the Covenant who is worthy of our trust. The story of the Israelites' relationship to God depicts the faith of several women and men. Among these are Sarah and Hannah. In faith, Sarah conceived the promised son, Isaac, in her old age and barrenness. Similarly, Hannah, who was barren, prayed to God with total trust. She gave birth to Samuel, who was known for his strength and wise judgment.

Two women of faith, Ruth and Esther, have Old Testament books named for them. Ruth entrusted her life to Naomi and the God of Israel. Instead of following custom and returning to the house of her father, Ruth pledged to follow Naomi, her people, and God. Ruth's faith was rewarded.

Her son Obed was part of the bloodline of David and Jesus.

Esther, a poor Jewess, led her people to trust in the power of God to protect them while living in exile in Persia. Esther's great beauty eventually opened the way for her to become queen. Queen Esther gained the love of the people and the confidence of the king. Her faith in God strengthened Esther to protect her people by saving them from certain massacre at the hand of Haman, the favored advisor of the king.

The stories of the faith of Sarah, Hannah, Ruth, and Esther were no doubt known to Mary and the first disciples of Jesus. They were for them, as they are for us, models of what it means to live a life of faith.

The Faith of Christians

The New Testament challenges the followers of Jesus to a life of faith that trusts and obeys the Father as he did. Such a faith transforms our hearts and minds and makes us Christ-like. For we all have been baptized into Christ and have clothed ourselves with Christ (See Galatians 3:27). Our continual conversion to Christ is the result of living such a life of faith.

The Christian faith is, above all, conversion to Jesus Christ,[1] full and sincere adherence to his person and the decision to walk in his footsteps.[2] Faith is a personal encounter with Jesus Christ, making of oneself a disciple of him. This demands a permanent commitment to think like him, to judge like him and to live as he lived.[3] In this way the believer unites himself to the community of disciples and appropriates the faith of the Church.[4]

GENERAL DIRECTORY FOR CATECHESIS 53

For Reflection

When can I recall that my faith in God led me to a deeper conversion to Christ?

Who has influenced my growth in faith? How do I share my faith with others?

Catechist to Catechist

Models of Faith

During this session, you and the children will come to know four faith-filled women of the Old Testament. Like Mary, they can become models of faith for you. In the course of this session, you might want to share the saints of the Church who are models of faith for you. This is one way of sharing your own faith story with the children. This will be a real gift to the children and help them learn to share their faith with others too.

A Holy Experience

As you share your faith story with the children, think of Moses before the burning bush. Moses took off his shoes to approach God. This is the attitude you need toward yourself and toward the children. The sharing of faith is a holy moment. Believing you too stand in God's presence, share your story and invite the children to share theirs with wonder, as did Moses.

The Church Teaches . . .

The *General Directory for Catechesis (GDC)* states:

> The historical character of the Christian message requires that catechesis attend to . . . presentation of salvation history by means of Biblical catechesis so as to make known the "deeds and the words" with which God has revealed himself to man. . . . This history, read within the perspective of faith, is a fundamental part of the content of catechesis.   *GDC* 108

For this reason, *Faith First* incorporates special Scripture chapters into every unit, as well as including Bible passages throughout the text.

See the Catechism . . .

For more on the teachings of the Catholic Church on Sacred Scripture and the saints, see *Catechism of the Catholic Church* 101–133 and 144–175.

CATECHIST PRAYER

Spirit of God,
who filled these four
women with faith, hope,
and love, help the
children and me grow
in faith, hope, and love.
Amen.

Footnote references on these two pages may be found on p. 456.

LESSON PLANNER

FOCUS To identify that the women of the Old Testament showed their faith in God

Engage

Page 37
Focus
To discover that the Bible tells us about people of faith

Opening Prayer

Discussion
Bible stories about people of faith

Teach and Apply

Pages 38–40
Focus
To explore that women of the Old Testament showed their faith in God

Presentation
Read, discuss, and summarize content.
Scripture
• Exodus 15:1
• Esther C:14, 25
Activities
• Complete the word search.
• Pray for people who are suffering.
• Write captions for photographs of people of faith.

Connect

Pages 41–42
Focus
To discover a woman of faith in today's times

Our Church Makes a Difference
Blessed Teresa of Calcutta was a woman of faith.
Our Catholic Faith
Prayer of the Faithful

What Difference Does Faith Make?
Activity
Draw or write about a hero of faith.
Faith Choice
Choose a way to show faith this week.

We Pray

Page 43
Prayer Form
Litany
Prayer
Choose volunteers to read petitions. Introduce the prayer and pray together.

We Remember

Review
• Complete the word puzzle activity.
• Read the "To Help You Remember" statements aloud.
Preview
Highlight features of the "With My Family" page.

Materials

• pens or pencils
• crayons or markers

Enriching the Session

Blackline Masters
Additional Activities booklet:
Chapter 4
Using symbols
Creating a drawing
Assessment Tools booklet:
Chapter 4 Test

Enriching the Lesson (CG page 93)
Telling Queen Esther's Story in Freeze Frames
Making a Cartoon Strip
Literature Connection

Music Connection (CG page 93)

www.FaithFirst.com

We update the *Faith First* Web site weekly. Check each week for new content and features. Here are some places to begin:

Catechists and Teachers
• Current Events
• Chapter Downloads
• Catechist Prayer

Faith First **for Families**
• Bible Stories
• Make a Difference

Kids' Clubhouse
• *Faith First* Activities
• Chapter Reviews
• Games
• Saints

Don't Forget! You can make lesson planning a breeze—check out the **Online Lesson Planner.**

Women of Faith
A Scripture Story

4

We Pray

Sing to the LORD,
for he is glorious!
Based on Exodus 15:1

Lord, we give our hearts to you. We trust you. We love you.   Amen.

Who do you know who has faith in God?

The Bible tells us about many men and women who had great faith in God.

What Bible stories have you heard about people of faith?

Queen Esther and
the king of Persia

(37)

Liturgy Tip

Prayer and Scripture. Using Scripture in prayer can help deepen a child's faith and spiritual life. By giving the children the frequent opportunity to quiet themselves and listen to the word of God, they can learn to listen to God's message. Using the *Lectionary for Masses with Children* when sharing Scripture will help the children better understand the context of the word. Like learning other forms of prayer, this form of prayer takes practice. The more familiar the children are with it, the more comfortable they will be in using it.

Engage

PRAY

- Gather the children for prayer.
- Invite one group to pray the Scripture verse and the second group to pray the prayer that follows.
- Begin and close with the Sign of the Cross.
- Pray together.

DISCOVER

Purpose: To assess what the children know about women of faith in the Bible

- Ask the children to name people they know who have faith in God. List their responses on the board.
- Read the introductory paragraph aloud and invite volunteers to respond to the question that follows.
- Invite the children to look carefully at the picture on this page.
- Tell them that the person on the right in the picture is Esther, a woman of great hope and trust in God. They will learn more about her in this chapter. Invite them to share what they think is happening in the picture. Affirm appropriate responses.

Teach

FOCUS

Read the "Faith Focus" question aloud. Share with the children that in this chapter they will discover how women of faith can help us grow in our own faith.

DISCOVER

- Remind the children that people of faith trust in God's love for them.
- Tell them that the Old Testament tells us about many men and women of faith.
- Read or tell the children the stories of Sarah, Hannah, and Ruth. Ask a volunteer to read the last paragraph.
- Ask how each of these women was a model of faith. Sarah believed in God's promise of a son; Hannah asked for God to give her a son; Ruth showed God's love by caring for her widowed mother-in-law.

Apply

REINFORCE

Read aloud together the faith word *trust* and its meaning. Have the children make a word card for *trust*.

INTEGRATE

- Have the children work with partners and tell each other one thing they learned from these women. Invite the children to do the word search puzzle.
- Ask the children to use each word they find in the puzzle in a sentence describing how they can live as people of faith.

Bible Background

Faith Focus

How did women of the Old Testament show their faith in God?

Faith Words

trust
To trust someone is to know that what the person tells us is true and that the person will always do what is good for us.

Sarah, Hannah, and Ruth

Mary, Jesus' mother, learned about God by hearing the stories of the Scriptures of the Jewish people. Mary heard the stories about Sarah, Hannah, and Ruth.

Sarah believed God's promise to her and gave birth to Isaac. Isaac became one of the great leaders of God's people. Hannah prayed to God for a child. Soon Hannah gave birth to Samuel. He became one of the judges of Israel. Ruth left her home to care for her husband's mother, Naomi, after both their husbands died.

Sarah, Hannah, and Ruth believed in God and had **trust** in his love. These women were models of faith for Mary and the Jewish people. They are models of faith for us too.

Find and circle the words in the puzzle that describe a person of faith.

Hannah

Sarah

Ruth

38

```
X L M T F Q B
C O U R A G E
B V R U I L I
Q E T S T O E
G H D T H A F
```

Background: Faith-Filled People

Sarah, Hannah, and Ruth. Sarah was married to Abraham. God promised them that they would have descendants more numerous than the stars. Hannah was the mother of Samuel. She took him to the shrine at Shiloh to serve God. When Ruth and Naomi, her mother-in-law, returned to Bethlehem, Ruth worked in the fields to obtain food for the two of them. Later she married Boaz, and their great-grandson was King David.

Reading the Word of God

Queen Esther

In Old Testament times God's people were sometimes forced to live away from their homeland. One time some Jewish people were forced to live in the ancient country of Persia.

Esther was a Jewish woman who became queen of that country. When she learned about a plot to kill her people, Queen Esther prayed,

"My LORD, you alone are God. Help me, for I am alone and I have no help but you. O God, remember us here. Save your people."

Based on Esther C:14, 25

With great courage, Esther told the king about the plot to kill her people. The king believed Esther, and God's people were saved. Each year the Jewish people remember and celebrate Queen Esther's faith and courage on the feast of Purim.

Think of someone or a group of people who is suffering. Quietly ask God to help them trust in his love for them.

Affirm appropriate responses.

39

Background: Scripture

Jewish Feast of Purim. The Book of Esther in the Old Testament recounts the story of Queen Esther and how her faith and action saved the Jewish people in Persia. It is the story that explains the origin and celebration of the Jewish holiday of Purim. *Purim* means *lots* and refers to the lots thrown by the evil Haman to determine which day the Jewish people should be defeated. Of course, this day never occurred and is the reason the Jewish people celebrate this feast of joy.

Teach

FOCUS
Remind the children that trust in God is the mark of a person of faith. Point out that they are going to learn about another woman of faith.

DISCOVER
- Tell the children that faith is tested when things are not going well. You may want to give an example from your own experience.
- Explain that Esther and her people faced a terrible situation.
- Tell the children to listen as you read for the problem Esther's people were having and how her faith in God helped her save them.

Apply

REINFORCE
- Map the story of Queen Esther on the board, asking the children to tell the events that mark the beginning, middle, and end of the story.
- Have the children look back to page 37 and ask which part of the story is represented by the stained-glass image.

INTEGRATE
- Talk with the children about people in our world today who are suffering. Ask: What would help these groups of people have faith in God's love for them? Affirm appropriate responses.
- Allow time for the children to offer a silent prayer for the suffering of the world.

Teach

FOCUS

Tell the children they are going to learn how the stories of faith in the Old Testament help us grow in faith and trust in God.

DISCOVER

- Remind the children that faith is a gift from God that helps us to believe all that he has revealed.
- Divide the children into groups of three. Have them make a list of people they know who are people of faith. Encourage them to think about one thing they have learned from these people.
- Read aloud "Praying the Scriptures."
- As you read, ask the class to listen for what Mary learned from the Old Testament women of faith.
- Ask: What does listening to stories about people of faith help us do? Helps us grow in faith and trust in God.

Apply

REINFORCE

Ask the children to share a story from Scripture that has taught them a lesson.

INTEGRATE

Direct the children's attention to the activity. Ask them to write how each person pictured is living as a person of faith.

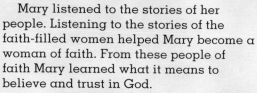

Understanding the Word of God

Praying the Scriptures

Mary listened to the stories of her people. Listening to the stories of the faith-filled women helped Mary become a woman of faith. From these people of faith Mary learned what it means to believe and trust in God.

Christians today prayerfully listen to the stories of the Old Testament and the New Testament. We continue to follow the examples of many of the faith-filled women of the Bible. Listening to the stories of these women helps us grow in faith and trust in God.

Under each picture, write how the people are living as people of faith.

Affirm appropriate responses.

Affirm appropriate responses.

Affirm appropriate responses.

40

Teaching Tip

Showing Our Faith. People of faith have a threefold way of showing their faith in God. First, the Holy Spirit guides them. Second, they are able, with God's grace, to express their convictions in actions. Third, their actions benefit others. Spend some time going over each way of showing faith, giving examples of each. Help the children make a list of biblical people of faith. Encourage the children to value these people as role models for them to follow.

Our Church Makes a Difference

Blessed Teresa of Calcutta

Blessed Teresa of Calcutta was a religious sister and a woman of faith. For over fifty years she took care of people who were homeless, sick, and dying in the city of Calcutta in India.

Many women and men wanted to join Mother Teresa in her work. She started the Missionaries of Charity. Today more than 4,000 women and men religious and 10,000 volunteers continue her work of prayer and of service to the poor. In 1997 Mother Teresa died in Calcutta at the age of 87.

In 1979 she was given the Nobel Peace Prize because of her service to the poor and suffering in the world. In 2003 Pope John Paul II beatified Mother Teresa. The Church now honors her as Blessed Teresa.

Why do you think so many men and women have chosen to continue the hard work of Blessed Mother Teresa?

Affirm appropriate responses.

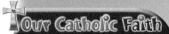

Our Catholic Faith

Prayer of the Faithful

At every Mass we celebrate the Liturgy of the Word. We listen to the Scriptures, profess our faith in God, and pray the Prayer of the Faithful. As God's people, we open our hearts to God in faith and trust as Mary, Queen Esther, and Blessed Teresa of Calcutta did.

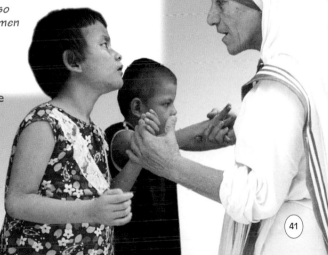

Blessed Mother Teresa talking with two blind children

41

HIGHLIGHT

Remind the children that people of faith are all around us today, helping us to grow in our own faith. Tell them they are going to learn more about another woman of faith.

DISCOVER

- Ask: Who is the person in this picture?
- Tell the children that in Blessed Teresa of Calcutta we have an example of a woman of faith who lived in our time. Have the children follow along as you read the story of Blessed Teresa.
- Ask: What helped Blessed Teresa do the difficult work she did for others? Her great faith in Jesus.
- Present "Our Catholic Faith." Ask why it is good to turn the needs of others over to God. Shows that we trust God to care for us and all those who are in need.

INTEGRATE

Ask a volunteer to answer the question. Be sure that students understand that we are all called to be witnesses to our faith in some way.

Background: Catholic Tradition

The Missionaries of Charity. Blessed Teresa of Calcutta, Mother Teresa, began the Missionaries of Charity in Calcutta, India. Their most important ministry is to care for those no one else will care for—the poorest of the poor. The missionaries' work has taken them to countries in Africa, Asia, and the Americas. The sisters' love and care is extended to include those suffering from the effects of natural catastrophes, such as floods, epidemics, and famine. As their foundress did, the Missionaries of Charity see Jesus in every person they care for. When they care for the least among people, they believe that they are caring for Jesus himself.

Connect

HIGHLIGHT

Invite a volunteer to give an explanation in their own words of what faith in God means. Let other children contribute their own ideas. List the children's ideas on the board.

RESPOND

- Invite the children to share ways they show their faith. *Words and actions.*
- Introduce the activity and give the children a few moments to consider a person of faith in their lives.
- Have the children complete the activity and invite volunteers to share their heroes of faith with the group.

CHOOSE

- Invite the children to respond to "My Faith Choice."
- After a moment of prayerful reflection have the children write their choices on the lines provided.
- Encourage the children to put their choices into practice this week.

What Difference Does Faith Make in My Life?

God gives you the gift of faith. The Holy Spirit and people of faith help you grow in faith. You show your faith by the way you act and pray.

Draw or write about a person of faith who has helped you grow in faith.

My Hero of Faith

Responses will vary.

My Faith Choice

I am a person of faith. This week I will show my faith in God by
Affirm appropriate responses.
_____
_____.

42

Teaching Tip

Take the Faith Challenge. Challenge the children to talk about faith with a friend. Divide the children into pairs and have them interview one another using these or similar questions.

- What is faith?
- Whom do you admire because of their faith in God?
- Whom do you know that has a strong faith?
- How does your faith in God affect what you do?

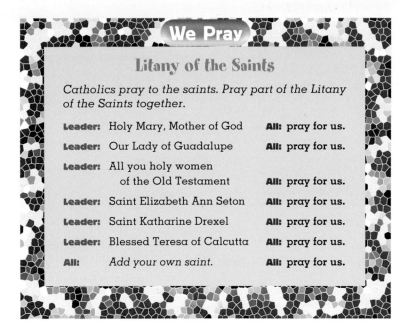

We Pray

Litany of the Saints

Catholics pray to the saints. Pray part of the Litany of the Saints together.

Leader: Holy Mary, Mother of God   **All:** pray for us.

Leader: Our Lady of Guadalupe   **All:** pray for us.

Leader: All you holy women
of the Old Testament   **All:** pray for us.

Leader: Saint Elizabeth Ann Seton   **All:** pray for us.

Leader: Saint Katharine Drexel   **All:** pray for us.

Leader: Blessed Teresa of Calcutta   **All:** pray for us.

All: *Add your own saint.*   **All:** pray for us.

We Remember

Choose one of the women of faith you learned about in this chapter. In this space describe why she is honored as a woman of faith.

Responses will vary.
Affirm appropriate responses.

To Help You Remember

1. Sarah and Hannah lived lives of faith and trust in God.

2. Ruth put her faith and trust in God and helped Naomi.

3. Queen Esther prayed and asked God to save her people.

Grade 3 • Chapter 4   43

Pray

WE PRAY

- Tell the children that today we will pray part of the Litany of the Saints together. Explain that litanies are prayers in which we repeat the same response after each petition.
- Gather the children in the prayer center. Choose volunteers to read each petition. Lead the children in the response "pray for us" after each one.
- Pray the "Litany of the Saints" together.

Review

WE REMEMBER

- Write the names *Sarah, Hannah, Ruth,* and *Queen Esther* on the board. Invite volunteers to share what they remember about each person.
- Complete the chapter review by inviting the children to complete the writing activity. Invite them to share what they have written with a partner.

Liturgy Tip

Expanding the Litany Prayer. In addition to the litany on page 43, you may wish to add a prayerful and interesting procession to the celebration. Consider adding music, such as "When the Saints Go Marching In." The children could proceed around the room singing the song and playing rhythm instruments. You may also invite a music minister to come to class and lead the children in singing the litany.

At Home

ENCOURAGE

Have the children carefully tear out pages 43 and 44 along the perforation. Encourage the children to share the pages with their families and to do the activities together. If they did not complete the review activity on page 43 by the end of the session, emphasize that they can complete it with their families.

VISIT FAITHFIRST.COM

- Share with the children the many activities on the *Faith First* Web site.
- Encourage the children to visit **www.FaithFirst.com.**

4 With My Family

This Week . . .

In chapter 4, "Women of Faith: A Scripture Story," your child listened to Bible stories from the Old Testament about women of faith: Sarah, Hannah, Ruth, and Queen Esther. These women of faith trusted God's love and prayed for God's help. Prayers of intercession were common to all these women. They prayed with deep trust in God. Hearing the stories of the faith-filled women of the Old Testament helped Mary become a woman of faith. The lives of the women and the lives of all the saints help us live a faith-filled life.

For more on the teachings of the Catholic Church on Sacred Scripture and the saints, see *Catechism of the Catholic Church* paragraph numbers 101–133 and 144–175.

44

Sharing God's Word

Read together the Bible story in Esther C:14–25 or the adaptation of the story on page 39. Emphasize that Queen Esther's faith and trust in God helped her people in their time of suffering.

Praying

In this chapter your child learned to pray part of the Litany of the Saints. Read and pray together the prayer on page 43.

Making a Difference

Choose one of the following activities to do as a family or design a similar activity of your own.

- Hannah, Sarah, Ruth, and Esther were models of faith for Mary. Invite each family member to share three people who have been models of faith for them. Be sure they explain why they chose each person.

- Make a faith tree. On the leaves of your faith tree, write the names of all of the people who have helped your family believe and trust in God.

- Choose one of the names from the Litany of the Saints on page 43. Find out more about this saint. You can look on the Internet, at the public library, or in your parish library.

For more ideas on ways your family can live your faith, visit the "Faith First for Families" page at **www.FaithFirst.com**. Click on the "Saints" page and discover other faith-filled people of the Church.

Before Moving On . . .

As you finish today's lesson, reflect on the following question before moving on to the next chapter.

Am I providing enough time to discuss the children's questions?

Evaluate

Take a few moments to evaluate this week's lesson.
I feel (circle one) about this week's lesson.

    a. very pleased

    b. OK

    c. disappointed

The activity the children enjoyed most was . . .

The concept that was most difficult to teach was . . .

because . . .

Something I would like to do differently is . . .

ENRICHING THE LESSON

Telling Queen Esther's Story in Freeze Frames

Purpose

To reinforce the story of Queen Esther (taught on page 38)

Directions

- Divide the children into groups of five.
- Have each group prepare to retell the story of Queen Esther in three freeze frames.
- Tell them to decide who will represent the Narrator, Queen Esther, the King, and the Jewish people celebrating the feast of Purim.
- Tell them that as the narrator slowly tells the story, they must create freeze frames with their bodies depicting each part of the story: Esther praying to God, talking with the King, and finally, all the Jewish people celebrating the outcome.

Materials

Making a Cartoon Strip

Purpose

To reinforce that we continue to follow the examples of models of faith in our lives (taught on pages 40–42)

Directions

- Children this age enjoy a good cartoon strip in a magazine or newspaper.
- Challenge the class to create cartoon strips that teach a lesson about faith and trust in God. Discuss with the children how a cartoon strip is set up. A cartoon usually includes at least two characters, and the characters' dialogue is drawn in speech balloons.
- Have the children work with partners to create their cartoons using four frames for the cartoon. The first will introduce the characters, the second will introduce the problem, the third will teach a lesson about trust in God, and the fourth frame will have the conclusion.

- When the children have completed their "faith" cartoon strips, display them in an area where others can enjoy the lessons to be learned about faith.

Materials

tag board
markers, pens or pencils

Literature Connection

Purpose

To reinforce that the women of the Old Testament believed in God and had trust in his love (taught on page 38)

Directions

The Song of the Temple Stones by Robert A. King is a terrific story about two large stones that are set aside during the building of a temple. The stones then teach a story of faith and trust.

- Read to the children *The Song of the Temple Stones* by Robert A. King (Pauline Books & Media, 1999) This book is a wonderful story about patience, faith, and trust in God's plan.
- Have the children choose one of the discussion questions found in the book to answer in small groups.

Materials

The Song of the Temple Stone by Robert A. King

Music Connection

- "Guide My Feet" (African-American traditional). *Singing Our Faith (SOF)* #206.
- "If Today You Hear God's Voice," M. Friedman. *Rise Up and Sing* #202.
- "Psalm 27: In the Land of the Living," C. Johengen. *Gather Comprehensive* #38.
- "Psalm 27: The Lord is My Light," D. Haas. *SOF* #17.

Jesus, the Son of God

Background

The Ministry and Mission of Jesus

The Good News of our liberation from sin and death through the life, Passion, death, and Resurrection of Jesus is at the heart of the Gospel proclamation.

The message of Jesus about God is Good News for humanity. Jesus proclaimed the Kingdom of God,[1] a new and definitive intervention by God, with a transforming power equal and even superior to his creation of the world.[2]

GENERAL DIRECTORY FOR CATECHESIS 101

At the beginning of his public life, Jesus proclaimed this Good News in the synagogue in Nazareth, announcing that his mission and ministry was the fulfillment of the promises of the prophet Isaiah. (See Luke 4:14–21.)

Jesus' entire life proclaimed and brought about this Good News of salvation. His mission was to bring good news to the poor, freedom to captives, sight to the blind, and liberation from everything and everyone that oppressed people. His healing enlightened the blind to see and the lame to walk with faith. His trusting obedience to the will of his Father

brought redemption to humanity and all of creation. Jesus' whole life revealed and restored humanity to the loving, merciful life of God the Father.

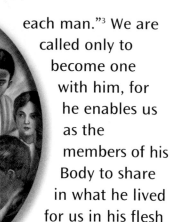

The Mission and Ministry of the Church

Through the original fall of the first parents, the original holiness that humanity had was lost, but not forever. The Good News is that "salvation is offered to all through Christ" (*Catechism of the Catholic Church* 389). "The victory that Christ has won over sin has given us greater blessings than those which sin has taken from us: 'where sin increased, grace abounded all the more'" [Romans 5:20] (*Catechism of the Catholic Church* 420). Through Baptism all believers share in the mission of Jesus Christ.

Christ enables us *to live in him* all that he himself lived, and *he lives it in us.* "By his Incarnation, he, the Son of God, has in a certain way united himself with

each man."[3] We are called only to become one with him, for he enables us as the members of his Body to share in what he lived for us in his flesh as our model.

CATECHISM OF THE CATHOLIC CHURCH 521

The Church is the sign and means of salvation for all people. We carry out this mission through the celebration of the sacraments and through the witness of our lives. In communion with Christ, the Head of his Body, the Church, and with one another, we proclaim the Good News of Jesus Christ through word and sacrament. We continue the work Jesus first announced in Nazareth and accomplished in the Paschal Mystery of his saving death, Resurrection, and glorious Ascension.

For Reflection

What Gospel stories illustrate the transforming power of Christ for me?

In what ways do my deeds and words proclaim and invite others to share in the Good News of salvation in Christ?

Catechist to Catechist

God's Constant Love

God does not pay attention to you sometimes and ignore you at other times. His love for you and the children is consistent, continual, and unconditional. His love does not alter when your faith or the children's faith vacillates. You can count on God.

Be Consistent

As you plan each session, look for ways to be consistent—in the way you greet the children, in the way you pray, in the way you call them to respect you and one 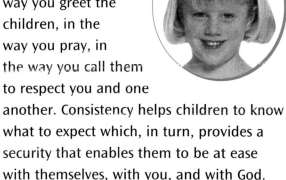 another. Consistency helps children to know what to expect which, in turn, provides a security that enables them to be at ease with themselves, with you, and with God. Your consistency shows the children God's constant and continual love for them.

The Church Teaches . . .

Pope John Paul II reminds us in his encyclical *On Catechesis in Our Time (CT)*:

> [A]t the heart of catechesis we find, in essence, a person, the Person of Jesus of Nazareth, "the only Son of the Father, full of grace and truth."[1]
>
> *CT 5*

You can help the children grow in their knowledge and relationship with Jesus, the Savior and Redeemer. Encourage the children to read the Bible and talk to Church leaders, ministers, and their families about Jesus Christ.

See the Catechism . . .

For more on the teachings of the Catholic Church on the mysteries of the infancy, hidden life, and public life of Christ, see *Catechism of the Catholic Church* 512–560.

CATECHIST PRAYER

God, our loving Father, you sent your son, Jesus, your Promised One and Messiah. Send the Holy Spirit to help us prepare for the coming of the kingdom Jesus announced. Amen.

Footnote references on these two pages may be found on p. 456.

LESSON PLANNER

Engage

Page 45
Focus

To recall that God the Father sent Jesus, his only Son, to save us from our sins

Opening Prayer

Discussion

What it is like to be saved from danger

Teach and Apply

Pages 46–48
Focus

To explain that Jesus is the Messiah who brought us the good news of the kingdom of God

Presentation

Read, discuss, and summarize content.

Scripture

- Psalm 79:9
- Luke 2:30, 46–47, 51–52

Activities

- Place yourself in the story of Jesus in the Temple.
- Follow a maze.
- Describe a good disciple.

Faith-Filled People

Saint Joseph

Connect

Pages 49–50
Focus

To demonstrate ways the Church proclaims the Good News by her actions

Our Church Makes a Difference

A third grade class continues the work Jesus began.

Our Catholic Faith

Holy Childhood Association

What Difference Does Faith Make?

Activity

Complete the survey, "Disciples of Jesus Today."

Faith Choice

Choose a way to live the Gospel this week.

We Pray

Page 51
  Prayer Form
  Prayer of petition for mercy
  Prayer
  Choose a leader. Pray together the "Lord, Have Mercy" that is prayed at Mass.

We Remember

Review
- Complete the matching activity.
- Read the "To Help You Remember" statements aloud.

Preview
Highlight features of the "With My Family" page.

Materials

- pens or pencils
- crayons or markers

Enriching the Session

Blackline Masters
  Additional Activities booklet:
    Chapter 5
      Following a maze
      Solving a puzzle
  Assessment Tools booklet:
    Chapter 5 Test

Enriching the Lesson (CG page 105)
  Learning a Rhyme about the Kingdom of God
  Designing a Web Page
  Literature Connection

Music Connection (CG page 105)

www.FaithFirst.com

We update the *Faith First* Web site weekly. Check each week for new content and features. Here are some places to begin:

Catechists and Teachers
- Current Events
- Chapter Downloads
- Catechist Prayer

Faith First **for Families**
- Bible Stories
- Make a Difference

Kids' Clubhouse
- *Faith First* Activities
- Chapter Reviews
- Games
- Saints

Don't Forget! You can make lesson planning a breeze—check out the **Online Lesson Planner.**

Jesus, the Son of God

5

We Pray

Help us, God our savior,
for the glory of your name. *Psalm 79:9*

God of love and mercy, open our hearts to welcome Jesus with joy. Amen.

Has anyone ever saved you from danger?

God promised to send a savior to save us from our sins.

Who did God send to be the Savior?

Christ and the Children of All Races by V. Horio Bianchini (45)

PRAY

- Gather the children for prayer.
- Pray the Sign of the Cross together.
- Pray Psalm 79:9 aloud.
- Invite the children to respond with the prayer.
- Close with the Sign of the Cross.

DISCOVER

Purpose: To discover what the children know about Jesus, the Son of God

- Discuss the illustration. Ask the children to tell about other images of Jesus they have seen. Ask them to tell how they imagine Jesus to look.
- Ask the opening question. Allow the children to share any experiences they may have had. Remind them that God promised to save us from our sins.
- Read aloud the final question and invite the children's responses.

Teaching Tip

Create a Time Line. Children in the third grade are beginning to develop a sense of history. To help them visualize the major events in the life of Jesus, create a time line large enough to be seen at a distance, and place it in front of the children as you teach this chapter. As the children learn more about his life, you may choose to add to the time line. The time line will set a foundation that will help the children recall the important events in the life of Jesus.

Teach

Read the "Faith Focus" question aloud. Share with the children that in this chapter they will discover that God the Father sent Jesus to be our Savior.

DISCOVER

- Talk with the children about some of the responsibilities of new parents.
- Point out that one of Mary's and Joseph's responsibilities was to raise Jesus in their Jewish faith.
- Have the children read silently "Jesus Is the Messiah" to find out what Mary and Joseph did as part of raising Jesus in their faith.

Apply

REINFORCE

- Point out the "Faith Words" *Jesus* and *Messiah*. Have a volunteer read the meanings.
- Invite the children to make word cards for these two words.

INTEGRATE

- Ask volunteers to share what they think Simeon meant when he said that he had seen God's salvation when he saw Jesus.
  Simeon recognized that Jesus was the promised Messiah.
- Ask the children to pretend they are greeting the Holy Family in the Temple. What would they say and do?

The Good News of Jesus Christ

Faith Focus

What is the Good News of Jesus Christ?

Faith Words

Jesus
The name *Jesus* means "God saves." Jesus is the Son of God and the Savior that God promised to send his people.

Messiah
The word *messiah* means "anointed one." Jesus is the Messiah, the Anointed One of God, the Savior God promised to send.

Jesus Is the Messiah

The angel Gabriel told Mary to name her baby **Jesus.** The name *Jesus* means "God saves." Jesus is the Savior God promised to send his people.

Soon after Jesus was born, Mary and Joseph took Jesus to the Temple in Jerusalem to dedicate him to God. Christians call this event in the life of Jesus the Presentation of the Lord.

When the Holy Family arrived at the Temple, they met Simeon and Anna. Simeon and Anna had been waiting all their lives for the **Messiah,** the Savior God promised to send. Simeon took Jesus in his arms, blessed God, and said,

"O God, my eyes have now seen your salvation." Based on Luke 2:30

Pretend you are in the Temple. How would you greet the Holy Family?

Affirm appropriate responses.

46

Faith Vocabulary

Jesus the Messiah. The word *Messiah* means "Anointed One." In the Old Testament, anointing a person with oil was a sign that a person had been chosen to serve, or help, God's people in a special way. Thus Jesus Christ means "Jesus, the Anointed One." God the Father sent Jesus, his only Son, to save his people from their sins.

The Holy Family

When Jesus was twelve years old, the Holy Family went to Jerusalem to celebrate Passover. Passover is a feast that the Jewish people celebrate each year. It celebrates God's mercy and love for his people. It especially celebrates God's freeing his people from slavery in Egypt.

When the Passover feast was over, Mary and Joseph could not find Jesus. The Bible tells us what happened.

> After searching the city for three days, Mary and Joseph found Jesus in the Temple. He was sitting with the teachers, listening to them and asking them questions.
>
> Jesus returned home to Nazareth with Mary and Joseph. He remained obedient to them. As the years passed, Jesus grew in wisdom, age, and grace.
>
> Based on Luke 2:46–47, 51–52

Faith-Filled People

Joseph

Saint Joseph is the foster father of Jesus and the husband of Mary. The Bible tells us that Joseph was a carpenter. Saint Joseph is the patron saint of workers. The Church celebrates the feast day of Joseph, husband of Mary, on March 19, and the feast day of Saint Joseph the Worker on May 1.

Follow the maze. Help Mary and Joseph find Jesus and bring him back home to Nazareth.

47

Background: Faith-Filled People

Saint Joseph. Though there is not much that is said about Joseph in the Scriptures, we do know that he was a man of great faith. He was also a kind and compassionate man. After an angel visited Joseph in a dream, Joseph did what was commanded of him. He willingly served the Lord and helped to bring Jesus into the world safely so that we might know salvation. Joseph took his duty to care for Jesus seriously, bringing Jesus to the Temple as well as teaching him a trade to support himself. Joseph is the patron saint of fathers and of workers.

Teach

FOCUS

Remind the children that Jesus' whole life on earth was dedicated to his Father.

DISCOVER

- Ask the children if they have ever been lost. What did their parents do?
- Read the first two paragraphs of "The Holy Family" aloud to the children.
- Have two volunteers proclaim the Scripture story of Jesus being found in the Temple based on Luke 2:46–47 and 51–52.
- Ask a volunteer to read "Faith-Filled People" aloud.
- Ask why Jesus was obedient to Mary and Joseph. What happened as a result of his obedience? Jesus grew in wisdom, age, and grace.

Apply

REINFORCE

Have the children do the maze at the bottom of the page.

INTEGRATE

Point out to the children that all families are called to be holy families. Invite them to share ways their family shows they are a holy family.

Teach

FOCUS

Point out that when Jesus grew up he shared the good news of the kingdom of God.

DISCOVER

- Talk with the children about how today good news is often spread by telephone, e-mail, in person or on television.
- Ask: In the time of Jesus, how do you think people spread good news? Travel in person from one place to another.
- Read aloud "Jesus Brings Good News."
- Have the children find and underline the meaning of the word *disciple*.
- Emphasize that Jesus' disciples came to know and believe that he was the Son of God and the Savior sent by God.

Apply

REINFORCE

Have the children work with partners and ask them to share two things they learned about Jesus on this page.

INTEGRATE

- Ask: When did you first become a disciple of Jesus? At Baptism.
- Explain the activity directions and have the children complete it.
- Write the word *disciple* on the board. Invite the children to help you create a word map by coming up one by one and writing one of the words they wrote in the activity.

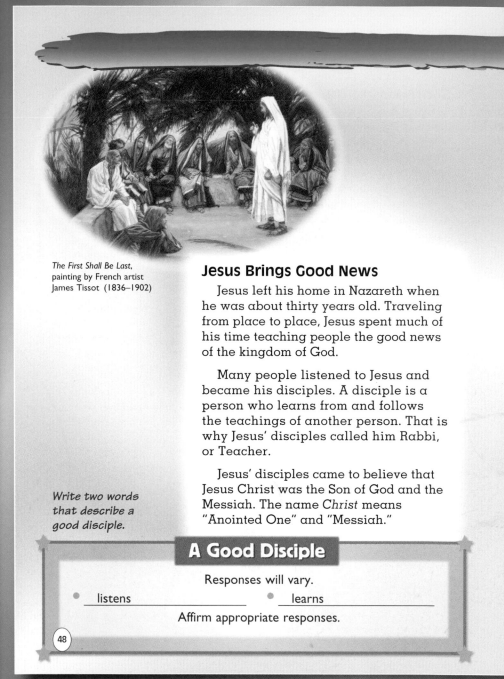

The First Shall Be Last, painting by French artist James Tissot (1836–1902)

Jesus Brings Good News

Jesus left his home in Nazareth when he was about thirty years old. Traveling from place to place, Jesus spent much of his time teaching people the good news of the kingdom of God.

Many people listened to Jesus and became his disciples. A disciple is a person who learns from and follows the teachings of another person. That is why Jesus' disciples called him Rabbi, or Teacher.

Jesus' disciples came to believe that Jesus Christ was the Son of God and the Messiah. The name *Christ* means "Anointed One" and "Messiah."

Write two words that describe a good disciple.

A Good Disciple

Responses will vary.

- listens
- learns

Affirm appropriate responses.

48

Teaching Tip

Sharing Hospitality. Point out to the children that living like Jesus and being his disciples means being kind to everyone. Share that the word *hospitality* includes providing shelter or a resting place for strangers or those who are traveling. If your parish has a Hospitality Committee, tell the children how they make others feel welcome. Point out your parish's greeters who welcome parishioners and visitors to Sunday Mass. Emphasize that by being kind to others, the Church community lives as Jesus lived.

Our Church Makes a Difference

Good News in Action

The third grade class at Saint Monica's Parish wanted to continue the work that Jesus began. They wanted to prepare the way for the coming of the kingdom of God. They thought about collecting food and clothing for the poor. They considered sending get-well cards to people who were sick. Finally, they decided to collect food when they heard the town food pantry was almost empty.

The class made posters to get other people involved. On the day of the collection, more than fifty people came to help. They filled twenty-eight boxes with food.

Describe one way that you can work with your friends to continue the work Jesus began.

Affirm appropriate responses.

Our Catholic Faith

Holy Childhood Association

The Holy Childhood Association helps young Catholics spread the Good News of Jesus. Children in religious education programs and in Catholic schools collect money. The money is used to provide food, clean water, medicine, places to live, and education to poor children in more than one hundred countries.

Catholic Social Teaching

Option for the Poor and Vulnerable. An inordinate and self-centered attachment to wealth and possessions is contrary to living as a disciple of Christ. The Catholic Church teaches this very principle: We are obligated to share our possessions, to be detached from them and to work for the elimination of the inequitable distribution of material and spiritual goods among peoples.

Tips: Help the children learn that part of being a disciple is sharing what we have with others. Pair your class with a parish-related mission group. Together, develop a plan for a food drive or other event that will help the needy of your parish. Pray together for the poor.

HIGHLIGHT

Remind the children that the Church helps us discover many ways of being good disciples.

DISCOVER

- Explain to the children that the story they are about to hear tells about a group of third graders who wanted to continue the work that Jesus began.
- Ask volunteers to read aloud "Good News in Action."
- Ask: How did these children spread the Good News?
- Have them read "Our Catholic Faith" to find out how the Holy Childhood Association helps young Catholics spread the Good News of Jesus.

INTEGRATE

Ask the children to name groups they know in their parish that help others. Point out that helping others is a way to spread the Good News of Jesus.

Connect

HIGHLIGHT

Remind the children that every time they live out their faith, they are announcing the coming of the kingdom of God.

RESPOND

- Read the opening paragraph.
- Explain the directions to the activity.
- Have the children complete the activity and share their responses with the group.

CHOOSE

- Invite the children to respond to "My Faith Choice."
- After a moment of prayerful reflection have the children write their choices on the lines provided.
- Encourage the children to put their choices into practice this week.

What Difference Does Faith Make in My Life?

Each time you put your faith in Jesus into action you announce the Good News announced by Jesus. You live the Gospel. You prepare for the coming of the kingdom of God.

Complete the survey. Circle the things that disciples of Jesus can do to live the Gospel today. Then discuss with a group some times and places you could do one of these things.

Disciples of Jesus Today

1. Come to know Jesus by reading the Bible.

(Agree)   Disagree

2. Welcome children who are new to our school or neighborhood.

(Agree)   Disagree

3. Help out at home more often.

(Agree)   Disagree

My Faith Choice

This week I will try to live as a disciple of Jesus. I will live the Gospel by

Affirm appropriate responses.

_____

_____ .

50

Background: Doctrine

The Kingdom of God. Jesus preached the Good News of the coming of the kingdom of God. As Jesus' announcement of the kingdom is made repeatedly in the Scriptures, we are reminded that we, as the Church, are called to continually prepare for this kingdom by living and proclaiming the Good News. Help the children see how the actions they take as disciples of Jesus can help prepare for the coming of the kingdom of God.

We Pray

Lord, Have Mercy

At Mass we ask God to bless us with the gift of his mercy. Pray this prayer, which we sometimes pray in the Introductory Rites of the Mass.

Leader: Lord Jesus, you came to gather all people into the peace of God's kingdom.

All: **Lord, have mercy.**

Leader: You come in word and sacrament to strengthen us in holiness.

All: **Christ, have mercy.**

Leader: You will come in glory with salvation for all your people.

All: **Lord, have mercy.**

We Remember

Match the people and places in the left column with the meanings in the right column.

People and Places	Meanings
__d__ 1. Anna and Simeon	**a.** People who are followers of Jesus
__a__ 2. disciples	**b.** The holy city of the Jewish people
__c__ 3. kingdom of God	**c.** The good news of God's mercy and love
__b__ 4. Jerusalem	**d.** People who recognized the infant Jesus to be the Messiah

To Help You Remember

1. Jesus Christ is the Messiah, the Savior God promised to send.
2. Jesus obeyed Mary and Joseph and grew in wisdom, age, and grace.
3. Jesus announced the good news of the kingdom of God.

Grade 3 • Chapter 5 — 51

Liturgy Tip

Lord Have Mercy. The "Lord, have mercy" is a prayer of petition. In a prayer of petition we ask God for forgiveness. God's mercy, his unconditional generosity and love, is the source of his forgiveness. The "Jesus Prayer," which is based on Luke 18:38, is an expanded form of the "Lord, have mercy" prayer. Read this Gospel story to the children. From time to time, use the "Lord, have mercy" prayer to augment the opening or closing prayer of the lesson.

Pray

WE PRAY

- Explain to the children that the prayer we will pray today is a prayer for mercy. We pray "Lord, have mercy" at the beginning of every Mass.
- Gather the children in the prayer center. Play an appropriate piece of music and lead the prayer, having the group respond "Lord, have mercy" or "Christ, have mercy" after each petition.

Review

WE REMEMBER

- With the children, create a word map around the word *Jesus.* Guide the children to include some of the key words found in the "To Help You Remember" statements, such as *Messiah, Savior, Mary* and *Joseph, good news.*
- Then invite volunteers to read each "To Help You Remember" statement aloud.
- Explain the directions for the activity. Allow the children time to complete it. Have them check their answers with a partner.

At Home

ENCOURAGE

Have the children carefully tear out pages 51 and 52 along the perforation. Encourage the children to share the pages with their families and to do the activities together. If they did not complete the review activity on page 51 by the end of the session, emphasize that they can complete it with their families.

VISIT FAITHFIRST.COM

- Share with the children the many activities on the *Faith First* Web site.
- Encourage the children to visit **www.FaithFirst.com**.

Before Moving On . . .

As you finish today's lesson, reflect on the following question before moving on to the next chapter.

Am I allowing quiet time for the children to think about the concepts I am presenting?

---

5 With My Family

This Week . . .

In chapter 5, "Jesus, the Son of God," your child learned that God sent Jesus Christ as the Messiah. He is the One anointed by the Holy Spirit to announce and share God's mercy and love with God's people. He is the Savior of the world. When Jesus was a baby, Mary and Joseph took him to the Temple in Jerusalem and dedicated him to God. At the Temple, Simeon and Anna recognized Jesus to be the Messiah. Life in the Holy Family prepared Jesus for his work as the Messiah. When he grew up, Jesus left his home in Nazareth, called disciples to follow him, and traveled about announcing the coming of the kingdom of God.

For more on the teachings of the Catholic Church on the mysteries of the infancy, hidden life, and public life of Christ, see *Catechism of the Catholic Church* paragraph numbers 512–560.

Sharing God's Word

Read together the Bible story in Luke 2:42–47, 51–52 about Jesus in the Temple or read the adaptation of the story on page 47. Emphasize that as Jesus grew up, he grew in wisdom and in faith.

Praying

In this chapter your child learned responses from the Act of Penitence we sometimes pray during the Introductory Rites of the Mass. In this prayer we ask God to bless us with his gift of mercy. Read and pray the prayer on page 51.

Making a Difference

Choose one of the following activities to do as a family or design a similar activity of your own.

- Talk about what it means to live as a disciple of Jesus. As a family, choose one thing you can do together this week to live as disciples of Jesus.

- When you take part in Mass this week, pay close attention to the response "Lord, have mercy" at the beginning of Mass. Use the response as your family prayer this week. Remember that God's mercy is a gift.

- Read together the Beatitudes on page 290. Talk about how living the Beatitudes prepares for the coming of the kingdom of God that Jesus announced.

For more ideas on ways your family can live your faith, visit the "Faith First for Families" page at **www.FaithFirst.com**. Visit the "Games" page. Ask your child to show you the game they most like.

Evaluate

Take a few moments to evaluate this week's lesson.
I feel (circle one) about this week's lesson.

    a. very pleased
    b. OK
    c. disappointed

The activity the children enjoyed most was . . .

The concept that was most difficult to teach was . . .

because . . .

Something I would like to do differently is . . .

ENRICHING THE LESSON

Learning a Rhyme About the Kingdom of God

Purpose

To reinforce the teaching that Jesus preached about the kingdom of God (taught on page 48)

Directions

Teach the following rhyme to reinforce the chapter's key concepts.

> Jesus traveled far and wide
> He did not go alone.
> He brought with him a bunch of folks
> He soon would call his own.
>
> Together Jesus and his friends
> Spoke of God's terrific plan
> To bring to earth the love of God
> For each woman, child, and man.
>
> Now it is our time to tell
> With words and actions, kind
> The message that we heard from him
> For every heart and mind.
>
> God's kingdom has begun, it's true!
> His peace and love are near!
> Let's shout it from the rooftops
> So everyone will hear!

Materials

copies of the rhyme

Designing a Web Page

Purpose

To reinforce that each time we put our faith into action we announce the Good News announced by Jesus (taught on pages 49–50)

Directions

- Brainstorm with the children ways they can prepare for the coming of the kingdom of God.
- In small groups have the children create their own web pages with drawings that illustrate what third graders can do.
- Encourage them to make their web pages attractive by using illustrations and bright colors.
- Display the completed web pages in an area where others can learn from them.

Materials

construction paper and crayons or markers

Literature Connection

Purpose

To extend the teaching about the Holy Family (taught on page 47)

Directions

In *The Family Under the Bridge* by Natalie Savage Carlson (HarperCollins Children's Books, 1989) Armand, a penniless hobo, is irritated to find that a single mother and her three children have claimed his "home" under a bridge. Gradually, he learns from them the true meaning of family love.

- Read the first chapter of the book to the children. Invite the children to predict what will happen next.
- Loan the book to an interested child and ask him or her to report the outcome to the class in a future session.
- Remind the children that the perfect model of love for all families is the Holy Family.

Materials

The Family under the Bridge by Natalie Savage Carlson

Music Connection

- "At the Name of Jesus," E. Bolduc. *Voices As One* #5.
- "I Want to Walk as a Child of the Light," K. Thomerson. *Gather Comprehensive (GC)* #507.
- "Jesus in the Morning" (African-American folk song). *Singing Our Faith* #168.
- "Sing Hey for the Carpenter," J. Bell. *GC* #692.

Jesus' Death and Resurrection

Background

The Paschal Mystery

The whole purpose of the Incarnation—the Son of God taking on flesh and becoming one of us in all things but sin—is the fulfillment of God's loving plan of salvation.

> He who is the "image of the invisible God" (Colossians 1:15)[1], is himself the perfect man who has restored in the children of Adam that likeness to God which had been disfigured ever since the first sin.
>
> PASTORAL CONSTITUTION OF THE CHURCH IN THE MODERN WORLD (GAUDIUM ET SPES) 22

Christ, the Incarnate Son of God, embraced suffering. He did so not without fear, not without sharing his inner "sorrow and distress" with his disciples and then with his Father. Seeking their presence and comfort, he said to his disciples:

> "My soul is sorrowful even to death. Remain here and keep watch with me." He advanced a little and fell prostrate in prayer, saying, "My Father, if it is possible, let this cup pass from me; yet, not as I will, but as you will." MATTHEW 26:38–39

The sacrifice of Jesus on the cross was a true sacrifice. It was Christ's free surrendering of his fears and distress and his very life, out of love for the Father who sent him and for those for whom he was sent. It was a full and true human expression of the depth of the Incarnate Son of God's love for God and for humanity.

New Life in Christ

Though Jesus was without sin, he suffered willingly for all sinners. In embracing his death on the cross, Jesus placed his life in complete conformity to the divine plan. In so doing, he gave glory to his Father and was in turn glorified by God.

> "Father, the hour has come. Give glory to your son, so that your son may glorify you. . . . I glorified you on earth by accomplishing the work that you gave me to do. Now glorify me, Father, with you, with the glory that I had with you before the world began." JOHN 17:1, 4–5

Through the Passion and death and Resurrection of Christ we are freed from the bondage of sin and evil. The doors to eternal life have been opened. We shall rise on the last day when Christ comes again in glory. For Christ has restored us to our place as sons and daughters of God. We are reconciled to God and to one another through his Paschal Mystery.

For Reflection

What experiences have I had that have made me aware that I share in the Paschal Mystery of Christ?

How can I be more ready to remain with and keep watch with others during times of their suffering?

Catechist to Catechist

The Heart of the Gospel

This week's lesson presents the heart of the Gospel message—the Paschal Mystery of Christ's Passion, death, Resurrection and Ascension. Jesus' trust in his Father's love is so complete that goodness triumphs over sin and death. In being raised from the dead, Jesus passes over from darkness to light, from death to new and glorious life.

A Message of Hope

Even though third graders cannot understand the deepest meaning of the Paschal Mystery, they can appreciate the message of hope that is at the heart of this central mystery of our faith in Christ. Even at the young ages of eight and nine, children are very aware of the suffering and violence that are part of our world. In teaching about Jesus' Resurrection and Ascension, you can share a much needed message of hope with the children. Help the children to know and trust in God's ever-present, infinite love and his promise of eternal life.

The Church Teaches . . .

The person of Jesus, the second Person of the Blessed Trinity, is revealed through one's interaction with others. The *General Directory for Catechesis* teaches:

> The relationship between the Christian message and human experience is not a simple methodological question. It springs from the very end of catechesis, which seeks to put the human person in communion with Jesus Christ. . . . Catechesis operates through this identity of human experience between Jesus the Master and his disciple and teaches to think like him, to act like him, to love like him.[1]   *GDC* 116

The children will come to know Jesus through their knowledge and experience of the Paschal Mystery. Share the mercy of Jesus with the children.

See the Catechism . . .

For more on the teachings of the Catholic Church on the mystery of Christ's Passion, death, Resurrection, and Ascension, see *Catechism of the Catholic Church* 599–655.

CATECHIST PRAYER

Spirit of God, breathe new life into me and into the children this week. Help us to serve you by following Jesus with joy. Amen.

Footnote references for these two pages may be found on p. 456.

LESSON PLANNER

To help the children discover the meaning of the Paschal Mystery

Engage

Page 53
Focus
To assess the children's knowledge about the death and Resurrection of Jesus

Opening Prayer

Discussion
How forgiveness is a sign of love

Teach and Apply

Pages 54–56
Focus
To identify the Paschal Mystery as the suffering, death, Resurrection and Ascension of Jesus Christ

Presentation
Read, discuss, and summarize content.
Scripture
• Psalm 33:22
• Luke 23:26, 33–34, 44, 46; Luke 24:50–51
• Matthew 27:59–60; 28:1, 5–7
Activities
• Discuss the meaning of "the sacrifice of the cross."
• Write a verse announcing the Resurrection.
• Design a Paschal Mystery emblem.
Faith-Filled People
Joseph of Arimathea

Connect

Pages 57–58
Focus
To discover one way the Church remembers the Paschal Mystery

Our Church Makes a Difference
As sharers in the Paschal Mystery we pray the Stations of the Cross as a community during Lent.
Our Catholic Faith
The Easter Candle
What Difference Does Faith Make?
Activity
Complete the New Life activity.
Faith Choice
Choose a way to share in the Paschal Mystery this week.

We Pray

Page 59
Prayer Form
Meditation
Prayer
Practice the responses. Lead the meditation of the Gospel of Matthew 28:1–10.

We Remember

Review
• Complete the scrambled letters activity.
• Read the "To Help You Remember" statements aloud.
Preview
Highlight features of the "With My Family" page.

Materials

• pens or pencils
• crayons or markers

Enriching the Session

Blackline Masters
Additional Activities booklet:
Chapter 6
Remembering the Resurrection
Talking with Jesus
Assessment Tools booklet:
Chapter 6 Test
Faith First Grade 3 Video
Segment 6: "Mrs. Pockets Story/ The Easter Story"
Enriching the Lesson (CG page 117)
Making Stations of the Cross Dioramas
Reenacting Events of the Paschal Mystery
Literature Connection
Music Connection (CG page 117)

www.FaithFirst.com

We update the *Faith First* Web site weekly. Check each week for new content and features. Here are some places to begin:

Catechists and Teachers
• Current Events
• Chapter Downloads
• Catechist Prayer
Faith First for Families
• Bible Stories
• Make a Difference
Kids' Clubhouse
• *Faith First* Activities
• Chapter Reviews
• Games
• Saints

Don't Forget! You can make lesson planning a breeze—check out the **Online Lesson Planner.**

Jesus' Death and Resurrection

We Pray

LORD, bless us with
your kindness.
We hope in you.
Based on Psalm 33:22

**God our Father,
you raised Jesus
from the dead.
Give us the gift
of eternal life.
Amen.**

*How does it feel when
someone forgives you?*

Forgiveness is a sign
of love. Jesus died on
the cross to forgive
our sins and make us
sharers in God's
forgiving love.

*What do you know
about the death and
Resurrection of Jesus?*

The Risen Christ (53)

PRAY

- Gather the children for prayer.
- Pray the Sign of the Cross together.
- Pray Psalm 33:22 aloud and have the children join you in praying the opening prayer.
- Close the prayer with the Sign of the Cross.

DISCOVER

Purpose: To assess what the children know about the Paschal Mystery

- Ask the children how they feel when someone forgives them.
- Read or summarize the introductory paragraph for the children and invite volunteers to respond to the question that follows. Affirm appropriate responses.

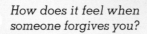

Background: Doctrine

Triumph over Death. The story of Jesus' death and Resurrection is a source of hope and consolation for all. Young children need to hear about the Risen Jesus walking and talking and spending time with his friends after his Resurrection. This will help them come to know that death is not the end of life, but rather it is the beginning of a new and better life—an eternal life of happiness with God and all the saints.

Teach

FOCUS

Share with the children that in this chapter they will learn more about the Paschal Mystery of Jesus and what it tells us about God's love.

DISCOVER

- Ask the children to give an example of making a sacrifice. Accept all answers that include doing something out of love for someone.
- Invite volunteers to read aloud "Jesus Dies on the Cross" to find out what happened to Jesus on the day he died.
- Ask: What do we call the death of Jesus on the cross? Crucifixion.
- Ask the children to share times when it is hard to be forgiving.
- Emphasize that the sacrifice Jesus made by dying on the cross was a free offering to God the Father for our sins.

Apply

REINFORCE

Ask volunteers to tell two things that Jesus said on the cross.

INTEGRATE

- Ask the children to look at the picture. Explain that Jesus had to carry his cross to the place where he was crucified.
- Read the question at the bottom of the page and invite responses. Jesus sacrificed his life on the cross so that we could live forever in heaven.

Jesus Dies and Is Risen

Jesus Dies on the Cross

After Jesus ate the Last Supper with his disciples, Judas brought the soldiers to arrest Jesus. The soldiers then brought Jesus to Pontius Pilate. Pilate ordered Jesus to be crucified, or put to death on a cross. This is what happened next.

The soldiers led Jesus outside of Jerusalem and nailed him onto a cross. Before he died, Jesus said, "Father, forgive them." At about three o'clock in the afternoon, Jesus said in a loud voice, "Father, I now give myself to you." Based on Luke 23:26, 33–34, 44, 46

Faith Focus

What does the Paschal Mystery of Jesus tell us about God's love?

Faith Words

Paschal Mystery
The Paschal Mystery is the Passion, death, Resurrection, and Ascension of Jesus Christ.

The death of Jesus on the cross is called the Crucifixion.

Jesus sacrificed his life to save all people from their sins so that we could live forever in heaven. The word *sacrifice* means "to give something that we value to God out of love."

Why do we call Jesus' dying on a cross "the sacrifice of the cross"?

Affirm appropriate responses.

Mary watching as Jesus passes by carrying his cross

54

Special Needs

Working with a Partner. Allow students to work with partners to create two-line verses for "Joyful People!" on page 55. Both students may write the same verse in their own books. When providing students with a partner, be sure to pair a student with weak writing skills with a student who is more proficient in this area.

Need: Children with writing deficits

God Raises Jesus to New Life

When Jesus died on the cross, Jesus' disciples thought they lost someone they loved. Three days later, they received some amazing good news. Here is their story.

After Jesus died on the cross, his disciple Joseph of Arimathea laid his body in his tomb. Three days later some of the women disciples of Jesus went to the tomb where he was buried. When the women looked in the tomb, Jesus' body was not there. The angel announced, "God has raised Jesus from the dead! Tell the other disciples to go to Galilee. Jesus will meet them there."

Based on Matthew 27:59–60; 28:1, 5–7

This event is called the Resurrection.

Jesus' suffering, death, Resurrection, and Ascension are known as the **Paschal Mystery**. It is the passover of Jesus from death to new life. Jesus won for us the promise of life everlasting with God. We believe that we too shall live after we die. We will live in happiness with God forever.

Create a two-sentence verse announcing the Resurrection.

Responses will vary.

Faith-Filled People

Joseph of Arimathea

Joseph of Arimathea was a disciple of Jesus. After Jesus died, Joseph asked Pilate for the body of Jesus. Joseph helped place Jesus' body in a new rock tomb in the side of a mountain.

Joyful People!

Example.

Jesus is Risen, Alleluia!

We will live with God

forever.

55

Background: Faith-Filled People

Joseph of Arimathea. The story of Joseph of Arimathea is told in all four Gospels (See Matthew 27:57–60; Mark 15:43; Luke 23:50–54; and John 19:38–42). The times were dangerous for followers of Jesus. Joseph of Arimathea teaches us that courage and faith go together. Faith helps us make decisions to live as God wants us to. The Holy Spirit's gift of courage can help one to stand up for what is right. Joseph of Arimathea was brave to speak up and identify himself as a disciple of Jesus.

Teach

FOCUS

Point out that God the Father raised Jesus from the dead to a new life.

DISCOVER

- Ask the children if they have experienced the death of a family member, friend, or pet. Ask the children to recall the sadness they felt. Emphasize that Jesus' friends felt very sad, too. They did not yet understand that Jesus would not leave them forever.
- Proclaim the Scripture based on Matthew 27:59–60; 28:1–7.
- Explain that we call Jesus' suffering, death, and Resurrection the Paschal Mystery.
- Emphasize that Jesus shares with all of us the same new life that God the Father gave to him when he was raised from the dead.
- Have the children read "Faith-Filled People" to discover what Joseph of Arimathea did after Jesus died.

Apply

REINFORCE

- Ask the children to read aloud the meaning of the faith word *Paschal Mystery.*
- Have them find these words in the text, underline them, and make a word card for this term.

INTEGRATE

Invite the children to complete the activity. Have them share their work with a neighbor.

(Student Page 55) 111

FOCUS

Remind the children that we believe that we too shall live in happiness with God forever. Tell them they are going to learn how Jesus returned to his Father in heaven.

DISCOVER

- Invite the children to describe a time when someone they love returned after being away. Discuss the feelings they had.
- Invite volunteers to read aloud "Jesus Returns to His Father."
- Ask: What did Jesus do before he returned to his Father? Blessed the disciples and sent them to share the Good News with the whole world.

Apply

REINFORCE

Ask the children to recall the four parts of the Paschal Mystery. Suffering, death, Resurrection, Ascension. Write them on the board.

INTEGRATE

- Divide children into pairs. Explain the activity and then complete it. Have volunteers share their symbols and words with the class.
- Remind them that the Paschal Mystery reminds us of God's promise of everlasting life.

Jesus Returns to His Father

After he was raised from the dead, Jesus came to the disciples and stayed with them for forty days. When the time came for Jesus to return to his Father in heaven, this is what happened.

Jesus blessed his disciples and sent them to share the Good News with the whole world. The Risen Jesus was then taken into heaven.
Based on Luke 24:50–51

We call Jesus' return to his Father the Ascension. The word *ascension* means "a going up." One day we too will return to our Father in heaven.

Design this emblem with symbols or words that tell about the Paschal Mystery of Jesus Christ.
Affirm appropriate responses.

56

Liturgy Tip

The Church's Happiest Word: Alleluia! Share with the children the meaning of the word *Alleluia*. Explain that it comes from a Greek form of a Hebrew word that means "Praise YHWH!" The Hebrew word, which is spelled *Hallelujah,* begins ten of the Psalms found in the Book of Psalms. The Greek form of the word is mentioned several times in the Book of Revelation. It has now become a formula of praise used by the Church. The Church does not say or sing "Alleluia" in the liturgy during the season of Lent as we prepare for Jesus' death and Resurrection, but we break out in Alleluia joy at Easter! Praise God! Jesus is risen! Sing out the Good News!

Our Church Makes a Difference

The Way of the Cross

You see the Way of the Cross, or the Stations of the Cross, in Catholic Churches. Catholics pray the Stations of the Cross as a community during the season of Lent. Praying the Way of the Cross helps us remember Jesus' suffering, death, and Resurrection. It helps us live Jesus' command, "Love one another as I have loved you" (based on John 13:34).

Turn to page 289 and prayerfully read the list of the Stations of the Cross. Thank Jesus for his love for you and for all people.

✚ Our Catholic Faith

The Easter Candle
The lighted Easter candle reminds us that Jesus was raised from the dead. We see the Easter candle in the place where the Church baptizes people and near the altar.

First Station:
Jesus condemned to death

Fifth Station:
Simon helping Jesus carry the cross

Twelfth Station:
Death of Jesus on the cross

57

💡 ## Teaching Tip

Teaching the Stations of the Cross. The story of the life of Jesus is very powerful, especially his Passion, death, and Resurrection. Become a storyteller and tell the children the stories of Jesus' public life, death and Resurrection. Use your knowledge of the Scriptures and the Stations of the Cross to tell the story. Let the power of God's word speak to the children. You may want to play a recording of one of the hymns suggested in "Music Connection" on page 117 of this guide as a beautiful way to share the sacrifice of Christ for each and every one of us.

Connect

HIGHLIGHT

Invite the children to explore with you a Catholic devotion that commemorates events in the Paschal Mystery of Jesus.

DISCOVER

- Invite volunteers to tell what they know about the Stations of the Cross.
- Present "The Way of the Cross" in your own words.
- Ask: What do the Stations of the Cross help us remember? When do Catholics especially pray the Stations of the Cross?
- Present "Our Catholic Faith." Remind the children that Jesus' story does not end with his death on the cross. The Easter candle reminds us that the story has a happy ending.

INTEGRATE

- Write this prayer on the board:

  We adore you, O Christ, and we bless you. Because by your holy cross you have redeemed the world.

- Direct the children to turn to the Stations of the Cross on page 289. Reinforce that the Stations of the Cross recall each step of Jesus' journey to Calvary where he died on the cross. Ask a child to read aloud each station. After each, pray the prayer on the board.

Connect

HIGHLIGHT

At Baptism we were made sharers in the Paschal Mystery.

RESPOND

- Invite the children to read silently the introductory paragraph.
- Ask the children to describe how the Holy Spirit helps us. The Holy Spirit gives us courage to make sacrifices; helps us love others.
- Explain the activity and give the children time to complete it. Invite volunteers to share their work.

CHOOSE

- Invite the children to respond to "My Faith Choice."
- After a moment of prayerful reflection have the children write their choices on the lines provided.
- Encourage the children to put their choices into practice this week.

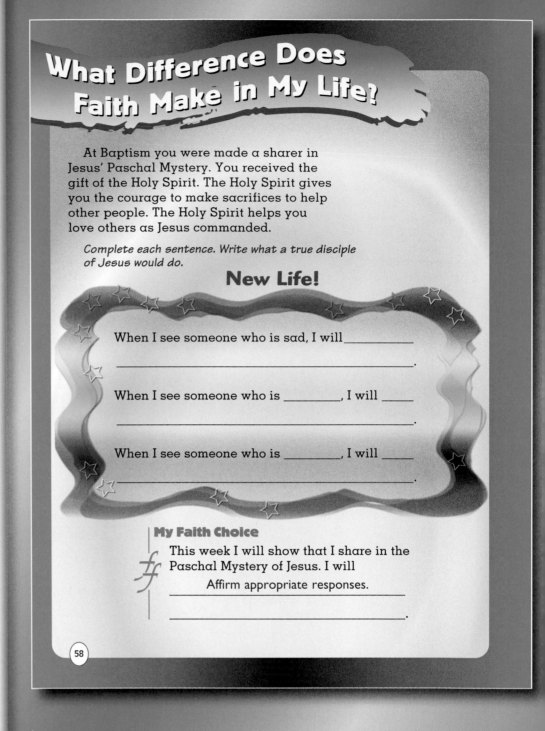

What Difference Does Faith Make in My Life?

At Baptism you were made a sharer in Jesus' Paschal Mystery. You received the gift of the Holy Spirit. The Holy Spirit gives you the courage to make sacrifices to help other people. The Holy Spirit helps you love others as Jesus commanded.

Complete each sentence. Write what a true disciple of Jesus would do.

New Life!

When I see someone who is sad, I will _____

_____.

When I see someone who is _____, I will _____

_____.

When I see someone who is _____, I will _____

_____.

My Faith Choice

This week I will show that I share in the Paschal Mystery of Jesus. I will _____

Affirm appropriate responses.
_____

_____.

58

Teaching Tip

The Paschal Mystery. Eight- and nine-year-olds are making the transition from literal and concrete thinking to a rational way of thinking. However, literal thinking still dominates this age group. Hence, their understanding of abstract and symbolic concepts will be limited. At this age, the goal is for them to learn the story of faith. Eight- and nine-year-olds cannot be expected to understand all the layers of meaning in a mystery as profound as the Paschal Mystery. But they can certainly understand that because of this event, they will live forever with God.

We Pray

Praying the Scriptures

We can use our imagination when we read and pray the Scriptures. We call this a prayer of meditation.

Leader: Close your eyes as I read a Gospel story about the Resurrection. Picture yourself in the room with the disciples.
A reading from the holy gospel according to Matthew. *Read Matthew 28:1–10.*

All: Glory to you, O Lord.

Leader: The Gospel of the Lord.

All: Praise to you, Lord Jesus Christ.

Leader: Talk with Jesus. *(Pause.)* Open your eyes. Let us all thank God.

We Remember

Unscramble the blue letters to find the words that complete the sentences. Write the words on the lines.

1. Jesus' death on the cross is the **ciCruionfix.**

   Crucifixion

2. Jesus' being raised by God to new life is the **surrecRetion.**

   Resurrection

3. Jesus' return to his Father in heaven is the **sionAscen.**

   Ascension

To Help You Remember

1. Jesus suffered and died on the cross to save all people from their sins.

2. Three days after Jesus died and was buried, God raised Jesus from the dead.

3. Forty days after he was raised from the dead, the Risen Jesus ascended, or returned, to his Father in heaven.

Grade 3 • Chapter 6 59

Pray

WE PRAY

- Gather with the children for prayer and explain that today they will meditate on a Gospel reading.
- Practice the responses with the children. When they are ready, lead them in the meditation "Praying the Scriptures."

Review

WE REMEMBER

- Write the words *Ascension, Resurrection,* and *Crucifixion* on the board. Ask a volunteer to rearrange the words in their correct sequence, as on a time line. Ask other children to describe what happened in each event.
- Introduce the unscrambling activity, and give the children time to complete it.

Liturgy Tip

Scripture and Meditation. Children can learn to use their imagination when they pray. The following are a few helpful hints for meditation. Give children a few moments of silence and remind them that they are in God's presence. Ask them to close their eyes and to imagine themselves in the story. Give them a little background on the Scripture story you are about to read so they are prepared. Use their own experiences to help them remember the story. Tell them to turn on imaginary video cameras or DVD recorders in their heads as you read so that they will remember the details.

At Home

ENCOURAGE

Have the children carefully tear out pages 59 and 60 along the perforation. Encourage the children to share the pages with their families and to do the activities together. If they did not complete the review activity on page 59 by the end of the session, emphasize that they can complete it with their families.

VISIT FAITHFIRST.COM

- Share with the children the many activities on the *Faith First* Web site.
- Encourage the children to visit **www.FaithFirst.com.**

Before Moving On . . .

As you finish today's lesson, reflect on the following question before moving on to the next chapter.

What have I learned about the different gifts and talents of the children?

---

6 With My Family

This Week . . .

In chapter 6, "Jesus' Death and Resurrection," your child learned about the Paschal Mystery of Jesus. The Paschal Mystery is the Passion, death, Resurrection, and Ascension of Jesus Christ. At Baptism we are made sharers in the Paschal Mystery of Jesus. We receive the promise of eternal life in heaven. Jesus suffered and died on the cross and was raised from the dead to save all people from sin. Forty days after the Resurrection Jesus returned, or ascended, to his Father. We await Christ's return in glory at the end of time when the kingdom he proclaimed will fully come about. We show our belief in these events by the way we live Jesus' new commandment of love.

For more on the teachings of the Catholic Church on the mystery of Christ's Passion, death, Resurrection, and Ascension, see *Catechism of the Catholic Church* paragraph numbers 599–655.

Sharing God's Word

Read together the Bible story in Luke 23:24–46 about Jesus' Crucifixion and burial or read the adaptation of the story on pages 54 and 55. Emphasize that even as Jesus was dying, he forgave those who had put him to death.

Praying

In this chapter your child prayed the Scriptures. Read and pray together the prayer on page 59.

Making a Difference

Choose one of the following activities to do as a family or design a similar activity of your own.

- Read together the Bible story about Jesus' Resurrection on page 55. Talk about how the women must have felt when they found the empty tomb.

- The Easter candle reminds us that the Risen Christ is with us. When you take part in Mass, look for the Easter candle.

- The next time you go to church, take some time to visit your parish's Stations of the Cross. Talk about what each station tells about Jesus' great love for your family and for all people.

For more ideas on ways your family can live your faith, visit the "Faith First for Families" page at **www.FaithFirst.com.** You will find the "Contemporary Issues" page helpful this week.

Evaluate

Take a few moments to evaluate this week's lesson.
I feel (circle one) about this week's lesson.

  a. very pleased
  b. OK
  c. disappointed

The activity the children enjoyed most was . . .

The concept that was most difficult to teach was . . .

because . . .

Something I would like to do differently is . . .

ENRICHING THE LESSON

Making Stations of the Cross Dioramas

Purpose

To reinforce the Way of the Cross (taught on page 57)

Directions

- Divide the children into groups of two. Assign each set of partners one of the Stations of the Cross. Invite the children to create a diorama, or scenic representation, of this station.
- Have the children color a background for the figures in their station on paper and glue it to the inside back of a shoe box.
- Provide them with a variety of materials from which to create figures, such as clay, pipe cleaners, and colored paper, to show the action of the station.
- When the dioramas are completed, display them around the classroom for the children to enjoy.

Materials

construction paper and colored paper
shoe boxes
clay
pipe cleaners
crayons

Reenacting Events of the Paschal Mystery

Purpose

To reinforce the events in the life of Jesus (taught on pages 54–56)

Directions

- Divide the class into four groups and assign one of the major events in the chapter to each group, namely, the Last Supper, the Crucifixion, the Resurrection, and the Ascension.
- Ask each small group to prepare a pantomime of their event in the Gospel story and perform it for the class.

- As an option, have the groups use words and pictures for their events and place their work on the mural they have created in the previous lesson.
- Display this mural in a place for everyone to enjoy.

Materials

pens or pencils
crayons or markers

Literature Connection

Purpose

To reinforce that Jesus sacrificed his life for us (taught on page 54)

Directions

- The book *If Jesus Came to My House* by Joan Gale Thomas (Harper Collins Publishers, 1976) brings home the message of Jesus to young and old alike.
- Read to the children this wonderful book that has survived generations.
- Have the children work with partners to write reviews of the book that would encourage others to read it.

Materials

If Jesus Came to My House by Joan Gale Thomas

Music Connection

- "Alleluia, Alleluia, Give Thanks," J. Berthier. *Singing Our Faith (SOF)* #132.
- "Dust and Ashes," D. Haas. *SOF* #120.
- "Jesus, You Love Us," C. Walker. *Rise Up and Sing* #224.
- "O How Good is Christ the Lord" (Puerto Rican traditional), acc. R. Batastini. *SOF* #124.

The Holy Spirit
A Scripture Story

The Outpouring of the Holy Spirit

The Holy Spirit mediates the continuing presence of Jesus in the Church and the world. Sacred Scripture tells us that the Holy Spirit was poured forth upon the followers of Jesus when they gathered in the Upper Room after his Ascension during the annual Jewish feast of Pentecost.

The Acts of the Apostles passes on to us that the presence of the Holy Spirit with the disciples was manifested by the signs of a "driving wind" and "tongues as of fire." Emboldened by the Holy Spirit, Peter and the others got up and followed the command of Jesus to take his mission into the world. On this feast of Pentecost, the Apostles began the work Jesus entrusted to them.

The Holy Spirit in the Life of Jesus

The Holy Spirit sparks faith in the hearts of those who believe in Jesus Christ. We come to know and believe in Christ through the influence of the Holy Spirit. This same Spirit, present from the moment of creation and in the hearts of the prophets and great leaders of the Israelites, overshadowed Mary, and she conceived her Son, Jesus.

The ascetic John, filled with the Holy Spirit, baptized Jesus in the Jordan River and prepared the way for his earthly ministry. The same Spirit led Jesus into the desert in order that he might prepare to do the work that the Father sent him to do. Throughout the ministry of Jesus, the Holy Spirit prompted and anointed Jesus for his redemptive mission. It is the same Spirit whom the Father sent in Jesus' name so the work of Christ would be continued until its completion at the end of time.

The Holy Spirit in the Life of the Church

The Holy Spirit dwells within our personal lives as well as in the life of the Church. "The mission of

Christ and the Holy Spirit is brought to completion in the Church, which is the Body of Christ and the Temple of the Holy Spirit" (*Catechism of the Catholic Church* 737). The ever-present Holy Spirit graces the Church with the gifts of healing, unity, and love. The Holy Spirit is the architect of the Church and a guide to those who pray. He is both Teacher, Advocate, and Sanctifier. The Holy Spirit is the animating breath of the liturgy and sacramental life of the Church. In the life of the baptized, the Holy Spirit pushes us out of complacency, empowering us with gifts and fruits to move beyond the comfortable, and challenging us with his amazing grace.

How often do I call upon the Holy Spirit to be my advocate and teacher?

In what ways has the Holy Spirit emboldened me to proclaim my faith in Jesus?

Catechist to Catechist

Come, Holy Spirit

As you plan and gather for each session throughout the year, remember to call upon the Holy Spirit to be with you. Trust the Holy Spirit to be your helper and your guide. Call upon the Holy Spirit in prayer. Ask for inspiration when you are at a loss for what to do, courage when you feel afraid, and patience when you seem to be having "one of those days."

A Helper and Guide

There are many ways that you can help the children learn to turn to the Holy Spirit, not only in formal prayer times, but also throughout the day. Value the things that the children make during the sessions as inspirations and gifts of the Holy Spirit. Decorate your prayer area with the children's creations. Invite the children to look at all these items and to recall what they have learned about God—Father, Son, and Holy Spirit. Help the children appreciate that the Holy Spirit is always with them to help them live as followers of Jesus each and every day.

The Church Teaches . . .

The *General Directory for Catechesis (GDC)* teaches:

> Jesus Christ, after his Resurrection together with the Father sent the Holy Spirit in order that he might accomplish from within the work of salvation and that he might animate his disciples to continue the mission to the whole world.   *GDC* 34

This chapter helps the children relate to the Holy Spirit as their advocate, helper, and guide along their journey of faith.

See the Catechism . . .

For more on the teachings of the Catholic Church on the mystery of the Holy Spirit, see *Catechism of the Catholic Church* 687–741.

CATECHIST PRAYER

*Holy Spirit,
descend upon my
eager heart. Give me
the strength and courage
needed to effectively
share your love with
the rest of the world.
Amen.*

LESSON PLANNER

Focus   To identify the work the Holy Spirit does in the Church

Engage

Page 61
Focus

To help the children identify what they have learned about the Holy Spirit

Opening Prayer

Discussion

Why we feel better when there is someone to help and guide us

Teach and Apply

Pages 62–64
Focus

To discover that the Holy Spirit came to the disciples, as Jesus promised on Pentecost and is with the Church as our advocate, helper, and guide

Presentation

Read, discuss, and summarize content.

Scripture

• Ezekiel 36:23, 27
• Acts of the Apostle 2:1–4, 14, 41

Activities

• Write or draw about the experience of the coming of the Holy Spirit.
• Name three qualities to help others learn about Jesus.
• Write a prayer to the Holy Spirit.

Connect

Pages 65–66
Focus

To identify the signs the New Testament names to show that the Holy Spirit is working in the Church

Our Church Makes a Difference

The Holy Spirit moves us to pray.

Our Catholic Faith

Fruits of the Holy Spirit

What Difference Does Faith Make?

Activity

Illustrate a way to cooperate with the Holy Spirit.

Faith Choice

Choose a way you will remember that the Holy Spirit will be with you this week.

We Pray

Page 67

Prayer Form

Prayer of petition to the Holy Spirit

Prayer

Introduce the prayer and pray together. Invite volunteers to share their own prayers to the Holy Spirit.

We Remember

Review

• Complete the crossword puzzle.
• Read the "To Help You Remember" statements aloud.

Preview

Highlight features of the "With My Family" page.

Materials

• pens or pencils
• crayons or markers
• music CD for prayer (optional)

Enriching the Session

Blackline Masters
Additional Activities booklet:
  Chapter 7
    Making a gift
    Playing a game
Assessment Tools booklet:
  Chapter 7 Test

Enriching the Lesson (CG page 129)
Creating Holy Spirit Word Puzzles
Making Paper Flames
Literature Connection

Music Connection (CG page 129)

www.FaithFirst.com

We update the *Faith First* Web site weekly. Check each week for new content and features. Here are some places to begin:

Catechists and Teachers
• Current Events
• Chapter Downloads
• Catechist Prayer

Faith First **for Families**
• Bible Stories
• Make a Difference

Kids' Clubhouse
• *Faith First* Activities
• Chapter Reviews
• Games
• Saints

Don't Forget! You can make lesson planning a breeze—check out the **Online Lesson Planner.**

The Holy Spirit
A Scripture Story

7

We Pray

Thus says the LORD God: . . . I will put my spirit within you.

Ezekiel 36:23, 27

Come, Holy Spirit, fill our hearts with the fire of your love.   Amen.

When have you felt better when someone was with you to help and guide you?

Jesus promised that the Holy Spirit would always be with the Church after he returned to his Father in heaven.

What do you know about the Holy Spirit?

Dove and flames of fire, symbols of the Holy Spirit 61

Engage

PRAY

- Play some soft music as you gather the children for prayer.
- Pray the Sign of the Cross together.
- Invite a volunteer to read aloud Ezekiel 36:23, 27.
- Pray the opening prayer to the Holy Spirit together.

DISCOVER

Purpose: To assess what the children know about the Holy Spirit

- Invite the children to describe what they see in the picture.
- Ask the opening question. Remind the children that Jesus promised that the Holy Spirit would always be with the Church to help and guide her.
- Ask the children what they know about the Holy Spirit.

Teaching Tip

Using Concrete Images. Remember that third graders are still concrete thinkers. To help the children understand and trust in the presence of the Holy Spirit in their lives, try to use concrete ideas that the children can relate to or are familiar with. For example, airplane pilots have all sorts of help that enables them to arrive safely at their destinations: radar equipment, flight crews, and weather reports, as well as judgment and experience. All of these factors require the use of listening skills, observing skills, and decision-making skills. Compare this to the Holy Spirit who guides us on our way to heaven.

Teach

FOCUS

Ask a volunteer to read the "Faith Focus" question aloud. Tell the children that they are going to discover more about the work of the Holy Spirit.

DISCOVER

- Ask volunteers to describe a time when they kept a promise.
- Explain that Jesus made an important promise to his friends on the night before he died.
- Have the children read silently "Jesus Promises the Holy Spirit" to learn more about Jesus' promise.
- Divide the class into three groups. Assign one of the paragraphs to each group and have the groups write two questions about their paragraphs.
- Collect the questions and write them on the board. Invite volunteers to answer each question.

Apply

REINFORCE

- Ask a volunteer to read aloud the definition of *Holy Spirit* in "Faith Words."
- Have the children make a word card for this term.

INTEGRATE

Ask the children what it is like to wait for something important to happen. Then introduce the activity and give the children time to complete it. Then ask the children to share their work.

Bible Background

Faith Focus

What work does the Holy Spirit do in the world?

Faith Words

Holy Spirit
The Holy Spirit is the third Person of the Holy Trinity.

Pentecost
Pentecost is the day on which the Holy Spirit came to the disciples of Jesus in Jerusalem fifty days after the Resurrection.

Jesus Promises the Holy Spirit

At the Last Supper Jesus told his disciples that he was going to return to his Father. Then he told them not to worry or be sad. Jesus promised that he would not leave them alone.

Jesus promised that God would send the **Holy Spirit** to his disciples. The Holy Spirit is the third Person of the Holy Trinity. The Holy Spirit would help them remember all that Jesus taught them. The Holy Spirit would always be with them. They would never be alone.

After Jesus died, he was raised from the dead. Forty days later he returned to his Father in heaven, and Mary and the disciples returned to Jerusalem. They went to a home and waited there for the coming of the Holy Spirit.

Pretend you are with Mary and the disciples in Jerusalem. In the flames write or draw what you might do while you are there.

62

Teaching Tip

Using Comparisons. By engaging their imagination, help the children understand what Jesus' disciples were likely feeling at the time of Pentecost. Ask the children to imagine that one of their parents suddenly went away for a long time and left them in charge of their house and their family. Discuss their fears, worries, and concerns. Relate this to the disciples' fears and worries after Jesus ascended into heaven. They too felt in need of guidance and help.

Reading the Word of God

The Spirit Comes on Pentecost

The Holy Spirit came to the disciples on the Jewish feast of **Pentecost.** The word *pentecost* means "fifty days." The Holy Spirit came to Mary and the disciples fifty days after Jesus' Resurrection. This is what the New Testament tells happened.

The disciples were gathered in a house. Suddenly, a sound like a strong wind filled the room. Small flames of fire settled over each disciple's head.

Peter and the other disciples went out into the street. Peter told everyone about Jesus. Many people became followers of Jesus that day.

Based on Acts of the Apostles 2:1–4, 14, 41

The Holy Spirit helped the disciples teach the people about Jesus. The Holy Spirit helped the people believe in Jesus.

Name three qualities you have that would help you tell other people about Jesus.

63

Background: Scripture

The Jewish Feast of Pentecost. The Jewish feast of Pentecost came to celebrate two great gifts from God: the grain harvest and the Law—the Ten Commandments, which God gave to Moses on Mount Sinai. Pentecost was celebrated fifty days after the feast of Passover. (*Pente* is the Greek word for "fifty.") This feast was the highlight of the year, and Jewish pilgrims from many parts of the known world would gather to celebrate the festival. They came from modern-day Turkey and Iran and from Libya, Italy, and Egypt. Travel was not easy since most walked; some rode on donkeys or camels, and others traveled by sea. You might use a map of the Mediterranean world to show the children the distance of these countries from Jerusalem.

FOCUS

Remind the children that Jesus promised to send the Holy Spirit. Tell them they are going to learn what happened when the Spirit came.

DISCOVER

- Talk with the children about events in their lives that are worth waiting for.
- Explain that Mary and the disciples waited for the Holy Spirit to come to them.
- Ask the children to follow along as you proclaim the Scripture based on Acts of the Apostles 2:1–4, 14, 41.
- Invite the children to read the last paragraph. Ask: How did the Holy Spirit help the disciples? By teaching the people about Jesus.

Apply

REINFORCE

Have the children read the definition of *Pentecost* in "Faith Words" on page 62 and create a word card for this word.

INTEGRATE

- Point out that the Holy Spirit filled the disciples with courage and enthusiasm to tell others about Jesus.
- Ask the children to name three qualities they have that would help them tell others about Jesus. Answers might include courage, knowledge, generosity.

Teach

FOCUS

Remind the children that the Holy Spirit helped the disciples to teach about Jesus. Tell them they are going to learn three names that the Church uses to teach us about how the Holy Spirit helps us to live as disciples of Jesus.

DISCOVER

- Invite the children to describe the kinds of help they have received from other people.
- Explain that the Holy Spirit helps us in many ways.
- Tell the children that the Church helps us understand the Spirit by giving the Holy Spirit other names.
- Write the three names for the Holy Spirit on the board as volunteers read aloud what these names tell us about the Holy Spirit.

Apply

REINFORCE

- Divide the children into three groups. Give each group one of the terms for Holy Spirit.
- Have them describe the work of the Holy Spirit by making comparisons. For example: The Holy Spirit is an Advocate like a parent who stands up for us or protects us.

INTEGRATE

- Explain the activity and give them sufficient time to complete it.
- Ask volunteers to share their prayers during today's prayer time.

Understanding the Word of God

The Holy Spirit Is with Us

Jesus promised that we would never be alone. We trust Jesus. We believe that the Holy Spirit is always with us.

The Church gives the Holy Spirit other names. Each name tells us something that we believe about the Holy Spirit.

_____

_____

_____

_____

_____

_____

_____

_____

_____

Amen.

Write a prayer to the Holy Spirit. Use the names of the Holy Spirit in your prayer.

 64

Advocate. An advocate speaks for another person. An advocate also defends people. The Holy Spirit is our advocate who speaks for us to God. The Holy Spirit defends us against danger and evil. Another word for advocate is *paraclete.*

Helper. A helper assists other people who need aid to understand or do something. The Holy Spirit helps us understand and live what Jesus taught.

Guide. A guide shows us the way. The Holy Spirit shows us the way to make good decisions to live as followers of Jesus.

The Holy Spirit helps us know, love, and serve God and our neighbor. The Holy Spirit is the Advocate, Helper, and Guide who is always with us.

Background: Doctrine

The Time of the Church. On Pentecost Sunday when the seven weeks of Easter come to an end, we celebrate the outpouring of the Holy Spirit and the birth of the Church. The gift of the Holy Spirit, promised by Jesus, is also given to us. We, as the Church, proclaim the Good News of Jesus' death and Resurrection. We do this by our good, helpful, and loving acts toward others. (See *Catechism of the Catholic Church* 731 and 732.)

Our Church Makes a Difference

Signs of the Holy Spirit

Every time we pray, the Holy Spirit moves our hearts to pray. The Church prays to the Holy Spirit. We ask the Holy Spirit to help us understand what Jesus taught and to live as Jesus' followers.

There are twelve signs that show the Holy Spirit is working in the Church. We call these the fruits of the Holy Spirit. The Holy Spirit helps us build a world with these qualities.

Our Catholic Faith

Fruits of the Holy Spirit

The fruits of the Holy Spirit are love, joy, peace, patience, kindness, goodness, generosity, gentleness, faithfulness, modesty, self-control, and chastity.

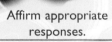

Look at each picture. On the line under each picture write the fruit of the Holy Spirit that is being used. Responses will vary.

Affirm appropriate responses.

Affirm appropriate responses.

Affirm appropriate responses.

Affirm appropriate responses.

65

HIGHLIGHT

The New Testament names twelve signs that the Holy Spirit is working in the Church.

DISCOVER

- Ask volunteers to read aloud "Signs of the Holy Spirit."
- Have the children read "Our Catholic Faith" silently to find out what the fruits of the Holy Spirit are.

INTEGRATE

- Point out that it is sometimes easy to think that we are doing everything on our own.
- Reinforce the belief that the Holy Spirit makes all the good things we do possible. The Holy Spirit helps us live as followers of Jesus.
- Direct the children's attention to the activity and read aloud the directions. Have the children work with partners to complete the activity and share their responses.
- Ask: Which fruits, or signs, of the Holy Spirit do you see in your own life and in the lives of others? Responses will vary. Affirm appropriate responses.

Background: Our Catholic Faith

Fruits of the Holy Spirit. The fruits of the Holy Spirit are signs that the kingdom of God is already at work in our midst. All are gifts from God. When we exhibit one of the fruits of the Spirit, our actions are a sign to others of his presence in the world. The goal in introducing the fruits of the Holy Spirit at this age is not to have the children commit them to memory but to recognize them. We know the fruits of the Holy Spirit because we see them in the actions of others. For example, a child who has finished a task but waits quietly while another child finishes is exhibiting patience. A child who holds his or her temper when things go wrong is showing self-control.

Connect

HIGHLIGHT

Remind the children that the Holy Spirit is always with us.

RESPOND

• Challenge the children to imagine what their lives might be like if they did not experience joy, kindness, and generosity, which are three of the fruits of the Holy Spirit. Explain that these are all gifts from God showing that the Holy Spirit is working in our lives.

• Point out that our lives would be much different and far more difficult if we were not blessed with the ability to be kind and generous.

• Explain the activity and ask the children to complete it.

CHOOSE

• Invite the children to respond to "My Faith Choice."

• After a moment of prayerful reflection have the children write their choice on the lines provided.

• Encourage the children to put their choice into practice this week.

What Difference Does Faith Make in My Life?

You can count on the Holy Spirit right now, later today, tomorrow, next month, next year, and when you are all grown up. The Holy Spirit will always be there as your advocate, helper, and guide.

Think of times when you were kind or generous. Write or draw about one of those times when you were cooperating with the Holy Spirit.

The Holy Spirit in My Life

My Faith Choice

This week I will remember that the Holy Spirit is with me. I will

Affirm appropriate responses.

_____

_____.

66

Teaching Tip

Reviewing Faith Choices. Each week the text asks the children to make a faith choice. After a child has written down what they hope to do for the week, it is easy for their promise to be forgotten, ignored, or neglected altogether. Call the children to responsibility by following up on their faith choice. Next week, begin your class by asking volunteers to share what they did during the week to fulfill the choice they made. Continue to do this each week, and more children will remember to follow through and put their faith into action.

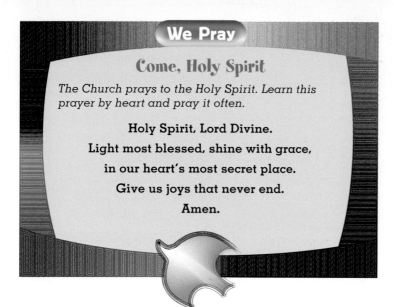

We Pray

Come, Holy Spirit

The Church prays to the Holy Spirit. Learn this prayer by heart and pray it often.

Holy Spirit, Lord Divine.

Light most blessed, shine with grace,

in our heart's most secret place.

Give us joys that never end.

Amen.

We Remember

Complete the puzzle. The clues point to our belief in the Holy Spirit.

Down

1. The Holy Spirit is the third Person of the Holy ___.
2. The Holy Spirit is the ___, or One who speaks for us.

Across

3. ___ is the day the Holy Spirit came to the disciples.
4. The Holy Spirit is the ___, or One who helps us understand Jesus' teachings.

Crossword answers: TRINITY (down), ADVOCATE (down), PENTECOST (across), HELPER (across)

To Help You Remember

1. God sent the Holy Spirit to always be with the Church.
2. On Pentecost the Holy Spirit helped the disciples teach about Jesus.
3. The Holy Spirit is our advocate, helper, and guide.

Grade 3 • Chapter 7 67

WE PRAY

- Remind the children that every time we pray, it is the Holy Spirit who moves our hearts to pray.
- Ask the children to bring the prayers they wrote on page 64 and gather in the prayer center.
- Help the children calm themselves for prayer by playing quiet music or sounding a chime.
- Invite anyone who wishes to share the prayer they wrote to the Holy Spirit on page 64.
- Close by praying the prayer to the Holy Spirit together.

Review

WE REMEMBER

- Ask volunteers to read aloud the three points from "To Help You Remember."
- Have the children work with partners to complete the crossword puzzle.

Liturgy Tip

The Prayer of the Holy Spirit. The Holy Spirit, the third Person of the Blessed Trinity, is the subject of many liturgical songs and the focus of a number of prayers. Help the children keep the Holy Spirit at the center of their lives. Teach the children the prayer on this page and use it often as part of an opening or closing prayer. Invoke the Holy Spirit and share with the children the melody to "Veni Sancte Spiritus" or "Come, Holy Spirit," arranged by Christopher Walker, OCP. This traditional hymn can be sung as part of an opening prayer or liturgical experience. See "Music Connection" on page 129 for other suggestions.

At Home

ENCOURAGE

Have the children carefully tear out pages 67 and 68 along the perforation. Encourage the children to share the pages with their families and to do the activities together. If they did not complete the review activity on page 67 by the end of the session, emphasize that they can complete it with their families.

VISIT FAITHFIRST.COM

- Share with the children the many activities on the *Faith First* Web site.
- Encourage the children to visit **www.FaithFirst.com.**

Before Moving On . . .

As you finish today's lesson, reflect on the following question before moving on to the next chapter.

How well am I allowing the children to use their talents in the various class activities?

With My Family

This Week . . .

In chapter 7, "The Holy Spirit: A Scripture Story," your child learned more about the Holy Spirit, the third Person of the Holy Trinity. Jesus promised that he and the Father would send the Holy Spirit to his disciples to be the Church's advocate, helper, and guide. The Holy Spirit came, as Jesus promised, to the disciples when they were in Jerusalem during the annual Jewish festival of Pentecost. After receiving the gift of the Holy Spirit, Peter the Apostle taught the people about Jesus. With the help of the Holy Spirit, many came to believe in Jesus and were baptized.

For more on the teachings of the Catholic Church on the mystery of the Holy Spirit, see *Catechism of the Catholic Church* paragraph numbers 687–741.

Sharing God's Word

Read together the Bible story in Acts 2:1–41 about Pentecost or read the adaptation of the story on page 63. Emphasize that the Holy Spirit came to the disciples on Pentecost.

Praying

In this chapter your child prayed to the Holy Spirit. Read and pray together the prayer on page 67.

Making a Difference

Choose one of the following activities to do as a family or design a similar activity of your own.

- Use the prayer to the Holy Spirit on page 67 as your family prayer this week. Talk about how you can count on the Holy Spirit to help you live as disciples of Jesus. Remember that the Holy Spirit is always with you.
- Make a banner with the words "Come, Holy Spirit" on it, and decorate the banner with symbols of the Holy Spirit. Hang the banner where it can remind the whole family that the Holy Spirit is always with you.
- Using the words *advocate*, *helper*, and *guide*, write a family prayer to the Holy Spirit. Include the prayer among your family prayers. Pray it regularly.

For more ideas on ways your family can live your faith, visit the "Faith First for Families" page at **www.FaithFirst.com.** Click on "Family Prayer" to find a special prayer to pray together this week.

68

Evaluate

Take a few moments to evaluate this week's lesson.
I feel (circle one) about this week's lesson.

- a. very pleased
- b. OK
- c. disappointed

The activity the children enjoyed most was . . .

The concept that was most difficult to teach was . . .

because . . .

Something I would like to do differently is . . .

ENRICHING THE LESSON

Creating Holy Spirit Word Puzzles

Purpose

To reinforce the faith terms *Advocate*, *Helper*, and *Guide* (taught on page 64)

Directions

- Invite the children to create word puzzles using the names of the Holy Spirit and the other faith words in this lesson or in previous lessons.
- Have the children create codes, jumbles, word searches, crossword puzzles, or any other type of word activity they enjoy doing. Make sure when doing word searches that they always write a direction to use the words in sentences to stress the meaning.
- Have them do this activity at home with their families and bring it to the next session. Provide time at the beginning of the next session for the children to swap their word puzzles with one another and complete them.

Materials

blank paper
rulers
pens or pencils

Making Paper Flames

Purpose

To reinforce that the Holy Spirit is always with us (taught on page 64)

Directions

- Divide the class into seven groups. Have each group choose one fruit of the Holy Spirit. On a paper "flame," have each group name their fruit.
- Using pictures from magazines, have the children develop a collage of pictures showing people living that fruit of the Holy Spirit. Have them decorate the flame in bright colors.

- Use the completed flames on a bulletin board or poster near the prayer table.

Materials

magazines
glue and scissors
colored paper
crayons or markers

Literature Connection

Purpose

To reinforce the teaching about the fruits of the Holy Spirit (taught on page 65)

Directions

The delightful book *The Quiltmaker's Journey* by Jeff Brumbeau (Orchard Books, 2005) tells how a self-centered and privileged young girl becomes the caring and generous old woman who changed the hearts of others.

- Read aloud a portion of *The Quiltmaker's Journey* to the class. Offer to lend the book to a volunteer who would like to read the rest of it during the week and share the rest of the story with the class the following week.
- Remind the children that all works of generosity are done through the power of the Holy Spirit.

Materials

The Quiltmaker's Journey by Jeff Brumbeau

Music Connection

- "Send Down the Fire," M. Haugen. *Singing Our Faith (SOF)* #176.
- "Send Us Your Spirit," D. Haas. *SOF* #171.
- "The Spirit is A-Movin'," C. Landry. *Rise Up and Sing (RUS)* #265.
- "We Are the Church," C. Walker. *RUS* #234.

We Are the Church

"Go to People of All Nations"

Jesus Christ is the first evangelizer, the first announcer of the Good News of the saving plan of the Father. Paul describes this Good News, saying, "[God] wills everyone to be saved and to come to the knowledge of the truth" (1 Timothy 2:4).

All of the baptized are charged with the responsibility to continue this mission of evangelization begun by Christ. We are to share and proclaim the Good News of salvation in Jesus Christ. We have been set free and saved from sin and death, a truth that every believer uncovers every day of his or her life. Each time we experience death—whether by means of a crisis, an illness, or a spiritual struggle—we die with Christ. Christ lifts us and raises us out of the struggle, and we discover a new way to live. We are transformed by our dying and rising. This is our good news!

There is a need for the explicit, public, and unequivocal proclamation of Jesus Christ. Paul the Apostle tells us why.

> But how can they call on him in whom they have not believed? And how can they believe in him of whom they have not heard? And how can they hear without someone to preach? And how can people preach unless they are sent? As it is written, "How beautiful are the feet of those who bring [the] good news!"
>
> ROMANS 10:14–15

The Temple of the Holy Spirit

The Holy Spirit has been given to the Church, the Temple of the Holy Spirit, to guide it in fulfilling its mission to spread the Good News of Jesus. Indeed, the Church "exists in order to evangelize," that is, "bringing the Good News into all the strata of humanity from within and making it new" (On Evangelization in the Modern World [Envangelii nuntiandi] 14, 18).

Moved by the Holy Spirit, the Church, through preaching, teaching, healing, and praying, has evangelization at its very core. All the ministry of the Church is to announce that Jesus has saved humanity through his birth, death, and Resurrection and make all peoples sharers in that salvation. With Paul we proclaim:

> Blessed be the God and Father of our Lord Jesus Christ, who has blessed us in Christ with every spiritual blessing in the heavens, as he chose us in him, before the foundation of the world. . . . In love, he destined us for adoption to himself through Jesus Christ.
>
> EPHESIANS 1:3–5

How do I experience the transforming power of the Good News in my life?

In what ways do I respond to Jesus' command to spread the Gospel to all people?

Catechist to Catechist

A Sense of Belonging

Belonging to groups and responsibly taking part in the activities of a group are very important to third graders. Many belong to teams or organizations that give them the opportunity to learn what it means to cooperate with others to reach a goal. They are beginning to recognize that they can contribute to the success of a group by sharing their talents. They are learning first-hand that good things happen when the members of a group work together and support one another's efforts.

The Church Community

In this session you will help the children better understand that the Church is not just a place of worship, but also a community of baptized Christians who use their gifts and talents to live as children of God and followers of Jesus Christ. Help the children see that they are living as members of the Catholic Church no matter where they are—at home, in school, on the playground, and in your sessions together.

The Church Teaches . . .

The *General Directory for Catechesis* (*GDC*) reminds us:

> Catechesis is an essentially ecclesial act.[1] The true subject of catechesis is the Church which, continuing the mission of Jesus the Master and, therefore animated by the Holy Spirit, is sent to be the teacher of the faith. *GDC* 78

In this chapter emphasis is placed on our Christian call to action as the Body of Christ, the Church. By following your Christian call to action, you become a living example of faith.

See the Catechism . . .

For more on the teachings of the Catholic Church on the mystery of the Church, see *Catechism of the Catholic Church* 668–679.

CATECHIST PRAYER

*Holy Spirit,
anoint me with the
oil of compassion
so that I may reach
out and share that
compassion with
others. Amen.*

Footnote references may be found on p. 456.

LESSON PLANNER

Focus To identify the work of the Church in the world

Engage

Page 69
Focus
To recall things Catholic do together

Opening Prayer

Discussion
Some things Catholics do together

Teach and Apply

Pages 70–72
Focus
To identify the Church as the People of God and Temple of the Holy Spirit

Presentation
Read, discuss, and summarize content.

Scripture
• Colossians 3:12, 15, 17
• Matthew 28:19–20
• 1 Corinthians 6:19

Activities
• Describe the work Jesus gave the Apostles, and tell who does that work in the Church today.
• Complete the drawing activity.
• Create a headline.

Faith-Filled People
Bishops and Priests

Connect

Pages 73–74
Focus
To discover that the Catholic Church is a worldwide community of the People of God

Our Church Makes a Difference
The Church helps us live the Gospel.

Our Catholic Faith
Works of Mercy

What Difference Does Faith Make?
Activity
Write about or draw how you can follow Jesus.
Faith Choice
Choose a way to live as a member of the holy People of God this week.

We Pray

Page 75
Prayer Form
Prayer of praise
Prayer
Use gestures to pray a prayer of praise.

We Remember

Review
• Complete the hidden message activity.
• Read the "To Help You Remember" statements aloud.
Preview
Highlight features of the "With My Family" page.

Materials

• parish bulletins for each child
• pens or pencils
• crayons or markers

Enriching the Session

Blackline Masters
Additional Activities booklet:
  Chapter 8
    Writing a story
    Writing a letter
Assessment Tools booklet:
  Chapter 8 Test

Enriching the Lesson (CG page 141)
Interviewing Disciples
Making Works of Mercy Posters
Literature Connection

Music Connection (CG page 141)

www.FaithFirst.com

We update the *Faith First* Web site weekly. Check each week for new content and features. Here are some places to begin:

Catechists and Teachers
• Current Events
• Chapter Downloads
• Catechist Prayer

Faith First for Families
• Bible Stories
• Make a Difference

Kids' Clubhouse
• *Faith First* Activities
• Chapter Reviews
• Games
• Saints

Don't Forget! You can make lesson planning a breeze—check out the **Online Lesson Planner.**

We Are the Church

We Pray

As God's holy people, live in peace, and do everything in Jesus' name. Based on Colossians 3:12, 15, 17

God our Father, may your Church always be your holy people. Amen.

What are some of the groups you belong to?

We are all members of a family. We are members of the community in which we live. We also belong to the Catholic Church. The Church is the holy People of God.

What are some of the things Catholics do together?

69

PRAY

- Gather the children for prayer.
- Pray the Sign of the Cross together.
- Ask the children to listen as you read aloud the Scripture passage based on Colossians 3:12, 15, 17.
- Pray the opening prayer together and close with the Sign of the Cross.

DISCOVER

Purpose: To discover what the children know about belonging to the Church

- Discuss the picture and ask the children to name some of the groups to which they belong.
- Tell the children that they also belong to the Catholic Church. Invite them to read the title of this chapter and think about what it might mean. Tell them that the Church is the holy People of God.
- Invite responses to the final question. Affirm appropriate responses.

 Liturgy Tip

Celebrate Diversity. During this session, emphasize that people of all nations make up the Catholic Church. Mass is celebrated in every language. If you have children in your class who speak a language other than English, invite them to lead the class in prayer in their native language.

Teach

FOCUS

Ask a volunteer to read the "Faith Focus" question aloud. Share with the children that in this chapter they will learn more about the Catholic Church and her work in the world.

DISCOVER

- Ask the children what it means to be responsible. To follow through on a task that you have been asked to perform.
- Proclaim the Scripture based on Matthew 28:19–20.
- Ask the children to describe Jesus' command. Go to the people of all nations, baptize them, and teach them Jesus' message.
- Invite the children to read silently the last paragraph to discover how the disciples responded.
- Ask: Who helped the disciples obey Jesus' command? The Holy Spirit.

Apply

REINFORCE

Have a volunteer read the meaning of the faith words *Apostles* and *Church* and make word cards for them.

INTEGRATE

- Ask the children what responsibility Jesus gave to the Apostles. Discuss who does that work in the Church today. Possible answers: priests, religious, catechists, deacons, missionaries.
- Read "Faith-Filled People" on page 71 to the children.

The Church Is the People of God

Faith Focus

What is the work of the Church in the world?

Faith Words

Apostles
The Apostles were the disciples of Jesus who witnessed his life, death, and Resurrection. They were chosen by Jesus to baptize and teach in his name.

Church
The Church is the People of God. It is the Body of Christ and the temple of the Holy Spirit.

Jesus Gives a Command

After the Resurrection, Jesus told his **Apostles** to invite all people to become his followers. He gave them this responsibility.

"Go to the people of all nations and make them my disciples. Baptize them in the name of the Father, and of the Son, and of the Holy Spirit. Teach them everything I have told you. I will be with you always."

Based on Matthew 28:19–20

With the help of the Holy Spirit, Jesus' Apostles and other disciples obeyed his command. They traveled by land and by sea to many parts of the world. Many people were baptized and became followers of Jesus Christ. They became the **Church.** Jesus is the Head of the Church. The Church is the Body of Christ. The Holy Spirit helps the Church grow.

Describe the responsibility Jesus gave to the Apostles. Who does that work in the Church today? Affirm appropriate responses.

70

Background: Doctrine

We Are One Body. The Church is the Body of Christ; it is one with him and unified in him. With Christ as the Head of the Body, all of its members are one. However, this unity does not take away from its great diversity. All are given different gifts by the Holy Spirit. Explore the different gifts the children have and help them see how these gifts contribute to the unity and diversity of the Church, the Body of Christ. Sharing Saint Paul's description of the Church as the Body of Christ will help the children come to appreciate this truth about the Church. (See 1 Corinthians 12.)

The Temple of the Holy Spirit

The New Testament describes the Church as the temple of the Holy Spirit. God is present with the Church. Saint Paul the Apostle taught,

"You are a temple of the Holy Spirit."
Based on Corinthians 6:19

Jesus promised that the Holy Spirit would always be present with the Church. The Holy Spirit is present in each of the followers of Jesus Christ. The Holy Spirit is present with the whole Church community too. The Holy Spirit gives the Church the grace to live as the holy People of God.

Write about or draw the members of your parish living as the holy People of God.
Responses will vary.

The Holy People Of God

Faith-Filled People

Bishops and Priests

The bishops of the Church are the successors of the Apostles. Bishops have the same responsibilities to preach, to teach, and to lead us in prayer that Jesus gave to the Apostles. Priests are helpers of the bishops.

Dove with flames, symbol of the Holy Spirit

71

Background: Faith-Filled People

Apostolic Tradition. Since the beginning of the Church, bishops, priests, and deacons have been ordained to serve the whole Church. Their vocation is a call from God to share in the life and work of Jesus that can be traced back to Peter the Apostle. Jesus asked Peter to show his love for him by feeding and tending his sheep. Before Jesus went to heaven to be with his Father, he gave Peter the Apostle and the other Apostles the responsibility to take care of the Church. Peter passed down his responsibility for Christ's sheep by anointing others to spread the Good News. Priests and bishops can trace their call to serve God and their anointing back to Peter and the other Apostles.

Teach

FOCUS

Remind the children that the Church is the Body of Christ. Tell them they are going to learn another expression that describes the Church.

DISCOVER

- Take a few moments to explain that a temple is a place where people believe God is present in a special way. Point out that for the Jewish people the holy Temple in Jerusalem was the holiest place in the known world. It was a place of worship and teaching.
- Invite volunteers to read aloud "The Temple of the Holy Spirit." Ask the children to listen for what Paul said about each of us.

Apply

REINFORCE

Emphasize that the Church is a special dwelling place for God. The term *Temple of the Holy Spirit* is used to describe the Church, or God's people.

INTEGRATE

- Point out that because the Holy Spirit dwells within each of us, we too are temples of the Holy Spirit.
- Ask: Since we are temples of the Holy Spirit, how should we treat one another? With dignity and respect.
- Have the children read the directions and complete the activity. Encourage them to share their work with their families.

(Student Page 71) 135

Teach

Remind the children that the Holy Spirit gives us the grace to live as the holy People of God. Point out that they are going to explore some ways to do this.

DISCOVER

- Write these questions on the board: When did the Catholic Church begin? When do we become members of the Church? Who are the People of God?
- Invite the children to read silently "The Catholic Church" and underline the answers to these questions. (1) at the time of the Apostles; (2) at Baptism; and (3) everyone who belongs to the Catholic Church.

Apply

REINFORCE

Ask the children to find and underline the word and meaning of *sanctifying grace*.

INTEGRATE

Provide the children with copies of a parish bulletin to help them complete the activity on the page. Ask the children which work of the parish they think they could help with.

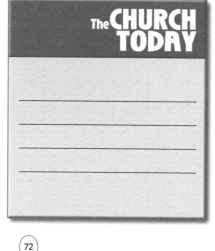

The Catholic Church

Create a headline for the front page of the newspaper The Church Today. Tell one way your parish is living as the community of God's holy people.
Responses will vary.

We belong to the Catholic Church. The Catholic Church goes all the way back to Jesus and the Apostles. The Catholic Church is made up of the pope and other bishops, priests, deacons, religious brothers and religious sisters, married and unmarried laypeople.

We become members of the Church through Baptism. At Baptism we receive the gift of sanctifying grace. The word *sanctifying* means "making holy." Sanctifying grace is the gift of God sharing his life with us. We become the holy People of God.

Everyone who belongs to the Catholic Church is part of the People of God. In the Church different people have different responsibilities and gifts. We all help others come to know Jesus and the good news of God's love for all people.

72

Catholic Social Teaching

Call to Family, Community, and Participation. The worldwide Catholic Church is a community of many races, languages, and ethnic groups; yet, we are one community of faith. As the People of God, we are concerned about issues affecting human dignity and the ability of all people to grow through equitable, just, and fair participation in the life of the community. We have an obligation and the responsibility to participate in society and to work to promote the common good.

Tip: Have the children take the parish bulletins home. Ask them to discuss with their families what parish activities they could participate in together.

Our Church Makes a Difference

✝ Our Catholic Faith

Works of Mercy

The Corporal Works of Mercy and the Spiritual Works of Mercy guide the Church in living as God's holy people. These works guide us in helping people care for the needs of their body and their soul.

The Church Today

The Catholic Church is a worldwide community of believers in Jesus Christ. A local church, or the church in a particular place, is called a diocese. A diocese has many parish churches and is led by a bishop.

All those who belong to a diocese help one another live the Gospel. Being active members of the Church enables us to be faithful followers of Jesus Christ. The way we act, the things we say, and even our attitudes show our love for God and people. The Church today helps us live as Jesus taught. When we live as a follower of Jesus, we build a kind, just, and peaceful world.

Name some of the people who help you live the Gospel. Responses will vary.

73

Connect

HIGHLIGHT

Point out that the place where we gather to worship is our parish church. Tell them they are going to learn more about the diocese to which they belong.

DISCOVER

• Write the name of your diocese on the board with the name of the bishop underneath. Ask the children the name of their parish. Explain that there are many parishes within a diocese.

• Ask the children to read "The Church Today" silently.

• Ask: What does being active in the Catholic Church help us to do? Helps us live as Jesus taught.

• Present "Our Catholic Faith." Explain that the people of the diocese are guided by the Works of Mercy which help them live as Jesus taught.

INTEGRATE

• Have the children turn to page 286 and check those Works of Mercy that they already do.

• Ask them to name some of the people that help them live the Gospel.

💡 Teaching Tip

Invite a Guest Speaker. Invite a parish priest or a priest from a religious order to speak to the children about the role of priests, deacons, and bishops. Inform the guest beforehand of what the children are learning in this chapter and have him speak to those concepts. Afterward, allow the children to ask appropriate questions.

Connect

HIGHLIGHT

Remind the children that we belong to the holy People of God through our Baptism.

RESPOND

- Talk with the children about what it means to be holy. Point out that to be holy means to share in the life and love of God and live as a child of God and follower of Jesus.
- Read aloud the directions to the activity and have the children complete it.

CHOOSE

- Invite the children to respond to "My Faith Choice."
- After a moment of prayerful reflection have the children write their choices on the lines provided.
- Encourage the children to put their choices into practice this week.

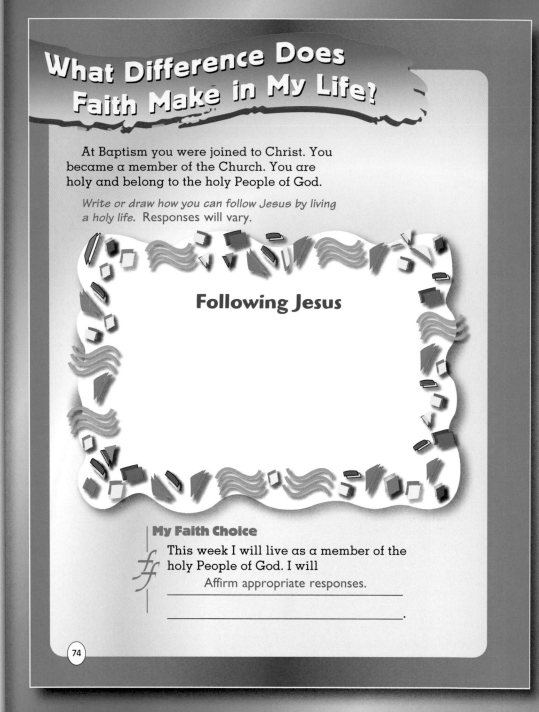

What Difference Does Faith Make in My Life?

At Baptism you were joined to Christ. You became a member of the Church. You are holy and belong to the holy People of God.

Write or draw how you can follow Jesus by living a holy life. Responses will vary.

Following Jesus

My Faith Choice

This week I will live as a member of the holy People of God. I will

Affirm appropriate responses.

_____

_____.

74

Teaching Tip

Sharing Faith. Teaching children how to be followers of Jesus by living holy lives is like mixing large amounts of sugar and water. It isn't easy to get the symbolic meaning of holiness to sink in. An effective way to tell the children how to live a holy life is by living a holy life yourself. You are one of the children's significant role models. Seeing you at Mass and at church functions and treating people with dignity and respect goes a long way in the heart of a child. Share your faith by living it, and you will encourage the children to do the same.

We Pray

We Are the Church

We use many gestures when we pray. Gestures help us pray.

Leader: We are the Church. We are the holy People of God.

All: **We raise our hands and say, "Alleluia!"**

Leader: We are the Church. We are the temple of the Holy Spirit.

All: **We bless ourselves and genuflect.**

Leader: We are the Church. We are the Body of Christ.

All: **We join our hands and say, "Amen!"**

We Remember

Find out the hidden message about the Church. Circle the first letter and then circle every other letter. Share the message with a friend.

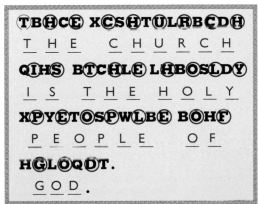

THE CHURCH

IS THE HOLY

PEOPLE OF

GOD.

To Help You Remember

1. The work of the Church is to help all people come to know Jesus and invite people to be followers of Jesus.

2. All the people of the Church help others come to know Jesus.

3. All the people of the Church live holy lives.

Grade 3 • Chapter 8   75

Liturgy Tip

Gestures. Prayer involves the whole person—our mind and heart, our bodies and our spirit. When we gather to take part in the celebration of Mass, we take part in a celebration that involves the whole person. Prayer gestures, such as kneeling and standing, walking in procession and raising our arms and hands, add to our participation. Explain the meaning of these gestures and practice them so that the children may understand their meaning and use them to actively participate in the celebration of Mass.

WE PRAY

- Remind the children that the Church uses gestures in prayer.
- Tell the children that the prayer today will include three gestures. Practice the gestures. Pay special attention to the correct form for genuflection, with the right knee touching the ground. Direct any children with injuries or disabilities to bow their heads reverently instead of genuflecting.
- Gather the children in the prayer center.
- Lead the prayer.

Review

WE REMEMBER

- Tell the children that we have learned three important things about the Church in this chapter. Ask them to recall what these three things are.
- Invite the children to check their answers in the "To Help You Remember" section.
- Introduce the activity and allow the children time to complete it. You may wish to put a word bank with key words on the board or on cards to assist some learners.

At Home

ENCOURAGE

Have the children carefully tear out pages 75 and 76 along the perforation. Encourage the children to share the pages with their families and to do the activities together. If they did not complete the review activity on page 75 by the end of the session, emphasize that they can complete it with their families.

VISIT FAITHFIRST.COM

- Share with the children the many activities on the *Faith First* Web site.
- Encourage the children to visit **www.FaithFirst.com.**

Before Moving On . . .

As you finish today's lesson, reflect on the following question before moving on to the next chapter.

What have I done to bring a spirit of Christian joy into my classroom?

---

8 With My Family

This Week . . .

In chapter 8, "We Are the Church," your child discovered more about the Catholic Church. The Catholic Church goes back to Jesus and the Apostles. Jesus is the Head of the Church. The Church is the Body of Christ. The Church is holy; it is the holy People of God. The Church is the temple of the Holy Spirit. The Holy Spirit is present within each of us and with the whole community of the Church. The Holy Spirit gives the Church the grace to live as the holy People of God.

For more on the teachings of the Catholic Church on the mystery of the Church, see *Catechism of the Catholic Church* paragraph numbers 668–679.

Sharing God's Word

Read together the Bible story in Matthew 28:19–20 about what Jesus told the disciples after the Resurrection or read the adaptation of the story on page 70. Emphasize the responsibility the Church has today to continue the work Jesus gave to the disciples.

Praying

In this chapter your child used different gestures for prayer. Read and pray together the prayer on page 75.

Making a Difference

Choose one of the following activities to do as a family or design a similar activity of your own.

- Jesus told the disciples to share the Good News with others. Talk about how your family can share the Good News with others.

- At Baptism we receive the gift of the Holy Spirit. We are made holy and become members of the holy People of God. As a family, choose one thing you can do this week to live as the holy People of God.

- Talk about how your parish community lives as followers of Christ. List the ways your parish helps your family live as followers of Jesus. Choose one of those things and join with your parish to do it.

For more ideas on ways your family can live your faith, visit the "Faith First for Families" page at **www.FaithFirst.com**. This week you will find it useful to look at "Questions Kids Ask."

76

Evaluate

Take a few moments to evaluate this week's lesson.
I feel (circle one) about this week's lesson.

a. very pleased
b. OK
c. disappointed

The activity the children enjoyed most was . . .

The concept that was most difficult to teach was . . .

because . . .

Something I would like to do differently is . . .

ENRICHING THE LESSON

Interviewing Disciples

Purpose

To reinforce the work that Jesus gave his Apostles and other disciples to do (taught on page 70)

Directions

- Have the children work with partners. Assign to some partners the role of people of the early Christian era who hear about Jesus and to other partners the role of the disciples. Have the people who want to know more about Jesus interview the Apostles or disciples. Provide the children with tags naming their roles.
- Before doing the interviews, have the children prepare questions they will ask the disciples about being followers of Jesus.
- Have the partners walk around the room and conduct their interviews.
- After they conduct their interviews, have some volunteers role-play their interviews for the class.

Materials

name tags with roles

Making Works of Mercy Posters

Purpose

To reinforce the Corporal Works of Mercy (taught on page 73)

Directions

- Provide the children with poster board, scissors, magazines and newspapers (especially Catholic or Christian publications), markers and crayons, and glue sticks.
- Invite the children to make posters that show one or more of the Corporal Works of Mercy and Spiritual Works of Mercy (See page 290).
- Have the children find and cut out pictures from the magazines or newspapers that depict the particular work or works of mercy they have chosen.
- Encourage them to identify the work of mercy with words and illustrations.

- Hang the completed posters where others can enjoy them.

Materials

poster board, magazines and newspapers
scissors and glue sticks
markers and crayons

Literature Connection

Purpose

To reinforce and extend the teaching about the Catholic Church as the People of God (taught on page 72)

Directions

Sister Anne's Hands by Marybeth Lorbiecki (Penguin Putnam Books for Young Readers, 2000), tells the story of a young African-American nun who comes to teach in a Catholic school in the 1960s. When a cruel note about her blackness lands on her desk one day, her dignified, gentle, and courageous reaction teaches in a way that can change children's perceptions forever.

- Read the story to the children and discuss times when the children may have felt suspicious or uncomfortable with someone different from themselves. Ask them to summarize what they think is the moral of this story.
- Offer to loan the book to any children who would like to re-read it with their families.

Materials

Sister Anne's Hands by Marybeth Lorbiecki

Music Connection

- "All Are Welcome," M. Haugen. *Singing Our Faith (SOF)* #185.
- "Bring Forth the Kingdom," M.Haugen. *SOF* #192.
- "We Are Many Parts," M. Haugen. *SOF* #182.
- "We Are the Church," C. Walker. *Rise Up and Sing* #234.

Paul the Apostle
A Scripture Story

Background

Conversion

While Baptism celebrates our initial conversion to faith in Christ, our conversion to him does not end there. In fact, it is only the beginning of a lifelong journey of conversion to him. "Adhering to Jesus Christ, in fact, sets in motion a process of continuing conversion, which lasts for the whole of life" (*General Directory for Catechesis* 56).

Conversion to Christ takes place within the Church, the Body of Christ. Because weakness and the tendency to sin can be experienced both individually and within groups and communities, we are all urged to seek that conversion of heart necessary for the perfection of our faith both as individuals, and with others. This ongoing process of conversion occurs in the ordinariness of daily living.

The word *metanoia* is often used to describe the depth of the interior conversion called for by Jesus. Metanoia is a radical turning around, a radical change of heart. It is the renewal of life for which all believers constantly strive. This reorientation of one's life becomes evident in the exterior good works and acts of love that point to our inner conversion.

The Work of the Holy Spirit

Conversion is not merely a matter of human determination and resolve. It is the work of the Holy Spirit, who empowers and sustains us to change our ways—the same Spirit who gifted us with God's life at Baptism. Without the Holy Spirit, true conversion is impossible. Saint Paul the Apostle names several signs, or Fruits of the Holy Spirit, that give evidence of our true conversion to Christ. He writes:

> [T]he fruit of the Spirit is love, joy, peace, patience, kindness, generosity, faithfulness, gentleness, self-control. GALATIANS 5:22

Paul's radical change from persecuting the early Church to becoming one of Christ's most fervent and fiery missionaries is an example of such radical conversion. As with Paul, the Holy Spirit is ever-present, moving and challenging us to serve the Lord with our whole heart, mind, soul, and strength—with our whole being.

As in the case of the conversion of Paul, we are filled with a new heart—our heart of stone is transformed into a heart of flesh. Spurred on by the strengthening of the Holy Spirit, we find the resolve to act in new and different ways. What once seemed impossible is now possible.

For Reflection

How can I be more aware of the movement of the transforming power of the Holy Spirit in my life?

How can I be a faithful companion to others as we make our journey of conversion to Christ?

Catechist to Catechist

A Change of Heart

The focus of this week's lesson is conversion. Conversion to Christ is the vocation of all Christians. The Greek term for "conversion" is *metanoia*. Metanoia is a profound transformation of mind and heart prompted and guided by the grace of the Holy Spirit. We are called throughout our whole life to open our mind and heart in response to the invitation to share in the very life and love of God the Father, Son, and Holy Spirit.

In the Footsteps of Jesus

In this chapter nurture the seeds of faith, hope, and love in the children's hearts. Help the children walk in the footsteps of Jesus and keep him at the center of their lives.  Remember that you can do this in many ways in addition to teaching them about their faith. The children learn how to follow Jesus by watching someone who is doing it already. When you speak kindly, listen carefully, respond patiently, or forgive quickly, they see what it means to follow Christ.

The Church Teaches . . .

Paul the Apostle was an evangelist who shared the Gospel message. You too are called to be an evangelist. The *General Directory for Catechesis* (GDC) reminds us:

> When catechesis transmits the mystery of Christ, the faith of the whole people of God echoes its message throughout the course of history: the faith received by the Apostles from Christ himself and under the action of the Holy Spirit . . . that of the saints who have lived it and live it profoundly . . . In truth there is present in catechesis the faith of all those who believe and allow themselves to be guided by the Holy Spirit. *GDC* 105

See the Catechism . . .

For more on the teachings of the Catholic Church on the mystery of the Church, see *Catechism of the Catholic Church* 737–741, 787–795, and 813–865.

CATECHIST PRAYER

*Holy Spirit,
who brought light to
Saul's darkness, enlighten
my mind. Help my heart
turn always, like a
flower in a garden, to
the light of your love.
Amen.*

LESSON PLANNER

To discover what Saint Paul did after he became a follower of Jesus

Engage

Page 77
Focus
To assess the children's knowledge of Saint Paul

Opening Prayer

Discussion
Times children have had to change their mind about something because someone wanted them to

Teach and Apply

Pages 78–80
Focus
To discover that Saint Paul loved God and his Law both as a Pharisee and after he became a follower of Jesus

Presentation
Read, discuss, and summarize content.
Scripture
• Psalm 9:2
• Acts of the Apostles 9:3–6, 8, 17–18
Activities
• Prepare a question to ask Jesus.
• Describe how Saul (Paul) might have felt when he heard the voice of Jesus.
• Write what Saint Paul might say to the people in his preaching about Jesus.

Connect

Pages 81–82
Focus
To discover how all members of the Church are missionaries

Our Church Makes a Difference
Saint John Neumann was a missionary.
Our Catholic Faith
Missionaries

What Difference Does Faith Make?
Activity
Complete the "Sharing the Good News" activity.
Faith Choice
Choose a way to share faith in Jesus with others this week.

We Pray

Page 83
Prayer Form
Memorial Acclamations
Prayer
Choose a leader. Divide the class into groups. Pray together.

We Remember

Review
• Complete the design activity.
• Read the "To Help You Remember" statements aloud.
Preview
Highlight features of the "With My Family" page.

Materials

• parish bulletin for each child
• pens or pencils
• crayons or markers

Enriching the Session

Blackline Masters
Additional Activities booklet:
  Chapter 9
    Drawing
    Writing
Assessment Tools booklet:
  Chapter 9 Test

Enriching the Lesson (CG page 153)
Presenting Skits about Saint Paul
Writing Letters to Missionary Orders
Literature Connection

Music Connection (CG page 153)

www.FaithFirst.com

We update the *Faith First* Web site weekly. Check each week for new content and features. Here are some places to begin:

Catechists and Teachers
• Current Events
• Chapter Downloads
• Catechist Prayer

Faith First **for Families**
• Bible Stories
• Make a Difference

Kids' Clubhouse
• *Faith First* Activities
• Chapter Reviews
• Games
• Saints

Don't Forget! You can make lesson planning a breeze—check out the **Online Lesson Planner.**

Paul the Apostle
A Scripture Story

9

We Pray

I will praise you,
Lord, with all
my heart.   Psalm 9:2

**God our Father,
help us tell others
about your Son,
Jesus, each day.
                    Amen.**

*When have you ever
changed your mind
about something?*

Each day we learn
new things. Learning
new things helps us
change the way to do
things. Paul changed
his entire life and
became a follower of
Jesus.

*What do you know
about Saint Paul?*

Saint Paul the Apostle   (77)

Engage

PRAY
- Gather with the children for prayer.
- Pray the Sign of the Cross together.
- Invite the children to raise their arms with you in praise to God as you pray Psalm 9:2.
- Pray the prayer aloud together and all respond "Amen."

DISCOVER
Purpose: To find out what the children know about Saint Paul the Apostle
- Ask the children the opening question. Tell them that Saint Paul changed his entire life and became a follower of Jesus.
- Ask them what they know about Saint Paul.

Background: Faith-Filled People

Saul of Tarsus. Tarsus was a city in the Roman province of Cilicia, which is in the southeast part of Asia Minor. It lies northwest of Jerusalem. Because it was a trading center, the city had many wealthy citizens. The city also had a university. But Saul probably went to school in Jerusalem, where he studied under Gamaliel, a famous rabbi. Saul also learned the trade of tent-making to support himself during this time. At the time Saul lived, tents were made from a cloth made from goats' hair. It was common for Jews who lived outside of Palestine to take Greek or Latin names. Paul, a Latin aristocratic name, is the one by which Saul was known throughout his ministry.

Teach

FOCUS

Have a volunteer read the "Faith Focus" question aloud. Share with the children that in this chapter they will learn more about Saul and how he changed.

DISCOVER

- Share the first paragraph in your own words.
- Ask a child to read the meaning of *Law of Moses* from "Faith Words."
- Point out that earlier in his life, Saul persecuted the followers of Jesus.
- Ask the children to read silently to find out why Saul opposed the Apostles' teachings. He thought the Apostles were speaking against the Law of Moses.

Apply

REINFORCE

Ask the children to underline the meaning of the words *Pharisee* and *Law of Moses* in the text. Have them make a word card for *Law of Moses*.

INTEGRATE

- Ask: Have you ever made fun of others or treated others unkindly because you did not understand them?
- Invite the children to look at the picture and respond to the question.
- Ask a group of volunteers to act out a conversation Paul and the Apostles might have.

Bible Background

Faith Focus

Who was Paul the Apostle?

Faith Words

Law of Moses
The Law of Moses is the Ten Commandments plus other important laws that guide the Jewish people in living the Covenant.

Saul Loved God and God's Law

Saul was a Pharisee. He became a follower of Jesus and one of the Apostles. The Pharisees were a group of Jewish people who lived the **Law of Moses** very strictly. The Law of Moses included the Ten Commandments and other laws that guided the Jewish people in living the Covenant.

Saul heard all about Jesus and his teachings. He knew about Jesus' death and his Resurrection. After the Risen Jesus returned to his Father, Saul heard what the Apostles of Jesus were teaching. This upset Saul because he thought Jesus' Apostles were speaking against the Law of Moses.

Pretend you are Saul. What question would you ask the followers of Jesus?

_____

_____ ?

78

Background: Doctrine

Faith in God. *The Catechism of the Catholic Church* (222–227) reminds us of the great consequences of believing in God: it means coming to know God's greatness and majesty; it means living in thanksgiving; it means knowing the unity and true dignity of all people; it means making good use of created things; it means trusting God in all things. Celebrate with the children the fact that, during this year, they will continue to deepen their own faith. Remind them that nourishing and growing in faith is a lifelong process.

Reading the Word of God

Jesus Calls Saul to Be an Apostle

One day Saul and some of his friends were traveling to the city of Damascus. They wanted to arrest the disciples of the Lord, bring them back to Jerusalem, and put them on trial. This is what happened next.

Suddenly, a great light shone around Saul, he was blinded, and he fell to the ground.

Saul heard a voice say, "Saul, why are you hurting me?" Saul asked, "Who are you?" The voice said, "I am Jesus. When you hurt my followers, you hurt me. Get up and go into Damascus."

When Saul and his friends arrived in the city of Damascus, Ananias, a follower of Jesus, came to Saul. Saul was baptized and became a follower of Jesus.

Based on Acts of the Apostles 9:3–6, 8, 17–18

Saul then became known as Paul. He became an Apostle and soon began to preach and teach all about Jesus.

Discuss how you think Saul felt when he first heard the voice of Jesus speak to him.

79

Teaching Tip

Bringing the Story to Life. Instead of reading the story of Saul, become Saul. Present the story in the first person by telling the story as if you were Saul. You may even wish to wear a simple costume, such as a large beach or bath towel tied at the waist with a rope for a tunic. Wear sandals on your feet and a headcovering made from a smaller towel, secured with another piece of rope or heavy yarn. Role-play the conversion of Saul with great enthusiasm and expression. You could also invite the children to take the roles of Jesus, Saul, and Ananias while you serve as the narrator.

Teach

FOCUS

Remind the children that after Jesus asked Paul to change his heart, Paul began to preach and teach about Jesus.

DISCOVER

- Share with the children that Paul's heart was changed by his encounter with Christ. This is what is meant by *conversion*.
- Use the image of a seed planted in the soil to discuss how Paul began to see with eyes of faith. List the phases of a seed's growth with a small illustration on the board: planting, growing, and sprouting.
- Challenge volunteers to match each phase of Saul's conversion to that of a seed being planted. Jesus appears to Paul; Paul is changed and begins to grow; Paul is baptized in Damascus and follows Jesus.

Apply

REINFORCE

Explain that Paul became one of the greatest Christian preachers. He traveled to faraway lands to share the Good News of the Risen Jesus.

INTEGRATE

- Introduce the activity and give the children some time to complete it.
- Ask volunteers to share what they wrote.

Understanding the Word of God

Paul's Faith

Jesus, the Son of God, called Saul to change and grow. Paul's heart was changed. He came to believe that Jesus was the fulfillment of all God's promises. We call this the conversion of Saint Paul.

Beginning on the road to Damascus, Jesus invited Paul to come out of darkness and see with the eyes of faith. That is how faith is. It is like a seed planted in dark ground. The seed grows through the darkness. Suddenly, it breaks through the earth into the light. The sun's light feeds the seed. The seed changes and grows.

Choose a partner. Imagine that you are with Paul the Apostle. You are visiting a town to tell people about Jesus. Write what Paul might be saying to the people.

Preaching the Gospel

_____

_____

_____

_____

_____

_____

80

Special Needs

Using Our Bodies to Learn. Some children are kinetic learners who understand a concept best when they become involved in it. To make the concept of the buried seed of faith come alive for the children, gather the children in an area where they have space to move about without bumping into each other. Then have them enact the different phases of growth beginning with the seed in the dark ground. Describe how the warmth of the sun draws the seed to crack open and grow, unbending and stretching toward the sun. Then the sprout bursts forth through the ground!

Need: Kinetic learners, all learners.

Our Church Makes a Difference

Saint John Neumann

Like Paul the Apostle, many Christians have traveled and preached the Good News of Jesus. John Neumann left his home in Europe and traveled across the Atlantic Ocean to New York. He became a priest and traveled to Maryland, Virginia, Pennsylvania, and Ohio, where he preached the Gospel.

Father John Neumann became an American citizen on February 10, 1848, and the bishop of Philadelphia on March 28, 1852. He built fifty churches and opened almost one hundred Catholic schools. He wrote newspaper articles and two catechisms. John Neumann was the first American bishop to be named a saint.

Describe ways your parish shares the Good News of Jesus with others. Clue: Look for the answer in your parish Sunday bulletin.

Saint Vincent de Paul Church, Philadelphia, 1851

Our Catholic Faith

Missionaries

Saint John Neumann was a missionary. Christian missionaries often travel to a country different than their own to teach about Jesus. Bishops, priests, deacons, religious brothers and sisters, and laypeople serve the Church as missionaries.

John Neumann, bishop of Philadelphia

81

Teaching Tip

Foster the Missionary Spirit. Missionaries often encounter cultures different from their own when they travel to other countries. We can encounter differences in our own families too. Share with the children that they can be missionaries to their families. They can share the love of Christ with those in need. Talk with the children about the elderly members of your own family and how they have helped you grow in your faith. Invite the children to share their own stories of grandparents and other relatives who helped them to know Jesus. Encourage the children to show respect and patience for all persons who are in their later years.

Connect

HIGHLIGHT

Help the children recall how living a life of faith is our baptismal call as Christians.

DISCOVER

- Tell the children that they are going to read about a saint who traveled and preached the Good News of Jesus.
- Have the children read silently "Saint John Neumann" and underline the places where John Neumann lived and preached. If possible, show the children where these places are on a map.
- Draw a Venn diagram on the board and ask the children to help you compare the work of Saint Paul and Saint John Neumann.
- Read aloud "Our Catholic Faith." Ask: What kind of missionary work did Saint John Neumann do?

INTEGRATE

- Invite the children to describe ways their parish shares the Good News of Jesus with others.
- Point out some of your parish's programs that share the Gospel with parishioners and others.
- Ask the children what work of sharing the Gospel they could begin now.

Connect

HIGHLIGHT

Help the children recall that it is the task of every Christian to teach about Jesus.

RESPOND

- Present the opening paragraph in your own words.
- Invite a volunteer to read aloud the directions for the activity on this page. Have the children complete the activity in small groups.
- Give each group time to share with the others.

CHOOSE

- Invite the children to respond to "My Faith Choice."
- After a moment of prayerful reflection have the children write their choices on the lines provided.
- Encourage the children to put their choices into practice this week.

What Difference Does Faith Make in My Life?

You do not have to travel far to be a missionary. You can be a missionary right where you live. You can share the Good News of Jesus with others every day.

Complete the following sentences to help you name ways you can share the Good News of Jesus.

Sharing the Good News

I can help my family know and love Jesus better when I _____ .

I can help my friends know and love Jesus better when I _____ .

I can help my neighbors know and love Jesus better when I _____ .

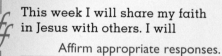

My Faith Choice

This week I will share my faith in Jesus with others. I will

Affirm appropriate responses.

_____ .

82

Teaching Tip

The Missionary Spirit. Paul's conversion opened him to a new vision and to new commitments. His world was turned upside down. No longer the determined persecutor of the followers of Christ, Paul became one of the Church's greatest missionaries and preachers. He traveled by land and boat to invite all people—Jews and Gentiles—to follow Christ. Invite the children to pray often for all missionaries.

Pray

We Pray

We Believe in the Paschal Mystery

Saint Paul believed in the Paschal Mystery of Jesus. He believed in the Passion, death, Resurrection, and Ascension of Jesus. At Mass we profess our faith in the Paschal Mystery.

Leader: Let us proclaim our faith in Jesus Christ.

Group 1: Christ has died,
All: **Christ has died,**

Group 2: Christ is risen,
All: **Christ is risen,**

Group 3: Christ will come again.
All: **Christ will come again.**

We Remember

Design this Good News CD cover. Use words that you learned in this chapter.

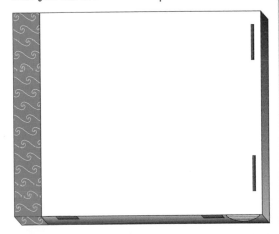

To Help You Remember

1. Saul was a Pharisee who loved God and lived the Law of Moses with all his heart and with all his strength.

2. Saul became one of Jesus' disciples and became known as Paul the Apostle.

3. Paul the Apostle preached and taught other people about Jesus.

Grade 3 • Chapter 9 83

WE PRAY

- Remind the children of the meaning of the Paschal Mystery.
- Invite the children to the prayer center and divide them into two groups. Invite a child to serve as the leader.
- Tell the children that today's prayer is one of the Memorial Acclamations from the Mass.
- Pray the Memorial Acclamation together.

Review

WE REMEMBER

- Create a T-chart on the board. Head each column with the words *Before* and *After*.
- Ask the children to recall what they know about Paul before and after his conversion using the "To Help You Remember" statements. Jot their answers on the chart.
- Introduce the activity and allow the children time to complete it. Invite the children to share their work with the class.

✝ Liturgy Tip

The Memorial Acclamation. The Eucharist is the celebration of the Paschal sacrifice of Jesus. At Mass, we profess our faith in the Paschal Mystery of Jesus during the Liturgy of the Eucharist. Following the words of consecration, or the Institution Narrative, we sing or pray aloud the Memorial Acclamation proclaiming our faith in Christ's death and Resurrection and the hope that he will come again. Familiarize the children with this acclamation before praying the prayer on this page. Discuss the meaning of this acclamation as a profession of faith. Encourage the children to pray this acclamation as part of their daily prayer as a helpful reminder of the Paschal Mystery.

At Home

ENCOURAGE

Have the children carefully tear out pages 83 and 84 along the perforation. Encourage the children to share the pages with their families and to do the activities together. If they did not complete the review activity on page 83 by the end of the session, emphasize that they can complete it with their families.

VISIT FAITHFIRST.COM

- Share with the children the many activities on the *Faith First* Web site.
- Encourage the children to visit **www.FaithFirst.com.**

Before Moving On . . .

As you finish today's lesson, reflect on the following question before moving on to the next chapter.

What opportunities have I provided for students to tell personal faith stories?

---

9   With My Family

This Week . . .

In chapter 9, "Paul the Apostle: A Scripture Story," your child was introduced to Paul the Apostle. Before he used his Roman name Paul, he was known as Saul. Saul was a Pharisee who loved God and lived the Law of Moses with his whole heart and strength. When Saul was traveling to Damascus, Jesus spoke to him, asking, "Why do you persecute me?" This experience began Saul's conversion from being a persecutor of Christians to living and dying as a great Apostle. Paul came to understand that Jesus and his followers are one.

For more on the teachings of the Catholic Church on the mystery of the Church, see *Catechism of the Catholic Church* paragraph numbers 737–741, 787–795, and 813–865.

Sharing God's Word

Read together the Bible story in Acts 9:1–20 about Jesus calling Saul to be his disciple or read the adaptation of the story on page 79. Emphasize that Paul became an Apostle and told others about Jesus with his whole heart and strength.

Praying

In this chapter your child prayed one of the memorial acclamations we pray at Mass. Read and pray together the acclamation on page 83.

Making a Difference

Choose one of the following activities to do as a family or design a similar activity of your own.

- Draw pictures that illustrate the Bible story about how Saul the Pharisee became known as Paul the Apostle. Display the pictures where they can serve as a reminder of the importance of teaching others about Jesus.
- Use the memorial acclamation your parish sings or prays aloud this week for your family prayer.
- When you take part in Mass this week, bring home the parish bulletin. Look through the bulletin to discover the many ways your parish shares the Good News of Jesus.

> For more ideas on ways your family can live your faith, visit the "Faith First for Families" page at **www.FaithFirst.com.** Check out "Bible Stories." Read and discuss the Bible story as a family this week.

✔ Evaluate

Take a few moments to evaluate this week's lesson. I feel (circle one) about this week's lesson.

    a. very pleased

    b. OK

    c. disappointed

The activity the children enjoyed most was . . .

The concept that was most difficult to teach was . . .

because . . .

Something I would like to do differently is . . .

ENRICHING THE LESSON

Presenting Skits about Saint Paul

Purpose

To reinforce the conversion of Paul (taught on page 79)

Directions

- In small groups have the children put together short skits that tell the conversion story of Paul.
- When the skits are ready to be presented, allow the groups to present their versions to the class.

Materials

Writing Letters to Missionary Orders

Purpose

To reinforce that some missionaries travel to countries other than their own to teach and share the Gospel of Jesus (taught on page 81)

Directions

- Research missionary orders, such as the Maryknoll Missionaries, the Franciscan Missionaries, and the Sisters of Charity, ahead of time. Write the names of these orders on the board.
- Have the children choose a missionary order and help them write a letter requesting information about the order's work. In the letter have the children thank the order for continuing the work of Saint Paul.
- As they receive information about their order, you might have the children design a poster that shows what they have learned.

Materials

note paper
pens or pencils
envelopes

Literature Connection

Purpose

To reinforce the meaning of conversion (taught on page 80)

Directions

The Advent season would be a good time to reinforce the teaching about conversion.

- Read to the children an adapted version of Charles Dickens' *A Christmas Carol*, such as the one adapted by Stephen Krensky (Harper Collins, 2004). Be sure the children understand that this is a work of fiction and not a true story.
- Tell the children to listen for how Scrooge had a change of heart.
- Discuss Scrooge's change of heart with the children.
- Remind them that each year we reflect on ways we can turn our hearts more fully toward the way of Jesus as Saint Paul did.

Materials

A Christmas Carol adapted by Stephen Krensky or another version of the story

Music Connection

- "As a Fire Is Meant for Burning," harmony by M. Haugen. *Singing Our Faith (SOF)* #190.
- "Bring Forth the Kingdom," M. Haugen. *SOF* #192.
- "Two By Two," R. Glover. *SOF* #188.
- "Who Am I," P. Freeburg/D. Walker. *Rise Up and Sing* #323.

The Communion of Saints

Background

Communion of Saints

We learn from reading the New Testament letters of Paul that the title of saint was initially given to all the baptized. Later, those who suffered martyrdom for their faith in Christ were called saints and became a source of inspiration and strength for Christians.

Popular devotions to particular saints began to grow in the early centuries of Church life. There is evidence in the third century that saints were considered to be intercessors before God. By the tenth century a formal papal procedure for bestowing this honor upon holy individuals was put into practice—canonization.

The saints of the Church are our companions in prayer, models of faith for us to emulate, patrons for those who are named in their honor, patrons of specific activities and places, and intercessors for us before the throne of God.

Some have confused the Church's veneration of the saints with her worship of God, seeing "veneration" and "worship" to be the same. This, of course, is not the case. God alone is worthy of our worship. The Second Vatican Council summarizes Catholic teaching on the saints:

The Church has always believed that the apostles and Christ's martyrs, who gave the supreme witness of faith and charity by the shedding of their blood, are closely united with us in Christ; she has always venerated them, together with the Blessed Virgin Mary and the holy angels, with a special love.

Dogmatic Constitution on the Church (Lumen gentium) 50

The Holy People of God

All Christians—and all people—are called to live a holy life. At Baptism we receive the gift of the Holy Spirit and sanctifying grace and are restored to holiness. The word *sanctifying* means "making holy." Joined to Christ, the holy One of God, and incorporated into the Church, the holy People of God, we are to live a life of holiness and prepare the way for the coming of the kingdom of heaven.

Now in heaven, Mary and all the saints share in the glory of Christ and wait for our coming to join them. We believe and hope with confidence that we are in "communion" with these holy men and women through our communion with Christ in the Holy Spirit. We believe and hope that we will one day live with them in everlasting life in the kingdom of heaven.

For Reflection

What saints inspire me to live my life in Christ? What aspect of their lives inspires me?

How might my life of holiness inspire others to live their lives in Christ?

Catechist to Catechist

Heroes of Our Faith

Third graders have a growing interest in learning about people who have accomplished great things. A good way to introduce this lesson is with a discussion of the heroes of our Catholic faith, the saints. The Catholic Church names saints from a diversity of times, places, and cultures.

Models of Faith

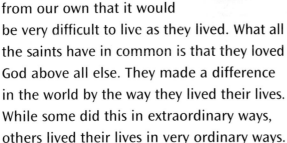

The life of every saint does not necessarily connect with the life of every Christian today. Some of the saints lived in times and places so different from our own that it would be very difficult to live as they lived. What all the saints have in common is that they loved God above all else. They made a difference in the world by the way they lived their lives. While some did this in extraordinary ways, others lived their lives in very ordinary ways.

The Church Teaches . . .

The catechetical document *To Teach as Jesus Did* reminds us:

> From the moment of Baptism [a person] becomes a member of a new and larger family, the Christian community. Reborn in Baptism, [a person] is joined to others in common faith, hope and love. This community is based . . . on the life of the Spirit which unites its members in a unique fellowship so intimate that Paul likens it to a body of which each individual is a part and Jesus Himself is the Head. *TJD 22*

In this chapter, the children learn that they belong to this greater and larger family of the Church, the Communion of Saints.

See the Catechism . . .

For more on the teachings of the Catholic Church on the mysteries of the Communion of Saints and everlasting life, see *Catechism of the Catholic Church* 946–959, 1172–1173, and 1402–1405.

CATECHIST PRAYER

*Holy Spirit,
inspire me to holiness.
Help me to live in
your love and to
share that love with
everyone I meet.
Amen.*

LESSON PLANNER

Engage

Page 85
Focus

To assess the children's knowledge about some of the heroes of the Church

Opening Prayer

Discussion

Personal heroes and heroes of the Church

Teach and Apply

Pages 86–88
Focus

To discover what it means to say that the Church is a Communion of Saints

Presentation

Read, discuss, and summarize content.

Scripture

• Psalm 24:5–6
• I Corinthians 12:12, 27

Activities

• Identify the way the Church honors all the saints in heaven.
• Write about or draw yourself as a member of the Communion of Saints.
• Name a personal gift from God.

Faith-Filled People

Souls in Purgatory

Connect

Pages 89–90
Focus

To discover ways the Church celebrates feasts of Mary and the other saints of the Church

Our Church Makes a Difference

We celebrate the feast of Our Lady of Guadalupe as patron of the Americas.

Our Catholic Faith

Holy People of God

What Difference Does Faith Make?

Activity

Tell what Saint Charles Lwanga teaches us about living our faith.

Faith Choice

Choose a saint to learn about this week.

We Pray

Page 91

Prayer Form

Prayer of intercession

Prayer

Choose a leader. Introduce the prayer and invite the children to add their own intercessions. Pray together.

We Remember

Review

• Complete the true or false activity.
• Read the "To Help You Remember" statements aloud.

Preview

Highlight features of the "With My Family" page.

Materials

• pens or pencils
• crayons or markers

Enriching the Session

Blackline Masters
Additional Activities booklet:
  Chapter 10
    Preaching the Good News
    Writing to share ideas
Assessment Tools booklet:
  Chapter 10 Test
  Unit 1 Test

Enriching the Lesson (CG page 165)
Role-Playing Phone Conversations
About Continuing Jesus' Work
Creating Heroes of the Faith
Character Maps
Literature Connection

Music Connection (CG page 165)

www.FaithFirst.com

We update the *Faith First* Web site weekly. Check each week for new content and features. Here are some places to begin:

Catechists and Teachers
• Current Events
• Chapter Downloads
• Catechist Prayer

Faith First **for Families**
• Bible Stories
• Make a Difference

Kids' Clubhouse
• *Faith First* Activities
• Chapter Reviews
• Games
• Saints

Don't Forget! You can make lesson planning a breeze—check out the **Online Lesson Planner.**

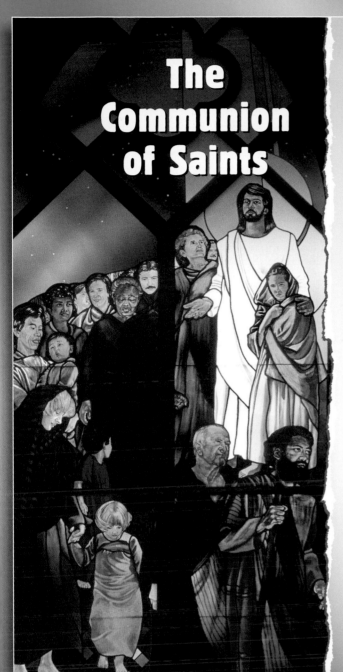

The Communion of Saints

We Pray

People who seek to see the face of God shall receive a blessing from God.
Based on Psalm 24:5–6

God our Father, may the Holy Spirit who blessed the lives of the saints bless our lives. Amen.

Who is one of your heroes? Why?

Our world has many heroes. The Church has heroes too.

Who are some of the heroes of the Church?

Christ reaching out to all people

85

Engage

PRAY

- Gather the children for prayer.
- Pray the Sign of the Cross together.
- Invite a volunteer to proclaim Psalm 24:5–6.
- Pray the opening prayer together and respond by saying "Amen."

DISCOVER

Purpose: To assess what the children know about the Church as the Communion of Saints

- Use the questions on the opening page to involve the children in a discussion of heroes. Begin with heroes in our world and lead them to heroes in the Church—the saints.
- Ask volunteers to share how the picture might help them to understand the title "Communion of Saints."

Teaching Tip

Heroes and Role Models. Children at this age are very enchanted by their heroes. They are familiar with both comic book or make-believe heroes, as well as ones who are in the spotlight because of their athletic abilities, singing talent, and so on. Carefully guide the conversation. When discussing heroes be sure to help the children recognize that not all of those they see on television are necessarily good role models. Children will likely be aware of the spotty record of a favorite sports hero from the news or elsewhere. Make a list of characteristics with the children that make someone a good role model and use that as the basis for your conversation.

Teach

FOCUS

Ask a volunteer to read the "Faith Focus" question aloud. Tell the children that in this chapter they will learn why the Church is a Communion of Saints.

DISCOVER

- Write the word *saint* on the board. Ask what words remind the children of saints. Jot those words around the word *saint*.
- Divide the class into three groups. Write these follow-up questions on the board.
(1) How do the saints help us? Pray for us; offer us guidance; protect us. (2) How does the Church honor saints? Feast days. (3) Who is the Church's greatest saint? Mary. Give each set of questions to a group to answer. Have a leader write the group responses to be shared with the entire class.
- Ask volunteers to read aloud "Heroes of the Faith." Ask the class to listen for ways the saints help us.

Apply

REINFORCE

Read aloud the faith word *saints* and its definition. Have the children make a word card for this term.

INTEGRATE

Ask the children what they can do when others are setting a bad example. Possible answers: pray to the Holy Spirit for strength; ask a wise person for advice; read the story of a saint's life for examples.

The Saints of the Church

Faith Focus

Why do we call the Church the Communion of Saints?

Faith Words

saints
The saints are people whose love for God is stronger than their love for anyone or anything else.

Communion of Saints
The Communion of Saints is the community of the faithful followers of Jesus, both those living on earth and those who have died.

Heroes of the Faith

The Church honors its heroes, the **saints,** for their holiness. Saints are people whose love for God is stronger than their love for anyone or anything else. Mary, the mother of Jesus, is our most holy saint.

From their place in heaven, the saints pray for us. They offer us guidance. They protect us. We too will live with God and all the saints forever.

One way the Church honors the saints is to set aside special days to celebrate their lives. These days are called the feast days of the saints. By honoring the saints, the Church helps us remember what it means to live as children of God. Whenever we live and love as Jesus taught us, we are living holy lives. We are living as saints.

Name the one day each year the Church honors all the saints in heaven. Describe how your parish celebrates that feast day.

86

Faith Vocabulary

Communion of Saints. The Church is a Communion of Saints. The Communion of Saints includes the faithful living on earth, those who have died and are being purified, and the blessed in heaven. As members of the Communion of Saints, we are all one body in Christ. When we suffer, we suffer for the good of all. What we do for the least of our brothers, we do for Christ. The exemplary lives of the saints can lead us to a deeper faith in Christ and commitment to live the Gospel in hope of joining the blessed in heaven.

The Communion of Saints

In the Apostles' Creed we pray, "I believe in the **Communion of Saints**." The Communion of Saints is made up of people living on earth who are trying to live holy lives. It also includes all the holy people who have died and are living in heaven. We honor all the saints in heaven on All Saints' Day.

Some people die and are not ready to receive the gift of heaven. They are still growing in their love for God. These people also belong to the Communion of Saints. On All Souls' Day the whole Church prays that God will welcome these people into heaven. Heaven is living in happiness with God forever.

We pray to the saints who live with God in heaven. This shows we believe that they have new life, life everlasting, as Jesus promised.

Faith-Filled People

Souls in Purgatory

The souls in purgatory are people who have died but still need to grow in their love for God before they enter heaven. November 2 is All Souls' Day. On that day the whole Church prays that the souls in purgatory receive the gift of heaven.

Write or draw some ways you can celebrate that you are a member of the Communion of Saints here on earth.

87

Background: Catholic Tradition

All Souls' Day. The Church has a long tradition of praying for all those who have died. On November 2 the Church celebrates All Souls' Day and prays that all the faithful who have died will one day share in the Resurrection of Jesus and live forever in heaven. We pray for the souls in purgatory that they will share in Christ's Resurrection and live in eternal happiness with the Holy Trinity and all the blessed.

FOCUS

Remind the children that the saints are with God in heaven. Tell them that they are going to learn more about others who wish to be holy.

DISCOVER

- Write the words *community* and *communion* on the board and ask a volunteer to tell how they are the same. Both words mean a group of people with common interests. The word *communion* suggests a more intimate relationship.
- Invite the children to read silently "The Communion of Saints" to discover who makes up the Communion of Saints.
- Draw three overlapping circles on the board. Ask the children to name the three groups who make up the Communion of Saints.
- Point out the difference between All Saints' Day and All Souls' Day.

Apply

REINFORCE

Read aloud "Faith-Filled People" to discover more about the souls in purgatory.

INTEGRATE

- Explain the activity at the bottom of page 87.
- Have the children complete the activity on their own.
- Invite volunteers to share their work.

Teach

FOCUS

Point out that we all belong to the Body of Christ.

DISCOVER

- Ask the children to listen carefully for the term Paul used for the Church as you read aloud "We Are One."
- Call on a volunteer to read the name Paul gave the Church. The Body of Christ.
- Explain that this term can help us understand how close we are to the saints and the souls not yet in heaven.
- Ask: What does it mean to be a part of the Body of Christ? We are all closely joined together to continue Christ's work on earth.

Apply

REINFORCE

Emphasize that we are joined most fully to Jesus and to the whole Communion of Saints when we receive the Eucharist.

INTEGRATE

- Write the words *eyes, mouth, hands, feet,* and *ears* on the board. Starting with the word *eyes,* invite volunteers to tell what they can do with their senses to help build up the Body of Christ.
- Have the children study the pictures. Then direct the children to complete the activity and share their responses.

We Are One

Paul the Apostle called the Church the Body of Christ. Each member of the Body of Christ is an important part of the Church. Saint Paul wrote,

The Body of Christ has many parts, just as any human body does. Together we are the Body of Christ. Each of us is an important part of his Body. Based on 1 Corinthians 12:12, 27

This teaching of Saint Paul helps us understand what it means to call the Church the Communion of Saints. At Baptism we are joined to Christ and become members of the Church, the Body of Christ. We belong to the Communion of Saints. When we receive the Body and Blood of Christ in Holy Communion, we are joined most fully to Jesus and to the whole Communion of Saints.

Name one gift you have. Tell how you can use it to work with other members of the Church.

Gift	How I Can Use It

88

Background: Catholic Tradition

Calendar of Saints. Over the centuries a calendar of saints has been added to the liturgical year. Usually these saints' days are celebrated on the anniversary date of the death of that particular saint. Obtain a liturgical calendar from your director of religious education. If one is not available, an inexpensive poster of the Church's year including the feast days of the saints is available through Liturgy Training Publications, 800 N. Hermitage Ave., Chicago, IL 60622; 1-800-933-1800. You may wish to mark on the calendar the name days of the children.

Our Church Makes a Difference

Our Lady of Guadalupe

The Church celebrates many feast days in honor of Mary. One of these is the feast of Our Lady of Guadalupe on December 12. On this feast we remember the story of Saint Juan Diego. We remember that Juan Diego spoke with a beautiful Aztec woman who told him she was Mary, the Mother of God. Mary's appearance to Juan Diego helps us believe that God's love is for everyone. People of every race and language are loved by God.

We honor Mary, Our Lady of Guadalupe, as the patron of the Americas. She prays in heaven for the people of North America and South America. We ask Mary to help us love all people and to live as the holy People of God.

Tell how the story of Saint Juan Diego and Our Lady of Guadalupe helps us treat all people with respect.

Affirm appropriate responses.

Our Catholic Faith

Holy People of God

The Church Jesus gave us is one, holy, catholic, and apostolic. These are the four marks, or essential qualities, of the Church Jesus gave us. The Church is holy because Jesus, the Holy One of God, is the Head of his Body, the Church.

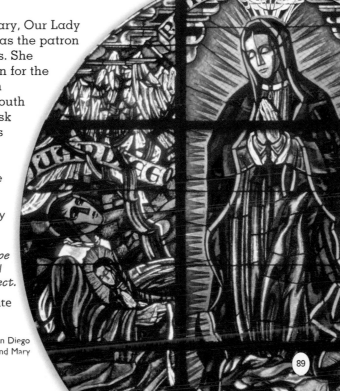

Saint Juan Diego and Mary

89

Liturgy Tip

The Feast of Our Lady of Guadalupe. The feast honoring Our Lady of Guadalupe each year is on December 12. Mary, Our Lady of Guadalupe, is both the patron saint of Mexico and the patron saint of the Americas. Consider celebrating this feast in your classroom in the session closest to the feast. Obtain the traditional image of the Virgin of Guadalupe and place it on the prayer table along with some roses that are so integral to the story. Lead the children in prayer, asking Mary to continue to bless all the people of the Americas.

Connect

HIGHLIGHT

The Church honors Mary as Our Lady of Guadalupe to remember Mary's appearance to Saint Juan Diego in Mexico.

DISCOVER

- Share with the children some titles for Mary, such as Mother of God, Queen of Heaven, and Our Lady of Peace.
- Tell or read the story of Our Lady of Guadalupe to the children.
- Invite volunteers to tell you the most important point of the story. People of every race and language are loved by God.
- Ask: What does Our Lady of Guadalupe do as patron of the Americas? Prays in heaven for the people of the Americas.
- Read "Our Catholic Faith" aloud to the children.
- Ask volunteers to name another important concept they have discussed that is related to the material in this box. The Body of Christ.

INTEGRATE

- Ask the children why they think Our Lady of Guadalupe appeared to a poor, uneducated person. To teach us that all people are important in God's eyes.
- Invite the children to share how the story of Saint Juan Diego and Our Lady of Guadalupe helps us treat all people with respect. Suggested answer: It reminds us that everyone, of every race and language, deserves our respect.

Connect

HIGHLIGHT

Remind the children that following the examples of the saints can help them to live as saints.

RESPOND

- Remind the children that saints are people whose love of God is stronger than anything else.
- Ask volunteers to read aloud the story of Saint Charles Lwanga.
- Help the children retell the saint's story. Draw three boxes on the board and have the children share with you three important events in the story of Charles Lwanga and his companions.
- Ask the children why Charles and his friends are honored as saints of the Church. They were martyrs for their faith in Jesus; they placed God first in their lives.
- Discuss with the children what the life of Saint Charles Lwanga or another saint teaches them about living their faith.

CHOOSE

- Invite the children to respond to "My Faith Choice."
- After a moment of prayerful reflection have the children write their choices on the lines provided.
- Encourage the children to put their choices into practice this week.

What Difference Does Faith Make in My Life?

You belong to the Communion of Saints. Following the example of the saints can help you live as a saint.

Read more about Saint Charles Lwanga or about another saint. Tell what the life of the saint teaches you about living your faith in Jesus Christ.

Saint Charles Lwanga

Charles Lwanga and his friends lived in the country of Uganda in Africa. They worked for a king who treated the people harshly. Charles and his friends learned about Jesus from missionaries working in their country. They asked to be baptized and became followers of Jesus Christ.

When the king forced the missionaries to leave the country, Charles began to teach others about Jesus. The king became angry and gave the order to have Charles and his friends killed.

Charles and his friends are martyrs of the Church. That means that they died for their faith. He is the patron saint of African youth and of all young people. We celebrate the feast day of Saint Charles and his friends on June 3.

My Faith Choice

This week I will learn more about a saint. The saint I will learn more about is

Affirm appropriate responses.
_____

90

Background: Doctrine

Intercession of the Saints. Explain to the children that all the saints in heaven are praying to God the Father to help the Church, the People of God, on earth. The saints are always listening to our prayers. Help the children learn more about some of the canonized saints by celebrating their particular feast days found on page 432 of this guide. Discuss some key characteristics of the saints and encourage the children to pray to them for wisdom, strength, and holiness.

We Pray

Prayer of Intercession

Prayers of intercession ask God to help other people.

Leader: Let us pray to God, our loving Father, who called us to be his Church.
For all the members of the Church on earth,

All: **Lord, hear our prayer.**

Leader: For all the members of the Church who have died and are waiting to be welcomed into heaven,

All: **Lord, hear our prayer.**

We Remember

Circle True under the true statements. Circle False under the false statements. Make the false statements true.

1. The saints are examples for us to follow.
   (True)   False

2. The saints pray for us.
   (True)   False

3. We pray for the saints.
   True   (False)

To Help You Remember

1. Saints are people whose love for God is stronger than their love for anyone or anything else.

2. The Communion of Saints is made up of holy people living on earth and those who have died.

3. The Church is the Body of Christ, the Holy One of God.

Teaching Tip

All Saints' Day. On November 1 we celebrate All Saints' Day. On this day we commemorate all saints, known and unknown. The Gospel reading for this day is about the Beatitudes. The word *beatitude* means "blessedness" or "happiness." Have the children turn to page 286 in their books and invite individuals to read the Beatitudes aloud. Ask the children to think about the answers to the following questions. Then encourage them to share their thoughts with the group.

- What clues do the Beatitudes give us about how to be holy?
- What clues do the Beatitudes give us about being happy?

Pray

WE PRAY

- Explain that today you will pray together a prayer of intercession. In prayers of intercession we pray for, or intercede with God for, the needs of others.
- Ask the children when we pray prayers of intercession as a parish community. In the Prayer of the Faithful at Mass.
- Gather the children in the prayer center.
- Invite a child to serve as the leader.
- Pray the prayer of intercession together. Invite the children to add their own intercessions to this prayer.

Review

WE REMEMBER

- Play the riddle game "Who am I?" to review the chapter concepts in the "To Help You Remember" section. Example: I am a faith hero of the Church. When I was on earth, I put God first in my life. Saint; the name of any particular saint.
- Introduce the activity. Invite the children to applaud if they agree with the statement and to remain silent if they disagree.

At Home

ENCOURAGE

Have the children carefully tear out pages 91 and 92 along the perforation. Encourage the children to share the pages with their families and to do the activities together. If they did not complete the review activity on page 91 by the end of the session, emphasize that they can complete it with their families.

VISIT FAITHFIRST.COM

- Share with the children the many activities on the *Faith First* Web site.
- Encourage the children to visit **www.FaithFirst.com.**

---

10 With My Family

This Week . . .

In chapter 10, "The Communion of Saints," your child learned that the Church is the Communion of Saints. The Communion of Saints is made up of those people living on earth, the faithful who have died and who have received the gift of heaven, and those faithful who have died who are not ready to receive the gift of heaven and are waiting to receive the gift of everlasting happiness. The Church honors the saints in heaven as heroes of our faith. Their lives are examples of how we can live a holy life as members of the Body of Christ, the Church. Sharing in the Eucharist unites us more closely with Jesus and the whole Communion of Saints and gives us the strength to live as a saint.

For more on the teachings of the Catholic Church on the mysteries of the Communion of Saints and everlasting life, see *Catechism of the Catholic Church* paragraph numbers 946–959, 1172–1173, and 1402–1405.

92

Sharing God's Word

Read together the Bible story in 1 Corinthians 12:12–13, 27 about what Paul the Apostle wrote about the Church or read the adaptation of the passage on page 88. Emphasize that Paul taught that every member of the Church is important.

Praying

In this chapter your child prayed a prayer of intercession. Read and pray together the prayer on page 91.

Making a Difference

Choose one of the following activities to do as a family or design a similar activity of your own.

- Find out more about Saint Juan Diego and Our Lady of Guadalupe. Read a children's book about Juan Diego to help you share more of this wonderful story together.
- Talk about the talents each member of your family has. As a family, choose one thing you can do this week to continue the work of Christ.
- Take some time this week to find out more about the patron saint of your parish or a saint who is special to your family. Visit www.FaithFirst.com or look in your public or parish library.

For more ideas on ways your family can live your faith, visit the "Faith First for Families" page at **www.FaithFirst.com.** Click on the "Saints" page and discover ways your family can live as followers of Jesus.

Before Moving On . . .

As you finish today's lesson, reflect on the following question before moving on to the next chapter.

How well have I modeled affirming comments and behaviors that I would like students to use with one another?

✔ Evaluate

Take a few moments to evaluate this week's lesson.
I feel (circle one) about this week's lesson.

    a. very pleased
    b. OK
    c. disappointed

The activity the children enjoyed most was . . .

The concept that was most difficult to teach was . . .

because . . .

Something I would like to do differently is . . .

ENRICHING THE LESSON

Role-Playing Phone Conversations about Continuing Jesus' Work

Purpose
To reinforce that whenever we live and love as Jesus taught us, we are living holy lives (taught on page 86)

Directions
- Bring in two real or play telephones for the children to use during this role-play.
- The call can be directed to any part of the world. The purpose of the phone call is to explain to the other party with as much imagination as possible how Christians today share in and continue the work of Jesus.
- Invite one person to make the call and the other person to respond with comments and questions.
- Provide time for the children to switch roles.
- Invite other pairs of children to repeat the process as time allows.

Materials
two real or play telephones

Creating Heroes of Faith Character Maps

Purpose
To reinforce that the Church honors heroes of faith (taught on page 86)

Directions
- Brainstorm with the children about the people in their lives who are heroes of faith for them.
- Have the children create a character map for one of their heroes of faith.
- Have them place the name of their hero in the center of a large piece of construction paper.
- Using three or four spokes, have them write the qualities that make this person a hero of faith for them.
- Beside each spoke have them write a situation in which this person illustrated this quality.
- Display these maps where everyone can enjoy them.

Materials
construction paper and markers or crayons

Literature Connection

Purpose
To extend the teaching about Our Lady of Guadalupe (taught on page 89)

Directions
You may wish to extend the teaching about Our Lady of Guadalupe by reading Tomie dePaola's beautifully illustrated story *The Lady of Guadalupe* (Holiday House, 1980).
- Read the story to the class, taking time to show the colorful illustrations.
- If you have children of Mexican origin in your class, ask them to share any memories they have of commemorating the feast day of Our Lady of Guadalupe.
- If time allows, list on the board three important things that happened in the story. Divide the children into groups and invite each group to prepare a small labeled poster illustrating one part of the story. Display the children's work.

Materials
The Lady of Guadalupe by Tomie dePaola

Music Connection
- "Chatter with the Angels" (African-American traditional), acc. R. Batastini. *Singing Our Faith (SOF)* #277.
- "Litany of Saints," J. Schiavone. *Rise Up and Sing (RUS)* #164.
- "Sing a Song to the Saints," J. Louden. *RUS* #166.
- "We Are Many Parts," M. Haugen. *SOF* #182.

Unit 1 Review

The unit review provides the opportunity to assess the children's understanding of the concepts presented in the unit and to affirm them in their growing knowledge and love of God. Here are a few suggestions for using these pages.

- Share that the next two pages are an opportunity to stop and review what they have learned.
- Provide time for the children to ask questions.
- Have the children complete the review alone or with a partner.

PART A:
The Best Word or Phrase

This section reviews the main concepts of the unit.

- Read the directions for section A. Illustrate what you expect the children to do by completing the first question together. By working together on the first question, you are teaching the children a strategy for answering these types of questions.
- When the children have finished this section, invite volunteers to share their answers. Review any question that the children seem to have difficulty answering.

FAMILY CONNECTION

Encourage the children to share the unit review pages with their families. This provides an excellent opportunity to involve the families in the faith formation of their children.

Review Unit 1

Name _____

A. The Best Word or Phrase

Complete the sentences. Circle the best choice under each sentence.

1. The gift of ___c___ helps us believe in God.
   a. love   b. hope   c. faith

2. The ___a___ is the mystery of one God in three Persons.
   a. Holy Trinity   b. Holy Family   c. Holy Spirit

3. God's love and care for creation is called ___a___ .
   a. divine Providence b. divine joy   c. stewardship

4. The ___b___ is the announcement to Mary that God chose her to be the mother of Jesus.
   a. Resurrection   b. Annunciation   c. Nativity

5. Jesus is called the ___b___ because he is the Anointed One of God who saves us from our sins.
   a. Son of God   b. Messiah   c. Christ the King

6. The ___a___ is the name for Jesus' Passion, death, Resurrection, and Ascension.
   a. Paschal Mystery   b. Crucifixion   c. Incarnation

7. The Holy Spirit came to the disciples on the Jewish feast of ___c___ .
   a. Pentecost   b. Easter   c. Passover

8. The Communion of ___c___ includes all the faithful followers of Jesus, including those on earth today and those who have died.
   a. Apostles   b. Bishops   c. Saints

(93)

Teaching Tip

Assessing Learning. Throughout the year use multiple forms of assessment. Children learn and communicate their learning in multiple ways. Some forms of communication, for example, writing paragraphs, work better for some children; other forms of communication, for example, artwork and verbal responses, work better for others. Asking questions, observing small group interactions, and using different activities throughout the sessions will provide you with multiple ways of identifying your young people's understanding of the truths of the faith of the Catholic Church.

B. Jesus and the Holy Spirit

Circle the † next to the words that tell about Jesus.
Circle the 🕊 next to the words that tell about the
Holy Spirit.

(†) 🕊 Messiah   † (🕊) Helper   † (🕊) Advocate

(†) 🕊 Savior   † (🕊) Guide   (†) 🕊 Son of God

C. What I Have Learned

1. *What are two new things you learned in this unit?*

   Responses will vary.

   Affirm appropriate responses.

2. *Look back at the list of faith words on page 12.*
   Circle the words you now know. Tell your group the
   meaning of two of the words.

D. From a Scripture Story

The story of Pentecost has a cause and an effect.
Write the effect of the story in the chart.

Cause	Effect
The Holy Spirit comes to the disciples.	The Holy Spirit helped the disciples teach the people about Jesus, and helped the people believe in Jesus.

PART B:
Jesus and the Holy Spirit

This section reinforces the unit vocabulary.

- Read the directions to the children and together do the first item in the activity. Have the children continue to work alone to finish the section.
- Invite volunteers to share their answers.

PART C:
What I Have Learned

This section provides the children with the opportunity to write or talk about what they have learned.

- Have the children share with a partner two things they remember from the chapters.
- Invite the children to return to the unit "Getting Ready" page and observe for themselves how they have grown in building a faith vocabulary.
- You may wish to have the children work with a partner and quiz each other on faith words using their word cards.

PART D:
From a Scripture Story

This section is a review of the Scripture story of Pentecost.

- Have the children work with a partner to retell the story and answer the question from the Scripture story.
- Have the children complete the activity and share their responses.

Teaching Tip

Sensitivity to All Learners. As you do this unit review, be sensitive to children with learning disabilities as well as to children who may have difficulty sharing their ideas aloud with a group. Remember that this formal review is only one way to assess the children's understanding of the concepts presented in the unit. Refer to the "Special Needs" boxes throughout this guide to learn some alternative ways of processing some of the review activities.

Unit 2 Opener

The unit opener pages are designed to assess, through a variety of questioning techniques, the children's prior knowledge about the key faith concepts presented in the unit. Processing these pages should not take more than ten or fifteen minutes.

USING ILLUSTRATIONS

The first page of the unit opener contains pictures that illustrate some of the important concepts in the unit. Pictures help stimulate the religious imaginations of the children.

- Invite the children to look at and think about the pictures.
- Ask volunteers to describe what each picture says to them.
- Invite the children to share a response to the question.

Unit 2 • We Worship

What are some times the Church celebrates as a community?

95

Background: Liturgy

Joined to Christ. Spend a few moments in prayerful reflection as you prepare for the teaching of this unit. Recall that when the Church gathers for worship and the celebration of the sacraments, the whole Church—Christ the Head and we the members of the Body of Christ—offers praise and thanksgiving to God the Father through the power of the Holy Spirit.

Getting Ready

What I Have Learned

What is something you already know about these faith words?

Paschal Mystery

Responses will vary.

_____

The liturgical year

Responses will vary.

_____

The Eucharist

Responses will vary.

_____

Words to Know

Put an X next to the faith words you know. Put a ? next to the faith words you need to know more about.

Faith Words   Responses will vary.

_____ liturgy

_____ Eucharist

_____ Blessed Sacrament

_____ parable

_____ Reconciliation

_____ Holy Orders

96

Questions I Have

What questions would you like to ask about the Eucharist?

Responses will vary.

_____

_____

A Scripture Story

THERE WAS A MARRIAGE IN CANA

Wedding in Cana

What did Jesus do at the wedding in Cana?

Affirm appropriate responses.

Teaching Tip

Sensitivity to Diversity. The faith life of the families of the children in your group is more than likely quite diverse. Some families may participate in the liturgy and the life of the Church on a very regular basis; others may participate mostly on special occasions, such as the Baptism of children, the marriage of family members, and so on. It is your responsibility to remind the children and their families of their obligation to take part in the celebration of Mass on Sundays and holy days of obligation. Be aware of this diversity as you call for a sharing of the children's faith experiences. Try to provide clear clues that will help the children respond to the questions.

GETTING READY

The "Getting Ready" page engages the children in sharing prior knowledge and aids you in planning your lessons to meet the needs of the children.

What I Have Learned

This section asks the children to share something they already know about the liturgy and the liturgical year. Read to the children the faith terms and ask volunteers to share ideas they know about each term.

Words to Know

This section is a quick assessment of the children's familiarity with some of the faith vocabulary they will be learning. Have them put an X next to terms they already know and a ? next to the terms they need to learn more about. At the end of this unit, the children will be asked to return to this page and once again share their understanding of these faith vocabulary terms.

Questions I Have

This section provides an opportunity for the children to ask questions that they have about the Eucharist. Write their questions on a chart. As you work through the unit always refer back to the chart and ask volunteers to answer the questions. This affirms for the children what they are learning about their faith.

A Scripture Story

This section uses the wedding in Cana to introduce Scripture used in this unit. Have the children look at the picture and answer the question. Their responses will help you become more aware of their knowledge of Scripture.

The Church's Year

A Celebration of the Paschal Mystery

The Church's year evolves in an annual cycle of seasons and feasts that celebrate Christ's birth, life, Passion, death, Resurrection, and Ascension. In each celebration and retelling of the mystery of Christ, the entire Christian story is remembered and its fountain of grace is continually poured out for all ages.

Sunday is the Lord's Day. The Church, since the days of the Apostles, has celebrated the Paschal Mystery of Christ on the first day of each week to commemorate the Lord's Resurrection. "Sunday must be ranked as the first holy day of all" (*General Norms for the Liturgical Year and Calendar* 4).

Advent-Christmas

The liturgical year begins with the first Sunday of Advent. During the season of Advent the Church reflects on and anticipates for four weeks the coming of Christ among us—past, present, and future. The Advent season, which is filled with joyful expectancy and hope, gives way to Christmas, a festive season lasting from the celebration of Christ's birth on December 25 through the Sunday after the feast of the Epiphany. Over the course of several weeks the Church celebrates the wonder of the Incarnation.

Lent–Easter

Lent is a period of prayer, fasting, and almsgiving that begins on Ash Wednesday. The weeks of Lent are a preparation for the celebration of the sacred Triduum and the Easter season. The Triduum is the sacred period of three days, beginning with the Evening Mass of the Lord's Supper on Holy Thursday and climaxing with the celebration of Evening Prayer on Easter Sunday.

Easter begins a season of fifty days, concluding with the celebration of Pentecost. Throughout Easter the Church rejoices. Joined to Christ in Baptism, we have passed from death to life, from slavery to freedom, and from sin to glory.

Ordinary Time

All the remaining weeks of the year—about 33 or 34 weeks— are known as Ordinary Time. Ordinary Time is a bridge, linking what has gone before and what is to come. Ordinary does not indicate that these weeks are

unimportant. Rather, the designation *ordinary* is derived from the Latin *ordo*, meaning "order." Ordinary Time indicates these Sundays and weeks are numbered in order.

In what ways does my participation in the seasons and feasts of the liturgical year enrich my life of faith?

What more can I do to make the Sunday celebration central to my life of faith?

Catechist to Catechist

Holidays and Holy Days

The liturgical year is a celebration of the faith of the Church. Season after season, week after week, day in and day out, the Church gathers to remember and share in the Paschal Mystery of Christ. For children, holidays and holy days mark the passage of time from one season to the next. The rituals connected with each holiday, holy day, and season become highlights in the lives of third graders. The way a family celebrates special days and times of the Church's year often includes customs, traditions, and rituals that are passed down from generation to generation.

Celebrate

One of the best ways you can teach children about the liturgical year is to celebrate it. As part of your discussion of each season of the Church's year, ask the children to share what their families do to celebrate this time of the year. By giving children a chance to share their family traditions, you are enriching the experience of all the children.

The Church Teaches . . .

The *Constitution on the Sacred Liturgy* reminds us:

> Holy Mother Church believes that it is for her to celebrate the saving work of her divine Spouse in a sacred commemoration on certain days throughout the course of the year. Once each week, on the day which she has called the Lord's Day, she keeps the memory of the Lord's resurrection. . . . In the course of the year, moreover, she unfolds the whole mystery of Christ. *SC* 102

That is why *Faith First* emphasizes the liturgical year through seasonal lessons and celebrations.

See the Catechism . . .

For more on the teachings of the Catholic Church on the liturgy and the liturgical year, see *Catechism of the Catholic Church* 1135–1186.

CATECHIST PRAYER

Spirit of God,
fill our hearts with
gratitude to the Father
for the gift of Jesus,
his only Son. Help
us to give thanks
for the gift of Jesus.
Amen.

LESSON PLANNER

Focus **To identify ways the Catholic Church celebrates its faith in Jesus Christ throughout the year**

Engage

Page 97
Focus
To assess the children's knowledge about the Church's year of worship

Opening Prayer

Discussion
Celebrating with family and the Church

Teach and Apply

Pages 98–100
Focus
To discover the meaning of the seasons and feasts of the liturgical year

Presentation
Read, discuss, and summarize content.
Scripture
Psalm 111:1
Activities
- Share how you celebrate Advent and Christmas.
- Identify the liturgical seasons.
- Choose a favorite Bible story and identify what it teaches about Jesus.

Faith-Filled People
The Elect

Connect

Pages 101–102
Focus
To discover ways the liturgical year helps us live our faith

Our Church Makes a Difference
The Catholic Church celebrates feasts of the Lord to remember that he is the Son of God and Savior of the world.

Our Catholic Faith
Liturgical Colors

What Difference Does Faith Make?
Activity
Complete the sentences about celebrating living as a follower of Jesus.
Faith Choice
Choose a way to celebrate that you are a follower of Jesus this week.

We Pray

Page 103
Prayer Form
Thanksgiving
Prayer
Practice signing the prayer; sing an appropriate hymn.

We Remember

Review
- Complete the crossword puzzle activity.
- Read the "To Help You Remember" statements aloud.

Preview
Highlight features of the "With My Family" page.

Materials

- Bible
- newsprint
- pens or pencils
- crayons or markers

Enriching the Session

Blackline Masters
Additional Activities booklet:
  Chapter 11
    Remembering God's love
    Writing a letter
Assessment Tools booklet:
  Chapter 11 Test

Enriching the Lesson (CG page 181)
Creating a Liturgical Dance
Celebrating the Triduum
Literature Connection

Music Connection (CG page 181)

www.FaithFirst.com

We update the *Faith First* Web site weekly. Check each week for new content and features. Here are some places to begin:

Catechists and Teachers
- Current Events
- Chapter Downloads
- Catechist Prayer

Faith First for Families
- Bible Stories
- Make a Difference

Kids' Clubhouse
- *Faith First* Activities
- Chapter Reviews
- Games
- Saints

Don't Forget! You can make lesson planning a breeze—check out the **Online Lesson Planner.**

The Church's Year

11

We Pray

With all my heart
I praise the LORD,
our God.
Based on Psalm 111:1

**Father, always
and everywhere
we give you
thanks through
Jesus Christ,
your Son. Amen.**

*What days do you
and your family like
to celebrate?*

Celebrating special
times is fun. The
Church celebrates
too. We gather to
celebrate our faith in
Christ.

*What are your
favorite celebrations
of the Church?*

97

PRAY
- Gather the children for prayer and pray the Sign of the Cross.
- Have a volunteer read the Psalm verse and then pray the opening prayer together.
- Conclude by praying the Sign of the Cross together.

DISCOVER
Purpose: To discover what the children know about the Church's year
- Invite the children to talk about celebrations they have with their families during the year.
- Read the introductory paragraph and invite responses to the question that follows.
- Invite the children to look at the picture. Ask them why they think this image of nature was chosen. Affirm appropriate responses.

Liturgy Tip

Celebrating the Church's Year. Children today live in a highly commercial culture. The strategies you choose to help the children observe each season of the Church's year are of tremendous value. Simple observances such as praying with Advent wreaths, choosing Lenten sacrifices, and venerating the cross can make lasting impressions. Connect Christmas gift-giving and dyed Easter eggs with the profound religious themes related to God's generosity in bringing us new life through Jesus.

Teach

FOCUS

Read the "Faith Focus" question aloud. Share with the children that the Church gathers all year long to celebrate faith in Jesus Christ. Tell them they are going to learn more about these seasonal celebrations.

DISCOVER

- Point out that the Church's year helps us recall the important events in the life of Jesus.
- Invite the children to read silently "The Liturgical Year" to discover the meaning of the term *liturgical year* and what seasons are a part of the *liturgical year*.
- Beginning with Advent, list the liturgical seasons on the board. Ask the children to tell you what the Church celebrates during each liturgical season.

Apply

REINFORCE

Ask volunteers to read the faith words *worship* and *liturgy* and their meanings. Have them make word cards for these terms.

INTEGRATE

Have the children look at the pictures and share with a partner how they celebrate Advent and Christmas.

The Church's Year

Faith Focus

How does the Church celebrate its faith in Jesus Christ throughout the year?

Faith Words

worship
Worship is the adoration and honor we give to God.

liturgy
The liturgy is the Church's work of worshiping God.

The Liturgical Year

The Church gathers all year long to celebrate its faith in Jesus Christ. We gather to **worship** God. We call this work of the Church the **liturgy.**

The Church's year of worship is called the liturgical year. The liturgical year is made up of the seasons of Advent, Christmas, Lent, Easter, and Ordinary Time.

Advent and Christmas

Advent begins the liturgical year. We prepare for Christmas. We wait in hope for Christ's return in glory at the end of time. During Christmas we praise and thank God for sending us Jesus, the Savior of the world.

Share with a partner how you like to celebrate Advent and Christmas. Responses will vary.

Advent

Christmas

98

 Liturgy Tip

A Year of Grace. The Church calls each liturgical year a year of grace. Grace is a free gift from God. Grace makes us sharers in the life of God and helps us live as children of God and followers of Jesus. We celebrate God's grace in our lives through the events of the Church's year. Use the liturgical lessons beginning on page 235 of the student text to enrich the children's understanding and celebration of the Church's year of grace.

Lent and Easter

During Lent we prepare for Easter. We join with those preparing for Baptism. We prepare to renew the promises we made at our Baptism. At the conclusion of Lent during Holy Week, the Church celebrates the Easter Triduum. The Easter Triduum is the center of the liturgical year. The word *triduum* means "three days."

The Easter Triduum begins on Holy Thursday evening and ends on Easter Sunday evening. It includes the celebrations on Holy Thursday, Good Friday, and the Easter Vigil/Easter Sunday. During these three days we celebrate and share in Jesus' Passion, death, and Resurrection.

The fifty days of the Easter season are celebrated next. During Easter we celebrate and remember Jesus' Resurrection and Ascension. The remaining weeks of the liturgical year are called Ordinary Time.

Faith-Filled People

The Elect

At the Easter Vigil you may see a special group of people. They are called the Elect. They have accepted God's invitation to become members of the Church. At the Easter Vigil they receive the sacraments of Baptism, Confirmation, and Eucharist.

Look at the four pictures. On the lines write the Church season each shows.

Easter

Lent

99

Background: Liturgy

The Elect. The Rite of Christian Initiation of Adults (RCIA) is a time of evangelization and conversion. It is a formation process by which adults and children are received into full communion with the Catholic Church. The word *elect* signifies that they have accepted God's invitation to be baptized. The rite of election takes place at the beginning of Lent. Thus Lent becomes a time of spiritual formation to help candidates prepare for full initiation into the Church at the Easter Vigil.

Teach

FOCUS

Point out that the highlight of the liturgical year is the Easter Triduum.

DISCOVER

- Ask the children if they have ever been to church services during Holy Week. Have them share what they remember about these liturgies.
- Write the word *triduum* on the board and next to it the words *three days*.
- Invite the children to read silently "Lent and Easter" to discover what three days make up the Easter Triduum. Explain that during these three special days we celebrate and share in Jesus' suffering, dying, and being raised from the dead to new life which is called the *Paschal Mystery*.
- Invite a volunteer to read about the Elect in "Faith-Filled People." You may wish to add material from the background box below.

Apply

REINFORCE

Have the children read the directions to the activity and complete it. Go over their responses together. Ask them to describe what each picture depicts.

INTEGRATE

Talk with the children about how their families might celebrate Lent and Easter. Sharing from your own experience may help to elicit the children's responses.

(Student Page 99) 175

Teach

FOCUS

Remind the children that the liturgical year has five seasons. Point out that Ordinary Time is the longest season in the Church's year.

DISCOVER

- Ask the children what the word *ordinary* means to them.
- Explain that the Church's longest season is called Ordinary Time. This does not mean that this season is less important.
- Tell the children it means that the weeks are numbered in order, such as the Fifteenth Sunday in Ordinary Time.
- Remind them that each Sunday is important because it is the Lord's Day, a celebration of the Paschal Mystery.
- Invite volunteers to read "Ordinary Time" to find out what stories of the Gospel tell us about Jesus.

Apply

REINFORCE

Have the children turn to page 236 in their text to look at "The Liturgical Year." Let them look at the pictures and notice how the pictures represent the seasons.

INTEGRATE

Explain the activity and encourage the children to complete it and share their favorite Gospel story.

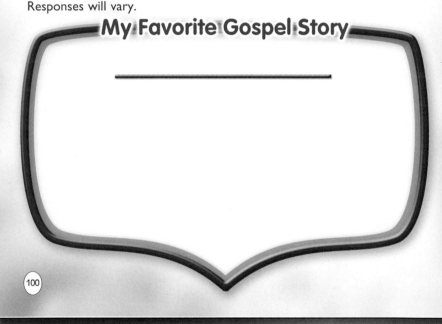

Ordinary Time

Ordinary Time is the longest part of the liturgical year. Ordinary Time includes the weeks that are not part of the seasons of Advent, Christmas, Lent, or Easter.

There are two parts of Ordinary Time. The first part begins after Christmas and continues to Lent. The second part begins after the fifty days of the Easter season and continues to Advent.

During Ordinary Time we listen to stories from the Gospels that tell us about Jesus' life and his saving work while he was on earth. We come to know Jesus more and more. We learn how we can live as his followers.

On the line write the title of one of your favorite Gospel stories. Draw or write something from the story in the space. Responses will vary.

My Favorite Gospel Story

100

Teaching Tip

Introduce Liturgical Colors. Ask the pastor or a parish staff member for permission to borrow a variety of the vestments worn during the liturgical seasons and special feasts. Share with the children the significance of each of the liturgical colors. Purple is the color of penance, white and gold signify rebirth and joyful celebration, and green is the color of life and hope. Cover your prayer table each week with a cloth that is the color of the liturgical season.

Our Church Makes a Difference

Feasts of the Lord

All throughout the liturgical year we celebrate the faith of the Church in Jesus Christ. In addition to Christmas and the saving events of Jesus' Passion, death, Resurrection, and Ascension, the Church celebrates other feasts of the Lord.

Epiphany

Baptism of the Lord

Annunciation

Transfiguration

Presentation of the Lord

Christ the King

These feasts of the Lord remember and proclaim that Jesus is the Son of God and Savior of the world. He is the new and everlasting Covenant of friendship that God has made with all people.

Talk about how celebrating these six feasts can help you grow in your faith in Jesus Christ.

(101)

Our Catholic Faith

Liturgical Colors

The Church uses colors to remind us of the liturgical seasons. Purple or violet is used for Advent and Lent. White or gold is used for Christmas and Easter. Green is used for Ordinary Time. On special days, such as Good Friday and Pentecost, red is used. The color white is used on the feasts of the Lord.

Connect

HIGHLIGHT

Help the children recall that we celebrate the faith of the Church in Jesus Christ throughout the liturgical year.

DISCOVER

- List on the board the six feasts of the Lord.
- Invite the children to read aloud "Feasts of the Lord" to discover what all these feasts have in common. They all proclaim that Jesus is the Son of God and the Savior of the world. He is the new and everlasting Covenant of friendship that God has made with all people.
- Ask a volunteer to read aloud "Our Catholic Faith."

INTEGRATE

- Ask the children to share with one another how celebrating the feasts of the Lord may help them to grow in faith.
- Tell the children what season the Church is now celebrating and ask them to notice what color the celebrant is wearing the next time they are at Mass.

Special Needs

Learning New Vocabulary. Play a game called *Rivet* to learn and reinforce the vocabulary for feasts of the Lord. For each word draw the appropriate number of blanks on the board for the letters in the word. Begin to write a word one letter at a time. Allow students to try to guess the word or words as more letters are revealed. As each word is guessed, talk about the feast. You will want to do this activity with student books closed so they do not have the words in front of them!

Need: Children with learning difficulties

Connect

HIGHLIGHT

Remind the children that the Church's liturgical year helps us to live as followers of Jesus.

RESPOND

- Read aloud the opening paragraph and introduction to the activity.
- Invite the children to complete the phrases that describe how the current season helps them to live as followers of Jesus.

CHOOSE

- Invite the children to respond to "My Faith Choice."
- After a moment of prayerful reflection have the children write their choices on the lines provided.
- Encourage the children to put their choices into practice this week.

What Difference Does Faith Make in My Life?

The Church's liturgical year helps you keep your faith alive. When you take part in the celebrations of the liturgical year, you share in God's love.

Describe how the liturgical season the Church is celebrating now helps you live as a follower of Jesus. Responses will vary.

Living as a Follower of Jesus

The Church is now celebrating the season of

_____.

During this season I will remember that Jesus

_____.

I will try to follow Jesus by _____

_____.

My Faith Choice

ƒc This week I will celebrate that I am a follower of Jesus. I will

_____ Affirm appropriate responses. _____

_____.

102

Teaching Tip

Focusing on the Season. Reflect for a moment on the current season of the Church's year. Think about how you are living the season in your day-to-day life. Consider how you might work to incorporate the lessons of the current liturgical season into lessons for the children. How can you highlight the season in prayer, through activities, and in discussion?

We Pray

Thank You, God

Learn to sign this prayer of thanksgiving. Pray it alone and with other people.

Thank you,   God,   for   everything.

We Remember

Use the clues to complete the puzzle.

DOWN

1. The Church's work of worshiping God.
2. We celebrate Jesus, the Son of God, coming to us as the Savior of the world.
3. We celebrate Jesus' being raised from the dead.
5. We prepare for Christmas.

ACROSS

4. The suffering, death, Resurrection, and Ascension of Jesus.
6. We get ready for Easter.

To Help You Remember

1. The Church's year of worship is called the liturgical year. The seasons of the liturgical year are Advent, Christmas, Lent, Easter, and Ordinary Time.

2. The center of the liturgical year is the Easter Triduum.

3. Ordinary Time is the longest part of the liturgical year.

Grade 3 • Chapter 11   103

Pray

WE PRAY

- Explain that the children are going to learn to sign a prayer of thanksgiving and pray it together.
- Have the children work with partners and practice the signs one word at a time.
- When they are ready, gather in the prayer center and pray the prayer together.

Review

WE REMEMBER

- Scramble the letters to the words *Advent, Triduum,* and *Easter.*
- Ask the children to unscramble the letters to name different parts of the Church year.
- Challenge the children to create a definition for each word.
- Introduce the crossword puzzle activity and invite the children to complete it on their own.

Liturgy Tip

Signs of the Liturgical Year. Teaching children the American Sign Language signs for simple prayers serves several purposes. First, from a liturgical standpoint, it stimulates participation by allowing the children to use their bodies in prayer. This especially appeals to kinesthetic learners. Second, it shows respect for an important segment of the faith community. If signing is used at Masses in your parish, ask the children to watch for signed prayers they have learned.

At Home

ENCOURAGE

Have the children carefully tear out pages 103 and 104 along the perforation. Encourage the children to share the pages with their families and to do the activities together. If they did not complete the review activity on page 103 by the end of the session, emphasize that they can complete it with their families.

VISIT FAITHFIRST.COM

- Share with the children the many activities on the *Faith First* Web site.
- Encourage the children to visit **www.FaithFirst.com.**

Before Moving On . . .

As you finish today's lesson, reflect on the following question before moving on to the next chapter.

What do I do to encourage and affirm the sense of humor I see in some of the students?

---

11 With My Family

This Week . . .

In chapter 11, "The Church's Year," your child learned about the Church's year of worship, or the liturgical year. Like the calendar year, the liturgical year is made up of a cycle of seasons and important days. The Easter Triduum, or the three days of Holy Thursday, Good Friday, and Easter Vigil/Easter Sunday, is the heart of the liturgical year. The seasons of Advent, Christmas, Lent, and Easter revolve around this solemn three-day celebration of Christ's Passion, death, and Resurrection. The remaining weeks of the liturgical year are called Ordinary Time.

For more on the teachings of the Catholic Church on the liturgy and the liturgical year, see *Catechism of the Catholic Church* paragraph numbers 1135–1186.

Sharing God's Word

Reread the Gospel passage that you heard proclaimed at Mass this week. You can find the reading by clicking "Gospel Reflection" at www.FaithFirst.com. Emphasize how the reading helps you grow and live your faith in Jesus Christ.

Praying

In this chapter your child learned to sign a short thanksgiving prayer. Ask your child to teach you the prayer on page 103. Pray the prayer together.

Making a Difference

Choose one of the following activities to do as a family or design a similar activity of your own.

- When you take part in Mass this weekend, look at the color of the vestments and identify what liturgical season it is. Look around the church for other clues that tell you about the liturgical season.
- At dinnertime talk about how celebrating the liturgical year helps you grow in and live your faith in Jesus Christ.
- Create place mats for the current season of the liturgical year. Use the place mats at family meals.

For more ideas on ways your family can live your faith, visit the "Faith First for Families" page at **www.FaithFirst.com**. This week take time to read an article from "Just for Parents."

✓ Evaluate

Take a few moments to evaluate this week's lesson.
I feel (circle one) about this week's lesson.

    a. very pleased
    b. OK
    c. disappointed

The activity the children enjoyed most was . . .

The concept that was most difficult to teach was . . .

because . . .

Something I would like to do differently is . . .

ENRICHING THE LESSON

Creating a Liturgical Dance

Purpose
To reinforce the different seasons of the liturgical year (taught on page 98)

Directions
- Brainstorm with the children some movements and gestures appropriate for each season.
- In small groups have the children create a dance for one of the seasons.
- Invite them to choose streamers appropriate for their season to use in their dance.
- Have the different groups present their dance and allow the other children to name the season.

Materials
crepe paper streamers

Celebrating the Triduum

Purpose
To reinforce that the Easter Triduum is the center of the liturgical year (taught on page 99)

Directions
- Help the children recall the events of each day of the Triduum.
- Have the children work with partners to create a diorama for one of the days of the Triduum.
- Using shoe boxes and colored paper, have the children create the background for one of these days.
- Then, using pipe cleaners and other art supplies, have the children place the people in the scene.
- Ask the children to display and describe their scenes.

Materials
colored paper and other art supplies
shoe boxes
pipe cleaners
scissors and markers

Literature Connection

Purpose
To reinforce that during Ordinary Time we listen to stories from the Gospels that tell us about Jesus' life and his saving work on earth (taught on page 100)

Directions
- The Gospels tell the story of Jesus Christ. Choose the Gospel that is being read during Ordinary Time of the current liturgical cycle to draw the children into the stories the Church is reflecting on this year.
- List several of the Gospel stories for the current year on the board.
- Pass out Bibles to the children and point out to them how to find the passages listed by using the guide words and numbers at the top of the pages.
- Have the children work in groups of three or four. Assign a Gospel story to each group.
- After the children have read their passage, have them prepare and perform a role-play of it for the class.
- Discuss the message of each story.

Materials
Bibles

Music Connection
- "I Come with Joy," A. Buchanan. *Singing Our Faith (SOF)* #184.
- "Pues Si Vivimos/If We Are Living" (Spanish traditional), arr. D. Kodner. *SOF* #180.
- "Walking By Faith," D. Haas. *SOF* #179.
- "We Are Many Parts," M. Haugen. *SOF* #182.

Celebrations of God's Love

Background

Signs of God's Love

The seven sacraments are the hub around which the faith and liturgical life of the Church revolve. The sacraments make the saving work present among us. Instituted by Christ, they are signs of God's love that make us sharers in the Paschal Mystery of Christ.

The sacraments are actions of the Church, the Body of Christ. Through the sacraments we are joined to Christ, the Head of the Church, and are made sharers in the life of God.

The purpose of the sacraments is to sanctify [people], to build up the Body of Christ, and, finally, to give worship to God. . . . They not only presuppose faith, but by words and objects they also nourish, strengthen, and express it.

CONSTITUTION ON THE SACRED LITURGY
(SACROSANCTUM CONCILIUM) 59

Baptism

Baptism is the gateway into the spiritual life and the doorway to the other sacraments. By Baptism we belong to Christ and to one another, pouring out our lives in service to one another. In Baptism we die with Christ, all past sinfulness is cleansed and destroyed, and we rise with Christ to newness of life. We receive the gift of the Holy Spirit and the grace to live holy lives as adopted sons and daughters of God the Father.

Confirmation

Confirmation is a sacrament of anointing that strengthens the graces of Baptism. We are sealed by the gift of the Holy Spirit for the mission to be a witness for Christ in the world. Confirmation, like Baptism, imparts a unique, indelible spiritual mark, or character, identifying us forever as belonging to Christ. These two Sacraments of Christian Initiation are received and celebrated only once.

Eucharist

Sharing in the Eucharist completes our initiation into Christ and the Church. The Eucharist is the source and summit of the Christian life and is to be received often throughout our lives. It renews our baptismal inheritance. Nourished by the Eucharist we go forth to live in service to others as bread broken and wine poured out for the life of the world.

Since 1972 when the rite for Christian initiation of adults (RCIA) was revised, the celebration of the sacraments of Baptism, Confirmation, and Eucharist was restored to the order they were celebrated in the early Church. All three sacraments are celebrated together at the Easter Vigil. The focus of this initiatory process for adults is one of discerning and ritualizing stages of conversion on the journey to full integration into the Catholic community of faith.

For Reflection

In what ways does my participation in the celebration of the sacraments nourish, strengthen, and express my faith and the faith of the Church?

How can the sacraments facilitate my ongoing conversion to Christ?

Catechist to Catechist

Touched by God

Our faith journey lasts a lifetime. Each stage of spiritual growth is unique as we grow in our personal relationship with the Trinity: Father, Son, and Holy Spirit. In the celebration of the sacraments, especially the Eucharist, we celebrate and are made sharers through the power of the Holy Spirit in the love that God the Father so freely shares with us through his Son, Jesus Christ.

Growing in Faith

As a catechist, you have a wonderful opportunity to help the children come to know of and respond to God's presence in their lives.  What they learn now can indeed influence the kind of committed Catholics they become. Help your third graders appreciate the importance of the sacraments in celebrating their Catholic identity. Emphasize that taking an active and conscious participation in the celebration of the sacraments is key to their growth as faith-filled children of God.

The Church Teaches . . .

The *National Catechetical Directory* reminds us:

> Catechesis has the task of preparing individuals and communities for knowing, active, and fruitful liturgical and sacramental celebration . . . The liturgy and sacraments are the supreme celebration of the paschal mystery. They express the sanctification of human life. . . . [and] accomplish the saving acts which they symbolize.
>
> *NCD 44*

This chapter helps the children grow in their appreciation for the sacraments and other liturgical celebrations of the Catholic Church.

See the Catechism . . .

For more on the teachings of the Catholic Church on the sacraments of Baptism and Confirmation, see *Catechism of the Catholic Church* 1135–1158, 1210–1211, 1212–1274, and 1285–1314.

CATECHIST PRAYER

*Spirit of God,
help me forgive anyone
who has hurt me.
And help me ask for
forgiveness from those
whom I have hurt.
Amen*

LESSON PLANNER

To explain that the sacraments are signs of God's love for us and that they help us live as followers of Jesus

Engage

Page 105
Focus

To assess the children's knowledge about the Church's celebration of the sacraments

Opening Prayer

Discussion
Family celebrations

Teach and Apply

Pages 106–108
Focus

To identify the seven sacraments and show how celebrating the sacraments of Baptism and Confirmation brings us closer to God

Presentation
Read, discuss, and summarize content.
Scripture
Psalm 66:1–2
Activities
• Write about a sacrament you have received.
• Talk about your Baptism with your family.
• Write and answer a question about Confirmation.
Faith-Filled People
The Apostles

Connect

Pages 109–110
Focus

To explain how the Church uses signs to help us pray and worship and identify ourselves as signs of God's love

Our Church Makes a Difference
Sacramentals are objects and blessings that we use in our worship and prayer.
Our Catholic Faith
Holy Water

What Difference Does Faith Make?
Activity
Write a letter to a friend about how a sacrament you have received helps you live as a follower of Jesus.
Faith Choice
Choose a way to show you are a follower of Jesus.

We Pray

Page 111
Prayer Form
Meditation
Prayer
Play appropriate background music, introduce the meditation, and lead the children step by step through the meditation.

We Remember

Review
• Complete the decoding activity.
• Read the "To Help You Remember" statements aloud.
Preview
Highlight features of the "With My Family" page.

Materials

• Bible
• paper
• pencils

Enriching the Session

Blackline Masters
Additional Activities booklet:
Chapter 12
Living a sacramental life
Writing a letter
Assessment Tools booklet:
Chapter 12 Test

Faith First Grade 3 Video
Segment 2: The Visual Bible™/
"The Baptism of Jesus"

Enriching the Lesson (CG page 193)
Reviewing Through Music
Making Sacrament Booklets
Literature Connection

Music Connection (CG page 193)

www.FaithFirst.com

We update the *Faith First* Web site weekly. Check each week for new content and features. Here are some places to begin:

Catechists and Teachers
• Current Events
• Chapter Downloads
• Catechist Prayer

Faith First for Families
• Bible Stories
• Make a Difference

Kids' Clubhouse
• *Faith First* Activities
• Chapter Reviews
• Games
• Saints

Don't Forget! You can make lesson planning a breeze—check out the **Online Lesson Planner.**

Celebrations of God's Love

We Pray

Sing to God with hearts full of happiness and joy; praise God and give him glory.

Based on Psalm 66:1–2

Father, you give us grace through the sacraments. Help us live as signs of your love for all people. Amen.

What makes family celebrations special?

Families celebrate special family times. Our Church family celebrates the sacraments to remember and share in God's love.

What sacraments have you celebrated?

Baptism of an infant (105)

PRAY

- Gather the children and invite them to quiet themselves for prayer. Pray the Sign of the Cross and have a volunteer read the Psalm verse.
- Pray the opening prayer together.

DISCOVER

Purpose: To discover what the children know about the sacraments

- Talk briefly with the children about the bonds of love within families.
- Discuss what makes a family celebration special.
- Invite them to look carefully at the picture and describe what they see happening. Baptism.
- Tell them that the Church's sacraments help us grow closer to God and to one another.
- Ask what sacraments they have celebrated.

Teaching Tip

Family Differences. At various times families experience stresses that can disrupt even the best intentions. When this happens, children in a family experience the stress. Acknowledge this reality with the children. In discussions about family life help the children recall their best family experiences. The memories of these positive experiences can help children cope with the rough spots in their family life.

Teach

FOCUS

Ask a volunteer to read aloud the "Faith Focus" question. Share with the children that in this chapter they will learn more about what the sacraments celebrate.

DISCOVER

- Ask the children to name as many of the seven sacraments as they can. Write their responses on the board. Invite them to read silently the first paragraph of "Jesus Gives Us the Sacraments" to help you fill in the list.
- Write *Holy Trinity* on the board. Ask three volunteers to read aloud the sentences on the page that tell what each Person of the Holy Trinity does through the sacraments.

Apply

REINFORCE

Together read aloud the definition of *sacraments* in "Faith Words."

INTEGRATE

- Have the children write the name of one sacrament they have received and a few sentences about the sacrament.
- Ask them to share the details or memories of the sacramental celebration with the class.

We Celebrate the Sacraments

Faith Focus

What do the sacraments do that brings us closer to Jesus?

Faith Words

sacraments
The sacraments are the seven special signs that make Jesus present to us and make us sharers in the life of the Holy Trinity.

Sacraments of Initiation
Baptism, Confirmation, and Eucharist are the Sacraments of Initiation.

On the top line write the name of one sacrament you have received. On the other lines write one thing about the sacrament.

Jesus Gives Us the Sacraments

Our Church celebrates the **sacraments.** There are seven sacraments. They are Baptism, Confirmation, Eucharist, Anointing of the Sick, Penance, Holy Orders, and Matrimony.

Jesus gave us the sacraments. The sacraments make us sharers in the life of the Holy Trinity. God the Father invites us to give him praise and thanksgiving. Jesus helps us bring the good news of God's love to others. The Holy Spirit helps us become more like Jesus.

Responses will vary.

Affirm appropriate responses.

(106)

Background: Doctrine

Baptism and Confirmation. Through the sacrament of Baptism (*baptize* meaning "to plunge" or "immerse") the Church celebrates the new life of the baptized as they emerge from the water, sharing in the Resurrection of Christ. This Sacrament of Christian Initiation unites new members of the Church with Christ and the mission of the Church. The sacrament of Confirmation strengthens the baptismal graces and empowers the confirmed to live as witnesses for Christ.

Baptism

Baptism is one of the three **Sacraments of Initiation.** They are Baptism, Confirmation, and the Eucharist. Baptism is the first sacrament we receive. If we are baptized as an infant, our parents and godparents, or sponsors, ask the Church to baptize us. Our godparents promise to help our parents teach us about Jesus and how to live as Jesus taught.

The priest, or deacon, uses water to baptize us. Through Baptism we are joined to Christ. We receive new life in Christ and are born into the Church family. Our sins are forgiven, and we receive the gift of the Holy Spirit.

In Baptism, we are marked with a lasting sign, or character. We are followers of Christ forever. That is why we can be baptized only one time.

Ask your family about your Baptism. If your family has your baptismal candle, use it at mealtime prayers this week.

Pouring water to baptize

Receiving a lighted baptismal candle

Anointing with chrism

107

Faith-Filled People

The Apostles

The Apostles were the disciples Jesus sent into the world to make disciples of all nations. Jesus gave the Apostles the work to baptize and to teach people all he had taught them.

Background: Catholic Tradition

The Apostles. When we say the Catholic Church is apostolic, we are saying the Catholic Church traces itself back to the Apostles whom Jesus gave the authority to teach in his name. Jesus sent the Holy Spirit to help the Apostles fulfill this call. Today the bishops are the successors of the Apostles. Together with priests, their coworkers, they continue the work Jesus gave to the Apostles.

Teach

FOCUS

Remind the children that the sacraments make us sharers in God's life and love. Tell the children they are going to learn more about the first sacrament Christians celebrate—Baptism.

DISCOVER

Ask the children to read silently to learn what happens to us through Baptism. Receive new life in Christ; born into the Church family; our sins are forgiven; receive the gift of the Holy Spirit.

Apply

REINFORCE

Ask a volunteer to read about *Sacraments of Initiation* in "Faith Words" on page 106. Have the children make a word card for this term.

INTEGRATE

- Ask the children what signs of Baptism they can see in the picture.
- Encourage the children to ask their family about their Baptism and to use their baptismal candle for mealtime prayer.

Teach

FOCUS

Remind the children that Baptism is the first sacrament we receive. Point out that the sacrament of Confirmation strengthens us to live our Baptism.

DISCOVER

- Ask volunteers to share what they know about Confirmation.
- Write two questions on the board: What does Confirmation strengthen us to do? What words does the bishop or priest, delegated by the bishop, pray at Confirmation?
- With a partner have the children read "Confirmation" together to find the answers to the two questions.

Apply

REINFORCE

Review Baptism and Confirmation by asking the children to complete these sentences.

- Through _____ we are born into the Church family.
- Through _____ the Holy Spirit makes us stronger followers of Jesus.

INTEGRATE

- Ask if any children in the class have celebrated Confirmation or attended the Confirmation of a family member. Ask them to share their memories of the sacrament.
- Invite them to write any question they may have about Confirmation on the page.

Confirmation

Confirmation completes and strengthens us to live our Baptism. Like Baptism, we can only receive this sacrament one time. In Confirmation, we are also marked with a permanent sign, or character.

Confirmation usually takes place at Mass. After the Gospel reading, the bishop, or the priest chosen by him, asks the candidates for Confirmation to renew their baptismal promises. He then extends his hands over all the candidates and prays, "Send your Spirit upon them to be their Helper and Guide."

Our sponsor, who can be one of our godparents, presents us to the bishop. The bishop lays his hand on our head and anoints us with the blessed oil of chrism, saying, "(Name), be sealed with the Gift of the Holy Spirit." The Holy Spirit strengthens us to bring Jesus to the world.

Write a question about Confirmation. This week try to find the answer to your question. Responses will vary.

108

Background: Liturgy

Sacramental Graces of Confirmation. Confirmation is one of the Sacraments of Christian Initiation. Like the other sacraments, Confirmation has specific sacramental graces. The sacramental graces, or effects, of Confirmation are:

- deepening our rebirth as God's adopted children.
- uniting us more closely to the Lord Jesus.
- increasing the gifts of the Holy Spirit within us.
- strengthening the bond of unity we experience with the Church.
- strengthening us to spread and defend the faith by word and deed.

(See *Catechism of the Catholic Church* 1302–1305.)

Our Church Makes a Difference

We Are Blessed by God

All believers ask for God's blessing. We ask God to be with us in all we say and do. Blessings of people, meals, objects, and places are sacramentals of the Church. Sacramentals are objects and blessings that we use in our worship and prayer.

Holy water, blessed oils, the crucifix, and blessed religious medals are sacramentals. The ashes we receive on our foreheads on Ash Wednesday are examples of objects that are sacramentals.

The Church asks for God's blessing in the name of Christ while making the sign of the cross of Christ. This shows that in Christ we are blessed by God the Father, God the Son, and God the Holy Spirit.

Our Catholic Faith

Holy Water

Water is one of the main sacramentals of the Church. Water reminds us that God is the giver of all life. He gives us the gift of life on earth and of eternal life in heaven.

What sacramentals do you use? Tell how they help you pray. Affirm appropriate responses.

109

Liturgy Tip

Sacramentals. Display a variety of sacramentals on the prayer table, such as a crucifix, a cross, rosary beads, a small glass jar of blessed oil, a Bible, or a bowl of holy water. Be sure to label each sacramental so the children will recognize what they are viewing. Take a few moments to explain how each of these sacramentals helps us recall signs of God's love in our lives. Invite the children to dip their fingers into the holy water and make the sign of the cross.

HIGHLIGHT

Tell the children that they are going to learn about blessings and other sacramentals.

DISCOVER

- Invite the children to silently read "We Are Blessed by God" and raise their hands when they find the meaning of the word *sacramentals*. Ask a volunteer to read the meaning and have everyone underline it.
- Ask volunteers to name any sacramentals that they have seen in their homes. Examples: holy water, crucifix, Bible.
- Remind the children that the sign of the cross is a sacramental too. We make it often to show that we are blessed by God.
- Have a volunteer read aloud the final paragraph.

INTEGRATE

Have the children look at the pictures. Ask the class if anyone has a sacramental with them today, and invite them to share it with the class. Show the children other sacramentals that you may have in the classroom.

Connect

HIGHLIGHT

Remind the children that they are signs of God's love.

RESPOND

Invite the children to read the directions to the activity and give them sufficient time to write their letters.

CHOOSE

- Invite the children to respond to "My Faith Choice."
- After a moment of prayerful reflection have the children write their choices on the lines provided.
- Encourage the children to put their choices into practice this week.

What Difference Does Faith Make in My Life?

You are a sign of God's love. By celebrating the sacraments you grow closer to God the Father, Jesus, and the Holy Spirit. You receive the grace to help others grow in their love for God.

Write a letter to a friend. Explain how one of the sacraments that you have received helps you live as a follower of Jesus. Affirm appropriate responses.

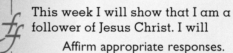

My Faith Choice

This week I will show that I am a follower of Jesus Christ. I will

Affirm appropriate responses.

110

Special Needs

Providing Writing Assistance. Children with difficulties in reading or writing will appreciate being offered alternative ways to participate in this activity. You might offer the children the option to role-play with a friend or draw a way that they are living as followers of Jesus. Have them share their responses with the class.

Need: Children with reading or writing deficits

We Pray

A Prayer of Meditation

A meditation is a prayer in which we use our imagination. Follow these directions and pray a prayer of meditation.

1. Close your eyes. Remember that the Holy Spirit lives within you.

2. Pretend you are sitting among a group of people on a mountainside listening to Jesus.

3. Listen as a reader reads Matthew 5:14–16.

4. Ask the Holy Spirit to help you learn how to be a light in the world.

5. Make a decision to live as a follower of Jesus.

We Remember

Use the code to discover a message about the sacraments.

A	B	C	D	E	F	G	H	I	J	K	L	M
1	2	3	4	5	6	7	8	9	10	11	12	13

N	O	P	Q	R	S	T	U	V	W	X	Y	Z
14	15	16	17	18	19	20	21	22	23	24	25	26

S A C R A M E N T S
19 1 3 18 1 13 5 14 20 19

M A K E U S
13 1 11 5 21 19

S H A R E R S I N
19 8 1 18 5 18 19 9 14

G O D'S L I F E
7 15 4 19 12 9 6 5

A N D L O V E.
1 14 4 12 15 22 5

To Help You Remember

1. The sacraments make Jesus present to us in a special way.

2. Baptism joins us to Christ and to the Body of Christ, the Church.

3. Confirmation strengthens our Baptism and helps us live as Jesus' followers.

Grade 3 • Chapter 12 111

Liturgy Tip

Meditation Takes Practice. The children might not be able to readily enter into meditation after a few moments of silence. Take your time getting started. Engage the children's imagination by elaborating on your description of the people on the mountainside listening to Jesus. Proclaim the Gospel yourself rather than asking a volunteer to read it. This will help keep the continuity of the prayer experience.

Pray

WE PRAY

- Tell the children that today they will meditate on a reading from Matthew's Gospel. Remind the children that in meditation they use their imaginations.

- Gather the children in the prayer center. Play appropriate background music as you have the children calm themselves for prayer.

- Lead them in the meditation following each of the five steps.

- Tell the children that they can repeat this meditation alone at home.

Review

WE REMEMBER

- Write the words *Baptism* and *Confirmation* on the board.

- Ask volunteers to tell you how each of these sacraments makes Jesus present to them in a special way.

- Invite them to check their responses with the "To Help You Remember" statements.

- Introduce the activity and allow the children time to complete it.

- Ask the children to read the message aloud together.

At Home

ENCOURAGE

Have the children carefully tear out pages 111 and 112 along the perforation. Encourage the children to share the pages with their families and to do the activities together. If they did not complete the review activity on page 111 by the end of the session, emphasize that they can complete it with their families.

VISIT FAITHFIRST.COM

- Share with the children the many activities on the *Faith First* Web site.
- Encourage the children to visit **www.FaithFirst.com.**

---

12 With My Family

This Week . . .

In chapter 12, "Celebrations of God's Love," your child learned about the sacraments. In particular your child explored the meaning of the celebration of Baptism and Confirmation. Jesus gave us the gift of the seven sacraments. Through taking part in the celebration of the sacraments we join with Christ and are made sharers in the very life of God—Father, Son, and Holy Spirit. Joined to Christ through Baptism and strengthened by the gift of the Holy Spirit, we give praise to the Father through a life of holiness.

For more on the teachings of the Catholic Church on the sacraments in general and on the sacraments of Baptism and Confirmation, see *Catechism of the Catholic Church* paragraph numbers 1135–1158, 1210–1211, 1212–1274, and 1285–1314.

Sharing God's Word

Read together the Gospel story in Matthew 28:16–20 about Jesus sending the disciples to baptize people. Emphasize that the sacrament of Baptism joins us to Christ and to the Body of Christ, the Church.

Praying

In this chapter your child prayed a prayer of meditation. Read and pray together the prayer on page 111.

Making a Difference

Choose one of the following activities to do as a family or design a similar activity of your own.

- Write the names of each of the seven sacraments on separate index cards. Have a member of the family choose a card and talk about why that sacrament is important to the Church. Continue until all the cards have been chosen.

- Find photos and other mementos of each family member's celebration of Baptism. One by one talk about each family member's Baptism.

- At dinnertime talk about how using oil in cooking helps prepare foods for meals. Then talk about how anointing in Baptism is a sign that the Holy Spirit helps us live as followers of Jesus.

For more ideas on ways your family can live your faith, visit the "Faith First for Families" page at **www.FaithFirst.com**. You're only a click away from taking a "Tour of a Church" with your child.

Before Moving On . . .

As you finish today's lesson, reflect on the following question before moving on to the next chapter.

Which child could use more attention from me?

Evaluate

Take a few moments to evaluate this week's lesson.
I feel (circle one) about this week's lesson.

    a. very pleased
    b. OK
    c. disappointed

The activity the children enjoyed most was . . .

The concept that was most difficult to teach was . . .

because . . .

Something I would like to do differently is . . .

ENRICHING THE LESSON

Reviewing Through Music

Purpose

To reinforce the seven sacraments (taught on page 106)

Directions

Sing this song with the children to the tune of "Frère Jacques." Together with the children devise additional verses to this song for other sacraments.

> Seven signs, seven signs
> Of God's love, of God's love.
> Jesus gives them to us.
> Jesus gives them to us.
> Sacraments, sacraments.
>
> We are baptized, we are baptized
> In God's love, in God's love.
> Making us all members,
> Making us all members
> Of Christ's Church, of Christ's Church.
>
> Sign of water, Sign of water,
> Sign of light, sign of light.
> Joined to Christ forever,
> Joined to Christ forever,
> Thank you, God. Thank you, God.

Materials

copies of the song

Making Sacrament Booklets

Purpose

To reinforce that our Church celebrates the sacraments of Baptism and Confirmation (taught on pages 107 and 108)

Directions

- Have the children develop a sacrament booklet using nine pieces of construction paper, one for each sacrament and a cover and final page. Have them staple the pages together.
- Ask the children to use words and pictures to create pages for Baptism and Confirmation and share what each sacrament celebrates.
- Encourage the children to take their booklets home to add pictures or drawings from family celebrations of the sacraments.

- The children might also design a cover that would be a collage of all the sacraments.
- Remind the children to bring the booklets to each session in order to complete them.

Materials

construction paper
markers or crayons
stapler

Literature Connection

Purpose

To reinforce and extend the teaching about the Apostles (taught on page 107)

Directions

Third graders will be interested in knowing more about the twelve Apostles. A book like *The Twelve Apostles: Their Lives and Acts* by Marianna Mayer (Penguin, 2000) recounts the story and contributions of each Apostle as gleaned from Scripture and Church legend.

- Ask the children to suggest an Apostle they would like to know more about and read his story to the class. Give them an opportunity to view and discuss the painting that accompanies the story.
- You also may wish to assign one of the Apostles to each member of the class for further research and invite them to give a report the following week.

Materials

The Twelve Apostles: Their Lives and Acts by Marianna Mayer

Music Connection

- "This Little Light of Mine" (African-American spiritual). *Singing Our Faith (SOF)* #208.
- "Walk, Walk in the Light," C. Landry. *SOF* #265.
- "We Are Marching" (South African). *SOF* #193.
- "We Are Walking in the Light," J. Moore. *SOF* #262.

We Celebrate the Eucharist

Background

The Source and Summit of the Christian Life

The Eucharist, "the source and summit of the Christian life," holds a preeminent place among the seven sacraments. In the Mass the whole of the Paschal Mystery—Jesus' Passion, death and Resurrection, and Ascension—is celebrated and remembered.

In the Mass we celebrate one liturgy consisting of two parts, the Liturgy of the Word and the Liturgy of the Eucharist. In the Liturgy of the Word we listen and respond to the word of God proclaimed and preached. In the Liturgy of the Eucharist we give thanks for all that God has done for us, especially for the gift of salvation.

In the Christian community the disciples of Jesus Christ are nourished at a twofold table: "that of the word of God and that of the Body of Christ."[1] The Gospel and the Eucharist are the constant food for the journey to the Father's House. The action of the Holy Spirit operates so that the gift of "communion" and the task of "mission" are deepened and lived in an increasingly intense way.

GENERAL DIRECTORY FOR CATECHESIS 70

Give Thanks and Praise to God

In the Eucharist the sacrifice of Jesus Christ on the cross is made present again, and we are made sharers in it. We join with Jesus, who offers this sacrifice of his very self on our behalf to save us from sin and death, and offer ourselves to God the Father.

> In the Eucharist the sacrifice of Christ becomes also the sacrifice of the members of his body.
>
> *CATECHISM OF THE CATHOLIC CHURCH 1368*

At the Eucharist the gifts of bread and wine become the Body and Blood of Jesus. Feeding on the Body and Blood of Christ, we are nourished for our own spiritual growth as well as for the work of participating in the mission of the Church.

Each and every time that we celebrate the Eucharist we are reminded that Jesus restores us to our rightful place as adopted children of the Father through the salvation he won for us. This free and generous gift of God's

love causes us to give thanks to him and to rejoice.

This sacrament of the mystery of our salvation in Christ concludes with the sending forth of the assembly to live and proclaim the Gospel. We are to be the leaven of the Good News in the world.

For Reflection

Why is my regular participation in Mass vital to my life?

How does my regular sharing in the Eucharist strengthen me to be leaven of the Good News in the world?

Catechist to Catechist

The Mystery of the Eucharist

This week strive to make the children's learning about the Eucharist more concrete. Concentrate on helping them use their five senses as they discover more about this great mystery of faith. Most of the children have been going to church and taking part in the celebration of the Eucharist. Help them think about what they see, hear, taste, touch, and smell at the Eucharist.

A Church Tour

A good way to help the children better understand the Mass is to give them the opportunity to experience up close the various places and things connected with the Sunday liturgy. If possible, arrange for a tour of the church and the sacristy. Point out the baptismal font or baptismal pool, tabernacle, sanctuary lamp, ambo, altar, crucifix, candles, chalice, ciborium, paten, altar cloths, and vestments. If such a tour is not possible, you can direct the children to the *Faith First* Web site to take a virtual tour of a church.

The Church Teaches . . .

The *General Directory for Catechesis* teaches:

> The sacraments . . . form "an organic whole in which each particular sacrament has its own vital place."[1] In this whole, the Holy Eucharist occupies a unique place to which all of the other sacraments are ordained. The Eucharist is to be presented as the "sacrament of sacraments."[2]
>
> *GDC* 115

In your teaching about the Eucharist, always emphasize its place as the "source and summit of Christian life"[3] *(CCC 1324)*.

See the Catechism . . .

For more on the teachings of the Catholic Church on the liturgical celebration of the Mass, see *Catechism of the Catholic Church* 1322–1405.

CATECHIST PRAYER

*Holy Spirit,
help me give
thanks each day
for the gift of
Jesus and for the
gift of others.
Amen.*

Footnote references may be found on p. 456.

LESSON PLANNER

Focus · To identify what we celebrate at the Eucharist

Engage

Page 113
Focus

To assess the children's knowledge about Mass

Opening Prayer

Discussion

Sharing special meals with families and sharing the Eucharist with the Church family

Teach and Apply

Pages 114–116
Focus

To explain that at Mass we do what Jesus did at the Last Supper—celebrate the Eucharist

Presentation

Read, discuss, and summarize content.

Scripture
- Psalm 92:2–3
- Matthew 26:26–28

Activities
- Name a way to be a peacemaker.
- Design a tabernacle for your church.

Faith-Filled People

Blessed Jeanne Jugan

Connect

Pages 117–118
Focus

To discover when the Church celebrates important events in God's plan of salvation

Our Church Makes a Difference

The Church celebrates the holy days of obligation throughout the year.

Our Catholic Faith

Precepts of the Church

What Difference Does Faith Make?

Activity

Check ways we love and serve the Lord.

Faith Choice

Choose to thank God for all his blessings this week.

We Pray

Page 119
Prayer Form
Preface
Prayer
Choose a leader. Divide the children into two groups. Introduce the prayer, and then pray together.

We Remember

Review
- Complete the writing activity.
- Read the "To Help You Remember" statements aloud.

Preview
Highlight features of the "With My Family" page.

Materials

- Bible
- pens or pencils
- crayons or markers

Enriching the Session

Blackline Masters
Additional Activities booklet:
Chapter 13
Leading a tour
Making a card
Assessment Tools booklet:
Chapter 13 Test

Faith First **Grade 3 Video**
Segment 3: The Visual Bible™: "Loaves and Fishes"

Enriching the Lesson (CG page 205)
Creating a Senses Chart for the Last Supper and Eucharist
Making Sacrament Booklets
Literature Connection

Music Connection (CG page 205)

www.FaithFirst.com

We update the *Faith First* Web site weekly. Check each week for new content and features. Here are some places to begin:

Catechists and Teachers
- Current Events
- Chapter Downloads
- Catechist Prayer

Faith First **for Families**
- Bible Stories
- Make a Difference

Kids' Clubhouse
- *Faith First* Activities
- Chapter Reviews
- Games
- Saints

Don't Forget! You can make lesson planning a breeze—check out the **Online Lesson Planner.**

We Celebrate the Eucharist

We Pray

LORD, our God, it is good to give you thanks all day long.
Based on Psalm 92:2–3

Father, all-powerful and ever-living God, we do well always and everywhere to give you thanks through Jesus Christ our Lord. Amen.

What important meals have you eaten with your family?

Sharing a meal strengthens the love of family members for one another. The most important celebration of the Church is the Eucharist.

What do we celebrate at the Eucharist?

Wheat and bread, symbols for the Eucharist

(113)

Engage

PRAY
- Gather the children and have them quiet themselves for prayer. Pray the Sign of the Cross.
- Invite a volunteer to read the Psalm verse. Read the opening prayer together.
- Close the prayer with the Sign of the Cross.

DISCOVER
Purpose: To discover what the children know about the Eucharist
- Ask the children to describe a special meal they shared with their families in the past year.
- Read the introductory paragraph.
- Invite the children to look at the picture and name the special meal that is represented in the stained glass. Eucharist.
- Remind the children that the Church family gathers for a special meal, the Lord's Supper.
- Ask the final question.

Liturgy Tip

Learning More About Liturgy. Do you want to know more about the liturgy? Are there things that you would like to be able to explain better? Two books by Liturgy Training Publications—*Children in the Assembly of the Church* by Eleanor Bernstein and John Brooks-Leonard, editors (1992) and *Preparing Liturgy for Children . . . and Children for Liturgy* by Gabe Huck (1989)—are good sources of information.

Teach

FOCUS

Ask a volunteer to read the "Faith Focus" question aloud. Share with the children that in this chapter they will learn what we celebrate at the Eucharist.

DISCOVER

- Invite a volunteer to read aloud the first paragraph of "Jesus Shares a Special Meal."
- Explain that the Last Supper was a very special meal.
- Ask the children to listen for what happened at the Last Supper as you proclaim the Scripture based on Matthew 26:26–28.
- Tell the children that at Mass we do the same things Jesus did at the Last Supper. We thank God the Father, and we share the Body and Blood of Jesus.

Apply

REINFORCE

Have the children underline the words Jesus said to his disciples when he gave them the bread and wine.

INTEGRATE

- Ask: When do you gather with your Church family to celebrate the Eucharist?
- Have the children work with partners and talk about the first time they received the Body and Blood of Christ.

We Give Thanks to God

Faith Focus

What do we celebrate at the Eucharist?

Faith Words

Eucharist
The Eucharist is the sacrament in which the Church gives thanks to God and shares in the Body and Blood of Christ.

Blessed Sacrament
The Blessed Sacrament is a name given to the Eucharist, the real presence of the Body and Blood of Jesus under the forms of bread and wine.

Jesus Shares a Special Meal

On the night before he died, Jesus shared his last meal with his disciples. We call this meal the Last Supper, or the Lord's Supper. This is what happened.

Jesus took bread, prayed a special blessing prayer, and broke the bread. He gave the bread to his disciples, saying, "Take and eat this. This is my body."

Then Jesus took a cup of wine and gave thanks to his Father. He gave the wine to his disciples, saying, "Drink from this cup, all of you, for this is my blood." Based on Matthew 26:26–28

The Church does what Jesus did at the Last Supper when we celebrate the Eucharist. We join with Jesus. We give thanks to God the Father. We share the Body and Blood of Jesus.

Talk about the first time you received the Body and Blood of Christ.

(114)

Teaching Tip

Understanding Passover. It may be helpful to share a little bit about the Jewish celebration of Passover when introducing the concept of the Last Supper. Helping the children understand why the Apostles gathered for this ritual meal will help them understand other aspects of the celebration of the Eucharist, such as the use of unleavened bread. Read Exodus 12:21–28, the promulgation of the Passover, to the children or share the story in your own words. Remind the children that Jesus is the Paschal Lamb who delivers us from the slavery of sin.

We Give Thanks

The Church celebrates the Eucharist at Mass. The Sunday celebration of the **Eucharist** is at the heart of our life as Catholics. The word *eucharist* means "to give thanks." Catholics have a serious duty, or obligation, to participate in the celebration of the Mass on Sundays.

The Liturgy of the Word is the first main part of the Mass. God is present with us. He speaks to us through the readings from Sacred Scripture.

The Liturgy of the Eucharist is the second main part of the Mass. The Church does what Jesus did at the Last Supper. We join with Jesus in offering himself to God. We remember and share in Jesus' life, Passion, death, and Resurrection. The bread and wine become the Body and Blood of Christ. We receive the gift of the Body and Blood of Christ in Holy Communion. This joins us more fully to Jesus Christ and to all the members of his Church.

Faith-Filled People

Jeanne Jugan

At the end of Mass, we hear the words, "Go in peace to love and serve the Lord." We can obey that command in many ways. Blessed Jeanne Jugan founded the Little Sisters of the Poor to take care of the elderly. She said, "Never forget that the poor are our Lord."

Decorate the poster.

> Jesus
> Is the
> Bread of Life

115

Teach

FOCUS

Remind the children that we join with Jesus when we celebrate the Eucharist. Tell the children they are going to review the main parts of the Eucharist.

DISCOVER

- Read aloud the meaning of the word *Eucharist*.
- Ask volunteers to read aloud "We Give Thanks."
- Have the children listen for and underline one new thing they learn in each paragraph.
- Divide the class into groups of four. Distribute newsprint and markers. Ask the groups to write *Liturgy of the Word* and *Liturgy of the Eucharist* at the top and then write four things that happen in these parts of the Mass. Invite all the groups to share their work.

Apply

REINFORCE

Have the children make a word card for the word *Eucharist*.

INTEGRATE

- Invite the children to decorate the poster at the bottom of the page.
- Ask the children to read "Faith-Filled People" to discover how Blessed Jeanne Jugan lived the Eucharist.

Teach

FOCUS

Remind the children that the hosts are consecrated during the Liturgy of the Eucharist. Tell them they are going to learn what happens to the hosts that are not used at Mass.

DISCOVER

- Invite the children to share what they know about the Blessed Sacrament.
- Write the word *tabernacle* on the board. Explain that after Mass the Church keeps consecrated hosts that are left over in the tabernacle.
- Tell the children that a lighted candle or sanctuary lamp lets us know that the Blessed Sacrament is in the tabernacle.
- Ask the children to read the third paragraph silently to learn why the Blessed Sacrament is kept in the tabernacle. To bring Holy Communion to those who are homebound or in hospitals, and so we can come to worship Jesus who is present there.

Apply

REINFORCE

If possible, bring the children to church to make a visit to the Blessed Sacrament.

INTEGRATE

Explain the activity. Ask the children to use their imaginations to design a tabernacle of their own.

The Blessed Sacrament

Sometimes there are consecrated hosts left over after the faithful have received Holy Communion at Mass. The consecrated hosts are brought to the tabernacle. The consecrated hosts are also called the **Blessed Sacrament.**

A special lighted candle is kept near the tabernacle. This candle is called the sanctuary lamp. This reminds us that the Blessed Sacrament is in the tabernacle. Jesus is truly present with us.

The Church brings the Blessed Sacrament as Holy Communion to people who are elderly, sick, or in the hospital. We also worship Jesus by praying before him present in the Blessed Sacrament.

Design a tabernacle for your church. Affirm appropriate responses.

116

Background: Liturgy

The Tabernacle. According to the document *Instruction on Eucharistic Worship (Eucharisticum Mysterium)*, each Catholic Church should have only one tabernacle which is placed in a location that is both prominent and conducive to private prayer and devotion. This tabernacle, in which the Blessed Sacrament is reserved, should also be strong and secured. Encourage the children to locate the tabernacle in the parish. You may also wish to gather the children before the Blessed Sacrament for a brief prayer or quiet reflection.

Our Church Makes a Difference

Holy Days of Obligation

Each year Catholics celebrate holy days of obligation that are not always celebrated on Sunday. These holy days celebrate very important events in God's plan of salvation. Catholics have the responsibility to participate in Mass on these holy days just as they do on Sundays.

There are six holy days of obligation that Catholics in the United States celebrate. They are the Solemnity of Mary, the Mother of God; the Ascension of Our Lord; the Assumption of the Blessed Virgin Mary into Heaven; All Saints; the Immaculate Conception of Mary; and Christmas Day. When we participate in Mass on these days, we help others see the difference that keeping God first in our lives makes.

Find out when the Church celebrates the six holy days of obligation this year.

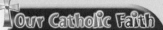

Our Catholic Faith

Precepts of the Church

The Church is our teacher and guide. One way the Church guides us is by giving us precepts, or rules, that state some of our responsibilities. One of the five precepts of the Church says that Catholics are to participate in the Eucharist on Sundays and on holy days of obligation.

117

Background: Catholic Tradition

Holy Days of Obligation. Feasts for remembering and honoring Jesus, Mary, and the saints were continually being added by local churches as days when the faithful were obligated to participate in Mass. As these feasts multiplied, the popes tried to bring some unified order to them. In 1917 the Code of Canon Law recognized ten holy days of obligation. Conferences of bishops, however, have the right to transfer and delete certain holy days—with the Vatican's approval. The number of holy days, therefore, varies by country. The United States Conference of Catholic Bishops has named six holy days of obligation in the United States.

Connect

HIGHLIGHT

Point out to the children that they are going to learn about days in the year other than Sundays when Catholics have the obligation to celebrate the Eucharist together.

DISCOVER

- Ask a volunteer to read aloud the first paragraph of "Holy Days of Obligation."
- Ask: What obligation, or responsibility, do Catholics have on these days?
- Ask the children to silently read the names of the holy days of obligation in the United States as you write them on the board.
- Explain that the Church gives us rules to remind us of our responsibilities as Catholics. We call these rules the precepts of the Church.
- Invite the children to read "Our Catholic Faith" to discover one of the precepts of the Church.

INTEGRATE

Ask the children to share a time they have been to church to celebrate a holy day. Let them know the date when the Church will celebrate the next holy day.

Connect

HIGHLIGHT

Remind the children that at the conclusion of Mass we are sent forth to live as children of God.

RESPOND

- Help the children prepare for the activity on this page by brainstorming with them some ways third graders can love and serve the Lord. Write the children's ideas on the board.
- Have the children complete the activity by using some of the recorded brainstorming ideas from the board.

CHOOSE

- Invite the children to respond to "My Faith Choice."
- After a moment of prayerful reflection have the children write their choices on the lines provided.
- Encourage the children to put their choices into practice this week.

What Difference Does Faith Make in My Life?

At the end of Mass the priest dismisses the people, using these or similar words, "Go in peace to love and serve the Lord."

Check three ways you can love and serve the Lord this week. Tell a partner exactly what you could do.

Love and Serve the Lord

- ☐ Help at home without being asked.
- ☐ Pray for someone.
- ☐ Cheer up someone.
- ☐ Share my games.
- ☐ Say I'm sorry.
- ☐ Help my teacher.

My Faith Choice

This week at Mass I will take time to thank God for all his blessings to me. I will thank God for

Affirm appropriate responses.

118

Teaching Tip

Developing "Soft Eyes." Baseball and football players are sometimes described as having soft hands. Many have the natural ability to catch a ball as if it falls softly and naturally into the glove. Suggest to the children that Christians have "soft eyes." Soft eyes help us to see God's presence in every aspect of life. Help the children list some of the ways the Holy Spirit helps them keep their soft eyes, for example, by inviting them to pray, to take part in the celebration of the sacraments, and to read the Bible. Discuss the places where they can see God's presence, such as in family members and friends and at church.

We Pray

Lift Up Our Hearts to God

At Mass we pray the preface. This prepares us to pray the Eucharistic Prayer. Pray this part of the preface.

Leader: Let us lift up our hearts and give thanks to God for the gift of the Eucharist.

All: Give thanks to the Lord our God. It is right to give him thanks and praise.

Group 1: Father, we give you thanks always and everywhere through Jesus Christ.

Group 2: With all the angels and saints, we give you thanks and praise.

All: Give thanks to the Lord our God. It is right to give him thanks and praise.

We Remember

Complete each sentence. Use the words in the word bank.

> **Eucharist   Word   Last Supper**

1. The _____Last Supper_____ is the meal at which Jesus gave us the Eucharist.

2. The Liturgy of the _____Word_____ is the first main part of the Mass.

3. The Liturgy of the _____Eucharist_____ is the second main part of the Mass.

To Help You Remember

1. At the Eucharist we celebrate what Jesus did at the Last Supper.

2. At Mass we listen to the word of God and we share the Eucharist.

3. At the Eucharist the bread and wine become the Body and Blood of Christ, through the words of the priest and the power of the Holy Spirit.

Grade 3 • Chapter 13 (119)

Pray

WE PRAY

- Divide the class into two groups. Tell the children which group they are in so they can follow along in their books.
- Lead the children in praying "Lift Up Our Hearts to God."

Review

WE REMEMBER

- Create a word map about the Eucharist. Write the word *Eucharist* on the board.
- Ask the children to name as many words and phrases as they can that tell things they have learned about the Eucharist. Jot their answers around the center word.
- Summarize by reading the "To Help You Remember" statements aloud.
- Introduce the activity and have the children complete it.

Liturgy Tip

The Preface. Share with the children that some books begin with a preface, a kind of introduction, to prepare the reader for what they are about to read. You may want to bring in a novel or book that has a preface and point it out to the children. Explain that at Mass we pray the Preface to prepare us for the celebration and praying of the Eucharistic Prayer. The words of the Preface state the reason we gather to give thanks and praise to God. For example, in the Preface for Pentecost, we pray in part, "Today we celebrate the great beginning of your Church."

At Home

ENCOURAGE

Have the children carefully tear out pages 119 and 120 along the perforation. Encourage the children to share the pages with their families and to do the activities together. If they did not complete the review activity on page 119 by the end of the session, emphasize that they can complete it with their families.

VISIT FAITHFIRST.COM

- Share with the children the many activities on the *Faith First* Web site.
- Encourage the children to visit **www.FaithFirst.com.**

Before Moving On . . .

As you finish today's lesson, reflect on the following question before moving on to the next chapter.

What opportunities am I giving the children to express themselves through prayer?

---

13 With My Family

This Week . . .

In chapter 13, "We Celebrate the Eucharist," your child learned more about the celebration of Mass and the mystery of the Eucharist. During the Liturgy of the Word at Mass we listen and respond to the word of God. During the Liturgy of the Eucharist we do what Jesus did at the Last Supper. We share in the Body and Blood of Christ and are made sharers in the Paschal Mystery of Jesus. After Mass the leftover consecrated bread is reserved in the tabernacle for distribution to the faithful who are sick or elderly and for the adoration of the faithful. The Blessed Sacrament is another name for the Eucharist.

For more on the teachings of the Catholic Church on the liturgical celebration of the Mass, see *Catechism of the Catholic Church* paragraph numbers 1322–1405.

Sharing God's Word

Read together the Bible story in Matthew 26:26–28 about the Last Supper or read the adaptation of this story on page 114. Emphasize that Jesus gave us the Eucharist at the Last Supper.

Praying

In this chapter your child prayed part of the preface that we pray at Mass. Read and pray together the prayer on page 119.

Making a Difference

Choose one of the following activities to do as a family or design a similar activity of your own.

- When you participate in Mass this week, join in with the assembly in praying the preface. Remember that we pray the preface to prepare for the Eucharistic Prayer.
- At the conclusion of Mass, the priest dismisses the assembly, using these or similar words, "Go in peace to love and serve the Lord." As a family, choose one thing you can do this week to love and serve the Lord.
- After you participate in Mass this week, make a visit to the Blessed Sacrament. Thank Jesus for sharing his life with us.

For more ideas on ways your family can live your faith, visit the "Faith First for Families" page at **www.FaithFirst.com.** This week share some of the family ideas on the "Gospel Reflections" page.

Evaluate

Take a few moments to evaluate this week's lesson.
I feel (circle one) about this week's lesson.

    a. very pleased
    b. OK
    c. disappointed

The activity the children enjoyed most was . . .

The concept that was most difficult to teach was . . .

because . . .

Something I would like to do differently is . . .

ENRICHING THE LESSON

Creating a Senses Chart for the Last Supper and Eucharist

Purpose

To reinforce what happened at the Last Supper (taught on pages 114 and 115)

Directions

- Write the names of the five senses on the board.
- Prepare a butcher paper chart by drawing two columns and labeling them *Last Supper* and *Eucharist Today*.
- Invite the children to name a way they would have used each of their senses at the Last Supper. For example, we would see Jesus, bread, disciples, and a cup of wine. We would hear Jesus speak and the sounds of Jesus and the disciples eating and drinking.
- Then challenge the children to name how they use their senses at the celebration of the Eucharist today. Remind them to share all the senses they use at both the Liturgy of the Word and the Liturgy of the Eucharist.
- Record their answers on the chart.
- Invite the children to decorate the chart with things they see at Mass.

Materials

butcher paper and pens or markers

Making Sacrament Booklets

Purpose

To reinforce the sacrament of the Eucharist (taught on page 115)

Directions

- Have the children continue to develop a sacrament booklet and complete the page on the Eucharist with words and drawings.
- Encourage the children to add pictures of their first Holy Communion to the booklet.
- Remind the children to bring the booklet back for the next session.

Materials

sacrament booklets and crayons or markers

Literature Connection

Purpose

To reinforce the teaching about the Mass (taught on page 115)

Directions

The gentle tale *The Weight of a Mass* by Josephine Nobisso (Gingerbread House, 2002) is an original story that is told as a medieval legend. It tells of a penniless old woman who begs for bread from a baker who is preparing delicious breads and pastries for the king's wedding. She promises that she will offer her prayers at the king's wedding Mass for the baker. Unimpressed, he writes the word Mass on a slip of paper, places it on a scale, and attempts to outweigh it with piles of pastries. When no amount can outweigh the weight of the Mass, he and the other townspeople, whose faith has grown weak, are transformed.

- Read the story to the children, giving them time to view the beautiful illustrations.
- Discuss the story, asking the children to comment on its message. Make a T-chart on the board and ask them to assess what is lost and what is gained when they miss a Sunday celebration of the Eucharist.

Materials

The Weight of a Mass by Josephine Nobisso

Music Connection

- "Friends, All Gather Round," J. Doucet/C. Landry. *Rise Up and Sing* #181.
- "Pan de Vida," B. Hurd/P. Moriarty. *Singing Our Faith (SOF)* #236.
- "Song of the Body of Christ/Canción del Cuerpo de Cristo" (Hawaiian traditional), arr. D. Haas. *SOF* #240.
- "We Come to Your Table," C. Landry. *SOF* #237.

The Pharisee and the Tax Collector A Scripture Story

Humility Before God in Prayer

Prayer is an expression of both our communion and covenant with God and raises our minds and hearts to him. As communication is to our relationships with family and friends, prayer is the lifeblood of our relationship with God.

Prayer is only possible because God invites us to pray, to share with him whatever is on our minds and in our hearts. Realizing that both the opportunity and the ability to pray are gifts from God, we approach him in thanksgiving and humility. We pray from the depths of a humble heart desiring to be with him who desires to be with us.

Meditation and Contemplation

Meditation and contemplation are two forms of prayer. In the prayer of meditation, we use our imaginations to learn about and commit ourselves to doing the will of God. We reflectively pray the Scriptures. Focusing on an icon or image of God, Mary, or a saint, retreating to a sacred space, journaling, lighting candles, and freeing our minds and hearts are

some of the practices that enhance meditation. Our hope is to be open to the movement of God in our hearts. When we place ourselves humbly before God, he leads us to discover the consolation of his presence in our prayer.

Contemplative prayer is wordless prayer. We open our empty hearts and the silent spaces of our being to God. In our prayer we humbly approach him as his trusting children, knowing full well that everything we are and have has been graciously bestowed upon us by divine love.

Contemplative prayer is the prayer of the child of God, of the forgiven sinner who agrees to welcome the love by which he is loved and who wants to respond to it by loving even more.[1] . . . Contemplative prayer is the poor and humble surrender to the loving will of the Father in ever deeper union with his beloved Son.
CATECHISM OF THE CATHOLIC CHURCH 2712

Total and complete surrender before God in contemplative prayer can be risky, for we open ourselves to be totally transformed by his will. This humble abandonment of everything to God's care deepens our union with God our Father through the power of the Holy Spirit in the redeeming love of Jesus.

Catechist to Catechist

A Look at Pride

The word *pride* has many different meanings for many people. It is both a virtue and a capital sin. Pride can be the cause of noble and magnificent achievements or the cause of great evil. Pride can be the source of a balanced self-esteem. It also can be the source of self-interest that has little regard for the good of other people. The latter is really "false pride."

Appreciating Talents

The Gospel story for this chapter tells us that true pride is based on the recognition that all our blessings are gifts from God. True pride gives rise to the virtue of humility. So 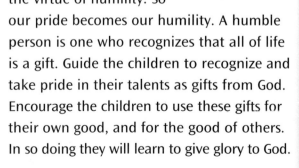 our pride becomes our humility. A humble person is one who recognizes that all of life is a gift. Guide the children to recognize and take pride in their talents as gifts from God. Encourage the children to use these gifts for their own good, and for the good of others. In so doing they will learn to give glory to God.

The Church Teaches . . .

The catechetical document *To Teach as Jesus Did* reminds us:

> In proclaiming all things which His Father commanded Him to reveal, Jesus used images from the lives of His hearers and spoke in the idiom of His day. The Church, too, must use contemporary methods and language to proclaim the message of Christ to men and women today.
>
> *TJD* 18

That is why *Faith First* consistently uses the retelling of parables in everyday terms as a method of transmitting the message of the Gospels.

See the Catechism . . .

For more on the teachings of the Catholic Church on the purpose of parables and the teaching of the parable of the Pharisee and the Tax Collector, see *Catechism of the Catholic Church* 546, 2607, 2613, and 2839.

CATECHIST PRAYER
*Lord God,
thank you for your
great goodness and
kindness to me.
Amen.*

Footnote references on these two pages may be found on p. 456.

LESSON PLANNER

To discover and put into practice what the parable of the Pharisee and the Tax Collector teaches

Engage

Page 121
Focus

To assess the children's knowledge about the parables Jesus told

Opening Prayer

Discussion

The stories you love to hear over and over again

Teach and Apply

Pages 122–124
Focus

To discover the parable of the Pharisee and the Tax Collector and its teachings about humility

Presentation

Read, discuss, and summarize content.

Scripture

• Psalm 25:2
• Luke 18:10–11, 13

Activities

• Write two things you learned about a Pharisee and a tax collector.
• Read the Scripture story.
• Write a four-line poem to share what you learned from the parable of the Pharisee and the Tax Collector.

Connect

Pages 125–126
Focus

To discover how the Church lives the virtue of humility

Our Church Makes a Difference

Discover what Saint Augustine teaches us about God's forgiveness.

Our Catholic Faith

Prayer Gestures

What Difference Does Faith Make?

Activity

Create a role-play about forgiving and asking for forgiveness.

Faith Choice

Choose a way you will be a "forgiveness" person this week.

We Pray

Page 127
Prayer Form
Petition
Prayer
Lead or choose a leader and pray together "Lord, Have Mercy."

We Remember

Review

• Complete the word search activity.
• Read the "To Help You Remember" statements aloud.

Preview

Highlight features of the "With My Family" page.

Materials

• Bible
• pens or pencils

Enriching the Session

Blackline Masters
Additional Activities booklet:
Chapter 14
Reciting a rap
Pantomiming
Assessment Tools booklet:
Chapter 14 Test

Enriching the Lesson (CG page 217)
Creating Storyboards
Making a Scroll
Literature Connection

Music Connection (CG page 217)

www.FaithFirst.com

We update the *Faith First* Web site weekly. Check each week for new content and features. Here are some places to begin:

Catechists and Teachers
• Current Events
• Chapter Downloads
• Catechist Prayer

***Faith First* for Families**
• Bible Stories
• Make a Difference

Kids' Clubhouse
• *Faith First* Activities
• Chapter Reviews
• Games
• Saints

Don't Forget! You can make lesson planning a breeze—check out the **Online Lesson Planner.**

The Pharisee and the Tax Collector
A Scripture Story

We Pray

LORD, my God, I place my trust in you.
Based on Psalm 25:2

God our Father, we know that you are good. You love us and do great things for us.   Amen.

What is one of your favorite stories?

There are many stories in the Gospels that Jesus told. We listen to these at Mass.

What stories do you know that Jesus told?

The Pharisee and the tax collector praying in the Temple in Jerusalem

121

PRAY

- Gather the children and have them quiet themselves for prayer.
- Pray the Sign of the Cross.
- Invite a volunteer to read the Psalm verse and then read the opening prayer together.

DISCOVER

Purpose: To assess the children's prior knowledge of stories that Jesus told

- Ask volunteers to share a story they have been told by their families that teaches a lesson.
- Tell the children that there are many stories like this in the Gospels that we enjoy hearing again and again.
- Invite the children to look at the picture of the stained-glass window. Point out that it shows Jesus' parable of the Pharisee and the Tax Collector.

Teaching Tip

Discovering God's Message. Jesus' merciful treatment of sinners is a sign of God's great compassion. The Gospel story for this lesson is a parable. As all parables do, it invites us to compare our own life with what is being taught in the parable and ask, What is it that Jesus is asking me to do? Help the children discover the importance of this dimension of a parable. A parable is far more than a story.

Teach

FOCUS

Ask a volunteer to read the "Faith Focus" question aloud. Share with the children that in this chapter they will learn what the parable of the Pharisee and the Tax Collector teaches about God's love.

DISCOVER

- Write the word *parables* on the board. Explain that Jesus often used parables to teach important lessons. Have the children make a word card for *parables*.
- Invite the children to read aloud the meaning of the faith word *parables*.
- Tell the children that the Scripture story is a parable about a Jewish leader, called a Pharisee, and a tax collector.
- Invite the children to read "Parables" silently to discover how these people were different.

Apply

REINFORCE

In partners have the children ask each other a "Who am I?" question relating to the Pharisee and the tax collector. Use the "Background" box on this page to give the children more information if necessary.

INTEGRATE

Have the children complete the activity. Then ask volunteers to share their responses as you list them on the board under the headings "Pharisee" and "Tax Collector."

Bible Background

Faith Focus

Why did Jesus tell the story about the Pharisee and the tax collector?

Faith Words

parables
Parables are stories that Jesus told to help people understand and live what he was teaching.

Parables

Jesus told stories called **parables** to teach people. In these stories Jesus included people and places his listeners knew. This helped the people listening to him understand what he was teaching.

Some of the many people who listened to Jesus were Pharisees. Pharisees were religious leaders of the Jewish people. Some Pharisees believed that they were better than other people.

Tax collectors also listened to Jesus. Some tax collectors took more money than people owed. They kept the extra money for themselves. Because of this, many Jewish people thought the tax collectors were sinners and they stayed away from them.

Name two things you have learned about Pharisees and two things about tax collectors in Jesus' time. Responses will vary.

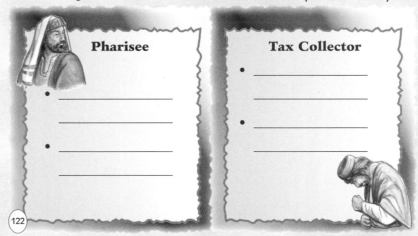

Pharisee

- _____
- _____
- _____

Tax Collector

- _____
- _____
- _____
- _____

122

Background: Scripture

The Pharisees. Pharisees observed the Law of Moses very strictly. They worked to make sure the beliefs and practices of the Jewish religion were not watered down by the values of the other cultures that surrounded the Jewish people. While some of the Pharisees' motives were good ones, their extreme focus on the letter of the Law led them to lose track of the spirit of the Law and the reason for it—to treat God, ourselves, and others with love and respect.

Reading the Word of God

The Pharisee and Tax Collector

One day Jesus told a parable about a Pharisee and a tax collector. Here is part of the parable Jesus told.

Two men went into the Temple in Jerusalem to pray. One was a Pharisee. The other was a tax collector. The Pharisee stood in the center of the Temple. He thanked God that he was not greedy or dishonest like other people. The tax collector stood toward the back of the Temple. He beat his chest with his hand to show he was sorry for his sins. He prayed, "God forgive me, for I am a sinner."

Based on Luke 18:10–11, 13

What prayer do you like to pray to ask God to help you live as a follower of Jesus?
Affirm appropriate responses.

123

💡 Teaching Tip

Humility, Trust, and Peace. In telling the parable about the Pharisee and tax collector, Jesus is teaching about prayer. Both the Pharisee and the tax collector went to the Temple to pray. The tax collector trusted in God's love. He honestly recognized that he was a sinner. He humbly asked for God's forgiveness. Invite the children to reread "The Pharisee and Tax Collector" with these two words in mind: *trust* and *peace*. Then discuss the tax collector's approach to praying. First, discuss how his trust in God helped him pray. Second, discuss why his prayer brought him peace.

FOCUS

Point out that Jesus had a very important lesson to teach when he told the parable of the Pharisee and the Tax Collector.

DISCOVER

- Have the children look at the picture as you read aloud "The Pharisee and Tax Collector."
- Ask the children to describe how the Pharisee prayed.
- Then ask the children to describe how the tax collector prayed.
- Invite volunteers to suggest what lesson they think Jesus is teaching in this parable. Every person needs God's forgiveness and mercy.

Apply

REINFORCE

Ask the children to underline the final sentence in the Scripture story. Tell them that these are very important words.

INTEGRATE

Invite the children to discuss the prayer they like to pray when asking God to help them live as followers of Jesus.

Teach

FOCUS

Point out that this parable also teaches that we are to humbly ask God's forgiveness. Tell them this page will teach them more about the meaning of humility.

DISCOVER

- Explain that all blessings come from God. A humble person recognizes this and is not unduly proud.
- Ask volunteers to read aloud "God Forgives the Humble."
- Ask the children to find evidence showing that the tax collector is humble.
- Have the children look at the picture on the page. Ask volunteers to share why they think this picture is on the page.

Apply

REINFORCE

Ask the children what they learned from the parable of the Pharisee and the Tax Collector.

INTEGRATE

- Have the children do the activity at the bottom of the page. They may share their poems with a partner.
- Point out to the children times you have seen them being humble.

Understanding the Word of God

God Forgives the Humble

The parable of the Pharisee and the Tax Collector teaches people that God wants people to be humble. A humble person believes that God is the giver of all gifts. Humble people also know they need God's mercy.

The tax collector in the parable is humble and honest. He knows and admits he has sinned. He knows he needs God's mercy. In deep sorrow, he trusts that God will hear his prayer and forgive him.

Everyone needs to be humble like the tax collector in the parable. Every person needs God's forgiveness and mercy. All our blessings, including God's forgiveness, are gifts from God. We humbly thank God for his great goodness and mercy to us. Affirm appropriate responses.

Write a four-line poem or song that tells what you learned from the parable of the Pharisee and the Tax Collector.

124

Teaching Tip

Living a Humble Life. Humility is the virtue whereby we recognize God as the source of all that is good. Because they do not have false pride, humble people are open to God, hear his call, and respond to it. In the Bible the parable of the Pharisee and Tax Collector ends with these words: "Everyone who exalts himself will be humbled, and the one who humbles himself will be exalted" (Luke 18:14). If we reflect on the meaning of these words and live by them, we will live and pray more authentically. Be willing to share your own faith with the children by modeling your own humility in prayer. Children do, indeed, learn from what they see.

Our Church Makes a Difference

ST. AUGUSTINE

Saint Augustine

Many saints show us what happens when we are humble. When he was young, Augustine was very proud like the Pharisee in the parable. He felt he didn't need forgiveness from God at all.

As Augustine got older, he came to believe that he really needed and wanted God's forgiveness. For the rest of his life, he prayed often and asked for forgiveness. The Holy Spirit helped Augustine change. He became a humble and happy man.

Saint Augustine shows us what can happen when we are humble. We can show others that happiness comes from trusting God and making God first in our lives.

What does Augustine teach us about being humble and happy?
Affirm appropriate responses.

✝ Our Catholic Faith

Prayer Gestures

Prayer gestures show that we believe and trust in God. Standing and kneeling, bowing our heads and genuflecting are four gestures we use during the liturgy. The tax collector touched his chest with his hand. This gesture showed he believed that he needed God's mercy and forgiveness.

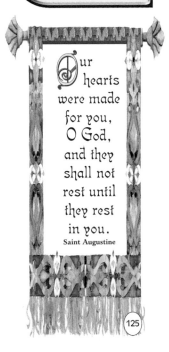

Our hearts were made for you, O God, and they shall not rest until they rest in you.
Saint Augustine

(125)

HIGHLIGHT

Remind the children that the Church honors saints who show us how to live as followers of Jesus.

DISCOVER

- Read to the children about Saint Augustine. Ask them to listen for how Saint Augustine became a humble and happy man.
- Ask the children to explain what Saint Augustine learned. *He learned to depend on God.*
- Point out that the Holy Spirit helped Saint Augustine change his heart and place God first in his life.
- Present "Our Catholic Faith." Point out that the prayer postures we use at liturgy express our humility before God. Remind the children that the tax collector stood at the back and beat his chest as a sign of his humility and desire for forgiveness.

INTEGRATE

- Help the children compare the tax collector in the parable and Saint Augustine.
- Invite responses to the question on the bottom of the page.

💡 Teaching Tip

Saint Augustine's Prayer. Saint Augustine's life is a story of conversion through prayer. Saint Augustine's conversion was brought about by the incessant prayer of Saint Augustine's mother, Saint Monica, who is credited with helping to turn her son's life around toward God. One prayer that Saint Augustine is known to have prayed after his conversion is: "Our hearts were made for you, O God, and they shall not rest until they rest in you." Take a few moments to pray this prayer with the children and explain its meaning. Copy the prayer for the children to take home and pray with their families.

Connect

HIGHLIGHT

Remind the children that each year we learn more of what it means to be a "forgiveness" person.

RESPOND

- Brainstorm with the children a list of forgiveness words and write them on the board.
- Direct the children's attention to the activity. Have them choose the words they wish to use and include them in what they write.

CHOOSE

- Invite the children to respond to "My Faith Choice."
- After a moment of prayerful reflection have the children write their choices on the lines provided.
- Encourage the children to put their choices into practice this week.

What Difference Does Faith Make in My Life?

Each year you are learning what a difference it makes to recognize and trust in God's forgiveness. You are learning to be humble.

Work with a partner. Create a role-play about asking for forgiveness or about forgiving others. Write your ideas here. Responses will vary.

Forgiveness

_____

_____

_____

_____

_____

_____

 My Faith Choice

This week I will be a "forgiveness" person. I will

Affirm appropriate responses.

_____.

126

Background: Doctrine

Call to Conversion. The call to conversion involves both external and internal dimensions. True conversion is first concerned with the internal aspects that involve a changed heart and a conscious turning away from sin. Only then do our outward actions of penance and change have ultimate meaning. Conversion is the work of God's grace, beckoning us back to the Father. Emphasize with the children the importance of forgiveness in the process of conversion that happens throughout our lives. (See *Catechism of the Catholic Church* 1427–1439.)

We Pray

Lord, Have Mercy

We pray the "Lord, have mercy" prayer at Mass. We show God that we are humble and need his mercy. Pray this prayer together.

Leader: Lord, you were sent to heal those who were sorry for their sins.

All: Lord, have mercy.

Leader: Lord, you came to call sinners.

All: Christ, have mercy.

Leader: Lord, you ask your Father to forgive us.

All: Lord, have mercy.

Leader: May almighty God have mercy on us, forgive us our sins, and bring us to everlasting life.

All: Amen.

We Remember

Circle the words in the puzzle that will help you remember the parable. Use the terms to retell it.

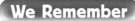

pray   humble   proud   Pharisee
tax collector   Temple   sin

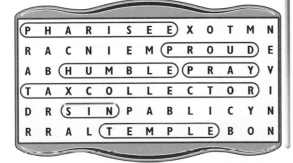

To Help You Remember

1. Jesus told parables to help his listeners understand what he was teaching.

2. The parable of the Pharisee and the Tax Collector teaches us to be humble.

3. The parable of the Pharisee and the Tax Collector teaches us that everyone needs God's forgiveness.

Grade 3 • Chapter 14 (127)

WE PRAY

- Gather the children in the prayer center.
- Explain that today we will pray a prayer of petition for God's mercy. Remind them that this prayer is based on one we pray at Sunday Mass.
- Invite a volunteer to lead the prayer. Invite all to respond to the petitions using the gesture suggested in the box on this page.

Review

WE REMEMBER

- Rephrase each "To Help You Remember" statement as a question. Have volunteers respond.
- Introduce the puzzle activity and give the children time to complete it. If time allows, invite volunteers to retell the story using the seven words they find.

Liturgy Tip

"Lord, Have Mercy." The version of the "Lord, Have Mercy" used for the closing prayer for this chapter is usually said during the Penitential Rite at Mass. This celebration of God's mercy is a reminder of God's unending love and forgiveness. It is not uncommon for persons to lightly strike their chests with their right fist as they recite this prayer, reflecting the same humility the tax collector expressed in the parable Jesus told.

At Home

Have the children carefully tear out pages 127 and 128 along the perforation. Encourage the children to share the pages with their families and to do the activities together. If they did not complete the review activity on page 127 by the end of the session, emphasize that they can complete it with their families.

VISIT FAITHFIRST.COM

- Share with the children the many activities on the *Faith First* Web site.
- Encourage the children to visit **www.FaithFirst.com.**

---

14 With My Family

This Week . . .

In chapter 14, "The Pharisee and the Tax Collector: A Scripture Story," your child listened to the parable of the Pharisee and the Tax Collector. A parable usually included people and places that the teacher's listeners knew well. This helped the listeners understand the message of the story. The teacher would use the people and places in such a way that the ending of the story would sometimes come as a surprise to the listeners. This too helped the teacher emphasize the point of the parable. The message of the parable of the Pharisee and the Tax Collector tells us that everyone is in need of God's forgiveness. We need to approach God humbly and with trust. This point is made by contrasting the attitude and actions of the Pharisee with those of the tax collector.

For more on the teachings of the Catholic Church on the purpose of parables and the teaching of the parable of the Pharisee and the Tax Collector, see *Catechism of the Catholic Church* paragraph numbers 546, 2607, 2613, and 2839.

Sharing God's Word

Read together the parable in Luke 18:9–13 about the Pharisee and the tax collector or read the adaptation of the parable on page 123. Emphasize the attitude of the tax collector.

Praying

In this chapter your child prayed a prayer of mercy based on a prayer we sometimes pray at the beginning of Mass. Read and pray together the prayer on page 127.

Making a Difference

Choose one of the following activities to do as a family or design a similar activity of your own.

- At dinnertime this week use appropriate prayer gestures. Talk about how our prayer gestures reflect and give expression to our attitudes or feelings about prayer.
- Pantomime the parable presented in this chapter. Take turns acting out the roles of the Pharisee and the tax collector.
- Create and display a poster that reminds your family to be a forgiving family.

For more ideas on ways your family can live your faith, visit the "Faith First for Families" page at **www.FaithFirst.com.** Check out "Bible Stories." Read and discuss the Bible story this week.

Evaluate

Take a few moments to evaluate this week's lesson.
I feel (circle one) about this week's lesson.

a. very pleased
b. OK
c. disappointed

The activity the children enjoyed most was . . .

The concept that was most difficult to teach was . . .

because . . .

Something I would like to do differently is . . .

Before Moving On . . .

As you finish today's lesson, reflect on the following question before moving on to the next chapter.

Am I flexible in adjusting time frames if children are working well on an activity?

ENRICHING THE LESSON

Creating Storyboards

Purpose

To reinforce the Gospel story "The Pharisee and Tax Collector" (taught on page 123)

Directions

- Tell the children that moviemakers often create a storyboard to help them visualize ahead of time the images they want to film.
- Invite the children to complete a storyboard of the parable of the Pharisee and the Tax Collector.
- Give them a sheet of paper (11" x 14" would be best) with three connected boxes drawn on it.
- Ask them to recall three important parts of the story. Draw one part in each box in the order in which they occurred.
- Encourage the children to write the title over their drawings.

Materials

large construction paper
crayons or markers

Making a Scroll

Purpose

To reinforce that everyone needs to be humble (taught on page 124)

Directions

- Micah 6:8 teaches about humility.
- Have the children make a scroll from a parchment-type paper and carefully print the words from Micah on it.
- Invite the children to decorate it, take it home, and display it where their family members can read it often.
- This will be a wonderful reminder of God's call to the children and their families to "walk humbly with God."

Materials

parchment-type paper
pens and crayons

Literature Connection

Purpose

To reinforce the concept of asking forgiveness (taught on page 124)

Directions

I'm Sorry, Almira Ann by Jane Kurtz (Scholastic, 2001) offers children the opportunity to explore the harder part of the concept of forgiveness—how to ask for it when our actions hurt others. Young Sarah is traveling west with her family in a covered wagon on the Oregon Trail. She has an impulsive nature, or what her family calls a "hasty spirit." When she breaks a rule and causes an accident that breaks her friend's leg, she looks for ways to repair the relationship she has damaged.

- Introduce the plot of the story to the children and read aloud the part where Sarah's impulsiveness causes the accident to Almira Ann.
- Invite the children to identify the causes of the situation and to suggest possible solutions.
- Ask a volunteer to take the book home, read to learn the outcome, and report back to the class.

Materials

I'm Sorry, Almira Ann by Jane Kurtz

Music Connection

- "Bring Forth the Kingdom," M. Haugen. *Singing Our Faith (SOF)* #192.
- "Good News," H. Olson. *SOF* #162.
- "The Pharisee and the Sinner," P. Freeburg/ C. Walker. *Rise Up and Sing* #326.
- "Walking by Faith," D. Haas. *SOF* #179.

We Celebrate God's Healing Love

Lord, Have Mercy

In Baptism we are joined to Christ, receive the gift of the Holy Spirit, and become adopted children of God the Father and heirs of heaven. It would be wonderful if we would always faithfully live our relationship with God and the Church. The reality is that we do not. We sometimes turn our hearts away from God and the gift of his love. We sin.

While we may be unfaithful to our covenant of love with God that we entered into at Baptism, he always remains true to his word and is always faithful in his love for us. Jesus, the Incarnate Son of God, has revealed that the love of God the Father is so merciful (unconditionally generous) that he is always open and ready to forgive us when we sin.

The Sacrament of Penance

We are made sharers in God's forgiveness and mercy in the sacrament of Penance, or Reconciliation. In this sacrament we receive forgiveness for the sins we commit after Baptism and are reconciled with God and the Church.

This sacrament goes by many names today. That is because it celebrates many things. Officially the rite is named the Rite of Penance because its authentic celebration always involves penitents taking action toward replacing their sinful behavior with new ways of living.

It is also called the sacrament of Reconciliation, a word that means "being made friends again," because through this sacrament the fullness of our relationship with God and the Church is restored by God's healing, forgiveness, and freeing us from sin.

Many refer to this sacrament as the sacrament of Confession. For example, some use the expression "going to confession" to describe their celebration of this sacrament. This is so because one of the essential elements of the celebration of this sacrament is the confessing of our sins individually to a priest who absolves us "in the name of the Father, and of the Son, and of the Holy Spirit."

The name Sacrament of Conversion is also used because this sacrament celebrates a change in the life of the believer who turns away from sin and back to God. The seeds of conversion take hold in the heart of the sinner.

The healing, liberation, and forgiveness brought about in this sacramental encounter work a

real change in the person. Led by the Holy Spirit and sustained in the same Spirit, we move toward holiness. Our relationship with God the Father, in Christ, and in unity with the Holy Spirit, and, correspondingly, with the Body of the Church is reconciled, or made right again.

Which of the names used for this sacrament of forgiveness helps me best appreciate the importance of this sacrament? Why?

In what ways am I an agent of reconciliation for my family, friends, and coworkers?

Catechist to Catechist

Accidents and Choices

There is a big difference between an accident and a deliberate choice. Many third graders are not exactly sure of the difference between the two. They often cannot differentiate between their responsibility for the consequences of accidents and the consequences of their deliberate choices. The manner in which you respond, or react, to the behaviors of the children can help them clarify this important difference.

The Forgiving Father

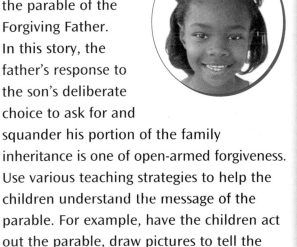

In this lesson, the children will hear the parable of the Forgiving Father. In this story, the father's response to the son's deliberate choice to ask for and squander his portion of the family inheritance is one of open-armed forgiveness. Use various teaching strategies to help the children understand the message of the parable. For example, have the children act out the parable, draw pictures to tell the story, make puppets and have a puppet show, or reread the parable from a children's Bible. In all cases, emphasize the father's forgiveness as a sign of God's forgiveness.

The Church Teaches . . .

The *General Directory for Catechesis* teaches:

> Jesus . . . proclaims and reveals that God is not a distant inaccessible Being, "a remote power without a name" but a Father, who is present among his creatures and whose power is his love. This testimony about God as Father, offered in a simple and direct manner, is fundamental to catechesis. *GDC* 102

By your communicating God's gentle love and mercy, the children will come to know the forgiving power of God.

See the Catechism . . .

For more on the teachings of the Catholic Church on the Sacraments of Healing, Reconciliation and Anointing of the Sick, see *Catechism of the Catholic Church* 1420–1484 and 1499–1525.

CATECHIST PRAYER

*God of forgiveness,
help me forgive
anyone who has hurt me.
Help me ask for
forgiveness from those
whom I have hurt.
Amen.*

LESSON PLANNER

Engage

Page 129
Focus

To assess the children's knowledge about how the Church celebrates God's forgiveness and healing

Opening Prayer

Discussion

Our need to forgive and to ask for forgiveness

Teach and Apply

Pages 130–132
Focus

To explain that we share in God's forgiving and healing love when we celebrate the sacraments of Reconciliation and Anointing of the Sick

Presentation

Read, discuss, and summarize content.

Scripture
- Psalm 51:1
- Luke 15:11–24

Activities
- Decode the message of the parable.
- Describe ways to show forgiveness.
- Draw or write something you could do if a family member were sick.

Faith-Filled People

Saint Peter

Connect

Pages 133–134
Focus

To discover ways we forgive and ask for forgiveness

Our Church Makes a Difference

Pope John Paul II taught us about forgiveness.

Our Catholic Faith

The Merciful

What Difference Does Faith Make?
Activity

Identify words you could use to ask forgiveness and words you could use to forgive someone else.

Faith Choice

Choose a way to bring God's healing love to someone this week.

We Pray

Page 135
Prayer Form
Prayer of sorrow
Prayer
Introduce the prayer and pray together.

We Remember

Review
- Complete the true or false activity.
- Read the "To Help You Remember" statements aloud.

Preview
Highlight features of the "With My Family" page.

Materials

- Bible
- pens or pencils
- crayons or markers

Enriching the Session

Blackline Masters
Additional Activities booklet:
  Chapter 15
    Unscrambling words and
    sentences
    Creating a design
Assessment Tools booklet:
  Chapter 15 Test

Enriching the Lesson (CG page 229)
  Making Sacrament Booklets
  Preparing Posters Announcing
   Sacraments of Healing
  Literature Connection

Music Connection (CG page 229)

www.FaithFirst.com

We update the *Faith First* Web site weekly. Check each week for new content and features. Here are some places to begin:

Catechists and Teachers
- Current Events
- Chapter Downloads
- Catechist Prayer

Faith First for Families
- Bible Stories
- Make a Difference

Kids' Clubhouse
- *Faith First* Activities
- Chapter Reviews
- Games
- Saints

Don't Forget! You can make lesson planning a breeze—check out the **Online Lesson Planner.**

We Celebrate God's Healing Love

15

We Pray

Have mercy on me, God, in your goodness.

Psalm 51:3

Father, we ask your mercy through Jesus Christ, your Son, our Lord. Amen.

When is a time you needed someone to forgive you?

Sometimes we need to ask God for forgiveness. We celebrate forgiveness in our families and in our Church.

When do we celebrate God's forgiveness with our Church?

129

Engage

PRAY

- Gather the children and have them quiet themselves for prayer.
- Pray the Sign of the Cross.
- Invite a volunteer to read the Psalm verse and then pray the opening prayer together.
- Close the prayer with the Sign of the Cross.

DISCOVER

Purpose: To assess what the children know about how the Catholic Church celebrates God's forgiveness

- Ask the children if they think it is harder to forgive someone or to ask for forgiveness. Why? Discuss a time when the children needed forgiveness.
- Invite the children to look at the picture and explain what they see. Tell them that a priest is leading a communal Reconciliation service for children.
- Ask a volunteer to tell when we celebrate forgiveness with our Church.

💡 Teaching Tip

The Healing Power of the Sacrament of Reconciliation. The experience of forgiving those who hurt us seems to be a necessary ingredient for our healing from personal injury. When we receive the sacrament of Reconciliation, we are made sharers in God's forgiveness. We receive the graces of being forgiven and the strength to forgive as we have been forgiven.

Teach

FOCUS

Have a volunteer read the "Faith Focus" question aloud. Share with the children that in this chapter they will learn how the sacraments of Reconciliation and Anointing of the Sick are connected.

DISCOVER

- Introduce the Scripture story by summarizing the story "The Forgiving Father" in your own words.
- Tell the children to imagine themselves as one of the characters in the story as you proclaim the Scripture based on Luke 15:16–24.
- Ask volunteers what they imagined as they listened to the story.

Apply

REINFORCE

Divide the class into groups of three. Have one person in each group be the narrator. Have the other two children mime the action in the story as the narrator speaks.

INTEGRATE

- Invite the children to do the decoding activity on their own.
- Discuss with the children how its message makes a difference in their lives.

God, Our Forgiving Father

Faith Focus

How do the Sacraments of Healing help us share in God's healing love?

Faith Words

sin
Sin is freely choosing to do or say something that we know is against God's Law.

Sacraments of Healing
Reconciliation and Anointing of the Sick are the two Sacraments of Healing.

The Forgiving Father

Do you remember hearing the parable of the Forgiving Father? It is also called the parable of the Prodigal Son. In this parable the younger son of a father demands his share of the family goods and money. He leaves home and wastes all his money. Here is what happens next.

The son was very hungry and sorry for what he had done. He decided to return home and ask his father for forgiveness. As he came near his father's home, the father ran down the road to greet his son. The father forgave his son and welcomed him home.
Based on Luke 15:16–24

| 1 = D | 2 = F | 3 = G | 4 = L | 5 = R |
| 6 = S | 7 = V | 8 = W | 9 = Y | |

G O D   A L W A Y S
3   1   4 8   9 6

F O R G I V E S   U S.
2   5 3 7   6   6

Use this code to discover the message of the parable of the Forgiving Father.

130

Teaching Tip

Celebrating Reconciliation. Number these steps in the individual rite for the sacrament of Reconciliation on poster board and place it on display for the next few weeks.

1. We prepare by examining our conscience.
2. The priest welcomes us. We may listen to a Scripture story about God's forgiveness.
3. We confess our sins. We begin by praying the Confiteor, or "I confess" prayer.
4. The priest gives us a penance, and we accept it.
5. We pray an act of contrition.
6. The priest absolves us.

Reconciliation

Every day we make choices just as the son made choices in the parable of the Forgiving Father. Most of the choices we make are good choices. Sometimes we make choices that are against God's laws. We **sin**. Sin always hurts our friendship with God and with other people. When we sin, we need to ask God for forgiveness.

Because we need forgiveness, Jesus gave us the sacrament of Reconciliation. This sacrament is also called the sacrament of Penance. It is one of the two **Sacraments of Healing.**

In Reconciliation we share in God's forgiveness and mercy. We are forgiven the sins we commit after we are baptized. We confess our sins to a priest. We show God we are sorry for our sins. Through the power of the Holy Spirit and the words and actions of the priest, God forgives us and heals us with his grace. The Holy Spirit helps us not to sin again. We are reconciled, or made friends again, with God and the members of the Church.

Describe one way you can show someone you forgive them. Affirm appropriate responses.

Faith-Filled People

Peter the Apostle

Saint Peter the Apostle knew how much Jesus forgave people. Once Peter denied he was a disciple of Jesus. Peter knew Jesus forgave him by the way Jesus looked at him. Jesus gave Peter and the other Apostles the power to forgive sins in his name. The Church celebrates the feast day of Saint Peter the Apostle on June 29.

(131)

Background: Faith-Filled People

Saint Peter the Apostle. Peter, a name meaning *rock*, was once called Simeon, or Simon. Peter left everything and willingly followed Christ. He had a strong undying faith and was the first to call Jesus the Messiah. He was chosen by Jesus to be the first among, or leader of, the Apostles. The popes are the successors of Saint Peter. There is an unbroken connection between Pope Benedict XVI, who was elected the 265th pope on April 19, 2005, and Saint Peter the Apostle.

Teach

FOCUS

Remind the children that God always forgives us when we truly are sorry for our sins.

DISCOVER

- Ask the children if they have ever made a bad choice.
- Invite the children to read the three paragraphs under "Reconciliation" silently and to look for the meanings of *sin* and *reconciliation*.
- Write the words *sin* and *Sacraments of Healing* on the board and ask the children what they learned about these words.
- Tell the children about Saint Peter by reading aloud "Faith-Filled People." Tell them to look for the connection of Saint Peter to the sacrament of Reconciliation as they read.

Apply

REINFORCE

Divide the class into groups and ask them to reread the last paragraph. Then have each group list ways we share in God's forgiveness and mercy in the sacrament of Reconciliation. Ask each group to share its answers.

INTEGRATE

Invite volunteers to role-play ways they can show someone forgiveness.

Teach

FOCUS

Remind the children that there are two Sacraments of Healing. The sacrament of the Anointing of the Sick is another Sacrament of Healing.

DISCOVER

- Ask the children to recall stories they know about Jesus healing the sick.
- Present "Anointing of the Sick" in your own words. Ask the children to listen for who may receive this Sacrament of Healing.
- Using the second paragraph, explain how the Anointing of the Sick is celebrated.
- Tell the children that the oil is a sign of this sacrament. Ask them if they remember which other sacraments have oil as a sign.

Apply

REINFORCE

Read the final paragraph to point out the effects of the sacrament of the Anointing of the Sick. Grace; strengthens our faith and trust in God; gives us strength, courage and peace.

INTEGRATE

Have the children complete the activity and share their work with a partner.

Anointing of the Sick

Jesus healed the sick during his life on earth. He healed their bodies and their souls. Jesus continues this work in a special way through the sacrament of the Anointing of the Sick. This sacrament is the second Sacrament of Healing.

When we are seriously ill or weak because of old age or in danger of dying, our Church family takes care of us. We celebrate the Anointing of the Sick. In this sacrament the Church prays for us. The Church shares God's word with us and with those who have gathered to share in the celebration. The priest anoints our hands and forehead with the oil of the sick. He prays that we will trust in God's care.

This sacrament brings us God's grace. This grace strengthens our faith and trust in God. It gives us strength and courage and peace.

Draw or write something you could do if a member of your family was sick. **Affirm appropriate responses.**

(132)

Background: Doctrine

Anointing of the Sick. Many people still believe that the sacrament of the Anointing of the Sick is reserved only for those who are very near death and can only be offered to someone one time. The *Catechism of the Catholic Church* (1514–1515) points out that this sacrament is for anyone who is seriously ill. If a person who was ill and received the sacrament regains their health and then becomes ill again, the sacrament may be offered again. Likewise, if a person has already received the sacrament and their condition becomes more serious, they may also receive the sacrament again.

Our Church Makes a Difference

The Pope Forgives

On May 13, 1981, in Saint Peter's Square in Rome, Italy, a large crowd was cheering for Pope John Paul II. A man fired two shots. The bullets hit the pope's arm, hand, and stomach. When people around the world wanted the man punished, the pope said, "Pray for the brother who shot me, whom I have sincerely forgiven."

Two years later Pope John Paul II visited the man in prison. They talked privately for twenty minutes. When the visit was over, the man leaned over and kissed the hand of the man he had tried to kill. He knew what it meant to be forgiven. Pope John Paul II was a living sign of God's mercy for the man who shot him.

What does this story teach you about the healing power of forgiveness?

Affirm appropriate responses.

Our Catholic Faith

The Merciful

Mercy brings us healing and forgiveness. In chapter 5 you learned about the Beatitudes. One of the Beatitudes tells us to be merciful to others. In this Beatitude Jesus taught us to share God's healing love with people as he did. When we do, we receive God's mercy.

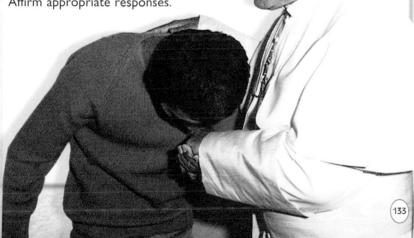

(133)

Teaching Tip

Being Merciful. One way to help the children understand the Beatitude "Blessed are the merciful, for they will be shown mercy" (Matthew 5:7) is to have them create a mercy collage. Provide magazines for the class. Have the children cut out pictures that depict actions showing mercy and paste them on a piece of newsprint. When all have pasted their pictures on the newsprint, use the finished collage as a discussion starter.

Connect

HIGHLIGHT

Point out that in 1981 the Church's leader—the pope—taught us a valuable lesson in forgiveness.

DISCOVER

- Talk with the children about their responsibility to forgive others and to show forgiveness.
- Read aloud "The Pope Forgives" and listen for ways Pope John Paul II showed forgiveness.
- Ask the children to tell what they think is so remarkable about this story of forgiveness.
- Have the children read "Our Catholic Faith."
- Point out that Pope John Paul II showed mercy to the man who tried to kill him.

INTEGRATE

- Invite responses to the question on page 133.
- Ask the children to think of someone they would like to forgive. As part of the celebration at the end of the lesson, invite the children to say silently to themselves, "I forgive ___," naming someone whom they need to forgive.

Connect

HIGHLIGHT

Remind the children that asking for and receiving forgiveness is an important part of their lives.

RESPOND

Separate the children into pairs. Explain the activity and have them complete it. Have the children share their role-play with the class.

CHOOSE

- Invite the children to respond to "My Faith Choice."
- After a moment of prayerful reflection have the children write their choices on the lines provided.
- Encourage the children to put their choices into practice this week.

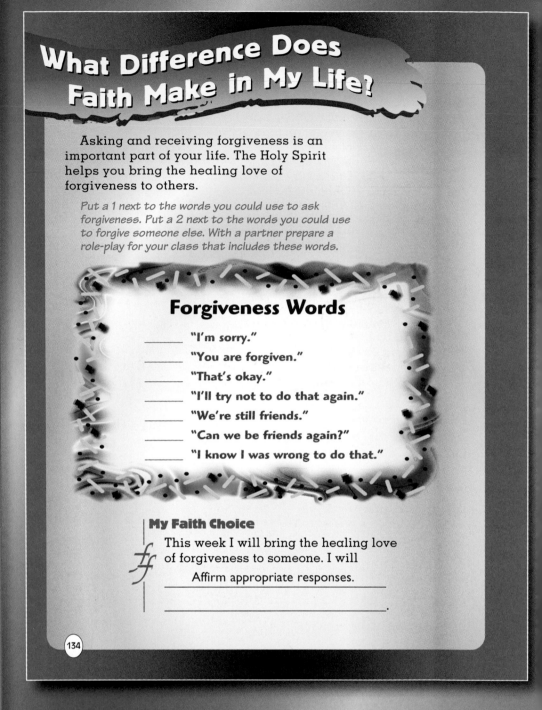

What Difference Does Faith Make in My Life?

Asking and receiving forgiveness is an important part of your life. The Holy Spirit helps you bring the healing love of forgiveness to others.

Put a 1 next to the words you could use to ask forgiveness. Put a 2 next to the words you could use to forgive someone else. With a partner prepare a role-play for your class that includes these words.

Forgiveness Words

_____ "I'm sorry."

_____ "You are forgiven."

_____ "That's okay."

_____ "I'll try not to do that again."

_____ "We're still friends."

_____ "Can we be friends again?"

_____ "I know I was wrong to do that."

My Faith Choice

This week I will bring the healing love of forgiveness to someone. I will _____ Affirm appropriate responses. _____

_____

134

Teaching Tip

The Umbrella of Friendship. Invite the children to think about friendship as a very large umbrella under which many things, such as family, friends, and acts of love, forgiveness, and kindness, can be gathered. Then have them imagine that outside the umbrella there are many things, such as gossip, jealousy, revenge, and selfishness, that can tear a friendship apart. Use this image to help the children live their faith. Have them come under the umbrella and think about what happens each day. Affirm the children in their efforts to live a life of forgiveness, love, and kindness and to keep things, such as gossip, jealousy, and revenge out of their lives.

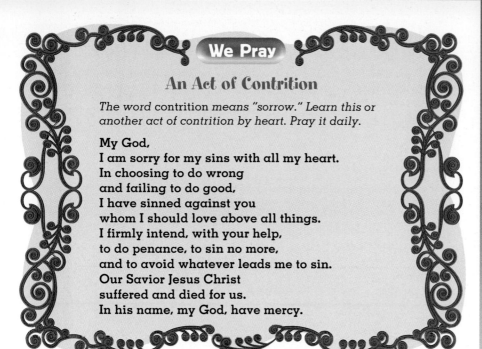

We Pray

An Act of Contrition

The word contrition *means "sorrow." Learn this or another act of contrition by heart. Pray it daily.*

My God,
I am sorry for my sins with all my heart.
In choosing to do wrong
and failing to do good,
I have sinned against you
whom I should love above all things.
I firmly intend, with your help,
to do penance, to sin no more,
and to avoid whatever leads me to sin.
Our Savior Jesus Christ
suffered and died for us.
In his name, my God, have mercy.

We Remember

Circle the T next to the true statements. Circle the F next to the false statements. Make each false statement true.

1. Sin hurts our friendship with God. **(T)** F
2. In the sacrament of Reconciliation we confess our sins to a priest. **(T)** F
3. We receive the sacrament of the Anointing of the Sick when we are healthy. T **(F)**
4. Jesus healed the sick during his life on earth. **(T)** F

To Help You Remember

1. In the sacrament of Reconciliation God always forgives us our sins when we are truly sorry.
2. In Reconciliation the Holy Spirit helps us to not sin again.
3. In the sacrament of the Anointing of the Sick, our faith and trust in God are made stronger.

Pray

WE PRAY

- Explain that our prayer today is an act of contrition.
- Pray the Act of Contrition together.
- Remind the children of God's forgiving love for us. Then ask them to take a moment to express in their hearts their forgiveness of the person whose name they thought of earlier in the lesson.

Review

WE REMEMBER

- Ask volunteers to read aloud each of the "To Help You Remember" statements to reinforce the lesson concepts.
- Introduce the activity. Ask volunteers to rephrase each false statement so that it is correct.

✝ Liturgy Tip

The Act of Contrition. Explain to the children that the prayer on this page is an act of contrition. An act of contrition is usually said during the sacrament of Reconciliation after we confess our sins to a priest. The version of the act of contrition in today's closing prayer is from the Rite of Penance and is the one commonly prayed in the celebration of the sacrament. The word *contrition* means "sorrow." Remind the children that true sorrow includes making a sincere effort not to repeat a sinful action and a promise to avoid actions that lead to sin. Go over each phrase of the act of contrition with the children. Devising gestures to accompany the prayer can help the children understand the meaning of the words. Send a copy home or use it often as a part of daily prayer.

At Home

ENCOURAGE

Have the children carefully tear out pages 135 and 136 along the perforation. Encourage the children to share the pages with their families and to do the activities together. If they did not complete the review activity on page 135 by the end of the session, emphasize that they can complete it with their families.

VISIT FAITHFIRST.COM

- Share with the children the many activities on the *Faith First* Web site.
- Encourage the children to visit **www.FaithFirst.com.**

Before Moving On . . .

As you finish today's lesson, reflect on the following question before moving on to the next chapter.

What am I doing to involve children who seldom volunteer for activities?

---

15 With My Family

This Week . . .

In chapter 15, "We Celebrate God's Healing Love," your child learned more about the forgiving and healing love of God. Through Christ we have been saved from sin and reconciled with God and with all creation. The sins we commit after Baptism are forgiven through the power of the Holy Spirit in the sacrament of Reconciliation. Christ's victory is also a victory over suffering and death. In the sacrament of the Anointing of the Sick, we receive the grace to join our sufferings to Christ's. Our faith and trust in God is strengthened.

For more on the teachings of the Catholic Church on the Sacraments of Healing, Reconciliation, and Anointing of the Sick, see *Catechism of the Catholic Church* paragraph numbers 1420–1484 and 1499–1525.

Sharing God's Word

Read together the parable of the Forgiving Father in Luke 15:11–24 or read the adaptation of the parable on page 130. Emphasize that the actions of the loving father in the parable tell us about God's love for us. God will always forgive us when we are sorry for our sins.

Praying

In this chapter your child prayed an act of contrition. Read and pray together the prayer on page 135.

Making a Difference

Choose one of the following activities to do as a family or design a similar activity of your own.

- Make a list of all the words you can use to ask for forgiveness or say to someone who asks for your forgiveness. Talk about how much better we feel after we ask to be forgiven or when someone forgives us.
- Recall that God always forgives us our sins when we are sorry. Invite family members to share their ideas on why forgiveness is an essential quality of the Christian family.
- Jesus often healed the sick during his life on earth. Talk about the ways your family cares for one another when someone in your family is sick.

For more ideas on ways your family can live your faith, visit the "Faith First for Families" page at **www.FaithFirst.com.** You are only a click away from "Family Prayer."

Evaluate

Take a few moments to evaluate this week's lesson.
I feel (circle one) about this week's lesson.

a. very pleased
b. OK
c. disappointed

The activity the children enjoyed most was . . .

The concept that was most difficult to teach was . . .

because . . .

Something I would like to do differently is . . .

ENRICHING THE LESSON

Making Sacrament Booklets

Purpose

To reinforce the Sacraments of Healing (taught on pages 131 and 132)

Directions

- Invite the children to complete the next two pages in their booklets using words and drawings to tell what they have learned about the sacraments of Reconciliation and the Anointing of the Sick.
- Remind the children to bring their sacrament booklets to the next session.

Materials

sacrament booklets
crayons or markers

Preparing Posters Announcing Sacraments of Healing

Purpose

To reinforce the Sacraments of Healing (taught on pages 131 and 132)

Directions

- In preparation for your parish's next communal Reconciliation service and its next celebration of Anointing of the Sick, invite the children to make posters announcing the two events.
- On the posters, have the children include all of the important information, such as the date, time, and place where the sacraments will be celebrated.
- Invite them to decorate the posters with symbols that remind them of the sacrament.
- In addition, have the children include reasons why parishioners might want to celebrate one or both of these sacraments. Make arrangements with the parish staff to post the children's announcements in places where parishioners will readily see them.

Materials

poster board
markers or crayons

Literature Connection

Purpose

To reinforce the teaching about the sacrament of the Anointing of the Sick (taught on page 132)

Directions

Some third graders have experienced the serious illness of a classmate, a friend, or relative. Joyce C. Mills' modern parable *Little Tree: A Story for Children with Serious Medical Problems* (American Psychological Association, 2003) presents the story of a tree that experiences severe storm damage but discovers that she still has strengths.

- Ask the children to tell about friends or relatives who have experienced, or are experiencing, serious illnesses or accidents.
- Read the book aloud to the children.
- Ask the children to describe what the tree comes to understand.
- Remind them that the sacrament of the Anointing of the Sick brings strength, courage, and peace.

Materials

Little Tree: A Story for Children with Serious Medical Problems by Joyce C. Mills

Music Connection

- "Hold Us in Your Mercy: Penitential Litany," G. Daigle. *Singing Our Faith (SOF)* #230.
- "Somebody's Knockin' at Your Door" (African-American spiritual). *SOF* #226.
- "Standin' in the Need of Prayer" (African-American spiritual). *SOF* #228.
- "We Come to Ask Forgiveness," C. Landry. *Rise Up and Sing* #190.

The Wedding Feast in Cana
A Scripture Story

Background

The Miracles of Jesus

Many of us have probably had something happen in our lives when we have prayed for a "miracle." We may also have had unforeseen things happen and said, "It's a miracle!" Stories of miracles fascinate us.

The Gospels share with us the accounts of many miracles Jesus performed. Some of the miracle stories in the Gospels leave us with more questions than answers. Upon hearing these miracle stories, our first response might be: How could water be changed into wine? A sea be calmed? A blind man see? A dead man live?

Of course, with miracles there is no natural explanation. A miracle is "a sign or wonder, such as healing or the control of nature, which can only be attributed to divine power. The miracles of Jesus were messianic signs of the presence of God's kingdom" (*Catechism of the Catholic Church* "Glossary"). As such, the miracle stories in the Gospels help us understand who Jesus is and the work that he came to do.

When the disciples of John asked if Jesus was the Messiah, Jesus replied:

"Go and tell John what you have seen and heard: the blind regain their sight, the lame walk, lepers are cleansed, the deaf hear, the dead are raised, the poor have the good news proclaimed to them. And blessed is the one who takes no offense at me."
LUKE 7:22–23

Jesus' miracles express the saving power of God. They proclaim that the power of God is present and active among us here and now.

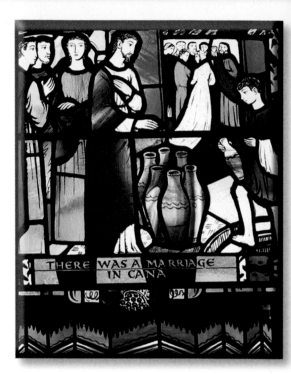

There was a marriage in Cana

The Miracle in Cana in Galilee

The miracle at the wedding feast in Cana occurs only in John's account of the Gospel. It is referred to as one of Jesus' signs and is the occasion for Jesus' glory to be revealed to his disciples so they will believe in him.

John places the Cana story at the beginning of his Gospel (John 2:1–12) to point to the fact that from the beginning of his public ministry, Jesus' disciples came to believe Jesus to be the Messiah. This is not the case in the other three accounts of the Gospel. In Matthew, Mark, and Luke the disciples only came to faith in Jesus as the Messiah at the conclusion of his public ministry.

We are like the first disciples of Jesus. Some of us come to faith in Jesus more slowly than others, as the disciples in Matthew's, Mark's, and Luke's accounts of the Gospel did. Others come to believe in Christ as the disciples in John's account did. But we all profess our faith in Christ and experience the miracle of the saving grace of God in our lives.

For Reflection

When have I experienced the wondrous and awesome presence of God with me?

What effect did my awareness of that presence have on me?

Catechist to Catechist

Signs of God's Love

Watching a good magician perform an array of magic tricks is fascinating. The act of creating illusions is captivating. As you present this lesson, be sure that you clearly teach that the miracles of Jesus are not magic of any kind. The miracles of Jesus are not acts of deception or illusions. The miracles performed by Jesus are astonishing signs of God's love in action. They are clear signs and testimonies of God's caring presence among us, apparent to those who see with eyes of faith and hear with ears of faith.

God's Caring Presence

If we look with eyes of faith, we will see other manifestations of God's caring presence in our daily lives. While not miracles in the sense of Jesus' changing water into wine, these manifestations are ever present in our midst. Help the children see and hear God at work in their lives. Help them marvel at God's constant, loving presence in our world.

The Church Teaches . . .

The *General Directory for Catechesis* teaches:

> Faith is a gift from God. It can only be born in the intimacy of Man's heart as a fruit of that "grace [which] moves and assists him,"[1] and as a completely free response to the promptings of the Holy Spirit who moves the heart and turns it toward God, and who "makes it easy for all to accept and believe the truth."[2]
>
> *GDC* 55

Through miracles Jesus invited a response of faith in his followers. His miracles continue to speak to our hearts today.

See the Catechism . . .

For more on the teachings of the Catholic Church on miracles, see *Catechism of the Catholic Church* 156, 515, 547–49, and 1335.

CATECHIST PRAYER

Holy Spirit,
help me recognize
the miracle
of your presence
in the lives
of the children.
Amen.

Footnote references may be found on p. 456.

LESSON PLANNER

Focus To discover what the wedding in Cana tells us about Jesus

Engage

Page 137
Focus
To assess the children's knowledge about miracles and the wedding in Cana

Opening Prayer

Discussion
Weddings and the wedding feast in Cana

Teach and Apply

Pages 138–140
Focus
To identify the miracle at Cana as a sign of God's power and presence among us

Presentation
Read, discuss, and summarize content.
Scripture
• Psalm 145:18
• John 2:3–11
Activities
• Describe why weddings are happy times.
• Pretend you are a disciple and write what you might have said to Jesus at Cana.
• Draw or write about another miracle story of Jesus.

Connect

Pages 141–142
Focus
To discover that the Church is a sign of God's love

Our Church Makes a Difference
One parish community is a sign that God is always at work in the world.
Our Catholic Faith
Collection at Mass

What Difference Does Faith Make?
Activity
Complete sentences to show how you come to know God's love.
Faith Choice
Choose a way to be a sign of God at work in the world this week.

We Pray

Page 143
Prayer Form
Intercession
Prayer
Divide the class into two groups. Introduce the prayer and pray together.

We Remember

Review
• Complete the scrambled words activity.
• Read the "To Help You Remember" statements aloud.
Preview
Highlight features of the "With My Family" page.

Materials

• Bibles
• pens or pencils

Enriching the Session

Blackline Masters
Additional Activities booklet:
Chapter 16
Solving and drawing
Creating and designing
Assessment Tools booklet:
Chapter 16 Test

Enriching the Lesson (CG page 241)
Retelling Miracles Stories
Having Fun with Words
Literature Connection

Music Connection (CG page 241)

www.FaithFirst.com

We update the *Faith First* Web site weekly. Check each week for new content and features. Here are some places to begin:

Catechists and Teachers
• Current Events
• Chapter Downloads
• Catechist Prayer

Faith First **for Families**
• Bible Stories
• Make a Difference

Kids' Clubhouse
• *Faith First* Activities
• Chapter Reviews
• Games
• Saints

Don't Forget! You can make lesson planning a breeze—check out the **Online Lesson Planner.**

The Wedding Feast in Cana

A Scripture Story

16

We Pray

The LORD, our God,
    is near
    to all who call
    upon him.
        Based on Psalm 145:18

God the Father, Son, and Holy Spirit, strengthen the faith of our families and through them, bless the Church. Amen.

Why are weddings such happy times?

The Gospel of John tells us that Jesus went to a wedding celebration in the village of Cana.

What do you remember about what happened at the wedding?

THERE WAS A MARRIAGE IN CANA

Jesus changing water into wine at the marriage celebration in Cana

137

PRAY

- Gather the children and have them quiet themselves for prayer.
- Pray the Sign of the Cross and have a volunteer read the Psalm verse.
- Say the opening prayer together.
- Close the prayer with the Sign of the Cross.

DISCOVER

Purpose: To discover what the children know about the story of the wedding feast at Cana

- Invite volunteers to share what they remember about a wedding they have attended. Ask: Why are weddings such happy times?
- Tell the children that Jesus once went to a wedding with his mother in the village of Cana.
- Ask the children to look at the picture of the stained-glass window. Invite volunteers to share what they see in the picture.

Teaching Tip

Wedding Ceremonies. Every culture has its own unique wedding customs. Have children share a unique custom from their own heritage or share the following customs with the children. In Vietnam the groom and his family go to the bride's house on the day of the wedding. The bride and groom pray at the altar of the ancestors in the home. They exchange rings and other jewelry. Afterward, everyone joins them at a restaurant. In Mexico during the wedding service a lasso is tied around the groom and bride as a symbol of their new union as husband and wife. They leave the church walking on rose petals that the guests have thrown in front of them.

Teach

FOCUS

Have a volunteer read the "Faith Focus" question. Share with the children that in this chapter they will learn what the story of the wedding at Cana tells us about God's love.

DISCOVER

- Have the children listen as you read "Jewish Weddings in Jesus' Time" to them. Have them listen to discover three facts about Jewish weddings in the time of Jesus.
- Ask volunteers to share one of the facts they found in the text about Jewish weddings in Jesus' time. Write the facts on the board.

Apply

REINFORCE

- Divide the class into small groups.
- Have the children compare a Jewish wedding in Jesus' time with a wedding they have attended.

INTEGRATE

Discuss with the children why the celebration of marriage is a happy and joyous celebration.

Bible Background

Faith Focus

What does the story of the wedding in Cana tell us about God?

Faith Words

miracle
A miracle is a sign of God's presence and power at work in our world.

Jewish Weddings in Jesus' Time

During Jesus' time many Jewish weddings took place in the fall of the year. The wedding began in the evening. The groom met the bride at her house. Then the wedding party walked from the bride's house to the groom's house for the ceremony.

The next day the bride and groom and everyone began celebrating the wedding. People danced and sang and opened presents. For seven days the bridegroom and his family provided food and wine for all the guests. The bridegroom kept the wine used at the wedding in large stone, or pottery, jars.

Why is the celebration of marriage a happy and joyous celebration?

Affirm appropriate responses.

138

Teaching Tip

Bible Atlas. Bring a Bible atlas to the session to show the children the various places they have learned about: Bethlehem, which is south of Jerusalem; Nazareth and Cana, which are in the area of the Holy Land known as Galilee. If a Bible atlas is not available, you may use a current globe marking Israel and the city of Jerusalem to give children perspective on the general area where the miracle in Cana took place.

Reading the Word of God

Jesus Helps a Newly Married Couple

Once Jesus, his mother, and the disciples went to a wedding in Cana in Galilee. During the wedding, Mary saw that the groom's family had run out of wine. Act out what happens next.

Mary: Jesus, they have no wine left.

Jesus: How can I help them, Mother?

Mary: (to the servants) Do whatever he tells you.

Jesus: (to the servants) Fill the six stone jars with water.

Narrator: The servants filled the six jars with water from a well. Each jar held twenty to thirty gallons of water.

Jesus: Take some of what is in the jars and give it to the head servant.

Head servant: (tastes wine and looks surprised) People serve their best wine first. Then after people eat, they serve their cheaper wine. But you have kept the best wine to serve last.

Narrator: Jesus changed the water into wine. Many of his disciples came to believe in Jesus because of what he did.

Based on John 2:3–11

Pretend you are one of Jesus' disciples at the wedding. Share what you might say to Jesus when you hear what he did.

Affirm appropriate responses.

139

Teaching Tip

Bring the Story to Life. Bring in props for the children to use when acting out the Bible passage. You might provide some old sheets, lengths of fabric, and headbands that can be used to dress up for the wedding. Collect six plastic pitchers. Have some water for the children to pour into the pitchers and a ladle to use to take some "wine" to the headwaiter. Invite the children to devise costumes from the box of props.

FOCUS

Share with the children that the Gospel of John tells us about a wedding that Jesus attended and an extraordinary thing he did there.

DISCOVER

- Set the scene by reading the first paragraph of "Jesus Helps a Newly Married Couple." Ask the children to listen for the problem at the wedding Jesus and Mary attended in Cana.

- Divide the class into three groups to present the story based on John 2:3–11 as a choral reading. You may take the part of the narrator.

Apply

REINFORCE

Have the children work with partners and share what they might say to Jesus if they had witnessed this miracle.

INTEGRATE

Ask the children to tell a friend what this story says to them about God.

Teach

FOCUS

Remind the children that after the waiters filled the jars with water as Jesus told them, the water became wine. Then point out that this work of Jesus is called a miracle.

DISCOVER

- Have the children turn back in their texts to page 138 and read aloud with you the faith word *miracle* and its meaning. Emphasize that miracles are extraordinary events that only God can do.
- Have the children read silently "God Is with Us" to learn more about how Jesus' miracles affected his followers.
- Ask the children to recall the purpose of the miracles Jesus performed. They invite people to believe and trust in God.

Apply

REINFORCE

Have the children make a word card for the faith term *miracle*.

INTEGRATE

- Brainstorm with the children other miracle stories they know from Scripture. Write their ideas on the board.
- Have the children complete the activity on the bottom of the page using the information from the board. Have them share their work with a partner.

Understanding the Word of God

God Is with Us

Jesus performed a **miracle** when he changed the water into wine. A miracle is a sign of God's presence and power at work in our world. Through miracles God invites us to believe and trust in him. Seeing this miracle of water changed into wine, Jesus' followers began to believe that he was sent by God.

The New Testament tells us that Jesus worked many other miracles. People came to have faith and trust in God because of the miracles Jesus performed.

The Healing of the Blind Beggar (Luke 18:35–43)

The pictures on this page show two other miracles of Jesus. In the box draw or write about another miracle story of Jesus that you know. Write the name of the story under the picture.

Responses will vary.

The Healing of a Paralyzed Man (Luke 5:17–20)

(140)

FAITH WORDS

Faith Vocabulary

Miracle. From the Latin *miraculum* meaning "a wonder or marvel," the English word *miracle* refers to an extraordinary event that reveals the presence and power of God at work in the world. The miracles in the Gospels invite us to place our faith and trust in God. They invite us to call upon the Lord to strengthen our trust in the healing love of God in our lives.

Our Church Makes a Difference

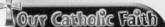
Our Catholic Faith

Collection at Mass

All Catholics are called to serve other people as the people of Saint Mark's parish do. The money that is collected at Mass during the collection is used by a parish to serve people in many ways. One way the money is sometimes used is to help people who are out of work. Serving people in this and other ways is a sign of God's love for them.

Signs of God's Love

The Catholic community of Saint Mark the Evangelist is a sign that God is always at work in the world. Each month the people of the parish collect canned food, used clothing, furniture, and everyday items such as soap, shampoo, and school supplies.

One Sunday each month, they fill a truck with the things the people of Saint Mark's wish to share with people in need. They bring everything they have gathered that month to the people of a parish they have adopted.

When we do these things, we are signs of God's love for people. Through the things we do and say God invites people to believe and trust in him.

Describe some of the ways your parish is a sign of God's love for people. How can you join with them in doing these things?

141

Special Needs

Alternative Responses. Help children who are shy to respond verbally to questions. Have the children use popsicle sticks and paper plates and draw a happy face on one side and a sad face on the other. Ask a series of yes or no statements about how your parish is a sign of God's love for people. Have the children respond by showing either a happy face or a sad face.

Need: Children who lack confidence or have a fear of public speaking

Connect

HIGHLIGHT

Remind the children that miracles are a sign of God's love. Tell them that the Church's work in the world today is another sign of God's love.

DISCOVER

- Tell the children they are going to read about the way one parish community is a sign of God's love.
- Invite the children to read silently "Signs of God's Love" to learn more about the Catholic community of Saint Mark.
- Tell the children there is another way the Church helps people. Ask a volunteer to read aloud "Our Catholic Faith."
- Ask the children if they know how their parish uses the money that is collected during Mass. Explain that some of that money goes to people in the community who are in need.

INTEGRATE

- Gather enough parish bulletins for the children to share.
- Tell them they may use the bulletins to help them answer the activity question.
- Ask the children how they can get involved in doing some of the activities.

Connect

HIGHLIGHT

Remind the children that God works in the world through us. Signs of his love are all around us.

RESPOND

- Write one activity sentence on the board and have the children suggest words that they might use to complete it.
- Then have the children complete two sentences with their own words.
- Have volunteers share their responses.

CHOOSE

- Invite the children to respond to "My Faith Choice."
- After a moment of prayerful reflection have the children write their choice on the lines provided.
- Encourage the children to put their choice into practice this week.

What Difference Does Faith Make in My Life?

God is at work in the world. When you help others, you help people come to know God's love. God works through you to invite people to believe and trust in him.

Complete these sentences to show how you come to know God's love.

Signs of God

Affirm appropriate responses.

Each time I see a _____
I believe God is at work in the world.

Each time I hear a _____
I believe God is at work in the world.

Each time I _____
I am a sign of God at work in the world.

My Faith Choice

This week I will be a sign of God at work in the world. I will

Affirm appropriate responses.
_____

_____

142

Background: Doctrine

At Work in the World. We profess faith in the truth that God acts through all of creation, including ourselves. Encourage the children to look for signs of God's work in the world and in each other. Have the group generate a list of positive things that have happened throughout the day and people for whom they are thankful. Then have them discuss how these could be seen as signs of God's work in the world.

We Pray

A Prayer for Families

God is always sharing his love with your family. Let us pray this prayer for our families and for all families.

All: **Bless our families.**

Group 1: O loving God,
you have made our families
signs of Jesus' love for the Church.

All: **Bless our families.**

Group 2: Send us the Holy Spirit to help us
grow in love for you, for each other,
and for all people.

All: **Bless our families.**

We Remember

Unscramble the purple words. Write the words on the lines to complete the sentences.

1. Jesus and his mother went to a wedding in the town of **nCaa**.

   CANA

2. At the wedding Jesus performed the **acmiler** of changing the water in six stone jars into wine.

   MIRACLE

3. When Jesus' disciples saw him change the water into wine, they came to **evebeli** he was sent to them by God.

   BELIEVE

To Help You Remember

1. Jesus performed a miracle at the wedding in Cana to show that God's power is at work in the world.

2. When Jesus changed water into wine, his disciples came to believe he was sent by God.

3. Jesus' miracle in Cana helped people trust in God.

WE PRAY

- Point out that the prayer today is a prayer of petition for families.
- Gather the children in the prayer center and divide them into two groups. Invite each group to read their part of the prayer.
- All say, "Amen."

WE REMEMBER

- Read the "To Help You Remember" statements aloud. Reword at least one of the statements so that it is incorrect. Ask a volunteer to correct the statement.
- Introduce the activity. Invite the children to read their completed sentences aloud.

Liturgy Tip

Signs of God's Love. Before concluding with this prayer for families, talk with the children about the signs of God's love they have been a witness to in their own families—the birth of a sibling or the recovery of a family member from a serious illness. Talk about the ways these things are signs of God's power and love. Then discuss ways their families can be signs of God's power and love in the world.

At Home

ENCOURAGE

Have the children carefully tear out pages 143 and 144 along the perforation. Encourage the children to share the pages with their families and to do the activities together. If they did not complete the review activity on page 143 by the end of the session, emphasize that they can complete it with their families.

VISIT FAITHFIRST.COM

- Share with the children the many activities on the *Faith First* Web site.
- Encourage the children to visit **www.FaithFirst.com.**

16 With My Family

This Week . . .

In chapter 16, "The Wedding Feast in Cana: A Scripture Story," your child learned the Gospel story about the wedding in Cana (John 2:1–11). The focus of this story is the miracle performed by Jesus of turning water into wine. The miracles in the Scriptures serve an important purpose. They are signs of God's power at work in the world. Miracles are divine invitations to believe and trust in God's goodness, which is always at work in the world. They are invitations to love God with our whole heart and to share that love with others.

For more on the teaching of the Catholic Church on miracles, see *Catechism of the Catholic Church* paragraph numbers 156, 515, 547–49, and 1335.

144

Sharing God's Word

Read together the Bible story in John 2:1–11 about the wedding in Cana or read the adaptation of the story on page 139. Emphasize that this miracle helped the disciples believe in Jesus and grow in their faith and trust in God.

Praying

In this chapter your child prayed a prayer for families. Read and pray together the prayer on page 143.

Making a Difference

Choose one of the following activities to do as a family or design a similar activity of your own.

- Jesus performed a miracle when he turned the water into wine. Read one or more of these miracle stories: Luke 18:35–43, Mark 4:35–41, or Luke 5:17–20. Share what each story helps you come to know about God.

- When we help people, we are signs of God's love. As a family, choose to do one thing this week to be a sign of God's love.

- At dinnertime this week think about and name the signs of God's love each family member has experienced that day. Include a prayer of thanksgiving as part of your mealtime prayer.

For more ideas on ways your family can live your faith, visit the "Faith First for Families" page at **www.FaithFirst.com.** Check out "Bible Stories." Read and discuss the Bible story together.

Before Moving On . . .

As you finish today's lesson, reflect on the following question before moving on to the next chapter.

How well do I communicate to the children how much I enjoy being their catechist?

Evaluate

Take a few moments to evaluate this week's lesson.
I feel (circle one) about this week's lesson.

    a. very pleased

    b. OK

    c. disappointed

The activity the children enjoyed most was . . .

The concept that was most difficult to teach was . . .

because . . .

Something I would like to do differently is . . .

ENRICHING THE LESSON

Retelling Miracles Stories

Purpose

To reinforce stories of the miracles of Jesus (taught on page 140)

Directions

- Have the children work with partners and choose one of the miracle stories on page 140 and read it in the Bible.
- Ask them to outline a short report telling the following: title, setting, characters, problem, action, and solution.
- Have the children share their retellings.

Materials

Bibles
blank paper
pens or pencils

Having Fun with Words

Purpose

To reinforce the teaching that through miracles God invites us to believe and trust in him (taught on page 140)

Directions

- Have the children find words in this chapter that either begin with one of the letters from the word *miracle* or that contain one of the letters.
- For the "m" in *miracle*, they could use the following words that begin with "m": Mary, month, Mass, mother, man; for words containing an "m": performed, Testament, groom.
- Have the class retell the story using as many words listed on the board as they can.

Materials

Literature Connection

Purpose

To reinforce the stories of the miracles of Jesus (taught on page 140)

Directions

- Using Tomie dePaola's book *The Miracles of Jesus* (Holiday House, Inc., 1987), read the story of "The Calming of the Storm."
- In small groups have the children do a choral reading of this story similar to the one they did for the wedding feast of Cana.
- Have each group present their miracle story.

Materials

The Miracles of Jesus by Tomie dePaola

Music Connection

- "I Say "Yes,"/Digo Sí, Señor," D. Peña. *Singing Our Faith (SOF)* #218.
- "We Are Many Parts," M. Haugen. *SOF* #182.
- "We Come to Share God's Special Gift," C. Walker. *Rise Up and Sing* #193.
- "You Are Mine," D. Haas. *SOF* #212.

The Sacraments of Service

Background

Love One Another

Love is our origin. We were created out of divine love and created to love God and others. Love is our constant calling. Love is our fulfillment in heaven. The kind of love that Christians are called to—the love that is celebrated in the sacraments—is a love that acts on behalf of others because of our love for God.

The Gospel account of Jesus washing the feet of the disciples at the Last Supper gives us insight into the meaning of Christian love. We are to love by serving others as Jesus did. Although serving others is at the heart of being a disciple of Christ, the Church has named two specific sacraments as Sacraments at the Service of Communion—Holy Orders and Matrimony—to build up the Church, the holy People of God.

Two other sacraments, Holy Orders and Matrimony, are directed toward the salvation of others; if they contribute as well to personal salvation, it is through service to others that they do so. They confer a particular mission in the Church and serve to build up the People of God.
CATECHISM OF THE CATHOLIC CHURCH 1534

Holy Orders

The sacrament of Holy Orders consecrates a baptized man for service to the Church, the People of God. "Those among the faithful who have received Holy Orders are appointed to nourish the Church with the word and grace of God in the name of Christ" *(Dogmatic Constitution on the Church 11).* All the ordained ministers of the Church—bishops, priests, and deacons—assist and serve the faithful in their pursuit of living the command to love and live a life of holiness. Ordination is a consecration, a setting aside and investing, of members of the Church who have been called by Christ for the sake of the whole Church. They act in the name and Person of Jesus Christ, Head and Shepherd of the Church. They have the responsibility to work to serve all the faithful.

Matrimony

Marriage between a baptized man and a baptized woman is a covenant. It is a pledge of committed love, publicly declared before God, family and friends, and the Church that cannot be dissolved until death. As Christ and his Church are united in a covenant of love, Christian spouses are united in Christ and share in this same covenant of love and unity. Chosen to be living signs of Christ's love for the Church, they receive the graces to help each other and their children to attain holiness.

For Reflection

Where am I called to service in my life as a disciple of Jesus?

Who are the priests and married couples I know who exemplify this kind of holiness?

Catechist to Catechist

Recognize Diversity

There is diversity in the backgrounds and experiences of the children in your group. This will shine forth in many ways as they interact with you and with one another. It is important to recognize, accept, and work with this diversity. The diversity among the children is at the root of the many gifts that they use now and will use in the future to serve the Church.

Support Each Child

Accept the children for who they are today, at this moment. Support each child's efforts. God's graciousness shines through your actions and those of the 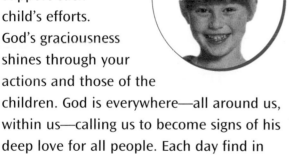 children. God is everywhere—all around us, within us—calling us to become signs of his deep love for all people. Each day find in the children's laughter and joy, sorrow and pain, failure and success, signs of God's presence in your midst.

The Church Teaches . . .

The General Directory for Catechesis teaches:

> Parents are the primary educators in the faith. . . . The family is defined as a 'domestic Church.'[1] . . . The family as a locus of catechesis has a unique privilege: transmitting the Gospel by rooting it in the context of profound human values.[2] . . . It is, indeed, a Christian education more witnessed to than taught, more occasional than systematic, more ongoing and daily than structured into periods.
>
> *GDC 255*

The family is to be a sign of God's love in the world.

See the Catechism . . .

For more on the teachings of the Catholic Church on the Sacraments at the Service of Communion, see *Catechism of the Catholic Church* 1533–1589 and 1601–1658.

CATECHIST PRAYER.

*Spirit of the Lord,
help me to serve others
and to teach the
children that joy
and fulfillment
are found in service
of others.
Amen.*

Footnote references may be found on p. 456.

LESSON PLANNER

To discover how ordained members of the Church and married people serve the People of God

Engage

Page 145
Focus
To assess the children's knowledge about the sacraments of Holy Orders and Matrimony

Opening Prayer

Discussion
Doing things for others and sacraments of service

Teach and Apply

Pages 146–148
Focus
To discover how bishops, priests, deacons, and married people are consecrated to serve the whole Church

Presentation
Read, discuss, and summarize content.
Scripture
• Psalm 119:34
• John 13:4–5, 15
Activities
• Write how you hope to live your vocation as a follower of Christ as an adult.
• Name ways a bishop, priest, or deacon serves people.
• Draw or write ways your family is a sign of God's love.

Faith-Filled People
Deacons

Connect

Pages 149–150
Focus
To discover how the Church serves people in need

Our Church Makes a Difference
Identify Catholic Relief Services as a Church organization that helps people in need.
Our Catholic Faith
The Pope

What Difference Does Faith Make?
Activity
Choose a quality that identifies a follower of Jesus and tell how you can serve others by living that quality.

Faith Choice
Name a quality that identifies a follower of Jesus that you will put into practice this week.

We Pray

Page 151
Prayer Form
Intercession
Prayer
Lead or choose a leader and pray together.

We Remember

Review
• Complete the sentence activity.
• Read the "To Help You Remember" statements aloud.

Preview
Highlight features of the "With My Family" page.

Materials

• pens or pencils
• crayons or markers

Enriching the Session

Blackline Masters
Additional Activities booklet:
   Chapter 17
      Solving riddles
      Writing a memo
Assessment Tools booklet:
   Chapter 17 Test
   Unit 2 Review

Enriching the Lesson (CG page 253)
Dramatizing the Scripture Story
Completing Sacrament Booklets
Literature Connection

Music Connection (CG page 253)

www.FaithFirst.com

We update the *Faith First* Web site weekly. Check each week for new content and features. Here are some places to begin:

Catechists and Teachers
• Current Events
• Chapter Downloads
• Catechist Prayer

Faith First **for Families**
• Bible Stories
• Make a Difference

Kids' Clubhouse
• *Faith First* Activities
• Chapter Reviews
• Games
• Saints

Don't Forget! You can make lesson planning a breeze—check out the **Online Lesson Planner.**

The Sacraments of Service

We Pray

LORD, help me understand how you want me to live.
Based on Psalm 119:34

Father, send the Holy Spirit to help your Church serve the People of God. Amen.

When have you done something really difficult to help someone else?

People do many things each day to help us. God calls some members of the Church to help and serve all the People of God.

What two sacraments dedicate people to serve the whole community of the Church?

145

Engage

PRAY

- Gather the children and have them quiet themselves for prayer.
- Pray the Sign of the Cross.
- Invite a volunteer to read the Psalm verse and then pray the opening prayer together.
- Close the prayer with the Sign of the Cross.

DISCOVER

Purpose: To discover what the children know about Holy Orders and Matrimony

- Ask the children to respond to the question about helping others. Read the introductory paragraph and invite responses to the question that follows.
- Invite the children to look at the picture on this page and describe what is happening.

Teaching Tip

Develop Listening Skills. Listening skills are an essential part of serving others. Jesus is a model of good listening. He teaches us how to listen to God, how to listen to others, and how to listen to ourselves. Help the children understand and practice their listening skills in the classroom.

Teach

FOCUS

Ask a volunteer to read the "Faith Focus" question aloud. Share with the children that in this chapter they will learn how bishops, priests, deacons, and married people serve the people of the Church.

DISCOVER

- Invite the children to read silently "Jesus Teaches Us to Serve." Have them circle the actions of Jesus in the Gospel story based on John 13:4–5,15. Got up, poured, washed, dried.
- Ask the children what Jesus meant when he said, "I have given you an example. Do what I have done." Do whatever it takes to serve one another, even if the task is hard.
- Ask the children to find and read the meaning of the word *vocation*. Remind them that at Baptism we are called to share in Jesus' life and work.

Apply

REINFORCE

Have the children look at the illustration and tell why they think this illustration was used here.

INTEGRATE

- Have the children complete the activity.
- Ask volunteers to share how they are living their vocations as followers of Christ now and how they plan to live them as adults.

We Are Called to Serve

Faith Focus

How do bishops, priests, deacons, and married people serve the people of the Church?

Faith Words

Holy Orders
Holy Orders is the sacrament in which a baptized man is ordained a bishop, priest, or deacon to serve the whole Church his whole life long.

Matrimony
Matrimony is the sacrament in which a baptized man and a baptized woman make lifelong promises to serve the Church as a married couple.

Jesus Teaches Us to Serve

Jesus served God and the People of God. God calls every baptized person to share in Jesus' life and work. At the Last Supper Jesus taught his Apostles to serve others as he did.

During the meal Jesus got up from the table. He poured water into a bowl and began to wash his disciples' feet. He dried their feet with a towel. When Jesus finished, he said, "I have given you an example. Do what I have done."

Based on John 13:4–5, 15

At Baptism we receive the vocation to share in Jesus' life and work. The word *vocation* means "a calling." We can live our vocation in many ways. You live that calling now. When you grow up, you will make a decision about how you will follow Christ as an adult.

Write how you are living your vocation as a follower of Christ now. Write how you might live it as an adult.

Affirm appropriate responses.

_____

_____

_____

_____

146

✦ Background: Scripture

Washing the Feet. In Jesus' time, washing feet was a common ritual for welcoming guests into one's home. Servants usually did this task. Jesus, whom the disciples respected and addressed as "Master," gave deeper meaning to this custom. The Master humbly served his followers. This took the disciples, especially Peter, by surprise. The Church reenacts Christ's washing of his disciples' feet in the liturgy of the Lord's Supper on Holy Thursday evening to remind the Church of Christ's command to serve as Jesus the Master did.

Holy Orders

God gives some members of the Church the vocation to be bishops, priests, or deacons. This vocation is celebrated in the sacrament of **Holy Orders.** Holy Orders is one of the two Sacraments at the Service of Communion. Like Baptism and Confirmation, Holy Orders cannot be repeated. It marks the man who receives this sacrament with a permanent, spiritual mark, or character.

Bishops, priests, and deacons are ordained to serve the whole Church. They have served the Church from the days of the Apostles. A baptized man is ordained forever. Only bishops can ordain other bishops, priests, and deacons.

Bishops lead the people in worshiping God. They teach people about the faith. They guide the Church to live as Jesus taught. Priests are coworkers with bishops in their work. Bishops and priests serve the Church in Jesus' name and live their life unmarried. Deacons are not priests. They help bishops and work with priests.

Name ways you have seen a bishop, priest, or deacon serve people.

Affirm appropriate responses.

A bishop ordaining a priest

147

Faith-Filled People

Deacons

Deacons assist at worship. They proclaim and preach the word of God. They minister the sacrament of Baptism and can lead the sacrament of Matrimony. They visit and pray with people who are sick. They help people who are in need of clothing, food, or a home.

Background: Faith-Filled People

Deacons. Every baptized person is called to serve others as Jesus did. The call of Jesus is the same for us today as it was 2,000 years ago for the first disciples. Bishops, priests, and deacons fulfill this call and serve God in a special way by serving the Church. Like priests and bishops, deacons are ordained ministers who serve the Church. They are helpers of bishops and priests. (See *Catechism of the Catholic Church* 1569–1571.)

FOCUS

Remind the children that all members of the Church have a vocation. Some are called to serve the whole Church through the sacrament of Holy Orders.

DISCOVER

- Direct the children's attention to the photograph on this page. Ask them to share what the bishop is doing.
- Read "Holy Orders" to the children and ask them to listen for what this sacrament celebrates. Discuss with the children how the sacrament of Holy Orders empowers those who celebrate it to strengthen the whole community of faith.
- Write the name of the present bishop (archbishop) of your diocese (archdiocese).
- Invite the children to read "Faith-Filled People" to learn how deacons serve the Church.

Apply

REINFORCE

- Divide the class into groups of three and have each group review one paragraph of the page together.
- Have each group list the main points of their paragraph and present them to the class.

INTEGRATE

Invite the children to describe how they or their families have been served by bishops, priests, and deacons.

Teach

FOCUS

Share with the children that married couples also serve God and the Church community through the sacrament of Matrimony.

DISCOVER

- Present "Matrimony" in your own words.
- Ask the children to read and underline in the text the words that tell what a baptized man and a baptized woman promise in the sacrament of Matrimony.

Apply

REINFORCE

Have the children make word cards for the faith terms *Holy Orders* and *Matrimony*.

INTEGRATE

- Draw the children's attention to the pictures on this page and ask them how the people in the picture are being signs of God's love for one another.
- Invite the children to share how their families are signs of God's love by completing the activity.
- Ask the children to share their drawings with a partner.

Matrimony

God calls some members of the Church to marry. A baptized man and a baptized woman celebrate marriage in the sacrament of **Matrimony.** They serve the Church as a married couple.

In Matrimony a man and a woman freely promise to always love and be faithful to each other. They accept the gift of children. They promise to treat each other with honor and respect.

The Holy Spirit helps husbands and wives love one another just as Jesus loves his Church. Parents and children work together to live the Gospel. Christian families have the vocation to be signs of God's love in the world.

Tell how the people in the pictures are being signs of God's love for one another. In the blank box draw or write about how your family is a sign of God's love. **Affirm appropriate responses.**

148

Teaching Tip

Families Are Holy. We learn to love and to forgive in our family. There are lots of ways you can emphasize this basic truth throughout the year. Start a list of family ideas and invite the children to add their ideas to your list. For example:

- Family members encourage one another.
- Family members trust one another.
- Family members celebrate important days together.

Our Church Makes a Difference

Catholic Relief Services

The Church serves everyone. At Baptism we receive a lighted candle and promise to live as lights in the world. The Catholic bishops in the United States have organized the Catholic Relief Services to help Catholics in America keep that promise.

Catholic Relief Services brings together the people of the Catholic Church in the United States to help people. Through the Catholic Relief Services' Thanksgiving Clothing Appeal, Catholics in America have shared millions of pounds of clothing with people in need.

Catholic Relief Services workers go wherever help is needed. They serve people in need in countries all over the world.

Describe one way you might serve people in your community.

Affirm appropriate responses.

Our Catholic Faith

The Pope

The pope is the pastor of the whole Church. Helped by the Holy Spirit, the pope guides the whole Church in serving people all over the world. The pope is the bishop of Rome. He is the successor of Saint Peter the Apostle. Jesus chose Peter the Apostle to be the first pastor of the whole Church.

Children in Burundi, East Africa, receiving help from Catholic Relief Services

149

Catholic Social Teaching

Rights and Responsibilities of the Human Person. The Catholic Church teaches that every human has fundamental human rights—a right to life, to the things required to live a decent and healthy life, to meaningful work, and to freedom—within the limitations required for the common good. Corresponding to our rights, of course, are responsibilities—to one another, to our families, and to our community. Catholic social teaching reminds us that these basic rights and responsibilities are not "either-or" choices. Both are necessary and must exist side by side.

Tip: Research a local current event and discuss with the children whether human dignity was helped or hampered.

Connect

HIGHLIGHT

Remind the children that the Church serves everyone. Point out that one way the Church serves others is through a service group called Catholic Relief Services.

DISCOVER

- Invite the children to name some organizations that help people in need.
- Invite the children to silently read "Catholic Relief Services" to discover how this group organized by the bishops helps Catholics live their baptismal promises.
- Read aloud "Our Catholic Faith." Ask the children to listen for who the pope is and what he does.
- Ask the children to name our present pope. Write his name on the board and have them read it aloud.

INTEGRATE

- Ask the children to share how the people in the pictures are being helped.
- Invite the children to describe ways they might serve people in their community.

Connect

HIGHLIGHT

Remind the children that the Holy Spirit helps them serve other people as Jesus taught us to do.

RESPOND

- Have the children complete the activity.
- Ask volunteers to share how they can serve others living the quality they chose.

CHOOSE

- Invite the children to respond to "My Faith Choice."
- After a moment of prayerful reflection have the children write their choice on the lines provided.
- Encourage the children to put their choice into practice this week.

You have been called by God to serve others as a follower of Jesus. The Holy Spirit helps you live that calling now in many ways.

The words in the border name some of the qualities of a follower of Jesus. Choose one of these qualities and color in the letters. Write or draw how you can serve others when you live that quality.

RESPECTFUL   GENEROUS

LOVING CARING   **Followers of Jesus**   PATIENT KIND

FORGIVING   HONEST

My Faith Choice

This week I will choose one of the words above and put it into practice to serve other people. I will

Affirm appropriate responses.

_____.

150

Teaching Tip

Interview Questions. Brainstorm a list of questions the children would like to ask your parish priest or deacon about his service to the Church. Compile a master list of questions and e-mail them to your parish priest or deacon. Ask him to respond to the questions either by e-mail or in writing.

We Pray

Bless Your Servants

Pray this prayer of intercession. In a prayer of intercession we ask God to bless others.

Leader: Let us pray for all who serve the Church. For all priests, deacons, and bishops,

All: **we ask your blessing, Lord.**

Leader: For all our parents and others who teach us how to love you and others,

All: **we ask your blessing, Lord.**

Leader: For everyone who works to build up the Church,

All: **we ask your blessing, Lord.**

Leader: We make our prayer in the name of your Son, Jesus.

All: **Amen.**

We Remember

Complete each sentence. Use the words in the word bank.

| Baptism | Holy Orders | Matrimony |

1. In _____Holy Orders_____ a baptized man is ordained a bishop, priest, or deacon.

2. At _____Baptism_____ all Christians receive the vocation to share in Jesus' work.

3. In _____Matrimony_____ a baptized man and a baptized woman promise to always love and be faithful to each other.

To Help You Remember

1. Bishops and priests lead people in worshiping God and learning and living their faith.

2. Deacons help bishops and work with priests.

3. A baptized man and a baptized woman who receive the sacrament of Matrimony are a sign of God's love in the world.

Background: Doctrine

The Domestic Church. The Church reminds us of the value and importance of parents in building the faith of children. It is in the life of the family that the faith of children is both fostered and nurtured through examples and experiences of love, forgiveness, prayer, and so on. This role is so primary that the Church, in its Vatican II document *Dogmatic Constitution on the Church* (*Lumen Gentium*), calls the family the domestic church. (See also *Catechism of the Catholic Church* 1655–1658.) By encouraging use of the "With My Family" pages, the family section of www.FaithFirst.com, or the *At-Home Family Guide*, you are supporting the families of your children as they grow in faith.

Pray

WE PRAY

- Invite the children to sit in a circle in the prayer center with their books.
- Explain that the prayer is a prayer of intercession, asking the Lord's blessing on those who serve in ministry, especially those who have celebrated the Sacraments at the Service of Communion.
- Practice the responses.
- Lead the prayer and invite all to respond to the petitions together.

Review

WE REMEMBER

- Introduce the activity. Invite the children to read their completed sentences aloud.
- Write the words *bishops, priests, deacons, Matrimony,* and *Holy Orders* on the board.
- Read aloud each "To Help You Remember" statement, leaving out one of the listed words when it appears in a statement.
- Ask volunteers to name the missing word(s) in each sentence. If they answer correctly, ask them to erase the appropriate word(s).
- Continue until all words are erased.

At Home

ENCOURAGE

Have the children carefully tear out pages 151 and 152 along the perforation. Encourage the children to share the pages with their families and to do the activities together. If they did not complete the review activity on page 151 by the end of the session, emphasize that they can complete it with their families.

VISIT FAITHFIRST.COM

- Share with the children the many activities on the *Faith First* Web site.
- Encourage the children to visit **www.FaithFirst.com.**

Before Moving On . . .

As you finish today's lesson, reflect on the following question before moving on to the next chapter.

What more could I do to incorporate music into our sessions?

---

17 With My Family

This Week . . .

In chapter 17, "The Sacraments of Service," your child learned that all the baptized have the vocation to serve God and other people as Jesus did. Some of the baptized are called to serve the whole Church. This call is celebrated in the two Sacraments at the Service of Communion, Holy Orders and Matrimony. Holy Orders is the sacrament through which a baptized man is ordained a bishop, a priest, or a deacon. Matrimony is the sacrament that unites a baptized man and a baptized woman forever in love as husband and wife.

For more on the teachings of the Catholic Church on the Sacraments at the Service of Communion, see *Catechism of the Catholic Church* paragraph numbers 1533–1589 and 1601–1658.

Sharing God's Word

Read together the Bible story in John 13:1–17 about Jesus washing the disciples' feet or read the adaptation of the story on page 146. Emphasize that at the Last Supper Jesus taught the disciples to serve others as he did.

Praying

In this chapter your child prayed a prayer of intercession asking God to bless all those who serve the Church. Read and pray together the prayer on page 151.

Making a Difference

Choose one of the following activities to do as a family or design a similar activity of your own.

- As a family, choose one thing you can do this week to serve others as Jesus did.

- Name some of the ways young people can keep the promises made at Baptism and live as signs of God's love in the world. Talk about how a family can help the young people in a family keep those promises.

- Talk about how your family can serve others and be a sign of God's love. Join with other members of your family and do one of those things.

For more ideas on ways your family can live your faith, visit the "Faith First for Families" page at **www.FaithFirst.com**. Visit the "Games" site this week. Ask your child to show you the game they like most. Play it together.

Evaluate

Take a few moments to evaluate this week's lesson.
I feel (circle one) about this week's lesson.

   a. very pleased
   b. OK
   c. disappointed

The activity the children enjoyed most was . . .

The concept that was most difficult to teach was . . .

because . . .

Something I would like to do differently is . . .

ENRICHING THE LESSON

Dramatizing the Scripture Story

Purpose

To reinforce that at the Last Supper Jesus taught his Apostles to serve others as he did (taught on page 146)

Directions

John 13:4–5, 15 is a wonderful Gospel story to have the children role-play.

- Have the children work with partners. Provide a bowl of water and a towel. Invite each pair to wash each other's hands.
- As the children finish washing their partner's hands, have them say in their own words Jesus' message of service, "I have given you an example. Do what I have done."

Materials

water
bowls
towels

Completing Sacrament Booklets

Purpose

To reinforce what the children have learned about the sacraments (taught in chapters 11 through 17)

Directions

- Have the children complete their sacrament booklets with words and drawings for the sacraments of Holy Orders and Matrimony.
- Have the children display their sacrament booklets in a place appropriate for everyone to enjoy.
- Remind the children to keep their sacrament booklets so that next year they can add more to the booklets.

Materials

sacrament booklets
construction paper
markers, pens or pencils

Literature Connection

Purpose

To reinforce the concept of serving others in need (taught on page 149)

Directions

- Ask children who are familiar with *The Quiltmaker's Gift* to tell about it. Point out that the new story is a prequel, describing events that happened earlier in the generous woman's life.
- *The Quiltmaker's Journey* (Orchard Books, 2005) tells the story of the wise woman's youth and how she turned from a selfish young woman into a wise and compassionate woman devoted to the needs of others.
- While the book is beautifully illustrated, it is a bit lengthy. Choose a few incidents from the woman's young life to read aloud that illustrate her selfishness. Be sure to show the illustrations.
- Read aloud one incident that shows how the woman's heart begins to change and then read the conclusion. Ask the children to work in small groups to name the main point of the story.

Materials

The Quiltmaker's Gift by Jeff Brumbeau

Music Connection

- "God Has Chosen Me," B. Farrell. *Singing Our Faith (SOF)* #204.
- "Here I Am, Lord," D. Schutte. *SOF* #211.
- "I Say 'Yes,'/Digo Sí, Señor," D. Peña. *SOF* #218.
- "Walk in the Light," C. Walker. *Rise Up and Sing* #282.

Unit 2 Review

The unit review provides the opportunity to assess the children's understanding of the concepts presented in the unit and to affirm them in their growing knowledge and love of God.

Here are a few suggestions for using these pages:
- Share that the next two pages are an opportunity to stop and review what they have learned.
- Provide time for the children to ask questions.
- Have the children complete the review alone or with a partner.

PART A:
The Best Word or Phrase

This section reviews the main concepts of the unit.
- Read the directions for section A. Illustrate what you expect the children to do by completing the first question together. By working together on the first question, you are teaching the children a strategy for answering these types of questions.
- When the children have finished this section, invite volunteers to share their answers. Review any questions that the children seem to have difficulty answering.

FAMILY CONNECTION

Encourage the children to share the unit review pages with their families. This provides an excellent opportunity to involve the families in the faith formation of their children.

 **Review Unit 2**   Name _____

A. The Best Word or Phrase

Complete the sentences. Circle the best choice under each sentence.

1. The Church gathers all year long to _____ God.
   (a. worship)   b. greet   c. sing to

2. The Church's year of worship is called the _____ .
   a. holy year   b. Christian year   (c. liturgical year)

3. _____ includes all the weeks of the Church's year that are not part of Advent, Christmas, Lent, or Easter.
   a. Springtime   b. Wintertime   (c. Ordinary Time)

4. _____ completes our Baptism and helps us bring Jesus to the world.
   (a. Confirmation)   b. Penance   c. Marriage

5. The Church brings the _____ to the elderly, sick, or those in the hospital.
   a. Bible   (b. Blessed Sacrament) c. collection

6. Reconciliation is one of the two Sacraments of _____ .
   a. Initiation   (b. Healing)   c. Service

7. A _____ is a sign of God's power at work in the world.
   (a. miracle)   b. parable   c. Bible

8. Holy Orders and _____ are the two Sacraments at the Service of Communion.
   a. Baptism   b. Confirmation   (c. Matrimony)

153

Teaching Tip

Assessment as Affirmation. Assessment is a time of affirmation. Affirm the children in all that they have learned. Point out their many positive efforts. Avoid criticizing them for the things you discover that they have not learned so well. Use these discoveries as opportunities to reinforce these concepts during the remaining sessions when it is appropriate. Remember that *Faith First* is a spiral curriculum. The children will be reintroduced to the key concepts of the faith year after year, building upon what has already been learned.

B. Words and Meanings

Draw a line to connect the words to their clues.

Words	Clues
Baptism	The grace of Baptism is strengthened.
Confirmation	Sins committed after Baptism are forgiven.
Eucharist	A person is born into the Church family.
Reconciliation	Bread and wine become the Body and Blood of Christ.
Anointing of the Sick	A baptized man and a baptized woman become husband and wife.
Matrimony	A baptized man becomes a bishop, priest, or deacon.
Holy Orders	We are strengthened in times of serious illness.

C. What I Have Learned

1. What are two new things you learned in this unit?

    Affirm appropriate responses.

    _____

2. Look back at the list of faith words on page 96. Circle the words you now know. Tell your group the meaning of two of the words.

D. From a Scripture Story

Complete the diagram. Tell how the Pharisee and the tax collector in the parable are alike and how they are different.

Pharisee   **Tax Collector**

Different — Alike — Different

Religious leader, Prayed in center of Temple

Listened to Jesus

Humble and honest, Prayed in back of Temple

Teaching Tip

Another Reminder. As you complete this unit, take the time to reinforce the importance of the faith choices. Have the children share their success stories and discuss with the children any challenges they may have had. Encourage them not to abandon their faith choices if they are not successful in keeping them the first time.

PART B:
Words and Meanings

This section further reinforces the children's understanding of the sacraments.

• Read the directions to the children and together do the first item. Have the children continue working with partners to finish the section.

• Invite volunteers to share their answers.

PART C:
What I Have Learned

This section provides the children the opportunity to write or talk about what they have learned.

• Have the children share with the group two things they remember from the unit chapters.

• Invite the children to return to the unit opener pages and affirm how they have grown in building a faith vocabulary.

PART D:
From a Scripture Story

This section is a review of the parable of the Pharisee and the Tax Collector. Have the children work with partners to retell the parable and complete the activity. Have each pair of students share their responses with the entire class.

Unit 3 Opener

The unit opener pages use a variety of questioning techniques to assess the children's prior knowledge about the key faith concepts presented in the unit. Processing these pages should not take more than ten or fifteen minutes.

USING ILLUSTRATIONS

Pictures help stimulate the religious imaginations of the children. The pictures on page 155 illustrate some of the important faith concepts in the unit.

- Invite the children to look at and think about the pictures.
- Ask volunteers to describe what each picture says to them.
- Invite the children to share a response to the question.

Unit 3 • We Live

What things do Christians do to live the Commandments?

155

Teaching Tip

Visual Learners. *Faith First Legacy* acknowledges that contemporary youth live in a visual world. The *Faith First Legacy* catechetical process builds on this characteristic of the twenty-first century learner. Throughout the *Faith First Legacy* texts, the minds of the young learners are first engaged by visuals that draw them into the mysteries of faith. The written text then opens up in more detail the teachings of the Catholic Church on the faith concepts presented in the lesson.

Getting Ready

What I Have Learned

What is something you already know about these faith words?

Loving God

Responses will vary.

_____

Loving others

Responses will vary.

_____

Words to Know

Put an X next to the faith words you know. Put a ? next to the faith words you need to know more about.

Faith Words   Responses will vary.

_____ Covenant

_____ Great Commandment

_____ Ten Commandments

_____ obey

_____ Psalms

_____ stewards

_____ grace

_____ heaven

Questions I Have

What question would you like to ask about living the Ten Commandments?

Responses will vary.

_____

A Scripture Story

Jesus teaching the Great Commandment

How does the Great Commandment help us live as followers of Jesus?

Responses will vary.
Affirm appropriate responses.

156

Faith Vocabulary

Religious Literacy. The "Faith Words" feature in each chapter is one way in which the children are building religious literacy as Catholics. Through the acquisition of a faith vocabulary the children develop the language to express Catholic belief. At the outset of each unit, the "Words to Know" feature forecasts the new words that the upcoming chapters will address. In each chapter the children will work with these words and create word cards for them. In the unit review they will have the opportunity to review the words once again. The Glossary on pages 297–301 of the student book contains all the faith words taught in the text.

GETTING READY

The "Getting Ready" pages help the children share prior knowledge and assist you in planning your lessons to meet the children's needs.

What I Have Learned

Ask the children to write one thing they know about loving God and loving others.

Words to Know

This section is a quick assessment of the children's familiarity with some of the faith vocabulary they will be learning. Have them put an X next to terms they already know and a ? next to the terms they need to learn more about. During the review for this unit, the children will be asked to return to this page and once again share their understanding of the "Faith Vocabulary" terms.

Questions I Have

Invite the children to write one question they have about the Ten Commandments. Ask volunteers to share their questions aloud. You may wish to write their questions on a chart. As you work through the unit, always refer back to the chart and ask volunteers to respond when they can answer the questions.

A Scripture Story

Unit 3 will review the Scripture story about Jesus teaching the Great Commandment. Have the children look at the picture and answer the question to help you assess their prior knowledge of this story.

Apprentices of Christ the Master

Disciples are apprentices. They are actively engaged in learning a trade, art, or calling by practice and experience under a skilled worker. Christian disciples are apprentices learning from Christ. There is comfort in knowing that disciples of Christ are lifelong apprentices. We are always learning from the Master. The call to be a disciple does not mean we have to be perfect now. It does mean that we are graced by the Holy Spirit to follow the ways of Jesus and strive for perfection.

Christian discipleship is rooted in the law of love. As disciples of Jesus, we are on the way of conversion. We are on the way of continuously deepening our union with Jesus and achieving the goal of living the law of love that Jesus taught us, especially among our families, friends, coworkers, and neighbors. Often it is these very people who, in turn, cause us to stop and think about how we are growing as disciples of Christ. They call us to a radical conversion of heart because of the very way they, too, are living the law of love.

Faith Without Works Is Dead

It is not enough for disciples of Christ to "be good;" we also have to "do good." It is in the doing that others are drawn into relationship with God who is the source of all love.

> Be doers of the word and not hearers only, deluding yourselves. What good is it, my brothers [and sisters], if someone says he has faith but does not have works? Can that faith save him? If a brother or sister has nothing to wear and has no food for the day, and one of you says to them, "Go in peace, keep warm, and eat well," but you do not give them the necessities of the body, what good is it? So also faith of itself, if it does not have works, is dead. JAMES 1:22, 2:14–17

The Church, through the activity of the Holy Spirit, helps us become and live as authentic disciples of Jesus. We are enriched and inspired by hearing the word of God; by celebrating the sacraments, especially the Eucharist; by becoming people of prayer; and by practicing the virtues.

The disciple of Christ is challenged to more than living a private life of holiness and virtue. The follower of Jesus is charged with the task of spreading the mission of Jesus Christ and making disciples of all peoples. We do this by professing our faith through both our words and our actions. Whenever we share our stories of God's presence and guidance in our lives, in good and difficult times, we proclaim the Good News. We continue the work of Christ, our Teacher and Master.

For Reflection

Who are some of the people who, by their words and example, have taught me to grow as a disciple of Christ?

What are some of the effective ways I have lived the law of love of Christ?

Catechist to Catechist

A Call to Love

There is an ancient prayer that gets right to the heart of the message of this chapter: "Lord, I want to go where you want me to go, do what you want me to do, be what you want me to be." The Great Commandment is the key to living this prayer. It calls us to love God wholly and to love our neighbor as we love ourselves. In teaching the Great Commandment, Jesus not only tells us about love, but also shows us how to love.

Jesus Our Teacher

Third graders put much faith and trust in their teachers. They have a right to expect that their teachers will guide them honestly and correctly. As you interact with the children, try to teach as Jesus did. Help the children come to appreciate Jesus as their greatest Teacher. Point out that Jesus' commandment of love is a commandment for us today and not just for the people of Bible times.

The Church Teaches . . .

Jesus taught us to live the covenant by his example. *Sharing the Light of Faith: National Catechetical Directory for Catholics in the United States*, which was published in 1979, teaches: "Love implies an absolute demand for justice, namely a recognition of the dignity and rights of one's neighbor."[1] Justice is therefore the foundation of charity. . . . It is impossible to give of oneself in love without first sharing with others what is due them in justice. This can be expressed very succinctly by saying that justice is love's absolute minimum. *NCD 165*

As Christians we are challenged to live the Great Commandment.

See the Catechism . . .

For more on the teachings of the Catholic Church on the Covenant and the Great Commandment, see *Catechism of the Catholic Church* 54–67, 2052–2055, and 2083.

CATECHIST PRAYER

Holy Spirit of divine love, grow strong within the children and me. Help me reach out to others and share the gift of your love. Amen.

Footnote references may be found on p. 456.

LESSON PLANNER

Engage

Page 157
Focus

To assess the children's knowledge about what the Bible tells us about God's promises

Opening Prayer

Discussion

Promises we make that are difficult to keep

Teach and Apply

Pages 158–160
Focus

To discover the meaning of the Covenant God made with his people and how Jesus taught us to live the Covenant

Presentation

Read, discuss, and summarize content.

Scripture

- Psalm 119:33, Matthew 22:35–40

Activities

- Explain how God kept his promise.
- Identify ways you can live the Great Commandment.
- Identify ways others are living the Great Commandment.

Connect

Pages 161–162
Focus

To discover ways the Church lives the Great Commandment

Our Church Makes a Difference

Some teachers of our Church have formed religious communities dedicated to teaching young people.

Our Catholic Faith
Cathedrals

What Difference Does Faith Make?
Activity

Draw yourself living the Great Commandment.

Faith Choice

Choose a way you will live the Great Commandment this week.

We Pray

Page 163
Prayer Form
Praise
Prayer
Play appropriate music. Introduce the prayer and pray together.

We Remember

Review

- Complete the true or false activity.
- Read the "To Help You Remember" statements aloud.

Preview

Highlight features of the "With My Family" page.

Materials

- music to play during celebration
- pens or pencils
- crayons or markers

Enriching the Session

Blackline Masters
Additional Activities booklet:
  Chapter 18
    Making a book
    Solving a code
Assessment Tools booklet:
  Chapter 18 Test

Enriching the Lesson (CG page 269)
Making Great Commandment Posters and Collages
Creating a Slogan
Literature Connection

Music Connection (CG page 269)

www.FaithFirst.com

We update the *Faith First* Web site weekly. Check each week for new content and features. Here are some places to begin:

Catechists and Teachers
- Current Events
- Chapter Downloads
- Catechist Prayer

Faith First **for Families**
- Bible Stories
- Make a Difference

Kids' Clubhouse
- *Faith First* Activities
- Chapter Reviews
- Games
- Saints

Don't Forget! You can make lesson planning a breeze—check out the **Online Lesson Planner.**

Jesus Teaches Us How to Love

A Scripture Story

We Pray

Teach me your ways,
O LORD.
Based on Psalm 119:33

**God of love,
may we do what
you ask of us.**
Amen.

*What promises have
you made?*

Promises are
important to keep.
The Bible tells us that
God made and keeps
his promises to us.

*What did God
promise us?*

157

Teaching Tip

The Love of Jesus. In the Great Commandment, Jesus reminds us of the heart of the Covenant God entered into with his people—love. Jesus not only tells us about love, but also shows us how to love. Jesus is the fullness of God's revelation. Keep in mind that as you teach the children, you are helping them come to know Jesus, our Teacher. Practice living Jesus' new commandment of love (see John 13:34–35) in the classroom, and create opportunities for the children to live it as well.

Engage

PRAY

- Gather the children and have them quiet themselves for prayer.
- Pray the Sign of the Cross.
- Ask a volunteer to read the Psalm verse.
- Pray the opening prayer together.
- Close the prayer with the Sign of the Cross.

DISCOVER

Purpose: To assess what the children know about the Great Commandment

- Ask: What promises have you made? Why are they sometimes difficult to keep?
- Invite the children to look at the picture. Ask the children what kinds of promises the two boys might have made to each other.
- Ask the children if they know what promise God made to us.

Teach

FOCUS

Ask a volunteer to read the "Faith Focus" question aloud. Share with the children that in this chapter they will learn how we show that we are friends of God.

DISCOVER

- Tell the children that the story on this page tells about God's greatest promise to us.
- Invite the children to silently read "God's Special Promise" to learn what this promise is called. The Covenant.
- Draw three boxes on the board. Ask volunteers to tell what happened in the beginning, middle, and end of the story. Adam and Eve sinned; God promised to make people and God friends again; God sent his Son, Jesus.

Apply

REINFORCE

Ask the children to read aloud together the faith word *covenant* and its meaning. Have the children make a word card for *covenant*.

INTEGRATE

Have the children complete the activity at the bottom of the page.

Bible Background

Faith Focus

How can we show that we are friends of God?

Faith Words

Covenant
The Covenant is the solemn agreement of friendship made between God and his people.

Great Commandment
The Great Commandment is the commandment of love that all of God's laws depend on.

God's Special Promise

In the very beginning of the Bible we read that our first parents made a promise to God. They promised to obey God. But our first parents, whom the Bible calls Adam and Eve, did not keep their promise and sinned. We call this broken promise original sin. They lost the happiness God had given them.

God made a promise to the first humans after they sinned. He would send someone to make people and God friends again. This promise is called the **Covenant.**

God kept his promise. He sent his Son, Jesus. Jesus made us friends with God again.

Put a ✔ next to the ways that show you are living as a friend of God. Then write two more ways you are living as a friend of God.

- ❏ Take part in Mass on Sunday.
- ❏ Honor my parents.
- ❏ Tell the truth.
- ❏ Play fairly at recess.
- ❏ Respect what belongs to others.

Responses will vary.

Affirm appropriate responses.

(158)

Background: Doctrine

First Promise of the Covenant. In the Bible we read about the Covenant with Noah, Abraham, and Moses, the leader of God's people, Israel. However, in the story of the fall of Adam and Eve from God's grace, the Church sees the first promise of the Redeemer. In that story God speaks to the serpent promising enmity between the offspring of the serpent and that of the woman. God says that while the serpent will strike at the heel, the woman's offspring (ultimately Jesus Christ) will strike at the head of the serpent, thus destroying it (see Genesis 3:15). Jesus is the everlasting Covenant, who overcomes evil and redeems humankind.

Reading the Word of God

The Great Commandment

Jesus taught what it means to live the Covenant. He reminded God's people to live the **Great Commandment.** Read what happened.

A teacher of the law asked Jesus, "Which of the commandments of God is the greatest commandment?"

Jesus answered, "'Love God with all your heart, soul, and mind.' This is the greatest and the first commandment."

Jesus did not stop there. He continued, "The second commandment is like it: 'You shall love your neighbor as yourself.' The whole law depends on these two commandments."

Based on Matthew 22:35–40

These two commandments of God make up the Great Commandment. When we live the Great Commandment, we live the Covenant. We keep our promises to God.

Name two ways the Church helps us live the Great Commandment.

Responses will vary. Affirm appropriate responses.

159

Teaching Tip

Classroom Rules. Make a list of your classroom rules and have the children tell how each rule helps us to show our respect and love for one another. Then have the children vote on the rule they think is the most important. After you tally the votes, print the rule with the most votes on poster board as a reminder for the children.

Teach

FOCUS

Remind the children that God always keeps his promises. Then point out that the Great Commandment helps us live the Covenant and keep our promises to God.

DISCOVER

- Set the scene for the Scripture story based on Matthew 22:35–40 by presenting the introductory paragraph in your own words.
- As you read the Scripture story, ask the children to listen for the answer Jesus gave the teacher of the law.
- Ask the children to underline the two parts of the Great Commandment and invite them to read it aloud with you.

Apply

REINFORCE

Ask the children what it means to love another person as you love yourself. To treat others with dignity and respect as children of God.

INTEGRATE

Challenge the children to name two ways in which the Church helps them live the Great Commandment. The Church teaches us and shows us by example how to live the Great Commandment.

Teach

FOCUS

Remind the children that the Great Commandment helps us live the Covenant. Tell them they are going to learn more about what it means to love God and others.

DISCOVER

- Ask the children to read silently the second paragraph of "Love God and Others."
- Ask the children why it is important to live both parts of the Great Commandment. The two parts form one Great Commandment.

Apply

REINFORCE

- Divide the class into groups of four and give each group a sheet of newsprint and markers.
- Assign one part of the Great Commandment to each group.
- Have them list ways to live their part of the Great Commandment.

INTEGRATE

- Ask the children to share what they discussed in their groups.
- Have the children complete the activity and then share their work with a partner.

Understanding the Word of God

Love God and Others

We keep our promises to God when we live the Great Commandment. The Great Commandment has two parts. The first part is that we are to love God. The second part is that we are to love others as we love ourselves. The two parts form one Great Commandment.

We need to live both parts of the Great Commandment. We cannot only show our love for God through prayer and worship. We also need to show our love for God by the way we treat ourselves and other people.

Jesus taught us that loving others includes loving our enemies. This is not an easy thing to do.

Tell how the children in the pictures are living the Great Commandment. In the space write about or draw yourself living the Great Commandment.

Affirm appropriate responses.

160

Teaching Tip

Group Work. Use group work as an opportunity for the children to show their love for their neighbors. Before dividing children into groups, remind them of the Great Commandment and then follow the helpful hints below.

1. Limit the size of the group to three or four children.
2. Give the children a specific task. If it has several parts, write them on the board.
3. Give the children a definite time limit to complete their work.
4. Assign a group leader to keep the task on track.
5. Always honor each group's work by asking for a report.

Our Church Makes a Difference

Teaching Communities

There have been many great teachers in our Church. Some of these teachers formed religious communities that are dedicated to teaching young people. Saint Angela Merici and Saint John Baptist de La Salle are two of these teachers.

Saint Angela Merici founded the Company of St. Ursula. The Ursuline Sisters were the first religious community of women dedicated to teaching.

Saint John Baptist de La Salle founded the Brothers of the Christian Schools. The Christian Brothers are dedicated to teaching young people, especially the poor. In 1950, the Church proclaimed de La Salle the patron of all teachers.

In all their teaching, the Ursulines and the Christian Brothers teach young people to grow in their love for Jesus. Their schools teach young people to prepare for the coming of the kingdom of God by living the Great Commandment.

Name someone who teaches you how to live the Great Commandment.

Our Catholic Faith

Virtues

You teach others by how you act. One way you do this is by living the virtues. Virtues are habits of doing good things. Living a life of virtue means getting into the habit of doing good things for others and for yourself. It is what living the Great Commandment is all about.

161

Background: Our Catholic Faith

Living a Life of Virtue. Virtues are spiritual powers or habits or behaviors that help us live the Great Commandment. The virtues help us build healthy relationships both with God and with other people. They are firm dispositions, or attitudes, that strengthen us to live the new life in Christ that we receive in Baptism.

Connect

HIGHLIGHT

Share that some members of the Church have formed religious communities dedicated to teaching us to live the Great Commandment.

DISCOVER

- Ask the children to answer the question on the bottom of the page by naming some of the people who have taught them about the Great Commandment.
- Introduce "Teaching Communities" by summarizing the first paragraph.
- Ask volunteers to read the next three paragraphs.
- Make a Venn diagram comparing Saint Angela de Merici and Saint John Baptist de la Salle. Draw two overlapping circles on the board with the names of the two saints above each circle. Write "Different" in the outside circles and "Alike" in the overlapping part. Ask the children to help you fill in the diagram.

INTEGRATE

- Have the children read "Our Catholic Faith" to discover what virtues are.
- Explain to the children that they, too, are teachers. They teach by acts of practicing the virtues.

Connect

HIGHLIGHT

Remind the children that the Holy Spirit gives them the grace to live the Great Commandment.

RESPOND

- Direct the children's attention to the activity while you explain the directions.
- Give the children time to draw themselves living the Great Commandment. Ask volunteers to share their work.

CHOOSE

- Invite the children to respond to "My Faith Choice."
- After a moment of prayerful reflection have the children write their choice on the lines provided.
- Encourage the children to put their choice into practice this week.

What Difference Does Faith Make in My Life?

The Holy Spirit is always teaching you to live the Great Commandment.

Draw or write about yourself living the Great Commandment. Share your story with someone.

Living the Great Commandment

My Faith Choice

This week I will try to live the Great Commandment. I will

Affirm appropriate responses.

162

Catholic Social Teaching

Solidarity of the Human Family. We are all a part of a single human family and are responsible for one another. Solidarity is an awareness of this interdependence that flows from our common dignity as humans and from Jesus' command to love our neighbors as ourselves. We are obligated to serve the common good and to protect the rights of each individual person.

Tip: Share with the children that the Great Commandment guides us in supporting the basic human rights of all people.

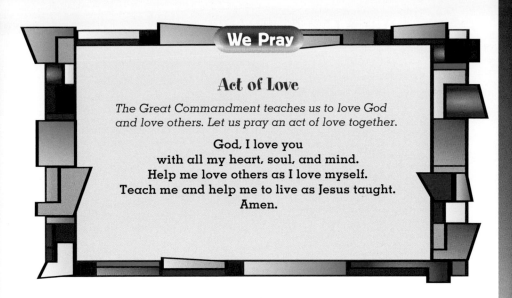

We Pray

Act of Love

The Great Commandment teaches us to love God and love others. Let us pray an act of love together.

**God, I love you
with all my heart, soul, and mind.
Help me love others as I love myself.
Teach me and help me to live as Jesus taught.
Amen.**

We Remember

*Circle the **T** next to the statement if it is true. Circle the **F** if the statement is false. Make any false statements true.*

1. Original sin is the name we give to Adam and Eve breaking their promise to God. (T) F

2. The Commandment is the solemn agreement of friendship made between God and his people. T (F)

3. The Great Commandment shows us how to find true happiness with God now on earth and forever in heaven. T (F)

To Help You Remember

1. We show we are friends of God when we keep our promise to live the Covenant.

2. We live the Covenant when we love God with our whole heart.

3. We live the Covenant when we love other people as we love ourselves.

Grade 3 • Chapter 18 163

Pray

WE PRAY

- Play a recording of appropriate background music as you gather the children for prayer.
- Explain that the prayer today is "Act of Love."
- Prepare the children by reading the opening paragraph.
- Lead the prayer and have the children echo each line after you. All respond "Amen" together.

Review

WE REMEMBER

- Ask: How are the faith words *Covenant* and *Great Commandment* connected?
- Check answers by asking volunteers to read aloud each "To Help You Remember" statement.
- Introduce the activity and allow time for the children to complete it. Ask the children to tell which statement is false and then correct it.

Liturgy Tip

Meditation. Encourage the children to use the Gospel story of the Great Commandment as a prayer meditation at home this week. Give them the following helpful hints on a separate sheet of paper.

- Be very quiet and still.
- Read the Scripture story silently.
- Place yourself in the Gospel story.
- Think about what God might be saying to you.
- Think about what you want to tell God.
- Share with Jesus how you will try to live as his follower.

At Home

ENCOURAGE

Have the children carefully tear out pages 163 and 164 along the perforation. Encourage the children to share the pages with their families and to do the activities together. If they did not complete the review activity on page 163 by the end of the session, emphasize that they can complete it with their families.

VISIT FAITHFIRST.COM

- Share with the children the many activities on the *Faith First* Web site.
- Encourage the children to visit **www.FaithFirst.com.**

18 With My Family

This Week . . .

In chapter 18, "Jesus Teaches Us How to Love: A Scripture Story," your child learned about the Covenant, or solemn agreement of friendship made between God and his people. The Covenant included the promise to send someone to restore all people to a life of friendship and happiness with God now and forever in heaven. God fulfilled this promise and sent his Son, Jesus, the new and everlasting Covenant. Jesus revealed that we live the Covenant when we live the Great Commandment.

For more on the teachings of the Catholic Church on the Covenant and the Great Commandment, see *Catechism of the Catholic Church* paragraph numbers 54–67, 2052–2055, and 2083.

Sharing God's Word

Read together the Bible story in Matthew 22:34–40 about the Great Commandment or read the adaptation of the story on page 159. Emphasize that Jesus taught that all of the Law of God depends on the Great Commandment.

Praying

In this chapter your child prayed an act of love. Read and pray together the prayer on page 163.

Making a Difference

Choose one of the following activities to do as a family or design a similar activity of your own.

- Invite each family member to share the names of people who have taught them to live the Great Commandment. Thank God for these wonderful people!

- Catechists, or religion teachers, live the Great Commandment when they teach us. Make thank-you cards for your catechists. Thank them for teaching you about the Great Commandment.

- Talk about how your family can live the Great Commandment. As a family, choose one thing you can do this week to live the Great Commandment.

For more ideas on ways your family can live your faith, visit the "Faith First for Families" page at **www.FaithFirst.com**. Click on "Make a Difference" for ideas on how your family can live the Great Commandment.

Before Moving On . . .

As you finish today's lesson, reflect on the following question before moving on to the next chapter.

How much of an effort do I make to reinforce and summarize before moving on to a new concept?

Evaluate

Take a few moments to evaluate this week's lesson.
I feel (circle one) about this week's lesson.

- a. very pleased
- b. OK
- c. disappointed

The activity the children enjoyed most was . . .

The concept that was most difficult to teach was . . .

because . . .

Something I would like to do differently is . . .

ENRICHING THE LESSON

Making Great Commandment Collages

Purpose

To reinforce living the Great Commandment (taught on pages 159 and 160)

Directions

- Invite the children to create a collage about living the Great Commandment.
- Have the children look through magazines and cut out pictures that show examples of people living the two parts of the Great Commandment.
- Then have them glue their pictures on a sheet of poster board. Have the children create a title for their posters using letters from the magazines.
- Display the posters where others can enjoy them.

Materials

magazines
scissors and glue sticks
poster board

Creating a Slogan

Purpose

To reinforce ways we live both parts of the Great Commandment (taught on page 160)

Directions

- Have the children work in small groups to reread Matthew 22:35–40 on page 159.
- Invite the children to create a catchy slogan that encourages people to live the Great Commandment.
- Distribute a sentence strip and markers to each group. Have the children write their slogans on the sentence strips.
- Discuss the slogans the groups have created.

Materials

Literature Connection

Purpose

To help the children understand in a more practical way the teaching of the Great Commandment (taught on page 160)

Directions:

- *Love Your Neighbor* by Melody Carlson (Broadman & Holman Publishers, (2002) is a wonderful story that teaches children how to truly love their neighbors even if they are not so easy to get along with.
- Invite the children to listen as you read the book aloud.
- Have the children work with partners to write another episode for the book using what they have learned about what Jesus would have said or done.
- If time allows have the children put their episode in cartoon format on construction paper for everyone to enjoy.

Materials

Love Your Neighbor by Melody Carlson
paper
crayons or markers

Music Connection

- "Come to My Heart," J. Pinson. *Rise Up and Sing (RUS)* #288.
- "God's Greatest Gift," O. Alstott. *RUS* #205.
- "No Greater Love," M. Joncas. *Gather Comprehensive* #628.
- "Shalom" (Jewish melody traditional). *RUS* #188.

The Ten Commandments Teach Us to Love

God Is Love

God created everything out of his goodness and love. For love of humankind, God the Father gave his only Son for our salvation, bringing us out of the bondage of sin and death. Both the Old Testament and the New Testament reveal that God is worthy of our complete and unconditional love. God, in whom we place our trust, is love.

> Whoever is without love does not know God, for God is love. In this way the love of God was revealed to us: God sent his only Son into the world so that we might have life through him. In this is love: not that we have loved God, but that he loved us and sent his Son as expiation for our sins. Beloved, if God so loved us, we also must love one another. No one has ever seen God. Yet, if we love one another, God remains in us, and his love is brought to perfection in us.   1 *JOHN* 4:8–12

How are we to respond to this Covenant?

Love of God

Our first response is to honor God by following his Commandments. The first three of the Ten Commandments are focused on love of God. Making God the prime focus of our lives, using his name with reverence and keeping the Lord's Day holy are the essence of these laws of love.

Our faith in God is evidenced by the ways in which divine love permeates our attitudes and actions. In word and deed we live in hope and confidence of divine goodness and mercy. Loving God as our response to his unfathomable love is demonstrated in our respect for him and our neighbors.

The biblical account of creation tells us when God's work of creation was finished, "he rested on the seventh day . . . [and] blessed the seventh day and

made it holy," (Genesis 2:2–3). Christians rest from their work on Sunday and keep it holy as the Lord's Day. On the Lord's Day, the Church gathers to worship God by celebrating the saving work of Jesus and giving thanks for the Resurrection. The Lord's Day is also observed by taking the time in our busy schedules to rest, to cultivate relationships, and to grow in the spiritual life.

Our love for God is initiated by his great love for us. We respond not only by following the letter of the Commandments, but also by cultivating the spirit of love for God in all our attitudes and actions.

For Reflection

What does God's revelation of himself, "God is love," say to me about my relationship with him?

What are some of the ways that I express my love for God? How are these related to the first three Commandments?

Catechist to Catechist

Keep Holy the Lord's Day

We live the Third Commandment by keeping the Lord's Day holy. Sunday is the Lord's Day for Christians. Catholics primarily keep Sunday holy by worshiping God by taking part in the celebration of Mass. We also spend time with our families and friends. In our contemporary society, finding time for family and friends seems to be getting more and more difficult to do. God's command to keep holy the Lord's Day addresses this issue. This Commandment includes both taking part in Mass and avoiding all that keeps us away from living as children of God. Keeping the Lord's Day holy calls us to take the time for one another and keep God at the center of our family life.

Family Time

Family time has become a precious commodity today. Many parents work long hours, and children are involved in numerous extra-curricular activities. Life just seems to be busier than ever. We need to find ways to make Sunday and our time with our families special. Help the children and their families grow in appreciating the wisdom of this Commandment. Families whose jobs involve unavoidable Sunday schedules can find another day or time to be together.

The Church Teaches . . .

One of the first catechetical documents after Vatican II, *To Teach as Jesus Did*, pointed out the need for catechists to do more than teach facts. It states:
Merely 'teaching about' religion is not enough. Instead such programs must strive to teach doctrine fully, foster community, and prepare their students for Christian service.   *TJD 87*

This is why it is important that you not only teach about the Ten Commandments but also help children practice applying them in daily life.

See the Catechism . . .

For more on the teachings of the Catholic Church on the Trinity as a divine communion of love and on the first three Commandments, see *Catechism of the Catholic Church* 218–221, 253–256, 2084–2132, 2142–2159, and 2168–2188.

CATECHIST PRAYER

*Spirit of God,
you led Moses up
Mount Sinai.
Lead me to
your love too.
Amen.*

LESSON PLANNER

FOCUS — To discover ways the First, Second, and Third Commandments teach us to love God

Engage

Page 165
Focus

To assess the children's knowledge about the Ten Commandments

Opening Prayer

Discussion

How the Ten Commandments help us love God, others, and ourselves

Teach and Apply

Pages 166–168
Focus

To identify the Ten Commandments and describe what the First, Second, and Third Commandments teach us

Presentation

Read, discuss, and summarize content.

Scripture
- Psalm 1:1–2
- Exodus 20:2–3, 7, 8

Activities
- Describe the importance of the Ten Commandments.
- Name a way to live each of the first three Commandments.
- Unscramble letters to discover how we are to love others.

Faith-Filled People
Saint John the Apostle

Connect

Pages 169–170
Focus

To discover how churches as we know them came about

Our Church Makes a Difference

Every church is a sign of the faith in God of the people who built it.

Our Catholic Faith
Cathedrals

What Difference Does Faith Make?

Activity

Identify ways you celebrate Sunday as a holy day.

Faith Choice

Choose a way to show God your love and respect for him this week.

We Pray

Page 171
Prayer Form
Adoration
Prayer
Lead or choose a leader. Play appropriate music. Introduce the prayer and assign roles. Pray together.

We Remember

Review
- Complete the fill-in activity.
- Read the "To Help You Remember" statements aloud.

Preview
Highlight features of the "With My Family" page.

Materials

- appropriate music
- pens or pencils

Enriching the Session

Blackline Masters
Additional Activities booklet:
Chapter 19
Making puppets
Presenting a play
Assessment Tools booklet:
Chapter 19 Test

Enriching the Lesson (CG page 281)
Reviewing the Ten Commandments
Making Commandment Signposts
Literature Connection

Music Connection (CG page 281)

www.FaithFirst.com

We update the *Faith First* Web site weekly. Check each week for new content and features. Here are some places to begin:

Catechists and Teachers
- Current Events
- Chapter Downloads
- Catechist Prayer

Faith First for Families
- Bible Stories
- Make a Difference

Kids' Clubhouse
- *Faith First* Activities
- Chapter Reviews
- Games
- Saints

Don't Forget! You can make lesson planning a breeze—check out the **Online Lesson Planner.**

The Ten Commandments Teach Us to Love

We Pray

Blessed is the child of God who finds happiness in the law of the LORD.
Based on Psalm 1:1–2

Lord God, thank you for sending us Jesus to teach us how to live as your friends. Amen.

Why do you think it is important to have rules or laws?

Everywhere we go there are rules and laws we must obey. God gave us the Ten Commandments to teach us to love God, others, and ourselves.

What are some of the Ten Commandments you already know?

Tablets containing the Ten Commandments

 165

PRAY

- Gather the children and have them quiet themselves for prayer.
- Pray the Sign of the Cross and invite a volunteer to read the Psalm verse aloud.
- Pray the opening prayer together.

DISCOVER

Purpose: To assess what the children may already know about the Ten Commandments

- Talk with the children about what rules and laws they know. Ask them why they think it is important to obey them.
- Ask the children which of the Ten Commandments they know.
- Invite the children to look at the picture of the stained-glass window. Ask them what the image represents. The Ten Commandments.

✝ Liturgy Tip

Prayer and Music. Children who are musically or rhythmically inclined love to use rhythm instruments. If you have rhythm or percussion instruments, such as drums, maracas, or chimes, you may want to use them as a way to begin the opening prayer. If no instruments are available, you can simply have the children beat out a rhythm for the whole prayer by clapping their hands or tapping on their books. You might also do this for the closing prayer when appropriate.

Teach

FOCUS

Ask a volunteer to read the "Faith Focus" question aloud. Share with the children that in this chapter they will learn how the Ten Commandments help us to love God.

DISCOVER

- Invite the children to read "God's Laws" and underline the name of the person God gave the Ten Commandments to. Moses.
- Assign the parts of the story to the children and invite them to pantomime the actions as you read it.
- Ask the children why God gave the Ten Commandments to the Israelites. To help them live as God's special people.

Apply

REINFORCE

Ask a volunteer to read aloud the faith words *Ten Commandments* and its meaning. Have the children make a word card for this term.

INTEGRATE

Point out the Ten Commandments on page 287 in the children's textbook. Have the children work with partners to complete the activity.

Living the Commandments

Faith Focus

How do the Ten Commandments help us to love God?

Faith Words

Ten Commandments
The Ten Commandments are the laws God gave to Moses on Mount Sinai. They guide us to love God and love others as we love ourselves.

God's Laws

The Bible tells many stories about the Covenant. We read about the covenants God made with Noah and with Abraham. Many years after Abraham, God made a covenant with Moses and God's people, the Israelites. God called Moses up to the top of Mount Sinai and gave him the **Ten Commandments.** Moses took the Commandments that God had given him and went down from the mountain. He explained the laws to the Israelites, who agreed to obey them. The Ten Commandments helped the Israelites to live as God's special people.

Read the Ten Commandments on page 287. Describe why living the Ten Commandments is important.

Responses will vary.
Affirm appropriate responses.

166

Teaching Tip

Pantomiming the Story. Some children express their learning best by using actions rather than words. The use of their bodies also helps them to reinforce key concepts. Occasionally, invite volunteers to take the parts of key characters in Scripture stories and to pantomime their actions as you read the story. You can add simple props to enhance the story, such as a box or crate for Moses to stand on in the story of the Ten Commandments. This reinforces the image of the mountain where God spoke to Moses.

Showing Our Love for God

The first three Commandments help us show our love for God. The First Commandment teaches that we are to worship only God. We are to love and honor God above all else. The First Commandment is

> "I am the LORD your God. You shall not have other gods before me."
>
> Based on Exodus 20:2–3

The Second Commandment teaches that we are to respect the name of God. We are to use God's name truthfully. The Second Commandment is

> "You shall not take the name of the LORD your God in vain." Exodus 20:7

The Third Commandment teaches that we are to keep Sunday holy. Sunday is the Lord's Day. Catholics must take part in the celebration of Mass on Saturday evening or Sunday. The Third Commandment is

> "Remember to keep holy the LORD's Day." Based on Exodus 20:8

✗ Faith-Filled People

John the Apostle
Saint John the Apostle was the brother of James the Apostle and the youngest disciple. John was also one of the Evangelists, or writers of the four Gospels. John taught "God is love." The Church celebrates the feast day of Saint John the Apostle on December 27.

Name one way you can live each of the first three Commandments.

Affirm appropriate responses.

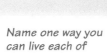

167

✚ Background: Faith-Filled People

Saint John the Evangelist. Saint John the Evangelist was a fisherman. He and his brother were called by Jesus to follow him (Matthew 4:21). Jesus rebuked both brothers with the nickname "Sons of Thunder" because they were eager to cast fire from heaven to punish those who did not welcome Jesus (Luke 9:54–55). Jesus took John, Peter, and James up a mountain to pray, and they saw the heavenly and transfigured glory of Jesus (Luke 9:28–36). Generations of Christians honor John the Evangelist as the "beloved disciple," a tradition based on Jesus entrusting John to take care of Mary at the Crucifixion (John 19:26).

Teach

FOCUS
Remind the children that the Ten Commandments help us love God. Then point out that the First, Second, and Third Commandments help us show our love for God.

DISCOVER
- Ask the children to read aloud together the First Commandment. Suggest that they highlight or underline it. Then have them read silently what the First Commandment teaches.
- Follow the same procedure for the Second and Third Commandments.

Apply

REINFORCE
- Have the children read silently "Faith-Filled People" to find out what Saint John the Apostle teaches about God.
- Ask volunteers to share how we show our love for God when we live the First, Second, and Third Commandments.

INTEGRATE
Have the children work with partners to name ways we can live each of the first three Commandments.

Teach

FOCUS

Remind the children that the first three Commandments help us show our love for God. Tell them they are going to learn more about who helps us to love one another.

DISCOVER

- Invite the children to read silently "God Is Love" to discover what the Holy Trinity teaches us about how to love.
- Ask: How should we love God and one another? We are to love God and others as God loves us.

Apply

REINFORCE

Tell the children that the word *love* is the word that tells us most about God. Ask them to make a list of other words that tell us about God. Possible answers: Creator, faithful, Covenant, Jesus, Mary, Church.

INTEGRATE

- Point out the "How to Love" activity and explain its directions. Be sure to tell the children to let the capital letters help them unscramble the words.
- When all of the children have completed the activity, ask volunteers to share their responses.

God Is Love

The Bible tells us that God is love. The three Persons in God the Holy Trinity love each other with a perfect love.

Jesus taught us that God loves us and shares his love with us. We share in the love of God the Father, God the Son, and God the Holy Spirit. We are to love God and one another as God loves us.

Unscramble the letters. Discover how we are to love others. Let the capital letters help you.

How to Love

evoL	sa
" Love	as

oGd	sevol	oyu.
God	loves	you ."

Based on Matthew 5:48

168

Special Needs

Unscrambling Words. Fill in several of the blanks to help students who have reading or writing deficits. Also provide them with the beginning letter for other words.

Needs: Children with learning deficits or reading deficits

Our Church Makes a Difference

Churches

In the first two hundred years after the first Pentecost, there were no churches like the ones we have today. The community of the Church gathered in homes to hear the Scriptures read, to learn the teachings of the Apostles, and to celebrate Eucharist. It was only after the emperor of Rome gave Christians permission to worship in public that Christians began to build churches.

The first churches were called basilicas. The basilica of Saint John Lateran is the oldest basilica in Rome. It is the cathedral of the bishop of Rome, the pope.

There are many different types of churches. Every church is a sign of the faith in God of the people who built it.

Take a tour of your church. How is your church a sign of the faith of the people of your parish community?

Affirm appropriate responses.

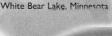

Our Catholic Faith

Cathedrals

The cathedral is the main church of the archdiocese or diocese. It is the archbishop's or bishop's church. The word *cathedral* comes from the word *cathedra* which means "chair." The bishop's chair is a symbol that the bishop is the chief teacher and celebrant of the liturgy of the diocese in the cathedral.

St. Mary of the Lake, White Bear Lake, Minnesota

St. John Lateran, Rome, Italy

St. Mary's, Miami, Florida

169

Teaching Tip

Role-Play Scenarios. Have the children take turns role-playing and then discussing the following scenarios about the first three Commandments.

- Juan likes his group of friends, but lately some of the boys are swearing. Juan knows it's wrong, but he wants to belong. What could Juan do?

- Sabrina and her brother are altar servers. Sabrina is respectful and attentive to the Mass, but her brother isn't. What could Sabrina do?

Connect

HIGHLIGHT

Point out that in the early Church there were no church buildings like we have today.

DISCOVER

- Invite the children to silently read the first paragraph of "Churches" to discover where the early Christians worshiped.
- Have volunteers share one thing they learned.
- Ask volunteers to read aloud the next paragraph and "Our Catholic Faith." Invite volunteers to describe in their own words basilicas and cathedrals.
- If you have pictures of your local cathedral or basilica, bring them in to share with the children. Ask volunteers to share their experiences if they have been to a basilica or cathedral.

INTEGRATE

- Remind the children that every church is a sign of the faith in God of the people who built it.
- If possible, take the children on a tour of the church.
- Divide the class into groups of four. Give the children drawing paper and crayons or markers. Ask them to draw an outline of a church and inside the outline write how their church is a sign of the faith for the people of their parish community.

Connect

HIGHLIGHT

Remind the children that Sunday is the Lord's Day. Each week we join our parish family to show our love and respect for God and one another.

RESPOND

- Read aloud the opening paragraph.
- Then explain the activity and invite the children to share their role-play with the group.

CHOOSE

- Invite the children to respond to "My Faith Choice."
- After a moment of prayerful reflection have the children write their choice on the lines provided.
- Encourage the children to put their choice into practice this week.

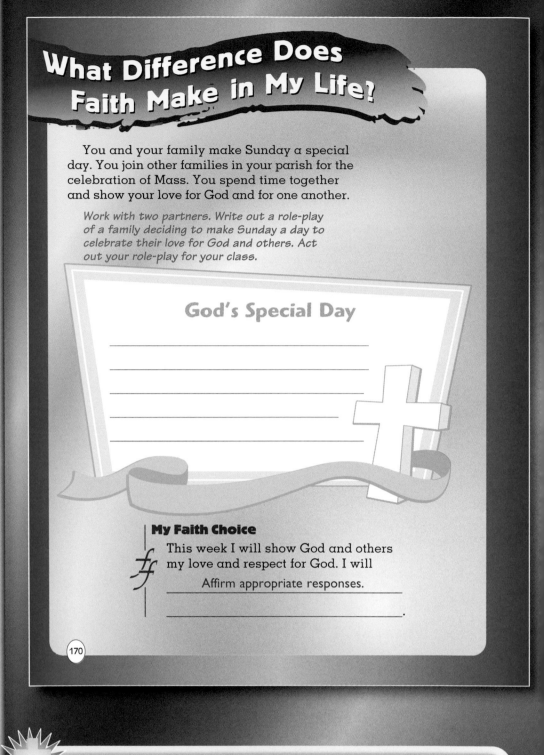

What Difference Does Faith Make in My Life!

You and your family make Sunday a special day. You join other families in your parish for the celebration of Mass. You spend time together and show your love for God and for one another.

Work with two partners. Write out a role-play of a family deciding to make Sunday a day to celebrate their love for God and others. Act out your role-play for your class.

God's Special Day

_____

_____

_____

_____

_____

My Faith Choice

This week I will show God and others my love and respect for God. I will

_____ Affirm appropriate responses. _____

_____.

170

Background: Doctrine

Reverence for the Sacred. The foundation for living the First and Second Commandments are the virtues of religion and reverence. Reverence and respect for the divine name is a respect and reverence for the mystery of God. The teachings of the First and Second Commandments include the respectful treatment in word and deed of all holy people and things. (See *Catechism of the Catholic Church* 2084–2159.)

We Pray

Prayer of Adoration

A prayer of adoration tells God that he alone is God. Pray this prayer together.

Leader: God, we cannot see you, yet we do believe.
All: **We adore you, O God.**

Leader: There is no other God but you.
All: **We adore you, O God.**

Leader: We know you are our God because your Son has told us so.
All: **We adore you, O God.**

Leader: We make our prayer in his name.
All: **Amen.**

We Remember

Complete the Commandments. Fill in the missing words.

1. I am the LORD your _____God_____.
   You shall not have other gods before me.

2. You shall not take the _____name_____ of the LORD your _____God_____ in vain.

3. Remember to keep _____holy_____ the _____Lord's_____ Day.

To Help You Remember

1. The First Commandment teaches us to love God above all else.

2. The Second Commandment teaches us to love God by honoring his name.

3. The Third Commandment teaches us to love God by keeping the Lord's Day holy.

Grade 3 • Chapter 19 (171)

WE PRAY

- Play a recording of appropriate background music as you gather the children in the prayer center.
- Explain that the prayer is a prayer of adoration. Ask four volunteers to pray the "Leader" parts during the prayer.
- Prepare the children by reading the opening paragraph.
- Pray the "Prayer of Adoration" together.

WE REMEMBER

- Introduce the activity and allow the children time to complete it.
- Ask a volunteer to read aloud the First, Second, and Third Commandments and then share what each of the first three Commandments tells us to do.
- Ask the children to check the answers by reading the "To Help You Remember" statements.

✝ Liturgy Tip

Sharing Our Love for God. There is an imaginative legend from Norway saying that God kisses us at the moment we are created. This legend tells us how much God loves us. God's love is so powerful that it helps us extend that love to others. Share this legend with the children to help remind them why we pray prayers of adoration.

At Home

ENCOURAGE

Have the children carefully tear out pages 171 and 172 along the perforation. Encourage the children to share the pages with their families and to do the activities together. If they did not complete the review activity on page 171 by the end of the session, emphasize that they can complete it with their families.

VISIT FAITHFIRST.COM

- Share with the children the many activities on the *Faith First* Web site.
- Encourage the children to visit **www.FaithFirst.com.**

---

19 With My Family

This Week . . .

In chapter 19, "The Ten Commandments Teach Us to Love," your child learned that God gave us the Ten Commandments. The Commandments teach us to love God, ourselves, and others. God gave the Commandments to Moses on Mount Sinai. The First, Second, and Third Commandments teach us to show our love and respect for God, who is love, above all else.

For more on the teachings of the Catholic Church on the Trinity as a divine communion of love and on the first three Commandments, see *Catechism of the Catholic Church* paragraph numbers 218–221, 253–256, 2084–2132 (First Commandment), 2142–2159 (Second Commandment), and 2168–2188 (Third Commandment).

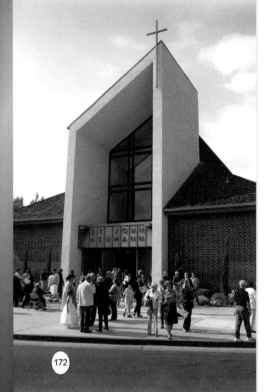

172

Sharing God's Word

Read together the story in Exodus 20:2–17 about the Ten Commandments. Emphasize that the Ten Commandments teach us how to live the Great Commandment.

Praying

In this chapter your child prayed a prayer of adoration. Read and pray together the prayer on page 171.

Making a Difference

Choose one of the following activities to do as a family or design a similar activity of your own.

- Catholics genuflect to show their adoration and respect for God. Share and talk about other prayer gestures the members of your family use to show your love, adoration, and respect for God.

- Invite each family member to share the feast day or holy day of obligation that is their favorite. Talk about how each of these feasts or holy days helps your family show love and respect for God.

- Talk about the ways your family lives the Third Commandment and keeps the Lord's Day holy. As a family, choose one thing you can do this coming Sunday to make the Lord's Day special.

For more ideas on ways your family can live your faith, visit the "Faith First for Families" page at **www.FaithFirst.com.** This week pay special attention to "Questions Kids Ask."

Before Moving On . . .

As you finish today's lesson, reflect on the following question before moving on to the next chapter.

What have I done to let the children know that they are helping me to grow in faith as I work with them?

Evaluate

Take a few moments to evaluate this week's lesson.
I feel (circle one) about this week's lesson.

    a. very pleased
    b. OK
    c. disappointed

The activity the children enjoyed most was . . .

The concept that was most difficult to teach was . . .

because . . .

Something I would like to do differently is . . .

ENRICHING THE LESSON

Reviewing the Ten Commandments

To reinforce the Ten Commandments (taught on page 166)

Directions

- State the first part of any one of the Ten Commandments taught on page 287, and have a child complete the Commandment.
- State the first part of another Commandment, and call on someone else to finish that Commandment.
- Continue the activity until all the Commandments have been reviewed.

Materials needed

Making Commandments Signposts

Purpose

To reinforce living the first three Commandments (taught on pages 167)

Directions

- Have the children work with partners to construct signposts for the first three Commandments.
- Tell the children that each signpost is to show other third graders how to live each of the first three Commandments.
- Using construction paper cut out three signposts for each pair of students. Have the children use words of the Commandments and pictures to create a signpost for each of the first three Commandments.

Materials needed

construction paper
markers or crayons

Literature Connection

Purpose

To reinforce the teaching about the role of churches as signs of faith (taught on page 169)

Directions

Log Cabin Church by Ellen Howard (Holiday House, 2002) tells the story of a young girl on the Michigan frontier who learns the importance of building a church building and why her family and community feel it is so important. As her siblings recall details of the church and its life that they left behind to move to the frontier, they help young Elvirey understand the role of the church as a sign of faith.

- Ask the children what they like best about their parish church.
- Read the story aloud to the children.
- Discuss with them what they would miss if they moved to a place where there were no place to gather as a community of faith.

Materials needed

Log Cabin Church by Ellen Howard

Music Connection

- "All You Works of God," M. Haugen. *Singing Our Faith (SOF)* #157.
- "Go Down, Moses" (African-American spiritual). *Rise Up and Sing* #141.
- "Psalm 119: Lord, I Love Your Commands," M. Guimont. *Comprehensive Gathering* #117.
- "Sing, Sing Praise and Sing" (South African traditional), arr. E. Syré. *SOF* #159.

20

We Love and Respect One Another

Background

Love One Another

As Christians we are infused with the gift of the Holy Spirit at Baptism. It is the Holy Spirit who urges us to live the command of Jesus to love our brothers and sisters as he loves us. Called by Jesus to love one another, followers of Jesus join with him in practicing the love he showed for humanity. This way of love is translated into action by the last seven Commandments.

The New Commandment of Love

In Matthew 25 Jesus gave a clear and concise statement of the importance of the Commandments for living our lives as his followers on earth and for enjoying ever-lasting life with him in heaven. Disciples of Jesus are to give drink to the thirsty, clothe the naked, shelter the homeless, visit the imprisoned, comfort the sick, and honor the dead. All these actions, which the Church enumerates as the Corporal Works of Mercy, are actions of the disciples of Jesus Christ. All these works of mercy implement Jesus' New Command-ment of love. In very concrete ways, we are to put our love for God and our neighbors into practice.

Graced sinners that we are, we cannot live out the fullness of the Law of Love on our own. Out of love God empowers us with the gift of the Holy Spirit, given at Baptism and strengthened at Confirmation. The gift of grace, strengthened by our sharing in the Eucharist and other sacraments, gives us the ability and power to put our faith into action (see *Catechism of the Catholic Church* 1972).

As members of the Church, the Body of Christ, we do not live the New Commandment alone. We are joined to Christ, who perfects and exemplifies this self-giving love, and to the other members of the Church.

[Jesus] made himself a catechist of the Kingdom of God for all categories of persons, great and small, rich and poor, healthy and sick, near and far, Jews and pagans, men and women, righteous and sinners, rulers and subjects, individuals and groups. He is available to all. He is interested in the needs of every person, body and soul. He heals and forgives, corrects and encourages, with words and deeds.

GENERAL DIRECTORY FOR CATECHESIS 163

For Reflection

Why is it important for me to be aware that Jesus always joins me as I try to love others?

What are some of the things I do to show my love for others?

Catechist to Catechist

Respectful Authority

Many adults bemoan the fact that young people do not seem to have the same respect for parents, teachers, and others as "they used to have." Respect flows from our belief in the dignity of each person as a child of God. Respect for authority is built upon the legitimate and not the abusive use of authority of parents, teachers, and others. As catechists we can help the children grow in the development and practice of the virtue of respect by the appropriate use of our authority—a use that always respects the dignity of each of the children entrusted to our care.

Words of Praise

This week, as often as possible, create opportunities for the children to recognize respectful actions. Start this habit by praising children when you see them treating one another with respect. The reward of receiving praise from a caring adult, especially on the issue of respect, is immeasurable. This type of affirmation is vital to their development.

The Church Teaches . . .

Pope Paul VI's encyclical on *Evangelization in the Modern World* teaches:

> Every evangelizer is expected to have a reverence for truth, especially since the truth that he [or she] studies and communicates is none other than revealed truth and hence, more than any other, a sharing in the first truth which is God himself. *EN 78*

An old adage says, "Practice what you preach." If you preach love and respect for the truth as a catechist, be sure your manner with the children is one of love and respect.

See the Catechism . . .

For more on the teachings of the Catholic Church on the Ten Commandments, see *Catechism of the Catholic Church* 2196, 2217–2246, 2258–2317, 2331–2391, 2401–2449, 2464–2503, 2514–2527, and 2534–2550.

CATECHIST PRAYER

Spirit of God, who guides us throughout our lives, be with us this week and help us praise you, the Father, and the Son through our work. Amen.

LESSON PLANNER

Focus   To discover what the last seven Commandments teach about loving and respecting all people

Engage

Page 173
Focus
To assess the children's knowledge about how the Ten Commandments teach us to love and respect one another

Opening Prayer

Discussion
What it would be like if everyone treated one another with love and respect

Teach and Apply

Pages 174–176
Focus
To describe what the Fourth through Tenth Commandments teach us about loving and respecting all people

Presentation
Read, discuss, and summarize content.

Scripture
- Psalm 119:10
- Exodus 20:12–18

Activities
- Identify ways family members honor one another.
- Rewrite a Commandment in your own words.
- Draw or write about a way to live one of the Commandments.

Faith-Filled People
Saint Frances Cabrini

Connect

Pages 177–178
Focus
To discover how our parish loves and respects all people

Our Church Makes a Difference
The Church and its members treat others with love because we are images of God.

Our Catholic Faith
The Christian Family

What Difference Does Faith Make?
Activity
Draw or write how living the Commandments can make your community a better place.

Faith Choice
Choose a way to show respect for yourself and others this week.

We Pray

Page 179
Prayer Form
Petition
Prayer
Choose a leader and pray the prayer of intercession together.

We Remember

Review
- Complete the numbering activity.
- Read the "To Help You Remember" statements aloud.
Preview
Highlight features of the "With My Family" page.

Materials

- appropriate music
- pens or pencils
- crayons or markers

Enriching the Session

Blackline Masters
Additional Activities booklet:
  Chapter 20
    Showing respect
    Designing a Web page
Assessment Tools booklet:
  Chapter 20 Test

Enriching the Lesson (CG page 293)
A Respecting New Life Project
Making Signposts for Living the Last Seven Commandments
Literature Connection

Music Connection (CG page 293)

www.FaithFirst.com

We update the *Faith First* Web site weekly. Check each week for new content and features. Here are some places to begin:

Catechists and Teachers
- Current Events
- Chapter Downloads
- Catechist Prayer

***Faith First* for Families**
- Bible Stories
- Make a Difference

Kids' Clubhouse
- *Faith First* Activities
- Chapter Reviews
- Games
- Saints

Don't Forget! You can make lesson planning a breeze—check out the **Online Lesson Planner.**

We Love and Respect One Another

20

We Pray

LORD, help me keep your Commandments with all my heart.
Based on Psalm 119:10

Father, Son, and Holy Spirit, help us live united in respect and love. Amen.

What would it be like if everyone treated one another with respect?

Each day we have many opportunities to treat one another with respect. God asks us to love and respect one another.

In what ways do the Ten Commandments teach us to show love and respect for one another?

173

PRAY

- Gather the children and have them quiet themselves for prayer.
- Pray the Sign of the Cross and invite a volunteer to read the Psalm verse.
- Say the opening prayer together.
- Close the prayer with the Sign of the Cross.

DISCOVER

Purpose: To assess what the children know about loving and respecting one another

- Read aloud the opening paragraph and invite responses to the questions.
- Invite the children to look at the picture and discuss how the mother and her daughter are showing love and respect for one another.

Teaching Tip

Interpreting Pictures. When the children are asked to describe pictures, they should look at the details not only with their eyes but also in terms of their other senses. Here are some key questions you might ask them: What do you see in the picture? Who are the people in the picture? What are they doing? What sounds do you hear when you look at this scene? Answering these types of questions will help the children give a clearer description of the picture.

Teach

Ask a volunteer to read the "Faith Focus" question aloud. Share with the children that in this chapter they will learn how the last seven Commandments help us to show our love and respect for one another and for ourselves.

DISCOVER

- Ask: What does the word *obey* mean? Read the meaning of the faith word *obey* together.
- Together read aloud the Fourth Commandment, which is highlighted in blue. Have the children read silently the three paragraphs of "The Fourth Commandment" to find out what the Fourth Commandment teaches.
- Ask the children to tell in their own words what the Fourth Commandment teaches us. List their responses on the board.

Apply

REINFORCE

Emphasize that our parents deserve our love and respect.

INTEGRATE

- Have the children share with a partner ways family members honor and respect one another.
- Ask the children to look at the picture. Discuss how the picture shows the meaning of the Fourth Commandment.

God Teaches Us the Way to Love

Faith Focus

How do the last seven Commandments help us show our love for one another and for ourselves?

Faith Words

obey
To obey means to choose to follow the guidance of someone who is helping us live according to God's laws.

covet
To covet means to wrongfully want something that belongs to someone else.

The Fourth Commandment

The last seven of the Commandments teach about living the second part of the Great Commandment. They name the ways God wants us to love and respect others and ourselves.

The Fourth Commandment teaches that we honor our parents. We honor our parents when we listen carefully to what they say and we **obey** them.

We honor our parents when we show them how much we appreciate what they do for us. We do this when we care for our clothes, our books, our food, our homes, and all the things they provide for us. The Fourth Commandment is

"Honor your father and your mother."
Exodus 20:12

Discuss some of the ways family members honor and respect one another.

Affirm appropriate responses.

174

Teaching Tip

Respect. When we use the word *honor*, we emphasize love and respect. Help the children learn ways they can show respect toward their parents and toward others in rightful authority. Talk about using a respectful tone of voice and respectful words.

Faith-Filled People

Frances Cabrini

Saint Frances Cabrini was the first American citizen to be named a saint. She lived the Ten Commandments in a special way. She built hospitals to care for the sick and homes to care for children without families. The Church celebrates the feast day of Saint Frances Cabrini on November 13.

The Fifth and Sixth Commandments

The Fifth Commandment teaches that all life is sacred and belongs to God. We are to treat our bodies and the bodies of others with respect and care. We are to avoid doing things that we know are dangerous and can harm us. The Fifth Commandment is
"You shall not kill." Exodus 20:13

The Sixth Commandment teaches that married people are to be faithful in their relationship. A husband and wife are always to love and honor each other. We live this Commandment when we respect our bodies and those of others. The Sixth Commandment is
"You shall not commit adultery."
Exodus 20:14

Choose one of the Commandments on these two pages and rewrite it in your own words.

What the Commandments Mean to Me

Affirm appropriate

responses.

175

Background: Faith-Filled People

Saint Frances Cabrini. Mother Cabrini (1850–1917) was born into a prosperous farm family in northern Italy. Despite suffering poor health, she was determined to become a missionary sister. In 1880 she established a religious community to serve the missions. Mother Cabrini and her small community traveled to the United States to serve Italian immigrant families living there. During her lifetime Mother Cabrini founded many schools, hospitals, and orphanages not only in the United States, but also in Europe and South America. Mother Cabrini was canonized in 1946 and is the patron saint of immigrants.

FOCUS
Remind the children that the Fourth Commandment teaches us to honor and obey our parents. Point out that they will learn next about the Fifth and Sixth Commandments.

DISCOVER
- Ask a volunteer to read aloud "The Fifth and Sixth Commandments." Ask the children to name the new things they learned.
- Read "Faith-Filled People" aloud together to discover how Saint Frances Cabrini lived the Fifth Commandment by respecting the lives of others.

Apply

REINFORCE
Ask the children to recite the Fifth and Sixth Commandments.

INTEGRATE
- Explain the directions to the activity and have the children complete it.
- Invite volunteers to share their understanding of the Fifth and Sixth Commandments.

Teach

FOCUS

Remind the children that the Fifth and Sixth Commandments show us ways to respect ourselves and others. Then point out that the last four Commandments teach us other ways that we are to love and respect all people.

DISCOVER

- Ask different volunteers to read each paragraph aloud.
- Discuss the last four Commandments using these or similar questions:
  —Besides stealing, what else is the Seventh Commandment about? Respect for the property of others, fairness and justice, thoughtfulness.
  —What are positive ways of keeping the Eighth Commandment? Honesty, truthfulness, and kindness in what we say about others.
  —When could it be wrong to want something that someone has? When we are greedy or jealous of others and want what is theirs.

Apply

REINFORCE

Turn back to page 174 and read the faith word *covet*. Have the children make word cards for *covet* and *obey*.

INTEGRATE

Have the children look carefully at the pictures on this page and then have them complete the activity.

The Seventh Through Tenth Commandments

The Seventh Commandment teaches that we respect what belongs to other people. We are to treat people fairly and justly. We use the things that we borrow properly and return them when we are finished. The Seventh Commandment is

"You shall not steal." Exodus 20:15

The Eighth Commandment teaches that we are to be honest and truthful. We are not to tell lies. We are not to hurt people by the things we say about them. The Eighth Commandment is

"You shall not bear false witness against your neighbor." Exodus 20:16

The Ninth Commandment teaches us to respect the marriage of a man and a woman. We are to help families grow in love. The Ninth Commandment is

"You shall not covet your neighbor's wife." Exodus 20:17

The Tenth Commandment teaches us not to be greedy or jealous. We are to share our things with people, especially with people in need. The Tenth Commandment is

"You shall not covet your neighbor's goods." Exodus 20:18

How are the actions of the children in the photos against the teachings of the Commandments? In the empty box, draw or write about children who are keeping the Tenth Commandment.

Responses will vary. Affirm appropriate responses.

Faith Vocabulary

Covet. The word *covet* comes from a Latin word *cupere,* meaning "to desire." In the Commandments, the meaning of the word *covet* refers to one's inordinate "desire" to possess that which belongs to someone else. Reflect on your own desire to possess goods. How does your desire for things affect your relationships with other people? How does it impact the way you live the Great Commandment?

Our Church Makes a Difference

Our Parish Family

We treat others with love because of who we are! We are images of God. What does that mean? It means that when people look at us, they should come to know and love God by the things we say and do.

Our parish family is a sign of God's love for the people who live in our community. People feel welcome to stop and pray in our parish church. They see us working very hard at getting along. They see us sharing food with those who are hungry and clothes with those who need them. They see us visiting and caring for people who are sick.

When our parish family does these and other kind and loving things, we are living the Commandments. We are living as Jesus taught. We are signs of God's love.

Describe things your parish family does that show it is an image of God.

Affirm appropriate responses.

Our Catholic Faith

The Christian Family

The Christian family is like a church. It is a small community of the People of God. That is why the Church says that the Christian family is a domestic church. The word *domestic* means "belonging to the home." Being a good Christian begins at home with our families.

Catholic Social Teaching

Life and Dignity of the Human Person. All human life is sacred. This is the source of our fundamental dignity as a human person. Here are some of the Catholic Church's teachings that flow from this principle: Direct abortion, euthanasia, suicide, and assisted suicide are inherently evil; human cloning and genetic engineering threaten the uniqueness of each human life; the death penalty can seldom if ever be justified; and war should be a last resort in the resolution of differences. (See *Catechism of the Catholic Church* 2258–2317.)

Tip: Help the children to develop good habits to care for their own lives.

Connect

HIGHLIGHT

Remind the children that the Church teaches us how to live the Commandments. We learn about living the Ten Commandments in our parish.

DISCOVER

- Invite the children to read the first paragraph of "Our Parish Family." Ask: What is the most important reason to treat others with love and respect? We are all created in God's image.
- Ask the children how their parish family is an image of God.
- Ask volunteers to read the rest of the page.
- Ask a volunteer to describe what is happening in the picture. Then invite volunteers to describe things they see their parish doing that shows it is an image of God.

INTEGRATE

- Ask the children if they ever thought of their family as being like a church.
- Have them read aloud together "Our Catholic Faith" to discover why the Church calls the family a domestic church.
- Ask: What work of the parish does your family do?

Connect

HIGHLIGHT

Share with the children that when they are living the Commandments as children of God, they are kind, loving, trustworthy, and honest.

RESPOND

- Invite the children to share times when they know they have lived the Ten Commandments well.
- Present the activity and have the children to complete it on their own.

CHOOSE

- Invite the children to respond to "My Faith Choice."
- After a moment of prayerful reflection, have the children write their choice on the lines provided.
- Encourage the children to put their choice into practice this week.

What Difference Does Faith Make in My Life?

Each day you are kind and generous. You are trustworthy and honest. You respect your family and your friends. You are living the Ten Commandments as a child of God.

In the box explain how living the Commandments can make your community a better place.

Responses will vary.

My Faith Choice

This week I will try to make good decisions to respect myself and others. I will

Affirm appropriate responses.

178

Background: Doctrine

Living the Ten Commandments. The Ten Commandments express our foundational and fundamental responsibilities toward God and neighbor. The Tradition of the Church, in accordance with Scripture and the example of Jesus, recognizes their utmost importance and reminds us that living the Commandments is facilitated by the grace of God. Help the children celebrate the different ways in which they are living the Commandments each day.

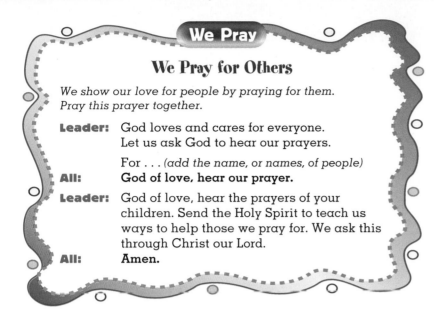

We Pray

We Pray for Others

We show our love for people by praying for them.
Pray this prayer together.

Leader: God loves and cares for everyone.
Let us ask God to hear our prayers.

For . . . *(add the name, or names, of people)*

All: **God of love, hear our prayer.**

Leader: God of love, hear the prayers of your
children. Send the Holy Spirit to teach us
ways to help those we pray for. We ask this
through Christ our Lord.

All: **Amen.**

We Remember

Read this list of ways we can show our love and respect for ourselves and others. Write the number of the Commandment being followed in each one.

7	We treat people fairly.
4	We listen carefully to our parents and obey them.
8	We tell the truth about others.
5	We avoid things that are dangerous and can harm us.

To Help You Remember

1. The last seven of the Ten Commandments teach us how to live the second part of the Great Commandment.

2. They teach us to honor and respect people and the things that belong to them.

3. They teach us to be honest and truthful, kind and generous.

Grade 3 • Chapter 20 (179)

Pray

WE PRAY

- Play appropriate background music as you gather the children in the prayer center.
- Explain that the prayer is a prayer of intercession. Invite a child to serve as the leader of the prayer.
- Prepare the children by reading the opening paragraph.
- Pray the prayer together. Let the children add the names of people for whom they wish to pray.

Review

WE REMEMBER

- Create a word map of ways to live the last seven Commandments.
- Tell the children they can look for clues in the "To Help You Remember" statements.
- Introduce the "We Remember" activity and allow the children time to complete it.

Liturgy Tip

Learning to Love. The Gospel talks about the hope of the kingdom of God and the need to prepare for the coming of that kingdom. Jesus told us that we both express our hope in and prepare the way for the coming of the kingdom by loving one another as he has loved us. One way we show our love for others is to pray for them as Jesus prayed for his disciples. Encourage the children to pray for those they love by sharing their names as part of the closing prayer.

At Home

ENCOURAGE

Have the children carefully tear out pages 179 and 180 along the perforation. Encourage the children to share the pages with their families and to do the activities together. If they did not complete the review activity on page 179 by the end of the session, emphasize that they can complete it with their families.

VISIT FAITHFIRST.COM

- Share with the children the many activities on the *Faith First* Web site.
- Encourage the children to visit **www.FaithFirst.com.**

Before Moving On . . .

As you finish today's lesson, reflect on the following question before moving on to the next chapter.

What have I done to let the children know that they are helping me to grow in faith as I work with them?

---

20 With My Family

This Week . . .

In chapter 20, "We Love and Respect One Another," your child learned that the last seven of the Ten Commandments teach us to live the second part of the Great Commandment. These Commandments teach us to treat all people and ourselves as images of God and children of God. They teach us to respect and honor ourselves and others. They teach us to be honest and truthful, kind and generous.

For more on the teachings of the Catholic Church on the Ten Commandments, see *Catechism of the Catholic Church* paragraph numbers 2196, 2217–2246 (Fourth Commandment), 2258–2317 (Fifth Commandment), 2331–2391 (Sixth Commandment), 2401–2449 (Seventh Commandment), 2464–2503 (Eighth Commandment), 2514–2527 (Ninth Commandment), 2534–2550 (Tenth Commandment).

Sharing God's Word

Read together 1 John 4:11 about God's love. Emphasize that God commands us to love and respect others and ourselves.

Praying

In this chapter your child showed his or her love for people by praying for them. Read and pray together the prayer on page 179.

Making a Difference

Choose one of the following activities to do as a family or design a similar activity of your own.

- To obey means to follow the guidance of someone who is helping us live according to the Law of God. Invite each family member to share the names of people who help them live the Ten Commandments.

- The Fifth Commandment teaches us not to kill. Talk about the ways your family lives the Fifth Commandment. Then rewrite the Fifth Commandment in your own words.

- Look through your parish bulletin or visit your parish web site and name the ways your parish shows its love and respect for people.

> For more ideas on ways your family can live your faith, visit the "Faith First for Families" page at **www.FaithFirst.com.** Click on "Contemporary Issues" for some interesting insights into living the Commandments.

Evaluate

Take a few moments to evaluate this week's lesson.
I feel (circle one) about this week's lesson.

- a. very pleased
- b. OK
- c. disappointed

The activity the children enjoyed most was . . .

The concept that was most difficult to teach was . . .

because . . .

Something I would like to do differently is . . .

ENRICHING THE LESSON

A Respecting New Life Project

Purpose

To reinforce that the last seven Commandments name the ways God wants us to love and respect others and ourselves (taught on page 174)

Directions

- Brainstorm with the children ways of sharing what is theirs with others.
- A wonderful project to consider with the children is a baby shower for a family in need.
- With the children, create a checklist of tasks that have to be accomplished to make this project a reality.
- Together have the children write a note to their parents detailing the project.
- Have each child bring a simple baby gift and some gift wrap to class.
- Help the children wrap the gifts and prepare a personal note to the parents of the baby, affirming God's gift of new life to the family.
- Take the gifts to your parish center to be delivered.

Materials

paper and pens or pencils

Making Signposts for Living the Last Seven Commandments

Purpose

To reinforce living the last seven Commandments (taught on pages 174–176)

Directions

- Have the children work with partners to construct signposts for the last seven Commandments. Assign a different Commandment to each pair of students.
- Using words and pictures have the children illustrate signposts for each of the last seven Commandments that show other third graders how to live them.

- Remind the children they may use their own words to rephrase the wording of the Commandments.

Materials

construction paper and markers or crayons

Literature Connection

Purpose

To reinforce the teaching about the Tenth Commandment (taught on page 176)

Directions

The witty and insightful Judy Moody series is popular with third graders. *Judy Moody Gets Famous* by Megan McDonald (Candlewick Press, 2001) illustrates the effects of jealousy and envy on Judy after the most "perfect" girl in the class achieves local fame by winning a spelling bee.

- Since this book is a chapter book, you will not have time to read all of it aloud to the students. Instead, describe the situation to the class and read aloud to them one or two of Judy's failed attempts to achieve fame.
- Ask the children to suggest endings of their own to the story.
- Then read aloud the author's conclusion. Discuss with the class why envy and jealousy get in the way of living as God desires.

Materials

Judy Moody Gets Famous by Megan McDonald

Music Connection

- "All Are Welcome," M. Haugen. *Singing Our Faith* #185.
- "No Greater Love," M. Joncas. *Comprehensive Gathering (CG)* #628.
- "These Are Our Gifts," J. Vogt. *Rise Up and Sing* #303.
- "We Have Been Told," D. Haas. *GC* #699.

The Psalms and Stewardship
A Scripture Story

Background

Caring for the Household of God

The Covenant of love between God and humankind binds us together in a web of mutual care. As members of God's family, created in his image and likeness, believers are to care for his creation and to see that the bounty of the earth's gifts is shared.

We all share a diversity of gifts, talents, skills, and physical abilities that differ from one person to another. These differences call us together—to share. For only in our mutual giving and receiving can we image the love and beauty of God and flourish physically, intellectually, and spiritually.

The concept of stewardship encapsulates the way in which we are to respond to God's love. As members of the family, or households of God, we have the responsibility to be good stewards of creation. A steward is one who manages a household or an estate. Christian stewardship refers to the care and good management of the household of God.

God's household includes all the gifts of creation and salvation. A good steward is one who receives these gifts in gratitude, cherishes them, and cares for them in a responsible manner. Our call to stewardship challenges us to share these gifts in justice and love with others, returning them with increase to God.

Christian Stewardship

We are moved to the vocation of Christian stewardship in the power of the Holy Spirit. Because of original sin, we need to work hard at avoiding the tendency to hoard our possessions, to place ourselves first, and to give only out of our excess. God's abundant outpouring of grace into our lives moves us to use our gifts to alleviate poverty, hunger, and human misery.

The bishops at the Second Vatican Council expressed the Church's vision of stewardship. They wrote:

> Christ is now at work in [human] hearts by the power of his Spirit; not only does he arouse in them a desire for the world to come but he quickens, purifies, and strengthens the generous aspirations of [humanity] to make life more humane and conquer the earth for this purpose.
>
> PASTORAL CONSTITUTION ON THE CHURCH IN THE MODERN WORLD (GAUDIUM ET SPES) 38

Jesus expects us to care for and increase the blessings of creation and the personal talents that are ours. We are to improve the communities to which we belong, as well as the wider human society of which we all are a part. As we grow in awareness of the global effects of the solidarity of all peoples, we will accept greater personal responsibility to become wise stewards of this earth.

For Reflection

What are some of the ways in which I have discovered the interdependence of all creation in the web of life?

What are some of my responsibilities as a steward of the household of God?

Catechist to Catechist

Pray as Jesus Prayed

Each week at Mass, you and the children sing or pray aloud a Psalm as a response to the first reading. So praying and singing verses from the Psalms is familiar territory for the children. What they may not know is that the Psalms were a basic part of Jesus' prayer life. It is important for the children to realize that when they pray the Psalms today, they are praying some of the same prayers that Jesus prayed.

A Psalm of Praise

Slowly and prayerfully read Psalm 104, which is the center of this chapter. Have the children imagine what is described in this Psalm of praise. Invite them to close their eyes and picture God's mighty deeds in creation. Give them the freedom to dance or clap to the rhythm of the Psalm. The cadence of this Psalm can catapult them into caring for creation!

The Church Teaches . . .

Sharing the Light of Faith: National Catechetical Directory for Catholics in the United States teaches:

> Catechesis seeks to help children make an increasingly personal response to God's word and gifts. This response is not just a matter of external expressions, however useful they may be, but is truly heartfelt and prayerful. Catechesis approaches young persons with reverence and aids them in discovering and developing their unique, God-given gifts with the help of the gospel.   *NCD* 178

Each child, by virtue of their Baptism, has been called to stewardship of all God's creation. Help foster their responses to that call through Scripture.

See the Catechism . . .

For more on the teachings of the Catholic Church on the role of the Psalms in the prayer life of the Church, see *Catechism of the Catholic Church* 716, 1176–1177, and 2585–2589.

CATECHIST PRAYER

Holy Spirit, you created mountains and mist, rivers and ravens, forest and fish. Create a new heart in me that I may become a steward of the children. Amen.

LESSON PLANNER

FOCUS
To identify how the Psalms help us to pray and live as children of God the Creator

Engage

Page 181
Focus
To assess the children's knowledge about the Psalms and why singing helps us pray

Opening Prayer

Discussion
Why people enjoy singing; What are the Psalms

Teach and Apply

Pages 182–184
Focus
To explain that the Psalms remind us to praise and thank God for creation

Presentation
Read, discuss, and summarize content.
Scripture
- Psalm 67:6
- Psalm 104:1, 10–12, 24, 31, 33
- Psalm 67:7
- Psalm 150:3–6

Activities
- Use a code to discover a verse from a psalm of thanksgiving.
- Pray Psalm 104.
- Complete a prayer of thanksgiving.

Connect

Pages 185–186
Focus
To discover how the Church is a good steward of creation

Our Church Makes a Difference
Farmers show us what it means to be good stewards.
Our Catholic Faith
Mealtime Prayers

What Difference Does Faith Make?
Activity
Decorate a poster with words and symbols of creation.
Faith Choice
Choose a way to be a good steward of God's creation this week.

We Pray

Page 187
Prayer Form
Psalm of praise
Prayer
Divide the children into three groups. Introduce the prayer and pray together.

We Remember

Review
- Complete the writing activity.
- Read the "To Help You Remember" statements aloud.

Preview
Highlight features of the "With My Family" page.

Materials

- appropriate music for prayer
- pens or pencils
- crayons or markers

Enriching the Session

Blackline Masters
Additional Activities booklet:
Chapter 21
Designing a sign
Being good stewards
Assessment Tools booklet:
Chapter 21 Test

Enriching the Lesson (CG page 305)
Giving Stewardship Speeches
Making a Psalm Booklet
Literature Connection

Music Connection (CG page 305)

www.FaithFirst.com

We update the *Faith First* Web site weekly. Check each week for new content and features. Here are some places to begin:

Catechists and Teachers
- Current Events
- Chapter Downloads
- Catechist Prayer

Faith First for Families
- Bible Stories
- Make a Difference

Kids' Clubhouse
- *Faith First* Activities
- Chapter Reviews
- Games
- Saints

Don't Forget! You can make lesson planning a breeze—check out the **Online Lesson Planner.**

The Psalms and Stewardship
A Scripture Story

21

We Pray

O God, the earth gives
us food.
You have blessed us.
Based on Psalm 67:6

**God the Creator,
we give you glory
for all the good
things we receive
from you.   Amen.**

*Why do people enjoy
singing?*

People sing about
many things and
for many reasons.
One way we can
pray is by singing.
The Psalms are
prayer songs in the
Bible.

*What do you know
about the Psalms?*

181

Liturgy Tip

Utilizing Chant in Prayer. Add music to your prayer by having the children sing a simple chant. Pick one musical note or tone and simply sing the words using that note. Or use one tone for the first part of the opening prayer and a different tone for the second part of the prayer. All the children will enjoy this form of prayer.

PRAY

- Gather the children and have them quiet themselves for prayer.
- Pray the Sign of the Cross together. Have a volunteer read aloud the Psalm verse.
- Lead the children in praying the opening prayer. Invite the children to read it aloud with you.
- Conclude by praying the Sign of the Cross together.

DISCOVER

Purpose: To discover what the children know about the Psalms

- Ask the children to name their favorite songs. Then ask them why they think people like to sing.
- Remind the children that the Psalms are prayer songs in the Bible written long ago. Ask volunteers to tell you what they know about the Psalms.
- Invite the children to look at the picture. Ask: If you were standing in a field full of flowers, what would you be thinking about?
- Share your own thoughts with the children and then invite volunteers to respond to the question.

Teach

FOCUS

Ask a volunteer to read aloud the "Faith Focus" question. Share with the children that in this chapter they will learn how the Psalms help us to pray and live as children of God the Creator.

DISCOVER

- Share with the children that singing can be a form of prayer. Ask them if they can recall a time when they have sung a prayer. Remind them that we sing Psalm verses at Sunday Mass.
- Present "Sacred Songs and Prayers."
- Ask the children to underline the four kinds of Psalms. Psalms of praise, lament, wisdom, and thanksgiving.

Apply

REINFORCE

Ask a volunteer to read the word *Psalms* and its meaning in "Faith Words." Have the children make a word card for this word.

INTEGRATE

- Have the children work with partners to do the decoding puzzle.
- When they are finished, encourage the children to pray Psalm 67:7 together.

Bible Background

Faith Focus

How do the Psalms help us pray and live as children of God the Creator?

Faith Words

Psalms
The Psalms are prayer songs found in the Bible in the Book of Psalms in the Old Testament.

stewards
Stewards are people who have the responsibility to care for things and to use them well.

Sacred Songs and Prayers

Long ago the Jewish people wrote sacred songs called Psalms. The Jewish people prayed these songs. Jesus learned the **Psalms** and prayed them all his life. The first Christians prayed the Psalms. Today Christians still pray the Psalms every day.

Some Psalms praise God and tell him about our needs. We call these laments. Other Psalms give practical advice about how we can live as God's children. We call these wisdom Psalms. We also pray the Psalms to thank God for the gifts of creation.

Use the code to discover one verse from a psalm of thanksgiving.

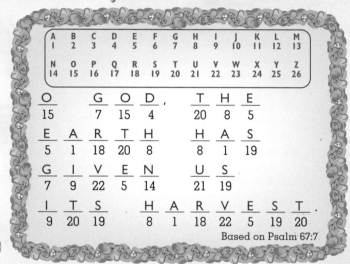

| A 1 | B 2 | C 3 | D 4 | E 5 | F 6 | G 7 | H 8 | I 9 | J 10 | K 11 | L 12 | M 13 |
| N 14 | O 15 | P 16 | Q 17 | R 18 | S 19 | T 20 | U 21 | V 22 | W 23 | X 24 | Y 25 | Z 26 |

O GOD, THE
15 7 15 4 20 8 5

EARTH HAS
5 1 18 20 8 8 1 19

GIVEN US
7 9 22 5 14 21 19

ITS HARVEST.
9 20 19 8 1 18 22 5 19 20

Based on Psalm 67:7

(182)

Teaching Tip

Introducing the Psalms. Remind the children that when they pray the Psalms, they are praying the same prayers Jesus prayed. Explain to the children that the Church prays the Psalms in the Liturgy of the Word at the Eucharist and in the Liturgy of the Hours, the daily prayer of the Church. Read to the children these examples of the different kinds of Psalms in the Bible: Psalm 148:1–5, a psalm of praise; Psalm 13:2–3, a psalm of lament; Psalm 1:1–3, a psalm of wisdom; and Psalm 92:2–5, a psalm of thanksgiving.

Reading the Word of God

Psalm 104

Here is part of Psalm 104. We pray it to praise God and thank him for creation. It reminds us that God cares for all creation.

O God, you are great!

You make small streams become
    mighty rivers.
They flow through the tall
    mountains.
They give drink to all animals.
Birds rest and sing beside your
    waters.

LORD, we cannot count all the good
    things you have created.
    The earth is full of your creatures.

May your glory shine forever;
    may you be happy with everything
    you have made.
I will sing to God all my life.
        Based on Psalm 104:1, 10–12, 24, 31, 33

Take a moment. Pray quietly in your heart the last seven lines from Psalm 104.

183

Background: Doctrine

The Prayer of the Psalms. The *Catechism of the Catholic Church* (2585–2589) reminds us that the Psalms are hymns that express different human experiences and reflect God's magnificent works in the history of his people. Have the children locate the Book of Psalms in the Bible. Point out that the Psalms are different lengths and that each has a title or subject. Remind them that the Psalms are often called "The Church's Prayer Book." Emphasize that Jesus prayed and sang these same Psalms throughout his life.

Teach

FOCUS
Remind the children that the people of the Old Testament wrote psalms to praise God and to tell him their needs.

DISCOVER
- Tell the children that you are going to read to them a psalm that praises and thanks God for the gift of creation. Ask the children to close their eyes and imagine the scene that is described in Psalm 104.
- Proclaim Psalm 104.

Apply

REINFORCE
- Have the children underline the part of Psalm 104 they liked best. Invite volunteers to share their favorite part with the entire class.
- Ask the children to underline the part that gives the psalmist's response to God's great gifts. "Sing to God all my life."

INTEGRATE
- Invite the children to silently pray the last seven lines from Psalm 104, which begin with "LORD, we."
- Ask the children to look at the pictures of creation on the page. Help them make up short verses that express their praise and thanks to God for what they see in the pictures.

Teach

FOCUS

Remind the children that many Psalms give praise to God. Then point out that we also praise God when we take care of creation.

DISCOVER

- Have the children turn back to page 182 and read aloud the faith word *stewards* and its meaning.
- Invite volunteers to read "Caring for God's World" to find out what good stewards do.
- Write the word *steward* on the board and create a word cluster. Ask the children to share words that describe good stewards. Write the children's responses on the board around the word *steward*.

Apply

REINFORCE

Ask the children how being a good steward is a way of living the Seventh Commandment. Have them make a word card for *steward*.

INTEGRATE

- Direct the children's attention to the activity while you explain its directions. Ask the children to brainstorm the names of animals that are part of God's creation. Choose animals whose names begin with the letters *p*, *a*, *i*, and *e*. List these words on the board.
- Invite the children to use some of the words on the board to complete their prayer of thanks.

Understanding the Word of God

Caring for God's World

All creation gives glory to God. We give glory to God both when we pray and when we take care of creation.

The Bible tells us that God gave us the responsibility to care for creation. When we care for God's creation and use it well, we are good **stewards** of creation.

Good stewards live the Seventh Commandment. They take care of creation so that all people can enjoy and share it. They do not waste or misuse the gifts of creation. They share the beauty and goodness of creation with everyone.

Complete this prayer of thanksgiving. Share your prayer with your family.
Affirm appropriate responses.

Thanking God for Creation

O God, you are great and wonderful!
I thank you
        Responses will vary.
        for puppies and p arrots   ,

        for antelope and a nt eaters   ,

        for iguanas and i mpalas   ,

        for elephants and e agles   .

                        Amen.

184

Teaching Tip

Chief Seattle. Chief Seattle was a great leader of the Duwamish tribe. He said these important words about caring for the earth: "Teach your children what we have taught our children, that the earth is our mother. Whatever befalls the earth, befalls the sons of the earth." Ask the children to share how Chief Seattle's wisdom is similar to the teaching of the Psalms about stewardship.

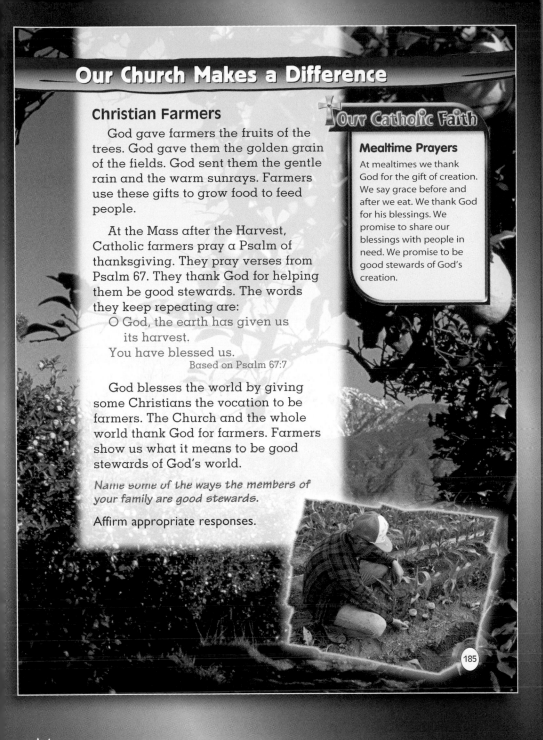

Our Church Makes a Difference

Christian Farmers

God gave farmers the fruits of the trees. God gave them the golden grain of the fields. God sent them the gentle rain and the warm sunrays. Farmers use these gifts to grow food to feed people.

At the Mass after the Harvest, Catholic farmers pray a Psalm of thanksgiving. They pray verses from Psalm 67. They thank God for helping them be good stewards. The words they keep repeating are:

O God, the earth has given us
     its harvest.
You have blessed us.
> Based on Psalm 67:7

God blesses the world by giving some Christians the vocation to be farmers. The Church and the whole world thank God for farmers. Farmers show us what it means to be good stewards of God's world.

Name some of the ways the members of your family are good stewards.

Affirm appropriate responses.

Our Catholic Faith

Mealtime Prayers

At mealtimes we thank God for the gift of creation. We say grace before and after we eat. We thank God for his blessings. We promise to share our blessings with people in need. We promise to be good stewards of God's creation.

185

Catholic Social Teaching

Dignity of Work and the Rights of the Worker. Work is one essential way that we participate in God's plan for creation. It is partly through our work that we fulfill our humanity and seek the happiness that God wishes us to have. Governments have the responsibility to guarantee their workers a just wage, to provide access to meaningful jobs, and to promote fairness in the workplace.

Tip: Call a local farmer or produce manager and invite them to come and speak to the children about being good stewards of nature and creation.

Connect

HIGHLIGHT

Christian farmers who use God's gifts for the good of others are good stewards of creation.

DISCOVER

- Discuss with the children what they know about the work of farmers.
- Read aloud "Christian Farmers." Have the children listen for how farmers show us what it means to be good stewards.
- Ask: How are farmers a blessing to the world? Farmers grow food to feed us.
- Ask the children to read together "Our Catholic Faith."
- Take a moment to review the "Grace Before Meals" and "Grace After Meals" on page 285.

INTEGRATE

- Ask the children how members of their family are good stewards. They recycle, plant flower and vegetable gardens, feed the birds and other wildlife, and keep their property free of trash.
- If time allows, give the children art paper and crayons or markers. Invite them to make bookmarks with the words of Psalm 67:7.

Connect

HIGHLIGHT

We give glory to God when we are good stewards.

RESPOND

- Read aloud the introductory paragraph and the directions for the activity.
- Give the children markers or crayons to use. If possible, give the children small pieces of poster board to create posters that can be hung in the classroom.
- Have the children complete the activity on their own.

CHOOSE

- Invite the children to respond to "My Faith Choice."
- After a moment of prayerful reflection have the children write their choice on the lines provided.
- Encourage the children to put their choice into practice this week.

What Difference Does Faith Make in My Life?

The Holy Spirit helps you live as a good steward of creation. When you are a good steward, your life is like a Psalm. It is a prayer that gives glory to God.

Decorate this poster with symbols of creation and your favorite words from Psalm 104.

My Faith Choice

This week I will be a good steward of God's creation. I will

Affirm appropriate responses.

186

Teaching Tip

Stewardship Survey. On sheets of paper list the following or similar questions.

- What is your favorite part of creation? Why?
- What is a problem you see in taking care of creation?
- What is one thing you think should be done to take better care of creation?

Ask the children to give the survey to one of their family members to answer and bring it back next week. Tally the results and share them with the class.

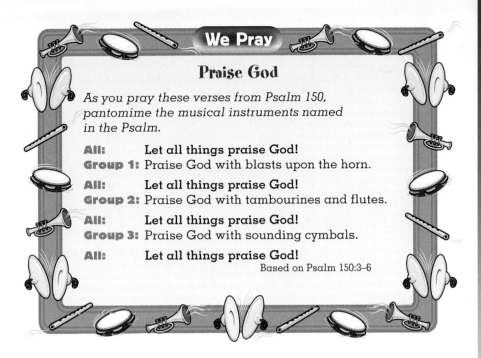

We Pray

Praise God

As you pray these verses from Psalm 150, pantomime the musical instruments named in the Psalm.

All: Let all things praise God!
Group 1: Praise God with blasts upon the horn.

All: Let all things praise God!
Group 2: Praise God with tambourines and flutes.

All: Let all things praise God!
Group 3: Praise God with sounding cymbals.

All: Let all things praise God!

Based on Psalm 150:3–6

We Remember

Write two ways you can be a good steward of God's creation.

Responses will vary.

Affirm appropriate responses.

To Help You Remember

1. Psalms help us pray many kinds of prayers.

2. Psalm 104 praises and thanks God for creation.

3. When we are good stewards of God's creation, we give praise and thanks to God.

Grade 3 • Chapter 21 **187**

Pray

WE PRAY

- Explain that the prayer is a psalm of praise.
- Prepare the children for prayer by reading the opening paragraph. Practice the suggested movements.
- Divide the children into three groups before moving to the prayer center.
- Lead the children in a procession to the prayer center. If possible, have some children play rhythm instruments, such as tambourines or cymbals.
- Pray Psalm 150:3–6 together.

Review

WE REMEMBER

- Read aloud the three "To Help You Remember" sentences to reinforce what the children learned in this chapter.
- Ask the children to recall the kinds of Psalms they have learned about in this chapter. *Psalms of lament, praise, thanksgiving, and wisdom.*
- Introduce the activity and invite the children to complete it. Ask volunteers to share their sentences.

† Liturgy Tip

Singing a Psalm. A prayer based on Psalm 150:3–6 has been written in the form of a hymn by Bob Hurd. Check with your director of religious education or your parish music director for a recording of "I Want to Praise your Name." You may also check the Oregon Catholic Press Web site for a link to a downloadable version that can be played on any Mp3 player. Have the children sing and pantomime the musical instruments while reinforcing that Psalms are often sung.

At Home

ENCOURAGE

Have the children carefully tear out pages 187 and 188 along the perforation. Encourage the children to share the pages with their families and to do the activities together. If they did not complete the review activity on page 187 by the end of the session, emphasize that they can complete it with their families.

VISIT FAITHFIRST.COM

- Share with the children the many activities on the *Faith First* Web site.
- Encourage the children to visit **www.FaithFirst.com.**

Before Moving On . . .

As you finish today's lesson, reflect on the following question before moving on to the next chapter.

What can I do to help the children who are more mathematically or scientifically inclined to bring their gifts to our religion activities?

---

21 With My Family

This Week . . .

In chapter 21, "The Psalms and Stewardship: A Scripture Story," your child learned about the Psalms. There are 150 Psalms in the Book of Psalms in the Old Testament. Praying the Psalms was part of the prayer life of Jesus and the first Christians. Christians today pray the Psalms every day. There are many types of Psalms. Each type of Psalm helps us share our thoughts and feelings with God. Psalm 150 is a Psalm giving praise and thanksgiving to God for the wonderful gift of creation. We become living Psalms of praise when we are good stewards of God's creation.

For more on the teachings of the Catholic Church on the role of the Psalms in the prayer life of the Church, see *Catechism of the Catholic Church* paragraph numbers 716, 1176–1177, and 2585–2589.

188

Sharing God's Word

Read together Psalm 104. You can find Psalm 104 in the Bible or an adaptation of several verses of Psalm 104 on page 183. Emphasize that this Psalm praises God and thanks God for creation.

Praying

In this chapter your child prayed Psalm 105:3–6. Read and pray together the prayer on page 187.

Making a Difference

Choose one of the following activities to do as a family or design a similar activity of your own.

- Design and make a poster that encourages people to be good stewards of God's creation. Try to come up with some creative slogans for your poster.
- Talk about how your family lives as good stewards of God's creation. As a family, choose to do one thing this week to be good stewards.
- Write a family prayer of thanksgiving. Thank God for all the wonderful gifts of creation. Use your prayer for family prayer this week.

For more ideas on ways your family can live your faith, visit the "Faith First for Families" page at **www.FaithFirst.com.** Click on the "Gospel Reflections" page this week and share some of the ideas together.

Evaluate

Take a few moments to evaluate this week's lesson.
I feel (circle one) about this week's lesson.

    a. very pleased
    b. OK
    c. disappointed

The activity the children enjoyed most was . . .

The concept that was most difficult to teach was . . .

because . . .

Something I would like to do differently is . . .

ENRICHING THE LESSON

Making a Psalm Booklet

Purpose

To reinforce the beautiful images that Psalm 104 paints (taught on page 183)

Directions

- Have each child make a Psalm 104 booklet.
- Brainstorm with the children images for the different lines of Psalm 104 on page 183.
- Invite the children to write each line of the Psalm on its own page.
- Have them draw an illustration or select a photo from a magazine that illustrates each line.
- Have the children gather their pages to form a booklet.
- Tell them to take their booklets home and use photos their families have taken to continue to design images for the Psalm as well as a cover for their booklet.
- Have the children bring their booklets to the next session and pass them around for the other children to observe.

Materials needed

construction paper
magazines
markers or crayons

Giving Stewardship Speeches

Purpose

To reinforce the importance of being good stewards of creation (taught on page 184)

Directions

- Talk with the children about what Chief Seattle said about creation, which can be found in the "Teaching Tip" box on page 300 of this guide.
- Invite the children to give a brief speech about being good stewards and caring for creation.
- Have the children focus their speeches on what people must do to care for and protect the earth.
- Have the children present their speeches.

Materials

Literature Connection

Purpose

To reinforce the concepts of stewardship and gratitude (taught on page 184)

Directions

- Read *Wonderful Earth* by Nick Butterworth (John Hunt Publishing, Limited, 2003) to the children.
- Have each child create a book report by telling what happened in the beginning, middle, and end of the book.
- Brainstorm the ways the story depicts the meaning of the word *stewardship* with the children. Write their responses on the board.
- Have the children choose one of their responses and draw a picture of it.
- Give volunteers a few moments to share their work.

Materials

Wonderful Earth by Nick Butterworth

Music Connection

- "All You Works of God," M. Haugen. *Singing Our Faith (SOF)* #157.
- "Canticle of the Sun," M. Haugen. *SOF* #14.
- "The Earth Is the Lord's," R. Oliano. *Gather Comprehensive* #495.
- "We Are the Family," R. Repp. *Rise Up and Sing* #232.

Background

Life Is Changed, Not Ended

The death of the human body is not an end of human life. It is the threshold through which we pass into a life for which we were created—life everlasting, or heaven. Heaven, the Beatific Vision, is our destiny. It is what God wants for us.

The term *Beatific Vision* is used to describe the total and complete union with God of those who die in the Lord, that is, those who die in friendship with him. This mystery of divine love defies description and human experience.

Scripture uses many images to convey this mystery, such as kingdom of God, kingdom of heaven, life, light, peace, banquet, mansions in the Father's house, paradise, and heavenly Jerusalem. We grope in hope with this vision of heaven while we journey on earth. Only after death will we fully grasp the life and glory God has ordained for those who love him. Only after death will we come to know the ultimate end and fulfillment of our deepest human longings and the happiness we spent a whole lifetime pursuing.

We Die and Rise in Christ

Christ came to open heaven's gates for all.

> In him, who rose from the dead, our hope of resurrection dawned. The sadness of death gives way to the bright promise of immortality. Lord, for your faithful people life is changed, not ended. When the body of our earthly dwelling lies in death we gain an everlasting dwelling place in heaven.
>
> ROMAN MISSAL, PREFACE FOR THE MASS OF CHRISTIAN BURIAL I

Christ will judge each of our individual lives at the moment of our death. He will make it clear to us whether we have chosen to cooperate with grace and grow in holiness and perfection or have rejected the gift of redeeming grace. Accordingly, each individual will receive judgment. Each individual will begin living in the eternal joy of heaven; in a state of purification, or purgatory, preceding entry into the eternal joy of heaven; or in the eternal punishment of hell.

At the end of time the Last, or Final, Judgment will occur. This judgment will be based upon the Gospel imperative of love for God and neighbor. The Last Judgment will reveal Christ's ultimate triumph over evil and manifest the ultimate meaning of all of creation.

For Reflection

How do I understand death to be the threshold of new and everlasting life?

How does the promise of heaven inspire me to live the law of love?

Catechist to Catechist

The Gift of Grace

Grace, while a wonderful gift from God, is certainly an extremely difficult concept for children—and for adults—to comprehend. Perhaps a good way to help third graders, who are still very concrete thinkers, gain some insights into the nature of grace is to give them a glimpse of the meaning of the gift of grace in action. The tone of your voice, the smile on your face, and the enthusiasm with which you share your faith will go a long way in helping the children understand that grace is sharing in God's life and love.

Eternal Life

Heaven has to do with the gift, or grace, of eternal life. As you present heaven in this chapter, emphasize that heaven is a life of eternal happiness with God and all the saints. It is the greatest happiness we can imagine. Remind the children of God's infinite love for them.

The Church Teaches . . .

The *General Directory for Catechesis* teaches that:

> The "providential plan"[1] of the Father, fully revealed in Jesus Christ, is realized by the power of the Holy Spirit. This implies . . . the offer of salvation to all men, as a gift of God's grace and mercy,[2] which implies freedom from evil, sin and death.[3]
>
> *GDC* 37

As a catechist and a follower of Christ, we continually deepen our understanding that salvation is not earned, but freely given by God.

See the Catechism . . .

For more on the teachings of the Catholic Church on life after death, true happiness, and grace, see *Catechism of the Catholic Church* 1020–1050, 1716–1724, and 1997–2016.

CATECHIST PRAYER

Spirit of God,
help us welcome your
presence in our lives.
Amen.

Footnote references may be found on p. 456.

LESSON PLANNER

Focus — To discover how God makes us sharers in his life and love now and forever in heaven

Engage

Page 189
Focus
To assess the children's knowledge about heaven

Opening Prayer

Discussion
How God shares his life with us

Teach and Apply

Pages 190–192
Focus
To explain that God shares his grace with us and calls us to share eternal life with him in heaven

Presentation
Read, discuss, and summarize content.
Scripture
- Psalm 27:13
- John 14:2–3
- Luke 14:16, 18–21, 23

Activities
- Describe the importance of prayer to the Holy Spirit.
- Work a word puzzle about heaven.
- Write how people show that they want to live in happiness with God.

Faith-Filled People
Patron Saints

Connect

Pages 193–194
Focus
To discover that the Church celebrates God's promise of everlasting life

Our Church Makes a Difference
At a Funeral Mass we celebrate the gift of eternal life with God.
Our Catholic Faith
Incense

What Difference Does Faith Make?
Activity
Write a message of hope.
Faith Choice
Choose a way you will show God this week that you want to be happy with him.

We Pray

Page 195
Prayer Form
Prayer of hope
Prayer
Introduce the prayer and pray "Act of Hope" together.

We Remember

Review
- Complete the crossword puzzle.
- Read the "To Help You Remember" statements aloud.
Preview
Highlight features of the "With My Family" page.

Materials

- appropriate music
- pens or pencils

Enriching the Session

Blackline Masters
Additional Activities booklet:
Chapter 22
Choosing to be happy
Loving God
Assessment Tools booklet:
Chapter 22 Test
Unit 3 Review

Enriching the Lesson (CG page 317)
Making Storyboards
Making Sympathy Cards
Literature Connection

Music Connection (CG page 317)

www.FaithFirst.com

We update the *Faith First* Web site weekly. Check each week for new content and features. Here are some places to begin:

Catechists and Teachers
- Current Events
- Chapter Downloads
- Catechist Prayer

Faith First **for Families**
- Bible Stories
- Make a Difference

Kids' Clubhouse
- *Faith First* Activities
- Chapter Reviews
- Games
- Saints

Don't Forget! You can make lesson planning a breeze—check out the **Online Lesson Planner.**

God Shares His Life with Us

22

We Pray

I believe I shall enjoy the LORD's goodness in the land of the living. Psalm 27:13

O Lord our God, may all live and be happy with you forever in heaven. Amen.

Who shares their life with you?

Our parents share their love and lives with us. God has made us sharers in his own life now and in heaven.

When you hear the word heaven, what do you think of?

189

PRAY

- Gather the children and have them quiet themselves for prayer.
- Pray the Sign of the Cross and Psalm 27:13 together.
- Lead the prayer and all say, "Amen."
- Begin and close with the praying of the Sign of the Cross together.

DISCOVER

Purpose: To assess what the children know about the gift of heaven

- Ask the children who they know who shares their life with them. God, their parents, other relatives.
- Read the introductory paragraph to the children.
- Ask: What do you think of when you hear the word *heaven?* Accept all appropriate responses.

Liturgy Tip

Praying for Those Who Have Died. In this chapter the children will discuss the meaning of eternal life. Explain to the children that it is a Catholic tradition to pray for the dead. Then teach the children the prayer from the Order of Christian Funerals:

Eternal rest grant unto them, O Lord. / And let perpetual life shine upon them. / May they rest in peace. / Amen.

Stress that the prayer is asking God to take care of the person who has died and to give the person happiness forever in heaven.

Teach

FOCUS

Ask a volunteer to read the "Faith Focus" question aloud. Share with the children that in this chapter they will learn how God makes us sharers in his life and love.

DISCOVER

- Draw a Venn diagram on the board. Label each circle at the top; label one circle *Sanctifying Grace* and the second circle *Actual Grace*. Write the word *Different* inside each circle. Label the overlapping part of the circles with the word *Same*.
- Ask the children to work with partners. Tell them to read "A Gift from God" together. Ask them to decide how the two kinds of grace are the same and how they are different.
- Give the groups five minutes to complete the task and ask them to share their results.
- Write their answers in the diagram on the board.

Apply

REINFORCE

Ask a volunteer to read the definition of the word *grace* in "Faith Words." Have them make a word card for this term.

INTEGRATE

- Ask volunteers to describe why they think it is important to ask the Holy Spirit to help us live as children of God.
- Summarize responses.

The Gift of Grace

Faith Focus

How does God make us sharers in his life and love?

Faith Words

grace
God's grace is the gift of God making us sharers in the life of the Holy Trinity. It is also the help God gives us to live a holy life.

heaven
Heaven is eternal life, or living forever in happiness with God after we die.

A Gift from God

God created us to share in the life and love of the Holy Trinity. Sharing in the life of God is a gift from God. We call this gift **grace.** The word *grace* means "gift" or "favor."

Sanctifying grace and actual grace are two kinds of grace. The word *sanctify* means "to make holy or sacred." Sanctifying grace is the grace we first receive at Baptism. It heals our soul of all sin and makes us holy. It makes us sharers in the very life of God.

Actual grace is the grace given to us by the Holy Spirit to help us make choices to live a holy life. Actual grace helps us overcome temptation. Temptation is everything that tries to lead us away from living as children of God. Actual grace helps us live as God wants us to live.

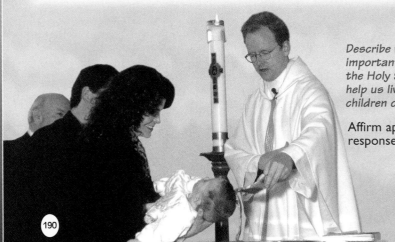

Describe why it is important to ask the Holy Spirit to help us live as children of God.

Affirm appropriate responses.

190

Teaching Tip

A Song of Grace. Sing the song "Frère Jacques" with the children to recall the melody. On the board, print the following words and have the children sing them to the melody of "Frère Jacques."

"God will help me. / God will help me / with his grace / with his grace. / Actual grace will help me. / Actual grace will help me / to choose well / to choose well."

Jesus Promises Us Eternal Life

You have learned that Jesus was raised from the dead and ascended, or returned, to heaven. He now lives with God the Father and the Holy Spirit. God wants you to be happy with him forever too.

When your body dies, your soul still lives. You will live in a different way. God created you to live forever.

At the Last Supper Jesus promised his disciples,

"I am going to prepare a place for you so that we can be together."
Based on John 14:2–3

We call this promise the promise of eternal life. The word *eternal* means "forever." We call our eternal life of happiness with God **heaven.**

Find and circle the words in the puzzle that describe heaven.

Faith-Filled People

Patron Saints

The Church names some saints as patron saints. Patron saints are saints in heaven who have been chosen to pray in a special way for a person, a country, a town, a local parish church, or a group of people. Patron saints pray that we join them in heaven.

D	X	D	M	S	J	T	V
H	O	L	P	T	O	W	Y
A	B	C	D	F	Y	M	N
P	E	A	C	E	F	U	L
P	B	L	C	O	U	G	G
Y	L	N	O	P	L	Q	T

HAPPY

PEACEFUL

JOYFUL

191

Background: Faith-Filled People

Patron Saints. Saints are heroes of faith. Their lives demonstrate holiness and prayer in action. Oftentimes we pray for their intercession with God—sometimes for a specific cause, other times for their help and guidance in general. Over the centuries, particular saints have been associated with specific causes or groups of people or places. For instance, the Catholic Church has officially designated Saint Francis of Assisi as the patron saint of ecologists.

FOCUS

Remind the children that grace is sharing in God's life. Share with them that they will learn about God's promise of eternal life.

DISCOVER

- Ask the children to share what they know about heaven.
- Ask volunteers to read aloud the first two paragraphs of "Jesus Promises Us Eternal Life." Have the children listen for what happens when our bodies die.
- Ask a volunteer to read aloud John 14:2–3.
- Make a word map with the children for the word *heaven*.
- Then have the children read aloud the meaning of the faith word *heaven* on page 190 in their text.
- Explain that when people who love God die, they go to heaven, and we call them saints.
- Invite the children to silently read "Faith-Filled People" to discover the meaning of *patron saints*.

Apply

REINFORCE

Remind the children that the word *eternal* means "forever." Jesus promises us an eternal life of happiness in heaven. Have the children make a word card for the word *heaven*.

INTEGRATE

Have the children complete the puzzle.

Teach

FOCUS

Remind the children that Jesus promises us eternal life in heaven. Then point out that God invites all people to a life of eternal happiness.

DISCOVER

- Read aloud "Some Choose to Turn Away" to the end of the Gospel story.
- Invite the children to share what they think Jesus was teaching us about eternal life.
- Invite the children to silently read the rest of the page to check understanding.

Apply

REINFORCE

Have the children underline the first sentence of the second paragraph, the important point of Jesus' story, and read it aloud together.

INTEGRATE

- Have the children work in groups to name two choices that bring us closer to God. Tell them to write these answers in the activity box.
- Ask volunteers to share what they have written.

Some Choose to Turn Away

Some people look for happiness that does not include God. Jesus told a story about people who do this. Jesus said, "A man had a banquet. The guests he invited chose not to come. The man then said to his servants, 'Go into the streets and invite everyone you meet.' Soon the banquet hall was filled with guests."

Based on Luke 14:16, 18–21, 23

What are some things people can do to show they want to live in happiness with God?

The important point of the story is that God invites everyone to be happy with him forever in heaven. But some people choose not to accept God's invitation. Living separated from God forever after we die is called hell.

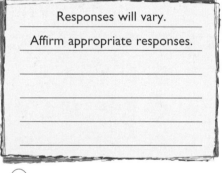

Responses will vary.

Affirm appropriate responses.

192

Teaching Tip

Role-Playing a Bible Story. Have the group gather into two small groups, and have each group present the Gospel story as a skit. You'll need children to play the roles of Jesus, the king, servants, guests who won't come, and guests who do. If you would like to use props, keep them simple. You can use sheets, fabric, and headbands for costumes, and white index cards for invitations.

Our Church Makes a Difference

The Funeral Mass

The Church celebrates when a Catholic dies. We celebrate the Funeral Mass. We share the gifts of comfort and hope with the family, friends, and neighbors of the person who has died.

We see many signs that we believe in the gift of eternal life. We see a large white cloth, or pall. This reminds us of Baptism and that we share in God's life. We see the lighted Easter candle. This reminds us that Jesus was raised from the dead and we will live with him forever in heaven.

Describe how our belief in God's promise of heaven can help us when someone we love dies.

Affirm appropriate responses.

Our Catholic Faith

Incense

The Church uses incense at the conclusion of the Funeral Mass. Incense is one of the Church's sacramentals. When it is burned, incense produces smoke and a sweet aroma. The smoke rises quickly as a sign of our prayers going to heaven. This is a sign that we believe God listens to our prayers.

Final prayers at the conclusion of the funeral liturgy, using holy water and incense

193

Background: Catholic Tradition

The Use of Incense. Made from the gums of resinous trees, burning incense was an ancient practice of many religions. It was used by the Jews in Jesus' time and burned on altars of sacrifice in the Temple of Jerusalem. Today it is sometimes used by the Catholic Church during the celebration of Mass.

HIGHLIGHT

Point out that one way the Catholic Church celebrates our faith in Jesus' promise of heaven is the Funeral Mass.

DISCOVER

- Ask the children if they have ever attended a funeral Mass. Invite volunteers to share what they saw and heard.
- Present "The Funeral Mass."
- Tell the children that the Funeral Mass celebrated by the Catholic Church recalls our faith and hope in Jesus' promise that we will share eternal life with God.
- Have the children work with partners to make a list of the things we see at a Funeral Mass that show we believe in the gift of eternal life. Have them tell each other what these signs mean.
- Read "Our Catholic Faith" to the children.

INTEGRATE

Ask: How does our belief in heaven help us when someone we love dies?

Connect

HIGHLIGHT

Help the children recall some of the ways the Holy Spirit helps us find happiness.

RESPOND

- Ask: How do you find true happiness?
- Direct the children's attention to the activity. Have them complete the invitation to someone they love.
- Give them sufficient time to complete the activity and invite volunteers to share their work.

CHOOSE

- Invite the children to respond to "My Faith Choice."
- After a moment of prayerful reflection have the children write their choice on the lines provided.
- Encourage the children to put their choice into practice this week.

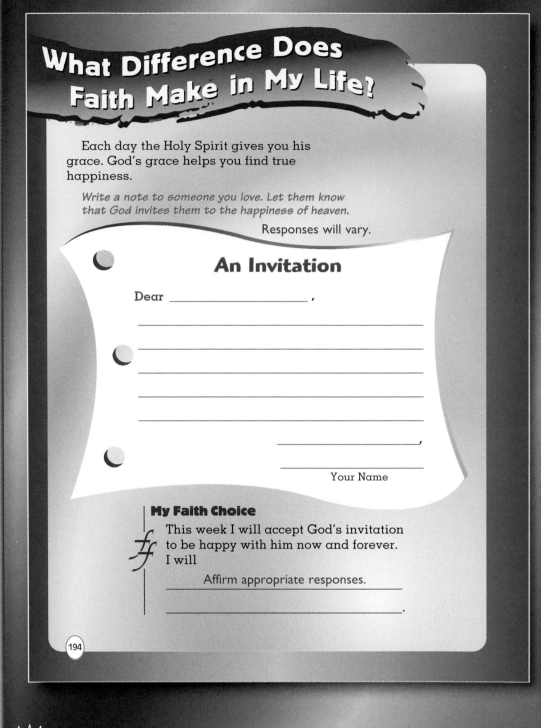

What Difference Does Faith Make in My Life?

Each day the Holy Spirit gives you his grace. God's grace helps you find true happiness.

Write a note to someone you love. Let them know that God invites them to the happiness of heaven.

Responses will vary.

An Invitation

Dear _____,

_____

_____

_____

_____,

_____
Your Name

My Faith Choice

This week I will accept God's invitation to be happy with him now and forever. I will

Affirm appropriate responses.

194

Teaching Tip

Experiencing Incense. Ask permission to take the hands-on approach to learning and burn a little bit of incense for the children to experience. Be careful not to use too much! Just a small amount burning while you and the children pray the closing prayer will help the children understand why the Church uses this very special sacramental as a reminder that God listens to our prayers.

We Pray

Act of Hope

Hope is a gift from God. Hope helps us want to live in happiness in heaven. Pray this act of hope.

God of love,
you are always good and kind.
I hope that with the help of your grace
I will live forever in happiness
with you in heaven.
Amen.

We Remember

Complete the crossword puzzle.

		¹H			²S		
³H		E		⁴G	R	A	C	E
E		L			N		
⁵A	C	T	U	A	L	G	R	A	C	E
V					T		
E					I		
N					F		
					Y		
					I		
					N		
					G		

DOWN
1. Living separated from God forever after death
2. The kind of grace that makes us holy
3. Eternal life with God

ACROSS
4. The gift of God's life and love to us
5. God's presence with us through the Holy Spirit, helping us live as children of God

To Help You Remember

1. God gives us the gift of grace to share in the life of God the Father, Son, and Holy Spirit.

2. God gives us the grace to live a holy life.

3. Jesus promised us the gift of eternal life and happiness in heaven.

Grade 3 • Chapter 22 (195)

Background: Liturgy

Christian Funerals. The funeral is a liturgical celebration of the Church. According to the *Order of Christian Funerals (Ordo Exsequiarum)*, it can be celebrated in the home, the church, and the cemetery. It is comprised of four elements: the Greeting of the Community, the Liturgy of the Word, the Liturgy of the Eucharist, and the Farewell. The Church accompanies the deceased at their journey's end and offers them to the Father proclaiming faith in eternal life.

Pray

WE PRAY

- Explain that the prayer is a prayer of hope.
- Play a recording of appropriate background music as you gather the children in the prayer center.
- Prepare the children by reading the opening paragraph. Remind them that Jesus' promise to us is the source of our hope in eternal happiness.
- Ask the children to kneel and raise their hands high, as if to heaven, as they pray.
- Pray the "Act of Hope" together.

Review

WE REMEMBER

- Scramble the letters of the words *eternal*, *grace*, and *heaven* and write the scrambled words on the board.
- Ask each child to write the words on a piece of paper and unscramble them at their desks. If you notice any children having trouble with the activity, circle the first letter in each scrambled word.
- Ask volunteers to use the unscrambled words in sentences.
- To reinforce learning, read the "To Help You Remember" statements aloud for the children.
- Introduce the crossword puzzle activity and give the children time to complete it.
- Have volunteers share their completed puzzle.

At Home

ENCOURAGE

Have the children carefully tear out pages 195 and 196 along the perforation. Encourage the children to share the pages with their families and to do the activities together. If they did not complete the review activity on page 195 by the end of the session, emphasize that they can complete it with their families.

VISIT FAITHFIRST.COM

- Share with the children the many activities on the *Faith First* Web site.
- Encourage the children to visit **www.FaithFirst.com.**

Before Moving On . . .

As you finish today's lesson, reflect on the following question before moving on to the next chapter.

How am I using the gifts of the artists in my class?

---

22   With My Family

This Week . . .

In chapter 22, "God Shares His Life with Us," your child learned about God's gifts of grace and eternal life. Sanctifying grace, which we first receive at Baptism, makes us holy and heals our soul of sin, both original sin and personal sins. Actual grace is the grace we receive from the Holy Spirit that strengthens us to live holy lives. Jesus promised the gift of eternal life and happiness with God, or heaven, to all who love God. Some people choose not to accept this gift and seek happiness apart from God. Some even choose to separate themselves from God's love forever. Living an eternal life of separation from God is called hell. Living an eternal life of happiness with God is called heaven.

For more on the teachings of the Catholic Church on life after death, true happiness, and grace, see *Catechism of the Catholic Church* paragraph numbers 1020–1050, 1716–1724, and 1997–2016.

Sharing God's Word

Read together the Bible story in Luke 14:15–24 about the man who had a banquet or read the adaptation of the story on page 192. Emphasize that Jesus is telling us that God invites everyone to live an eternal life of happiness in heaven.

Praying

In this chapter your child prayed an act of hope. Read and pray together the act of hope on page 195.

Making a Difference

Choose one of the following activities to do as a family or design a similar activity of your own.

- Watching incense rise toward heaven reminds us that God listens to our prayers. Talk about times that incense is used in your parish.

- In the Bible story about the man who had a banquet, Jesus teaches us that some people choose not to accept God's invitation to live an eternal life of happiness in heaven. Talk about how family members help one another live a holy life.

- The Resurrection shows us that life does not end for a person who has died. Talk about how your family can comfort those who have lost a loved one.

For more ideas on ways your family can live your faith, visit the "Faith First for Families" page at **www.FaithFirst.com.** Click on "Games" and make learning fun for your child.

Evaluate

Take a few moments to evaluate this week's lesson.
I feel (circle one) about this week's lesson.

    a. very pleased

    b. OK

    c. disappointed

The activity the children enjoyed most was . . .

The concept that was most difficult to teach was . . .

because . . .

Something I would like to do differently is . . .

ENRICHING THE LESSON

Making Storyboards

Purpose
To reinforce that grace is a gift of God that helps us live a holy life (taught on page 190)

Directions
- Play for the children a CD of the song "Amazing Grace."
- Provide each child a copy of the lyrics of this hymn.
- Have the children work with partners to make storyboards that visualize one of the verses of the song.
- Display the children's completed work in a place where others can enjoy it.

Materials
lyrics of the hymn
poster board or construction paper
markers or crayons

Making Sympathy Cards

Purpose
To reinforce what the Church celebrates at a Funeral Mass (taught on page 193)

Directions
- Have the children brainstorm phrases or sentences that are words of comfort and hope to families or friends that have had someone die.
- Invite the children to write a card that they can use that will share these words of comfort or hope.
- Have the children share their cards.
- Gather the cards and give them to the appropriate parish staff person to send to families who experience the death of a loved one.

Materials
paper for notes
pens or pencils
envelopes

Literature Connection

Purpose
To reinforce the Church's teaching about eternal life (taught on pages 191 and 193)

Directions
The topic of death and eternal life may raise questions for third graders who have experienced the serious illness or death of a friend or relative. Rabbi Marc Gellman's book *And God Cried, Too* (HarperCollins, 2002) tells the story of a young fictional angel-in-training who is troubled about problems on earth and asks questions of the angel Gabriel. Their conversations explore questions as basic as why a pet dies and as complex as the terrorist attack on September 11, 2001. The book presents a strong Judaeo-Christian image of a compassionate and loving God and encourages acts of kindness to all.

- Begin by asking children to share their experiences of illness or death.
- Choose an appropriate chapter and read it aloud. Remind the children that the characters in the story are imaginary, but the truths that Gabriel shares are important.
- Ask the children to share what they learned about God from the story.

Materials
And God Cried, Too by Marc Gellman

Music Connection
- "Eat This Bread," J. Berthier. *Rise Up and Sing* #201.
- "I Received the Living God," arr. R. Proulx. *Singing Our Faith (SOF)* #239.
- "Song of the Body of Christ/Canción del Cuerpo de Cristo" (Hawaiian traditional), arr. D. Haas. *SOF* #240.
- "Walking By Faith," D. Haas. *SOF* #179.

Unit 3 Review

The unit review provides the opportunity to assess the children's understanding of the concepts presented in the unit and to affirm them in their growing knowledge and love of God.

Here are a few suggestions for using these pages:

- Share with the children that the next two pages are an opportunity for them to stop and review what they have learned.
- Provide time for the children to ask questions.
- Have the children complete the review alone or with a partner.

PART A:
The Best Word or Phrase

This section reviews the main concepts of the unit.

- Read the directions for section A. Illustrate what you expect the children to do by completing the first question together.
- When the children have finished this section, invite volunteers to share their answers. Review any questions that the children seem to have had difficulty answering.

FAMILY CONNECTION

Encourage the children to share the unit review pages with their families. This provides an excellent opportunity to involve the families in the faith formation of their children.

Review Unit 3

Name _____

A. The Best Word or Phrase

Complete the sentences. Circle the best choice under each sentence.

1. The _____ is the solemn agreement God made with Moses and the Israelites.
   (a.)Covenant   b. Beatitudes   c. Great Commandment

2. The Great _____ tells us to love God and love our neighbor as ourselves.
   a. Covenant   b. Communion   (c.)Commandment

3. The _____ are the laws that teach us how to live the Covenant.
   (a.)Ten Commandments   b. parables   c. Psalms

4. Jesus learned and prayed sacred songs called _____ .
   a. lyrics   (b.)psalms   c. poems

5. The _____ Commandment teaches us to worship God.
   (a.)First   b. Second   c. Third

6. The _____ Commandment teaches us to respect all human life as sacred.
   a. Third   b. Fourth   (c.)Fifth

7. The _____ Commandment teaches us to honor our parents.
   (a.)Fourth   b. Fifth   c. Sixth

8. The _____ Commandment teaches us to be honest and tell the truth.
   a. Sixth   b. Seventh   (c.)Eighth

(197)

Teaching Tip

Assessment of Learners = Assessment of Catechists.
Value these unit reviews as an opportunity for your own assessment. Sharing the faith of the Catholic Church with the children and facilitating their growth as Catholics is an important ministry. Listen carefully to the children's responses. Their incorrect responses or their inability to respond can give you insights on ways to improve your presentation. Realize that the children's growth in faith is not your work alone—the Holy Spirit is truly the primary catechist during your sessions.

B. Making Sentences

Draw a line to connect the sentence parts in Column A with the sentence parts in Column B to make correct sentences.

Column A

1. The first three Commandments
2. The last seven Commandments
3. Good stewards
4. Sanctifying grace is the grace that
5. Actual grace is the grace that

Column B

a. makes us holy.

b. are people who use creation wisely and fairly.

c. teach us to love God.

d. teach us to love and respect others.

e. helps us live a holy life.

C. What I Have Learned

1. *What are two new things you learned in this unit?*

Responses will vary.

Affirm appropriate responses.

2. *Look back at the list of faith words on page 156. Circle the words you now know. Tell your group the meaning of two of the words.*

D. From a Scripture Story

Psalm 104 teaches us to praise and thank God for creation. Write two things this psalm teaches us about giving praise and thanks to God.

It reminds us that God cares for all creation.

It reminds us of the many things God created

that we have to be thankful for.

PART B:
Making Sentences

This section reinforces the unit faith vocabulary.

- Read the directions to the children and together match the first item. Have the children continue working with partners to finish the section.
- Invite volunteers to share their answers.

PART C:
What I Have Learned

This section provides the children with the opportunity to write or talk about what they have learned.

- Have the children share with the group two things that they remember from the chapters.
- Invite the children to return to the unit opener pages for unit 3 and observe for themselves how they have grown in building a faith vocabulary.

PART D:
From a Scripture Story

This section is a review of the children's understanding of Psalm 104. Have the children work with partners to do the activity. Have each pair share their responses.

Teaching Tip

Pick a Section. It is not necessary, and perhaps it is not even desirable, to use all sections of the unit review during the session. Choose one of the review sections to process during the session. Send the review home with a note to the families, encouraging them to complete the unit review and use it as a faith-sharing tool with their children.

Unit 4 Opener

The unit opener pages use a variety of questioning techniques to assess the children's prior knowledge about the key faith concepts presented in the unit. Processing these pages should not take more than ten or fifteen minutes.

USING PICTURES

Pictures help stimulate the religious imaginations of the children. The pictures on page 199 illustrate some of the important faith concepts in the unit.

- Invite the children to look at and think about the pictures.
- Ask volunteers to describe what each picture says to them.
- Invite the children to share a response to the question.

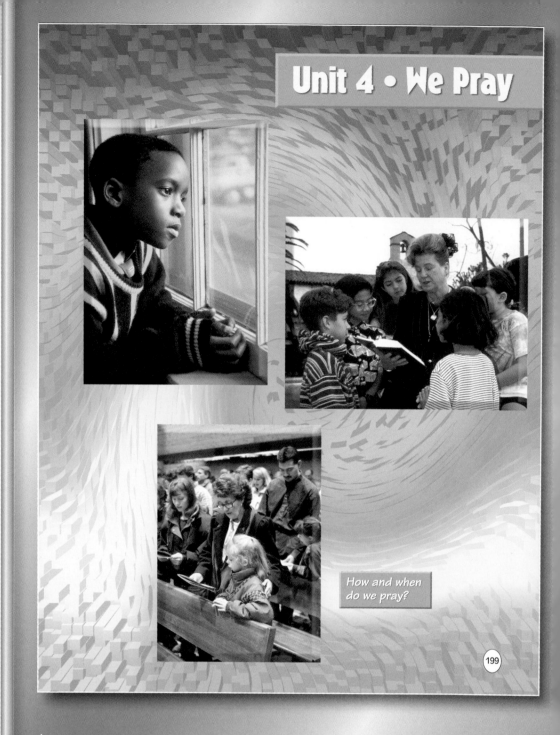

Unit 4 • We Pray

How and when do we pray?

199

Teaching Tip

A Person of Prayer. Prepare for presenting this unit on prayer by taking time to reflect on the role of prayer in your daily life. Identify the rhythm prayer has in your life: When do you pray during the day? What forms of prayer are you most comfortable praying? Being in touch with yourself as a person of prayer will help you share the Church's teaching on prayer and the prayers of the Church with the children. As you begin this unit, have the children turn to the "Catholic Prayers and Practices" section of their books. Review the prayers in the section. Have the children identify the prayers they know. Share a few thoughts about the prayers they do not know.

Getting Ready

What I Have Learned

What is something you already know about these two faith terms?

Personal prayer
Responses will vary.

_____

_____

Public prayer
Responses will vary.

_____

Words to Know

Put an X next to the faith words you know. Put a ? next to the faith words you need to know more about.

Faith Words   Responses will vary.

_____ prayer

_____ Abba

_____ petition

_____ intercession

_____ creed

_____ Hail Mary

Questions I Have

What questions would you like to ask about praying?

_____

Responses will vary.

_____

A Scripture Story

Mary visiting Elizabeth

Why did Mary visit Elizabeth?

Responses will vary.
Affirm appropriate responses.

200

Liturgy Tip

Memorizing Prayers. Memorizing prayers can improve our prayer life. The prayers become part of us and are always there when we need them. The key to memorizing is repetition. Saying the same prayer for several classes will set the prayer in the children's memory. Encourage the children to memorize Psalm verses and traditional Catholic prayers. When they are faced with a situation where they have difficulty praying in their own words, memorized prayers will facilitate their ability to pray.

GETTING READY

The "Getting Ready" page engages the children in sharing prior knowledge and aids you in planning your lessons to meet the needs of the children.

What I Have Learned

Ask the children to write one thing they know about personal prayer and public prayer.

Words to Know

This section is a quick assessment of the children's familiarity with some of the "Faith Words" they will be learning. Have them put an X next to terms they already know and a ? next to the terms they need to learn more about. During the unit review for this unit, ask them to return to this page and once again share their understanding of the faith words.

Questions I Have

Invite the children to write one question they have about praying. Ask volunteers to share their questions aloud. You may wish to write their questions on a chart. Refer back to the chart from time to time and ask volunteers to respond when they can answer the questions.

A Scripture Story

Unit 4 will review the Scripture story about Mary's visit to Elizabeth. Have the children look at the picture and answer the question to help you assess their prior knowledge of this story.

Jesus Teaches Us to Pray

Background

The Prayer of Jesus

When we use the term *Good News*, we are really talking about the Person and message of Jesus Christ, the eternal Word of God. Jesus, in his Person, his ministry, and his teaching most fully and clearly revealed the Good News of God the Father's love for us. The Lord's Prayer, which Jesus gave the Church, is a summary of that Good News, or Gospel.

> The Our Father gathers up the essence of the Gospel. . . . This prayer, given by Jesus to his disciples, makes clear the childlike trust and the deepest desires with which one can turn to God.[1]
>
> GENERAL DIRECTORY FOR CATECHESIS 115

Jesus understands the needs of our hearts. In giving us the Lord's Prayer, he gave us a means to express our innermost longings to God the Father. "When Jesus openly entrusts to his disciples the mystery of prayer to the Father, he reveals to them what their prayer and ours must be." (*Catechism of the Catholic Church* 2614).

The words of the Our Father are animated and brought to life in the light of Jesus' teaching, ministry, Passion, death, and Resurrection. When we pray as Jesus taught, we unite our petitions and hopes to the very Person of Jesus under the power of the Holy Spirit. The Holy Spirit prays within us, giving us the words, the thoughts, and the desire to turn our minds and hearts to the Father. In this way we come to know prayer as our communion in love with the Holy Trinity.

The Prayer of God's People

As the People of God we gather to offer our communal prayers, particularly at the Eucharist, to God the Father. Other traditional forms of communal prayer include the Liturgy of the Hours, Benediction, novenas, and holy hours, as well as the informal ways we pray with other believers in small groups and at parish gatherings.

Whether we pray alone or together, we raise our minds, hearts, and prayers to the Father, trusting that he knows what we will ask for even before we are aware of those petitions ourselves.

"Ask and it will be given to you; seek and you will find; knock and the door will be

opened to you. For everyone who asks, receives; and the one who seeks, finds; and to the one who knocks, the door will be opened."

MATTHEW 7:7–8

For Reflection

As I come before God in prayer, why is it significant that Christ joins me and that I pray in his name?

What hope and trust is engendered in me when I join with others in prayer?

Catechist to Catechist

Diversity in Prayer

Congratulate yourself and the children today for being open to so many different ways of praying this year. You have used liturgical gestures, body movements, songs, chants, words in another language, and meditation. Through this emphasis on diversity in prayer, you have helped these third graders share their lives with God.

A Story of Prayer

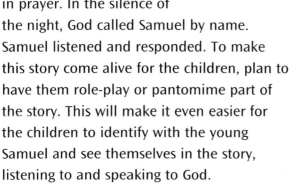

This is a good time to recall the story in 1 Samuel 3:1–10 of God calling Samuel. This is a wonderful story about listening and responding to God in prayer. In the silence of the night, God called Samuel by name. Samuel listened and responded. To make this story come alive for the children, plan to have them role-play or pantomime part of the story. This will make it even easier for the children to identify with the young Samuel and see themselves in the story, listening to and speaking to God.

The Church Teaches . . .

The *General Directory for Catechesis* teaches:

> When catechesis is permeated by a climate of prayer, the assimilation of the entire Christian life reaches its summit. *GDC 85*

Beginning and ending your sessions with prayer surrounds your lesson with a prayerful atmosphere. In this way children will understand that all catechesis has as its goal the deepening of one's relationship with God the Father, through Jesus, in the Holy Spirit.

See the Catechism . . .

For more on the teachings of the Catholic Church on prayer, see *Catechism of the Catholic Church* 2558–2567, 2598–2619, and 2700–2719.

CATECHIST PRAYER

Spirit of God,
help the children
and me stay in touch
with your love for us.
Amen.

Footnote references on these two pages may be found on p. 456.

LESSON PLANNER

To identify ways Jesus taught us to pray

Engage

Page 201
Focus
To assess the children's knowledge about the importance of praying

Opening Prayer

Discussion
When we spend time with God

Teach and Apply

Pages 202–204
Focus
To discover how Jesus prayed and what Jesus' prayer life teaches us about prayer

Presentation
Read, discuss, and summarize content.

Scripture
- Psalm 5:2, 3
- Luke 23:34, 46

Activities
- Write ways we show our trust in God.
- Name times we pray the Our Father.
- Draw or write about yourself praying.

Faith-Filled People
Saint Teresa of the Andes

Connect

Pages 205–206
Focus
To explain how the Church uses sacramentals and how the Holy Spirit helps the Church to pray

Our Church Makes a Difference
The Church uses objects, such as crucifixes and statues, to help us pray.

Our Catholic Faith
Churches

What Difference Does Faith Make?
Activity
Identify ways you pray now and ways you would like to try to pray.

Faith Choice
Choose how you will listen to the Holy Spirit and pray every day this week.

We Pray

Page 207
Prayer Form
The Our Father
Prayer
Introduce the Our Father and pray it together.

We Remember

Review
- Complete the matching activity.
- Read the "To Help You Remember" statements aloud.

Preview
Highlight features of the "With My Family" page.

Materials

- appropriate music
- pens or pencils
- crayons or markers

Enriching the Session

Blackline Masters
Additional Activities booklet:
  Chapter 23
    Designing a prayer aid
    Praying in different ways
Assessment Tools booklet:
  Chapter 23 Test

***Faith First* Grade 3 Video**
Segment 7: "Story of Faith"
Segment 8: "Our Father"

Enriching the Lesson (CG page 333)
Making Prayer Coupons
Making Prayer Spinners
Literature Connection

Music Connection (CG page 333)

www.FaithFirst.com

We update the *Faith First* Web site weekly. Check each week for new content and features. Here are some places to begin:

Catechists and Teachers
- Current Events
- Chapter Downloads
- Catechist Prayer

***Faith First* for Families**
- Bible Stories
- Make a Difference

Kids' Clubhouse
- *Faith First* Activities
- Chapter Reviews
- Games
- Saints

Don't Forget! You can make lesson planning a breeze—check out the **Online Lesson Planner.**

Jesus Teaches Us to Pray

23

We Pray

Hear my words,
O LORD.
To you I pray.

Psalm 5:2, 3

Our Father, who art in heaven, hallowed be thy name.   Amen.

Why is it important to spend time talking with those we care about?

God wants us to spend time talking with him.

When are some of the times you spend time with God?

201

PRAY

- Gather the children and have them quiet themselves for prayer.
- Pray the Sign of the Cross together. Choose a volunteer to read Psalm 5:2, 3.
- Lead the opening prayer.
- All say "Amen" together.

DISCOVER

Purpose: To assess what the children know about prayer

- Invite the children to share why it is important to spend time talking with those they care about, even those who live far away.
- Read aloud the introductory paragraph. Begin and end by inviting responses to the questions.
- Invite the children to look at the picture and ask them to consider what the child might be doing.

Teaching Tip

Making Room for Prayer. In a very real sense, prayer is much more an action than words. Words are important, but there is something even more important about prayer. Whenever we pray, we are responding to God's invitation to share our thoughts and feelings with him. We are growing in our relationship with him. Before you begin teaching this chapter on prayer, reflect for a moment on your own relationship with Jesus. Where is there room for improvement? Think about ways you can include more time for prayer into the rhythm of your daily life.

Teach

FOCUS

Ask a volunteer to read the "Faith Focus" question aloud. Share with the children that in this chapter they will learn some ways Jesus teaches us to pray.

DISCOVER

- Ask the children to read "The Prayer of Jesus" and underline the times Jesus prayed.
- Ask: When do you pray?
- Have the children respond in their prayer journals or have them reflect on the question for a few moments and share their thoughts with a partner.

Apply

REINFORCE

- Have the children make a prayer chart with the two columns "When I Pray" and "Where I Pray."
- Encourage the children to fill it each day this week to track the times and places that they pray.

INTEGRATE

- Have the children look at the picture as you proclaim Jesus' prayer when he was dying on the cross.
- Invite the children to complete the activity on the page.

Trusting God

Faith Focus

What are some ways Jesus teaches us to pray?

Faith Words

personal prayer
Personal prayer is spending time alone with God.

public prayer
Public prayer is praying with other people.

The Prayer of Jesus

When Jesus was on earth, he often spent time with God his Father in prayer. He prayed when he began his work on earth. He prayed when he chose his disciples. On the night before he died, Jesus prayed with his disciples at the Last Supper.

When Jesus was dying on the cross, he prayed,

"Father, forgive them. They do not know what they are doing." Just before he died, Jesus said, "Father, I give myself to you."

Based on Luke 23:34, 46

All Jesus' prayers show how much he trusts his Father. Trust is believing that a person loves us and will always be good and kind to us.

Jesus showed he trusted God the Father. Name some of the ways that you show your trust in God.

Responses will vary.

Affirm appropriate responses.

202

Teaching Tip

Creating a Prayer Life. Prayer is vital to our life with God. In a sense prayer is asking God to help us see things the way he does. As prayer becomes a part of who we are and a daily habit, we see God's point of view more and more clearly. Invite the children to pray frequently. Brainstorm with the children ways and times a person can pray. This will help them create their charts for the "Reinforce" activity.

Jesus Teaches Us the Our Father

When Jesus prayed to his Father, he sometimes used the word *Abba*. *Abba* is a word meaning "daddy" in the language Jesus spoke. It is a word that showed how much children trusted a parent. It showed they knew that the parent loved them.

One day Jesus' disciples were with him when he was praying. When he was finished, they asked Jesus to teach them to pray. Jesus said, "When you pray, say, 'Our Father'" (based on Matthew 6:9).

We call the prayer that Jesus taught the disciples the Lord's Prayer, or the Our Father. In this prayer we call God "Abba," our own Father.

The Church prays the Our Father every day. Name the times when you pray the Our Father.

Affirm responses.

Background: Faith-Filled People

Saint Teresa of the Andes (1900–1920). Saint Teresa of the Andes is the first Chilean and first American Discalced Carmelite to be named a saint of the Church. As a teenager she enjoyed playing the piano and swimming and was a parish catechist. At the age of nineteen on October 14, she fulfilled her calling and she began her novitiate as a Discalced Carmelite nun. Less than a year later she died on April 12, 1920, three months before her twentieth birthday. Throughout her life, Teresa reveals in her writings she had a very strong sense of God's presence with her.

Teach

FOCUS

Remind the children that Jesus showed his trust in his Father through prayer.

DISCOVER

- Ask the children what they think of when they hear the word *daddy*. Explain that Jesus sometimes used a word that means "daddy" when he prayed.
- Invite the children to silently read "Jesus Teaches Us the Our Father."
- Ask: What did Jesus teach his disciples to say when they pray? What do we call the prayer Jesus taught his disciples?
- Invite a volunteer to read "Faith-Filled People" to learn the story of a person of prayer.

Apply

REINFORCE

Emphasize that we are to pray the way Jesus prayed. We are to place our trust in God's love and care for us.

INTEGRATE

- Ask volunteers to share when and how often they pray the Our Father.
- Invite the children to form a circle and hold hands and pray the Our Father together.

Teach

FOCUS

Remind the children that Jesus taught us how to pray. Then point out that today they will learn about two kinds of prayer.

DISCOVER

- Talk with the children about times they like to be alone and times they like to pray with a group of people.
- Invite volunteers to read aloud "Praying Alone and with Others" to discover the meaning of personal prayer and public prayer.
- Ask the children to explain their understanding of personal prayer and public prayer.

Apply

REINFORCE

Have the children turn to page 202 and have a volunteer read the "Faith Words" and their meanings. Have the children make word cards for these faith terms.

INTEGRATE

- Explain the activity and invite the children to complete it.
- Invite volunteers to share responses.

Praying Alone and with Others

Jesus often left his disciples and went off to be alone with his Father. We, like Jesus, pray this way too. We enjoy being alone with God in prayer. We call this **personal prayer.**

Jesus also prayed with other people. Jesus prayed with people in Nazareth. He prayed with people in the Temple in Jerusalem. Praying with others is called **public prayer.** We pray this way too. We pray with our family at home. We pray with our Church community at Mass and at other times.

Draw a picture or write about yourself praying.

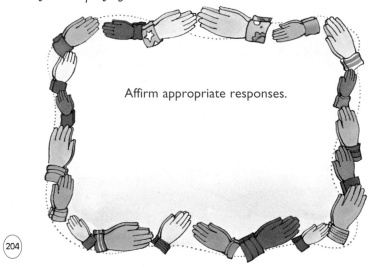

Affirm appropriate responses.

204

Teaching Tip

Brainstorming Two Ways of Praying. Divide the class into two groups. Assign one group "praying alone" and the other group "praying with others." Have each group brainstorm ways of praying the way assigned to it. Invite volunteers from each group to come forward and share ways to pray alone or with others. List the responses on the board. Encourage the children to choose one or several ways to pray alone and with others and to put their choices into practice this week.

Our Church Makes a Difference

A People of Prayer

The Catholic Church uses many objects that help us pray. The crucifix reminds us that Jesus died for us and loves us. Lighted candles remind us that Jesus was raised from the dead. Statues of Joseph, of Mary, and of the other saints remind us that we belong to a community of people on earth and in heaven.

Our Catholic Faith

Churches

Churches are sometimes called "houses of prayer." They are also called "houses of God." We gather in our church to pray together and to pray alone. Our parish church reminds us that the followers of Jesus are a people of prayer.

All these things are sacramentals. They help us raise our minds and hearts to God in prayer.

Name and describe the things that help you pray.

Affirm appropriate responses.

205

HIGHLIGHT

Remind the children that the Church is a people of prayer. Point out that they are going to learn about objects that help Catholics pray.

DISCOVER

- Read "A People of Prayer" and ask the children to listen for the objects Catholics use to pray.
- Ask the children how these items help us pray. They remind us of Jesus and the community of saints in heaven and on earth.
- Have the children read "Our Catholic Faith" aloud together. Explain that churches remind us that we are people of prayer.

INTEGRATE

Ask the children to name and describe sacramentals that help them to pray. Ask them to name sacramentals they have in their homes.

Liturgy Tip

Statues and Icons. Images of holy people help us to honor the holy persons they represent. It is important to remember that we do not pray to the statues. Statutes remind us of the holy people to whom we are praying. When preparing your prayer table this week, include sacramentals the children will recognize. Go over each item in the prayer center and discuss how it helps you pray.

Connect

HIGHLIGHT

Remind the children that the Holy Spirit teaches and helps us to pray.

RESPOND

- Introduce the activity on this page. Ask a volunteer to read the directions aloud.
- Invite the children to complete the activity on their own. When they are finished, invite volunteers to share their choices with the group.

CHOOSE

- Invite the children to respond to "My Faith Choice."
- After a moment of prayerful reflection have the children write their choice on the lines provided.
- Encourage the children to put their choice into practice this week.

What Difference Does Faith Make in My Life?

The Holy Spirit teaches you to pray. Every time you pray you show that you trust in God and God's love for you.

Put a ✔ next to the ways you now pray. Put a ★ next to the ways you would like to try to pray.

When, Where, How

Responses will vary.

___ 1. In my home

___ 2. At my parish church

___ 3. With my friends

___ 4. Kneeling down

___ 5. With my arms extended

___ 6. Every day

My Faith Choice

This week I will listen to the Holy Spirit and pray every day. I will
Affirm appropriate responses.

_____

_____

206

Liturgy Tip

Public and Private Intentions. As part of your visit to the parish church or during your sessions with the children, lead the children in praying a prayer of intercession. Invite them to name the intentions or people for whom they want to pray. Use the response, "We pray for this, O God." See this as an opportunity to demonstrate the difference between personal prayer and public prayer.

Pray

We Pray

Our Father

The Our Father is the prayer of all Christians.
The words of the Our Father teach us how to pray.

Leader: Let us raise our hands and pray as Jesus taught us.

All: Our Father, who art in heaven,
hallowed be thy name;
thy kingdom come;
thy will be done on earth as it is in heaven.
Give us this day our daily bread;
and forgive us our trespasses
as we forgive those who trespass against us;
and lead us not into temptation,
but deliver us from evil. Amen.

We Remember

Match the words in Column A with the words in Column B.

Column A		Column B	
d	1. Abba	a.	Prayer Jesus gave us
a	2. Our Father	b.	Praying alone
b	3. private prayer	c.	Praying with others
c	4. public prayer	d.	A word that means "Father"

To Help You Remember

1. Jesus taught us to talk and listen to God the Father.

2. Jesus taught us to pray with trust.

3. Like Jesus, we pray alone with God and we pray together with other people.

Liturgy Tip

The Orans Posture. During prayer we sometimes stretch out our arms and hands with palms facing up when we pray. This prayer gesture is called the *Orans* posture. This gesture is both a sign of our receptiveness to the Father and a symbol of the Risen Lord. Demonstrate the *Orans* posture for the children. Invite them to use it during the closing prayer.

Pray

WE PRAY

- Play a recording of appropriate background music as you gather the children in the prayer center.
- Explain to the children that the prayer today is well known to them. It is the Our Father.
- Introduce the prayer by inviting the children to raise their hands as they pray.
- Pray the Our Father together.

Review

WE REMEMBER

- Review the key concepts of the chapter by asking these questions based on the "To Help You Remember" statements:
  —What is prayer?
  —What are two ways we can pray?
- Introduce the matching activity and give the children time to complete it.
- Invite volunteers to share responses.

At Home

ENCOURAGE

Have the children carefully tear out pages 207 and 208 along the perforation. Encourage the children to share the pages with their families and to do the activities together. If they did not complete the review activity on page 207 by the end of the session, emphasize that they can complete it with their families.

VISIT FAITHFIRST.COM

- Share with the children the many activities on the *Faith First* Web site.
- Encourage the children to visit **www.FaithFirst.com.**

---

23 With My Family

This Week . . .

In chapter 23, "Jesus Teaches Us to Pray," your child learned about the prayer of Jesus and that Jesus taught us to pray. With trust, Jesus shared his thoughts and feelings with his Father. Jesus prayed for himself and for others. When his disciples asked Jesus to teach them to pray, he taught them to pray, "Our Father. . ." When we pray to God our Father, we pray with childlike trust and address God as Abba. We pray as children reaching out to parents who they know love them with a love that knows no limits.

For more on the teachings of the Catholic Church on prayer, see *Catechism of the Catholic Church* paragraph numbers 2558–2567, 2598–2619, 2700–2719.

Sharing God's Word

Read together the Bible story in Matthew 6:9–13 about Jesus teaching the disciples the Our Father. Emphasize that Jesus' prayers show how much he trusts his Father.

Praying

In this chapter your child prayed the Our Father. Read and pray together the Our Father on page 207.

Making a Difference

Choose one of the following activities to do as a family or design a similar activity of your own.

- When Jesus prayed, he placed his trust in God the Father. Invite family members to talk about how they show their trust in God.
- When you take part in Mass this week, spend time in the church after Mass. Look at the statues and all the other sacramentals that help you pray. Talk about how these things help you remember that God is always with you.
- Talk about the ways the members of your family pray alone and the ways you pray together. As a family, take time to pray each day this week.

For more ideas on ways your family can live your faith, visit the "Faith First for Families" page at **www.FaithFirst.com.** Click on "Family Prayer" to find a special prayer to pray together this week.

Before Moving On . . .

As you finish today's lesson, reflect on the following question before moving on to the next chapter.

What can I do to make sure that the children leave the session feeling more positive about themselves as faith-filled people?

Evaluate

Take a few moments to evaluate this week's lesson.
I feel (circle one) about this week's lesson.

   a. very pleased
   b. OK
   c. disappointed

The activity the children enjoyed most was . . .

The concept that was most difficult to teach was . . .

because . . .

Something I would like to do differently is . . .

ENRICHING THE LESSON

Making Prayer Coupons

Purpose
To reinforce the importance of spending time in prayer (taught on page 202)

Directions
Explain to the children that often we want to help people in need, but think that there is nothing we can do. Point out that we can always pray.

- Provide the children with a sheet of art paper. Have them fold the paper into four boxes to make prayer coupons.
- Print on the board, "_____ is praying for you."
- Have the children copy the sentence in each of the four sections of their paper, filling their name in the blank space.
- Encourage the children to decorate the coupons.
- Finally, have the children cut the coupons apart.
- Encourage the children to give the prayer coupons to people in their families or to their friends or neighbors.

Materials
paper
scissors
markers or crayons

Making Prayer Spinners

Purpose
To reinforce the teaching about personal prayer and public prayer (taught on page 204)

Directions
- Have the children brainstorm all the places they go during the week.
- Then, have the children make a spinner.
- Around the edge of the spinner, have them draw or write times and places they visit during the week.

- Invite the children to spin the arrow to identify a time and place they will remember to pray this week.
- Encourage the children to take the spinners home and spin them once a day to remind themselves of a place to pray.

Materials
construction paper
sheet of bendable plastic for spinners
scissors
paper fasteners
markers or crayons

Literature Connection

Purpose
To reinforce the prayer that Jesus taught the disciples (taught on page 203)

Directions
- Read *The Lord's Prayer* by Tim Ladwig, (Wm. B. Eerdmans Publishing Co. 2000).
- Ask volunteers to share how the young girl and her father lived the Our Father.
- Next ask the children to name some ways they live the Our Father in their lives.

Materials
The Lord's Prayer by Tim Ladwig

Music Connection

- "If You Believe and I Believe" (Zimbabwean traditional), arr. J. Bell. *Singing Our Faith (SOF)* #258.
- "Lord's Prayer," D. Haas. *Gather Comprehensive (GC)* #7.
- "O Lord, Hear My Prayer," J. Berthier. *SOF* #130.
- "The Lord's Prayer," M. Joncas. *GC* #16.

The Church Is a People of Prayer

Communion with God

Prayer is one of the ways in which we both express and deepen our relationship with God. As our hearts are transformed by the love of God, we long to respond to his gracious love. We respond by communicating with him and opening our hearts to further transformation through a life of prayer.

God longs for us, and we yearn to be united with him. Prayer is an expression of our thirst for God. It is also a source of strength as we face the temptations and evils of this world. Prayer is our hearts expressing themselves in gratitude for God's generosity.

Prayer is a fountain of humility. In prayer we surrender our struggles to God, acknowledging our power-lessness. Ultimately, prayer is our communion with God who formed us and breathed life into us.

Ways to Pray

Our whole life is to be a prayer to God, who desires that we communicate with him. Just as we keep our relationships with people alive by communication, we have the need to do the same to deepen our relationship with God.

The *Catechism of the Catholic Church* speaks of five basic types of prayer which have been revealed in Sacred Scripture. They are the prayer of blessing and adoration, the prayer of petition, the prayer of intercession, the prayer of thanksgiving, and the prayer of praise. Using all these types of prayer helps us express our thoughts and feelings to God amid varying circumstances of our lives.

When we stand before the beauty of creation, we may, for example, find the prayers of praise and thanksgiving on our lips. At those times in our lives when great needs press upon us, our prayer is one of petition. Most often, the form of our prayer is a mix of the various types of prayer. We believe that on our own we cannot pray; it is the Holy Spirit, the third Person of the Trinity, dwelling within us who urges us to pray. The Holy Spirit moves us to pray. Because of the impor-tance of prayer, it is vital that we respond to the Holy Spirit and pray without ceasing. As Saint Paul the Apostle reminds us, "Persevere in prayer, being watchful in it with thanksgiving" (Colossians 4:2).

For Reflection

How would I describe my life of prayer?

How can I apply Paul's teaching on prayer to my life?

Catechist to Catechist

Kinds of Prayer

This week you will talk about several prayer terms that name types of prayers that the children have already prayed and with which they are familiar. They are prayers which are rooted in the Psalms. They are prayers of praise, blessing, thanksgiving, petition, and intercession. Spend time making sure they can identify all five types of prayer. When the children are able to identify all five kinds of prayer, they will be better able to include them in their own prayer lives.

Heart to Heart

Some have described prayer as a heart-to-heart talk between friends. Provide time during this session to foster this personal communion between the children and God. It is important to nurture the gift of going down into the deep center of ourselves where God dwells. There we metaphorically kneel before him in wonder and awe.

The Church Teaches . . .

The *General Directory for Catechesis* teaches:

> Genuine catechesis is that catechesis which helps to perceive the action of God throughout the formative journey. It encourages a climate of listening, of thanksgiving and of prayer.[1]   *GDC* 145

Help the children recognize and respond to God's love. Encourage grateful thanksgiving through communal prayer during your sessions.

See the Catechism . . .

For more on the teachings of the Catholic Church on prayer, see *Catechism of the Catholic Church* 2598–2691.

CATECHIST PRAYER

God of love,
be with us
this week.
Help us discover
that we are
people of prayer.
Amen.

LESSON PLANNER

To discover ways the Bible teaches us to pray

Engage

Page 209
Focus

To assess the children's knowledge about the five ways we pray

Opening Prayer

Discussion

What we can share with God in prayer

Teach and Apply

Pages 210–212
Focus

To explain the five traditional expressions of prayer

Presentation

Read, discuss, and summarize content.

Scripture
- Psalm 92:2
- Luke 17:15–16

Activities
- Use a picture to help identify ways people talk to God.
- Finish a prayer of blessing.
- Add to a prayer of praise.

Faith-Filled People

Blessed Damien of Molokai

Connect

Pages 213–214
Focus

To discover that prayer groups help us pray

Our Church Makes a Difference

Prayer groups help us pray.

Our Catholic Faith

Liturgy of the Hours

What Difference Does Faith Make?
Activity

Decorate a prayer poster.

Faith Choice

Choose to pray a prayer of thanksgiving this week.

We Pray

Page 215
Prayer Form

Praise and blessing

Prayer

Introduce the prayer and pray together.

We Remember

Review
- Complete the word puzzle.
- Read the "To Help You Remember" statements aloud.

Preview

Highlight features of the "With My Family" page.

Materials

- appropriate music
- pens or pencils
- crayons or markers

Enriching the Session

Blackline Masters
  Additional Activities booklet:
    Chapter 24
      Planning a project
      Marking a bookmark
  Assessment Tools booklet:
    Chapter 24 Test

Enriching the Lesson (CG page 345)
  Taking a Nature Walk
  Performing a Gospel Skit
  Literature Connection

Music Connection (CG page 345)

www.FaithFirst.com

We update the *Faith First* Web site weekly. Check each week for new content and features. Here are some places to begin:

Catechists and Teachers
- Current Events
- Chapter Downloads
- Catechist Prayer

Faith First **for Families**
- Bible Stories
- Make a Difference

Kids' Clubhouse
- *Faith First* Activities
- Chapter Reviews
- Games
- Saints

Don't Forget! You can make lesson planning a breeze—check out the **Online Lesson Planner.**

The Church Is a People of Prayer

We Pray

LORD our God, it is good to praise you.
Based on Psalm 92:2

Holy, holy, holy Lord, God of power and might. Heaven and earth are full of your glory.

What do you talk about with your family and friends?

People talk about many things with one another. We can talk to God about these and many other things.

What do you share with God when you pray?

(209)

PRAY

- Play a recording of appropriate background music as you gather the children and have them quiet themselves for prayer.
- Pray the Sign of the Cross together and invite a volunteer to read Psalm 92:2 aloud.
- Pray the opening prayer aloud with the children.
- Conclude with praying the Sign of the Cross together.

DISCOVER

Purpose: To assess ways that the children pray

- Ask: What kinds of things do you talk to others about?
- Read the introductory paragraph and invite responses to the question that follows.
- Invite the children to look at the picture of the assembly. Ask them to describe the feelings these people may have.

Liturgy Tip

The Mass Acclamations. The Eucharistic Prayer begins with an introductory dialogue and the Preface. The priest and the people pray the acclamation together: "Holy, holy, holy, Lord." Frequently, the assembly sings this acclamation. If possible, sing the opening prayer using a simple melody that is sung in your parish. Encourage the children to raise their arms in praise of God as they sing.

Teach

FOCUS

Ask a volunteer to read the "Faith Focus" question aloud. Share with the children that in this chapter they will learn about five different kinds of prayer the Church prays.

DISCOVER

- Ask the children to name some things or people for whom they pray.
- Invite them to read "We Pray for Ourselves and for Other People" and underline the two kinds of prayer they find in the reading.
- Draw a T-chart on the board with the two headings "Prayer of Petition" and "Prayer of Intercession." Invite the children to help you fill in facts about these two kinds of prayer.

Apply

REINFORCE

Invite volunteers to read aloud the two terms in "Faith Words" and their meanings. Have them make word cards for these terms.

INTEGRATE

Call the children's attention to the pictures on the page. Ask the activity question and have them share their responses with their partners.

The Prayers of the Church

Faith Focus

What are some of the ways we pray?

Faith Words

prayers of petition
Prayers of petition are prayers in which we ask God to help us.

prayers of intercession
Prayers of intercession are prayers in which we ask God to help others.

We Pray for Ourselves and for Other People

Jesus prayed in many ways. He prayed for himself and for other people. Like Jesus, we ask God to bless and help us. We ask God for forgiveness. We ask God to teach us how to live the Great Commandment. We pray that we will live in happiness with God and all the saints in heaven. We call these prayers for ourselves **prayers of petition**.

At other times we pray for other people. We pray for our family and friends. We pray for all people. We call these prayers for other people **prayers of intercession**.

When we pray for ourselves and for other people, we trust God listens to our prayers.

Look at the pictures on this page. With a partner talk about what the people in the pictures might be saying to God.
Affirm appropriate responses.

210

Faith Vocabulary

Prayers of Intercession. When we think of sharing with people in need, we most often think about the physical needs of people, such as housing, food, shelter, and clothing. The Church clearly teaches that we are to work toward the sharing of spiritual goods among people as well. When we share our spiritual goods by praying for others, we are saying prayers of intercession. Whether we make these prayers together as a community during Sunday Mass or at home with our families, we trust that God is listening.

We Bless God

The bread and the wine we use at Mass are God's gifts to us. They are also our gifts to God. At Mass the priest takes the plate holding the bread that we have just brought to the altar. Lifting it up he prays a prayer of blessing. He prays,

Blessed are you, Lord, God of all creation. Through your goodness we have this bread to offer, which earth has given and human hands have made. It will become for us the bread of life.

We respond, "Blessed be God for ever."

The priest then holds up the cup of wine and prays another prayer of blessing. In a prayer of blessing, we tell God we know that everything good we have is God's gift to us. God blesses us, and we bless God.

✗ Faith-Filled People

Damien of Molokai
Blessed Damien of Molokai helped people who had a serious skin disease called leprosy. Nobody wanted to be near these people. Father Damien lived with them in their village so he could take care of them. We bless God for the gift of Blessed Damien of Molokai.

Finish this prayer of blessing.

Blessed are you, God.

Affirm appropriate

responses.

_____

_____

_____.

Amen.

 211

Background: Faith-Filled People

Damien of Molokai. Before the birth of Blessed Damien, few had any firsthand knowledge of leprosy (Hansen's disease). By the time he died of leprosy at the age of 49, people all over the world knew about this disease. Damien, forced to quit school at a young age, worked his family farm until he entered the Congregation of the Sacred Hearts of Jesus and Mary. In May 1864, Damien was ordained a priest in Honolulu and assigned to the island of Hawaii. In 1873 he went to the Hawaiian government's leper colony on the island of Molokai and volunteered to remain there permanently, caring for the people's physical, medical, and spiritual needs. In time he became their most effective advocate to obtain promised government support.

Teach

FOCUS
Remind the children that we pray prayers of petition and prayers of intercession. Point out that the prayer of blessing is another kind of prayer the Church prays.

DISCOVER
- Invite a volunteer to read the first paragraph of "We Bless God."
- Read the words from the Preparation of the Gifts, which begins the Liturgy of the Eucharist, and have the children respond, "Blessed be God forever."
- Invite a volunteer to read the last paragraph. Ask: What do we mean when we say "Blessed be God?" We are telling God that we know that everything good we have is his gift to us.
- Explain to the children that there are many people the Church recognizes as blessings from God.
- Read aloud "Faith-Filled People."
- Ask the children to explain how Blessed Damien was a blessing to the people he cared for.

Apply

REINFORCE
Invite the children to reflect on their experiences that are a gift from God. Ask the children to name what they thought of, and after each child has a chance to share, say together, "Blessed be God forever."

INTEGRATE
Invite the children to complete the prayer.

Teach

FOCUS

Remind the children that they have learned about three of the five kinds of prayer the Church prays. Point out that the prayer of thanksgiving and the prayer of praise are two other kinds of prayer the Church prays.

DISCOVER

- Ask the children to name the kinds of prayer they have already learned. Petition, intercession, blessing.
- Then ask them why we say "thank you" to people.
- Read aloud to the children "We Praise God." Ask them what they think the message of the story is.
- Ask the children to explain what it means to praise God.
- Have the children read silently "We Thank God."

Apply

REINFORCE

Ask the children to name a special holiday when we thank God.

INTEGRATE

- Ask the children to think of what they are thankful for.
- Have them complete the activity on their own.
- Invite volunteers to share responses.

We Praise God

There is only one God who is Father, Son, and Holy Spirit. We pray a prayer of praise when we tell God that only he is God. We love him above all else.

We Thank God

One day ten people who had a serious skin disease called leprosy came to Jesus. They asked Jesus to cure them of their sickness. Jesus cured all ten people. Here is what happened.

Only one of the ten thanked Jesus. He said, "Glory to God! I am healed!" Based on Luke 17:15–16

Invite all creation to praise God. Add to this prayer of praise.

God has done many wonderful things. It is important to say thank you to God for his blessings. When we do this, we are praying a prayer of thanksgiving.

> ### Praise God
>
> Praise God, sun and moon!
>
> Praise God, ___Affirm appropriate responses.___
>
> Praise God, _____.
>
> Praise God, _____.

212

Teaching Tip

An Act of Gratitude. Jesus cured ten lepers (see Luke 17:11–19). Yet only one returned to thank him. Jesus praised this person. We know God is pleased when we thank him for the blessings in our lives. Have the children write a prayer thanking God for someone who has blessed their lives. Helping children acquire the habit of expressing gratitude to God (and to people), whether in writing or in spoken words, is one of the most important things you can accomplish this year.

Our Church Makes a Difference

Prayer Groups

When we come together to pray, Jesus tells us he is there with us. He said, "When you gather as my disciples, I am there with you" (based on Matthew 18:20). Prayer groups help us remember that Jesus is always with us when we pray together. Jesus is part of everything we do in his name. When we remember this, it makes a difference. Our whole life becomes a prayer.

Many parishes have prayer groups. Parishioners gather at the parish church or in homes to read the Scriptures and to pray together. They ask God's help for themselves and others. They bless God and ask God's blessing. Together they pray prayers of praise and thanks.

Describe some of the ways the people of your parish come together to pray.

Responses will vary.

Our Catholic Faith

Liturgy of the Hours

The Church gathers many times each day to pray. The Church celebrates the Eucharist and prays the Liturgy of the Hours. The Liturgy of the Hours is the official daily prayer of the Church.

213

Teaching Tip

Forming a Prayer Group. Give the children the opportunity to experience a prayer group. Read a Scripture story that the children have read this year, such as The Great Commandment (Matthew 22:34–38). Then have the children gather into groups. Have each group choose a leader who will ask the members of their group to tell one thing they learned from the reading. Monitor each group. Give help when needed. Then have each group pray together in any way they wish.

Connect

HIGHLIGHT

Remind the children that sometimes we pray alone and sometimes we pray with others. Point out that prayer groups give us a special opportunity to pray with our parish family.

DISCOVER

- Ask the children if they know anyone who belongs to a prayer group at their parish.
- Read "Prayer Groups" aloud to the children. Ask them to listen for what Jesus told us about praying together.
- Have the children name the prayers prayed in prayer groups. Prayers of blessing, intercession, petition, thanks, and praise.
- Then have the children read "Our Catholic Faith" to discover the official daily public prayer of the Church, the Liturgy of the Hours.

INTEGRATE

- Ask the children to look at the pictures and tell what kind of prayers the people might be praying.
- Divide the class into groups and have them describe some of the ways the people of their parish come together to pray.

Connect

HIGHLIGHT

Remind the children that the Holy Spirit helps us pray.

RESPOND

- Emphasize that every time we pray, it is the Holy Spirit who gives us the ability to pray and teaches us to pray.
- Give the children crayons and markers to decorate the prayer poster on this page.

CHOOSE

- Invite the children to respond to "My Faith Choice."
- After a moment of prayerful reflection have the children write their choice on the lines provided.
- Encourage the children to put their choice into practice this week.

What Difference Does Faith Make in My Life?

When you pray prayers of petition, intercession, blessing, praise, and thanksgiving, it is the Holy Spirit who is helping you pray.

Decorate this prayer poster.

Lord, hear my prayer.

My Faith Choice

This week I will pray every day. I will say a prayer of thanksgiving for

Affirm appropriate responses.

_____ .

(214)

Background: Doctrine

Pray at All Times. Prayer is vital to our life as a Christian. Through the rhythm of daily prayer we keep God at the center of our life. Every event of each day becomes a moment for prayer. (See *Catechism of the Catholic Church* 2697–2699 and 2742–2745.)

We Pray

Blessed be God

The Divine Praises is a prayer the Church gives us. Pray this part of the Divine Praises.

Leader: Let us praise God. Let us join together and tell God he is wonderful and great. Blessed be God.

All: **Blessed be his holy name.**

Leader: Blessed be Jesus Christ, true God and true man.

All: **Blessed be the name of Jesus.**

Leader: Blessed be the Holy Spirit the Paraclete.

All: **Blessed be God in his angels and in his saints.**

We Remember

Find and circle the prayer words hidden in the puzzle. Use the words to tell a partner about prayer. Affirm appropriate responses.

> blessing   intercession   thanks
> petition   praise

Q	W	W	B	P	E	T	I	T	I	O	N
L	K	Z	L	P	C	Z	O	I	U	Y	T
I	N	T	E	R	C	E	S	S	I	O	N
W	E	H	S	A	P	S	Q	W	E	R	T
R	W	A	S	I	O	S	A	D	F	G	H
T	Q	N	I	S	I	I	Z	X	C	V	B
Y	P	K	N	E	U	R	J	H	G	F	D
U	O	S	G	M	Y	G	U	Y	T	R	E

To Help You Remember

1. We pray for ourselves and for other people.

2. We bless God who gives us all our blessings.

3. We thank and praise God for all our blessings.

Grade 3 • Chapter 24　215

Liturgy Tip

Prayers of the Faithful. Every Sunday at Mass, immediately after praying the Profession of Faith, we pray the Prayer of the Faithful, or general intercessions. Remind the children that they should listen carefully to these prayers and silently add their own prayers for others. This is one way we bring our prayers to Jesus, who is present in the Eucharist and in the entire faith community.

WE PRAY

- Play appropriate background music as you gather the children for prayer.
- Explain that the prayer is a prayer of praise and blessing. It is part of a prayer called the Divine Praises that is sometimes prayed when the Church worships Jesus in the Blessed Sacrament during the Benediction.
- Choose a volunteer to be the leader.
- Remind the children that when we come together to pray, Jesus is with us. Then introduce the prayer and pray the Divine Praises together.

Review

WE REMEMBER

- Ask volunteers to recall the five kinds of prayer they have learned. Write their answers on the board.
- Ask them to find the statement in "To Help You Remember" that contains a definition for each kind of prayer.
- Introduce the word search activity. Invite volunteers to use the hidden prayer words in sentences.

At Home

ENCOURAGE

Have the children carefully tear out pages 215 and 216 along the perforation. Encourage the children to share the pages with their families and to do the activities together. If they did not complete the review activity on page 215 by the end of the session, emphasize that they can complete it with their families.

VISIT FAITHFIRST.COM

- Share with the children the many activities on the *Faith First* Web site.
- Encourage the children to visit **www.FaithFirst.com.**

Before Moving On . . .

As you finish today's lesson, reflect on the following question before moving on to the next chapter.

What activities have I included that involve movement for those children who learn best that way?

---

24 With My Family

This Week . . .

In chapter 24, "The Church Is a People of Prayer," your child learned that the Church is a people of prayer. Prayer is at the heart of living and growing in our relationship with God. When we read the Bible and look at the life of Jesus, we discover five basic ways that the People of God express their prayers. We pray prayers of blessing and adoration, of petition, of intercession, of thanksgiving, and of praise. We pray to acknowledge and thank God the Creator and Savior and Sanctifier. We pray for ourselves and for others.

For more on the teachings of the Catholic Church on prayer, see *Catechism of the Catholic Church* paragraph numbers 2598–2691.

Sharing God's Word

Read together the Bible story in Matthew 18:20 about Jesus telling his disciples he is always with them when they gather in his name. Emphasize that Christians make their prayer in the name of Jesus.

Praying

In this chapter your child prayed a prayer of blessing God. Read and pray together the prayer on page 215.

Making a Difference

Choose one of the following activities to do as a family or design a similar activity of your own.

- When we pray for ourselves, we pray prayers of petition. When we pray for others, we pray prayers of intercession. As a family, take turns offering prayers of petition and intercession.

- When you take part in Mass this week, pay close attention to the prayer of the faithful. At dinnertime this week include a prayer of the faithful in your mealtime prayers.

- Find out if your parish has a prayer group who prays each day for the needs of your parish community. Contact the person in charge of the group. Have them include your family as a member of the group.

For more ideas on ways your family can live your faith, visit the "Faith First for Families" page at **www.FaithFirst.com**. Read this week's "Bible Story." Talk about the Bible story with your child.

Evaluate

Take a few moments to evaluate this week's lesson.
I feel (circle one) about this week's lesson.

   a. very pleased
   b. OK
   c. disappointed

The activity the children enjoyed most was . . .

The concept that was most difficult to teach was . . .

because . . .

Something I would like to do differently is . . .

ENRICHING THE LESSON

Taking a Nature Walk

Purpose
To reinforce the many blessings God has given us (taught on page 211)

Directions
Nature manifests the wonderful blessings from God.

- Take the children on a nature walk around the church property to find God's blessings in nature.
- Stop on occasion and pray a short prayer of blessing, such as "God, we bless you for the gift of flowers."
- When you and the children return from your walk, have them try to list all the wonderful blessings they saw, heard, touched, and smelled.
- Have the children decorate a prayer card with a short prayer of blessing and pictures of what they observed during the nature walk.

Materials
construction paper
scissors
crayons or markers

Performing a Gospel Skit

Purpose
To reinforce that it is important to say "thank you" to God for his blessings (taught on page 212)

Directions
- Read the full story of the ten lepers to the children from Luke 17:11–19.
- Have ten children take the parts of the ten people with the skin disease and one child take the part of Jesus.
- Have them tell the story in their own words.
- Then have the one who was thankful come back and thank Jesus in his or her own words.

- If possible, provide the children with simple props and costumes.

Materials
simple props (optional)

Literature Connection

Purpose
To reinforce the concept of expressing our thanks to God in prayer (taught on page 212)

Directions
Most children are aware of the hard work of custodians at their schools. In *The A+ Custodian* by Louise Borden (Simon & Schuster Children's Books, 2004) two children whose mother teaches in the school arrive early each day with her and observe the work of their custodian, Mr. Carillo. They initiate a school-wide project to show their appreciation to Mr. Carillo.

- After reading the book aloud, have the children describe how the members of the school expressed their thanks and why this was an important thing to do.
- Brainstorm with the children the many things that they have to thank God for.
- Invite the children to work alone or in small groups to express their thanksgiving to God, through words, gestures, song, or art. Be sure to invite them to perform or display their prayers.

Materials needed
The A+ Custodian by Louise Borden

Music Connection
- "All You Works of God," M. Haugen. *Singing Our Faith (SOF)* #157.
- "Amen Siakudumisa/Amen, We Pray to You" (South African traditional). *SOF* #284.
- "How Shall I Sing to God," D. Haas. *Gather Comprehensive* #591.
- "Prayer of Peace," D. Haas. *SOF* #248.

We Profess Our Faith

Faith and Belief

Faith is God's free gift to us, inviting us to freely enter into a relationship of trusting love with him. The gift of faith unites us in a covenant relationship with God. The gift of faith helps sustain us in a life of communion with God, who has been most fully revealed in Jesus, the Word of God. Through prayer we express our trust in God whom we have come to know in faith as Truth and Love.

We profess our Catholic faith in numerous ways. As we celebrate the Mass, we profess our faith by praying the creed. The words of the creed summarize the foundational beliefs of the Catholic Church. Praying the creed helps us express our faith with others, grow in our identity as Catholics, and hand the faith of the Church on to others.

Baptismal Profession of Faith

The first profession of faith we make is at Baptism. This profession is made within the community of believers and underscores the importance of the Church community in the life of faith.

At the Baptism of an infant, the community pledges to support the parents of the child as the child grows in faith. In the initiation of an adult through Baptism, Confirmation, and Eucharist, the public proclamation of faith is renewed by the whole assembly at the Easter Vigil and at all the Easter celebrations of the Eucharist.

Faith is a personal act—the free response of the human person to the initiative of God who reveals himself. But faith is not an isolated act. No one can believe alone, just as no one can live alone.

CATECHISM OF THE CATHOLIC CHURCH 166

The Apostles' Creed

The baptismal creed is founded on the Apostles' Creed, which is a summary of the faith handed on to the early Church by the Apostles. The Apostles' Creed contains three major expressions of belief.

- First, it professes the faith of the Church in God the Father, the Creator of all that is.
- Second, it professes the faith of the Church in God the Son, who became one of us through his Incarnation, and in the saving work of our redemption through his death and Resurrection.
- Third, it professes the faith of the Church in God the Holy Spirit, who is continually present in the Church, sanctifying and guarding the faith of the People of God as we journey toward life everlasting.

"This Creed," Saint Ambrose said, "is the spiritual seal, our heart's meditation and an ever-present guardian; it is, unquestionably, the treasure of our soul."

How does praying the Nicene Creed at Mass help me participate more fully in the Eucharist?

How has the gift of faith grown and matured in my life?

Catechist to Catechist

The Apostles' Creed

Summer and vacation time are approaching, and your time as a catechist with this group of children, this year, is coming to an end. Take time during these last few sessions to help the children recognize the good things they have shared and experienced as a small community this year.

Learn and Live

Learning about the Apostles' Creed gives you an opportunity to think back over the entire year. Choose from the suggested activities or  create your own to help the children draw together the learning of the whole year. In your activities help the children see that professing our faith in God is more than praying a creed. It is living that faith by putting it into action. This will help the children discover the difference faith truly does make in their lives.

The Church Teaches . . .

The *General Directory for Catechesis* teaches:

> In fusing his [or her] confession of faith with that of the Church, the Christian is incorporated into her mission: to be the "universal sacrament of salvation" for the life of the world. *GDC* 83

This chapter explains the importance of the creed and the mission of all those who believe.

See the Catechism . . .

For more on the teachings of the Catholic Church on prayer, see *Catechism of the Catholic Church* 2650–2672.

CATECHIST PRAYER

Holy Spirit,
teach us how to pray
the Apostles' Creed
with all our hearts and
with all our minds
and with all our souls.
Help us mean
what we pray.
Amen.

LESSON PLANNER

Focus   **To discover why we pray with creeds**

Engage

Page 217
Focus
To assess the children's knowledge about the creeds of the Church

Opening Prayer

Discussion
Our personal beliefs and the beliefs of the Church expressed in the creeds

Teach and Apply

Pages 218–220
Focus
To explain that the creeds of the Church help us express our faith in God

Presentation
Read, discuss, and summarize content.
Scripture
- Psalm 106:12
- Romans 8:26
- 1 Corinthians 12:3

Activities
- Fill in a prayer chart.
- Tell what beliefs the Church expresses in the Nicene Creed.
- Write three things the Apostles' Creed professes about Jesus.

Faith-Filled People
The Apostle Paul

Connect

Pages 221–222
Focus
To discover ways the Church lives the faith she professes in the creeds

Our Church Makes a Difference
We pray and live the words of the creeds.
Our Catholic Faith
Baptism Promises

What Difference Does Faith Make?
Activity
Design an "I Believe" banner.
Faith Choice
Choose a way you will pray and live what the Church believes this week.

We Pray

Page 223
Prayer Form
Prayer of praise
Prayer
Pray the prayer based on the *Te Deum* together.

We Remember

Review
- Complete the completion activity.
- Read the "To Help You Remember" statements aloud.

Preview
Highlight features of the "With My Family" page.

Materials

- appropriate music
- pens or pencils
- crayons or markers

Enriching the Session

Blackline Masters
Additional Activities booklet:
  Chapter 25
    Making time for prayer
    Cracking a code
Assessment Tools booklet:
  Chapter 25 Test

Faith First **Grade 3 Video**
Segment 7: "Story of Faith"

Enriching the Lesson (CG page 357)
Making Heart-Shaped Symbols
Making Collages
Literature Connection

Music Connection (CG page 357)

www.FaithFirst.com

We update the *Faith First* Web site weekly. Check each week for new content and features. Here are some places to begin:

Catechists and Teachers
- Current Events
- Chapter Downloads
- Catechist Prayer

Faith First **for Families**
- Bible Stories
- Make a Difference

Kids' Clubhouse
- *Faith First* Activities
- Chapter Reviews
- Games
- Saints

Don't Forget! You can make lesson planning a breeze—check out the **Online Lesson Planner.**

We Profess Our Faith

We Pray

They believed God's word and sang his praise.
Based on Psalm 106:12

I believe in God the Father, God the Son, and God the Holy Spirit. Amen.

What are some of the things that you believe?

The creeds of the Church are summaries of what the Church believes. Each week we pray the creed at Mass.

What are two creeds the Church prays?

Priests In procession during the celebration of Easter Mass by the pope at St. Peter's Basilica in Rome (217)

PRAY

- Gather the children and have them quiet themselves for prayer.
- Divide the class into two groups. Ask one group to pray aloud Psalm 106:12 and the other group to pray aloud the opening prayer.
- Pray the Sign of the Cross together.
- Begin the opening prayer by saying, "Let us pray," and then pray together as planned.
- Close the prayer with the Sign of the Cross.

DISCOVER

Purpose: To assess what the children know about our Church's creeds

- Ask: What are some of the things you believe? Read the opening paragraph and invite responses to the second question.
- Invite volunteers to share their thoughts about the picture.

† Liturgy Tip

Taught by the Holy Spirit. We need to be able to pray with trust and confidence. Sometimes, however, we may find it too difficult to pray. We might not know what to say. Remind the children that the Holy Spirit teaches us to pray. With the grace of the Holy Spirit, we can pray with confidence and trust. We can pray anytime and anyplace knowing that God is with us and listening to us. (See *Catechism of the Catholic Church* 2670–2672 and 2734.)

Teach

FOCUS

Have a volunteer read the "Faith Focus" question aloud. Share with the children that in this chapter they will learn why we pray with creeds and how the Holy Spirit helps us pray.

DISCOVER

- Read aloud the opening paragraph and Scripture verse of "The Holy Spirit Helps Us Pray."
- Emphasize that learning to pray is one of the most important things we do as Catholics.
- Ask a volunteer to read the final paragraph aloud.

Apply

REINFORCE

Emphasize that we could never pray without the prompting of the Holy Spirit.

INTEGRATE

- Invite volunteers to name things they can pray for during the day.
- Have the children fill in the chart at the bottom of the page. Ask them to share their work with a partner.

We Give Our Hearts to God

Faith Focus

Why do we pray with creeds?

Faith Words

creeds
Creeds are statements of what a person or a group believes.

Apostles' Creed
The Apostles' Creed is a brief summary of what the Church has believed from the time of the Apostles.

The Holy Spirit Helps Us Pray

Learning to pray is one of the most important things we do as Catholics. Saint Paul the Apostle said,

"We do not know how to pray as we ought." Romans 8:26

The Holy Spirit who is in our hearts helps and teaches us to pray. Every moment of every day, the Holy Spirit helps us give our hearts to God. The Holy Spirit is always praying in us and through us.

Fill in the chart by naming something you can pray about at different times during the day. Affirm appropriate responses.

Praying During the Day

Morning	_____
Noon	_____
Afternoon	_____
Evening	_____
Bedtime	_____

218

 FAITH WORDS

Faith Vocabulary

Creeds. Mission statements are used to clarify what a group believes and to identify values and priorities that guide their mission. From the Latin *Credo* meaning "to believe," the creeds of the Church are summaries of the beliefs of the Church. When we pray the creeds of the Church, we profess our faith.

We Pray the Creed at Mass

Saint Paul the Apostle told us, "No one can believe and say Jesus is God without the help of the Holy Spirit" (based on 1 Corinthians 12:3). The Church says what we believe in the **creeds** of the Church. When we pray the creeds of the Church, we profess our faith.

At Mass on Sundays, we make a profession of faith. We stand and pray the creed. The creed we usually pray is called the Nicene Creed.

Look up the Nicene Creed on page 284. Talk about what the Nicene Creed tells about what the Church believes.
Affirm appropriate responses.

Faith-Filled People

Paul the Apostle
Saint Paul became an Apostle after Jesus returned to heaven. Paul traveled by land and by sea to teach people about Jesus and to invite them to believe in Jesus. The Church celebrates the feast day of Saint Paul the Apostle on June 29.

"We believe in one God . . ."

Praying the Nicene Creed at Mass

219

Background: Faith-Filled People

Saint Paul the Apostle. The story of Paul's (Saul's) conversion (Acts 9:1–20) is one of the most famous conversion stories in history. Paul is completely transformed, no longer speaking out against the Good News of Jesus. Instead he proclaims the Good News with great energy and conviction. He travels to many distant places to tell the people that in Jesus all are invited to share in the gift of salvation. Perhaps there is no greater explanation of the qualities of the love Christians are called to live than Saint Paul's own description in 1 Corinthians 13:4–7.

Teach

FOCUS
Tell the children that the Holy Spirit teaches and helps us profess our faith.

DISCOVER
- Have the children read "Faith-Filled People" and underline three action words that tell what Paul did for the people he visited. Traveled, taught, invited. Use the background box at the bottom of the page for additional facts about Paul to share with the children.
- Read the Scripture passage from Saint Paul based on 1 Corinthians 12:3 aloud to the children.
- Invite the group to read silently "We Pray the Creed at Mass" to discover how the Church expresses what she believes.

Apply

REINFORCE
Ask the children to read aloud the faith word *creeds* and its meaning. Have them make a word card for this term.

INTEGRATE
Ask volunteers to share what the Nicene Creed tells about what the Church believes.

Teach

FOCUS

Remind the children that the Church's creeds express the faith of the Church. Point out that one of the main creeds of the Church is the Apostles' Creed.

DISCOVER

- Invite volunteers to read "The Apostles' Creed" to discover where the Apostles' Creed got its name.
- Point out that the Apostles' Creed contains beliefs that the Church has held since the time of the Apostles.

Apply

REINFORCE

- Tell the children to turn to page 284. Then divide the class into four groups.
- Assign one part of the creed to each group and have them read the Apostles' Creed as a choral reading.
- Encourage each group to devise a gesture to accompany their part of the creed.

INTEGRATE

Have the children complete the activity and invite volunteers to share their responses.

The Apostles' Creed

The **Apostles' Creed** and the Nicene Creed are the two main creeds of the Church. The Apostles' Creed is a brief summary of what the Church has believed from the time of the Apostles.

We pray the Apostles' Creed and the other creeds alone and together as a Church community. Praying the creeds of the Church helps us grow as a Church family. It helps us remember who we are as a Church.

Look up and read the Apostles' Creed on page 284. Fill in the blanks with three things the Apostles' Creed professes about Jesus.

I Believe in Jesus Christ

I believe in God, the ___Father___ almighty, creator of heaven and earth.

I believe in Jesus Christ, his only Son, our Lord.
Responses will vary.

- He was conceived by the power of the Holy Spirit and born of the Virgin Mary.

- He was crucified, died, and was buried.

- On the third day he rose again.

220

Background: Doctrine

The Nicene Creed. Among the Church's earliest professions of faith in Jesus was "Jesus is Lord." In the first centuries of the Church, some Christians were falsely teaching that Jesus Christ was not true God and true man. Some falsely thought that Jesus was really God and only pretended to be a man; others thought the opposite. The Ecumenical Council of the Church held at Nicaea, in what is now Turkey, in A.D. 325, affirmed the apostolic teaching that Jesus Christ is true God and true man. This teaching and other apostolic teachings about the Trinity were further affirmed at the First Council of Constantinople in 381 and the Council of Chalcedon in 451. The creed we pray at Mass is based on the teachings of these councils.

Our Church Makes a Difference

Living What We Believe

You have heard the saying, "Actions speak louder than words." Many people first come to know Jesus and follow him because of the deeds, or actions, of Christians.

The New Testament tells us how the first Christians lived their faith in Jesus. One writer wrote, "See how they love one another. See how they are ready even to die for one another." Many people admired the way the Christians lived their faith. They asked to be baptized and became followers of Jesus.

We not only pray the words of the creed, we also live what we say we believe. When our actions speak louder than our words, we make a difference in the world.

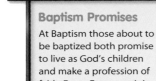

Our Catholic Faith

Baptism Promises

At Baptism those about to be baptized both promise to live as God's children and make a profession of faith. Every Easter we join with the whole Church and renew the promises we made at Baptism. We promise to live our faith.

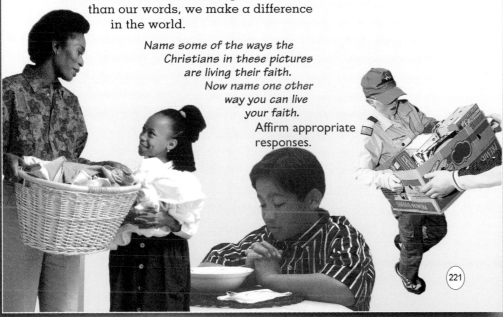

Name some of the ways the Christians in these pictures are living their faith. Now name one other way you can live your faith. Affirm appropriate responses.

221

Teaching Tip

An Evangelizing Faith. We can all be evangelists of our faith. Tap the talents and gifts of the youth in your parish. Invite a young person to a class session to speak with the children about their faith and how they live it. It will be more interesting for the children to hear an older child explain the faith of the Catholic Church. Sharing their faith will have an impact that can bring the younger children to stronger faith.

Connect

HIGHLIGHT

Remind the children that the Apostles' Creed summarizes the teachings of the Apostles. Remind the children that we must also live what we believe.

DISCOVER

- Write the saying "Actions speak louder than words" on the board. Ask the children what they think this means.
- Invite volunteers to read the first two paragraphs of "Living What We Believe." Point out the actions of the first Christians that led others to ask to be baptized. Loved one another; ready to die for one another. Have the children underline them in the text.
- Ask the children what living the words of the creed shows others. When we live the words of the creed, we live as followers of Jesus.
- Read aloud "Our Catholic Faith."
- Ask: How is the renewal of our baptismal promises like a creed? We say again what we believe. Both are a profession of faith.

INTEGRATE

Direct the children's attention to the pictures as you ask them to name some of the ways the Christians in the pictures are living their faith. Then ask the children to name other ways they can live their faith.

Connect

HIGHLIGHT

We belong to the Catholic Church. When we live the faith of the Church, we give ourselves to God.

RESPOND

Have the children complete the banner activity and have volunteers share their work.

CHOOSE

- Invite the children to respond to "My Faith Choice."
- After a moment of prayerful reflection have the children write their choice on the lines provided.
- Encourage them to put their choice into practice this week.

What Difference Does Faith Make in My Life?

You belong to the community of the Catholic Church. When you live the faith of the Church, you are giving your heart to God.

Design a banner that tells who you are and what you believe as a Catholic.

I Believe

My Faith Choice

This week I will pray and live what the Church believes. I will

Affirm appropriate responses.

222

💡 **Teaching Tip**

Word Play. Print *Apostles' Creed* on the board in a vertical column. Challenge the children to go through the text in this chapter and find words that begin with or contain each letter in *Apostles' Creed*. The words must say something about the creed. Have the children tell how the words they choose are related to the Apostles' Creed.

We Pray

You Are God

Hymns are songs of faith. The Church sings hymns to praise God and profess our faith in God. Pray this hymn together.

Group 1: You are God: we praise you;

Group 2: You are the Lord: we honor you;

Group 1: You are the eternal Father:

Group 2: All creation worships you.

Group 1: The holy Church everywhere honors you,

Group 2: Mighty Father, true and only Son, and Holy Spirit, helper and guide.

All: **Come then, Lord, help your people, and bring us to everlasting life. Amen.** Based on the Te Deum

We Remember

Use the letters in the word PROFESS to write words about what the Church believes.

Responses will vary.

Scri **P** tures

Chu **R** ch

S **O** n

F ather

et **E** rnal life

Holy **S** pirit

Re **S** urrection

To Help You Remember

1. We profess what we believe about God when we pray the creeds of the Church.

2. The Apostles' Creed is a brief summary of what the Church has believed from the time of the Apostles.

3. Praying the creeds of the Church helps us grow as a Church family.

Grade 3 • Chapter 25 **223**

Liturgy Tip

Praying with Gestures. Consider dividing the first lines from the Nicene Creed into the following five sections: (1) "We believe in one God, the Father, the Almighty," (2) "maker of heaven and earth." (3) "We believe in one Lord, Jesus Christ," (4) "the only Son of God," and in (5) "the power of the Holy Spirit." Encourage each of the five groups to create a prayerful gesture for its section. As you finish this chapter about the Creed we profess at Mass, incorporate a recitation of the Nicene Creed into a final prayer and include the gestures they have devised.

Pray

WE PRAY

- Play a recording of appropriate background music as you gather the children for prayer.
- Divide the children into two groups for prayer. Tell the children to raise their hands and arms in praise when they read their part of the prayer.
- Explain that the prayer is an ancient prayer of praise. It also tells some of the things we believe about God.
- Begin with the Sign of the Cross and then pray "You Are God" together.

Review

WE REMEMBER

- Write the words *creeds, Catholic Church,* and *Holy Spirit* on the board. Read the three "To Help You Remember" statements, leaving out the key words.
- Ask volunteers to fill in the missing words, using the words on the board.
- Invite the children to complete the "We Remember" activity. Then stand and pray the Apostles' Creed together.

At Home

ENCOURAGE

Have the children carefully tear out pages 223 and 224 along the perforation. Encourage the children to share the pages with their families and to do the activities together. If they did not complete the review activity on page 223 by the end of the session, emphasize that they can complete it with their families.

VISIT FAITHFIRST.COM

- Share with the children the many activities on the *Faith First* Web site.
- Encourage the children to visit **www.FaithFirst.com**.

---

25 With My Family

This Week . . .

In chapter 25, "We Profess Our Faith," your child learned about the creeds of the Church. The creeds of the Church summarize the faith of the Church. The Apostles' Creed is one of the main creeds of the Catholic Church. It is called the Apostles' Creed not because it was written by the Apostles but because it is a summary of the faith handed on to the early Church from apostolic times. When we profess our faith, we do not profess it simply on our own. We profess our faith in prayer with the help of the Holy Spirit.

For more on the teachings of the Catholic Church on prayer, see *Catechism of the Catholic Church* paragraph numbers 2650–2672.

Sharing God's Word

Read together the Bible passage 1 Corinthians 15:3–11. Emphasize that Paul wrote one of the earliest creeds of the Church.

Praying

In this chapter your child prayed part of the hymn "Te Deum." Read and pray together the prayer on page 223.

Making a Difference

Choose one of the following activities to do as a family or design a similar activity of your own.

- Pray the Apostles' Creed every day this week for family prayer. Praying this prayer daily will help your family grow in your identity as a Catholic family.
- Compare the Apostles' Creed and the Nicene Creed on page 284. Talk about what the two creeds have in common and how they are different from each other.
- Write a family creed. Be sure to include your beliefs about God the Father, God the Son, God the Holy Spirit, the Catholic Church, and life after death. Pray your family creed at dinnertime this week.

For more ideas on ways your family can live your faith, visit the "Faith First for Families" page at **www.FaithFirst.com**. Click on "Make a Difference." Discover ways for your family to live your faith.

(224)

Before Moving On . . .

As you finish today's lesson, reflect on the following question before moving on to the next chapter.

How well am I providing activity options so that all the children get a chance to express themselves in the way that is best for them?

Evaluate

Take a few moments to evaluate this week's lesson.
I feel (circle one) about this week's lesson.

   a. very pleased
   b. OK
   c. disappointed

The activity the children enjoyed most was . . .

The concept that was most difficult to teach was . . .

because . . .

Something I would like to do differently is . . .

ENRICHING THE LESSON

Making Heart-Shaped Symbols

Purpose

To reinforce the importance of professing our faith in the creeds (taught on page 220)

Directions

- Provide the children with heart shapes cut from colorful construction paper.
- Tell them that the heart shapes can remind them that they believe in God and love him with their whole heart.
- Have the children write on their heart shapes statements that tell the beliefs of the Church in their own words.
- Hang the hearts in a place where others can enjoy them.

Materials

construction paper for the heart shapes
crayons or markers

Making Collages

Purpose

To reinforce the importance of living our faith (taught on page 221)

Directions

- Have the children use newspapers and magazines and cut out headlines that tell about people living the faith of the Church.
- Invite the children to also cut out letters and make their own headlines for people living their faith.
- Have the children work in small groups to create collages of their headlines and title the collage.
- Have the different groups share their collages with the entire class.

Materials

newspapers
magazines
construction paper
scissors
glue sticks

Literature Connection

Purpose

To reinforce the teaching about living our faith (taught on page 221)

Directions

The Three Questions by John J. Muth (Scholastic, 2002) is a retelling of a tale by Leo Tolstoy. Nikolai wants to lead a good life but is unsure how to make the right choices that will help him to do so. He seeks the answers to three questions: When is the best time to do something? Who is the most important person to help? What is the right thing to do? Through his conversation with a wise old turtle, Nikolai learns the answers.

- Read the story aloud to the children.
- Give them some imaginary dilemmas to test the book's wisdom. Here is an example: Tom is looking forward to an afternoon baseball game with friends. His mother asks him to stay home to care for his brother while she runs an errand. Tom's friends will not have enough players for the game now. What can Tom do?
- Ask the children to work in groups to create similar scenarios.
- Point out that we express our beliefs when we recite the creed at Mass and then we live our faith day by day.

Materials

The Three Questions by John J. Muth

Music Connection

- "O Bless the Lord," J. Michaels. *Rise Up and Sing (RUS)* #243.
- "One Bread, One Body," J. Foley. *Singing Our Faith (SOF)* #242.
- "We Are Many Parts," M. Haugen. *SOF* #182.
- "We Believe, We Believe in God," C. Landry. *RUS* #279.

The Hail Mary
A Scripture Story

Background

The Faith of Mary

The first two chapters of the Gospel according to Luke give us a mosaic of stories about Jesus' infancy. In these chapters the stories of the Annunciation and the Visitation paint a vivid picture of the faith and humility of Mary.

Mary's yes to the angel's announcement is an act of faith and trust in God's providential plan. All of her privileges, including her choice to become the Mother of God, come from her faithful obedience to God's word, spoken to her by the angel. Graced by the Holy Spirit, Mary put aside everything to say yes to God, the response that opened the way for our salvation through Jesus. Her free and total assent to the seemingly impossible makes her the model of faith for us today.

Devotion to Mary

Mary has always had a central role in the life of the Church. Through the years the Church has placed her trust in Mary as the Mother of God, the Mother of Jesus, and the Mother of the Church.

From the cross, Jesus saw his mother and the disciple whom he loved. "[H]e said to his mother, 'Woman, behold your son.' Then

he said to the disciple, 'Behold, your mother.' And from that hour the disciple took her into his home" (John 19:26–27).

From that hour Christians have honored and trusted Mary as our mother. Mary intercedes for us, gives us a model of faith, and guides us in following Jesus, her Son. Mary's inseparable link to the saving work of Jesus has given rise to many expressions of reverence and devotion throughout Christian history. Meditation on the mysteries of the Rosary, and the Marian appearances at Lourdes, Fatima, Guadalupe, and other

places, along with so many other special Marian devotions, serve to indicate the high esteem Christians place on this woman of faith.

Multiple forms of devotion to the Mother of God have developed in different circumstances of time and place, in response to popular sensibilities and cultural differences. Certain forms of Marian devotion however, because of long usage, require a renewed catechesis to restore to them elements that have become lost or obscured. By such catechesis the perennial value of Marian devotion can be emphasized, doctrinal elements gleaned from theological reflection and the Church's Magisterium assimilated.

GENERAL DIRECTORY FOR CATECHESIS 196

For Reflection

How might I describe my trust as I address Mary, "Holy Mary, Mother of God, pray for us"?

What influence does the model of Mary's complete surrender to the love of God have on my faith decisions?

Catechist to Catechist

Faith Shared

Throughout this year you have shared your faith with the children, and they have shared their faith with you. You have been a model of faith for one another. With this lesson you end this year of faith with the children by focusing on Mary, who is a model of faith for us all. This week help the children come to see Mary's great faith in God's love and the difference Mary's faith has made for the world.

Thank You, God

Spend some quiet time this week thanking God for the wonder and the gift of this year of faith. Thank the Holy Spirit for being with you and the children and for helping you come to know and believe in Jesus more. Thank Jesus for being with you and teaching you how to love in deed and truth. Let this session be one of thanksgiving as you pray the Hail Mary together. Congratulations! You and the children have journeyed together this year and grown in faith!

The Church Teaches . . .

The *General Directory for Catechesis* teaches:

> Today as ever, all laborers of catechesis, trusting in her intercession, turn to the Blessed Virgin Mary, who saw her Son grow "in wisdom, age and grace" *(Luke 2:52)*. They find in her the spiritual model for carrying out and strengthening the renewal of contemporary catechesis, in faith, hope and love.
>
> GDC 291

As you study this chapter with the children, pray the Hail Mary with renewed hope. Through the intercession of Mary may you find strength and renewal of your vocation.

See the Catechism . . .

For more on the teachings of the Catholic Church on the Hail Mary, see *Catechism of the Catholic Church* 2673–2679.

CATECHIST PRAYER

*Spirit of God,
you spoke through Mary.
Speak through me this
week so that I may be a
model of faith for the
children as they are for me.
Amen.*

LESSON PLANNER

Engage

Page 225
Focus

To assess the children's knowledge about why the Church prays the Hail Mary

Opening Prayer

Discussion

Why we ask people to do favors for us and what we ask Mary

Teach and Apply

Pages 226–228
Focus

To explain that the Hail Mary tells us about God's love for Mary and helps us express our love for her

Presentation

Read, discuss, and summarize content.

Scripture

• Luke 1:42, 56

Activities

• Color the stained-glass window of Mary.
• Read the Scripture story of the Visitation.
• Decorate the initial cap of the Hail Mary as monks did many years ago.

Connect

Pages 229–230
Focus

To discover that one way the Church honors Mary is by praying to her

Our Church Makes a Difference

We can best imitate Mary by saying yes to God as she did.

Our Catholic Faith
The Rosary

What Difference Does Faith Make?
Activity

Write a prayer asking Mary to help you say yes to God.

Faith Choice

Choose a time when you will say the Hail Mary this week.

We Pray

Page 231
  Prayer Form
    Mary's prayer, the Magnificat
  Prayer
    Play appropriate background music. Divide the children into four groups. Introduce the prayer and pray together.

We Remember

Review
• Complete the number code activity.
• Read the "To Help You Remember" statements aloud.

Preview
Highlight features of the "With My Family" page.

Materials

• appropriate music; enough missalettes for the children to us for words to hymns
• pencils, crayons or markers

Enriching the Session

Blackline Masters
Additional Activities booklet:
    Chapter 26
      Drawing and coloring
      Completing a picture
Assessment Tools booklet:
    Chapter 26 Test
    Unit 4 Review

Enriching the Lesson (CG page 369)
  Making a Prayer Puzzle
  Sharing What You Have Learned
  Role-Playing/Favorite Scripture Stories

Music Connection (CG page 369)

www.FaithFirst.com

We update the *Faith First* Web site weekly. Check each week for new content and features. Here are some places to begin:

Catechists and Teachers
• Current Events
• Chapter Downloads
• Catechist Prayer

Faith First **for Families**
• Bible Stories
• Make a Difference

Kids' Clubhouse
• *Faith First* Activities
• Chapter Reviews
• Games
• Saints

Don't Forget! You can make lesson planning a breeze—check out the **Online Lesson Planner.**

The Hail Mary
A Scripture Story

26

We Pray

"Mary, most blessed are you among women." *Luke 1:42*

Holy Mary, Mother of God, pray for us.

Amen.

When have you asked someone to do a favor for you?

People turn to one another when they need help. Catholics ask Mary to pray to God for them.

What prayer asks Mary to pray for us?

Elizabeth greeting Mary (225)

PRAY

- Gather the children and have them quiet themselves for prayer.
- Pray the Sign of the Cross and have a volunteer pray aloud Luke 1:42.
- Pray the opening prayer together.
- Close the prayer with the Sign of the Cross.

DISCOVER

Purpose: To assess what the children know about the Hail Mary

- Ask the children when they have asked someone to do a favor for them. Discuss the reasons why they asked for the favor.
- Read the introductory paragraph and invite responses to the question that follows.
- Invite the children to look at the picture of the stained-glass window of Mary. Ask them why they think we find windows like this in churches.

Teaching Tip

Mary's Example of Faith. Mary's example of faith teaches us to say yes to God, especially when we don't fully understand his plan for us. Share with the children that praying the Hail Mary during these moments is a great way to deepen our faith in God. The Holy Spirit can give us the wisdom and the courage to answer God's call and to do his will.

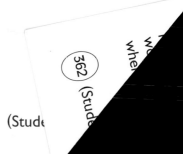

362 (Stude

Teach

FOCUS

Ask a volunteer to read the "Faith Focus" question aloud. Share with the children that in this chapter they will learn why we pray to Mary.

DISCOVER

- Invite the children to tell you what they already know about Mary and her faith in God. Write appropriate responses on the board.
- Have the children silently read "The Annunciation." Ask volunteers what parts of this page they have heard before.
- Have the children work with partners to discuss the following questions. Write the questions on the board for clarity.
  —Where did Mary first learn about her religion and customs?
  —Where did you first learn about your religion?
  —Who did Mary and all Jewish girls of her time wait and pray for?

Apply

REINFORCE

Write the events of the Annunciation out of order on the board and ask the children to put them into the correct order.

INTEGRATE

Have the children color the stained-glass window of Mary praying. As the children are working, ask them to name times when they could pray like Mary.

(Student Page 226)

Bible Background

Faith Focus

Why do we pray the Hail Mary?

Faith Words

Visitation
The Visitation is the visit of Mary, the mother of Jesus, with Elizabeth, the mother of John the Baptist.

Hail Mary
The Hail Mary is a prayer based on the Gospel stories of the Annunciation and the Visitation.

Color the stained-glass window of Mary praying.

The Annunciation

Mary and other young Jewish girls of her time first learned about their religion and customs at home. They learned God would some day send God's people the Messiah, who would be their Savior. They came to hope that one of them would be the mother of the Messiah.

Mary, like the Jewish people of her time, prayed for the coming of the Savior. The angel Gabriel came to Mary while she was praying. Gabriel greeted Mary, saying,

"Hail, you are full of grace, for God is with you." Based on Luke 1:30

The angel told Mary that God had chosen her to be the mother of the Savior. We call this the Annunciation. Mary is the mother of Jesus. Jesus is the Savior and Messiah God promised to send.

226

Background: Doctrine

The Immaculate Conception. The solemnity of the Immaculate Conception is celebrated on December 8th. The dogma of the Immaculate Conception states that Mary was free from all sin, both original and personal, from the very first moment of her conception. (See *Catechism of the Catholic Church* 490—493.)

Reading the Word of God

Wood carving of Elizabeth greeting Mary

The Visitation

The angel Gabriel told Mary that her relative Elizabeth was also going to have a son. So Mary went to visit Elizabeth. Here is what happened.

When Elizabeth saw Mary, she greeted Mary. Elizabeth said, "Blessed are you among women, and blessed is the child you carry within your womb." Mary stayed with Elizabeth for three months and then returned home. Based on Luke 1:41–42, 56

The visit of the Virgin Mary to Elizabeth is called the **Visitation.**

Work with two partners. Prepare a role-play of the Visitation. Act it out for your group.

(227)

Teach

FOCUS

Remind the children of the angel's greeting to Mary at the Annunciation. Tell the children they are going to hear the story of something Mary did a few months after the angel's visit.

DISCOVER

- Explain that the angel Gabriel also told Mary that her relative Elizabeth was also going to have a son.
- Tell the children to listen to what happened when Mary visited Elizabeth. Proclaim the Scripture based on Luke 1:41–42, 56.

Apply

REINFORCE

- Ask: What do we call Mary's visit to Elizabeth?
- Ask a volunteer to read aloud the definition of the word *Visitation* in the "Faith Words." Have them make a word card for this term.

INTEGRATE

- Invite two sets of volunteers to prepare role-plays of the Annunciation and Visitation to perform for the whole group.
- Ask the class to guess which story the children are performing.
- Conclude by asking the children to repeat after you this statement from the Apostles' Creed: "He was conceived of the Holy Spirit and born of the Virgin Mary."

(Student Page 2

Teach

FOCUS

Remind the children of both the angel's words and Elizabeth's words to Mary. Point out that it is with these words that we greet and honor Mary in the first part of the Hail Mary.

DISCOVER

- Ask a volunteer to read the first paragraph of "The Hail Mary."
- Explain that the Church added the second part of the prayer.
- Ask: Why does the Church pray to Mary? What do we ask Mary in the second part of the prayer?

Apply

REINFORCE

- Review the definition of the Hail Mary in "Faith Words" and have the children make a word card for this term.
- Emphasize that by praying the Hail Mary we show our respect and love for Mary.

INTEGRATE

- Read the directions for the activity and have the children complete it on their own.
- Pray aloud the Hail Mary together.

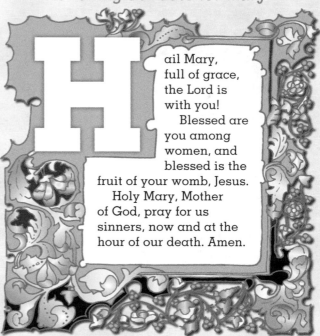

Understanding the Word of God

The Hail Mary

We honor Mary for her great faith. One way we show we honor Mary is by praying the **Hail Mary.** The Hail Mary has two parts. In the first part we greet and honor Mary as Gabriel and Elizabeth did.

The Church has added the second part of the prayer. In this part, we ask Mary to help us live as followers of Jesus. We pray that Mary will greet us and welcome us to heaven.

Showing Our Love for Mary

Decorate the letter H to show your love for Mary.

Hail Mary, full of grace, the Lord is with you! Blessed are you among women, and blessed is the fruit of your womb, Jesus. Holy Mary, Mother of God, pray for us sinners, now and at the hour of our death. Amen.

228

Teaching Tip

Using Gestures. Invite the children to pray the Hail Mary with gestures. Use gestures such as the following:

Hail Mary, (*Lift hands upward.*)
full of grace, (*Cross arms over chest.*)
the Lord is with you. (*Rotate arms over head.*)
Blessed are you (*Extend arms outward.*)
among women, (*Cross one hand over the other over heart.*)
and blessed is the fruit of your womb, Jesus. (*Hold arms as if cradling a baby.*)

Have the children create gestures of their own for the rest of the prayer.

Our Church Makes a Difference

Say Yes to God

The Jewish name *Mary* means "excellence." Mary is "full of grace." She is the greatest of the saints. Mary said yes to God and became the mother of Jesus, the Son of God. That is why Mary is the Mother of God.

Throughout her whole life, Mary always gave her whole heart to God. We ask Mary to pray for us. We ask her to help us grow in our love for God. We ask her to help us say yes to God as she did.

Tell about how you join with the other people of your parish to honor Mary.

Our Catholic Faith

The Rosary

We pray the Hail Mary when we pray the rosary. The rosary is a prayer of the Church. It helps us remember the important events in the lives of Jesus and Mary. We learn what it means to say yes to God. We honor Mary. We pray that we share in the love God shares with us in Jesus.

(229)

Background: Our Catholic Faith

The Rosary. This lesson encourages us to pray the rosary and to ask Mary to help us be people of faith. Tell the children that we have been praying the rosary in its present form since the sixteenth century. Other interesting facts about the rosary are:

- The origin of the rosary is attributed to Saint Dominic (1170–1221).
- The use of beads as a guide in prayer is found in many religious traditions.
- The Church has honored Mary as Our Lady of the Rosary since 1573.

This would be a good time to turn to page 288 and review how to pray the rosary.

HIGHLIGHT

Tell the children they are going to learn why Mary is the greatest saint and is a model of faith for the whole Church.

DISCOVER

- Ask a volunteer to read the first paragraph of "Say Yes to God."
- Emphasize that Mary is the greatest of saints.
- Ask the children to read silently to learn what we ask Mary to do for us when we pray. We ask her to help us grow in our love for God. We ask her to help us say yes to God.
- Ask the children what it means to say that Mary gave her whole heart to God. She always put God first.

INTEGRATE

- Read aloud "Our Catholic Faith."
- Tell the children that one way we can honor Mary is by praying the rosary. We say the Hail Mary when we pray the rosary.
- Ask the children how they join with others in their parish to honor Mary.

Connect

HIGHLIGHT

Recall with the children that Mary's faith in God helps us to have faith in God too.

RESPOND

- Read the introductory paragraph.
- Before they do the activity, ask the children if they have any questions about what they have learned this year about their Catholic faith. You may wish to invite class members to answer the questions as well.
- Read the introduction to the activity and have the children complete it.

CHOOSE

- Invite the children to respond to "My Faith Choice."
- After a moment of prayerful reflection have the children write their choice on the lines provided.
- Encourage the children to put their choice into practice this week.

EVALUATE

Have the children evaluate the choices they have made this year. Have them turn to the "Faith Choice" activity in each chapter and identify those faith choices that they have successfully implemented and that have become a part of their lives. Celebrate their success and remind them to pray to the Holy Spirit to help them make good faith choices and put those choices into action.

What Difference Does Faith Make in My Life?

Mary had great faith and trust in God. Mary said yes to God. It is because of your faith and trust in God that you say yes to God too.

Write a prayer asking Mary to help you say yes to God.

Saying Yes to God

_____
_____
_____
_____
_____
_____
_____

My Faith Choice

 This week I will ask Mary to help me say yes to God. I will pray the Hail Mary when

Affirm appropriate responses.

_____ .

230

Teaching Tip

Litany of the Blessed Virgin Mary. Mary's great faith in God and infinite wisdom is summarized in the Litany of the Blessed Virgin Mary. In this prayer the Church honors Mary with many different titles. Brainstorm with the children the many different names the Church uses to honor Mary. Write them on the board. As the children brainstorm, give them a few hints. Remind the children that many parishes have names that honor Mary. You might use your diocesan directory to point out the titles for Mary often used as names of parishes.

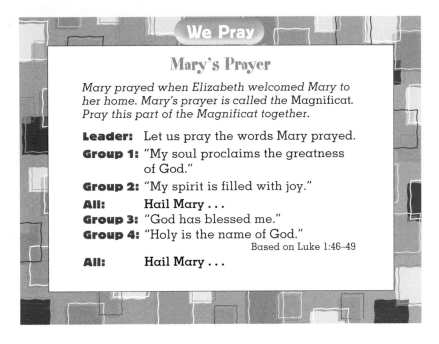

We Pray

Mary's Prayer

Mary prayed when Elizabeth welcomed Mary to her home. Mary's prayer is called the Magnificat. Pray this part of the Magnificat together.

Leader: Let us pray the words Mary prayed.

Group 1: "My soul proclaims the greatness of God."

Group 2: "My spirit is filled with joy."

All: Hail Mary . . .

Group 3: "God has blessed me."

Group 4: "Holy is the name of God."

Based on Luke 1:46–49

All: Hail Mary . . .

We Remember

Discover the hidden message. Use the number code.

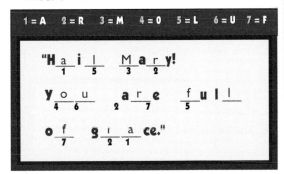

To Help You Remember

1. The Hail Mary remembers Mary's faith in God.

2. The Hail Mary remembers God's love for Mary.

3. The Church honors Mary by praying the Hail Mary.

Pray

WE PRAY

- Since this is the final celebration for the year, make the prayer special. See the liturgy tip below for some suggestions.
- Share with the children that in this prayer, Mary is filled with joy as she proclaims the greatness of God.
- Divide the class into four groups and then pray the prayer together.

Review

WE REMEMBER

- Write *Hail Mary* on the board. Ask the children to tell you three facts about the Hail Mary. Then have them read aloud the "To Help You Remember" statements.
- Introduce the hidden message activity. Allow the children time to complete it.

Liturgy Tip

Closing Prayer Variations. The end of the year celebration should be special. Here are some suggestions for the closing prayer.

- Play a recording of appropriate background music as you and the children proceed together to the prayer center. Have a child carry a statue of Mary to the center before you proceed and have the children wave streamers of blue ribbon as they walk.
- Have the children stand in four separate groups around the prayer table.
- Introduce the prayer and after you pray together, sing a hymn about Mary. (See "Music Connection" on page 369 of this guide.)

At Home

Have the children carefully tear out pages 231 and 232 along the perforation. Encourage the children to share the pages with their families and to do the activities together. If they did not complete the review activity on page 231 by the end of the session, emphasize that they can complete it with their families.

VISIT FAITHFIRST.COM

- Share with the children the many activities on the *Faith First* Web site.
- Encourage the children to visit **www.FaithFirst.com.**

With My Family

This Week . . .

In chapter 26, "The Hail Mary: A Scripture Story," your child learned that Mary and other Jewish girls of her time learned about their religion and customs and prayer at home. Mary, like all her people, prayerfully waited in expectation for the coming of the Messiah God promised to send his people. When the time came for God to fulfill that promise, he sent the angel Gabriel to Mary to ask her to be the mother of his Son, Jesus. Mary, giving her whole heart to God, said yes. The Church uses the words of Gabriel and of Elizabeth in the Hail Mary.

For more on the teachings of the Catholic Church on the Hail Mary, see *Catechism of the Catholic Church* paragraph numbers 2673–2679.

Sharing God's Word

Read together the Bible story in Luke 1:26–38 about the Annunciation and the story of the Visitation in Luke 1:39–56 or read the adaptation of one of these stories on pages 226 and 227. Emphasize Mary's faith, hope, and love for God.

Praying

In this chapter your child prayed part of the Magnificat, Mary's prayer of praise of God. Read and pray together the prayer on page 231.

Making a Difference

Choose one of the following activities to do as a family or design a similar activity of your own.

- Show your respect and love for Mary as a family. Use the Hail Mary for family prayer this week.

- When you take part in Mass this week, spend some time in church after Mass. Look around for any pictures or statues of Mary. Talk about what these works of art tell us about Mary.

- Make a Hail Mary puzzle. Write the Hail Mary on a piece of paper and cut the paper into strips. Assemble the strips over and over. As you assemble the puzzle, talk about how Mary is a model of faith, hope, and love for Christian families.

For more ideas on ways your family can live your faith, visit the "Faith First for Families" page at **www.FaithFirst.com.** "Gospel Reflections" will continue to change each week over the summer. Don't forget to check it out.

Looking Back . . .

As you finish today's lesson, reflect on the following question.

In what ways could the classroom environment I have created this year be described as positive?

Evaluate

Take a few moments to evaluate this week's lesson.
I feel (circle one) about this week's lesson.

    a. very pleased
    b. OK
    c. disappointed

The activity the children enjoyed most was . . .

The concept that was most difficult to teach was . . .

because . . .

Something I would like to do differently is . . .

ENRICHING THE LESSON

Making a Prayer Puzzle

Purpose
To reinforce the teaching about the Hail Mary (taught on page 228)

Directions
This activity can help the children learn or practice the Hail Mary.

- Have the children put together a "Hail Mary" puzzle. On a sheet of paper, have them write the words of the Hail Mary.
- Next, have them cut the sheets of paper into several puzzle pieces and put the pieces into envelopes.
- Finally, have the children take the puzzle pieces home and put the puzzle together for their family. Ask the children to lead their families in praying aloud the Hail Mary.

Materials needed
art paper
scissors
envelopes
pencils
crayons or markers

Sharing What You Have Learned

Purpose
To reinforce the many concepts that children have learned this year

Directions
- Divide the class into six groups. Assign several chapters from the book to each group.
- Ask the children to review their chapters and list one main idea that they have learned from each of those chapters.
- Have the groups write their main ideas on the board.
- Then individually have the children write a letter to the second graders telling them what they will learn in the third grade.
- Have the third graders deliver the letters.

Materials
paper
pens or pencils

Role-Playing Favorite Scripture Stories

Purpose
To reinforce the many Scripture stories (taught in the 26 chapters)

Directions
Instead of using a story from literature to reinforce learning this week, use Bible stories the children learned this year.

- Have the children work in small groups to select their favorite Scripture story and prepare a role-play for the story.
- Have the children present their role-play, and have the other groups name the Scripture story. (You might also want the children to present their role-plays to the second graders to share what they will be learning next year.)
- Remind the children what great learners they were and encourage them to continue to live the choices they made this year to show what difference faith makes in their lives.

Materials needed
Bible

Music Connection

- "Ave Maria," D. Kantor. *Singing Our Faith (SOF)* #266.
- "Hail Mary: Gentle Woman," C. Landry. *Gather Comprehensive* #782.
- "Holy Is Your Name" (Irish traditional), arr. D. Haas. *SOF* #269.
- "Mary's Song," M. Rieth. *Rise Up and Sing* #175.

Unit 4 Review

The unit review provides the opportunity to assess the children's understanding of the concepts presented in the unit and to affirm them in their growing knowledge and love of God. Here are a few suggestions for using these pages.

- Share that the next two pages are an opportunity to stop and review what the children have learned.
- Provide time for the children to ask questions.
- Have the children complete the review alone or with a partner.

PART A:
The Best Word or Phrase

This section reviews the main concepts of the unit.

- Read the directions for section A. Illustrate what you expect the children to do by completing the first question together. By working together on the first question you are teaching the children a strategy for answering these types of questions.
- When the children have finished this section, invite volunteers to share their answers. Review any questions that the children had difficulty answering.

FAMILY CONNECTION

Encourage the children to share the unit review pages with their families. This provides an excellent opportunity to involve the families in the faith formation of their children.

Review Unit 4

Name _____

A. The Best Word or Phrase

Complete the sentences. Circle the best choice under each sentence.

1. The _____ is the prayer Jesus taught his disciples.
   a. Hail Mary   b. Apostles' Creed   (c. Our Father)

2. The _____ is Gabriel's telling Mary that God had chosen her to be the mother of Jesus, the Son of God.
   a. Visitation   b. Resurrection   (c. Annunciation)

3. Jesus used the word *Abba*, which means "_____," to show his love for God the Father.
   a. Holy One   b. Almighty   (c. Father)

4. Praying alone is called _____ prayer.
   (a. personal)   b. public   c. quiet

5. Praying with others is called _____ prayer.
   a. personal   (b. public)   c. private

6. Prayers for ourselves are called prayers of _____.
   a. praise   (b. petition)   c. thanksgiving

7. When we pray the creeds of the Church, we profess our _____.
   (a. faith)   b. hope   c. love

8. The _____ Creed is the creed we usually profess at Mass on Sunday.
   a. Apostles'   (b. Nicene)   c. Catholic

233

Teaching Tip

Affirm Everyone. Use this final unit review to deepen the children's sense of accomplishment this year. Share how much they have learned and what a difference they have made in your life. Take time to remind the children that Jesus spent many years in Nazareth with Mary, Joseph, and the people of his synagogue and village learning the teachings, prayers, and practices of the Jewish religion. Encourage the children to pray each day during the summer that they might come to know and love Jesus more and more.

B. Petitions and Intercessions

Put a ✔ in the box next to the examples of petitions.
Put an ✗ in the box next to the examples of intercessions.

☑ "Forgive me, Lord." ☒ "Lord, help Jenny who is sick."

☑ "Give me courage, Lord." ☒ "Lord, help the leaders of the Church."

C. What I Have Learned

1. What are two new things you learned in this unit?

_____ Responses will vary. _____

_____ Affirm appropriate responses. _____

2. Look back at the list of faith words on page 200. Circle the words you now know. Tell your group the meaning of two of the words.

D. From a Scripture Story

Name the person who said these words to Mary. Put an **E** for Elizabeth. Put a **G** for the angel Gabriel.

__G__ 1. "Hail, you are full of grace."

__G__ 2. "God is with you."

__E__ 3. "Blessed are you among women."

__E__ 4. "Blessed is the child you carry within your womb."

PART B:
Petitions and Intercessions

This section reinforces the unit vocabulary.

• Read the directions to the children and together do the first item in the "Petitions and Intercessions" activity. Have the children continue working with partners to finish the section.

• Invite volunteers to share their answers.

PART C:
What I Have Learned

This section provides the children with the opportunity to write or talk about what they have learned.

• Have the children share with the group two things that they learned from the chapters in this unit.

• Invite the children to return to the "Getting Ready" page for this unit and observe for themselves how they have grown in building a faith vocabulary.

PART D:
From a Scripture Story

This section is a review of the Scripture stories of the Annunciation and the Visitation. Have the children complete the activity and share their responses.

Teaching Tip

Family Faith Sharing. Send a note home with the children that encourages their families to use the "Catholic Prayers and Practices" section of the student book with their children over the summer. For example, families might use the:

• "Glossary" to share about some of the key faith concepts the children learned this year.

• "We Celebrate the Mass" section to talk about the Mass, using the pictures of the Mass.

• "Rosary" section to help the children continue to honor Mary and remember the important events in the lives of Jesus and Mary.

We Celebrate

How does the Church celebrate its faith all year long?

235

The Liturgical Year

We call the Church's celebration of the liturgy the liturgical year. The seasons of the liturgical year are Advent, Christmas, Lent, Easter, and Ordinary Time.

Advent
Advent begins the liturgical year. For about four weeks the Church prepares for God's coming among us. We get ready to celebrate Christmas.

Christmas
During the Christmas season, we celebrate that the Son of God came and lived among us.

Lent
During Lent we prepare for Easter. It is a time to prepare to welcome new members into the Church. It is a time to renew our own baptismal promises.

Triduum
Holy Thursday, Good Friday, and Easter Vigil/Easter Sunday are the most important days of the liturgical year. We call these three days the Triduum.

Easter
The Easter season lasts fifty days. We celebrate the Resurrection of Jesus from death to new life.

Ordinary Time
The other weeks of the year are called Ordinary Time. We remember Jesus' work on earth and his teachings.

236

The Liturgical Year/Ordinary Time

Background

Seasons and Feasts

We all know that we need consistency in our lives. But we also need a break from consistency; we need surprises and festive days. Absolute consistency introduces monotony and makes us a dull people. Endless festivity dissipates the spirit and wears us down. Experience teaches us the value of balancing the daily and the festive or the ordinary and the extraordinary.

The Church is uniquely positioned to gather us for celebration. It does this through liturgy. The liturgical year provides a wonderful balance of ordinary and festive time. Filled with anticipation during Advent, we prepare to celebrate the festive season of Christmas. The traditional Lenten practices of fasting, praying, and almsgiving prepare us to enter into Triduum and the Easter season.

Easter is central to the liturgical year. Because Jesus was raised from the dead on Sunday, the Church gathers to celebrate each week on that day. Every Sunday is a memorial of the Paschal Mystery and a commemoration of Easter.

Festive seasons, such as the Easter season, stand in contrast

to the long, steady season of Ordinary Time. Generally, of the thirty-four Sundays in Ordinary Time, about ten occur on the Sundays between the seasons of Christmas and Lent. The remainder of the Sundays in Ordinary Time are celebrated after the Solemnity of the Body and Blood of Christ (two weeks after Pentecost) and culminate in the feast of Christ the King. This late autumn feast brings the liturgical year to a close.

The Rhythm of the Liturgical Year

The seasons of the liturgical year help us keep balanced as nature's seasons pass. Through the seasons of autumn, winter, spring, and summer, significant changes occur. As time passes from season to season, the Church provides a steady rhythm.

Sunday after Sunday, we are reminded and called to live out the reality of the abiding presence of the Risen Lord among us. Sunday after Sunday from the extremes of deep winter to high summer, we remember with gratitude that all time and all ages belong to Christ, who is yesterday and today, the beginning and the end.

The liturgical year is our way to remember with gladness and joy that every day is the day the Lord has made. We remember that we are called to rejoice in this.

For Reflection

How does the liturgical year provide a wonderful balance of ordinary and festive time for my life of faith?

Which of the liturgical seasons is my favorite? Why?

Catechist to Catechist

Ordinary Time

The word *ordinary* which is used to designate this time of the liturgical year is a misnomer that might lead us to undervalue the importance of Ordinary Time. The word *ordinary* is not used to describe the value of Ordinary Time. It is used to indicate that these Sundays are identified by numbers or ordos; for example, Second Sunday in Ordinary Time, Third Sunday in Ordinary Time, and so on. During this time of the liturgical year we develop the daily, or ordinary, habit of integrating God's word into our daily lives—turning ordinary lives into extraordinary lives of faith.

Signs of the Liturgical Year

Display signs of the liturgical year in your learning space. Surround the children with reminders that will help set the tone of both the seasons and feasts of the liturgical year. For example, consider using a table runner the color of each liturgical season in the prayer area. Place a Bible opened to the Sunday Gospel reading on the prayer table.

The Church Teaches . . .

During Ordinary Time and the other seasons of the liturgical year, the feast days of many of the canonized saints are remembered in the celebration of the liturgy. The *Catechism of the Catholic Church* points out,

> When the Church keeps the memorials of martyrs and other saints during the annual cycle, she proclaims the Paschal Mystery in those "who have suffered and have been glorified with Christ."[1] CCC 1173

You may wish to celebrate the feast days of some of the saints during your sessions, particularly those who may be the patron saints of the children.

See the Catechism . . .

For more on the teachings of the Catholic Church on the liturgical year, see *Catechism of the Catholic Church* 1168–1171, and 1172–1173.

CATECHIST PRAYER

God, Father and Creator, you always watch over your people. Through the prayer of Jesus, your Son, may your blessings be poured out on us and keep us safe in your care. Amen.

[BASED ON THE OPENING PRAYERS FOR FIFTH SUNDAY IN ORDINARY TIME]

Footnote references may be found on p. 456.

Teach

FOCUS

Ask a volunteer to read the "Faith Focus" question aloud. Share with the children that the Church has seasons as the calendar year does.

DISCOVER

- Invite the children to name the seasons of the year and the time of year each season occurs. Then have them name as many seasons of the Church year as they can.
- Ask: What season of the calendar year and what season of the Church year do you like best?
- Have the children silently read "Seasons of the Church Year."
- Write the names of the Church seasons on the board. Ask the children to name some of the ways that they and their families participate in the celebration of these seasons. List all of the responses on the board under the appropriate season.
- Ask the children to look at the photo and share what colors they see in the banners and what color the priest is wearing. Remind the children that the color for Ordinary Time is green.

Ordinary Time

Faith Focus

How do we celebrate our faith all year long?

The Word of the Lord

Choose this year's Gospel reading for the Sixteenth Sunday in Ordinary Time. Read and discuss it with your family.

Year A
Matthew 13:24–43

Year B
Mark 6:30–34

Year C
Luke 10:38–42

Seasons of the Church Year

The Church has special seasons just as the calendar year does. They are times of preparation and celebration. The seasons in the Church year are Advent, Christmas, Lent, Easter, and Ordinary Time. Ordinary Time is the longest time in the Church year.

Each week of the Church year we gather at Mass to celebrate and pray. We listen to the Scripture readings to hear God's message to us. We hear about Jesus and what he taught us by his words and actions.

Each of the seasons of the Church year has a special color. During Advent and Lent the color purple or violet is used. During Christmas and Easter either white or gold is used. On some days like Palm Sunday, Good Friday, and Pentecost the color red is used. Green is the color used during Ordinary Time.

237

Teaching Tip

Liturgical Calendar. Work with the group to create a large circular graphic to display in the classroom. Divide the circle into proportional parts representative of the size and sequential order of the seasons of the liturgical year: Advent, Christmas, Ordinary Time, Lent, Easter Triduum, Easter, and Ordinary Time. Color each of the liturgical seasons with the appropriate liturgical color. Add names of specific feasts within each of the seasons, for example, Mary, the Mother of God, (January 1, Christmas season), and so on.

The Seasons of the Church's Year

Use the colors gold or white, purple or violet, and green that go with the different seasons of the Church's year. Color the stoles that the priest wears.

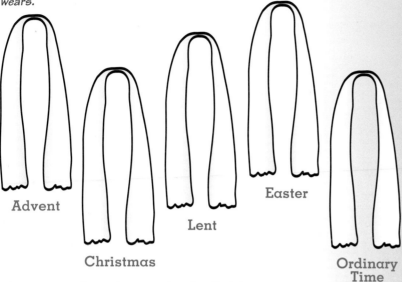

Advent

Christmas

Lent

Easter

Ordinary Time

What can you do to show your love for God during these seasons? Responses will vary. Affirm appropriate responses.

Season	What I Can Do
Advent	_____
Christmas	_____
Lent	_____
Easter	_____
Ordinary Time	_____

(238)

Teaching Tip

The Prayer Area. Decorate the prayer area so that it reflects the current season of the liturgical year. For example, during Ordinary Time use a green runner to cover the prayer table. Keep green potted plants mixed with the usual autumn flowers in the prayer area. On the table place a Bible opened to the current Sunday Gospel reading. As the year progresses change the display appropriately.

Apply

REINFORCE

Ask volunteers to recall the colors for the different seasons of the Church's year. Advent and Lent = purple or violet, Christmas and Easter = white or gold, Ordinary Time = green.

INTEGRATE

- Invite the children to color the stoles the appropriate color in "The Seasons of the Church's Year" activity.
- Then encourage the group to think of different ways they can show their love for God during the different seasons and write their responses on the lines provided.
- After the children have completed the activity, invite volunteers to share how they can show their love for God during the different seasons.
- Identify for the children the current season of the liturgical year that the Church is celebrating. If it is Ordinary Time, name the Sunday and week of Ordinary Time for the children.

PRAY

- Gather the children in the prayer space which has previously been highlighted with the color of the current Church season.
- Distribute copies of the *Faith First* booklet, *Called to Prayer*, for grades 1–3. Have the children turn to "Morning Prayer: Ordinary Time" (pages 6–7) or "Evening Prayer" (pages 7–8).
- Ask the children to quiet themselves for prayer. After a moment of prayerful reflection, lead the class in prayer.

The Season of Advent

Hope-Filled Expectation

Advent begins the liturgical year. The expectation of the coming of the Lord literally colors the season. Advent's violet, or purple, color is reminiscent of the sky just before dawn. After a long night, we naturally look to the east and long for the dawn. We are able to do this because we are sure the sun will rise. Our certitude is based on past experience.

In Advent we prepare for the coming of the Incarnate Son of God among us. Our confidence about his coming is based on faith. Through faith we can be even more sure of his coming than we are of the rising of the sun in the east.

Faith-Filled Anticipation

During Advent the Church urges us toward quiet meditation as we make the necessary practical preparations to welcome the Savior at Christmas. We prepare for his coming by recalling the Incarnation. We live with the mystery and grace of his presence with us now. And, lastly, we look to his coming in majesty at the end of time as the Lord of all time and all space.

God Fulfills Our Hope

The opening Gospel readings of the Advent season in each of the three cycles proclaim the Day of the Lord. The Gospel readings awaken us to our present Christian life and our promised future.

The Sunday Gospel readings then move ever closer to the birth of Jesus. John the Baptist announces his coming. Finally, Elizabeth, Mary, and Joseph prepare themselves—and us—as the time of the celebration of Jesus' birth draws near.

Throughout the four Sundays of Advent, the Old Testament prophets, who longed for Emmanuel, also accompany us. As we pray for the Savior's arrival among us, we prepare our homes and hearts for the gift of his presence.

For Reflection

How does celebrating Advent help me live in the mystery of God's presence?

What are my hopes for this Advent season? How can I prepare to welcome the fulfillment of those hopes?

Catechist to Catechist

The Three Comings of Christ

Advent is a time of joyful preparation. There is a fascination created by our preparation for Christmas that captures the imaginations and hearts of all Christians. This fascination can narrow our celebration of Advent to the point that we mistakenly only focus on Christ's birth and his coming to us in the past.

We constantly need to prepare our hearts to welcome Christ who comes to us each and every moment of our lives. We need to prepare ourselves throughout our entire life, each and every day, to be ready to welcome him when he comes again in glory at the end of time.

Waiting in Silence

Advent favors quiet anticipation. An extra effort is needed to offset the pre-Christmas holiday bustle of this season. Whatever you do this season, do it patiently, quietly, and with the awareness of the coming of Jesus Christ right here, right now. Be sure to add moments of quiet and silent prayer to your classroom prayer, to balance the hectic nature of the secular Christmas season.

The Church Teaches . . .

The *Catechism of the Catholic Church* teaches:

> When the Church celebrates the *liturgy of Advent* each year, she makes present this ancient expectancy of the Messiah, for by sharing in the long preparation for the Savior's first coming, the faithful renew their ardent desire for his second coming.[1]
> CCC 524

Preparing for Christ in prayer and liturgy each week during Advent heightens expectation among the children and helps them focus on the true meaning of the season.

See the Catechism . . .

For more on the teachings of the Catholic Church on Advent, John the Baptist, and Jesus the Messiah, see *Catechism of the Catholic Church* 522–524, 748, and 2466.

CATECHIST PRAYER

Father in heaven, increase our longing for your Son, Christ our Savior. Give us strength to grow in love. Open our minds and hearts to welcome the light of his truth. Amen.

[BASED ON THE OPENING PRAYERS FOR THE MASS ON SECOND SUNDAY OF ADVENT]

Footnote references may be found on p. 456.

Teach

FOCUS

Ask a volunteer to read the "Faith Focus" question aloud. Remind the children that Advent has four Sundays.

DISCOVER

- Have three volunteers read the paragraphs of "A Jesse Tree" on page 239. When they finish reading, ask a volunteer to share with the group what a Jesse tree is.
- Point out the picture on page 239 to see how one class made their own Jesse tree to remember those who prepared the way for Jesus.
- Explain to the group that they will now make their own Jesse tree. Show them the tree you have made out of construction paper in advance (see photo on page 239 for example).
- Distribute art materials and have the children work in pairs to create symbols or pictures for some of the people who prepared the way for Jesus. Ask them to use the people of the Bible who are named on page 239.
- Ask volunteers to share their symbols or pictures with the large group.
- Brainstorm with the children how they can work together as a class to prepare to welcome Jesus into the class. Write their suggestions on the board.
- Share "What You See" with the group to help them learn about the Advent wreath.

The First Week of Advent

Faith Focus

Who are some of the people that prepared us for Jesus' coming?

The Word of the Lord

Choose this year's Gospel reading for the First Sunday of Advent. Read and discuss it with your family.

Year A
Matthew 24:37–44

Year B
Mark 13:33–37

Year C
Luke 21:25–28, 34–36

What You See

The Advent wreath is made of evergreens and four candles. Each week we light another candle as we wait for the coming of Christ at Christmastime.

A Jesse Tree

You know the names of your parents and grandparents and aunts and uncles. They are part of your family tree. A family tree helps you remember the people in your family.

During Advent we make a family tree to prepare for Christmas. It helps us remember the people who prepared the way for Jesus. We call this tree a Jesse tree. Jesse was a shepherd from Bethlehem. He was also the father of King David, an ancestor of Jesus. We hang symbols on the Jesse tree to remind us of the people who prepared the way for Jesus.

We remember Adam and Eve and Noah. We remember Abraham and Sarah and Moses and David. We remember John the Baptist, Mary, and Joseph.

(239)

Teaching Tip

Jesse Tree. At the beginning of Advent, place an airy, broad-branched bare or evergreen tree in a prominent place in your learning area. Post a list with the names of the people of the Bible who prepared the way for Jesus, together with an idea for a symbol; for example: Adam and Eve (an apple or garden), Abraham and Sarah (a star), Moses (two tablets for the Ten Commandments), David (a king's crown or a harp), Isaiah (a quill or pen), John the Baptist (a river), and so on. During each week of the Advent season, invite the children to hang the traditional symbols used to decorate the Jesse tree.

Welcoming Jesus

Decorate the Christmas tree. Under each star write the name of someone who helps you prepare for the coming of Jesus at Christmas. Send each of the people you name a thank-you card. **Responses will vary.**

240

REINFORCE

Ask the children why we make Jesse trees during Advent. To prepare for Christmas by remembering the people of the Bible who prepared the way for Jesus.

INTEGRATE

- Introduce the "Welcoming Jesus" activity on page 240. Give the children time to decorate their trees and write some names of people who help them prepare for Christmas.
- Invite the children to share some of the names they wrote on the lines with the class and how those people help them prepare for the coming of Jesus at Christmas.
- Provide a sample thank-you card for the group so they have an example of what they might write. If they do not complete the thank-you card activity during the session, encourage them to complete it at home with their families.

PRAY

- Invite the children to quietly place their symbols or pictures for Adam and Eve, Noah, and Abraham and Sarah on the Jesse tree, thinking of these people who prepared the way for Jesus.
- Gather the children in the prayer area around an Advent wreath which you have set up in advance and lead the children in singing the refrain from "O Come, O Come, Emmanuel" as the closing prayer.

Teaching Tip

Making an Advent Chain. Tell the children that they are going to make an Advent chain at home, representing the days that we prepare for Christmas Day. Give each child an envelope that contains 24 six-inch strips (one for each day from December 1 to December 24) made from purple construction paper, which are individually numbered 1 through 24. Tell the children to make and connect the links one at a time each day during Advent. Suggest that they write on each link either a short prayer or one way they can prepare for Christmas.

Teach

FOCUS

Ask a volunteer to read the "Faith Focus" question aloud. Remind the children that purple is the color used during the Church's season of Advent.

DISCOVER

- Ask the children to share how their families get ready for Christmas.
- Invite the children to discover how John the Baptist prepared to welcome the Messiah. Ask them to silently read "Prepare the Way!" on page 241.
- Give each child a piece of art paper. Invite them to draw scenes from John the Baptist's life.
- Encourage the group to use the ideas from "Prepare the Way!", such as John's birth, John in the desert as a young man, and John on the bank of the Jordan River speaking and baptizing people.

The Second Week of Advent

Faith Focus

Who was John the Baptist?

The Word of the Lord

Choose this year's Gospel reading for the Second Sunday of Advent. Read and discuss it with your family.

Year A
Matthew 3:1–12

Year B
Mark 1:1–8

Year C
Luke 3:1–6

Prepare the Way!

Our parents and our teachers help us get ready for big celebrations. They help us prepare when someone comes to visit our home or classroom. John the Baptist helped people prepare for the coming of Jesus. When John was born, his father said,

"And you, child, will be called prophet of the Most High,
for you will go before the Lord
to prepare his ways." Luke 1:76

John called people to prepare to receive the Messiah promised by God. Many changed their ways, and John baptized them. They waited with great hope for the Messiah. They knew he was coming soon.

Jesus, the Messiah, came. After his death and Resurrection, he returned to his Father in heaven. During Advent, we look forward to Jesus coming again in glory at the end of time.

241

Teaching Tip

Including All Learners. Remember that children learn in a variety of ways. Some children express themselves best through art and not so easily verbally. This is a wonderful season to invite the children who are artistically talented to work with children who are less artistically talented and together create a Christmas creche and other Advent and Christmas decorations. You might also locate the source for American Sign Language (ASL) and learn and teach the children how to sign such words as *joy, celebrate, Advent, Christmas, Mary,* and *Jesus*. Then you could invite the children to sign these words when they pray or use them in discussions during the Advent and Christmas sessions.

Get Ready

There are _____ days until Christmas. How will you prepare for Christmas? **Affirm appropriate responses.**

December

I can pray for

_____

by _____

_____

_____

I can make up with

_____

by _____

_____

_____

I can offer to help

_____

by _____

_____

_____

I can make a gift for

_____

by _____

_____

_____

(242)

Background: Advent Saints

Saint Nicholas. Saint Nicholas is one of the most popular saints even though very little is known about him. He was the bishop of Myra (in what is now the country of Turkey) and died in the fourth century. Saint Nicholas inspired our modern figure of Santa Claus. He is the patron saint of children because so many legends surround his generosity. His feast day is December 6.

Our Lady of Guadalupe. The feast of Our Lady of Guadalupe is December 12. Mary, Our Lady of Guadalupe, is the patron saint of the Americas. Share the story of Saint Juan Diego and the miracle of the roses with the children.

Apply

REINFORCE

Ask the children to recall what John the Baptist did. He helped people prepare for Jesus. He announced the coming of God's promised One, the Messiah, and baptized people.

INTEGRATE

- Invite the children to find out how many days are left until Christmas. Provide them with a calendar so that they can count the days.
- Have the group put the number of days left until Christmas in the appropriate space in the "Get Ready" activity.
- Then invite them to finish the sentences on page 242 with names of people and the actions they are going to take to prepare for Christmas.
- After they have completed the activity, give them time to share their responses with one another.

PRAY

- Gather the children in the prayer space by humming the tune to "O Come, O Come, Emmanuel."
- If time allows, pray aloud the prayer from Luke 1:76 for each child, inserting their name in the prayer. Have each child respond, "Lord, help me prepare for your coming."
- If time does not allow, pray aloud the prayer from Luke 1:76 on page 241 as it is written. Invite the children to respond, "Lord, help us prepare for your coming."

Teach

FOCUS

Ask a volunteer to read the "Faith Focus" question aloud. Share with the children that they will learn that Jesus is the Messiah promised by God.

DISCOVER

- Have the children work in small groups to create mimes for ways they can show their love for others. Offer examples from everyday life. For example: A child is sitting alone in the school lunchroom and another child sits beside him or her and proceeds to talk and be friendly.
- Have volunteers read the three paragraphs of "The Messiah" and encourage the children to listen for the different ways people were prepared by the prophets to welcome the Messiah.
- Place the children in groups of three and invite each group to think of one way the class can prepare for Jesus' coming.
- Write the groups' answers on the board. Together decide which would be the best way the entire class could prepare for Jesus during the time that is left in this Advent season.

The Third Week of Advent

Faith Focus

How does God speak to us?

The Word of the Lord

Choose this year's Gospel reading for the Third Sunday of Advent. Read and discuss it with your family.

Year A
Matthew 11:2–11

Year B
John 1:6–8, 19–28

Year C
Luke 3:10–18

The Messiah

God speaks to us in many ways. Long ago God chose good and holy people to speak in his name. We call these people prophets. Isaiah the Prophet said that God would send his people a new leader who would bring peace and justice.

Jeremiah the Prophet said that God's Promised One would be a shepherd. He would do what is right and just. Micah the Prophet said that God's Promised One would be born in Bethlehem.

The words of the prophets came true when Jesus was born. As Christmas draws near, we look forward to the peace of Christ, God's Promised One.

243

Background: Liturgy

Celebrating Reconciliation. Participating in the sacrament of Penance, or Reconciliation, regularly is highly recommended by the Church as a vital way to prepare our minds and hearts for the coming of the Lord into our lives each day. When we celebrate Reconciliation, we strengthen our baptismal promises to reject evil and live as children of God. Parishes commonly celebrate the communal rite of this sacrament during Advent. Check the parish bulletin for the date and time of this celebration in your parish. Write the information in large letters on the board. Encourage the children to take part in the celebration.

The Lord Is Near

Here is a prayer you and your family may use as Christmas draws near. As a family complete the prayer. Pray it together each day this week.
Responses will vary.

Leader: As we wait for the coming of Jesus, let us also prepare to welcome him.

All: **To welcome Jesus we will**

_____

_____.

Leader: You are near to us. We rejoice in you, Lord Jesus.

All: **To show our joy that Jesus is near, we will**

_____

_____.

Leader: You are near to us. We offer our prayer to you, Lord Jesus.

All: **You are near to us. We wait in hope. Amen.**

244

Teaching Tip

Making Changes. Saint John the Baptist announced the coming of Jesus by inviting people to repent. Repenting involves making decisions to live our faith in Jesus. This Advent you might look at the group behaviors of the class and discuss ways the group might "change their ways." For example, consider inviting the group to work at changing inappropriate and harmful behaviors, such as teasing and using insulting words and bullying actions and replacing them with acts of kindness and words that compliment people.

Apply

REINFORCE

Ask volunteers to respond to the question: What is a prophet? *Prophets are good and holy people whom God chose to speak in his name.*

INTEGRATE

- Direct the children's attention to the prayer activity "The Lord Is Near." Brainstorm with the group ways they might complete the two unfinished sentences or use ideas already listed on the board.
- Choose two of the ideas and highlight them for use in the closing prayer.
- Encourage the children to take this activity home to complete with their families.
- Tell the children they can invite their families to pray this prayer together each day in the coming week.

PRAY

- Have the children bring their books opened to page 244 and gather the group in the prayer area around the Advent wreath.
- Adapt Isaiah 61:1–2, 11 using language third graders will easily understand.
- After the reading from Isaiah, tell the children that the group will now pray "The Lord Is Near."
- Read the "Leader" parts and the beginning of the "All" parts inviting the children to finish the sentences with the two chosen ideas from the board.

Teach

FOCUS

Ask a volunteer to read the "Faith Focus" question aloud. Tell the children that they will learn about some of the Bible stories we hear during Advent.

DISCOVER

- Read aloud the first five sentences of "All Is Ready." Have the children share how they and their families prepare to celebrate a birthday.
- Read aloud the rest of "All Is Ready" and have the children listen for stories about the family of Jesus.
- Point out the picture of Mary and Elizabeth on page 245.
- Ask the children to name the people closest to Jesus and to tell how they may have prepared for the day of his birth.
- Invite the children to share how angels helped Mary and Joseph.
- Read the Gospel reading for the appropriate year found in "The Word of the Lord" to the group for further insight into these Scripture stories.

The Fourth Week of Advent

Faith Focus

How do we prepare for Jesus?

The Word of the Lord

Choose this year's Gospel reading for the Fourth Sunday of Advent. Read and discuss it with your family.

Year A
Matthew 1:18–24

Year B
Luke 1:26–38

Year C
Luke 1:39–45

Mary and Elizabeth

All Is Ready

We know how to get ready to celebrate a birthday. We may decorate the house. We may bake a cake. We may wrap gifts. We may even plan a favorite meal. During the last days of Advent, we prepare our hearts to welcome Jesus. The Church invites us to read the stories of the family of Jesus.

We read about the angel Gabriel who announced the news of Jesus' birth to Mary. The angel said, "Hail, favored one! The Lord is with you" (Luke 1:28). We also read about Mary's visit with Elizabeth. Elizabeth said to Mary, "Most blessed are you among women" (Luke 1:42). We read that an angel helped Joseph to understand that Mary's child would save all people from their sins. The angel asked Joseph to take care of Mary. Joseph said yes, and he took Mary into his home.

(245)

Teaching Tip

Lights and Candy Canes. Help the children use the common decorations of lights and candy canes to focus on Advent as a time of preparation for the coming of Jesus. Brainstorm some of the many uses of light; for example, some lights, such as headlights, guide us as we travel. Discuss how lights help us prepare for Christmas. Show the group a candy cane and explain its meaning. The modern-day candy cane traces its origin to Germany in the 1670s. The bent shape of the cane represents a shepherd's staff. The flavor is peppermint, which is similar in taste to the Old Testament spice called hyssop. Discuss how seeing a candy cane reminds us to prepare for the coming of Jesus.

We Are Ready

Readings from the Bible are God's word to us. When we listen to the Bible, we need to be ready to respond to God's word. Listen to these readings and tell God you are ready for Christmas.

Reader 1: Isaiah the Prophet said, "The virgin shall be with child, and bear a son, and shall name him Immanuel" (Isaiah 7:14).

All: **We are ready!**

Reader 2: Mary said, "Behold, I am the handmaid of the Lord. May it be done to me according to your word" (Luke 1:38). Mary was ready.

All: **We are ready!**

Reader 3: Elizabeth said of Mary, "Most blessed are you among women" (Luke 1:42). Elizabeth was ready.

All: **We are ready!**

Reader 4: Paul said to us, "Rejoice in the Lord always. I shall say it again: rejoice! Your kindness should be known to all. The Lord is near" (Philippians 4:4–5).

All: **We are all ready! Come, Lord Jesus!**

(246)

Teaching Tip

Songs of the Season. Teach the children a few lines of several Christmas carols, such as "Silent Night" or "Joy to the World." When Christmas Day comes, the children will be able to join the worshiping community in singing these hymns at Mass, or as they are sung on the radio, on television, and at family gatherings. Appropriate music for all the liturgical seasons can be found on **www.FaithFirst.com.**

Apply

REINFORCE

Ask the children one important way the Church asks us to prepare for the coming of Jesus. Invite them to find the answer on page 245. The Church invites us to read the stories of the family of Jesus.

INTEGRATE

- Introduce the prayer service "We Are Ready" and read the introductory paragraph.
- Choose volunteers for the four reader parts and allow them time to practice reading their parts aloud.
- Practice the unison parts with the rest of the group.

PRAY

- Have the children gather in the prayer space to some quiet instrumental music.
- Invite the group to take a minute of silence to tell God, in their hearts, that they are ready for the coming of Jesus at Christmas.
- Lead the group in praying "We Are Ready" with the help of the four readers.

The Season of Christmas

Background

The Light of the World

The celebration of the Incarnation is suffused with light. In the third century, missionaries to Britain encountered festivals of light celebrated in the dark December night. The Church supplanted these light rituals with the celebration of the "Christ Mass" and the feast honoring the birth of Jesus, the true "sun of justice" (Malachi 3:20) and "light of the world" (John 8:12).

The Church in the East preferred to celebrate Epiphany as the major feast commemorating the coming of the Savior into the world. This celebration focused on the manifestation of Emmanuel to the whole world, represented by the Magi. Today the liturgical season of Christmas enfolds these two feasts and more.

The Season of Christmas

Though the Christmas season begins with the Mass of the Vigil of Christmas, most Catholics begin the season by celebrating one of the three Masses of Christmas: the Mass at Midnight, the Mass at Dawn, or the Mass During the Day. The Gospel for the Mass at Midnight is the account of the birth of Jesus in the stable. The Gospel for the Mass at Dawn tells the story of the shepherds. The Gospel for the Mass During the Day begins with the towering account: "In the beginning was the Word" (John 1:1).

The Christmas season continues with the celebration of the feast of the Holy Family on the Sunday after Christmas (or on December 30); the Solemnity of Mary, Mother of God (January 1); Epiphany (the Sunday between January 2 and 8); and the Baptism of the Lord on the Sunday following Epiphany. The celebrations of the Christmas season cover the entire spectrum, from the intimacy of the Bethlehem story on Christmas night to the proclamation to the whole world at the liturgical celebration of the Baptism of Jesus that Jesus is the beloved Son on whom the Father's favor rests.

A Season of Light and Abundance

The season of Christmas is very dear to the hearts of Christians. In the birth of the child Jesus, who is named Savior and Emmanuel, Christ and Lord, we are made new. The whole earth rejoices. Delightful traditions are evident along our streets and in our homes. Gifts abound. Evergreens are strung with lights and ornaments. Delicious baked goods are given and received. Special meals are shared. This season of light and blessing reminds us of our vocation to be light, to bear gifts, to share our blessings both during this season and throughout the year.

For Reflection

In what ways does my celebration of the birth of Jesus, who is named Savior and Emmanuel, renew my life of faith?

How can I best celebrate the Christmas gift, the grace of God's presence?

Catechist to Catechist

Lift up Your Hearts

Christmas is a natural time of the year to grow in our love for God, the giver of all good gifts. It is the time of the year to grow in our awareness and acknowledgment that all our blessings are from God. Paul urged the Colossians to sing with gratitude in their hearts (Colossians 3:16). Christians are a people of gratitude. We are a eucharistic people, a people whose hearts are filled with thanks and praise of God.

It Is Right to Give God Thanks and Praise

Mary's yes to God is at the heart of the Christmas story. Rarely does an artist depict Christmas without Mary, the Mother of Jesus. Mary is a model of gratitude. Share with the group Mary's wonderful hymn of gratitude and praise of God, the Magnificat (Luke 1:46–55). Pray it in a variety of ways, silently, antiphonally, as a choral reading, and so on. Have the children work in small groups to create Magnificat bookmarks or prayer cards.

The Church Teaches . . .

In *Music in Catholic Worship* (1972) the U.S. Bishops' Committee on the Liturgy states:
Among the many signs and symbols used by the Church to celebrate its faith, music is of preeminent importance. As sacred song united to words it forms a necessary or integral part of the solemn liturgy. . . . The quality of joy and enthusiasm which music adds to community worship cannot be gained in any other way.
Music in Catholic Worship 23

Make sure that the children have an opportunity to sing their favorite traditional Christmas hymns throughout the Christmas season during the prayer celebrations.

See the Catechism . . .

For more on the teachings of the Catholic Church on the Incarnation, see *Catechism of the Catholic Church* 359, 456–463, and 484–507.

CATECHIST PRAYER

God of mercy, open our hearts in welcome. Remove everything from our hearts and minds that closes them to receive your Son, the Light of the world. May we look forward in joy to celebrating the day of his birth and his coming in glory at the end of time. Amen.

[BASED ON THE OPENING PRAYER FOR MASS ON THE SECOND SUNDAY OF ADVENT]

Teach

FOCUS

Ask a volunteer to read the "Faith Focus" question aloud. Tell the children that Christmas is a season of celebration for the Church.

DISCOVER

- Have the children silently read "Shout for Joy!" to discover some of the many ways that we celebrate the birth of Jesus.
- Have the children list the different ways we might celebrate the birth of Jesus and write their responses on the board.
- Read Isaiah 11:6 aloud and ask: What do you think Isaiah is telling us? He is saying that people will live in harmony and we will all be happy together.
- Invite a volunteer to read aloud "What You See" on page 247 to help the children learn more about the Church's use of Nativity scenes.
- Give each child a piece of green construction paper folded in half lengthwise. Teach them how to cut out a Christmas tree.
- Invite them to decorate their trees with symbols of peace and joy.

The First Week of Christmas

Faith Focus

How do we celebrate the arrival of Jesus?

The Word of the Lord

This is the Gospel reading for the Mass on Christmas Day. Read and discuss it with your family.

Years A, B, and C
John 1:1–18 or
John 1:1–5, 9–14

What You See

The Nativity scene (or crèche) has a new addition. It is baby Jesus! Nativity scenes usually remain on display until the feast of the Epiphany on January 6.

The Holy Family of Jesus, Mary, and Joseph

Shout for Joy!

Christmas is a time to rejoice! When Jesus was born, angels and shepherds rejoiced. The Masses for Christmas Day invite us to rejoice too.

During Christmastime we use the gifts of creation to help us rejoice. We decorate bread and cookies. We wrap packages. We put lights on our trees. We want the whole earth to rejoice and be glad. We want heaven and nature to sing.

On Christmas we rejoice. We invite the whole world to celebrate the birth of the newborn King and Savior. We remember that all creatures will happily live with one another. We read,

> The wolf shall be a guest
> of the lamb, . . .
> The calf and the young lion shall
> browse together,
> with a little child to guide them.
> Isaiah 11:6

(247)

Teaching Tip

Jesus, the Savior of All People. Children are interested in learning languages other than their own. Invite the children who can speak or write the name *Jesus* in a language other than English to do so for the class. This is a memorable and engaging way to help the group come to know that Jesus is the Savior of all people. You might wish to learn in advance how to write and say the name *Jesus* in several languages. This activity can be enhanced by including the singing of Christmas carols in a variety of languages and by inviting the children to share the special Christmas customs of their cultural heritage, for example, Las Posadas.

A Blessing for Trees

Here is a prayer you and your family may use to bless your Christmas tree on Christmas Day.

Leader: Our help is in the name of the Lord.

All: **Who made heaven and earth.**

Reader 1: Sing to the Lord a new song. Sing to the Lord, all the earth. Bless his name; announce his salvation day after day.

All: **Sing to the Lord a new song.**

Reader 2: Let the heavens be glad and the earth rejoice; let the sea and what fills it resound; let the plains be joyful and all that is in them.

All: **Sing to the Lord a new song.**

Reader 3: Let all the trees of the forest rejoice before the Lord who comes, who comes to govern the earth.

Leader: O Lord, bless this tree. Let it shine with light. May its decorations celebrate your coming among us. We ask this in the name of Jesus your Son, born of the Virgin for us.

All: **Amen.** Based on Psalm 96:1, 2, 11–13

248

Teaching Tip

Dramatize the Christmas Story. Use the children's familiarity with the Christmas story as the foundation to have them dramatize it. Look over the infancy stories in both Matthew's Gospel and Luke's Gospel and combine them into a simple one-act play. Place the children's names in a box and randomly select the players for the main roles. Provide simple costumes, such as old colored sheets for clothes.

Apply

REINFORCE

Ask the children to name another word for *celebrate* that we frequently hear during Christmastime. Rejoice. Invite the children to look at page 247 for the answer.

INTEGRATE

- Introduce the prayer service "A Blessing for Trees." Explain how this prayer service, which focuses on creation, praises God.
- Divide the group into three parts and assign each group one of the three reader parts.
- Invite each group to create gestures to use for praying the part assigned to them.
- Practice the "All" parts with the whole group.

PRAY

- When everyone is ready, ask the children to gather in the prayer center.
- Lead the group in praying aloud the prayer service. Have each group read their section at the appropriate time and use the gestures they have created.
- Close by singing "Joy to the World!" with the group.

Teach

FOCUS

Ask a volunteer to read the "Faith Focus" question aloud. Share with the children that in this lesson they will learn what the name *Jesus* means.

DISCOVER

- Ask the children to tell what they know about the origin or meaning of their first names. Try to discover who was named after someone in his or her family, after a saint, and so on.
- Read the section "Jesus Our Savior" to the children. Ask the children to listen as you read to find out how Jesus received his name and what the name *Jesus* means.
- Invite volunteers to tell the story of why Mary called her baby *Jesus*.
- Have the children name the people in the Gospel story who understood that Jesus was the Savior. As volunteers offer these names, write them on the board.
- When all the names from page 249 have been written down, invite the children to come to the board and add their own names to the list.
- Invite a volunteer to read "What You Hear" on page 249 to help the children learn more about the Church's use of the word *Alleluia*.

The Second Week of Christmas

Faith Focus

Why do we call Jesus our Savior?

The Word of the Lord

This is the second reading for the Second Sunday of Christmas. Read and discuss it with your family.

Years A, B, and C
Ephesians 1:3–6, 15–18

What You Hear

When we celebrate Jesus' birth, we often hear the word *Alleluia*. *Alleluia* means "Praise God." We give praise to God for sending his only Son, Jesus, the Savior of the world, who saves us from sin.

Jesus Our Savior

During Christmastime we give and receive gifts. We feel happy because God's Promised One is with us. Jesus has come to be the Savior of the world. The name *Jesus* means "God saves."

The angel Gabriel told Mary that she would give birth to God's Son. His name would be Jesus because he would save his people from their sins. Later, shepherds heard angels announce that the Savior was born in Bethlehem. Some wise men, called Magi, brought gifts to the Savior.

When Mary and Joseph brought Jesus to the Temple in Jerusalem, Simeon and Anna rejoiced. Simeon blessed the child. He praised God and said,

"My eyes have seen your salvation."
Luke 2:30

During Christmas the Church honors Jesus as the Savior of the world. We remember that Jesus' birth is part of the great mystery of salvation.

249

Teaching Tip

The Epiphany Story. The yearly telling of the story of the Magi always fascinates the imaginations of children. Enrich their appreciation of the visit of the three kings by playing the CD soundtrack of *Amahl and the Night Visitors* (Jay Records 1998). This wonderful retelling of the story will capture the imaginations of the children.

Celebrating the Birth of Jesus

Write a poem by following these steps. Line 1: one word telling about Jesus. Line 2: the names of Jesus' mother and foster father. Line 3: three other names for Jesus. Line 4: two words about the first Christmas. Line 5: one word about your Christmas celebration.

Jesus

Responses will vary.

Messiah

Mary   Joseph

Savior   King   Lord

Peace   Joy

Alleluia!

250

Teaching Tip

Sunday Gospel Readings. Provide the children with a list of the Gospel readings for the main liturgical celebrations during the Christmas season. This will help enrich their appreciation that Christmas is not simply a one-day celebration of the Church but a full season, which begins with Christmas Day and concludes with the feast of the Baptism of the Lord. On the list include the Gospel readings of the current year for the feast of the Holy Family; the Solemnity of Mary, Mother of God; Epiphany; and the Baptism of the Lord.

Apply

REINFORCE

Ask the children why the name *Jesus* was chosen as the name for Mary's baby. Answers might include: *Jesus* is the name the angel told Mary to give to her baby, the name *Jesus* tells everyone that he is the Savior, *Jesus* means "God saves."

INTEGRATE

- Read the directions for the "Celebrating the Birth of Jesus" activity. Make sure the children understand what they are to write for the different lines of their poems.
- Invite the children to work with partners to create their poems.
- When they have finished, encourage several volunteers to share their poems with the entire class.

PRAY

- Tell the children to listen as you read the story of Simeon and Anna in Luke 2:25–32.
- Have the children close their eyes and imagine they are standing near Simeon or Anna when Mary and Joseph bring the infant Jesus to the Temple.
- When you finish reading the Gospel story, ask the children to silently say a prayer thanking God for the gift of Jesus, using their own words.

The Season of Lent

Life in Christ

The season of Lent prepares us for the celebration of the Triduum and the Easter season during which we initiate new members into the Church, the Body of Christ. Throughout Lent the Church constantly reminds us that through the Passion, death, and Resurrection of Christ, joy came to the whole world. Self-denial and struggle are for the sake of life. By dying Jesus taught us how to live.

Lent begins on Ash Wednesday. On this day we are reminded of our vulnerability and need for redemption. We are invited to enter into the company of the faithful who willingly and whole-heartedly take on the Lenten work of deepening their life in Christ through prayer, fasting, and almsgiving.

We ask the Holy Spirit's guidance and help to enter fully into the death and new life of the Lord. As the Church, the new People of God, we support one another and work together to welcome new members into the Church at the Easter Vigil through the celebration of the three Sacraments of Christian Initiation—Baptism, Confirmation, and Eucharist.

God's Word to Us

The goal of our Lenten journey is to celebrate and deepen our new life in Christ. The Gospel readings for the first two Sundays of Lent speak of the Temptation of Christ and his Transfiguration. We journey with Jesus into the desert and confront both our weakness and our strength. Moved by the Holy Spirit we confront sin and evil in our lives, renewing our commitment to reject sin and the glamour of evil and to live as children of the Father.

We journey up the slopes of the Mount of the Transfiguration and listen, as Saints Peter, James, and John did, to the words of the Father, "This is my beloved Son, with whom I am well pleased; listen to him" (Matthew 17:5). We are privileged to do so that we may be transformed into his faithful and faith-filled disciples of his Son. The Gospel readings assigned for the remaining Sundays of Lent shine with images of living water, of restored sight, and of life. We cannot miss the allusion to the Easter sacraments here.

Finally, the Mass of Palm Sunday of the Lord's Passion introduces us to the holiest week of the liturgical year. We remember and celebrate Jesus' final entrance into the city of Jerusalem, his celebration of Passover for the last time with his disciples, and his journey up the hill of Calvary to the place of his death. As we enter into this week of Jesus' Passion and death, we look forward to his Resurrection.

For Reflection

As I journey through Lent and remember that through the cross of Christ joy came to the whole world, how am I strengthened?

What can I do to deepen my life in Christ during this holy season?

Catechist to Catechist

Garden of Faith

Lent is a season of new life, a season of hope, a season of spiritual growth and renewal. Imagine yourself as a spiritual gardener using the threefold Lenten discipline of prayer, almsgiving, and fasting to care for your garden of faith, your spiritual life. Fasting, almsgiving, and prayer all help us live the Great Commandment. Prayer focuses on our life with God and deepens our intimacy with him. Almsgiving is a concrete, practical way to express our love for our neighbor. Fasting strengthens the virtue of detachment in us, guiding us to see that God and the things of God alone are the treasures our hearts should seek.

Working at the Lenten Disciplines

All three Lenten practices are spiritual skills that need to be used appropriately throughout one's lifetime. This Lent offer the children opportunities to develop the habit of prayer. Encourage their participation in the celebration of the sacrament of Penance and the praying of the Stations of the Cross. Encourage the giving up of "little things" and the doing of "little extras" to show their love for God and others.

The Church Teaches . . .

In the *Ceremonial of Bishops* we read: The faithful are to be encouraged to participate in an ever more intense and fruitful way in the Lenten liturgy and in penitential celebrations. They are to be clearly reminded that both according to the law and tradition they should approach the sacrament of penance during this season so that with purified heart they may participate in the paschal mysteries.

CB 251

During Lent your parish probably will celebrate the communal rite of the sacrament of Penance. This always includes the confession of sins by individuals to the priest. Take the time to review the examination of conscience and rites for the celebration of Penance with the class.

CATECHIST PRAYER

*God of compassion,
you invite us to turn to
prayer, fasting, and sharing
with our brothers and sisters.
Let your compassion fill
us with hope and lead us to
the beauty of Easter joy.*

[BASED ON THE ALTERNATIVE OPENING PRAYER FOR
THE MASS FOR THE THIRD SUNDAY OF LENT]

Teach

FOCUS

Ask a volunteer to read the "Faith Focus" question aloud. Point out to the children that they will begin to find out the answer to this question in the lesson.

DISCOVER

- Read the first paragraph of "The Season of Lent" to the group.
- Have the children think about a special event they have celebrated (or soon will be celebrating) with their families.
- Ask: How did you get ready (or are you getting ready) for that special family event?
- Have the children work with partners to finish reading "The Season of Lent."
- Write the headings "Give to Others," "Give Up," and "Pray" on the board. As a class, discuss examples of ways the children can give to others, can give something up, or can improve their prayer lives during Lent.
- Invite the children to come forward one at a time and write their ideas under one or more of the headings.
- Then ask the children to choose one specific thing they will do during the Lenten season.

The First Week of Lent

Faith Focus

How do we spend our time during Lent?

The Word of the Lord

Choose this year's Gospel reading for the First Sunday of Lent. Read and discuss it with your family.

Year A
Matthew 4:1–11

Year B
Mark 1:12–15

Year C
Luke 4:1–13

The Season of Lent

Think of a wonderful thing that will happen soon in your life. Will you celebrate your birthday? Will you go on a trip? Will you see a friend again? What will you do to prepare for this event?

During Lent we prepare for a wonderful happening. We get ready for Easter. We try extra hard to give time and effort to help others. We also fast, or give up something, and we try to pray more.

During Lent we also get ready to welcome new members into the Church at the Easter Vigil. We prepare ourselves to renew our baptismal promises and to become more like Jesus.

In these ways we prepare for the wonderful celebration of Easter.

(251)

Teaching Tip

Celebrating Lenten Resolutions. Lent is a time to reflect on our own Baptism and to welcome new members into the Church. It is also a season during which we make serious decisions, or resolutions, to renew living our life in Christ. Invite the children to make Lenten resolutions and write them on a piece of paper, place their written resolutions in envelopes, and seal their envelopes. Walk among the children and seal each envelope again with tape. Then have the children walk in procession as they carry the sealed envelopes to the prayer area and place them in a shoebox. Seal the shoebox with tape and keep it on the prayer table during your Lenten sessions with the group.

On the Way to Easter

Put a ✔ next to the things in each box that you will do during Lent to prepare for Easter. Keep a list of all things you will do. Hang it where you will see it each day.

Responses will vary. Affirm appropriate responses.

I will give

____ a smile to someone who looks sad.

____ kind words to someone who loves me.

____ help to someone in need.

____ thanks to someone who has helped me.

____ other _____.

I will give up

____ a snack during the day.

____ a favorite TV show.

____ arguing.

____ a bad habit.

____ other _____.

I will pray for

_____,

_____,

_____,

_____.

252

Apply

REINFORCE

Ask the children to suggest three ways we can try to become more like Jesus during Lent. Answers might include: We give our time and effort to help others; we give up something; we pray more.

INTEGRATE

- Direct the children's attention to the activity on page 252.
- Read the directions and give the group time to put a check next to the things they will do during Lent to prepare for Easter.
- Encourage the children to tear out this page and hang it somewhere in their home where they will see it each day to remind them of what they will do to prepare for Easter.

PRAY

Invite the children to the prayer area. When all have gathered, read Colossians 3:12–15 to the children.

Teaching Tip

Respecting the Dignity and Difference of Each Person. Invite the children to open their hearts and treat each other with respect and acceptance. Every person is an image of God and a child of God. Each person is unique. Each and every one of us has our own unique gifts, talents, and limitations. Each person is blessed by God who invites us to share our differences as gifts with one another. The Lenten discipline of almsgiving, which is the sharing of "money or goods to the poor as an act of penance or fraternal charity" (*CCC* page 865), is rooted in our love and respect for one another, especially the poor and those most in need among us, as children of God and brothers and sisters in Christ.

Teach

FOCUS

Ask a volunteer to read the "Faith Focus" question aloud. Explain to the children that during Lent we are encouraged to be cheerful.

DISCOVER

- Invite the children to describe in detail what they see in the photos on page 253.
- Read the first paragraph of "A Cheerful Giver" to the children. Invite volunteers to describe times they were cheerful givers.
- Invite three volunteers to read the remaining three paragraphs from "A Cheerful Giver" to the group. Have everyone listen and learn what it means to be a cheerful giver.
- After the reading, invite the children to share what they learned from the reading.
- Distribute paper and invite the children to quiet themselves and write a short prayer asking God to help them be cheerful givers. Collect the children's prayers and put them on the table in the prayer area.

The Second Week of Lent

Faith Focus

What does it mean to be a "cheerful giver"?

The Word of the Lord

Choose this year's Gospel reading for the Second Sunday of Lent. Read and discuss it with your family.

Year A
Matthew 17:1–9

Year B
Mark 9:2–10

Year C
Luke 9:28–36

A Cheerful Giver

Sometimes we may have to give time to our younger brother or sister when we would like to play with friends. We may have to give something away that we want to keep. At these times it is not always easy to be cheerful.

During Lent we choose to give up things. Jesus asks us to be quiet and cheerful givers. He teaches us to give away money and goods without telling everyone about our good deeds. Paul the Apostle adds to this idea. He tells us, "God loves a cheerful giver" (2 Corinthians 9:7).

Jesus also asks us to fast, or give up things. He wants us to be bright and cheerful when we do this. When we fast without looking gloomy, we follow Jesus.

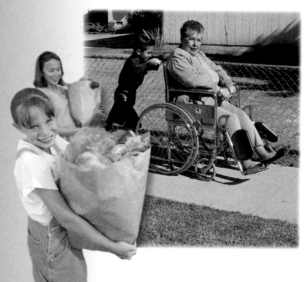

Jesus also asks us to pray simply and confidently to God. We pray from the deepest part of our heart. Jesus reminds us that God, our Father, knows our needs.

 253

Teaching Tip

Affirm the Children's Efforts. Encourage the children to recall the things they said they would try to do this Lent. Affirm the children in all their Lenten efforts. Affirmation is a strong motivator. When children are affirmed in their efforts at doing good, they will value their efforts and grow in the conviction that living their faith makes a difference.

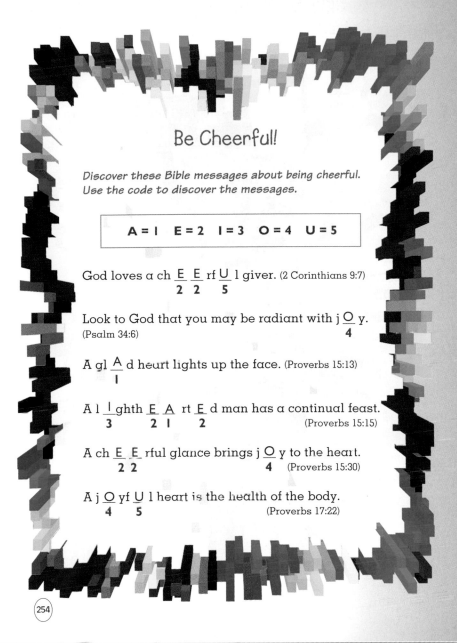

Be Cheerful!

Discover these Bible messages about being cheerful. Use the code to discover the messages.

A = 1	E = 2	I = 3	O = 4	U = 5

God loves a ch E E rf U l giver. (2 Corinthians 9:7)
2 2 5

Look to God that you may be radiant with j O y.
(Psalm 34:6) 4

A gl A d heart lights up the face. (Proverbs 15:13)
1

A l I ghth E A rt E d man has a continual feast.
3 2 1 2 (Proverbs 15:15)

A ch E E rful glance brings j O y to the heart.
2 2 4 (Proverbs 15:30)

A j O yf U l heart is the health of the body.
4 5 (Proverbs 17:22)

254

Apply

REINFORCE

Ask the children to share how we are to pray during Lent. Our prayers should be simple, trusting, and from our hearts.

INTEGRATE

- Have the children complete the "Be Cheerful!" activity by using the code given.
- Provide several Bibles so that children who finish early can look up the five Scripture verses.
- After the children have filled in the missing letters to discover the Bible messages, go over the answers together.

PRAY

- Gather the children in the prayer center which has been highlighted with the color and symbols of Lent.
- Allow volunteers to pray aloud the prayers they wrote.

Background: Our Catholic Identity

The Sacrament of Penance. Lent is a traditional time to strengthen our efforts to renew living our Baptism by participating in the sacrament of Penance, or Reconciliation. Share with the children the date and time for your parish celebrations both of the communal rite and of the individual rite of this sacrament. Enhance the children's preparation for their celebration by sharing several of the prayers of sorrow that are in the Book of Psalms, for example, Psalm 24:8–11, Psalm 32:1–2, and Psalm 51:11–14.

Teach

FOCUS

Ask a volunteer to read the "Faith Focus" question aloud. Remind the children that Christians are people of prayer.

DISCOVER

- Invite the children to name their favorite prayers and their favorite times to pray.
- Have the children read "Praying Alone and Together" with a partner.
- Reread the "Faith Focus" question to the children and invite volunteers to respond to it.
- Divide the children into three groups. Distribute art paper, magazines with pictures of people, scissors, and paste or tape.
- Invite the children to find pictures of people or events that they would like to pray for.
- Ask each group to use their pictures to make a collage and write a prayer for all those pictured on the collage. For example: "For these people who are hungry, God, watch over them and show us how to help them."
- When all the groups have finished their collages, ask a volunteer from each group to share its collage with the class.

The Third Week of Lent

Faith Focus

How do we know God is near?

The Word of the Lord

Choose this year's Gospel reading for the Third Sunday of Lent. Read and discuss it with your family.

Year A
John 4:5–42 or
John 4:5–15, 19–26, 39, 40–44

Year B
John 2:13–25

Year C
Luke 13:1–9

What You Hear

During Lent we do not sing the Alleluia. This is because we will not rejoice until we celebrate Jesus being raised from the dead on Easter.

Praying Alone and Together

We like to talk to our friends, but sometimes they are too busy. God is never too busy. God is one friend we can always talk to. We can thank and praise God and tell him our needs anytime and anywhere.

Faith tells us that God is always near. Prayer helps us to be aware that God is near. Psalm 37:7 tells us,

> "Be still before the LORD;
> wait for God."

During Lent we ask God to draw near us.

We are a people of prayer. On Sunday we gather to give praise and thanks to God. The Eucharist is our shared prayer to God. When we pray together, we celebrate our friendship with God.

During Lent we also pray alone. In the silence of our heart, we pray to God. When we pray alone, we celebrate our friendship with God.

Teaching Tip

The Elect and Candidates. Share with the children that there is a special group of people in our parish who are preparing to become members of the Catholic Church at the celebration of the Easter Vigil on Holy Saturday night. These people are called the Elect, or candidates for full communion if they were previously validly baptized in another Christian denomination. Make a list of the names of the Elect and the candidates written in bold letters and post the list of names in the prayer area. Invite each of the children to choose the name of one of these people and pray for that person during Lent. This is one way you can help the children develop the habit of practicing the Lenten discipline of prayer.

The Lord Is Near

Create the second verse to this prayer.
Sing it to the tune of "Kumbaya."

Verse 1
Someone's praying, Lord,
The Lord is near.
Someone's praying, Lord,
The Lord is near.
Someone's praying, Lord,
The Lord is near.
O Lord, you are near.

Verse 2   Responses will vary.
Someone's _____ , Lord,
You are here.
Someone's _____ , Lord,
You are here.
Someone's _____ , Lord,
You are here.
O Lord, you are here.

256

REINFORCE

Ask the children to share what we are doing when we pray together and aloud. Answers might include: We celebrate our friendship with God.

INTEGRATE

- Practice humming the tune to "Kumbaya," which provides the basic melody and lyrics for "The Lord Is Near" activity.
- Read and explain the directions for the activity and give the children time to complete the missing lines in verse 2. You might wish to have the children work with partners or in small groups to complete the activity.
- Invite volunteers to offer their versions of the lyrics to "The Lord Is Near."

PRAY

Use one or several of the children's completed "The Lord Is Near" songs as a closing prayer. Lead the group in singing both verses.

Liturgy Tip

Enhancing Prayer with Gestures. The simplest prayer experience is enhanced by music and ritual action. The more of our senses that we use in prayer, the richer the experience can be. For example, the children could place their hands over their heart or point to their heart as they sing the words "The Lord is near."

Teach

FOCUS

Ask a volunteer to read the "Faith Focus" question aloud. Tell the children that in this lesson they will learn about Lent as a time for giving to others.

DISCOVER

- Ask the children to help you rearrange the room to clear a space so that they will be able to perform a short play later in the lesson.
- Make a point of thanking the children for helping.
- Invite the children to look at the photo on page 257 and describe what they think is happening.
- Have the children silently read "A Time to Give" on page 257.
- When they have finished reading, ask the children to name the helping actions Jesus asked his followers to do.
- List the children's responses on the board.
- Emphasize that Jesus said that to help another person is the same as helping Jesus himself.

The Fourth Week of Lent

Faith Focus

How does Jesus want us to help people?

The Word of the Lord

Choose this year's Gospel reading for the Fourth Sunday of Lent. Read and discuss it with your family.

Year A
John 9:1–41 or
John 9:1, 6–9, 13–17, 34–38

Year B
John 3:14–21

Year C
Luke 15:1–3, 11–32

A Time to Give

Sometimes we see people who need our help. Helping may not seem important to us at that time. "Someone else will help," we say.

Jesus said that when we care about people who need help, we care about him. When we feed someone who is hungry, we feed Jesus. When someone is thirsty and we offer them a drink, we offer Jesus a drink. When someone is alone or imprisoned and we visit them, we visit Jesus.

During Lent we make extra effort to help people. We remember that even the smallest things we do for those in need really do make a difference.

257

Teaching Tip

Reaching Out to People in Need. Almsgiving is one of the three traditional Lenten practices. Invite the children to brainstorm ways that they can do a special act of kindness with their families for another person. Some families might make sandwiches and take them to a shelter for people who are homeless. Other families might choose to eat less for dinner one day a week for a month and give the money saved to an organization that helps people. Remind the children that when we do these helping things, it is the Lord himself whom we are serving (see Matthew 25:31–46).

Saint Martin and the Beggar

Read this story. Write the ending yourself.
Clue: Read Matthew 25:35–40.

Once upon a time, Martin the soldier came upon a cold, shivering beggar on the side of the road.

Martin reined in his horse and drew his sword. He cut his wool cloak in two and gave half to the beggar.

The beggar wrapped himself in the warm cloak. He grew warm with joy and happiness.

That night Martin dreamed that Jesus stood before him on the roadway, wrapped in the part of the warm cloak Martin had given away.

Responses will vary.

Suddenly, Martin knew he was helping Jesus too.
_____
_____ .

258

REINFORCE

Ask the children to share ways in which they can help others this Lent. Affirm all appropriate responses.

INTEGRATE

- Read and explain the directions for the "Saint Martin and the Beggar" activity on page 258. Have the children look up the Scripture passage in a Bible and write an ending to the story.
- When they have finished, choose several volunteers to play the parts of Martin and the beggar. Have the volunteers act out the story, using the words they wrote to end the play.
- Be creative and allow many children to take turns performing for the class.
- Emphasize that what we do for others we do for Jesus.

PRAY

- Gather the children in the prayer space.
- Invite them to take a moment to remember that when we help others, we are helping Jesus.
- Use the entire reading from Matthew 25:35–40 in a closing prayer of meditation.

Teaching Tip

FaithFirst.com. Remind the children and their families to visit RCL's Web site, FaithFirst.com. Emphasize that FaithFirst.com provides a wide variety of resources for all family members. There are pages for the adults, for the children, and for the whole family. Encourage your families to integrate visiting FaithFirst.com into their family routine of growing in faith together. Point out that the "Make a Difference" page will give them ideas of ways to live their faith in concrete, practical ways.

Teach

FOCUS

Ask a volunteer to read the "Faith Focus" question aloud. Have the children look at the photo on page 259 and share with them that Lent is also a time of forgiveness and reconciliation.

DISCOVER

- Encourage the children to give examples of being forgiven and asking for forgiveness. Stress that forgiving others and accepting the forgiveness of others are among the most important things we can do.
- Ask the children to follow along as you read aloud "Be Reconciled."
- Help the children appreciate that Jesus asks us to forgive others as God forgives us.
- Identify the sacrament of Reconciliation as a celebration of forgiveness. Ask the children why Reconciliation is like coming home to God. Affirm appropriate responses.
- Invite volunteers to mime the situations mentioned in "Be Reconciled." Summarize by emphasizing that God always forgives us our sins when we are truly sorry for them. He welcomes us back and rejoices with us.

The Fifth Week of Lent

Faith Focus

Why is it important to forgive?

The Word of the Lord

Choose this year's Gospel reading for the Fifth Sunday of Lent. Read and discuss it with your family.

Year A
John 11:1–45 or
John 11:3–7, 17,
20–27, 33–45

Year B
John 12:20–33

Year C
John 8:1–11

Be Reconciled

Sometimes a friend hurts our feelings. Forgiving that friend can be difficult. But Jesus shows us that God is always ready to forgive. We must always be ready to forgive also.

During Lent the Scripture readings remind us about God's forgiveness. God seeks us the way a shepherd seeks lost sheep. God rejoices like a woman who finds a lost coin. God welcomes us home the way a father welcomes his wandering child.

During Lent the Church invites us to celebrate God's forgiveness. The Church encourages us to celebrate our return to God through the sacrament of Reconciliation.

When we have been lost and alone, God rejoices at our return. God welcomes us back. We find peace with God and with one another.

(259)

Liturgy Tip

The Rite of Penance. This would be a good time to review with the children the steps in both the communal and the individual rites for the celebration of the sacrament of Penance, or Reconciliation. Use the outline of the rites for celebrating this sacrament found in the "Catholic Prayers and Practices" section on page 296 of the student text.

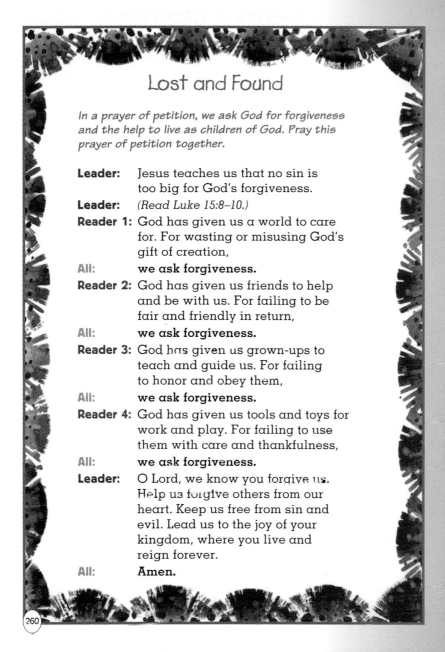

Lost and Found

In a prayer of petition, we ask God for forgiveness and the help to live as children of God. Pray this prayer of petition together.

Leader: Jesus teaches us that no sin is too big for God's forgiveness.

Leader: *(Read Luke 15:8–10.)*

Reader 1: God has given us a world to care for. For wasting or misusing God's gift of creation,

All: **we ask forgiveness.**

Reader 2: God has given us friends to help and be with us. For failing to be fair and friendly in return,

All: **we ask forgiveness.**

Reader 3: God has given us grown-ups to teach and guide us. For failing to honor and obey them,

All: **we ask forgiveness.**

Reader 4: God has given us tools and toys for work and play. For failing to use them with care and thankfulness,

All: **we ask forgiveness.**

Leader: O Lord, we know you forgive us. Help us forgive others from our heart. Keep us free from sin and evil. Lead us to the joy of your kingdom, where you live and reign forever.

All: **Amen.**

260

Apply

REINFORCE

Ask the children to share when we need forgiveness. Affirm appropriate responses.

INTEGRATE

- Talk to the children about experiences of being lost and found. Include your own appropriate personal stories. Emphasize the feeling of joy when someone who is lost has been found.
- Preview the "Lost and Found" prayer of petition with the children.
- Choose volunteers for the four "Reader" parts.
- Allow the children selected to be readers to practice their parts. Go over the "All" parts with the other children.

PRAY

Gather the children in the prayer center and lead them in praying the "Lost and Found" prayer service.

Teaching Tip

Singing About God's Gifts of Peace and Justice. Help the children prayerfully reflect on their call to bring justice and peace to the world. Expand their understanding of their responsibility to live as peacemakers by having them write new lyrics to a song, such as "Let there be justice on earth" or "Let there be love on earth." Other songs you might use are "He's Got the Whole World in His Hands" and "Make Me a Channel of Your Peace." Most will be available in your parish hymnal.

Holy Week

The Easter Triduum

The Easter Triduum is the center of the Church's year. The celebration of the Triduum begins with the celebration of the Evening Mass of the Lord's Supper on Holy Thursday and concludes with Evening Prayer, or Vespers, on Easter Sunday. "Christ redeemed us all and gave perfect glory to God principally through his Paschal Mystery: dying he destroyed our death and rising he restored our life. Therefore the Easter triduum of the passion and resurrection of Christ is the culmination of the entire liturgical year."

"GENERAL NORMS FOR THE LITURGICAL YEAR AND THE CALENDAR," ROMAN MISSAL 18

Holy Thursday

The first day of the Triduum begins with the Evening Mass of the Lord's Supper. (The term *day* is somewhat misleading if one thinks of days as independent twenty-four-hour periods of time. The Triduum in reality is a three-day-long celebration and participation in this great mystery of our faith—the Paschal Mystery.) Celebrating this liturgy for Holy Thursday marks our entrance into the solemn observance of the Triduum. We join Christ at the Passover meal. We watch and listen in amazement. We learn what it means to serve

as Jesus did. We receive the gift of his Body and Blood, the Eucharist.

Good Friday

On the second day of the Triduum, Good Friday, we gather for the celebration of the Lord's Passion. Celebrating this liturgy occurs ideally at about three o'clock in the afternoon, the traditional hour of Jesus' death. However, this time is often altered to reflect pastoral needs.

Holy Saturday

The third day of the Triduum begins with the celebration of the Easter Vigil on Holy Saturday evening and ends with the celebration of Vespers, or Evening Song, on Easter Sunday. The

Easter Vigil, during the holy night when Christ rose from the dead, ranks as the "mother of all vigils."

Keeping watch, the Church awaits Christ's resurrection and celebrates it in the sacraments. Accordingly, the entire celebration of this vigil should take place at night, that is, it should either begin after nightfall or end before the dawn of Sunday.

"GENERAL NORMS FOR THE LITURGICAL YEAR AND THE CALENDAR," ROMAN MISSAL 21

The Easter Vigil summons us to enter into the Service of Light, with the singing of the Easter Proclamation, and the celebration of the Liturgy of the Word, the Liturgy of Baptism, and the Liturgy of the Eucharist. We initiate and welcome new members into the Church, the Body of Christ, and renew our Baptism. Together we rejoice:

Jesus Christ, our King, is risen!
Sound the trumpet
of salvation! *EASTER PROCLAMATION*

For Reflection

How does my taking part in the celebration of the Easter Triduum strengthen my identity as a follower of Jesus Christ?

What can I do to observe these days as the holiest time of the Church's year?

Catechist to Catechist

The Paschal Mystery

The Paschal Mystery of Christ is the heart of the work his Father sent him to do. "Christ redeemed us all and gave perfect glory to God principally through his Paschal Mystery: dying he destroyed our death and rising he restored our life" ("General Norms for the Liturgical Year and the Calendar," 18). Through the celebration of Holy Week, especially the three-day feast of the Easter Triduum, we remember and enter into the power of the Paschal Mystery and are further transformed by the love and sacrifice of Christ.

Celebrate the Rites

The liturgical rites of Palm Sunday and the Easter Triduum open up the meaning of our faith in Christ in dramatic ways. Have your group try their hand at announcing these events. You might divide your group into smaller groups. Have one group present a live newscast of the crowd welcoming Jesus into Jerusalem. Have another group pantomime the Last Supper; be sure they include the washing of the feet. Ask a third group to present a tableau vivant of the Passion story. Have the final group role-play Mary Magdalene and the other women reporting to the disciples the news that Jesus' tomb was empty and he would meet them in Galilee.

The Church Teaches . . .

In *Paschale Solemnitatis,* the 1988 circular letter concerning the preparation and celebration of the Easter feast, written by the Congregation for Divine Worship and the Discipline of Sacraments, we read:

> The greatest mysteries of redemption are celebrated yearly by the church, beginning with the evening Mass of the Lord's Supper on Holy Thursday and ending with Vespers of Easter Sunday. This time is called "the triduum of the crucified, buried and risen."[1]
>
> *PS* 38

Ideally, the children would have an opportunity for catechesis on the Easter Triduum immediately before its celebration. If this is not possible, encourage the families to use the Triduum lessons at home.

CATECHIST PRAYER

God, Father of compassion, send your blessing down upon us who celebrate the death of your Son in the hope of his Resurrection. Amen.

[BASED ON "PRAYER OVER THE PEOPLE" FROM THE LITURGY OF GOOD FRIDAY, ROMAN MISSAL.]

Footnote references may be found on p. 456.

Teach

FOCUS

Ask a volunteer to read the "Faith Focus" question aloud. Share with the children that Palm Sunday of the Lord's Passion is the beginning of Holy Week.

DISCOVER

- Invite the children to name a well-known person—for example, the mayor, the bishop, the president, or the pope—and describe how they would welcome that person to their city, neighborhood, parish, or school.
- Have the children look at the photo on page 261 and describe what they see happening.
- Have the children work with partners to read "Hosanna!" to discover more about what the Church celebrates on Palm Sunday of the Lord's Passion.
- Invite the children to tell how the people welcomed Jesus. List the children's responses on the board.
- Use "What You See" to help the children recall why we use palm branches on this Sunday.

Palm Sunday of the Lord's Passion

Faith Focus

What event do we remember on Palm Sunday of the Lord's Passion?

The Word of the Lord

Choose this year's Gospel reading for Palm Sunday of the Lord's Passion. Read and discuss it with your family.

Year A
Matthew 26:14–27:66 or Matthew 27:11–54

Year B
Mark 14:1–15:47 or Mark 15:1–39

Year C
Luke 22:14–23:56 or Luke 23:1–49

What You See

On this day palm branches are held high during the reading of the Passion of our Lord. We do this to re-create and remember Jesus' entry into Jerusalem.

Hosanna!

When someone important comes to your school, you celebrate. You greet the person and do special things.

Many years ago children welcomed Jesus to Jerusalem. They did this on the day we call Palm Sunday of the Lord's Passion.

The celebration of Palm Sunday of the Lord's Passion begins Holy Week. On that day we carry palms and remember the day Jesus came into the city of Jerusalem. People welcomed him and cheered. They called out, "Hosanna!" They waved palm branches. They spread their cloaks on the road to make the path smooth and less dusty for Jesus.

261

Background: Scripture

Palm Sunday of the Lord's Passion. Share these biblical facts with the children to help them enter into the liturgical celebration of Palm Sunday: (1) Three of the four accounts of the Gospel mention that the people waved branches from the trees. Only John's account mentions palm branches. Many of the trees were palms, but willows and other trees with supple small switches also grew in Palestine. (2) As a sign of respect for military leaders and other dignitaries traveling the road, people spread their cloaks on the roadway to keep the dust down. (3) In Jesus' time, military rulers usually rode into the city on horses. Jesus came on a donkey. This was a sign that he was a leader who would triumph with love and compassion, and not with military might.

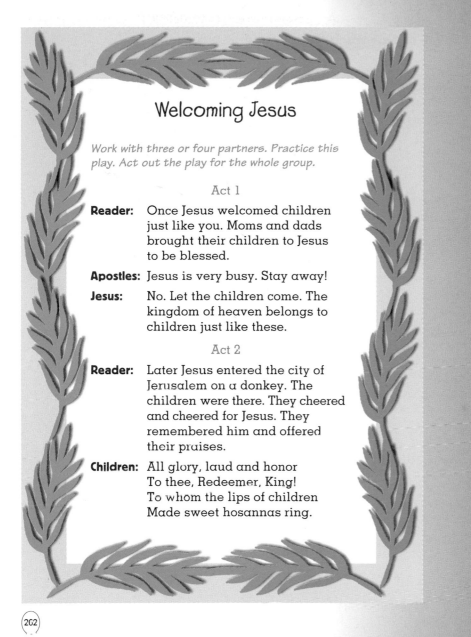

Welcoming Jesus

Work with three or four partners. Practice this play. Act out the play for the whole group.

Act 1

Reader: Once Jesus welcomed children just like you. Moms and dads brought their children to Jesus to be blessed.

Apostles: Jesus is very busy. Stay away!

Jesus: No. Let the children come. The kingdom of heaven belongs to children just like these.

Act 2

Reader: Later Jesus entered the city of Jerusalem on a donkey. The children were there. They cheered and cheered for Jesus. They remembered him and offered their praises.

Children: All glory, laud and honor
To thee, Redeemer, King!
To whom the lips of children
Made sweet hosannas ring.

262

Apply

REINFORCE

Ask the children what the great welcome on Palm Sunday of the Lord's Passion reminds us about Jesus. Answers might include: Our celebration of Palm Sunday of the Lord's Passion reminds us that Jesus is the King and Savior of all.

INTEGRATE

- Introduce the "Welcoming Jesus" play to the children.
- Have the children work with three or four partners to act out this play for the whole class.
- Emphasize the importance of welcoming people in the name of the Lord.

PRAY

- Invite a music minister to join the group or obtain a copy of the song used in your parish during the procession of palms on Palm Sunday.
- Sing the hymn with the children as a closing prayer.

Teaching Tip

Making Crosses from Palm Branches. Many Christians have the custom of making crosses, using the palm branches that they receive on Palm Sunday. Invite someone from the parish who knows how to weave the palm fronds into designs of crosses to visit with the children and teach them to weave the palms. The children will learn to participate in this custom and share it with their families.

Teach

FOCUS

Ask a volunteer to read the "Faith Focus" question aloud. Explain that the celebration called the Easter Triduum begins on Holy Thursday.

DISCOVER

- Write the words *The Lord's Supper* on the board.
- Read aloud "Called to Serve" and ask the children to identify the two actions that happened at the Last Supper that we celebrate on Holy Thursday. Responses might include: We remember that Jesus gave us the Eucharist; The washing of the disciples' feet shows us that Jesus served others.
- Give the children pieces of art paper. Ask them to fold the piece of paper in four sections. Ask the children to create an invitation for their family to the celebration of the Evening Mass of the Lord's Supper. Use the ideas in the box on page 411 of this guide to enhance this activity.
- After the children write and decorate their invitations, have them share them with one other person in the class.

Triduum/Holy Thursday

Faith Focus

What do we celebrate at the Mass of the Lord's Supper?

The Word of the Lord

Choose one of the Scripture readings for Holy Thursday. Read and discuss it with your family.

First Reading
Exodus 12:1–8, 11–14

Second Reading
1 Corinthians 11:23–26

Gospel
John 13:1–15

Called to Serve

The three days just before Easter Sunday are one big celebration. They are called the Easter Triduum. The word *triduum* means "three days."

The celebration of the Easter Triduum begins on Holy Thursday with the evening Mass of the Lord's Supper. The Church remembers the first time that Jesus took bread and wine and said, "This is my body," and "This is my blood." We remember that Jesus gave us the Eucharist.

The Gospel reading tells us that Jesus washed the feet of his disciples at the Last Supper. The washing of the disciples' feet shows us that Jesus served others. All of us who share in the Body and Blood of Christ Jesus are also to serve others as Jesus did.

The Last Supper

Teaching Tip

Write Invitations to Celebrate Holy Thursday as a Family. Work with the children to write invitations to their family members to participate in the liturgy on Holy Thursday evening. Write the time and other pertinent information about the liturgy on the board. Discuss with the children ideas about symbols they can use to decorate their invitations; for example, a cup or chalice or unleavened bread on a plate.

Hands to Serve

Trace an outline of your hand over the words on this page. Think of ways to serve using your hands. Write them in the lines provided. Then say this prayer together.

Reader 1: When my hands comfort others,
All: God is truly here.

Reader 2: When my hands help others,
All: God is truly here.

Reader 3: When my hands open and close in prayer,
All: God is truly here.

Reader 4: When my hands hold on tight,
All: God is truly here.

Reader 5: _____ *Affirm appropriate responses.* _____

_____ ,

All: God is truly here.

Reader 6: _____ *Affirm appropriate responses.* _____

_____ ,

All: God is truly here.

264

REINFORCE

Ask volunteers to share what the Gospel reading on Holy Thursday tells us. The Gospel reading at Mass on Holy Thursday tells about Jesus washing the feet of the disciples at the Last Supper and giving us the Eucharist.

INTEGRATE

- Have the children trace an outline of one of their hands over the "Hands to Serve" prayer.
- Read the prayer service together. Then pause and give the children time to write the two ways they can use their hands to follow Jesus' command to serve others as he did.
- Have volunteers share their ideas with the class.

PRAY

- As a group, come up with actions that can demonstrate each of the statements in the "Reader" parts. Choose two statements from the group for Reader 5 and Reader 6.
- Lead the children in praying "Hands to Serve," using the actions chosen for each statement.

Teaching Tip

Washing of the Feet: Helping Hands. The rite of washing of feet is an integral part of the Holy Thursday evening liturgy. Guide the children to grasp the essence of this rite, namely, we are to serve others as Jesus did. To extend the activity on this page, have the children trace and cut out outlines of both of their hands on art paper. In the outline of one hand, have them write their name. In the outline of the other hand, have them write or draw one way they can serve, or help, people at home. Encourage the children to put their faith choices into action and make a difference.

Teach

FOCUS

Ask a volunteer to read the "Faith Focus" question aloud. Ask the children to look at the stained-glass image and describe what they see. Remind the children that the second day of the Triduum is Good Friday.

DISCOVER

- Have volunteers read the paragraphs of "We Remember" for the entire class.
- Invite the children to share what they remember about Palm Sunday of the Lord's Passion. Write the key words of their responses on the board.
- Ask volunteers to share what happened to Jesus on Good Friday. Write the key words of their responses on the board.
- Invite volunteers to share what they think Jesus and his followers must have been feeling on each of these days.
- Ask: What did Jesus do before he died? Forgave. What does Jesus ask us to do when others hurt us? Forgive.

Triduum/Good Friday

Faith Focus

Why do we remember Good Friday?

The Word of the Lord

Choose one of the Scripture readings for Good Friday. Read and discuss it with your family.

First Reading
Isaiah 52:13–53:12

Second Reading
Hebrews 4:14–16, 5:7–9

Gospel
John 18:1–19:42

We Remember

On Good Friday we remember that Jesus died on the cross because he loved all of us. When someone is put to death on a cross, it is called a crucifixion.

Jesus was accused of being a criminal. Even though he was innocent, some people wanted him to die on the cross anyway. They shouted, "Crucify him!" The soldiers took Jesus away. They made Jesus carry his cross along the road to the place where criminals were put to death.

Jesus carrying his cross

Before Jesus died, he forgave the people who hurt him. He asked his Father to forgive them. He prayed, "Father, forgive them for they know not what they do" (based on Luke 23:34).

Whenever we see a cross or a crucifix, we thank God for loving us so much. We remember to forgive those who have hurt us.

Teaching Tip

The Cross: A Symbol of Jesus' Love. The rite of the Veneration of the Cross is unique to the celebration of the liturgy on Good Friday. Emphasize for the children that the cross is a symbol of Jesus' love for them and for all people. Remind the children that Jesus said that there is no greater sign of a person's love than to give up one's life for others. Display a cross in a prominent place in your learning area or in your prayer area. During Easter decorate the cross with flowers, for example, daffodils or Easter lilies. These visuals will help the children grow in their understanding that Jesus' death was a source of new life for all people.

Apply

Reminders of God's Love

Write or draw something you can do this Good Friday to thank Jesus for giving his life for you.

Responses will vary.

Affirm appropriate responses.

266

REINFORCE

Ask the children to share how Jesus showed his love for us. Answer might include: He showed his love for us in many ways but especially by dying on the cross for us.

INTEGRATE

- Read aloud the directions for the "Reminders of God's Love" activity. Give the children time to write down or draw something they can do to thank Jesus for giving his life for us.
- Invite volunteers to share their responses.

PRAY

- Select a child to carry a cross to the prayer area.
- Direct the child to hold the cross in both hands above his or her head, saying in a loud voice, "This is the wood of the cross."
- Ask the class to respond, "Come, let us worship."
- Ask the child to place the cross in the prayer area. Invite the children to gather around and to silently pray, remembering the events of Good Friday.

Liturgy Tip

Holy Communion. Point out that the celebration of the Lord's Passion on Good Friday does not include the Liturgy of the Eucharist as the celebration of Mass always does. The Communion Rite, however, is part of the liturgy for Good Friday. Explain to the children that the Eucharist we receive on Good Friday has been reserved in the tabernacle from the celebration of Mass on Holy Thursday evening.

Teach

FOCUS

Ask a volunteer to read the "Faith Focus" question aloud. Point out that Easter is the greatest feast of the Church and the third and final day of the Triduum.

DISCOVER

- Ask the children how they show they are happy.
- Encourage them to describe actions as well as identify words they use to express their happiness.
- Write this incomplete sentence on the board, "Christians celebrate the happiness of Easter by . . ."
- Read "Praise the Lord!" and ask the children to listen for ways to complete the sentence.
- Invite the children to tell how many days the Church celebrates Easter. Fifty days or seven Sundays.
- Ask: What does the word *Alleluia* mean? Praise God!
- Invite the children to copy the sentence-starter "Christians celebrate the happiness of Easter by . . ." on strips of paper. Have them complete the sentence by telling how they can join the Church and celebrate Easter.
- Ask the children to share their ideas with one another in small groups.

Triduum/Easter

Faith Focus

Why are Christians especially happy at Easter?

The Word of the Lord

Choose this year's Gospel reading for Easter Sunday. Read and discuss it with your family.

Year A
John 20:1–9 or
Matthew 28:1–10 or
Luke 24:13–35

Year B
John 20:1–9 or
Mark 16:1–7 or
Luke 24:13–35

Year C
John 20:1–9 or
Luke 24:1–12 or
Luke 24:13–35

Praise the Lord!

Think of a time when something wonderful happened and you were really happy. Did you want to sing or shout or jump for joy? What happy words came to you? For Christians, *Alleluia* is a happy word.

We are Easter people. Alleluia is our song. We are people of the Resurrection.

Every Sunday we praise and thank God for the new life of the Resurrection. The responsorial psalm sung on Easter reminds us, "This is the day the Lord has made; let us be glad and rejoice in it."

During the fifty days of the Easter season, the Church sings Alleluia over and over. *Alleluia* means "Praise the Lord!" We praise God because we are new in the Lord. We walk in the light of the new day of the Resurrection.

267

Teaching Tip

The Prayer Area. Saint Paul the Apostle tells us that if Christ did not rise from the dead, our faith is in vain. Easter is the central liturgical time of the Church's year. And every Sunday is a celebration of the Resurrection, a little Easter. Take the time to decorate your prayer area with the symbols and colors of Easter. Cover the prayer table with a white cloth, place a golden bookmark in the Bible to mark the Gospel reading for each Sunday of the Easter season, decorate the prayer table with colorful fresh flowers, and keep a bowl of holy water on the table to remind the children of their Baptism. Encourage the children to use the holy water to bless themselves throughout the Easter season.

Praise the Lord. Alleluia!

Divide into two groups. Face each other and take turns praying the verses of this psalm.

All: **Alleluia!**

Group 1: Praise the LORD from the heavens;
             give praise in the heights.

Group 2: Praise him, all you   ;
             give praise, all you hosts.

All: **Alleluia!**

Group 1: Praise him,   and   ;
             give praise, all shining   .

Group 2: You   and hail,   and   ,
             storm winds that fulfill his command;

All: **Alleluia!**

Group 1: You   and all hills,

             fruit   and all cedars;

Group 2: You   wild and tame.
             You kings of the   and all   .

All: **Praise the LORD. Alleluia!**

Based on Psalm 148:1–3, 7–11

(268)

REINFORCE

Ask the children to explain why Easter is the most important time of the Church's year. Easter is the day on which Jesus was raised from the dead.

INTEGRATE

- Read the directions for the "Praise the Lord. Alleluia!" activity. After dividing the children into two groups, give each group time to practice saying their verses in unison.
- Remind the children that this lesson's prayer is a rebus. Explain that when we use words and pictures to tell a story or prayer, it is called a rebus.

PRAY

Lead the children in praying "Praise the Lord. Alleluia!" as your closing prayer.

Teaching Tip

Recognize the Cultural Diversity within Your Group.
Gather a variety of ethnic traditions for celebrating Easter. Some nationalities prepare special foods; others bless Easter baskets, and so on. Include some of the ethnic traditions of the children in your class or of the people in your parish in sessions with the children during the Easter season. Invite guests who represent a variety of ethnic backgrounds to visit with the children and share their Easter customs with the group.

The Season of Easter

The Great Sunday

The fifty days from Easter Sunday to Pentecost are celebrated as one feast day, sometimes called the great Sunday (see "General Norms for the Liturgical Year and the Calendar," *Roman Missal* 22). The Easter season, which includes the feasts of the Ascension and Pentecost, is a time of praise, assurance, and mission. With our insistent "Alleluias" we lift up praise to God for the new life that comes to us in the Resurrection of Jesus Christ, our Lord and Savior. We cannot but marvel before this great mystery of our Redemption. The only fitting or, indeed, possible response is one of praise and thanksgiving.

The Scripture readings and the prayers of the Easter season reassure the hope of all believers. The story of the Risen Jesus encountering the two disciples on the road to Emmaus (see Luke 24:13–35) confirms the continuing presence of the Lord in his Church. In word and sacrament, through the proclamation of the Scriptures (see Luke 24:32) and the celebration of the Eucharist (see Luke 24:35), Jesus, the Risen One, abides with his community of faithful believers. The Easter readings and prayers that present Jesus as the Good Shepherd assure us of his continuing presence, love, and care for us, the sheep he claims as his own.

Proclaim the Resurrection

The Easter season renews the whole People of God and each individual believer in their sense of mission. The Risen Lord promised us that the Father would send the Holy Spirit. That promise was fulfilled on Pentecost, and the Holy Spirit continues to empower and encourage believers to proclaim the Gospel and to invite all people to repentance and Baptism. Those who are sealed with the Easter sacraments of Baptism, Confirmation, and Eucharist continue the mission of Jesus until he returns again in glory. During the Easter season, the liturgy rekindles the sense of holy responsibility to both celebrate and extend to others

the saving mysteries of Christ's death and Resurrection.

How does singing "Alleluia" for fifty days move me to share the good news of the Resurrection with others?

What are some practical, age-appropriate ways that young people can share in the mission of the Church?

Catechist to Catechist

A Period of Mystagogy

The Easter season is a period of mystagogy, or post-baptismal catechesis. It is a time for the newly initiated members of the Church, the neophytes, and the whole community to reflect on the meaning of the Easter sacraments. On Easter Sunday the rite of "Renewal of Baptismal Promises" replaces the praying of the creed. If you were baptized as an infant, take the experience of the Easter renewal of your baptismal promises to a new level. Use the Easter season to reflect on that experience as an extension of your Baptism.

Easter Renewal of Baptism

Reinforce the children's identity as an Easter people. Remind them that in Baptism they were joined to Christ. They died to sin and rose to new life in Christ. Make this Easter season a period of mystagogy for the children and their families. Send the *Faith First* seasonal lessons home. The first time you do so, send a brief note with a suggested way that families can use these lessons to focus better on the liturgical year.

The Church Teaches . . .

Paschale Solemnitatis, the 1988 circular letter concerning the preparation and celebration of the Easter feast, written by the Congregation for Divine Worship and the Discipline of the Sacraments, reminds us:

> The celebration of Easter is prolonged throughout the Easter season. The fifty days from Easter Sunday to Pentecost Sunday are celebrated as one feast day, the "great Sunday."[1]
>
> *PS* 100

Because of the importance of the Easter season, incorporate at least part of each of these lessons for Easter into your sessions. You might wish to include the seasonal prayer celebrations to conclude your sessions during Easter.

See the Catechism . . .

For more on the teachings of the Catholic Church on the Resurrection and Easter, see *Catechism of the Catholic Church* 638–655, 1166, and 1168–1169.

CATECHIST PRAYER

God of mercy,
as we celebrate
Christ's Resurrection
renew your gift of
life within us. Amen.

[OPENING PRAYER OF THE MASS FOR THE SECOND SUNDAY OF EASTER.]

Footnote references may be found on p. 456.

Teach

FOCUS

Ask a volunteer to read the "Faith Focus" question. Explain to the children that they will learn how they are like the disciples who witnessed the Risen Jesus.

DISCOVER

- Invite the children to tell a brief story about an interesting or exciting event they saw.
- Tell the children the people who see and tell others what they have seen are called witnesses.
- Invite volunteers to read "Witnesses for Christ" to the group.
- Ask: How can you show that you believe in the Risen Lord?
- Have the children brainstorm words and actions they can perform that give witness, or show others, that they are followers of the Risen Jesus.
- Write the children's ideas on the board. Look for words that suggest welcome, hospitality, forgiveness, and justice.

The Second Week of Easter

Faith Focus

What did the first witnesses of the Resurrection tell us about Jesus?

The Word of the Lord

This is the Gospel reading for the Second Sunday of Easter. Read and discuss it with your family.

Years A, B, and C
John 20:19–31

What You See

One of the Easter symbols is the Paschal, or Easter, candle. The candle is lighted at the Easter Vigil and during the celebration of the liturgy throughout the Easter season.

Witnesses for Christ

When we witness something, we tell other people what we have seen. Many people witnessed the new life of Jesus. They told others about the Risen Lord.

Mary Magdalene saw the Risen Jesus and proclaimed the good news to the disciples: "I have seen the Lord" (John 20:18). Two other disciples knew the Risen Lord in the breaking of the bread.

The Risen Jesus appeared many times to his Apostles. He gave them peace and the gift of the Holy Spirit. Thomas the Apostle professed his faith in Jesus as his Lord and God.

These witnesses believed in Jesus as the Risen Lord. They were the first witnesses. By what you say and do, you are also a witness to the Risen Lord today.

269

Liturgy Tip

Easter Music. Easter is a time to celebrate with music. During Lent the music of the Church was somewhat subdued. During Easter our voices break out in joyful song, "Alleluia! Alleluia! He is Risen." Include appropriate Easter music in your sessions, especially your prayer time, during the Easter season. Visit **FaithFirst.com** to find a list of suggested hymns to use with the children.

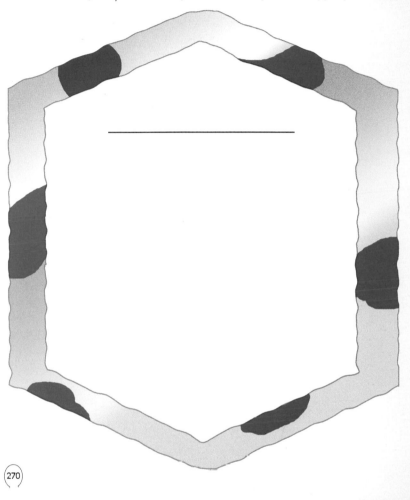

Today's Witnesses

Mary Magdalene and Thomas the Apostle were witnesses to the Risen Lord. Draw a picture of how you can be a witness to the Risen Lord. On the line write a title for your picture. **Responses will vary. Affirm appropriate responses.**

_____

270

REINFORCE

Ask the children to share who some of the first witnesses of the Resurrection were. Answers might include: Mary Magdalene, two disciples in the breaking of the bread, Thomas the Apostle.

INTEGRATE

- Direct the children to the "Today's Witnesses" activity. Read the directions aloud and give them time to draw their pictures and write a title for their pictures.
- Invite volunteers to share their completed activities with the entire class.

PRAY

- Gather the group together in the prayer area.
- Lead the children in a prayer of meditation, using simplified accounts of Matthew 28:1–10, Mark 16:1–8, Luke 24:1–12, or John 20:1–10.
- Invite the children to sing an Easter Alleluia, preferably one sung at the Sunday celebration of the Eucharist.

Teaching Tip

A Church Tour. Visit your parish church with the children during the Easter season and have them look for and identify the signs and symbols the Church uses during this season. Provide the children with a list of items to look for; for example, the Easter candle, the Easter water, the decorated crucifix, flowers, banners and other decorations that use the liturgical color for Easter. If possible, lead a brief prayer service in the church near the Easter candle or in the baptistry.

Teach

FOCUS

Ask a volunteer to read the "Faith Focus" question aloud. Tell the children that they will learn more about our call as Christians to serve one another.

DISCOVER

- Ask the children to tell how they are good caretakers of the earth, of pets, of one another, and so on.
- Have the children silently read "Ministry" on page 271.
- Ask the children to share their ideas about why the idea of a good shepherd helps us understand how Jesus cares for others.
- Explain that we call the leaders of our Church who serve the people "shepherds."
- Identify the bishop of your diocese or archdiocese. Point out that when the bishop enters the church to celebrate liturgy, he carries a staff, or crosier. This reminds everyone that he is a shepherd who cares for his flock, the people of the diocese or archdiocese.

The Third Week of Easter

Faith Focus

How does Jesus ask us to serve others?

The Word of the Lord

Choose this year's Gospel reading for the Third Sunday of Easter. Read and discuss it with your family.

Year A
Luke 24:13–35

Year B
Luke 24:35–48

Year C
John 21:1–19 or
John 21:1–14

Ministry

When we care for others, we minister to them. We take care of their needs and help them. Jesus asks us to do this. He asks us to serve one another.

Jesus said, "I am the good shepherd" (John 10:14). He is a leader who serves others. During the Easter season we think about Jesus as a good shepherd. Jesus is a shepherd who gave his life for his sheep.

The first Christians ministered to those in need. They were willing to serve others as Jesus taught them to do.

During Easter we think about our faith in Jesus. We think about how living our faith in Jesus makes a difference. We think about Baptism and how we meet Jesus in the other sacraments. We think about how we can serve others as Jesus did.

271

Liturgy Tip

Creating an Easter Banner. Take the time to add new Easter decorations to the prayer area or to your learning area. This will refresh the children's focus on Easter. Have the children create one or several Easter banners, using Easter symbols, appropriate Gospel stories of the Risen Jesus appearing to his disciples, or other Easter messages, such as, "This is the day the Lord has made!" or "Alleluia!" Display the banners during your sessions throughout the remaining weeks of the Easter season.

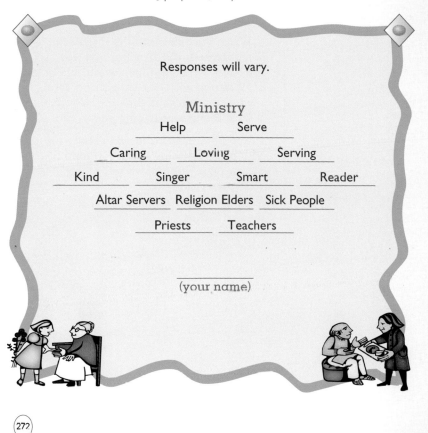

Sharing in Ministry

Create a diamond shaped poem by writing the following:
- Line 2: two words to describe "ministry"
- Line 3: three "-ing" words about how you can minister to others
- Line 4: four words naming skills and talents you have to give
- Line 5: three needs in your parish
- Line 6: two ministering people in your parish

Responses will vary.

Ministry

Help   Serve

Caring   Loving   Serving

Kind   Singer   Smart   Reader

Altar Servers   Religion Elders   Sick People

Priests   Teachers

(your name)

272

Apply

REINFORCE

Ask the children to share how they think the first Christians ministered to those in need. Answers might include: The first Christians shared their possessions and money and ministered to all in need. No one was needy or alone.

INTEGRATE

- Read the directions for the "Sharing in Ministry" activity.
- Invite the children to complete the activity by choosing words for each line.
- Give the children time to complete their work. Then invite them to share their poems with the whole group.

PRAY

- Gather the children in the prayer area.
- Lead the children in a prayer asking God to bless all the ministers of the Church.
- Ask volunteers to call out the names or ministries of these people. After each name or ministry, together pray, "Thank you, God, for your love and care."

Teaching Tip

Sign Language. Have the children learn to sign *joy, Alleluia, new life, peace, happiness,* and other Easter terms, and share the Easter message with others. Local libraries have books on American Sign Language that have simple illustrations for signing. If possible, research to see if there is a parishioner who can sign. Invite that person to teach the signs of the Easter words to the children.

Teach

FOCUS

Ask a volunteer to read the "Faith Focus" question aloud. Explain to the children that in this lesson, they will learn how we are called to be "lights in the world."

DISCOVER

- Read "Welcome to the Table" to the group.
- Ask the children why the Eucharist is so important to the Church. Review that we all share in the Body and Blood of Christ at Mass.
- Read "What You See" and look at the picture. Point out the white vestments and the Easter candle.

The Fourth Week of Easter

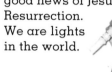

Faith Focus

What does the Eucharist call us to share?

The Word of the Lord

Choose this year's Gospel reading for the Fourth Sunday of Easter. Read and discuss it with your family.

Year A
John 10:1–10

Year B
John 10:11–18

Year C
John 10:27–30

What You See

The priest wears white vestments during the Easter season. White is a symbol of joy and life. We rejoice in Jesus' Resurrection.

Welcome to the Table

The Church welcomes new members by celebrating the three sacraments of Baptism, Confirmation, and Eucharist. The Church washes them in the waters of Baptism. The Church lays hands upon them and anoints them with oil at Confirmation. The Church invites them to share in the Body and Blood of Christ in the Eucharist.

When we celebrate the Eucharist, we participate in the Paschal Mystery. Together, we sometimes say aloud or sing,
"When we eat this bread and drink this cup, we proclaim your death, Lord Jesus, until you come in glory."

The Eucharist calls us to share our life with others. When we help others by sharing our talents, we tell others the good news of Jesus' Resurrection. We are lights in the world.

Lighting the Easter candle

273

Teaching Tip

The Newly Initiated. Share with the children that Easter is a special time to show hospitality and welcome to those newly initiated into the Church. Parishes often post the names of the people who were initiated into the Church at the Easter Vigil. Work with the children and create cards that share words of hospitality and welcome with the newly initiated. Have the children print a simple Scripture verse, for example, "One Lord, One Faith, One Baptism" on the cover and write a brief note welcoming the new members to the Church. Read all the cards and be sure to mail them.

Love and Serve the Lord

Read this rhyme about the celebration of the Eucharist. Then add a verse of your own. Tell how you love and serve the Lord.

The Lord's Day

Each week upon the Lord's Day,
We remember Jesus in a special way.

Many gather to sing and praise,
To hear and heed God's saving ways.

We celebrate together the great story,
How Jesus died and was raised to glory.

We share Body broken and Blood outpoured.
His gift is himself, our Savior and Lord.

The Lord we receive; the Lord we share.
We love and serve every day and everywhere.

Affirm appropriate responses.

_____

_____

274

REINFORCE

Ask the children what the Eucharist calls us to be. Answers should reflect an awareness that followers of Jesus are faithful, sharing, hopeful, loving, and life-giving people.

INTEGRATE

- Give the children time to read through the rhyme on page 274.
- Tell the children to add a verse of their own to tell how they love and serve the Lord.
- Invite the children to share with the whole class their ideas about loving and serving the Lord by having them read the whole rhyme with their verses included.

PRAY

- Gather with the children in the prayer area.
- Distribute copies of the *Faith First* booklet, *Called to Prayer*, for grades 1–3 and have the children turn to the section "Seasonal Prayers for Easter and Pentecost."
- Have the children quiet themselves for prayer. After a moment of prayerful reflection, pray the "Easter Psalm" (Psalm 23) together.

Teaching Tip

First Communion Cards. During the Easter season many parishes continue the initiation of those children who were baptized as infants with their celebration of First Holy Communion. Talk with your parish coordinator and then with the catechists preparing children for First Holy Communion. Pair the children in your group as pen pals with the children receiving Holy Communion for the first time. Set aside time for your group to make cards to send to those children who have celebrated or will be celebrating First Communion this year.

Teach

FOCUS

Ask a volunteer to read the "Faith Focus" question aloud. Explain that this lesson will focus on what it means to be a follower of Jesus.

DISCOVER

- Invite the children to name people whose good example shows them how to be loving people.
- Ask: Which is more powerful, our actions or our words? Have the children give a reason for their responses.
- Have volunteers read "Faith in Action" on page 275.
- Invite the children to put into their own words the words of James the Apostle that invite Christians to act in love and not just talk about it.
- Write the sentence "Actions speak louder than words" on the board.
- Invite volunteers to role-play the following with partners:
  One child makes a statement; the other child role-plays the opposite. For example: first child says, "You are my good friend." Second child says, "Would you help me with this math problem?" First child says, "Not now. I want to go play."
- Emphasize that our words *and* our actions, not only our words, need to show we are followers of Jesus.

The Fifth Week of Easter

Faith Focus

How do Christians show their faith in Jesus?

The Word of the Lord

Choose this year's Gospel reading for the Fifth Sunday of Easter. Read and discuss it with your family.

Year A
John 14:1–12

Year B
John 15:1–8

Year C
John 13:31–35

Faith in Action

When someone is a good leader, we follow that person. We do what our leader does. Our actions show that we are good followers. As Christians we follow Jesus.

James the Apostle says that our good words and works witness to Jesus' new life. James says that we show our faith in Jesus through our actions.

If we see someone without food or clothing, we must do something to help. James reminds us that we cannot just say, "Go in peace, keep warm, and eat well" (James 2:16). John the Apostle says the same thing. "Children, let us love not in word or speech but in deed and truth" (1 John 3:18).

Today we are called to be witnesses to the good news of Jesus' Resurrection. God calls us to put our faith into action. The Holy Spirit helps us do this.

(275)

Teaching Tip

Great Commandment Stories. The theme of this lesson is related to the Great Commandment that the children studied in chapter 18. Have the children gather in small groups. Then distribute to each group several copies of newspapers and periodicals. Be sure to include copies of your diocesan newspaper. Have each group identify stories that tell about people living the Great Commandment. Then invite each group to present its Great Commandment stories to the class.

Living Our Faith

Pretend a new family with a third grader moves into your neighborhood. Create a skit showing how you will welcome the new boy or girl. Write a title and describe two scenes for your skit.

Affirm appropriate responses.

TITLE: _____

Scene 1: _____

_____

_____

_____

_____

_____

_____

Scene 2: _____

_____

_____

_____

_____

_____

_____

276

REINFORCE

Ask the children to share some ways that they can put their faith into action. Affirm appropriate responses.

INTEGRATE

- Read aloud the directions for the "Living Our Faith" activity.
- Invite the children to work with partners or in small groups.
- After they have written their skits, invite the partners or groups to practice their skits.
- Invite volunteers to present their skits to the entire class.

PRAY

- Invite the children to gather in the prayer center.
- Have them form a circle, face one another, and pray for one another, saying, "Lord, we choose to show our love for these people. Bless us and help us love them as you love us. Amen."
- Lead the group in singing an "Alleluia" sung in the parish.

Background: Scripture

Kindness, or Mercy. The Hebrew word in the Bible that we translate into English as mercy is *hesed*. This Hebrew word is often connected to the Covenant God entered into with his people. It is used to describe the "unconditional kindness" with which God reaches out to his people, despite their unfaithfulness to him. Such is the mercy or kindness that we petition for when we pray, "Lord, have mercy." Such is the kindness and mercy that we are to offer to one another, especially those who "trespass against us."

Teach

FOCUS

Ask a volunteer to read the "Faith Focus" question aloud. Explain to the children that they will learn how followers of Jesus help the Church grow.

DISCOVER

- Invite the children to think about the people they like to be with. Help them to name the reasons this is so.
- Have the students work with partners to read "The Growing Church" on page 277.
- Emphasize that followers of Jesus passed on the good news of the Risen Lord by their words and actions.
- Show the children the Acts of the Apostles in a Bible. Tell the children that this book has many stories that tell what actions helped the Church grow after Jesus returned to his Father in heaven.
- Display a piece of poster board on which you have written the title "Acts of Third Graders." Remind the children that they are called to put their faith in Jesus into action.
- Distribute pieces of art paper. Have the children draw pictures of loving, faith-filled actions they do. As they finish their drawings, have the children tape or glue their pictures to the poster board.

The Sixth Week of Easter

Faith Focus

What did the followers of Jesus do to help the Church grow?

The Word of the Lord

Choose this year's Gospel reading for the the Sixth Sunday of Easter. Read and discuss it with your family.

Year A
John 14:15–21

Year B
John 15:9–17

Year C
John 14:23–29

The Growing Church

When we do good, others want to do good too. When we do good, we become good news for others. That is what the followers of Jesus are. They are good news!

During the Masses of the Easter season, the first reading at Mass is from the Acts of the Apostles. We learn how the early Church grew under the guidance of the Holy Spirit.

The first followers of Jesus welcomed others. They shared food and clothing with people in need. They prayed for one another. They cared for people who were sick. People who did not believe in Jesus saw this faith in action. They wanted to do good too.

Followers of Jesus do more than talk about the good news of Jesus' Resurrection. They show that they are good news themselves! People see this. They want to follow Jesus too. The Church grows and grows.

(277)

Background: Scripture

The Acts of the Apostles. The Acts of the Apostles continues the story that Luke began in his Gospel. Luke wants us to see how God's plan of salvation continued to be accomplished through particular people and events. As we read through the Acts of the Apostles, we notice that the message of Jesus was delivered first to the Jews and only later to Gentiles. From this we see God's great love for the Jewish people. That is one reason the Church condemns any form of anti-Semitism.

Who's Who?

Find these passages in the Bible. Write down the name of the follower of Jesus.

I was chosen to take the place of Judas.

I am _____Matthias_____ .
(Acts of the Apostles 1:24–26)

I was a deacon. I gave my life for Christ.

I am _____Stephen_____ .
(Acts of the Apostles 7:54–60)

Once I persecuted Christians. Then I became an apostle and a missionary.

I am _____Paul_____ .
(Acts of the Apostles 9:1–8)

My husband and I welcomed Paul to our home. We were tentmakers.

I am _____Priscilla_____ .
(Acts of the Apostles 18:1–4)

Teaching Tip

Creating a Word Map. Guide the young people to a deeper understanding of what it means to be a follower of Jesus by having them work in groups to create a word map. Have each group draw a circle with four lines coming out of it on a piece of art paper or poster paper. Have each group write the word *DISCIPLE* within the outline of the circle. Then discuss with the group that a disciple of a person is "one who learns from and follows the teachings of that person." On each of the four lines coming from the circle with the word *DISCIPLE* in it, have each group write words that tell about the actions of a disciple of Jesus.

Apply

REINFORCE

Invite volunteers to share what some of the early followers of Jesus did to be "good news." Answers might include: They offered clothing and shelter to the needy. They prayed for the sick.

INTEGRATE

- Ask the children to gather in four groups and distribute a Bible to each group.
- Read aloud the directions to the "Who's Who?" activity and assign one of the passages from Acts of the Apostles to each group.
- Give the groups time to find and read their passage.
- Have the groups call out the name of the follower of Jesus they discovered. Invite all the children to complete the activity.

PRAY

- Tell the children that the closing prayer for the lesson will be a litany of saints.
- Explain that you will say the name of each saint and they will respond, "pray for us."
- Gather the children in the prayer area and lead them in the litany.

> Leader: Holy Mary, Mother of God,
>
> **All: pray for us.**
>
> Leader: Saint Joseph,
>
> **All: pray for us.**
>
> Leader: Saint Peter and all the Apostles,
>
> **All: pray for us.**
>
> Leader: (*Invite the children to name saints. After each saint's name, invite everyone to respond,*)
>
> **All: pray for us.**

Teach

FOCUS

Ask a volunteer to read the "Faith Focus" question aloud. Explain to the children that this lesson will help them further understand the Good News that we are called to share with others.

DISCOVER

- Invite the children to silently read "Sharing the Good News of the Resurrection" on page 279.
- Have volunteers pick out sentences or ideas that could be proclaimed as good news. For example: Jesus promised always to be with his followers. The Holy Spirit guided and helped them.
- As each volunteer finds a good news sentence, have him or her go to the front of the room and announce his or her sentence very dramatically. Ask the entire class to proclaim, "Jesus is risen!"

The Seventh Week of Easter

Faith Focus

What is the Good News that Christians share with others?

The Word of the Lord

Choose this year's Gospel reading for the Seventh Sunday of Easter. Read and discuss it with your family.

Year A
John 17:1–11

Year B
John 17:11–19

Year C
John 17:20–26

The Risen Christ

Sharing the Good News of the Resurrection

We smile when we have good news. We share it with others. Our good news is that God has raised Jesus to new life. We share this good news by the way we live.

Before Jesus returned to his Father, he told his Apostles to share this good news with everyone. He told them to baptize and teach people. Jesus promised always to be with his followers.

After the Risen Jesus returned to his Father, the Holy Spirit came to his followers as Jesus promised. The Holy Spirit guided and helped them. They lived joyful lives. They became generous and loving. Their actions showed others that they were a joyful, generous, and loving people.

279

Background: Doctrine

The Assumption of Mary. God blessed Mary at the end of her life on earth in a unique way. Mary was assumed into heaven, body and soul, where she is honored as Queen of Heaven and Earth. The Assumption of Mary into heaven is a dogma of the Catholic Church "which recognizes the Blessed Virgin Mary's singular participation in her Son's Resurrection by which she was taken up both body and soul into heavenly glory, when the course of her earthly life was finished" (*Catechism of the Catholic Church* 966). The Church celebrates the feast of the Assumption on August 15.

Love in Action

Jesus calls us to share the good news of his Resurrection with people. We do this both by our words and by our actions. Color in all the parts that name actions that are good news to others with one color. In the empty space write one thing you can do. Choose other colors for the rest of the boxes.

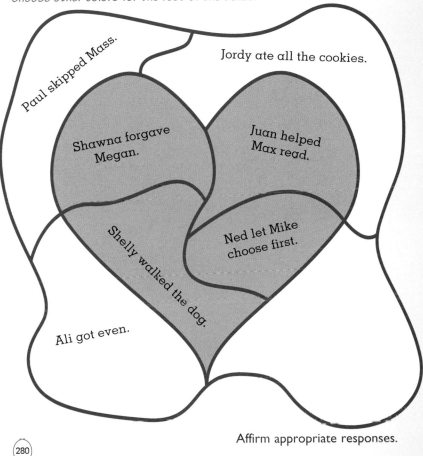

Paul skipped Mass.

Jordy ate all the cookies.

Shawna forgave Megan.

Juan helped Max read.

Shelly walked the dog.

Ned let Mike choose first.

Ali got even.

Affirm appropriate responses.

REINFORCE

Ask volunteers to share how the Holy Spirit helped the Apostles. The Holy Spirit guided and helped the Apostles to spread the Good News and to be joyful, generous, and loving people.

INTEGRATE

- Read the directions for the "Love in Action" activity.
- After the children complete the activity, go over each situation with them. Ask them to change the unloving situations in such a way that each shows love in action.
- Have volunteers share the ideas they wrote in the empty space.

PRAY

- Gather with the children in the prayer area.
- Teach them the Easter mantra, "Christ is risen, Alleluia." Explain that a mantra is a prayer we pray over and over again.
- Play a recording of appropriate Easter instrumental music.
- Ask the children to close their eyes and pray the Easter mantra.

Liturgy Tip

Prayer Center. Next Sunday is the Solemnity of Pentecost. Take the time to redecorate the prayer area with symbols and colors the Church uses to help us celebrate this feast. Change the liturgical color from white to red; add symbols the Church uses for the Holy Spirit, for example, the dove and flames of fire; include red-colored flowers; have the Bible opened to the Pentecost story in the Acts of the Apostles, and mark the page with a red- or gold-colored ribbon or narrow piece of cloth.

Teach

FOCUS

Ask a volunteer to read the "Faith Focus" question aloud. Explain to the children that this lesson will help them learn more about the feast of Pentecost.

DISCOVER

- Invite the children to name something that they find difficult to do. Discuss: Who encourages and helps you to do this thing?
- Ask three volunteers to read the three paragraphs of "Pentecost."
- Invite the children to identify the signs the writer of the Acts of the Apostles uses for the coming of the Holy Spirit on the disciples. Wind and fire.
- Write on the board the gifts of the Holy Spirit named in the "Come, Holy Spirit" prayer on page 282.
- Emphasize that we receive the gifts of the Holy Spirit at Baptism.
- Give each child a pre-cut flame made out of construction paper. Ask each to pick out the gift of the Holy Spirit that they think would most help them live as a follower of Jesus. Have each child write the gift of the Holy Spirit they chose on the flame.

Pentecost

Faith Focus

How does the Holy Spirit help the Church?

The Word of the Lord

Choose this year's Gospel reading for Pentecost. Read and discuss it with your family.

Year A
John 20:19–23

Year B
John 20:19–23 or
John 15:26–27,
16:12–15

Year C
John 20:19–23 or
John 14:15–16, 23–26

Pentecost

When we have difficult things to do, the Holy Spirit helps us. We can depend on the Holy Spirit. We can grow in faith, hope, and love with the help of the Holy Spirit.

On the feast of Pentecost the disciples were gathered in Jerusalem. As they prayed together, they heard the sound of a great wind. Flames gently settled over their heads. Filled with the Holy Spirit, they boldly proclaimed the Risen Lord.

Peter stood in front of the people. Everyone understood his words even though everyone did not speak the same language as Peter. He told them about Jesus' life, death, and Resurrection. He wanted everyone to know that the Risen Jesus was Messiah and Lord. Many people became followers of Jesus. Those who were baptized received the Holy Spirit. They grew into the new People of God who followed the Risen Lord. The People of God is another name for the Church.

A dove, a symbol for the Holy Spirit

281

Background: Scripture

Mary and the Holy Spirit. Point out to the children that Mary was with the disciples in the upper room in the house in Jerusalem when the Holy Spirit came to them as Jesus promised. This is an important detail of the Pentecost story that we often miss. Relate this detail to the role the Holy Spirit played in the Gospel story of the Annunciation: The angel told Mary, "The Holy Spirit will come upon you, and the power of the Most High will overshadow you. Therefore the child to be born will be called holy, the Son of God" (Luke 1:35).

Come, Holy Spirit

Saint Paul tells us that we are temples of the Holy Spirit. The Holy Spirit lives within us. Pray this prayer to the Holy Spirit.

LEADER: The Holy Spirit has always been at work in the world.

GROUP 1: The spirit of the LORD shall rest upon us:
a spirit of wisdom and of understanding,

GROUP 2: A spirit of right judgment and courage,

GROUP 3: A spirit of knowledge and reverence. *Based on Isaiah 11:2*

ALL: **Come, Holy Spirit, fill the hearts of your faithful.**

GROUP 1: I am David. When I was a young shepherd boy, Samuel anointed me with oil. The spirit of the Lord rushed upon me. *Based on 1 Samuel 16:12–13*

GROUP 2: I am Mary. The angel told me the Holy Spirit would come upon me. I would be Jesus' mother. *Based on Luke 1:26–38*

GROUP 3: We are the Church. Jesus told the Apostles, "I am sending the promise of my Father upon you; but stay in the city until you are clothed with power from on high." *Luke 24:49*

ALL: **Come, Holy Spirit, fill the hearts of your faithful.**

282

Apply

REINFORCE

Ask the children to share what the Holy Spirit helps us do. Answers might include: The Holy Spirit helps us do things to live as followers of Jesus.

INTEGRATE

- Look at the prayer service "Come, Holy Spirit." Have the children underline the gifts of the Holy Spirit that are named in the prayer.
- Divide the children into three groups and choose one child to be the leader of each group. Allow everyone a chance to practice their parts, including the "All" part.

PRAY

- Gather the children in the prayer space which is now decorated with the color and symbols of Pentecost.
- Lead the children in praying the "Come, Holy Spirit" prayer together.

Teaching Tip

A Pentecost Walkway. Discuss this project with the appropriate person in your parish for permission. Create a Pentecost walkway to the parish church. Distribute red, orange, and yellow ribbons or streamers and one sturdy dowel to each child. Have the children cut the ribbon or streamers into various lengths, curl them, and attach them to the top or near the top of the dowel. Plant the dowels into the ground along the walkway to the church, creating a Pentecost walk to the main entrance of the church. This is an appropriate project to coordinate with other classes and in which to involve families.

Saints for All Seasons

Here is a reference chart of all the canonized saints taught in the third grade book, arranged according to their feast days. Since you may not teach the chapter in which the saint is taught during the month when the saint's feast day is celebrated, this chart will allow you to honor these saints as their feasts occur in the Proper of the Saints throughout the school year. Saints who are not in the Proper of the Saints are also listed by their traditional celebration days. You may also wish to prepare a chart of the saints for whom the children in the class are named and honor these saints as well.

January

5 Saint John Neumann

27 Saint Angela Merici

February

3 Saint Blase

11 Our Lady of Lourdes

March

17 Saint Patrick

19 Saint Joseph, husband of Mary

April

7 John Baptiste de La Salle

29 Saint Catherine of Siena

May

1 Saint Joseph the Worker

10 Saint Damien of Molokai

June

3 Saint Charles Lwanga and companions

24 Birth of Saint John the Baptist

29 Saints Peter and Paul, Apostles

July

3 Saint Thomas the Apostle

13 Saint Teresa of the Andes

22 Saint Mary Magdalene

25 Saint James the Apostle

August

15 Assumption of Mary

28 Saint Augustine

September

8 Birth of Mary

20 Saint Andrew Kim Taegon and companions

October

4 Saint Francis of Assisi

15 Saint Teresa of Avila

November

1 All Saints

2 All Souls

5 Saint Elizabeth

13 Saint Frances Cabrini

30 Saint Andrew the Apostle

December

9 Saint Juan Diego

27 Saint John, Apostle and Evangelist

Catholic Prayers and Practices

Sign of the Cross

In the name of the Father,
and of the Son,
and of the Holy Spirit. Amen.

Glory Prayer

Glory to the Father,
    and to the Son,
    and to the Holy Spirit:
as it was in the beginning, is now,
    and will be for ever. Amen.

Lord's Prayer

Our Father, who art in heaven,
hallowed be thy name;
thy kingdom come;
thy will be done on earth
    as it is in heaven.
Give us this day our daily bread;
and forgive us our trespasses
as we forgive those who trespass
    against us;
and lead us not into temptation,
but deliver us from evil.
Amen.

Prayer to the Holy Spirit

Come, Holy Spirit, fill the hearts
    of your faithful.
And kindle in them the
    fire of your love.
Send forth your Spirit and
    they shall be created.
And you will renew the
    face of the earth.

Hail Mary

Hail Mary, full of grace,
the Lord is with you!
Blessed are you among women,
and blessed is the fruit
    of your womb, Jesus.
Holy Mary, Mother of God,
pray for us sinners,
now and at the hour of our death.
Amen.

Act of Contrition

My God,
I am sorry for my sins
    with all my heart.
In choosing to do wrong
and failing to do good,
I have sinned against you
whom I should love above all things.
I firmly intend, with your help,
to do penance,
to sin no more,
and to avoid whatever leads me to sin.
Our Savior Jesus Christ
suffered and died for us.
In his name, my God, have mercy.

(283)

This section contains some of the major traditional prayers and practices of the Catholic Church. Refer to these pages during your sessions and integrate them into your presentations and your prayer time with the children. Encourage families to use them with their children as an aid to developing their children's Catholic identity.

MEMORIZATION

The memorization of prayers facilitates our ability to pray them spontaneously. Use the prayers on page 283 regularly throughout your sessions. Encourage the children to pause throughout the day and spontaneously pray. This will deepen their awareness that God is always with them as their divine Companion and Friend.

APOSTLES' CREED

The word *creed* comes from two Latin words that mean "I give my heart to" that have been joined together to form one word that means "I believe." In the creed we believe in and give our hearts to God. The Apostles' Creed is one of the earliest creeds of the Church. It is called the Apostles' Creed because the teachings in this creed date back to the main beliefs that the Church has professed since the days of the Apostles. Read the words of the Apostles' Creed one line at a time, and have the children echo, or repeat, the words after you.

NICENE CREED

The praying of the creed, or the profession of faith, is part of the worshiping assembly's response to the word proclaimed during the Liturgy of the Word. The Roman Missal states: "The purpose of the *Symbolum* or Profession of Faith, or Creed, is that the whole gathered people may respond to the word of God proclaimed in the readings taken from Sacred Scripture and explained in the homily and that they may also call to mind and confess the great mysteries of the faith by reciting the rule of faith in a formula approved for liturgical use, before these mysteries are celebrated in the Eucharist" (*General Introduction to the Roman Missal* 67).

The Nicene Creed, or more correctly, the Nicene-Constantinople Creed, is the creed regularly professed at Mass on Sundays. For this reason it is important

---

Apostles' Creed

I believe in God,
  the Father almighty,
  creator of heaven and earth.

I believe in Jesus Christ,
  his only Son, our Lord.
  He was conceived by the power
    of the Holy Spirit
    and born of the Virgin Mary.
  He suffered under Pontius Pilate,
    was crucified, died, and was buried.
  He descended to the dead.
  On the third day he rose again.
  He ascended into heaven,
    and is seated at the right hand
    of the Father.
  He will come again to judge
    the living and the dead.

I believe in the Holy Spirit,
  the holy catholic Church,
  the communion of saints,
  the forgiveness of sins,
  the resurrection of the body,
  and the life everlasting. Amen.

Nicene Creed

We believe in one God,
  the Father, the Almighty,
  maker of heaven and earth,
  of all that is, seen and unseen.

We believe in one Lord, Jesus Christ,
  the only Son of God,
  eternally begotten of the Father,
  God from God, Light from Light,
  true God from true God,
  begotten, not made, one in Being
    with the Father.

Through him all things were made.
For us men and for our salvation
  he came down from heaven:

by the power of the Holy Spirit
  he was born of the Virgin Mary, and
    became man.

For our sake he was crucified under
  Pontius Pilate;
  he suffered, died, and was buried.
  On the third day he rose again
    in fulfillment of the Scriptures;
  he ascended into heaven
    and is seated at the right hand
    of the Father.
  He will come again in glory to judge
    the living and the dead,
    and his kingdom will have no end.

We believe in the Holy Spirit, the Lord,
  the giver of life,
  who proceeds from the Father
    and the Son.
  With the Father and the Son he is
    worshiped and glorified.
  He has spoken through the Prophets.
We believe in one holy catholic and
  apostolic Church.
We acknowledge one baptism for
  the forgiveness of sins.
We look for the resurrection
  of the dead,
  and the life of the world to come.
  Amen.

Morning Prayer

Dear God,
as I begin this day,
keep me in your love and care.
Help me to live as your child today.
Bless me, my family, and my friends
   in all we do.
Keep us all close to you. Amen.

Grace Before Meals

Bless us, O Lord,
   and these your gifts
which we are about to receive
   from your goodness.
Through Christ our Lord.
Amen.

Grace After Meals

We give you thanks for all your gifts,
   almighty God,
living and reigning now and for ever.
Amen.

Evening Prayer

Dear God,
I thank you for today.
Keep me safe throughout the night.
Thank you for all the good I did today.
I am sorry for what I have chosen
   to do wrong.
Bless my family and friends. Amen.

A Vocation Prayer

God, I know you will call me
for special work in my life.
Help me follow Jesus each day
and be ready to answer your call.

285

to guide the children to become familiar with its words so that they can join in professing the creed at Mass. You might slowly introduce it to the children by integrating the use of this creed into your lessons. For example: Point out its Trinitarian structure when you present the Holy Trinity in chapter 1, "God Speaks to Us."

RHYTHM OF PRAYER

Praying is to the spiritual life as breathing is to our physical life. Saint Paul captures the truth of this adage when he recommends that we pray always. Guide the children to pray always by helping them develop the habit of prayer. Suggest appropriate times in the day for prayer. Help the children establish a rhythm of daily prayer.

LIVING OUR LIFE IN CHRIST

This page and the next page contain a brief summary of the ways we are to implement God's Law of Love into daily living. Use these pages to:

• Introduce the children to Unit 3, "We Live," to provide the big picture of what it means to live as a child of God.

• Reinforce the teaching of chapters 18 through 22 and prepare the children for the unit review.

THE BEATITUDES AND WORKS OF MERCY

While the Beatitudes are not taught in Grade 3, you may want to point them out to the children when you teach the Works of Mercy.

The Beatitudes and Works of Mercy are based on the teachings and life of Jesus. As disciples of Jesus we listen and learn from him so we may live as he taught. Emphasize to the children that when we carefully read and reflect on Matthew 25:31–46, we realize quickly the importance of living these moral teachings of the Gospel.

The Letter of James gets right to the point, admonishing Christians of every age, "If a brother or sister has nothing to wear and has no food for the day, and one of you says to them, 'Go in peace, keep warm, and eat well,' but you do not give them the necessities of the body, what good is it? So also faith of itself, if it does not have works, is dead" (James 2:15–17).

The Beatitudes

"Blessed are the poor in spirit,
   for theirs is the kingdom of heaven.
Blessed are they who mourn,
   for they will be comforted.
Blessed are the meek,
   for they will inherit the land.
Blessed are they who hunger
      and thirst for righteousness,
   for they will be satisfied.
Blessed are the merciful,
   for they will be shown mercy.
Blessed are the clean of heart,
   for they will see God.
Blessed are the peacemakers,
   for they will be called children of God.
Blessed are they who are
      persecuted for the
      sake of righteousness,
   for theirs is the kingdom of heaven.

"Blessed are you when they insult you and persecute you and utter every kind of evil against you [falsely] because of me. Rejoice and be glad, for your reward will be great in heaven."

Matthew 5:3–12

Corporal Works of Mercy

Feed people who are hungry.
Give drink to people who are thirsty.
Clothe people who need clothes.
Visit prisoners.
Shelter people who are homeless.
Visit people who are sick.
Bury people who have died.

Spiritual Works of Mercy

Help people who sin.
Teach people who are ignorant.
Give advice to people
   who have doubts.
Comfort people who suffer.
Be patient with other people.
Forgive people who hurt you.
Pray for people who are alive and for
   those who have died.

286

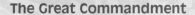

The Ten Commandments

1. I am the LORD your God: you shall not have strange gods before me.
2. You shall not take the name of the LORD your God in vain.
3. Remember to keep holy the LORD's Day.
4. Honor your father and your mother.
5. You shall not kill.
6. You shall not commit adultery.
7. You shall not steal.
8. You shall not bear false witness against your neighbor.
9. You shall not covet your neighbor's wife.
10. You shall not covet your neighbor's goods.

Based on Exodus 20:3, 7–17

The Great Commandment

"You shall love the Lord, your God, with all your heart, with all your soul, and with all your mind. . . . You shall love your neighbor as yourself."

Matthew 22:37, 39

Precepts of the Church

1. Participate in Mass on Sundays and holy days of obligation and rest from unnecessary work.
2. Confess sins at least once a year.
3. Receive Holy Communion at least during the Easter season.
4. Observe the prescribed days of fasting and abstinence.
5. Provide for the material needs of the Church, according to one's abilities.

287

THE GREAT COMMANDMENT AND THE TEN COMMANDMENTS

Jesus clearly made the connection between the Ten Commandments and the Great Commandment. Young people sometimes mistakenly think that Jesus gave us the Great Commandment. The truth is that the two parts of the Great Commandment are clearly found in the Old Testament in the Book of Deuteronomy and the Book of Leviticus. When presenting the Ten Commandments, connect each of the Commandments to the Great Commandment and focus on the foundational virtues that help us live as followers of Christ.

PRECEPTS OF THE CHURCH

These concisely stated guidelines outline concrete ways Catholics are to integrate Church practices into their living of the Ten Commandments.

DEVOTION TO MARY

The Blessed Virgin Mary has a favored and unique place in God's loving plan of salvation for the world. The twenty mysteries of the rosary summarize Mary's role in God's plan as intrinsically related to the mysteries of the life of Christ.

Connect the rosary with your sessions. For example, when a chapter talks about a mystery from the life of Mary and Jesus, such as the Annunciation, the Nativity, the Crucifixion, the Resurrection, the Ascension, or the descent of the Holy Spirit on Pentecost, make the connection with the rosary.

Introduce the children to the praying of the rosary. With a rosary, use the information on page 288 to demonstrate to the children how the rosary is prayed. Point out the centrality of the praying of the Hail Mary as part of the rosary. Draw their attention to the Hail Holy Queen prayer which has been placed on this page so the children can begin to become familiar with it.

Rosary

Catholics pray the rosary to honor Mary and remember the important events in the life of Jesus and Mary. There are twenty mysteries of the rosary. Follow the steps from 1 to 5.

5. Pray the Hail, Holy Queen prayer. Make the Sign of the Cross.

3. Think of the first mystery. Pray an Our Father, 10 Hail Marys, and the Glory Prayer.

2. Pray an Our Father, 3 Hail Marys, and the Glory Prayer.

4. Repeat step 3 for each of the next 4 mysteries.

1. Make the Sign of the Cross and pray the Apostles' Creed.

Joyful Mysteries

1. The Annunciation
2. The Visitation
3. The Nativity
4. The Presentation
5. The Finding of Jesus in the Temple

Mysteries of Light

1. The Baptism of Jesus in the Jordan River
2. The Miracle at the Wedding at Cana
3. The Proclamation of the Kingdom of God
4. The Transfiguration of Jesus
5. The Institution of the Eucharist

Sorrowful Mysteries

1. The Agony in the Garden
2. The Scourging at the Pillar
3. The Crowning with Thorns
4. The Carrying of the Cross
5. The Crucifixion

Glorious Mysteries

1. The Resurrection
2. The Ascension
3. The Coming of the Holy Spirit
4. The Assumption of Mary
5. The Coronation of Mary

Hail, Holy Queen

Hail, holy Queen, mother of mercy,
hail, our life, our sweetness,
    and our hope.
To you we cry, the children of Eve;
to you we send up our sighs,
mourning and weeping
    in this land of exile.
Turn, then, most gracious advocate,
your eyes of mercy toward us;
lead us home at last
and show us the blessed fruit
    of your womb, Jesus:
O clement, O loving, O sweet
    Virgin Mary.

288

Stations of the Cross

1. Jesus is condemned to death.

2. Jesus accepts his cross.

3. Jesus falls the first time.

4. Jesus meets his mother.

5. Simon helps Jesus carry the cross.

6. Veronica wipes the face of Jesus.

7. Jesus falls the second time.

8. Jesus meets the women.

9. Jesus falls the third time.

10. Jesus is stripped of his clothes.

11. Jesus is nailed to the cross.

12. Jesus dies on the cross.

13. Jesus is taken down from the cross.

14. Jesus is buried in the tomb.

Some parishes conclude the Stations by reflecting on the Resurrection of Jesus.

(289)

STATIONS OF THE CROSS

When we pray the Stations of the Cross, we are making a mini-pilgrimage. We walk in prayer from station to station visiting the final places on earth that Jesus walked on his way to Calvary. In the fourteenth century, the Franciscans introduced the Stations of the Cross to meet the desire of those Christians who wanted to visit Jerusalem but were unable to do so.

LIVING STATIONS OF THE CROSS

Have the young people develop a dramatic presentation of the Stations of the Cross. One way they might design their presentation is to create a single shadow tableau for each station. Have the young people stand behind a large white sheet to form their tableau. Shine a bright white light on the young people, creating a shadow on the sheet. The people sitting in front of the sheet will then see only the shadows creating the scene for each station. Have a narrator describe each event. Include a prayer for each of the Stations of the Cross. Present the drama for other classes or groups of young people, or present it for parishioners one night during Lent.

THE SEVEN SACRAMENTS

This page presents an overview of the seven sacraments of the Church. As a reinforcement exercise at the conclusion of Unit 2, you might have the children create a mural showing a panorama of the seven sacraments.

- Invite different groups to draw a picture illustrating the celebration of one of the sacraments.
- Have the children use the title and first sentence from the text on this page to label their sacrament drawing.

The Seven Sacraments

Jesus gave the Church the seven sacraments. The sacraments are the main liturgical signs of the Church. They make the Paschal Mystery of Jesus, who is always the main celebrant of each sacrament, present to us. They make us sharers in the saving work of Christ and in the life of the Holy Trinity.

Sacraments of Initiation

Baptism

Through Baptism we are joined to Christ and become members of the Body of Christ, the Church. We are reborn as adopted children of God and receive the gift of the Holy Spirit. Original sin and all personal sins are forgiven.

Confirmation

Confirmation completes Baptism. In the sacrament the gift of the Holy Spirit strengthens us to live our Baptism.

Eucharist

Sharing in the Eucharist most fully joins us to Christ and to the Church. We share in the one sacrifice of Christ. The bread and wine become the Body and Blood of Christ through the power of the Holy Spirit and the words of the priest. We receive the Body and Blood of Christ.

Sacraments of Healing

Reconciliation

Through the ministry of the priest we receive forgiveness of sins committed after our Baptism. We need to confess all mortal sins.

Anointing of the Sick

Anointing of the Sick strengthens our faith and trust in God when we are seriously ill, dying, or weak because of old age.

Sacraments at the Service of Communion

Holy Orders

Through Holy Orders a baptized man is consecrated to serve the whole Church as a bishop, priest, or deacon in the name of Christ. Bishops, who are the successors of the Apostles, receive this sacrament most fully. They are consecrated to teach the Gospel, to lead the Church in the worship of God, and to guide the Church to live holy lives. Bishops are helped by priests, their coworkers, and by deacons.

Matrimony

Matrimony unites a baptized man and a baptized woman in a lifelong bond of faithful love to always honor one another and to accept the gift of children from God. In this sacrament the married couple is consecrated to be a sign of God's love for the Church.

We Celebrate the Mass

THE INTRODUCTORY RITES

We remember that we are the community
of the Church. We prepare to listen to the word of God
and to celebrate the Eucharist.

The Entrance

We stand as the priest, deacon, and
other ministers enter the assembly. We
sing a gathering song. The priest and
deacon kiss the altar. The priest then
goes to the chair where he presides
over the celebration.

Greeting of the Altar
and of the People Gathered

The priest leads us in praying the Sign
of the Cross. The priest greets us, and
we say,

"And also with you."

The Act of Penitence

We admit our wrongdoings.
We bless God for his mercy.

The Gloria

We praise God for all the good
he has done for us.

The Collect

The priest leads us in praying the
Collect, or the opening prayer.
We respond, **"Amen."**

(291)

WE CELEBRATE THE MASS
Use "We Celebrate the Mass"
on pages 291–296 of the
children's book to help the
children participate fully and
actively in the celebration of
the Mass. This section of the
children's book includes photos
that will help the children identify
with the rites of the Mass,
descriptions of the Mass parts,
and responses used during the
Mass.

ADDITIONAL SUGGESTIONS

- Have the children examine the photographs of the Mass. Relate what is happening in the photographs with the prayers and explanations. Point out that although there may be some differences in the way each parish celebrates Mass, the main rites of the Mass—the responses, prayers, and actions—always remain the same.

- Review the parts of the Mass in relationship to each other. This will help the children see that all the parts of the Mass fit together as one whole prayer.

- Integrate RCL's *Eucharist* music CD, which contains appropriate songs for each part of the Mass. Be sure to incorporate hymns from the "Music Connection" feature at the end of each chapter in this guide. The hymns and refrains included there are all appropriate choices for liturgy.

The Liturgy of the Word

God speaks to us today.
We listen and respond to God's word.

The First Reading from the Bible

We sit and listen as the reader reads from the Old Testament or from the Acts of the Apostles. The reader concludes, "The word of the Lord."
We respond,
    "Thanks be to God."

The Responsorial Psalm

The song leader leads us in singing a psalm.

The Second Reading from the Bible

The reader reads from the New Testament, but not from the four Gospels. The reader concludes, "The word of the Lord." We respond,
    "Thanks be to God."

Acclamation

We stand to honor Christ present with us in the Gospel. The song leader leads us in singing, **"Alleluia, Alleluia, Alleluia"** or another chant during Lent.

The Gospel

The deacon or priest proclaims, "A reading from the holy gospel according to (name of Gospel writer)." We respond,
    "Glory to you, O Lord."
He proclaims the Gospel. At the end, he says, "The gospel of the Lord." We respond,
    "Praise to you, Lord Jesus Christ."

The Homily

We sit. The priest or deacon preaches the homily. He helps the whole community understand the word of God spoken to us in the readings.

The Profession of Faith

We stand and profess our faith. We pray the Nicene Creed together.

The Prayer of the Faithful

The priest leads us in praying for our Church and its leaders, for our country and its leaders, for ourselves and others, for the sick and those who have died. We can respond to each prayer in several ways. One way we respond is,
    "Lord, hear our prayer."

292

The Liturgy of the Eucharist

**We join with Jesus and the Holy Spirit
to give thanks and praise to God the Father.**

The Preparation of the Gifts

We sit as the altar table is prepared and the collection is taken up. We share our blessings with the community of the Church and especially with those in need. The song leader may lead us in singing a song. The gifts of bread and wine are brought to the altar.

The priest lifts up the bread and blesses God for all our gifts. He prays, "Blessed are you, Lord, God of all creation . . ."
We respond,
   "Blessed be God for ever."

The priest lifts up the cup of wine and prays, "Blessed are you, Lord, God of all creation . . ."
We respond,
   "Blessed be God for ever."

The priest invites us,
   "Pray, my brothers and sisters, that our sacrifice may be acceptable to God, the almighty Father."

We stand and respond,
   "May the Lord accept the sacrifice at your hands for the praise and glory of his name, for our good, and the good of all his Church."

The Prayer over the Offerings

The priest leads us in praying the Prayer over the Offerings. We respond, **"Amen."**

293

ADDITIONAL SUGGESTIONS

- Take the children on a visit to the parish church. Show them the things that are used in the celebration of the Mass. Let the children see and touch the vestments, books, vessels, and other items used for the celebration of Mass. Allow the children to stand at the altar, the ambo, and the presider's chair so that they can experience the church from that perspective.

- Briefly talk about the vestments. Share these ideas: The three basic vestments worn by the priest at Mass are an alb, a stole, and a chasuble. **Alb:** A long, white vestment tied at the waist with a cincture, a sash made of cord or cloth. **Stole:** A long strip of cloth worn over the alb in the color of the liturgical season. Priests hang the stole around the neck. The deacon's stole hangs over the left shoulder and is fastened on the right side. **Chasuble:** The outer liturgical garment worn over the alb and stole. It matches the liturgical color of the season. It is a poncho-like garment that developed from the cloak or poncho-like garment that workers wore.

ADDITIONAL SUGGESTIONS

- Explain the prayers, responses, and actions of the Mass so that the children understand what is happening throughout the Mass.
- Review with the children your parish's directions for receiving Holy Communion.

How to Receive Holy Communion

- Reverently walk in procession to the altar, singing the communion song, to receive Holy Communion from the priest, deacon, or extraordinary minister of Holy Communion.
- You may receive Holy Communion either in your hand or on your tongue.
- The consecrated bread, or host, is offered to you with the words "The body of Christ." You respond, "Amen."
- If you choose to receive Holy Communion in your hand,
  —place one hand underneath the other hand,
  —hold your hand out with palms facing up, and
  —bow and receive the consecrated bread in the palm of your hand.
  —Step to the side and briefly stop,
  —slowly and reverently take the consecrated bread from the palm of your hand, using the hand that is underneath the other, and put the consecrated bread in your mouth.
  —Chew and swallow the consecrated bread, the Body of Christ.

Preface

The priest invites us to join in praying the Church's great prayer of praise and thanksgiving to God the Father.

Priest: "The Lord be with you."
Assembly: "And also with you."
Priest: "Lift up your hearts."
Assembly: "We lift them up to the Lord."
Priest: "Let us give thanks to the Lord our God."
Assembly: "It is right to give him thanks and praise."

After the priest sings or prays aloud the preface, we join in acclaiming,

"Holy, holy, holy Lord, God of power and might.
Heaven and earth are full of your glory.
Hosanna in the highest.
Blessed is he who comes in the name of the Lord.
Hosanna in the highest."

The Eucharistic Prayer

The priest leads the assembly in praying the Eucharistic Prayer. We call upon the Holy Spirit to make our gifts of bread and wine holy and that they become the Body and Blood of Jesus. We recall what happened at the Last Supper. The bread and wine become the Body and Blood of the Lord. Jesus is truly and really present under the appearances of bread and wine.

The priest sings or says aloud, "Let us proclaim the mystery of faith." We respond using this or another acclamation used by the Church,

"Christ has died, Christ is risen, Christ will come again."

The priest then prays for the Church. He prays for the living and the dead.

Doxology

The priest concludes the praying of the Eucharistic Prayer. He sings or prays aloud,

"Through him, with him, in him, in the unity of the Holy Spirit, all glory and honor is yours, almighty Father, for ever and ever."

We respond, "Amen."

294

THE COMMUNION RITE

The Lord's Prayer

We pray the Lord's Prayer together.

The Rite of Peace

The priest invites us to share a sign of peace, saying, "The peace of the Lord be with you always." We respond, **"And also with you."** We share a sign of peace.

The Fraction, or the Breaking of the Bread

The priest breaks the host, the consecrated bread. We sing or pray aloud,

**"Lamb of God, you take away the sins of the world:
    have mercy on us.
Lamb of God, you take away the sins of the world:
    have mercy on us.
Lamb of God, you take away the sins of the world:
    grant us peace."**

Communion

The priest raises the host and says aloud,

"This is the Lamb of God who takes away the sins of the world.
Happy are those who are called to his supper."

We join with him and say,

"Lord, I am not worthy to receive you, but only say the word and I shall be healed."

The priest receives Communion. Next, the deacon and the extraordinary ministers of Holy Communion and the members of the assembly receive Communion.

The priest, deacon, or extraordinary minister of Holy Communion holds up the host. We bow and the priest, deacon, or extraordinary minister of Holy Communion says, "The body of Christ." We respond, **"Amen."** We then receive the consecrated host in our hand or on our tongue.

If we are to receive the Blood of Christ, the priest, deacon, or extraordinary minister of Holy Communion holds up the cup containing the consecrated wine. We bow and the priest, deacon, or extraordinary minister of Holy Communion says, "The blood of Christ." We respond, **"Amen."** We take the cup in our hands and drink from it.

The Prayer after Communion

We stand as the priest invites us to pray, saying, "Let us pray." He prays the Prayer after Communion. We respond, **"Amen."**

295

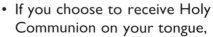

- If you choose to receive Holy Communion on your tongue,
  —fold your hands, bow, and open your mouth and put your tongue out to receive the consecrated bread.
  —Chew and swallow the consecrated bread.
- You may also receive the consecrated wine, the Blood of Christ. The cup of consecrated wine will be offered to you with the words "The blood of Christ." You respond, "Amen."
- If you choose to receive the Blood of Christ at Holy Communion,
  —bow and take the cup of consecrated wine firmly in both hands,
  —using both hands, reverently bring the cup to your mouth,
  —take a small sip of the consecrated wine from the cup, and
  —carefully give the cup back, using both hands.
- Reverently return to your place, singing the communion hymn.
- Continue singing with the assembly. Then spend some time in quiet prayer and reflection after you have received Holy Communion.

SACRAMENT OF RECONCILIATION

Review with the children the two rites of Reconciliation. Take the children to church to walk them through the rites of this sacrament. Point out the similarities and differences between the individual and communal rites.

We are sent forth to do good works, praising and blessing the Lord.

Greeting

We stand. The priest greets us as we prepare to leave. He says, "The Lord be with you." We respond, **"And also with you."**

Blessing

The priest or deacon may invite us, "Bow your heads and pray for God's blessing." The priest blesses us, saying, "May almighty God bless you, the Father, and the Son, and the Holy Spirit." We respond, **"Amen."**

Dismissal of the People

The priest or deacon sends us forth, using these or similar words, "The Mass is ended, go in peace." We respond, **"Thanks be to God."**

We sing a hymn. The priest and the deacon kiss the altar. The priest, deacon, and other ministers bow to the altar and leave in procession.

The Sacrament of Reconciliation

Individual Rite

Greeting

Scripture Reading

Confession of Sins and Acceptance of Penance

Act of Contrition

Absolution

Closing Prayer

Communal Rite

Greeting

Scripture Reading

Homily

Examination of Conscience, a litany of contrition, and the Lord's Prayer

Individual Confession and Absolution

Closing Prayer

296

Glossary

A

Abba [page 200]
The word *Abba* means "Father" in the language Jesus spoke. Jesus used this word when he prayed to God the Father.

actual grace [page 190]
Actual grace is the grace given to us by the Holy Spirit to help us make choices to live a holy life.

Advocate [page 64]
Advocate is a name for the Holy Spirit that means "one who speaks for another person."

angels [page 30]
Angels were created by God. They have no bodies. They give honor and glory to God. Sometimes God sends angels to us as his messengers.

Annunciation [page 30]
The Annunciation is the announcement the angel Gabriel made to the Blessed Virgin Mary that God had chosen her to be the mother of Jesus, the Son of God.

Apostles [page 70]
The Apostles were the disciples of Jesus who witnessed his life, death, and Resurrection. They were chosen by Jesus to baptize and teach in his name.

Apostles' Creed [page 218]
The Apostles' Creed is a brief summary of what the Church has believed from the time of the Apostles.

Ascension [page 56]
The word *ascension* means "a going up." The Ascension is the return of the Risen Jesus to his Father in heaven forty days after the Resurrection.

B

Baptism [page 25]
Baptism is the Sacrament of Initiation in which we are joined to Christ. Through Baptism we become members of the Church and followers of Jesus, our sins are forgiven, and we receive the gift of the Holy Spirit.

> The words in boldface type are Faith Words in the text.

Bible [page 15]
The Bible is the written word of God that the Holy Spirit helped God's people to write. The Bible is also called Sacred Scripture.

bishops [page 71]
The bishops of the Church are the successors of the Apostles.

Blessed Sacrament [page 114]
The Blessed Sacrament is a name given to the Eucharist, the real presence of the Body and Blood of Jesus under the forms of bread and wine.

Body of Christ [page 111]
The Church is the Body of Christ.

C

canticle [page 31]
A canticle is a song of praise to God.

Catholic Church [pages 16 and 71]
The Catholic Church is the Church founded by Jesus and whose leaders go back to the Apostles.

Christ [page 48]
The name *Christ* means "the Anointed One" and "Messiah."

Christians [page 9]
People who are baptized and believe in Jesus Christ.

Church [page 70]
The Church is the People of God. It is the Body of Christ and the temple of the Holy Spirit.

Communion of Saints [page 86]
The Communion of Saints is the community of the faithful followers of Jesus, both those living on earth and those who have died.

Confirmation [page 99]
Confirmation is the Sacrament of Initiation in which baptized people receive and celebrate the strengthening of the gift of the Holy Spirit within them.

contrition [page 135]
Contrition is the sorrow we feel when we have done something wrong.

conversion [page 80]
The experience of changing one's heart and turning back to God is called conversion.

(297)

Covenant [page 158]
The Covenant is the solemn agreement of friendship made between God and his people.

covet [page 174]
To covet means to wrongfully want something that belongs to someone else.

creation [page 22]
Creation is all that God has made out of love and without any help.

creeds [page 218]
Creeds are statements of what a person or a group believes.

crucified [page 54]
To be crucified means to be put to death on a cross.

Crucifixion [page 54]
The Crucifixion is the death of Jesus on the cross.

D-E

diocese [page 73]
A diocese is a local church, or church in a particular area. A diocese has many parish churches and is led by a bishop.

disciple [page 48]
A disciple is a person who learns from and follows the teachings of another person. The people who followed Jesus were called his disciples.

divine Providence [page 22]
Divine Providence is God's caring love for all his creation.

Easter [page 98]
Easter is the time of the year Christians celebrate and remember the Resurrection of Jesus.

Easter Triduum [page 99]
The Easter Triduum (or "three days") is the center of the liturgical year. It begins on Holy Thursday evening and ends on Easter Sunday evening.

Eucharist [page 114]
The Eucharist is the sacrament in which the Church gives thanks to God and shares in the Body and Blood of Christ.

eternal [page 53]
The word *eternal* means "forever.

Evangelists [page 15]
The writers of the four Gospels are called the Evangelists. Their names are Saint Matthew, Saint Mark, Saint Luke, and Saint John.

F-G

faith [page 14]
Faith is a gift from God. It helps us believe in God and all that he has revealed.

feasts [page 23]
Feasts are special days of the Church's year on which we honor the saints.

forgive [page 53]
To forgive is to pardon someone for the wrong they have done.

fruits of the Holy Spirit [page 65]
The fruits of the Holy Spirit are twelve signs that the Holy Spirit is working in the Church. They are love, joy, peace, patience, kindness, goodness, generosity, gentleness, faithfulness, modesty, self-control, and chastity.

Good Friday [page 99]
Good Friday is the Friday before Easter Sunday. It is the day when we remember Jesus was crucified and died.

Gospels [page 16]
The Gospels are the first four books of the New Testament.

grace [page 190]
God's grace is the gift of God making us sharers in the life of the Holy Trinity. It is also the help God gives us to live a holy life.

Great Commandment [page 158]
The Great Commandment is the commandment of love that all of God's laws depend on.

H-I

Hail Mary [page 226]
The Hail Mary is a prayer based on the Gospel stories of the Annunciation and the Visitation.

heaven [page 190]
Heaven is eternal life, or living forever, in happiness with God after we die.

298

hell [page 192]
> Hell is life separated from God forever after death.

Holy Family [page 47]
> The Holy Family is the family of Jesus, Mary, and Joseph.

Holy Orders [page 146]
> Holy Orders is the sacrament in which a baptized man is ordained a bishop, priest, or deacon to serve the whole Church his whole life long.

Holy Spirit [page 62]
> The Holy Spirit is the third Person of the Holy Trinity.

Holy Trinity [page 14]
> The Holy Trinity is the mystery of one God in three divine Persons—God the Father, God the Son, and God the Holy Spirit.

honor [page 17]
> Honor means "to show respect and love for someone."

Incarnation [page 30]
> The Incarnation is the Son of God becoming a man and still being God.

intercession [page 210]
> The word intercession means "to make a request for someone else."

J-K-L

Jerusalem [page 46]
> Jerusalem is the holiest city of the Jewish people.

Jesus [page 46]
> The name Jesus means "God saves." Jesus is the Son of God and the Savior who God promised to send his people.

Joseph [page 47]
> Joseph is the foster father of Jesus and the husband of Mary.

kingdom of God [page 48]
> The time when people will live in peace and justice with God, one another, and all of God's creation is known as the kingdom of God.

Last Supper [page 54]
> The Last Supper is the meal that Jesus and his disciples ate together on the night before he died.

Law of Moses [page 78]
> The Law of Moses is the Ten Commandments plus other important laws that guide the Jewish people in living the Covenant.

liturgical year [page 98]
> The liturgical year is the cycle of seasons and feasts that make up the Church's year of worship.

liturgy [page 98]
> The liturgy is the Church's work of worshiping God.

Liturgy of the Eucharist [page 115]
> The Liturgy of the Eucharist is the second part of the Mass.

Liturgy of the Word [page 42]
> The Liturgy of the Word is the first part of the Mass.

Lord's Prayer [page 203]
> The Lord's Prayer is another name for the Our Father. It is the prayer that Jesus gave us.

M-N

Magnificat [page 31]
> The Magnificat is Mary's canticle of praise to God.

Mary [page 30]
> The Virgin Mary is the mother of Jesus, the Son of God who became like us.

Mass [page 9]
> Mass is the celebration of listening to God's word and giving thanks and praise to God for the gift of Jesus.

Matrimony [page 146]
> Matrimony is the sacrament in which a baptized man and a baptized woman make lifelong promises to serve the Church as a married couple.

Messiah [page 46]
> The word messiah means "anointed one." Jesus is the Messiah, the Anointed One of God, the Savior God promised to send.

miracle [page 138]
> A miracle is a sign of God's presence and power at work in the world.

(299)

missionaries [page 81]
Christian missionaries often travel to countries different from their own to teach about Jesus.

mystery of God [page 14]
We say that God is a mystery because we can never fully know God. God has to reveal, or tell us, about himself.

Nativity [page 32]
The Nativity is the story of the birth of Jesus.

New Testament [page 15]
The New Testament is the second main part of the Bible. It tells us about Jesus, his teachings, and the early Church.

obey [page 174]
To obey means to choose to follow the guidance of someone who is helping us live according to God's laws.

Old Testament [page 15]
The Old Testament is the first main part of the Bible. It tells the story of God's people who lived before Jesus was born.

Ordinary Time [page 100]
Ordinary Time includes the weeks of the liturgical year that are not part of the seasons of Advent, Christmas, Lent, or Easter.

Our Father [page 24]
Another name for the Lord's Prayer is the Our Father.

parables [page 122]
Parables are stories that Jesus told to help people understand and live what he was teaching.

Paschal Mystery [page 54]
The Paschal Mystery is the Passion, death, Resurrection, and Ascension of Jesus Christ.

Passover [page 47]
Passover is the feast that the Jewish people celebrate each year to celebrate God's freeing his people from slavery in Egypt.

patron saints [page 191]
Saints who have been chosen to pray in a special way for people, countries, parishes, and for other reasons are called patron saints.

penance [page 106]
A penance is a prayer or good deed that the priest in the sacrament of Reconciliation asks us to do.

Pentecost [page 62]
Pentecost is the day on which the Holy Spirit came to the disciples of Jesus in Jerusalem fifty days after the Resurrection.

People of God [page 11]
The Church is the People of God.

personal prayer [page 202]
Personal prayer is spending time alone with God.

petition [page 210]
The word *petition* means "to make a solemn request."

pray [page 8]
To pray is to talk and listen to God.

prayers of blessing [page 25]
Prayers of blessing are prayers in which we honor that God is the Creator of everything good and the source of all our blessings.

prayers of intercession [page 210]
Prayers of intercession are prayers in which we ask God to help others.

prayers of petition [page 210]
Prayers of petition are prayers in which we ask God to help us.

prayers of praise [page 213]
Prayers of praise are prayers in which we show our love and respect for God.

prayers of thanksgiving [page 213]
Prayers of thanksgiving are prayers in which we thank God for every blessing.

psalms [page 182]
The Psalms are prayer songs found in the Bible in the Book of Psalms in the Old Testament.

public prayer [page 202]
Public prayer is praying with other people.

300

purgatory [page 87]
Purgatory is growing in love for God after we die so we can live forever in heaven.

Q-S

Reconciliation [page 130]
Reconciliation is the sacrament that brings us God's forgiveness and mercy. This sacrament is also called the sacrament of Penance.

respect [page 10]
Respect means "to look up to," "to honor," or "to admire."

Resurrection [page 55]
The Resurrection is God the Father's raising Jesus from the dead to new life by the power of the Holy Spirit.

sacraments [page 106]
The sacraments are the seven special signs that make Jesus present to us and make us sharers in the life of the Holy Trinity.

Sacraments at the Service of Communion [page 147]
The Sacraments at the Service of Communion are Matrimony and Holy Orders.

Sacraments of Healing [page 130]
Reconciliation and Anointing of the Sick are the two Sacraments of Healing.

Sacraments of Initiation [page 106]
Baptism, Confirmation, and Eucharist are the Sacraments of Initiation.

Sacred Scriptures [page 15]
The words *Sacred Scriptures* mean "holy writings." The Sacred Scriptures are also called the Bible.

sacrifice [page 54]
To sacrifice is to give something that we value to God out of love.

saints [page 86]
The saints are people whose love for God is stronger than their love for anyone or anything else.

sanctifying grace [page 71]
Sanctifying grace is the grace we receive at Baptism. It makes us holy. It is the gift of God's sharing his life with us.

sin [page 130]
Sin is freely choosing to do or say something that we know is against God's Law.

soul [page 23]
Our soul is that part of us that lives forever. It gives us the power to know, love, and serve God.

stewards [page 182]
Stewards are people who have the responsibility to care for things and to use them well.

T-U

tabernacle [page 116]
The tabernacle is the special place in which the Blessed Sacrament is kept.

Ten Commandments [page 166]
The Ten Commandments are the laws God gave to Moses on Mount Sinai. They guide us to love God and love others as we love ourselves.

Temple in Jerusalem [page 47]
The Temple in Jerusalem is the holy place where the Jewish people worshiped God.

temple of the Holy Spirit [page 70]
The Church is the temple of the Holy Spirit.

trust [page 38]
To trust someone is to know that what the person tells us is true and that the person will always do what is good for us.

V-Z

Visitation [page 226]
The Visitation is the visit of Mary, the mother of Jesus, with Elizabeth, the mother of John the Baptist.

vocation [page 146]
Our call from God to share in Jesus' life and work is called our vocation. We live this call in many ways.

works of mercy [page 73]
The works of mercy guide the Church in living as God's holy people. They guide us in caring for the needs of both the body and soul.

worship [page 98]
Worship is the adoration and honor we give to God.

(301)

Index

A-B

Abba, 203
Abraham, 166
actual grace, 190
Advent, 98,101, 236, 239–246
Angelus, 36
Anna and Simeon, 46, 249
Annunciation, 30, 33, 101
Anointing of the Sick, 106, 132, 135
Apostles, 16, 70, 71, 78, 107, 131
Apostles' Creed, 87, 218, 220, 284
Ascension, 56

Baptism, 58, 71, 74, 88, 99, 106–107, 111, 146, 149
Beatitudes, 286
Bible, 15, 37, 47, 50, 157
bishops, 71, 73, 108, 147
Blessed Sacrament, 114, 116, 119–120
Body and Blood of Christ, 88, 114–115, 119

C

Cana, 137–139, 143–144
canticle, 31
cathedrals, 169
Catholic Church, 16, 69, 71, 73, 76, 205, 222
Catholic Relief Services, 149
children of God, 86
Christmas, 98, 101, 236, 247–250
Church, 69–76, 85–92
    becoming member of, 71, 74, 88, 107
    as Body of Christ, 70, 75, 84, 88, 92
    as Communion of Saints, 85–92
    as Easter people, 267–268
    early days of, 16, 169, 221, 277
    family as domestic, 177
    as People of God, 69–76
    as people of prayer, 205, 209–216, 256
    as temple of Holy Spirit, 70, 72, 75
    work of, 69–75, 98
collection at Mass, 141
Communion of Saints, 85–92
Confirmation, 99, 106, 108, 111
contrition, 135
conversion, 80
Corporal Works of Mercy, 286
Covenant, 78, 158–159, 168
covet, 174, 176
creation, 21–27, 182–187
creeds, of Church, 19, 217–223
crucifix,109, 205, 266
Crucifixion, 54, 265

D-E

David, King, 239
deacons, 71, 147
diocese, 73
disciples of Jesus, 48
divine Providence, 22, 24
domestic church, 177

Easter, 98–99, 101, 236, 267–280
Easter candle, 57, 193, 269
Easter Triduum, 99, 103–104, 236, 263–267
Easter Vigil, 99, 252, 269
Elect, the, 99
Esther, Queen, 39
eternal life, 53–56, 87, 191–195
Eucharist, 99, 106, 113–120, 263–264, 293–295
Eucharistic Prayer, 294
Evangelists, 15

F-G-H-I

faith, 13–20, 30–35, 37–40, 43, 219, 221, 246, 277–278
family, Christian, 170, 177
fasting during Lent, 251, 254
feast days of saints, 33, 86, 89, 90
feasts of the Lord, 101
forgiveness, 53, 83, 107, 124–127, 129–131, 133–135, 210, 259–260
fruits of the Holy Spirit, 65
Funeral Mass, 193

Gabriel, angel, 29–30, 46, 226–227, 249
Galilee, 55, 139
God, Father and Creator, 21–28, 182–187. See also Holy Spirit, Holy Trinity, Jesus Christ.
Good Friday, 99, 101, 265–266
Gospel, 15, 32, 100
grace, 190, 194, 195
Great Commandment, 158–163, 287
greed, 176

Hail Mary, 29, 225–231, 283
Hannah, 38
heaven, 54–56, 86–87, 89, 92, 189–195
hell, 192
Holy Childhood Association, 49
Holy Communion, 88, 115–116
holy days of obligation, 117
Holy Family, 46–47
Holy Orders, 106, 146–147
Holy Spirit, 61–68
    Church as temple of, 70, 72
    coming upon disciples, 63, 281
    in life of Christians, 70, 72, 107–108, 110, 134, 150, 162, 186, 190, 194, 206, 214, 218–219, 276
    prayer to, 282, 283
    symbols for 72

Holy Thursday, 99, 263–264
Holy Trinity, 14, 19, 62, 168
Holy Week, 261–266
humility, 124–125, 127–128

image of God, people as, 23, 177
Incarnation, 30, 32, 35
incense, 193
Isaac, 38
Isaiah the Prophet, 243, 246, 247
Israelites, 166

J

jealousy, 176
Jeremiah the Prophet, 243
Jerusalem, 47, 54, 62, 79, 261, 281
Jesse Tree, 239
Jesus, meaning of name, 46, 249
Jesus Christ, 45–52, 53–60, 137–144
    announcement of birth of, 30, 245
    Ascension of, 56, 59, 60, 62
    birth of, 32, 247–248
    death of, 53–55, 57, 59, 60
    entry of, into Jerusalem, 261–262
    finding of, in Temple, 47
    as Good Shepherd, 271
    as Messiah, 46, 48, 51, 241–244
    miracles of, 137–144
    at prayer, 202–204
    preparing way for coming of, 239–246
    presentation of, in Temple, 46, 249
    promise of, to send Holy Spirit, 61–62, 64
    Resurrection of, 53–55, 57, 59, 60, 98
    as Savior, 31–32, 46, 53–55, 98, 101, 249–250
    as Son of God, 19, 30, 32, 35, 45–46, 48, 51, 101, 219
    as Teacher, 48, 157–164, 197–208
John Paul II, Pope, 133
Joseph of Arimathea, 55

K-L-M

kingdom of God, 48–51

Last Supper, 54, 62, 114–115, 119, 146, 191, 263
Law of Moses, 78.
Lent, 57, 98, 101, 236, 251–260
life, human, 22–23, 175
liturgical year, 97–104, 236, 235–282
liturgy, 98
Liturgy of the Eucharist, 293–295
Liturgy of the Word, 116, 292
Lord's Day, 167, 171
Lord's Prayer, 203, 207, 283

Credits

Guide Credits

Cover Design: Kristy Howard
Cover Illustration: Amy Freeman

Photo and Art Credits

Abbreviated as follows: (bkgd) background, (t) top, (b) bottom, (l) left, (r) right, (c) center.

Page 17, Amy Freeman; 18 (all), © Photodisc; 19 (l), © Tony Freeman/Photoeditinc; 19 (r), © Bill Wittman; 20 (t), © Lawrence Migdale/Stock, Boston; 20 (bl), © Myrleen Ferguson Cate/Photoeditinc; 20 (br), © Punchstock; 21, © Michael Krasowitz/FPG International; 22, © Bob Daemmrich/Stock, Boston; 23, © Donald F. Wristin/RCL; 28 (t, b), © Banana Stock/Punchstock; 28 (cr), © Comstock Klips; 28 (cl), © Photodisc; 29 (t, cl), © Banana Stock/Punchstock; 29 (cr), © Comstock Klips; 29 (b), © Photodisc/Punchstock; 30 (t), © Jon Feingersh/Corbis; 30 (bl), © Gabe Palmer/Corbis; 30 (br), © LWA-Dan Tardif/Corbis; 31, © Bill Wittman; 32, © Sam Martinez/RCL; 33, © Larry Williams/Corbis; 46, The Crosiers/Gene Plaisted, OSC; 58, © Joseph Van Os/The Image Bank; 70, © The Crosiers/Gene Plaisted, OSC; 82, Mari Goering; 94, © SuperStock, Inc.; 106, © Bill Wittman; 118, 130, 142, 154, © The Crosiers/Gene Plaisted, OSC; 170, © Bill Wittman; 182, 194, © The Crosiers/Gene Plaisted, OSC; 206, Mari Goering; 218, 230, © The Crosiers/Gene Plaisted, OSC; 242, © James Shaffer; 258, © John Terence Turner/Gettyimages; 270, © Spencer Grant/Photoeditinc; 282, © Ariel Skelley/Corbis; 294, © Corbis Images; 306, © Novastock/Stock Connection; 322, © Michael Newman/Photoeditinc; 334, © Joe Sohm/Chromosohm/PictureQuest; 346, © Bill Wittman; 358, © The Crosiers/Gene Plaisted, OSC; 374, © Anthony Jambor/RCL; 378, The Crosiers/Gene Plaisted, OSC; 388, © SuperStock, Inc.; 394, 406, © The Crosiers/Gene Plaisted, OSC; 416, © Bill Wittman.

Footnotes

Front Matter
Page 22
  1 Cf. *John* 17:4.

Chapter 1
Page 46
  1 *Dei Verbum*: The Dogmatic
    Constitution on Divine
    Revelation 21.
Page 47
  1 Cf. St. Iraneus of Lyons, "*Adversus*
    haereses" III, 20, 2. Sources
    chrétiennes 211, 389-393. *Dei*
    verbum: The Dogmatic Constitution
    on Divine Revelation 15; *Catechesi*
    Tradendae: On Catechesis in Our
    Time 58; *Christifiedeles Laici* 61;
    Catechism of the Catholic Church 53
    and 122; and also Part III, chap. 1.
  2 *Catechism of the Catholic Church*
    54–64.

Chapter 3
Page 71
  1 Cf. Paul VI, Apostolic Exhortation
    Marialis cultus (2 February 1974),
    nn. 24, 25, 29, *Acta Apostolicae*
    Sedis 66 (1979) pp. 134-136, 141.

Chapter 4
Page 82
  1 Cf. *Ad Gentes*: On Missionary
    Activity in the Church 13a.
  2 Cf. *Catechesi Tradendae*: On
    Catechesis in Our Time 5b.
  3 Cf. *Catechesi Tradendae*: On
    Catechesis in Our Time 20b.
  4 Cf. *Catechism of the Catholic*
    Church 166-167.

Chapter 5
Page 94
  1 Cf. *Evangelii nuntiandi*: On
    Evangelization in the Modern
    World 11-14; Roman Missal 12-20;
    cf. *Catechism of the Catholic Church*
    541-556
  2 In the liturgy of the Church it is
    expressed in the Easter Vigil:
    "Almighty and eternal God you
    created all things in wonderful
    beauty and order. Help us now to
    perceive how still more wonderful
    is the new creation by which in the
    fullness of time you redeemed your
    people through the sacrifice of our
    Passover, Jesus Christ, who lives
    and reigns forever and ever"
    (Missale Romanum, Easter Vigil,
    prayer after the first reading).
  3 *Gaudium et spes*: The Pastoral
    Constitution on the Church in the
    Modern World 22 ¶ 2.
Page 95
  1 Cf. *John* 1:14.
Page 102
  1 *Evangelii nuntiandi*: On
    Evangelization in the Modern
    World 14.

  2 *Evangelii nuntiandi*: On
    Evangelization in the Modern
    World 18.

Chapter 6
Page 107
  1 Cf. *Catechesi Tradendae*: On
    Catechesis in Our Time 20b.

Chapter 8
Page 131
  1 As has been stated in chapter I of
    this part in "The transmission of
    Revelation by the Church, the work
    of the Holy Spirit" and in part II,
    chapter I in "The ecclesial nature of
    the Gospel message." Cf. *Evangelii*
    Nuntiandi: On Evangelization in
    the Modern World 60 which speaks
    of the ecclesial nature of any
    evangelizing activity.

Chapter 9
Page 142
  1 Cf. *Roman Missal* 46b.

Chapter 13
Page 194
  1 Cf. *Dei Verbum*: The Dogmatic
    Constitution on Divine
    Revelation 21.
Page 195
  1 *Catechism of the Catholic Church*
    1211.
  2 *Catechism of the Catholic Church*
    1211.
  3 *Lumen gentium*: The Dogmatic
    Constitution on the Church 11.

Chapter 14
Page 206
  1 Cf. *Lk* 7:36-50; 19: 1-10.

Chapter 15
Page 219
  1 *Evangelii nuntiandi*: On
    Evangelization in the Modern
    World 26.

Chapter 16
Page 231
  1 *Dei Verbum*: The Dogmatic
    Constitution on Divine Revelation
    5; cf. *Catechism of the Catholic*
    Church 153.
  2 *Dei Verbum*: The Dogmatic
    Constitution on Divine Revelation
    5; cf. *Catechism of the Catholic*
    Church 153.

Chapter 17
Page 243
  1 Cf. *Lumen gentium*: The Dogmatic
    Constitution on the Church 11;
    Apostolicam actuositatem: The
    Decree on the Apostolate of the
    Laity 11; *Familiaris consortio*: On
    the Family 49.

  2 Cf. *Gaudium et spes*: The Pastoral
    Constitution on the Church in the
    Modern World 52; *Familiaris*
    consortio: On the Family 37a.
Page 259
  1 Justice in the World, II, The
    Gospel Message and the Mission
    of the Church, The Saving Justice
    of God Through Christ.

Chapter 22
Page 307
  1 Cf. *Eph* 2:8; *Evangelii nuntiandi*:
    On Evangelization in the Modern
    World 27.
  2 Cf. *Evangelii nuntiandi*: On
    Evangelization in the Modern
    World 9.

Chapter 23
Page 322
  1 The Our Father is, in truth, the
    summing up of the entire Gospel
    (Tertullian, *De oratione*, 1, 6).
    "*Go through all the prayers in the*
    Scriptures and I do not believe that it
    is possible to find anyone, anywhere,
    that is not included in the Lord's
    Prayer" (St Augustine, *Epistolas*,
    130, 12; PL, 33, 502); Cf. *Catechism*
    of the Catholic Church 2761.

Chapter 24
Page 335
  1 Cf. General Catechetical Directory
    (1971) 10 and 22.

Chapter 26
Page 358
  1 Cf. Paul VI, Apostolic Exhortation
    Marialis cultus (2 February 1974),
    nn. 24, 25, 29, *Acta Apostolicae*
    Sedis 66 (1979) pp. 134-136, 141.

Ordinary Time
Page 375
  1 *Sacrosanctum Concilium*: The
    Constitution on the Sacred Liturgy
    104; cf. *Sacrosanctum Concilium*:
    The Constitution on the Sacred
    Liturgy 108,111.

Advent
Page 379
  1 Cf. *Rev.* 22:17.

Holy Week
Page 407
  1 Cf. *Maxima Redemptionis Nostrae*
    Mysteria; St. Augustine, *Epistolas*
    55, 24, PL, 35, 215.

Easter
Page 417
  1 Cf. Roman Missal, Easter Vigil, 53;
    Roman Missal, Ritual Masses, 3,
    Baptism.